AF270256

Ephesians

An Exegetical Guide
for Preaching
and Teaching

Ephesians

An Exegetical Guide for Preaching and Teaching

Benjamin I. Simpson

HERBERT W. BATEMAN IV, SERIES EDITOR

Ephesians: An Exegetical Guide for Preaching and Teaching
© 2020 by Benjamin I. Simpson

Published by Kregel Academic, an imprint of Kregel Publications, 2450 Oak Industrial Dr. NE, Grand Rapids, MI 49505-6020.

This book is a title in the Big Greek Idea Series, edited by Herbert W. Bateman IV.

The Hebrew font, NewJerusalemU, and the Greek font, GraecaU, are available from www.linguistsoftware.com/lgku.htm, +1-425-775-1130.

Nestle-Aland, Novum Testamentum Graece, 28th Revised Edition, edited by Barbara and Kurt Aland, Johannes Karavidopoulos, Carlo M. Martini, and Bruce M. Metzger in cooperation with the Institute for New Testament Textual Research, Münster/Westphalia, © 2012 Deutsche Bibelgesellschaft, Stuttgart. Used by permission.

The translation of the New Testament portions used throughout the commentary is the author's own English rendering of the Greek.

Scripture quotations marked NET are from the NET Bible® copyright ©1996–2006 by Biblical Studies Press, LLC (www.bible.org). Scripture quoted by permission. All rights reserved.

Scripture quotations marked NLT are from the Holy Bible, New Living Translation, copyright © 1996, 2004, 2007 by Tyndale House Foundation. Used by permission of Tyndale House Publishers, Inc., Carol Stream, Illinois 60188. All rights reserved.

ISBN 978-0-8254-4543-9

Printed in the United States of America

20 21 22 23 24 / 5 4 3 2 1

To Amber, Madison, and Eli

Contents

Paul identifies his credentials as an apostle through the will of God and greets the church in Ephesus by wishing them grace and peace from both the Father and the Lord Jesus Christ.

God deserves praise because he blesses believers in Christ by choosing them for adoption, by redeeming them through the death of Christ, and by giving them the Holy Spirit, who serves as a guarantee of God's salvation in the future.

Paul prays that through spiritual insight God reveals the hope of the believers' call, the depth of his inheritance, and his immeasurable power available to them; the same power through which God raised Christ from the dead and gives him dominion over all the authorities of the world.

Despite once being dead in sins and under satanic control, God demonstrates his mercy to the world by saving believers, making them alive, and giving them a seat in the heavenlies with Christ— an act of grace—so that they might walk in the good works that he has prepared for them.

Even though Gentiles were once without hope and alienated from
the covenantal promises that God gave to Israel, Christ destroyed
the hostility between the two groups through his death by nullifying the law and granting peace and access to God for both groups.
As a result he created a new people group out of the two, the
church, founded on Christ, and in which the Spirit of God dwells.

According to his plan, God reveals the mystery of Christ to Paul,
along with the apostles and prophets, in order to proclaim this
mystery to the rulers and authorities of this world, namely that
Gentiles have become fellow heirs and fellow partakers of the
promise of Christ with the Jews.

God, who is able to do more than anyone can imagine, deserves
all glory for strengthening the believers and for allowing them
to grow in ways that are inconceivable, since they have a firm
foundation.

Believers should walk in a manner worthy of their Christian faith by
keeping the unity of the community, which God made possible by
appointing Christian leaders to train the body, and which is essential for the growth of the body to withstand attacks of the evil one.

Believers should walk in holiness, recalling the change in their
lives in light of their new identity as Christians; and as a result,
they should build up the community through their behavior and
cease any conduct that breaks down the community.

Believers should imitate God by loving one another like Christ,
who loved us by sacrificing himself for us. They should abstain
from any sign of sexual deviancy or harsh words, since these types
of people will not inherit the kingdom; rather, believers should be
known for thanksgiving.

Believers should walk as children of light, characterized by goodness, justice, and truth, not associating with those who do shameful deeds of evil, but rather exposing them.

Preface to the Series

The Big Greek Idea Series: An Exegetical Guide for Preaching and Teaching is a grammatical-*like* commentary with interlinear-*like* English translations of the Greek text that provides expositional-*like* commentary to guide a pastor and teacher in their sermon and teaching preparations. Every volume of this series has a threefold audience in mind: the busy pastor, the overworked professor of an academic institution, and the student with demanding Greek professors.

WHY PASTORS, PROFESSORS, AND STUDENTS

First and foremost, the Big Greek Idea Series is for the busy *pastor* who desires to use their Greek text in their sermon preparation. Most preachers who have earned a Masters of Divinity degree and who have taken some New Testament Greek have not had a lot of exposure in studying books of the New Testament in Greek. If they were fortunate, they may have studied two New Testament books in Greek. Furthermore, many preachers who desire to work in the Greek New Testament do not have the luxury to study and work in the Greek on their own in any great detail. They need a tool to guide them in their use of New Testament Greek in their sermon preparation. This series is meant to be that tool.

> THE BIG GREEK IDEA: A GUIDE FOR PREACHING AND TEACHING was *written for* three groups of people:
> 1. the busy *pastor*,
> 2. the overloaded *professor*,
> 3. and the *student* with demanding New Testament Greek professors.

Second, the Big Greek Idea Series is for the overloaded *professor* of an academic institution. Institutional demands are high and expectations at times appear overwhelming. On the one hand, many academies expect faculty to teach Greek exegesis with minimal time to prepare, forgetting that such courses differ from courses requiring only English language aptitude. On the other hand, students anticipate a great deal of explanation from those who teach them. Often the professor is merely one step ahead of their students. This tool is intended to streamline class preparation and perhaps even serve as a required or recommended textbook to help take a load off the professor.

Finally, the Big Greek Idea Series is for the *student* with demanding Greek professors. What a student puts into a course is what a student will get and retain from a course. Students who have professors with great expectations are blessed, though the student may feel cursed (at the time). This tool will provide answers that will impress your professor, but more importantly provide information that will build confidence in handling the Greek New Testament. The Big Greek Idea Series will be a tool students will use in ministry long after the course is over.

WHAT CAN BE EXPECTED

Each volume of the Big Greek Idea Series features one or more New Testament books in Greek. It is a series for people who have studied basic New Testament Greek grammar and intermediate Greek syntax and grammar. Each volume provides an introduction that features information crucial for understanding each New Testament book while making minimal assumptions about the reader's capabilities to work in the New Testament Greek text. After the introduction, the volume has three distinct features.

First, each featured New Testament book is broken into units of thought. The units open with a big Greek idea. Professors sometimes refer to the big Greek idea as the exegetical idea of a passage. The big Greek idea is followed by a summary overview underscoring verbs and key transitional and structural markers. The section closes with a simple outline for the unit.

Second, the Nestle-Aland 28th edition Greek text is broken into independent and dependent clauses that reveal visually the coordination and subordination of thought based upon key structural markers. Verbs and key structural markers are often in bold and always underlined. Under each Greek clause is an original English translation. The interlinear-*like* English translations of the Greek helps readers spot the words they know and those they do not.

Finally, each unit closes with an analysis of the clausal outline. It explains the various contemporary author's syntactical understanding of clausal relationships, their semantical rendering of all Greek verbs, verbals, and key structural markers, and an interpretive translation of the text. Interspersed throughout this closing section are grammatical, syntactical, semantic, lexical, theological, and text-critical nuggets of information. They are expositional-*like* commentary to enhance an understanding of selected issues that surface in the text.

HOW TO USE THE SERIES

The Big Greek Idea Series has the potential for a threefold usage.

First, use it as a grammatical commentary because it is a grammatical-*like* commentary. Every volume represents the early stages of Bible study in New Testament Greek. Identifying clauses is a first step typically practiced in exegesis. Yet, every independent and dependent Greek clause has a corresponding explanatory discussion that underscores the grammatical, syntactical, and semantic functions of their respective Greek structural markers that are <u>underlined</u> and often in **bold** print for easy interpretation. Unlike computer programs that present a New Testament Greek text with English translations and parsing capabilities, the Big Greek Idea Series discusses syntax and semantic options important for exegesis yet not available with computer programs . . . but I'm sure that too will change.

Second, use it as an interlinear because it has an interlinear-*like* presentation of the Nestle-Aland 28th edition of the Greek New Testament text with a corresponding English translation. Yet, the Big Greek Idea Series offers far more than a traditional interlinear. The Greek text is presented in a clausal outline format that provides the twenty-first-century reader a visual of the biblical author's flow of thought. More importantly, it causes a person to *slow down* and *look at the text* more closely.

- What does the text say . . . not what *I* remember about the text.
- What does it mean . . . not what *I* want it to mean.
- What do we need to believe . . . not *my* theological pet peeves.
- How should we then live for God . . . not according to *my* preconceived ideas.

Third, use it as a commentary because interwoven throughout every volume are expositional-*like* nuggets. Expositional-like nuggets are comments that underscore a grammatical, syntactical, semantic, lexical, theological, or text-critical issue. Typical of any expositional commentary, if time is taken to discuss an issue, it's probably important and warrants some special attention. Similarly, the expositional-*like* nuggets point the reader to important interpretive issues.

Yet, the Big Greek Idea Series is not meant to replace current commentaries. Commentators generally begin commentary preparation on the clause level, but a publisher's page restriction often makes it difficult to visualize clausal parallels, coordination, and subordination of thought. Descriptions are at times ambiguous and

> THE BIG GREEK IDEA: A GUIDE FOR PREACHING AND TEACHING FEATURES
> 1. Units of Thought
>   *Big Greek Idea*
>   *Summary Overview*
>   *Outline*
> 2. Clausal Outlines
>   *Clausal Relationships Visualized*
>   *Structural Markers Identified*
>   *English Translation Provided*
> 3. Explanations
>   *Syntax Explained*
>   *Semantical Decisions Recognized*
>   *Interpretive Translation Justified*
>   *Expositional Comments Provided*

perhaps even ignored, due to the difficulty in presenting a syntactical situation. This tool cannot hide ambiguities and difficulties of coordination or subordination of thought, because clauses are clearly reproduced and explained for readers to evaluate a contemporary author's decisions. Thus, the Big Greek Idea Series is meant to complement critical commentaries like Baker's Exegetical Commentary, Word Biblical Commentary, Anchor Bible, and others.

I trust the Big Greek Idea Series will be a rewarding tool for your use in studying the New Testament.

HERBERT W. BATEMAN IV
SERIES EDITOR

Author's Acknowledgments

Few people actually set out to learn Greek and Hebrew for the sake of learning the language itself. I certainly did not. I began learning Greek to come to a better understanding of the New Testament. Learning any language can be arduous, even impossible. And yet, for serious Bible study having some kind of access to Greek and Hebrew is essential. The ability to work with the language opens up a tool to craft dynamic sermons. Tracing the thoughts of the biblical writers not only will shape you, the reader, but it will shape how you minister to others and how you preach and teach the message. The Greek language asks students to make a steep payment but pays significant dividends. The more you can invest, the more it will return.

A project like this is not possible without several people behind it. First of all, I am grateful to Herb Bateman for developing the idea for this series. A tool like this helps students engage with the world of the Scripture. I am particularly thankful for the team at Kregel, who are dedicated to giving students tools to study the Bible well and teach its message with accuracy.

This project would certainly not be possible without the support of the New Testament department at Dallas Theological Seminary. I learned Greek exegesis at their feet. I first learned how to identify Greek markers from Dan Wallace and Hall Harris. Later I worked with John Grassmick to grade the work for first-year Greek students. I took electives from Darrell Bock, Harold Hoehner, Jay Smith, and Buist Fanning. And now as a colleague, I have had the unique opportunity to continue learning from them and others in the department, particularly Michael Burer, Will Johnston, and Joe Fantin. I have profited from both their insight and encouragement.

I am also grateful for my students. Much of the work in this book has been developed from class notes and worked out in lectures. My students in Dallas, Houston, and Washington, D.C. are the primary audience that I have in mind as I write this book. My sole desire in writing a book like this is to see more students engage with the text of the New Testament.

Finally, I am grateful for my family. Not only did I take time to work on this project, but I constantly asked my wife, Amber, about exegetical problems and theological themes in the book. She graciously read over stilted technical prose and offered feedback. It is to her, and my children, Madison and Eli, that I dedicate this book.

Benjamin I. Simpson

Abbreviations

Bible Translations

ASV	American Standard Version
CJB	Complete Jewish Bible
CNT	Comprehensive New Testament
CSB	Christian Standard Bible
ESV	English Standard Version
GNT	Good News Translation
HCSB	Holman Christian Standard Bible
KJV	King James Version
LEB	Lexham English Bible
NASB	New American Standard Bible
NET	New English Translation. First Beta ed. (Biblical Studies Press, 2001)
NIRV	New International Reader's Edition
NIV	New International Version (2011)
NKJV	New King James Version
NLT	New Living Translation
NRSV	New Revised Standard Version
RSV	Revised Standard Version
WEB	World English Bible

General Abbreviations

AB	Anchor Bible
BECNT	Baker Exegetical Commentary on the New Testament
BHGNT	Baylor Handbooks to the Greek New Testament
BLG	Biblical Languages: Greek
BNTC	Black's New Testament Commentaries
BSac	*Bibliotheca Sacra*
BSL	Bible Study Library
BST	Bible Speaks Today
EEC	Evangelical Exegetical Commentary
EGGNT	Exegetical Guide to the Greek New Testament
HeTr	Helps for Translators
HNTE	Handbook for New Testament Exegesis
HThKNT	Herders Theologischer Kommentar zum Neuen Testament
ICC	International Critical Commentary
JBL	*Journal of Biblical Literature*
JTS	*Journal of Theological Studies*

LCL	Loeb Classical Library
LEC	Library of Early Christianity
LHJS	Library of Historical Jesus Studies
LNTS	Library of New Testament Studies
MT	Hodges, Zane C., and Arthur L. Farstad. *The Greek New Testament according to the Majority Text*. 2nd ed. Nashville: Nelson, 1985.
NA[28]	Aland, Barbara, et al. *Novum Testamentum Graece*. 28th ed. Stuttgart: Deutsche Bibelgesellschaft, 2012.
NSBT	New Studies in Biblical Theology
NTL	New Testament Library
OTM	Oxford Theological Monographs
PNTC	Pillar New Testament Commentaries
RP[2005]	Robinson, Maurice A., and William G. Pierpont. *The New Testament in the Original Greek: Byzantine Textform, 2005*. Southborough, MA: Chilton, 2005.
SBL	Holmes, Michael W. *The Greek New Testament SBL Edition*. Atlanta: Society of Biblical Literature; Bellingham, WA: Logos Bible Software, 2010.
SBLDS	Society of Biblical Literature Dissertation Series
SNTMS	Society for New Testament Studies Monograph Series
SP	Sacra Pagina
SubBi	Subsidia Biblica
THGNT	Jongkind, Dirk, Peter J. Williams, Peter M. Head, and Patrick James. *The Greek New Testament: Produced at Tyndale House, Cambridge*. Wheaton, IL: Crossway, 2017.
TNTC	Tyndale New Testament Commentaries
WBC	Word Biblical Commentary
ZECNT	Zondervan Exegetical Commentary of the New Testament

TECHNICAL ABBREVIATIONS

ca.	circa
CE	Common Era (equivalent to AD)
cf.	*confer*, compare
ed(s).	editor(s)
e.g.	*exempli gratia*, for example
esp.	especially
ET	English translation
etc.	*et cetera*, and the rest
H	Hebrew
i.e.	*id est*, that is
lit.	literally
n(n).	note(s)

p(p).   page(s)
s.v.   *sub verbo*, under the word
TSKS   article-substantive-καὶ-substantive
v(v).   verse(s)

Apocrypha, Pseudepigrapha, and Apostolic Fathers

1 En.   First Enoch
Barn.   Barnabas
Let. Aris.   Letter of Aristeas
Mart. Pol.   Martyrdom of Polycarp

Rabbinic Literature

m. ʾAbot   Mishnah ʾAbot

Ancient Writings

Aristotle
       Eth. nic.   *Nicomachean Ethics*

Chrysostom
       Hom. Eph.   *Homilies on Ephesians*

Herodotus
       Hist.   *Histories*

Josephus
       Ant.   *Jewish Antiquities*
       J.W.   *Jewish War*

Periodical, Reference, and Serial

Arnold   Arnold, Clinton E. 2010. *Ephesians*. ZECNT 10. Grand Rapids:
               Zondervan.

Barth   Barth, Marcus. 1974. *Ephesians 1–3: A New Translation with Intro-
               duction and Commentary;* and *Ephesians 4–6: A New Translation
               with Introduction and Commentary.* AB 34–34a. Garden City, NY:
               Doubleday.

Baugh   Baugh, Steven M. *Ephesians*. 2016. EEC. Bellingham, WA: Lex-
               ham.

BDAG　　Danker, Frederick W., Walter Bauer, William F. Arndt, and F. Wilbur Gingrich. 2000. *A Greek–English Lexicon of the New Testament and Other Early Christian Literature*. 3rd ed. Chicago: University of Chicago Press.

BDF　　Blass, Frederich, Albert Debrunner, and Robert W. Funk. 1961. *A Greek Grammar of the New Testament and Other Early Christian Literature*. 3rd ed. Chicago: University of Chicago Press.

Best　　Best, Ernest. *A Critical and Exegetical Commentary on Ephesians*. ICC. Edinburgh: T&T Clark,

Bullinger　　Bullinger, E. W. 1986. *Figures of Speech Used in the Bible: Explained and Illustrated*. Grand Rapids: Baker.

DPL　　Hawthorne, Gerald F., Ralph P. Martin, and Daniel G. Reid, eds. 1993. *Dictionary of Paul and His Letters*. Downers Grove, IL: InterVarsity Press.

Hoehner　　Hoehner, Harold W. 2002. *Ephesians: An Exegetical Commentary*. Grand Rapids: Baker Academic.

GE　　Montanari, Franco. 2015. *The Brill Dictionary of Ancient Greek*. Translated and edited by Madeleine Goh and Chad Schroeder. Boston: Brill.

KMP　　Köstenberger, Andreas J., Benjamin L. Merkle, and Robert L. Plummer. 2016. *Going Deeper with New Testament Greek: An Intermediate Study of the Grammar and Syntax of the New Testament*. Nashville: B&H Academic.

Larkin　　Larkin, William J. 2009. *Ephesians: A Handbook on the Greek Text*. BHGNT. Waco, TX: Baylor University Press.

Lincoln　　Lincoln, Andrew T. 1990. *Ephesians*. WBC 42. Dallas: Word.

L&N　　Louw, Johannes P., and Eugene A. Nida, eds. 1989. *Greek-English Lexicon of the New Testament: Based on Semantic Domains*. 2nd ed. New York: United Bible Societies.

LSJ　　Liddell, Henry George, Robert Scott, and Henry Stuart Jones. 1996. *A Greek-English Lexicon*. 9th ed. with rev. sup. Oxford: Clarendon.

M   Mounce, William D. 2009. *Basics of Biblical Greek Grammar*. 3rd ed. Grand Rapids: Zondervan.

Merkle   Merkle, Benjamin L. 2016. *Ephesians*. EGGNT. Nashville: B&H Academic.

Metzger   Metzger, Bruce M. 1994. A *Textual Commentary on the Greek New Testament*. 2nd ed. Stuttgart: Deutsche Bibelgesellschaft.

MM   Moulton, James Hope, and George Milligan. 1930. *The Vocabulary of the Greek Testament: Illustrated from the Papyri and Other Non-literary Sources*. Grand Rapids: Eerdmans.

Moule   Moule, C. F. D. 1959. *An Idiom Book of the Greek New Testament*. 2nd ed. Cambridge: Cambridge University Press.

Osborne   Osborne, Grant R. 2017. *Ephesians: Verse by Verse*. Bellingham, WA: Lexham.

Porter   Porter, Stanley E. 1994. *Idioms of the Greek New Testament*. 2nd ed. BLG 2. Sheffield: JSOT Press.

Robertson   Robertson, A. T. 1934. *A Grammar of the Greek New Testament in the Light of Historical Research*. Nashville: Broadman.

TDNT   *Theological Dictionary of the New Testament*. 1964–1976. Edited by Gerhard Kittel and Gerhard Friedrich. Translated by Geoffrey W. Bromiley. 10 vols. Grand Rapids: Eerdmans.

Thielman   Thielman, Frank. 2010. *Ephesians*. BECNT. Grand Rapids: Baker Academic.

Turner[1]   Turner, Nigel. 1963. *Grammar of the New Testament Greek: Volume 3: Syntax*. Edinburgh: T&T Clark.

Turner[2]   Turner, Nigel. 1976. *A Grammar of the New Testament Greek: Volume 4: Style*. Edinburgh: T&T Clark.

W   Wallace, Daniel B. 1996. *Greek Grammar Beyond the Basics: An Exegetical Syntax of the New Testament*. Grand Rapids: Zondervan.

Zerwick   Zerwick, Maximilian. 1963. *Biblical Greek: Illustrated by Examples*. Translated by Joseph Smith. SubBi 41. Rome: Pontifical Biblical Inst.

Introduction

Ephesians: An Exegetical Guide for Preaching and Teaching guides pastors and teachers in their understanding on Paul's Greek structure, his use of Greek clauses, his Greek syntax, and his Greek writing style with this single intention: to underscore Paul's numerous big Greek ideas.[1] Tracing the various big Greek ideas in Ephesians is possible by recognizing Paul's thought process evident in the co-ordination and subordination of the Greek clauses he employs within each of his letters. We do not assume that pastors and teachers remember everything learned during their initial study of New Testament Greek in their college or seminary classes. We strive to define and explain Paul's use of Greek in ways that help pastors and teachers recall what was once learned, refresh and expand an appreciation for Paul's presentation in Koine Greek, and underscore the value to engage the Greek text when preparing to preach and teach Ephesians.

We construct the Greek words from Ephesians in 109 independent clauses and 255 dependent clauses and arrange them into clausal outlines. Each clause is translated and then explained for interpretive recognition, comprehension, and communication. The clausal outlines represent an early stage in preparing to preach and teach the text.[2] All the clauses appear in Greek from NA[28] along with an interpretive translation for easy usage. The clausal outlines make it possible for pastors to visualize the relationship clauses have to one another in order to trace Paul's flow of thought and ultimately his big idea.

Number of Greek Words in Ephesians				
Chapter	**NA28**	**SBL**	**RP2005**	**MT**	**THGNT**
Ephesians 1	401	401	405	405	402
Ephesians 2	362	362	361	361	362
Ephesians 3	325	324	334	334	325
Ephesians 4	483	482	486	487	482
Ephesians 5	457	455	471	471	457
Ephesians 6	394	393	402	401	394

---

1. Portions of this work are excerpted from Simpson 2015; used by permission of the Cyber-Center for Biblical Studies.
2. For nine steps of exegesis, see Bateman 2013.

THE CLAUSAL OUTLINE

The clausal outlines for Ephesians are based on a variety of Greek clauses employed throughout the letter. By nature, a Greek clause has a subject and a predicate, which may be a verb, a participle, or an infinitive. They may be independent or dependent Greek clauses. Whereas independent clauses can stand alone, dependent clauses have a subordinate relationship to another clause.

Other terminology exists for this same process. Mounce (1996, xvi–xxiii) calls it "phrasing," Guthrie (Guthrie and Duvall 1998, 27–42) calls it "grammatical diagram," and MacDonald (1986, 145–52) calls it "textual transcription." While these other works tend to break sentences into clauses and phrases, *Ephesians* concentrates on the clause level. As you work your way through the clauses in Paul's letter to the Ephesians, you can expect the following.

1. Every clause reproduces the Greek text in the exact word order of NA[28] even when syntax is less than clear. Every attempt is made to make sense of Paul's syntax in Ephesians regardless of the occasional lack of clarity.

2. Every Greek clause underscores the Greek words deemed as important structural markers. A structural marker is always a verb, which may be a verbal (participle or infinitive). Other important structural markers are conjunctions, relative and demonstrative pronouns, and a select number of prepositional phrases that introduce clauses. Structural markers are always <u>underlined</u> and often in **bold** print. For instance:

   [5:28a] (ὁ κλέπτων) μηκέτι **κλεπτέτω**
   [5:28a] (The one who steals) must no longer **steal**

   The major structural marker is the imperative **κλεπτέτω**, and therefore underlined and in bold type. The substantival participle κλέπτων is an important verbal, but not the structural maker, so the parentheses offset it for visual purposes.

3. Every Greek structural marker serves to distinguish different types of independent and dependent clauses. The chart below summarizes the types of independent and dependent Greek clauses found in Ephesians and the means by which they are introduced.

Types (Classifications) of Independent and Dependent Clauses[3]	
Three Types of Independent Clauses	**Four Types of Dependent Clauses**
Conjunctive clauses are introduced by simple connective (καί or δέ), contrastive conjunction (ἀλλά, δέ, πλήν), correlative conjunction (μὲν … δέ, or καὶ … καί), explanatory conjunction (γάρ), inferential conjunction (ἄρα, διό, οὖν, or γάρ), or transitional conjunction (καί, δέ, or οὖν).	Pronominal clauses are introduced by a relative pronoun (ὅς, ἥ, ὅ), a relative adjective (οἶος, *such as*; ὅσος, *as much/many as*), a relative adverb (ὅπου, *where*; ὅτε, *when*), or a demonstrative pronoun (οὗτος).
Prepositional clauses are introduced by "for this reason" (διὰ τοῦτο), "for this reason" (ἐπὶ τοῦτο), "as a result of this" (ἐκ τούτου), "why" (εἰς τί), or "in this" (ἐν τούτῳ).	Conjunctive clauses are introduced by a subordinate conjunction that denotes semantical concepts such as time (ὅτε, ὅτον), reason and cause (διό, ὅτι, ἐπεί), purpose and result (ἵνα, ὥστε), or comparison (καθώς, ὡς, ὡσεί, ὥσπερ), etc.
	Participial clauses are introduced by participles. Their objects may be a noun, pronoun, prepositional phrases, etc.
Asyndeton clauses are not introduced by a conjunctive word or phrase.	Infinitival clauses are introduced by infinitives.

4. Every independent Greek clause (the main thought) is placed farthest to the left of the page. Dependent Greek clauses that directly modify a Greek word in another clause are either placed in parentheses or positioned under (or above if necessary) the word it modifies for easy identification. This positioning of a clause *visualizes* the *subordination* and *coordination* of Ephesians' basic grammatical and syntactical relationships, parallelisms, and emphases.

5. Every independent and dependent Greek clause has an interpretive English translation provided under the Greek text. Every translated structural marker is also <u>underlined</u> and often in **bold** print for easy recognition, use, and evaluation.

---

3.   W, 656–65. There is a difference between the chart above and Wallace. Whereas the pronominal clause represents both the relative and demonstrative pronoun in the chart on this page, Wallace limits the category to a relative pronoun.

One to Five Exemplified

An example of what to expect is nicely illustrated with a verse from Ephesians 1:15–16.

> [15] Διὰ τοῦτο κἀγὼ **ἀκούσας** τὴν καθ' ὑμᾶς πίστιν ἐν τῷ κυρίῳ Ἰησοῦ καὶ τὴν ἀγάπην τὴν εἰς πάντας τοὺς ἁγίους
> [15] <u>For this reason</u>, **after hearing** about your faith in the Lord Jesus and your love for all of the saints

[16a] οὐ **παύομαι**
[16a] **I do** not **cease**

> [16b] **εὐχαριστῶν** ὑπὲρ ὑμῶν
> [16b] **giving thanks** on your behalf

> [16c] μνείαν **ποιούμενος** ἐπὶ τῶν προσευχῶν μου
> [16c] while **remembering** you in my prayers,

1. The order of the Greek sentence is followed.

2. Every Greek clause underscores the Greek words deemed as important structural markers.

3. Every Greek structural marker distinguishes the different types of independent and dependent clauses. Ephesians 1:15–16 has three dependent participle Greek clauses; verse 16a is an independent conjunctive clause introduced by Διὰ τοῦτο.

4. The independent clause (v. 16a) is placed to the extreme left. The three dependent participle clauses function adverbially modifying the main verb. The participles are indented to show their relationship to the main verb. Since the adverbial participles are the major structural markers, they are clearly identified.

5. Every Greek clause has a corresponding English translation and all the translated structural markers are identified for easy recognition.

---

6. Every independent and dependent Greek clause has a corresponding explanatory discussion that underscores the grammatical, syntactical, and semantic functions of their respective Greek structural markers that are <u>underlined</u> and often

in **bold** print. Thus, not every word within a clause is discussed; explanatory discussions major on the structural makers in order to underscore Paul's point. Yet if a structural marker is not in bold, it is often for easier visual distinctions.

> **Grammatical Function:** Grammatical function identifies the Greek *structural marker* as to whether it is pronominal, conjunctive, a verb, or verbal (participle or infinitive). If the marker is a verb or verbal, it is parsed with an appropriate lexical meaning provided from BDAG. If it is pronominal or conjunctive, a lexical definition is also provided based upon BDAG.

> **Syntactical Function:** Syntactical function first draws attention to the independent or dependent clause's type. If it is a *dependent clause*, its syntactical function within a sentence is underscored. All clauses are identified as either substantival, adjectival, or adverbial, as well as the word or words the clause modifies.

> **Semantic Function:** Semantic functions are by nature interpretive suggestions whereby a Greek structural marker is explained based upon its literary context. Semantic interpretations employ the categories listed and defined in Wallace's *Greek Grammar beyond the Basics* (1996), many of which are discussed in critical commentaries, and reflected in English Bible translations.

7. Explanatory discussions about Greek structural markers are interspersed with commentary-*like* remarks identified as *nuggets*. Numerous text-critical, grammatical, syntactical, structural, theological, and lexical nuggets appear between clausal presentations that delve deeper into and expand on issues in order to advance your appreciation for Ephesians, its readers, and its message.

8. All independent and dependent Greek clauses are grouped into units of thought. Ephesians is broken into seventeen units of thought.

9. Every unit opens with a structural overview that provides a synopsis for the unit's structure and each summary is followed with a "Big Greek Idea" statement.

10. An interpretive English translation of Ephesians concludes *Ephesians: An Exegetical Guide for Preaching and Teaching.*

All ten expectations are intended to help pastors and teachers recall and refresh their previous training in Greek, to expand a person's understanding of Koine Greek, and to encourage personal engagement with the Greek text. Hopefully the process in this book will increase confidence in understanding and appreciating Ephesians for preaching and teaching it.

Yet *Ephesians* is not a guide for translation. There are works designed for that task (Larkin; Simpson 2015; Merkle). This book is a grammatical-*like* commentary with interlinear-*like* English translations of the Greek text that provides expositional commentary-*like* comments to guide a pastor and teacher in their sermon and teaching preparations.

But before delving into examining the "Big Greek Idea" in Ephesians, it may be helpful to pause, define, and illustrate the different types of Greek clauses typically found in the letter.

Pauline Independent Clauses

Independent Greek clauses are rather important in determining Paul's main thought in a given sentence. There are *three types of independent Greek clauses* found in the Greek New Testament: conjunctive, prepositional, and asyndetic. All three types of independent clauses appear in Ephesians.

The first and most common type of independent Greek clause in Ephesians is the *independent Greek conjunctive clause*. This clause is introduced by a Greek conjunction (καί, δέ, γάρ, ἀλλά, ἄρα, διό, οὖν, πλήν). Sometimes the Greek conjunction starts the independent clause. Other times it appears in a postpositive position. The independent conjunctive clause dominates Ephesians. In fact, independent conjunctive clauses appear in Ephesians *at least* sixty-eight times. The following are a few representative samples worthy of mention.

2:8a Τῇ **γὰρ** χάριτί ἐστε σεσῳσμένοι διὰ πίστεως·
2:8a **For** you are saved by grace through faith;

2:14a Αὐτὸς **γάρ** ἐστιν ἡ εἰρήνη ἡμῶν,
2:14a **For** he is our peace,

2:19a **ἄρα οὖν** οὐκέτι ἐστὲ ξένοι καὶ πάροικοι,
2:19a **So then**, you are no longer strangers and aliens

3:13a **διὸ** αἰτοῦμαι μὴ ἐγκακεῖν ἐν ταῖς θλίψεσίν μου ὑπὲρ ὑμῶν,
3:13a **Therefore**, I ask that you not be discouraged because of my suffering on your
    behalf,

4:1a Παρακαλῶ **οὖν** ὑμᾶς ἐγὼ ὁ δέσμιος ἐν κυρίῳ
4:1a **Therefore**, I, a prisoner in the Lord, urge you

⁴:²⁰ ὑμεῖς **δὲ** οὐχ οὕτως ἐμάθετε τὸν Χριστόν,
⁴:²⁰ **But** you have not learned Christ in such a manner,

⁴:³⁰ᵃ **καὶ** μὴ λυπεῖτε τὸ πνεῦμα τὸ ἅγιον τοῦ θεοῦ
⁴:³⁰ᵃ **And** do not grieve the Holy Spirit of God,

⁵:¹ γίνεσθε **οὖν** μιμηταὶ τοῦ θεοῦ, ὡς τέκνα ἀγαπητά,
⁵:¹ **Therefore** be imitators of God, as beloved children,

⁵:³³ᵃ **πλὴν** καὶ ὑμεῖς οἱ καθ' ἕνα ἕκαστος τὴν ἑαυτοῦ γυναῖκα οὕτως ἀγαπάτω
⁵:³³ᵃ **Nevertheless** each of you, love your own wife

⁶:⁴ᵃ **Καὶ** οἱ πατέρες, μὴ παροργίζετε τὰ τέκνα ὑμῶν,
⁶:⁴ᵃ **And** fathers, do not anger your children,

Naturally, these Greek conjunctive clauses are independent because they contain a subject and predicate, present a complete thought, and can stand alone. While it is not evident above, in the pages to follow all independent clauses will be placed farthest to the left of the page because they are independent. Each of the independent clauses above begins with a Greek conjunction that makes some sort of connection with a previous clause or transitions to a new thought. Also, as you can see from the samples above, conjunctions sometimes appear in the postpositive position (Eph. 2:8a, 14a; 4:1a, 20; 5:1) but not always (Eph. 2:19a; 3:13a; 4:30a; 5:33a; 6:4a).

The most frequent independent Greek conjunctive clauses in Ephesians are those introduced with καί. Of the sixty-seven conjunctive independent clauses in Ephesians, 35 percent begin with "and" (καί). Even though Paul's favored conjunction is καί, five other Greek conjunctions appear in Ephesians: ἀλλά, ἄρα οὖν, γάρ, δέ, διό, and οὖν. The following chart not only lists the Greek conjunction and where they appear in Ephesians, it identifies how the conjunction has been interpreted semantically in our interpretive English translation for Ephesians.

Conjunctions in Ephesians						
	καί	ἀλλά	δέ	γάρ	διό	ἄρα οὖν	οὖν
Ascensive The conjunction provides a point of focus "even"	5:31c						

Conjunctions in Ephesians						
	καί	ἀλλά	δέ	γάρ	διό	ἄρα οὖν	οὖν
Connective or **Coordinate** The conjunction adds an additional element to the discussion "and, also"	1:22a, 22b 2:6a, 6b, 17b 4:11, 17b, 26b, 30a 5:4a, 11a, 14d, 14e, 18a, 29c, 31b, 33a 6:17a		5:33c				
Contrastive or **Adversative** The conjunction provides an opposing thought to the idea to which is connected "but, yet"		2:19b 5:4c, 17b, 18c, 29b 6:4b	2:5b, 13 4:7, 20, 28b, 32 5:3a, 8b, 11b, 13, 32b				
Emphatic The conjunction intensifies the discussion "indeed"							
Explanatory Following verbs of emotion, the conjunction provides additional information "for"	2:8b 5:2a		4:9a	2:8a, 10a, 14a 5:9, 12, 14a, 29a			
Inferential The conjunction signals a conclusion or summary of a discussion "therefore, thus"				5:5a, 6b, 8a	2:11a 3:13a 4:8a, 25b 5:14b	2:19a	4:1a, 17a 5:1, 7, 15a 6:14a
Transitional The conjunction moves the discussion in a new direction "now"	6:4a, 9a		3:21 6:21b				

The second type of independent Greek clause in Ephesians is the *independent Greek prepositional clause*. This clause is introduced by a Greek preposition (διὰ τοῦτο, τούτου χάριν, ἀντὶ τοῦτο). There are *at least* six independent clauses in Ephesians introduced with a Greek prepositional phrase.

1:15 **Διὰ τοῦτο** … 16aοὐ παύομαι
1:15 For this reason, … 16aI do not cease

3:1 **Τούτου χάριν** ἐγὼ Παῦλος ὁ δέσμιος τοῦ Χριστοῦ Ἰησοῦ ὑπὲρ ὑμῶν τῶν ἐθνῶν
3:1 **For this reason**, I Paul, a prisoner of Christ Jesus on behalf of you, the Gentiles

3:14 **Τούτου χάριν** κάμπτω τὰ γόνατά μου πρὸς τὸν πατέρα,
3:14 **For this reason**, I bow my knees before the Father,

5:17a **διὰ τοῦτο** μὴ **γίνεσθε** ἄφρονες,
5:17a **For this reason**, do not become foolish,

5:31a **ἀντὶ τούτου** καταλείψει ἄνθρωπος τὸν πατέρα καὶ τὴν μητέρα
5:31a **For this reason**, a man shall leave his father and mother

6:13a **διὰ τοῦτο** ἀναλάβετε τὴν πανοπλίαν τοῦ θεοῦ,
6:13a **For this reason**, take up the whole armor of God

Like the independent Greek conjunctive clauses, these Greek prepositional clauses are independent because they contain a subject and predicate, present a complete thought, and can stand alone. In the pages that follow, all independent prepositional clauses will be placed farthest to the left of the page because they too are independent.

Ephesians 5:31a is part of an Old Testament quotation and 3:14 resumes Paul's argument from 3:1. This suggests that Paul predominantly uses the phrase διὰ τοῦτο in the letter of Ephesians. The significant interpretive issue that the reader faces is the referent to the prepositional phrase. Generally, in Ephesians, Paul uses the preposition inferentially, stating an implication.

The third type of independent Greek clause is the *independent Greek asyndeton clause*. This clause has neither an introductory Greek conjunction nor an opening Greek prepositional phrase. Yet it too is an independent clause with only a verb as its structural marker. It appears at least thirty-five times in Ephesians. Of these, a few are worthy of mention because they exemplify what to expect when studying Ephesians. There is but one structural marker, the verb, which is <u>underlined</u> and in **bold** print.

^{1:3a} Εὐλογητὸς [**ἔστιν**] ὁ θεὸς καὶ πατὴρ τοῦ κυρίου ἡμῶν Ἰησοῦ Χριστοῦ,
^{1:3a} Blessed [**be**] the God and Father of our Lord Jesus Christ

^{2:5c} —χάριτί **ἐστε σεσωσμένοι**—
^{2:5c} —**you are saved** by grace—

^{4:5a} [**ἔστιν**] εἷς κύριος,
^{4:5a} there [**is**] one Lord;

^{4:5b} [**ἔστιν**] μία πίστις,
^{4:5b} there [**is**] one faith;

^{4:5c} [**ἔστιν**] ἓν βάπτισμα·
^{4:5c} there [**is**] one baptism;

^{4:10a} (ὁ καταβὰς αὐτός) **ἐστιν** καὶ (ὁ ἀναβὰς) ὑπεράνω πάντων τῶν οὐρανῶν,
^{4:10a} (The very one who descended) **is** also (the one who ascended) above all of the heavens

^{5:14c} **Ἔγειρε**, (ὁ καθεύδων,)
^{5:14c} **Get up**, (sleeper,)

^{5:22a} Αἱ γυναῖκες [**ὑποτάσσεσθε**] τοῖς ἰδίοις ἀνδράσιν
^{5:22a} Wives, [**submit**] to your own husbands

^{5:25a} Οἱ ἄνδρες, **ἀγαπᾶτε** τὰς γυναῖκας,
^{5:25a} Husbands, **love** your wives,

^{6:11a} **ἐνδύσασθε** τὴν πανοπλίαν τοῦ θεοῦ
^{6:11a} **Put on** the whole armor of God

Once again, these Greek asyndeton clauses are independent clauses because they contain a subject and predicate, present a complete thought, and can stand alone. In the pages that follow, they too will be placed farthest to the left of the page because they are independent. Yet they differ from one another, making a significant rhetorical thrust.

> **Ellipsis Defined**
> An ellipsis is the omission of a word or any element of the Greek language that renders a sentence "ungrammatical," yet the missing element or word is from the context.

First, it is important to recognize that not all asyndeton clauses contain a verb. There are five occurrences of these elliptical clauses from our examples above (Eph. 1:3a; 4:5a, 5b, 5c; 5:22a). In English, we have to supply a verb, which raises the question about the nature of the clause. The clause might make a simple statement, in which case we would use an equative verb. For example, in Ephesians 4:5 Paul makes a series of assertions that require us to use the verb *is* in English: "there *is* one Lord; there *is* one faith; there *is* one baptism." In Ephesians 4:10a, Paul supplies the equative verb. On the other hand, another clause may insinuate an imperative. In Ephesians 1:3a, we might insert some form of εἰμί, but the context suggests an imperatival idea: "Blessed *be* God" or "God *should be* blessed." Similarly, in Ephesians 5:22a, the verb is of this asyndeton clause is implied from the participle in verse 21, but the context suggests that the force of the verb is imperative: "Wives, *submit* to your own husbands."

Second, the challenge with interpreting asyndeton clauses is understanding their relationship to the context. Some of these clauses are straightforward; some begin a new thought and do not require any additional link. For example, in the household code, Paul addresses various members of the family. Each section begins with an asyndeton (Eph. 5:22, 25a above, cf. 6:1, 5). He begins the body of the letter with an asyndeton (Eph. 1:3a). At times the asyndeton might simply be an aside. For example, in Ephesians 2:5c, Paul interrupts his statement about how God treats the believer to make a statement about the believer. He repeats the phrase in verse 8 but introduces it with a conjunction (γάρ). And at times, the connection is not clear. For example, in Ephesians 4:4–6 he makes a series of asyndetic statements with no connection, leaving the reader to make the connection.

Finally, since there are no other markers, we would expect to find only the verb of an asyndeton clause marked. However, in our examples above, we have three clauses with additional markers (Eph. 2:5c; 4:10a; 5:14c). Two of these involve substantival participles. In Ephesians 4:10a, Paul equates "the one who comes down" (ὁ καταβὰς αὐτός) with "the one who goes up" (ὁ ἀναβάς). Similarly in Ephesians 5:14c, Paul uses the substantival participle as a vocative: "Get up, sleeper!" We have marked the substantival participles because of their importance, but they do not merit being placed on their own line. Ephesians 2:5c merits our attention as well. The verb in the clause is periphrastic. Even though there are two verbs, they create one verbal idea: "you are saved by grace." Because they represent a single verbal idea we have placed a contiguous line under both verbs.

In summary, independent Greek clauses are rather important in determining Paul's main thought of a given sentence. There are 109 independent clauses in Ephesians. While the *independent Greek conjunctive clause* dominates Ephesians with sixty-eight occurrences, the *independent Greek asyndeton clause* appears thirty-five times. The *independent Greek prepositional* clause occurs merely six times and only in Ephesians.

The chart below identifies where the 109 independent Greek clauses appear in Ephesians.

Chapter	Conjunctive Independent Clauses	Prepositional Independent Clauses	Asyndeton Independent Clauses
1	22a, 22b	16a	1a, 2, 3a
2	5b, 6a, 6b, 8a, 8b, 10a, 11a, 13, 14a, 17b, 19a, 19b		5c, 8c, 9a
3	13a, 21	1, 14	8a
4	1a, 7, 8a, 9a, 11, 17a, 17b, 20, 25b, 26b, 28b, 30a, 32		4a, 4b, 5a, 5b, 5c, 6, 8c, 8d, 10a, 26a, 26c, 27, 28a, 29a, 31
5	1, 2a, 3a, 4a, 4c, 5a, 6b, 7, 8a, 8b, 9a, 11a, 11b, 12, 13, 14a, 14b, 14d, 14e, 15a, 17b, 18a, 18c, 29a, 29b, 29c, 31b, 31c, 32b, 33a, 33c	17a, 31a	6a, 8d, 14c, 22a, 25a, 28c, 32a
6	1b, 4a, 4b, 9a, 10a, 14a, 17a, 21b	13a	1a, 2a, 5a, 11a, 23, 24

Throughout *Ephesians: An Exegetical Guide for Preaching and Teaching*, independent Greek clauses will appear to the extreme left of the page with their verbs <u>underlined</u> and often in **bold** print. Yet just as there are different types of independent clauses, there are various types of dependent clauses in Ephesians worthy of introduction because they expand Paul's initial thoughts expressed in his independent clauses.

PAULINE DEPENDENT CLAUSES

There are *four types of dependent Greek clauses*: (1) Greek pronominal clauses are introduced by a relative pronoun (ὅς, ἥ, ὅ), relative adjective (οἷος, *such as*; ὅσος, *as much/many as*), relative adverb (ὅπου, *where*; ὅτε, *when*), or sometimes a demonstrative pronoun (οὗτος), (2) Greek conjunctive clauses are introduced by a subordinate Greek conjunction (ἵνα, ὅτι, καθώς, εἰ, ἐάν, etc.), (3) Greek participial clauses are introduced by a participle, and (4) Greek infinitival clauses are introduced by certain infinitives or infinitives with a preposition (e.g., διά, μετά, εἰς + infinitive). Regardless of its type, dependent clauses generally modify a word or possible concept in another clause.

Procedurally, *the type of dependent clause* is first identified, and then the relationship of the dependent Greek clause to words in other clauses (i.e., the *syntactical function*) is determined. The syntactical function of a Greek clause may be *adverbial, adjectival,* or *substantival.* Once the syntactical relationship of a dependent clause is determined, it is positioned in the outline for easy identification. If *adverbial,* the first word of the dependent clause is positioned under the Greek verb it modifies; if *adjectival,* the first word of the dependent clause is positioned under the Greek noun or pronoun it modifies; if *substantival,* the clause is often placed in parentheses.

> **Steps for Identifying Dependent Clauses**
> 1. Take note of the type of dependent clause it is.
> 2. Be aware of the clause's syntactical function.
> 3. Identify the verb, noun, or pronoun the clause modifies.

The first type of dependent Greek clause is the *dependent Greek pronominal clause.* There are *at least* forty-six examples of the dependent Greek pronominal clause in Ephesians. Naturally all begin with a Greek pronoun. Of these, thirty-eight relative pronouns are *adjectival.* In Ephesians, Paul uses the interrogative pronoun τίς *substantivally* eight times. In the samples below, the *adjectival* relative clause is positioned under or just above the noun or pronoun it modifies. All *substantival* relative clauses functioning as either the subject or direct object of a clause are placed in parentheses or on their own line. All relative pronouns are <u>underlined</u> and at times in **bold** print along with their respective verbs. Below are extensive examples from Ephesians 1:5–9, 18–19; and 2:4 that illustrate how Paul uses pronominal clauses in the letter.

[1:5a] **προορίσας** ἡμᾶς [5b]εἰς υἱοθεσίαν διὰ Ἰησοῦ Χριστοῦ εἰς αὐτόν, κατὰ τὴν εὐδοκίαν τοῦ θελήματος αὐτοῦ [6a]εἰς ἔπαινον δόξης τῆς χάριτος αὐτοῦ

[1:5a] <u>**while predestining**</u> us for adoption through Jesus Christ to himself according to his pleasurable will for the praise for his glorious grace,

[1:6b] <u>ἧς</u> **ἐχαρίτωσεν** ἡμᾶς ἐν (τῷ ἠγαπημένῳ).
[1:6b] <u>which</u> **he gave** to us in (the beloved).

[1:7] ἐν <u>ᾧ</u> **ἔχομεν** τὴν ἀπολύτρωσιν διὰ τοῦ αἵματος αὐτοῦ τὴν ἄφεσιν τῶν παραπτωμάτων κατὰ τὸ πλοῦτος τῆς χάριτος αὐτοῦ

[1:7] In <u>whom</u> <u>**we have**</u> the redemption through his blood the forgiveness of our trespasses according to his rich grace

[1:8] <u>ἧς</u> **ἐπερίσσευσεν** εἰς ἡμᾶς, ἐν πάσῃ σοφίᾳ καὶ φρονήσει,
[1:8] <u>which</u> **he lavished** on us in all wisdom and insight,

1:9a **γνωρίσας** ἡμῖν τὸ μυστήριον τοῦ θελήματος αὐτοῦ, κατὰ τὴν εὐδοκίαν αὐτοῦ
1:9a **by making known** to us the mystery of his will, according to his pleasure

1:9b ἣν **προέθετο** ἐν αὐτῷ 10aεἰς οἰκονομίαν τοῦ πληρώματος τῶν καιρῶν
1:9b which **he intended** in him10afor the administration of the fullness of time

1:18b **εἰς τὸ εἰδέναι** ὑμᾶς
1:18b **so that** you may **know**

1:18c τίς **ἐστιν** ἡ ἐλπὶς τῆς κλήσεως αὐτοῦ,
1:18c what **is** the hope of his calling

1:18d τίς [**ἐστιν**] ὁ πλοῦτος τῆς δόξης τῆς κληρονομίας αὐτοῦ ἐν τοῖς ἁγίοις,
1:18d what [**is**] the wealth of his glorious inheritance among the saints,

1:19 καὶ τί [**ἐστιν**] (τὸ ὑπερβάλλον μέγεθος τῆς δυνάμεως αὐτοῦ) εἰς (ἡμᾶς τοὺς πιστεύοντας) κατὰ τὴν ἐνέργειαν τοῦ κράτους τῆς ἰσχύος αὐτοῦ.
1:19 and what [**is**] (his surpassingly great power) for (us who believe) according to the working of his strong might.

2:4aὁ δὲ θεὸς πλούσιος **ὢν** ἐν ἐλέει, διὰ τὴν πολλὴν ἀγάπην αὐτοῦ
2:4a but God, **because he is** rich in mercy, because of his great love

2:4b ἣν **ἠγάπησεν** ἡμᾶς,
2:4b **with which he loved** us,

These Greek pronominal clauses are representative of what to expect in Ephesians. The pronominal clause that dominates Ephesians is the Greek relative clause (ὅς, ἥ, ὅ). They are unable to stand alone and thereby are dependent clauses. Yet they contribute grammatically to the sentence either as a subject or direct object of a clause (substantival) or as a modifier of a noun or pronoun within another clause (adjectival).

Paul predominantly uses the interrogative pronoun (τίς) substantivally. For example, in Ephesians 1:18b–19, Paul repeats the interrogative pronoun three times, each functioning as the direct object of the infinitive εἰδέναι ("know"). The substantival clauses express what Paul wants these believers to know: the hope of God's calling, the wealth of his inheritance, and his power at work within those who believe. Due to Paul's extensive sentence, we have placed each substantival clause on its own line. Each clause has its own grammatical issues. The first substantival clause is straightforward. The last two are elliptical—in English, we have to supply the verb is: "what *is*." The last clause contains two substantival participles. The first substantival participle functions as the subject of the clause. The second substantival participle functions as the object of the preposition εἰς—this power is *for* "us, who believe."

Paul predominantly uses the relative pronoun *adjectivally*. He is able to string together long sentences with the relative pronoun. For example, he uses the relative pronoun eight times in Ephesians 1:3–14, a text that makes up a single sentence. In contrast, he uses the relative pronoun only twelve times throughout the second half of the letter (Eph. 4–6), where he uses shorter sentences. Even though Ephesians 1:5–9 is part of the sentence, it provides a good insight into how Paul uses the relative pronoun. The first relative pronoun appears in verse 6b. It modifies the object of the preposition at the end of verse 6a: "grace" (χάριτος). The relative clause is aligned under the word it modifies. Even though the case of the pronoun is genitive, it functions as the direct object, but due to attraction (BDF §294.2), the case of the pronoun shifted to agree with the case of the antecedent. The relative pronoun agrees with the number (singular) and gender (feminine) with the noun that it modifies. As we will see in the examples below, this is more common in Paul's writing.

> ## The Relative Pronoun
>
> ### Regular Usage
> A relative pronoun usually agrees in number and gender with its antecedent and thereby links the noun or pronoun to the dependent relative clause to describe, clarify, or restrict its antecedent.
>
> ### Unusual Usage
> Sometimes the relative pronoun's gender does not match its antecedent because sense agreement supersedes syntactical agreement (*construction ad sensum*).
>
> Other times the case of the relative pronoun is attracted to that of its antecedent. Often referred to as "attraction" or "direct attraction."

The second relative pronoun appears in verse 7. The pronoun functions as the object of the preposition ἐν: "in whom." The antecedent of the pronoun is the substantival participle τῷ ἠγαπημένῳ from verse 6b, a reference to Christ. The pronoun retains the number (singular) and gender (masculine) from the antecedent, but unlike our first pronoun, the case is determined by its function within the relative clause.

The third relative pronoun appears in verse 8. The antecedent of the pronoun is at the end of verse 7, a repeated reference to "grace" (χάριτος). The relative clause gives the reader more information about this grace, namely that God lavishes it on the believer. The pronoun agrees with the antecedent in number (singular) and gender (feminine), but again, the case shifts. We would anticipate the case to be accusative since it functions as the direct object, but the case shifts to genitive to agree with the antecedent.

The final relative pronoun appears in verse 9b. The antecedent of the pronoun is God's "pleasure" (εὐδοκίαν). The relative clause gives a further description of God's pleasure—he intended it in Christ for his plan for the fullness of time. The pronoun agrees with the number (singular) and gender (masculine) of the antecedent, but its case is determined by its function in the clause. In this case, it is accusative since it is the direct object of the verb προέθετο ("he established").

The last relative clause in our examples above illustrates how Paul can emphasize an element with a redundant relative clause. For example, in Ephesians 2:4 he uses a relative clause to modify "love" (ἀγάπην). The pronoun agrees with the antecedent in number (singular) and gender (feminine). The pronoun is instrumental, so we would expect it to be dative, but due to attraction the case shifted to accusative, the case of the antecedent. In this example, Paul uses the cognate verb in the relative clause. He describes a love "with which he loved us." By using a verb within the same semantic family, Paul emphasizes God's love for us.

The second type of dependent Greek clause is the *dependent Greek conjunctive clause*. There are *at least* seventy-six examples of dependent Greek conjunctive clauses in Ephesians. The following are a few representative samples worthy of mention. The Greek conjunctions with their respective verbs are <u>underlined</u> and in **bold** print for easy recognition.

2:11a <u>Διὸ **μνημονεύετε**</u>
2:11a <u>Therefore, **remember**</u>

       |

    2:11b **ὅτι** ποτὲ ὑμεῖς τὰ ἔθνη ἐν σαρκί, (οἱ λεγόμενοι ἀκροβυστία)
        ὑπὸ (τῆς λεγομένης περιτομῆς) ἐν σαρκὶ χειροποιήτου,
    2:11b **that** once you—Gentiles in flesh, (the ones called "uncircumcised")
        by (the so-called "circumcised") done by hand in the flesh—

       |

    2:12a **ὅτι ἦτε** τῷ καιρῷ ἐκείνῳ χωρὶς Χριστοῦ,
    2:12a **that <u>you were</u>** at that time without the Messiah,

[εὐαγγελίσασθαι ... καὶ φωτίσαι (3:8–9)]
[to proclaim the gospel . . . and enlighten (vv. 8–9)]

       ^{3:10}**ἵνα γνωρισθῇ** νῦν ταῖς ἀρχαῖς καὶ ταῖς ἐξουσίαις ἐν τοῖς
       ἐπουρανίοις διὰ τῆς ἐκκλησίας ἡ πολυποίκιλος σοφία τοῦ
       θεοῦ, ^{11a}κατὰ πρόθεσιν τῶν αἰώνων
       ^{3:10}**so that** the multifaceted wisdom of God **might** now **be made
       known** to the rulers and authorities in the heavenly places through
       the church, ^{11a}according to his eternal purpose,

^{4:20}ὑμεῖς δὲ οὐχ οὕτως **ἐμάθετε** τὸν Χριστόν,
^{4:20}But you **have not learned** Christ in such a manner,

    ^{4:21a}εἴ γε αὐτὸν **ἠκούσατε**
    ^{4:21a}**if indeed you heard** about him

      ^{4:21b}καὶ ἐν αὐτῷ **ἐδιδάχθητε**,
      ^{4:21b}and **were taught** in him,

^{5:16a}**ἐξαγοραζόμενοι** τὸν καιρόν,
^{5:16a}**by making the most of** the opportunity,

  ^{5:16b}**ὅτι** αἱ ἡμέραι πονηραί **εἰσιν**.
  ^{5:16b}**because** the days **are** evil.

^{5:25a}Οἱ ἄνδρες, **ἀγαπᾶτε** τὰς γυναῖκας,
^{5:25a}Husbands, **love** your wives,

    ^{5:25b}**καθὼς** καὶ ὁ Χριστὸς **ἠγάπησεν** τὴν ἐκκλησίαν
    ^{5:25b}**just as** Christ **also loved** the church

    ^{5:25c}καὶ ἑαυτὸν **παρέδωκεν** ὑπὲρ αὐτῆς,
    ^{5:25c}and **gave** himself for her,

[προσευχόμενοι (v. 18a)]
[by praying (v. 18a)]

  ^{6:19b}**ἵνα** μοι **δοθῇ** λόγος ἐν ἀνοίξει τοῦ στόματός μου,
  ^{6:19b}**that** a word **may be given** to me when I speak

6:21a Ἵνα δὲ εἰδῆτε καὶ ὑμεῖς τὰ κατ᾽ ἐμέ, (τί πράσσω),
6:21a Now **that** you also **might know** about my circumstances (what I am doing),

6:21b πάντα **γνωρίσει** ὑμῖν Τυχικὸς ὁ ἀγαπητὸς ἀδελφὸς καὶ πιστὸς διάκονος ἐν κυρίῳ,
6:21b Tychicus, the beloved brother and faithful servant in the Lord, **will make known** all things to you

Like the dependent Greek pronominal clauses, these Greek conjunctive clauses are unable to stand alone and thereby are dependent clauses. Of these examples, five are clearly adverbial and two are substantival. The first word of the adverbial and adjectival conjunctive clauses is positioned either under or above the word it modifies. The substantival clauses are placed in parentheses or placed on their own line.

Even though most of the conjunctive clauses in Ephesians are adverbial, Paul uses at least fourteen conjunctive clauses substantivally. There are two examples from the above (Eph. 2:11–12; 6:19b). In Ephesians 2:11–12, the conjunction ὅτι in verse 11b and 12a function as the direct object of the verb μνημονεύετε ("remember") in verse 11a. The conjunctions introduce what Paul wants these Gentile believers to remember: that they were alienated from the people of God. Because of this, the conjunction introduces indirect discourse.

The second substantival clause is in Ephesians 6:19b. The conjunction ἵνα introduces a clause that functions as the direct object of the participle προσευχόμενοι ("praying") in verse 18. The conjunction introduces the specific requests in Paul's prayer. In verse 19, his request is that God might give him a word when he speaks. He makes a second request in verse 20b: to boldly proclaim the gospel. He regularly uses ἵνα to introduce prayer requests (cf. 1:17; 3:16a, 18a, 19b).

In Ephesians, Paul uses sixty-one adverbial conjunctive clauses in a number of different ways. The first example comes from Ephesians 3:10. Paul introduces the clause with the conjunction ἵνα. The conjunction modifies both infinitives from verses 8b and 9a. Since there is an intervening clause in verse 9b, we have repeated the infinitives to make the relationship clear. The conjunction expresses the purpose of the infinitives. Paul's ministry is to preach the gospel and enlighten people *so that* God's wisdom might be made known to the rulers and authorities in the heavenly places. The last example, Ephesians 6:21a, is a similar use of ἵνα. Paul is sending Tychicus to the Ephesians to give them a report *so that* they will know about Paul's circumstances. In this instance, the conjunctive clause precedes the independent clause. In normal circumstances, it follows the independent clause. Finally, in Ephesians 5:16, he introduces a conjunctive clause with ὅτι. The clause modifies the participle in verse 16. The conjunctive clause gives the reason why believers should redeem the time: "*because* the days are evil."

In Ephesians 4:21, the third example above, the conjunction introduces a conditional clause. In this instance, the clause is dependent on the independent clause in verse 20—the apodosis of the conditional statement. The conjunctive clauses in verse 21 are the protasis: "*if* indeed you heard about him (v. 21a) and were taught in him (v. 21b), *then* you did not learn Christ in such a manner (v. 20)." This is a first class conditional statement, which puts forward a statement of truth for the sake of an argument (W, 690–94). By framing the conditional statement this way, Paul assumes that the Ephesians have indeed learned Christ.

The final example comes from Ephesians 5:25. The conjunctive clauses in verses 25b and 25c modify the verb of the independent clause in verse 25a: Paul's command for husbands to love their wives. The conjunctions express a comparison describing how husbands should love their wives, namely in the same way Christ loved the church—by giving himself up for her.

The third type of dependent Greek clause is the *dependent Greek participial clause*. There are at least one hundred dependent Greek participial clauses in Ephesians. The most prominent dependent Greek participial clause is the adverbial participle, which modifies another verb. Paul uses fifty-six participles adverbially. There are twenty-three adjectival participles modifying other nouns and twenty-one substantival participles, which function as a noun. The following examples are worthy of mention with all participles <u>underlined</u> and in **bold** print, and at times placed in parentheses for easy grammatical identification.

2:17a καὶ <u>**ἐλθὼν**</u>
2:17a <u>and</u> **when he came**,

2:17b <u>**εὐηγγελίσατο**</u> εἰρήνην ὑμῖν τοῖς μακρὰν καὶ εἰρήνην τοῖς ἐγγύς·
2:17b <u>**he proclaimed the good news**</u> of peace to you who were far off and peace to those who were near.

3:9b τίς [<u>**ἐστιν**</u>] ἡ οἰκονομία (τοῦ μυστηρίου τοῦ <u>**ἀποκεκρυμμένου**</u>) ἀπὸ τῶν αἰώνων ἐν (τῷ θεῷ τῷ τὰ πάντα <u>**κτίσαντι**</u>),
3:9b <u>what</u> [<u>**is**</u>] the administration of (the mystery <u>**that was hidden**</u>) for ages in (God <u>**who created**</u> all things),

^{4:28a} (ὁ **κλέπτων**) μηκέτι **κλεπτέτω**,
^{4:28a} (The one who **steals**) must no longer **steal**,

^{4:28b} μᾶλλον δὲ **κοπιάτω**
^{4:28b} but rather **must do work**

^{4:28c} **ἐργαζόμενος** ταῖς ἰδίαις χερσὶν τὸ ἀγαθόν,
^{4:28c} **by producing** what is good with his own hands,

^{4:28d} ἵνα **ἔχῃ** μεταδιδόναι (τῷ χρείαν **ἔχοντι**).
^{4:28d} that **they may have** something to share with (the one who has need).

^{5:18c} ἀλλὰ **πληροῦσθε** ἐν πνεύματι,
^{5:18c} but **be filled** by the Spirit,

^{5:19a} **λαλοῦντες** ἑαυτοῖς ἐν ψαλμοῖς καὶ ὕμνοις καὶ ᾠδαῖς πνευματικαῖς,
^{5:19a} **with the result of speaking** to one another with psalms, hymns, and spiritual songs,

^{5:19b} **ᾄδοντες**
^{5:19b} **with the result of singing**

^{5:19c} καὶ **ψάλλοντες** τῇ καρδίᾳ ὑμῶν τῷ κυρίῳ,
^{5:19c} and **with the result of making music** with your heart to the Lord,

^{5:20} **εὐχαριστοῦντες** πάντοτε ὑπὲρ πάντων ἐν ὀνόματι τοῦ κυρίου ἡμῶν Ἰησοῦ Χριστοῦ τῷ θεῷ καὶ πατρί,
^{5:20} **with the result of giving thanks** always for all things in the name of our Lord Jesus Christ to the God and Father,

^{5:21} **ὑποτασσόμενοι** ἀλλήλοις ἐν φόβῳ Χριστοῦ.
^{5:21} **with the result of submitting** to one another in the fear of Christ.

^{6:14a} **στῆτε** οὖν
^{6:14a} Therefore, **stand**

^{6:14b} **περιζωσάμενοι** τὴν ὀσφὺν ὑμῶν ἐν ἀληθείᾳ,
^{6:14b} **by girding** your waist with truth,

6:14c καὶ **ἐνδυσάμενοι** τὸν θώρακα τῆς δικαιοσύνης,
6:14c and **by putting on** the breastplate of righteousness,

6:15 καὶ **ὑποδησάμενοι** τοὺς πόδας ἐν ἑτοιμασίᾳ τοῦ εὐαγγελίου
τῆς εἰρήνης,
6:15 **by binding** your feet with the preparation of the gospel of peace,

6:16a ἐν πᾶσιν **ἀναλαβόντες** τὸν θυρεὸν τῆς πίστεως,
6:16a in all things, **by taking up** the shield of faith,

These examples are representative of what to expect when translating dependent participial clauses in Ephesians. As was the case for the Greek pronominal and Greek conjunctive dependent clauses, these Greek participial clauses cannot stand alone. They are dependent.

Most of the participles in Ephesians are adverbial. There are several examples of this above. First, in Ephesians 2:17, the participle ἐλθών modifies the following verb εὐηγγελίσατο. The participle expresses a temporal element, describing when Christ preached peace: "*when* he came." Another example is in Ephesians 5:18b–20. Paul uses five participles to modify the main verb in the independent conjunctive clause: "and be filled by the Spirit." These participles most likely describe the *result* of being filled by the Spirit: speaking to one another in psalms, singing, praising the Lord, giving thanks, and submitting to one another. Finally in Ephesians 6:14–16a, Paul gives a similar string of participles that adverbially modify the verb "stand." These participles describe the *means* by which a believer stands against the evil one: "*by* girding their waist with truth, putting on the breastplate of righteousness, binding their feet with the gospel, and taking up the shield of faith." Adverbial participles are set on their own line in the clausal layout and usually in bold and underlined.

Substantival participles function as a noun in the sentence. They are placed in parentheses in order to visualize the contribution the dependent Greek participle makes to the clause. In Ephesians 4:28, Paul uses two substantival participles. First, he tells those who steal to steal no longer. The substantival participle ὁ κλέπτων ("the one who steals") functions as the subject of the imperatives "no longer steal" and "must do work." The second substantival participle τῷ χρείαν ἔχοντι ("the one who has need") functions as the indirect object of the infinitive μεταδιδόναι ("to share"). He commands these thieves to work with their hands so that they might have something to share with those who have need. The accusative χρείαν ("need") is the direct object of the substantival participle: "the one who has *need*." In the clausal outline, substantival participles are marked with parentheses marked with parentheses, but retained on the same line with the major structural marker. In contrast, the participle in verse 28c is adverbial. It modifies the imperative κοπιάτω, describing how these former thieves should work—by laboring with their hands.

Adjectival participles modify other nouns. These participles are placed in parentheses, normally with the noun that they modify, in order to visualize their contribution to the clause. A good example comes from Ephesians 3:9b, the second example above. The participles are a part of a clause describing what Paul was making known as a part of his ministry: "what is the administration of the mystery that was hidden for ages in God who created all things." The first participle modifies "mystery" (τοῦ μυστηρίου), the second participle modifies "God" (τῷ θεῷ). Both participles agree with the noun's case, number, and gender. The noun is included with the participle within the parentheses and the participle itself is underlined. Articular participles will always be substantival or adjectival; anarthrous participles will generally adverbial but can be adjectival (see, e.g., Eph. 1:21b; 4:14a; 5:27) (W, 617).

The fourth type of dependent Greek clause is the *dependent Greek infinitival clause*. There are twenty-nine dependent Greek infinitival clauses in Ephesians. Most of these infinitives are adverbial, making up seventeen instances. There are eight instances of infinitives functioning substantivally (Eph. 1:10b; 3:13b, 16b; 4:17c, 22, 23, 24; 5:12) and four instances of infinitives functioning adjectivally (Eph. 3:6b, 8b, 9a, 17a). The Greek substantival infinitives below are <u>underlined</u> and are in **bold** type, with their respective clauses placed in parentheses for easy identification.

3:8a ἐμοὶ τῷ ἐλαχιστοτέρῳ πάντων ἁγίων **ἐδόθη** ἡ χάρις αὕτη,
3:8a This grace **was given** to me, the very least of all of the saints,

    3:8b τοῖς ἔθνεσιν **εὐαγγελίσασθαι** τὸ ἀνεξιχνίαστον πλοῦτος τοῦ Χριστοῦ,
    3:8b **to proclaim the good news** of the unfathomable wealth of Christ to the Gentiles,

[ἐδιδάχθητε (v. 21b)]
[you were taught (v. 21b)]

    4:22 **ἀποθέσθαι** ὑμᾶς κατὰ τὴν προτέραν ἀναστροφὴν (τὸν παλαιὸν ἄνθρωπον τὸν φθειρόμενον) κατὰ τὰς ἐπιθυμίας τῆς ἀπάτης,
    4:22 **that you put off** (the old man who is corrupted) according to the former behavior according to the desires from deceit,

    4:23 **ἀνανεοῦσθαι** δὲ τῷ πνεύματι τοῦ νοὸς ὑμῶν,
    4:23 but **you are being renewed** in your spirit, your mind

^{4:24} καὶ **ἐνδύσασθαι** (τὸν καινὸν ἄνθρωπον τὸν κατὰ θεὸν κτισθέντα)
ἐν δικαιοσύνῃ καὶ ὁσιότητι τῆς ἀληθείας.
^{4:24} and **you put on** (the new self, created according to God's likeness) in
righteousness and holiness from truth.

^{6:11a} **ἐνδύσασθε** τὴν πανοπλίαν τοῦ θεοῦ
^{6:11a} **Put on** the whole armor of God

^{6:11b} **πρὸς τὸ δύνασθαι** ὑμᾶς ^{6:11c} **στῆναι** πρὸς τὰς μεθοδείας τοῦ
διαβόλου·
^{6:11b} **so that** you **can** ^{6:11c} **stand** against the schemes of the devil

These examples are representative of what to expect when translating dependent infinitival clauses in Ephesians. Like the other dependent clauses, Greek infinitival clauses cannot stand on their own. They have dependent relationships with other clauses.

Most of the infinitives in Ephesians are adverbial, modifying another verb. This is the case in the final example above. In Ephesians 6:11b, the infinitive δύνασθαι ("can") modifies the verb in the independent clause ἐνδύσασθε ("put on"). The infinitive expresses the purpose for putting on the whole armor of God. The second infinitive in the verse (v. 11c) is also adverbial, modifying the first infinitive. This infinitive is complementary, completing the verbal idea of the infinitive. The purpose for putting on the whole armor of God is so that the believer *can stand* against the schemes of the devil. In Ephesians, out of the seventeen adverbial infinitives, eleven are complementary.

The adjectival infinitive modifies a noun in another clause. We see a good example of this in Ephesians 3:8. In verse 8a, Paul describes his ministry as grace, which God gave to him. In verse 8b, he uses the infinitive to describe this grace, namely to proclaim the good news of Christ's unfathomable wealth to the Gentiles. Since the infinitive clause modifies a noun, it is adjectival. The infinitival clause is epexegetical, giving more definition to God's grace (W, 607). Even though we have placed the infinitival clause on a line by itself, we have visually shown that it modifies the noun χάρις ("grace").

Finally, the infinitive can function substantivally. The infinitival clause can function as a noun. In Ephesians 4:22–24, Paul gives three infinitives that function as the direct object of the verb "you were taught" (ἐδιδάχθητε) from verse 21. The infinitives express indirect discourse, giving what the Ephesian believers were taught, namely that they took off the old self (v. 22), renewed their minds (v. 23), and put on the new self (v. 24).

In summary, there are four types of dependent Greek clauses: pronominal, conjunctive, participial, and infinitival. These dependent clauses are extremely important because they provide additional information about the independent clause that helps trace Paul's flow of thought. The most frequent type of dependent Greek clause in Ephesians is the *dependent Greek participle clauses* with *at least* one hundred examples. Paul regularly uses *dependent Greek conjunctive clauses* with *at least* seventy-six examples in Ephesians. Even though it is significantly fewer, Paul still regularly uses *dependent Greek pronominal clauses* with *at least* forty-six examples in Ephesians. Finally, he uses *at least* twenty-nine *dependent Greek infinitival clauses* in the letter.

The following chart lists the types of dependent clauses in Ephesians, their syntactical function, and their semantical category is identified as we have interpreted them.

Syntactical Function	Four Types of Dependent Clauses and Verbal Usage in Ephesians

Substantival Clauses	Pronominal
	
	    Interrogative Relative Pronoun Clause: **1**:18c, 18d, 19; **3**:9b, 18c; **5**:10, 17b; **6**:21a
	
	    Conjunctive ὅτι Direct Object: **2**:11b, 12a; **3**:3a; **4**:9b; **6**:8b, 9d, 9e
	
	    ὅτι Appositional: **5**:5b
	
	    ἵνα Direct Object: **1**:17; **3**:16a, 18a, 19b; **6**:19b, 20b
	
	Participial Subject: **4**:10a, 28a; **5**:28c
	
	    Predicate nominative: **4**:10a
	
	    Objective (direct object, indirect object, object of the preposition): **1**:1b, 6b, 11b, 21b, 23; **3**:20a; **4**:28d; **5**:12; **6**: 24
	
	    Appositional: **1**:3b, 12, 19; **2**:11b, 13, 14b (2x)
	
	    Vocative: **5**:14c
	
	Infinitive Direct Objects: **3**:13b, 16b; **4**:17c, 22, 23, 24; **5**:12
	
	    Appositional: **1**:10b

Syntactical Function	Four Types of Dependent Clauses and Verbal Usage in Ephesians
Adjectival Clauses	Pronominal Relative Pronoun Clause: **1**:6b, 7, 8, 9b, 11a, 13a, 13b, 14, 20a; **2**:2, 3a, 3c, 4b, 10c, 21b, 22; **3**:4, 5a, 7, 11b, 12, 15, 20b, 20c; **4**:1c, 15c, 16, 30b; **5**:4b, 18b; **6**:16b, 17b, 20a, 22a Indefinite Relative Pronoun Clause: **1**:23; **3**:13c; **4**:19b; **6**:2b Conjunctive: None Participial Attributive: **1**:19, 21b; **2**:2, 7 (2x), 11b; **3**:2, 7, 9b (2x), 19a, 20c; **4**:14a (2x), 16 (2x), 18b, 22, 24; **5**:13, 14a, 27; **6**:16b Infinitive Epexegetical: **3**:6, 8b, 9a, 17a
Adverbial Clauses	Pronominal: None Conjunctive ὅτι + Indicative Mood Clauses: **2**:18; **4**:25c; **5**:16b, 23a, 30; **6**:12 ἵνα + Subjunctive Mood Clauses: **2**:7, 9b, 10d, 15b, 16a; **3**:10; **4**:10b, 14a, 15b, 28d, 29c; **5**:26a, 27; **6**:3a, 3b, 13b, 21a, 22b, 22c οὕτως, πῶς; καθώς; ὡς: **1**:4a; **2**:3d; **3**:3b, 5b; **4**:4c, 17d, 21c, 32c; **5**:2b, 2c, 3b, 8c, 15b, 15c, 15d, 22b, 23b, 24a, 24b, 25b, 25c, 28a, 28b, 29d, 33b; **6**:5b, 6b, 6c, 7b, 20c εἴ (first class condition): **3**:2; **4**:21a, 21b, 29b ἐάν (third class condition): **6**:8c εἰ μή: **4**:9b μέχρι (temporal): **4**:13 Participial Temporal: **1**:5a, 13a, 13b, 15, 16b; **2**:17a; **3**:4; **4**:8b; **6**:13d Causal: **1**:11b, 18a; **2**:4a, 10b, 20a; **3**:17b, 17c; **4**:19a, 25a; **6**:8a, 9c Means: **1**:9a, 20b, 20c; **2**:15a, 16b, 21a; **4**:2b, 3a, 15a, 28c, 32b; **5**:10, 16a, 26b; **6**:14b, 14c, 15, 16a, 18a, 18b Manner: **2**:3b, 12b, 12d; **4**:18a, 18b; **6**:6d, 7a, 9b Concessive: **2**:1, 5a Result: **2**:15c; **5**:19a, 19b, 19c, 20, 21 Genitive Absolute: **2**:20b Infinitive Purpose: **1**:4b, 12, 18b; **4**:28d; **6**:11b Result: **6**:19c Complementary: **3**:4, 18b, 19a, 20a; **4**:1b, 3b; **5**:28a; **6**:11c, 13c, 13e, 20d

Paul's Style and Vocabulary in Ephesians

Every author of the Greek New Testament has a writing style that exhibits features readily repeated or perhaps even unique to their letters. Speaking very simplistically, the author of Hebrews likes chiastic structures, Peter somewhat idiomatically employs Greek imperatival participles, Jude favors the use of adjectival Greek participles, and the adverbial Greek participle abounds in Paul. The authors of Hebrews, Peter, and Jude often appeal to the Old Testament either by direct quotation or allusion. The authors of Hebrews, Peter, and Jude are at times difficult to read due to their complex writing styles. Although there are other stylistic issues that could be listed for each of these authors, the point to be made here is that Paul also exhibits several stylistic features in Ephesians worth highlighting.

For example, several commentators have noted Paul's verbosity within the letter (Turner[2], 83). In fact, some of the longest sentences in the Greek New Testament are found in Ephesians. A number of things in Paul's writing style leads to this wordiness. He tends to create genitive strings and amass prepositional phrases creating lengthy clauses. On occasion he seems to move away from his main point, creating a digression. The focus of this section is to look at some of the features that are peculiar to Ephesians.

Paul's Style in Ephesians

The first stylistic element that stands out when reading Ephesians is the length of the sentences. The first sentence in the body of the letter (Eph. 1:3–14) is the longest in the Greek New Testament, spanning 202 words. In fact there are eight lengthy sentences throughout the letter:

1:3–14	202 words
1:15–23	169 words
2:1–7	124 words
3:2–13	189 words
3:14–19	126 words
4:1–6	71 words
4:11–16	125 words
6:14–20	113 words[4]

These eight sentences alone make up 46 percent of the letter. Most of these sentences come from the first half of the book. These long sentences account for the dearth of independent clauses, particularly in the first half of the book. There are only twenty-six independent clauses in Ephesians 1–3, compared to eighty-three

---

4. These totals come from Hoehner, 153, 247, 306, 417, 472, 501, 538, 837, respectively.

in Ephesians 4–6, giving a total of 109 independent clauses. These results are stark when we compare this to another book, such as 1 John, which is a little shorter than Ephesians. First John uses *at least* 179 independent clauses (Bateman 2017, 32–36).

Besides using extensive dependent clauses to extend these sentences, two other features of these sentences stand out: genitive chains and prepositional phrases. Genitive chains are several genitives, usually modifying the one before it. Below is a sample of a genitive chain and the exegetical issues that they raise. The genitive chains are underlined.

> 1:6a: εἰς ἔπαινον <u>δόξης τῆς χάριτος αὐτοῦ</u>
> 1:6a: for the praise <u>for his glorious grace</u>

The difficulty with genitive chains is understanding the relationship between the genitives. In Ephesians 1:6 the genitive δόξης could be an attributive genitive: "*glorious* praise." Another option is that it could function as an objective genitive—the reason for our praise. In this case, the genitive χάριτος would be attributive: "for the praise of his *gracious glory*." Finally, the δόξης could be attributive and χάριτος could be objective: "for the praise of his *glorious grace*." While teasing out the semantics of the genitive might seem tedious, there is exegetical value to determine the object of praise in Ephesians 1.

Prepositional phrases also raise similar types of questions. Understanding what each prepositional phrase modifies is essential to understand Paul's argument. Throughout the letter, Paul modifies a clause with several prepositional phrases. For example, in Ephesians 1:3–14 Paul uses thirty-five prepositions. Two examples highlight the issues.

One example comes from Ephesians 1:4. The prepositional phrase at the end of verse 4, "in love" (ἐν ἀγάπη) could modify either the participle in verse 5, "predestining" (προορίσας), describing how God predestined us. If this is the case, then this most likely refers to God's love for the believer. Most English translations render the phrase this way (cf. ESV, NIV, HCSB, RSV, NRSV). On the other hand, the prepositional phrase could modify the previous clause: "he chose us to be holy and blameless *in love*." this suggests that Paul is referring to the believer's love (see Syntactical Nugget at 1:4b).

Our second example comes from Ephesians 4:12, which contains three prepositional phrases that modify the verb in verse 11 ἔδωκεν ("appointed"). God appointed these Christian leaders "*to* equip the saints *for* the work of service." If the prepositions are parallel to one another, then the grammar suggests that Paul intends for these Christian leaders to both equip the saints and do the work of service. On the other hand, if the second prepositional phrase modifies the first, then Paul intends these leaders to equip the saints so that the saints can do the work of the ministry—no small difference in meaning. The phrases could be outlined in the following ways (see Syntactical Nugget at 4:11).

v. 11: καὶ αὐτὸς <u>ἔδωκεν</u> ...
  <u>πρὸς</u> τὸν καταρτισμὸν τῶν ἁγίων
  <u>εἰς</u> ἔργον διακονίας,
  <u>εἰς</u> οἰκοδομὴν τοῦ σώματος τοῦ Χριστοῦ

v. 11: "and he <u>gave</u> ..."
  "<u>for</u> the equipping of the saints"
  "<u>for</u> the work of ministry"
  "<u>in</u> the building up of the body of Christ"

v. 11: καὶ αὐτὸς ἔδωκεν ...
  <u>πρὸς</u> τὸν καταρτισμὸν τῶν ἁγίων
   <u>εἰς</u> ἔργον διακονίας,
    <u>εἰς</u> οἰκοδομὴν τοῦ σώματος τοῦ Χριστοῦ

v. 11: "and he <u>gave</u> ..."
  "<u>for</u> the equipping of the saints"
   "<u>for</u> the work of ministry"
    "<u>in</u> the building up of the body of Christ"

Both genitive chains and prepositional phrases are important to Paul's argument. However, they are not structural markers. In the clausal layout, you will find genitive chains and prepositional phrases on the same line as the structural marker that it modifies. The examples above show the complexity and exegetical options that these phrases present. More discussion is given to these and other phrases in the syntactical explanation.

Another stylistic feature that lends itself to Paul's lengthy sentences in Ephesians is digression. At times in the letter, it appears that Paul moves away from his main point to either change his subject or add something beyond the topic of speech (Bullinger, 906). Modern readers may conclude that Paul is absentminded, but the letter would have been carefully crafted. Paul uses the digression for rhetorical effect. We find digression in two texts. The first example is in Ephesians 2:1–7. The subject of the sentence, ὁ θεός ("God"), appears in verse 4. The sentence is complex with three verbs: συνεζωοποίησεν, συνήγειρεν, συνεκάθισεν. God "made us alive" "raised," and "seated us" with Christ. The verbs appear toward the end of the sentence (vv. 5b–6). Paul begins the sentence by addressing the readers: "And even though you were dead in your trespasses and sins." But he goes into a long description of their former life as unbelievers and God's mercy

(vv. 1–4). He picks up his original thread in verse 5 by repeating the phrase but he changes the pronoun: "And even though we were dead in our trespasses." The repetition suggests that verses 1–4 create a digression. Another digression appears in Ephesians 3. In verse 1, Paul begins his prayer that concludes the first half of the book with the phrase: "For this reason, I, Paul, a prisoner of Christ Jesus on behalf of you, the Gentiles." However, in verse 2 he begins a long discussion about the gospel ministry that God gave him. Finally, in verse 14 he returns to the benedictory prayer that ends the chapter (3:14–21).

Within the context of these lengthy sentences, Paul's short pithy sentences have a rhetorical effect. Both elliptical and asyndetic clauses have additional punch. For example, after one of his lengthy sentences (Eph. 2:1–7), Paul gives four short sentences (Eph. 2:8–9). The first sentence is an independent conjunctive clause summarizing God's salvation described in verses 1–7. The next three sentences are elliptical, emphasizing that this salvation is a gift from God. The third and fourth sentences are asyndetons creating a contrast.

2:8a Τῇ γὰρ χάριτί **ἐστε σεσωσμένοι** διὰ πίστεως·
2:8a For **you are saved** by grace through faith;

2:8b καὶ τοῦτο [**ἐστίν**] οὐκ ἐξ ὑμῶν·
2:8b and this [**is**] not from yourselves,

2:8c θεοῦ τὸ δῶρον· [**ἐστίν**]
2:8c it [**is**] a gift from God;

2:9a οὐκ ἐξ ἔργων [**ἐστίν**],
2:9a it [**is**] not from works,

2:9b **ἵνα** μή τις **καυχήσηται**.
2:9b **so that** no one **can boast**.

One more final stylistic element to point out is the Hebraic influence on Paul. Turner notes that perhaps "some of the clearest Semitisms occur in this epistle" (Turner[2], 84). This fact is hardly surprising since Paul himself was Jewish; nonetheless, it is worth highlighting some of these peculiar idioms within Ephesians. The first example is that Paul uses an attributive genitive with υἱός or τέκνα to refer to a group of people associated with a specific quality (Moule, 174). For example, in Ephesians 2:2–3, Paul refers to unbelievers as "sons of disobedience" (τοῖς υἱοῖς τῆς ἀπειθείας) and "children of wrath by nature" (τέκνα φύσει ὀργῆς). The first phrase insinuates that disobedience characterizes these people; the second phrase suggests that they are destined for wrath. In Ephesians 5:6, he states that God's wrath will come upon these "sons of disobedience" and contrasts them with believers, whom he calls "children of light" (Eph. 5:8). Other attributive genitives such as "the promised Holy Spirit" (τῷ πνεύματι τῆς ἐπαγγελίας τῷ ἁγίῳ) indicate a Semitic influence as well (W, 86–88).

Second, Paul makes indirect, or redundant statements. On two occasions he uses circumlocution with mouth to refer to speech (Eph. 4:29; 6:19) (Turner[2], 84). There is possibly a Semitic idiom behind his use of the redundant relative pronoun. In Ephesians 2:4, he refers to God's great love "with which he loves us." Again in Ephesians 4:1, he encourages believers to walk according to the call "by which you were called." By using a cognate verb in a relative clause to modify a word, Paul places emphasis on the element.

Finally, Paul's use of πᾶς ... μή to mean "no one," instead of οὐδείς, reflects a Hebrew idiom. For example, in Ephesians 4:29 he writes: πᾶς λόγος σαπρὸς ἐκ τοῦ στόματος ὑμῶν μὴ ἐκπορευέσθω. Instead of "all words," we might translate the phrase: "do not let any unwholesome words come out of your mouth." We find a similar construction in Ephesians 5:5. Instead of inserting the negative first, we have πᾶς: πᾶς πόρνος ἢ ἀκάθαρτος ἢ πλεονέκτης ... οὐκ ἔχει κληρονομίαν. Literally, the phrase means that "*all* immoral, unclean, or greedy person has no inheritance," but it might be best rendered: "*no* immoral, unclean, or greedy person has an inheritance." The construction emphasizes each member of a particular class (Hoehner, 660).

The Vocabulary of Ephesians

There are some words in the letter of Ephesians that are unique. They do not appear elsewhere in the New Testament. The following chart identifies forty *hapax legomena* in the book of Ephesians. The following list was composed with the help of Burer and Miller's *A New Reader's Lexicon of the Greek New Testament* (2008, 362–71) and Sakae Kubo's *A Reader's Greek-English Lexicon of the New Testament* (1975, 181–87).

Hapax Legomena in Ephesians				
Verse	*Hapax Legomenon*	English Translations	Lexical Form	Lexical Meaning
1:11	ἐκληρώθημεν	"we have obtained an inheritance" (ESV, NRSV, NASB, NKJV, KJV; cf. CSB, HCSB, NLT) "we were chosen" (NIV; cf. RSV)	κληρόω	"obtain by lot" BDAG, s.v. 2, p. 549

Hapax Legomena in Ephesians				
Verse	*Hapax Legomenon*	English Translations	Lexical Form	Lexical Meaning
1:12	προηλπικότας	"the first to hope" (ESV, GNB, NASB) "the first to set our hope" (NRSV, NET) "the first to put our hope" (NIV) "first trusted" (KJV, NKJV) "first hoped" (RSV) "already put our hope" (HCSB)	προελπίζω	"to hope before" or "be the first to hope" BDAG, s.v., p. 868
1:19	μέγεθος	"greatness" (ESV, CSB, HSCB, NKJV, KJV, NET, NASB, NRSV, RSV, NLT) "great" (NIV)	μέγεθος	"greatness" BDAG, s.v. 2, p. 624
2:12	ἄθεοι	"without God" (ESV, RSV, NRSV, NIV, NET, CSB, HCSB, NASB, NKJV, KJV, CJB)	ἄθεος	"without God" BDAG, s.v. 1, p. 24
2:14	μεσότοιχον	"middle wall" (NET, KJV, NKJV) "dividing wall" (ESV, LEB, NRSV, RSV, CSB, HCSB) "barrier" (NIV, NASB) "wall" (NLT)	μεσότοιχον	"dividing wall" BDAG, s.v., p. 635
2:19	συμπολῖται	"fellow citizens" (ESV, RSV, NIV, NET, CSB, HCSB, NASB, NKJV, KJV) "citizens" (NRSV) "citizens along with" (NLT)	συμπολίτης	"fellow-citizen" or "compatriot" BDAG, s.v., p. 959
2:21 4:16	συναρμολογουμένη, συναρμολογούμενον	"joined together" (ESV,RSV, NRSV, NIV, NET, NLT) "fitted together" (NASB, NKJV) "put together" (CSB, HCSB)	συναρμολογέω	"fit" or "join together" BDAG, s.v., p. 966

Hapax Legomena in Ephesians				
Verse	*Hapax Legomenon*	English Translations	Lexical Form	Lexical Meaning
2:22	συνοικοδομεῖσθε	"built together" (ESV, RSV, NRSV, NIV, NET, CSB, HCSB, NASB, NKJV, KJV) "made part of" (NLT)	συνοικοδομέω	"to build up" BDAG, s.v. 1, p. 974
3:6	σύσσωμα	"members of the same body" (ESV, RSV, NRSV, CSB, HCSB) "of the same body" (NKJV, KJV) "fellow members of the body" (NET, NASB)	σύσσωμος	"belonging to the same body" BDAG, s.v., p. 978
3:6 5:7	συμμέτοχα, συμμέτοχοι	"partakers" (ESV, RSV, NKJV, KJV) "partners" (CSB, HCSB) "sharers together" (NIV) "fellow partakers" (NET NASB)	συμμέτοχος	"sharing with" BDAG, s.v., p. 958
3:10	πολυποίκιλος	"manifold" (ESV, RSV, NIV, NASB, NKJV, KJV) "multifaceted" (NET, CSB, HCSB) "in its rich variety" (NRSV, NLT)	πολυποίκιλος	"(very) many-sided" BDAG, s.v., p. 847
3:18	ἐξισχύσητε	"have the power" (NIV, RSV, NRSV, NLT) "have the strength" (ESV) "be able" (CSB, HCSB, NASB, NKJV, KJV, NET)	ἐξισχύω	"to be able," "to be strong enough," or "be in a position" BDAG, s.v., p. 350
4:3 4:13	ἑνότητα	"unity" (ESV, RSV, NRSV, NIV, NET, CSB, HCSB, NASB, NKJV, KJV) "united in" (NLT)	ἑνότης	"unity" BDAG, s.v., p. 338

Hapax Legomena in Ephesians				
Verse	*Hapax Legomenon*	English Translations	Lexical Form	Lexical Meaning
4:8	ἠχμαλώτευσεν	"he led a host of captives" (ESV, RSV, NLT; cf. NASB) "he took many captives" (NIV) "he captured captives" (NET) "he made captivity itself a captive" (NRSV; cf. NKJV, KJV) "he took the captives captive" (CSB, HCSB)	αἰχμαλωτεύω	"to capture" or "take captive" BDAG, s.v., p. 31
4:9	κατώτερα	"lower" (ESV, RSV, NRSV, NIV, NET, CSB, HCSB, NASB, NKJV, KJV) "lowly" (NLT)	κατώτερος	"lower" BDAG, s.v., p. 535
4:12	καταρτισμόν	"equip" (ESV, RSV, NRSV, NIV, NET) "equipping" (CSB, NASB, NKJV) "training" (HCSB) "perfecting" (KJV)	καταρτισμός	"equipment" or "equipping" BDAG, s.v., p. 526
4:14	κλυδωνιζόμενοι	"tossed to and fro" (RSV, NRSV, NKJV, KJV) "tossed to and fro by waves" (ESV) "tossed back and forth by the waves" (NIV, NET) "tossed by the waves" (CSB, HCSB) "tossed here and there by waves" (NASB) "tossed" (NLT)	κλυδωνίζομαι	"to be tossed here and there by waves" BDAG, s.v., p. 550
4:14	κυβείᾳ	"sleight" (KJV) "cunning" (ESV, CSB, HCSB, NIV, RSV) "trickery" (NET, NASB, NRSV, NKJV)	κυβεία	"craftiness" or "trickery" BDAG, s.v., p. 573

Hapax Legomena in Ephesians				
Verse	*Hapax Legomenon*	English Translations	Lexical Form	Lexical Meaning
4:14 6:11	μεθοδείαν, μεθοδείας	"schemes" (ESV, NET) "scheming" (NASB, NIV, NRSV) "techniques" (CSB, HCSB) "wiles" (RSV) "plotting" (NKJV)	μεθοδεία	"scheming" or "craftiness" BDAG, s.v., p. 625
4:19	ἀπηλγηκότες	"callous" (ESV, RSV, NET, CSB, HCSB) "lost all sensitivity" (NIV, NRSV) "past feeling" (NKJV, KJV) "have no sense of shame" (NLT)	ἀπαλγέω	"to become callous," "dead to feeling," or "be despondent" BDAG, s.v., p. 96
4:23	ἀνανεοῦσθαι	"renewed" (ESV, RSV, NRSV, NET, CSB, HCSB, NASB, KJV, NKJV, NLT) "made new" (NIV)	ἀνανεόω	"to renew" BDAG, s.v. 1, p. 68
4:26	ἐπιδυέτω	"go down" (ESV, RSV, NRSV, NIV, NET, CSB, HCSB, NASB, NKJV, KJV, NLT)	ἐπιδύω	"to sink down" or "to set (upon)" BDAG, s.v., p. 371
4:26	παροργισμῷ	"anger" (ESV, RSV, NRSV, NET, CSB, HCSB, NASB) "wrath" (NKJV, KJV) "angry" (NIV, NLT)	παροργισμός	"angry mood" or "anger" BDAG, s.v., p. 780
5:4	αἰσχρότης	"filthiness" (ESV, RSV, NASB, NKJV, KJV) "obscene" (NRSV, CSB, NLT) "obscenity" (NIV) "vulgar speech" (NET)	αἰσχρότης	"shamefulness" or "obscenity" BDAG, s.v., p. 29
5:4	μωρολογία	"foolish talk" (ESV, NIV, NET, NLT; cf. CSB, HCSB, NKJV, KJV) "silly talk" (RSV, NRSV, NASB)	μωρολογία	"foolish talk" or "silly talk" BDAG, s.v., p. 663

Hapax Legomena in Ephesians				
Verse	*Hapax Legomenon*	English Translations	Lexical Form	Lexical Meaning
5:4	εὐτραπελία	"crude joking" (ESV, CSB, HCSB) "coarse joking" (NIV; cf. NLT) "coarse jesting" (NET, NASB, NKJV; cf. KJV) "levity" (RSV)	εὐτραπελία	"course jesting" or "risqué wit" BDAG, s.v. xx, p. 414
5:12	κρυφῇ	"in secret" (ESV, RSV, NIV, NET, CSB, HCSB, NASB, NKJV, KJV, NLT) "secretly" (NRSV)	κρυφῇ	"in secret" BDAG, s.v., p. 572
5:14	ἐπιφαύσει	"will shine" (ESV, NRSV, NIV, NET, CSB, HCSB, NASB) "will give light" (RSV, NKJV, KJV, NLT)	ἐπιφαύσκω	"to arise," "appear," or "shine" BDAG, s.v., p. 386
5:15	ἄσοφοι	"fools" (NKJV, KJV, NLT) "unwise" (ESV, NIV, NET) "unwise people" (NRSV, HCSB, CSB) "unwise men" (RSV, NASB)	ἄσοφος	"unwise" or "foolish" BDAG, s.v., p. 144
5:27	ῥυτίδα	"wrinkle" (ESV, RSV, NRSV, NIV, NET, CSB, HCSB, NASB, NKJV, KJV, NLT)	ῥυτίς	"a wrinkle" BDAG, s.v., p. 908
5:29 6:4	ἐκτρέφει, ἐκτρέφετε	"nourishes" (5:29; ESV, RSV, NRSV, NASB, NKJV, KJV) "feeds" (5:29; NET, NLT; cf. NIV) "provides" (5:29; CSB, HCSB) "bring up" (6:4)	ἐκτρέφω	"to nourish," "to rear," or "bring up" BDAG, s.v., p. 311
6:3	μακροχρόνιος	"live long" (ESV, RSV, NRSV, NASB, NKJV, KJV) "long life" (NIV, CSB, HCSB, NLT) "a long time" (NET)	μακροχρόνιος	"long-lived" BDAG, s.v., p. 613

\multicolumn{5}{c}{***Hapax Legomena* in Ephesians**}				
Verse	*Hapax Legomenon*	English Translations	Lexical Form	Lexical Meaning
6:7	εὐνοίας	"a good will" (ESV, RSV, NASB, NKJV, KJV) "enthusiasm" (NRSV, NET, NLT) "good attitude" (CSB, HCSB) "wholeheartedly" (NIV)	εὔνοια	"good attitude" or "willingness" BDAG, s.v. 2, p. 409
6:12	πάλη	"struggle" (NRSV, NIV, NET, CSB, NASB) "wrestle" (ESV, NKJV, KJV) "battle" (HCSB) "contending" (RSV)	πάλη	"struggle against" BDAG, s.v., p. 752
6:12	κοσμοκράτορας	"world rulers" (NET, RSV) "world forces" (NASB) "rulers" (KJV, NKJV) "cosmic powers" (ESV, NRSV, CSB) "world powers" (HCSB) "powers of this dark world" (NIV)	κοσμοκράτωρ	"world-ruler" BDAG, s.v., p. 561
6:15	ἑτοιμασίᾳ	"preparation" (KJV, NKJV, NET, NASB) "readiness" (ESV, CJB, GNT, CSB, HCSB, NIV) "whatever will make you ready" (NRSV)	ἑτοιμασία	"readiness" or "preparation" BDAG, s.v., p. 401
6:16	θυρεόν	"shield" (ESV, RSV, NRSV, NIV, NET, CSB, HCSB, NASB, NKJV, KJV, NLT, LEB)	θυρεός	"shield" BDAG, s.v., p. 462
6:16	βέλη	"arrows" (NRSV, NIV, NET, CSB, HCSB, NASB, NLT) "darts" (ESV, RSV, NKJV, KJV)	βέλος	"arrow" BDAG, s.v., p. 174

<table>
<tr><td colspan="5">Hapax Legomena in Ephesians</td></tr>
<tr><td>Verse</td><td>Hapax Legomenon</td><td>English Translations</td><td>Lexical Form</td><td>Lexical Meaning</td></tr>
<tr><td>6:18</td><td>προσκαρτερήσει</td><td>"perseverance" (ESV, CSB, HCSB, KJV, NKJV, LEB, NET, NASB, RSV)

"always persevere" (NRSV)

"always keep on" (NIV)</td><td>προσκαρτέρησις</td><td>"perseverance" or "patience" BDAG, s.v., p. 881</td></tr>
<tr><td>6:19</td><td>ἀνοίξει</td><td>"opening" (ESV, NASB, RSV)

"when I open" (CSB, HCSB)

"when I speak" (NRSV; cf. NET)

"whenever I speak" (NIV)

"I may open" (NKJV, KJV)</td><td>ἄνοιξις</td><td>"opening" BDAG, s.v., p. 85</td></tr>
</table>

In summary, there are a number of *hapax legomena* in Ephesians that add to the unique stylistic features of the letter. The amount of variation in Paul's word choice does not exceed the unique vocabulary we find in his other letters. The statistics alone do not seem to rule out Pauline authorship of the letter (Hagner 2012, 591). Paul uses all three *independent* Greek clauses, but he uses both the independent Greek asyndeton and the independent Greek conjunctive clauses with regularity. The independent Greek prepositional clause is more exceptional. The frequency of these clauses highlight Paul's style in Ephesians. Less than 25 percent of the independent clauses occur in the first half of the book (Eph. 1–3), where we find the lengthier sentences in the book.

Paul uses a number of *dependent* clauses that make up these long sentences. While Paul uses a variety of dependent clauses, both the dependent Greek participle clauses and dependent conjunctive clauses appear with the most frequency throughout Ephesians. Besides these dependent clauses, Paul uses genitive chains and prepositional phrases to make longer sentences. Finally, he uses digression to both reinforce and reiterate points essential to the book. These lengthy sentences help to frame Paul's shorter, pithy statements. While his long sentences may add rhetorical flourish, they make the simple sentences in the book stand out.

All English translations reflect the interpretive decisions of the translator or committee. The same is true throughout this work. Keep this in mind as you use this tool to study the text of Ephesians and compare it with other translations and commentaries. Remember to think critically as you sift through the issues. Although we are confident in our conclusions, we take no offence if you differ from them. We do, however, take offence if you just accept our conclusions at face value. Our goal is for you to delve into the Greek text of Ephesians. Engage the Scripture. As a Bible student, you will get no bigger payoff than when you actively wrestle with the Greek and Hebrew text of the Bible. And remember to have fun as you pursue the language.

Ephesians

Paul wrote the letter to the Ephesians to give them an update on his situation in prison. At the end of the letter, he says that he sent Tychicus to provide an update about his current situation (Eph. 6:21–22), and yet he does not want them to lose heart concerning his present situation. Paul most likely intended the letter to be read in several churches throughout the Lycos Valley. The broad themes and omission of specific greetings suggest that he has a wider audience in mind. Regardless, the letter has a coherent message for his readers (or more likely "hearers").

It is popular to divide Ephesians into two parts: the first half (Eph. 1–3) addresses doctrinal issues, and the second half (Eph. 4–6) addresses ethical implications. It is true that Paul defines the relationship between the believers and God in the first half; the second half rests on this theological foundation. However, it might put too much weight on a dichotomy between theology and ethics. Paul looks forward to the second half of the letter, and he certainly continues to develop theological themes throughout the second part.

Perhaps the most dominant theme in the book is that God saves the believer as an act of grace, as a gift, apart from works (Eph. 2:8–9). Through this act of salvation, God shows his power to the world—the same power at work in Christ when he raised him from the dead and enthroned him in heaven. This resurrection power is available to believers through their relationship with Christ (Eph. 1:19–23; 3:20–21; 6:10–20).

From this main theme, Paul develops two more additional and integrally related themes that are essential to his argument. The first is that God created a new humanity out of two distinct and antagonistic groups of people (Eph. 2:14–16). The believers are able to partake in the promises of God due to their relationship with Christ, regardless of their ethnicity. This new humanity makes up the church. Paul uses two key metaphors to describe the church. In Ephesians 2:20–22, he describes a building, or a temple, in which the Spirit dwells. A more dominant metaphor is the church as a body, of which Christ is the head (Eph. 1:22–23; 4:15–16; 5:29–32). The metaphors imply that unity is vital to the health of the church (Eph. 4:1–6). These metaphors make two implications: the church as an organism will mature, and we are interconnected. According to Paul, we will become more like Christ and our choices and behavior affect one another.

The church plays a significant role in God's plan. In Ephesians 3:10, Paul indicates that God reveals his "multifaceted wisdom" to the rulers and authorities through the church. This complex piece of wisdom is the unification of Gentiles with Jews, a reference itself to the church. This looks forward to the second half of the book, where Paul describes how believers should conduct their lives in this world.

The second related theme is that God has secured victory through Christ. Ironically, Paul, who characterizes himself as an ambassador for God, preaches this message of victory from prison. This apparent defeat is not surprising. Despite this triumph, the church resides in a space dominated by those who have rebelled against God (Eph. 2:2). Throughout the letter, Paul refers to a number of rulers, authorities, and powers (Eph. 1:21; 3:10). In Ephesians 6:12, he describes them as openly hostile to believers (cf. Eph. 4:15). As we read the letter, it becomes clear that these powers are angelic or spiritual, cosmic forces that reside in the "heavenly places." The chief of these hostile figures is the devil (Eph. 4:27; 6:22). The implication is clear: even though God has achieved victory for the believer through Christ, we must watch how we live in this foreign world filled with enemy forces (Eph. 5:15–16).

In the second half of the letter, Paul shows how this theological reality impacts the believer. As members of a new humanity, believers have a new ethic. As a result of their new relationship with God, they should become holy, set apart from the world in which they live. Paul organizes the second half of the book around the Greek word περιπατέω ("walk"), a metaphor for how one behaves. He uses the verb six times in the second part of the letter to describe how the believer should "walk" (Eph. 4:1, 17 [2x]; 5:2, 8, 15). Believers should abstain from behavior that tears down the community: lying, stealing, slander, obscene joking, unbridled anger, sexual immorality, greed. Rather believers should characterize themselves with kindness, generosity, love, and thanksgiving, which reflect how God treated them (Eph. 5:1). This does not mean that Paul calls the church out of the world, but to live in a way that exposes the evil in the world (Eph. 5:12).

Finally, Paul ends the letter with an extensive description of the "full armor of God" (Eph. 6:10–20), which ties these themes together. He tells believers "to put on" the armor to withstand the attacks of the devil (Eph. 6:11–12, 16). The imperative "put on" alludes to the believer's initiation into the Christian community (cf. Eph. 4:24). Each piece of armor draws the reader back to the Christian faith: the belt of truth, the breastplate of righteousness, shodding their feet with the gospel of peace, the shield of faith, the helmet of salvation, and the sword of the Spirit. God has given believers the provision that they need for victory against Satan; they find it in the Christian community.

In short, the letter of Ephesians is Paul's call for this new community without ethnic distinction to live differently in a hostile world in light of the radical change that God accomplished in their lives. God himself provides the power for this new life, a power that he demonstrated through the resurrection and ascension of Christ.

Ephesians 1:1–2

Big Greek Idea: Paul identifies his credentials as an apostle through the will of God and greets the church in Ephesus by wishing them grace and peace from both the Father and the Lord Jesus Christ.

Structural Overview: Paul begins his letter with a normal three-part greeting that we find in other first-century letters (for more information on ancient letters, see O'Brien 1993b, 550–53). First, Paul identifies himself as the author and describes his apostolic office. He states that the authority of his position comes "through the will of God" (Eph. 1:1). Second, he identifies his audience, the community of believers in Ephesus. He calls them both "saints" (ἁγίοις) and "the faithful" (πιστοῖς) in Christ Jesus (Eph. 1:1). Third, he concludes the greeting with a wish for their health. Paul replaces the conventional health wish, "Rejoice!" (χαίρειν) (cf. Acts 15:23; 23:26), with two nouns: grace (χάρις) and peace (εἰρήνη). He prays that these come from both the Father and the Lord Jesus Christ (v. 2).

Outline:
>   Paul greets the believers in Ephesus (v. 1)
>   Paul wishes the believers a blessing (v. 2)

Clausal Outline for Ephesians 1:1–2

1:1a Παῦλος ἀπόστολος Χριστοῦ Ἰησοῦ διὰ θελήματος θεοῦ
1:1a Paul, an apostle of Christ Jesus by the will of God
>   1:1b (τοῖς ἁγίοις τοῖς οὖσιν ἐν Ἐφέσῳ) καὶ πιστοῖς ἐν Χριστῷ Ἰησοῦ·
>   1:1b (to the saints who are in Ephesus) and the faithful in Christ Jesus;

1:2 χάρις ὑμῖν καὶ εἰρήνη ἀπὸ θεοῦ πατρὸς ἡμῶν καὶ κυρίου Ἰησοῦ Χριστοῦ.
1:2 grace and peace to you from God our Father and the Lord Jesus Christ.

Syntax Explained for Ephesians 1:1–2

1:1a Παῦλος: The proper noun "Paul" is in the singular nominative form. This is a normal way for a letter writer to identify himself. **Syntactically**, Παῦλος is the subject of the sentence ("I, Paul, send greeting to the Ephesians"). Conventional letters do not include a verb. They follow a three-part structure (A to B, Greetings! See above **Structural Overview**). **Semantically**, Παῦλος is a nominative absolute and does not require a verb (W, 49–51). The nominative absolute regularly appears in phrases not normally construed as a sentence, such as titles, headings, or salutations.

ἀπόστολος: ἀπόστολος is a singular nominative masculine from the noun ἀπόστολος that means "apostle" (BDAG, s.v. "ἀπόστολος" 2c, p. 122). **Semantically**, ἀπόστολος is in apposition to Παῦλος and retains the same syntactical relationship to the rest of the clause: "Paul, an apostle of Christ Jesus." (W, 48–49). The title adds formality to his letter. The following genitive (Χριστοῦ Ἰησοῦ) could either be a genitive of possession ("an apostle belonging to Christ Jesus") or subjective genitive ("an apostle sent by Christ Jesus") (W, 82 n. 30).

Lexical Nugget: What does Paul mean when he calls himself an "apostle" (ἀπόστολος)? The term "apostle" (ἀπόστολος) occurs eighty times in the New Testament, thirty-four times in Paul's writings, and four times in Ephesians. The term literally means an "envoy," "delegate," or "messenger" (BDAG, s.v. "ἀπόστολος" 1, p. 122); however, New Testament writers use the term to describe a specific group who functioned as God's messengers. The basic characteristic of an apostle is having seen the risen Lord (1 Cor. 9:1). This group surely included the Twelve, but was most likely larger (cf. 1 Cor. 15:5–9). Paul himself describes his own apostleship as one "untimely born" (1 Cor. 15:8), most likely referring to his Damascus road experience (cf. Gal. 1:13–17; Acts 9:1–19; 22:1–21; 26:9–18) (Barnett 1993, 45–51). In Galatians 1–2, Paul defends his apostolic authority with the authenticity of the gospel message that he preached creating a link between the office of an apostle and the content of the gospel message (Dunn 1998, 572–73). Paul normally begins his letters by pointing to his apostolic authority (1 Cor. 1:1; 2 Cor. 1:1; Col. 1:1; 2 Tim. 1:1; cf. Rom. 1:1; Gal. 1:1). The reference serves a specific purpose in each book. In Ephesians, Paul describes the apostles as the foundation of the church, of which Jesus Christ is the cornerstone (Eph. 2:20; cf. Heb. 3:1). God reveals his good news to the world through the apostolic proclamation (Eph. 3:5). This proclamation of the gospel lies at the core of Paul's apostolic ministry (Eph. 3:8–13). Finally, it is through his apostolic ministry that the believers are equipped for the work of service (Eph. 4:11–12).

Paul states that this apostleship comes "through the will of God" (διὰ θελήματος θεοῦ). The preposition διά marks the intermediate agent (W, 433–35, specifically 434 n. 79; BDAG, s.v. "διά" 3d, pp. 224–25). He regularly uses the phrase to describe the source of his apostlicity (1 Cor. 1:1; 2 Cor. 1:1; Col. 1:1; 2 Tim. 1:1; cf. Gal. 1:1). Most English versions translate the preposition as "by the will of God" (ESV, NIV, RSV, NRSV, CSB, NASB, NKJV, KJV). The genitive θεοῦ can express possession: "God's will" (CSB, HCSB); or as a subjective genitive: an apostleship that "God wills." The following section argues that all that God has done for the believer through Christ is a part of his plan (Eph. 1:5). This includes Paul's role as an apostle.

Text-Critical Nugget: Is Paul an "apostle of Christ Jesus" or "of Jesus Christ"? A number of Alexandrian (א, A, 1175, 1739, 1881), Western (F, G), and Byzantine (𝔐, K, L) manuscripts invert Jesus's name and title: Ἰησοῦ Χριστοῦ (cf. MT; RP[2005]; THGNT). On the other hand, the earliest Alexandrian manuscripts (𝔓[46] B) and a key Western manuscript (D) follow the NA[28] reading: Χριστοῦ Ἰησοῦ. In his salutations, Paul normally refers to Jesus as Χριστοῦ Ἰησοῦ (Rom. 1:1; 1 Cor. 1:1; 2 Cor. 1:1; Col. 1:1; Phil. 1:1; 1 Tim. 1:1; 2 Tim. 1:1; Titus 1:1; Philem. 1). This suggests that the reading "Jesus Christ" (Ἰησοῦ Χριστοῦ) is harder (Hoehner, 133 n. 2). This fact along with the superior external support suggests that the original reading is "Jesus Christ" (Ἰησοῦ Χριστοῦ), though there is little difference in meaning. The structural layout follows the NA[28].

[1:1b] ἁγίοις: The Greek word ἁγίοις is a masculine dative plural adjective from the noun ἅγιος. The substantival form of the adjective means "holy ones" or "saints" (BDAG, s.v. "ἅγιος" 2dβ, p. 11). Paul regularly refers to believers this way (Eph. 1:15, 18; 3:8, 18; 4:12; 5:3; 6:18). **Syntactically**, ἁγίοις functions as a substantival adjective. The Old Testament regularly uses the term in reference to the nation of Israel (LXX Exod. 22:31; Pss. 15:3; 34:10; cf. Lev. 11:45; 19:2). By referring to believers as saints, Paul identifies Gentiles as the people of God (Arnold, 69). The NIV renders the adjective as "God's holy people" (cf. NLT). **Semantically**, ἁγίοις is a dative of recipient, which appears in verbless constructions. In this case, the dative identifies the saints in Ephesus as the recipients of the letter. This type of dative regularly occurs in salutations (W, 148–49). Holiness is an important theme for Paul in the letter. The believers are called to holiness (Eph. 1:4; 5:27; cf. 2:20). Holiness is not just a description of the state of the believer, but a process. Later in the letter, Paul describes Christ sanctifying the church by cleansing her (Eph. 5:26). Paul imagines that the believer will grow into the full stature of Christ (Eph. 4:13). On the one hand, Paul describes the believers as holy, but on the other, he directs them to live in a manner worthy of that status (see Porter 1993, 401).

οὖσιν: The Greek word οὖσιν is a masculine plural dative present active participle from the verb εἰμί that means "to be" (BDAG, s.v. "εἰμί" 3a, p. 284). Most English translations render the participle as "who are" (ESV, RSV, NRSV, NASB; BDAG, s.v. "εἰμί" 3a, p. 284). **Syntactically**, οὖσιν is an attributive participle modifying "the saints" (τοῖς ἁγίοις). **Semantically**, οὖσιν is an equative present tense, describing the believers as those who reside in Ephesus (ἐν Ἐφέσῳ).

Text-Critical Nugget: Should the prepositional phrase "in Ephesus" (ἐν Ἐφέσῳ) be included in the text? Several significant Alexandrian manuscripts have omitted the prepositional phrase ἐν Ἐφέσῳ (𝔓46, א, B, 1739). The prepositional phrase occurs in most Western (D, F, G, latt) and Byzantine

manuscripts (K, L, 𝔐). Even though the omission of the phrase is supported by the most significant manuscripts, the participle phrase (τοῖς οὖσιν)
and conjunction (καί) do not make sense without the prepositional phrase.
Without the prepositional phrase, we might translate the phrase as "to the
saints who are also faithful." Many commentators suggest that Ephesians was
an encyclical letter, a letter sent to several communities. As the letter came
to different communities in Asia Minor, around Ephesus, the reader could
add the name of the community. This would account for the omission of
the phrase in the earliest manuscripts and the addition of the phrase in later
manuscripts. The more general message of Ephesians accounts for a broader
audience than a single town. However, while the insertion may not be original, Paul most likely intended that Ephesus be a part of the larger audience.
The grammar requires a place name to be inserted, so we have included it.
Throughout the book, we will refer to the recipients as the "Ephesians." (For
more information see Metzger, 532; NET note for Eph. 1:1).

καί: The Greek word καί is a conjunction that means "and" (BDAG, s.v. "καί"
1bα, p. 494). **Syntactically**, καί introduces a dependent coordinating clause "and
the faithful in Christ Jesus" (καὶ πιστοῖς ἐν Χριστῷ Ἰησοῦ). The conjunction
joins this clause to the previous clause: "the saints who are in Ephesus" (τοῖς
ἁγίοις τοῖς οὖσιν ἐν Ἐφέσῳ), referring to the same group (W, 270–86, specifically 282). Because of this, many translations omit the conjunction ("to the
saints in Ephesus, the faithful," NET, NIV) or treat the adjective attributively ("to
the faithful saints," CSB) (Barth, 67–69). **Semantically**, since Paul is referring to
the same group of people, καί is best understood as epexegetical (Merkle, 13).

πιστοῖς: The Greek word πιστοῖς is a dative plural masculine from the adjective πιστός that means "faithful" or "trusting." In this context, the adjective
is used substantivally to refer to believers (BDAG, s.v. "πιστός" 2, p. 821).
Syntactically, πιστοῖς is parallel with ἁγίοις, giving a further description of
the believers: "the saints … and faithful." **Semantically**, like ἁγίοις, πιστοῖς
is a dative of recipient. The prepositional phrase "in Christ Jesus" (ἐν Χριστῷ
Ἰησοῦ) expresses sphere. The Ephesian believers' faith is in Christ Jesus (Hoehner, 143; Thielman, 34; Arnold, 69; cf. Col. 1:2).

Syntactical Nugget: How does the repeated preposition "in" (ἐν) relate to
the context? Paul addresses his letter to the saints in Ephesus, the faithful
in Christ Jesus:

    τοῖς ἁγίοις τοῖς οὖσιν
       ἐν Ἐφέσῳ
    καὶ πιστοῖς
       <u>ἐν</u> Χριστῷ Ἰησοῦ

> The saints who are
> > in Ephesus
> > and the faithful
> > > in Christ Jesus

The repetition of the prepositional phrase gives balance to the recipients. Both prepositions convey the idea of sphere. The first preposition provides the literal location of the believers; whereas the second preposition provides the location of their faith, which will dominate Paul's blessing in the next major section (Eph. 1:3–14). God's blessing comes to the believers because they are "in Christ" (see Theological Nugget at 1:4a).

1:2 χάρις … καὶ εἰρήνη: The Greek word χάρις is a nominative singular feminine from the noun χάρις that means "grace" or "favor" (BDAG, s.v. "χάρις" 2c, p. 1079). The Greek word εἰρήνη is a nominative singular feminine from the noun εἰρήνη that means "peace" (BDAG, s.v. "εἰρήνη" 2a, pp. 287–88). **Syntactically**, the two nouns are nominative absolutes, an independent use of the nominative in introductory material that is not a sentence (W, 49–51). It is possible that we assume the presence of the optative form of εἰμί (εἴη) (Arnold, 69). Most major translations translate the phrase without the verb: "Grace to you and peace" (ESV, RSV, NRSV, HCSB, NASB, NKJV). The KJV includes it: "Grace be to you, and peace."

Paul states that this grace and peace come "from God our Father and the Lord Jesus Christ" (ἀπὸ θεοῦ πατρὸς ἡμῶν καὶ κυρίου Ἰησοῦ Χριστοῦ). The preposition ἀπό conveys the idea of source: "from" (ESV, NIV, RSV, NRSV, CSB, NASB, NKJV; BDAG, s.v. "ἀπό" 5d, pp. 106–7). Paul concludes the letter with a similar wish for peace, love, and faith from God the Father and the Lord Jesus Christ (Eph. 6:23–24) (Lincoln, 6; Arnold, 69–71). By stating that this blessing comes from both God the Father and Jesus Christ, Paul implicitly places Jesus and God on equal footing and reflects the early Christian devotion of Jesus (Hurtado 2018, 54–55).

Theological Nugget: Why does Paul greet his readers with "grace and peace"? This is a standard greeting in Paul's letters (Rom. 1:7; 1 Cor. 1:3; 2 Cor. 1:2; Gal. 1:3; Phil. 1:2; Col. 1:2; 1 Thess. 1:1; 2 Thess. 1:2; Philem. 3; cf. 1 Tim. 1:1; 2 Tim. 1:2; Titus 1:4). The greeting is identical in Romans, 1 Corinthians, 2 Corinthians, Galatians, Ephesians, Philippians, 2 Thessalonians, and Philemon:

χάρις ὑμῖν καὶ εἰρήνη ἀπὸ θεοῦ πατρὸς ἡμῶν καὶ κυρίου Ἰησοῦ Χριστοῦ

In Colossians, he omits the reference to Christ: χάρις ὑμῖν καὶ εἰρήνη ἀπὸ θεοῦ πατρὸς ἡμῶν, but in 1 Thessalonians he omits the entire prepositional phrase: χάρις ὑμῖν καὶ εἰρήνη. Titus gives a similar greeting, but he refers to Jesus as: "Christ Jesus our savior" (χάρις καὶ εἰρήνη ἀπὸ θεοῦ πατρὸς καὶ Χριστοῦ Ἰησοῦ τοῦ σωτῆρος ἡμῶν). Finally, both 1 and 2 Timothy offer a unique greeting, but add "mercy" (ἔλεος): χάρις ἔλεος εἰρήνη ἀπὸ θεοῦ πατρὸς καὶ Χριστοῦ Ἰησοῦ τοῦ κυρίου ἡμῶν ("grace, mercy, and peace from God the Father and Christ Jesus our Lord").

Romans 1:7
1 Corinthians 1:3
2 Corinthians 1:2
Galatians 1:3   χάρις ὑμῖν καὶ εἰρήνη ἀπὸ θεοῦ πατρὸς ἡμῶν
Ephesians 1:2   καὶ κυρίου Ἰησοῦ Χριστοῦ
Philippians 1:2
Philemon 3
2 Thessalonians 1:2

Colossians 1:2   χάρις ὑμῖν καὶ εἰρήνη ἀπὸ θεοῦ πατρὸς ἡμῶν

1 Thessalonians 1:1   χάρις ὑμῖν καὶ εἰρήνη

1 Timothy 1:1   χάρις καὶ εἰρήνη ἀπὸ θεοῦ πατρὸς καὶ Χριστοῦ
2 Timothy 1:2   Ἰησοῦ τοῦ σωτῆρος ἡμῶν
Titus 1:4

Conventional letters in antiquity use the infinitive χαίρειν (cf. Acts 15:23; 23:26) (Klauck 2006, 18–19), but Paul uses the nominal form (χάρις) and adds εἰρήνη, a Greek translation of the standard Jewish greeting: "peace" ("shalom"; םולש). Paul may alter the standard greeting to allude to larger themes that appear throughout the letter. Grace is the basis of our salvation (Eph. 2:5, 8–9; cf. Rom. 3:24). Through this salvation, believers have peace with one another and with God (Eph. 2:14–15, 17; 4:3; cf. Rom. 5:1).

EPHESIANS 1:3–14

Big Greek Idea: God deserves praise because he blesses believers in Christ by choosing them for adoption, by redeeming them through the death of Christ, and by giving them the Holy Spirit, who serves as a guarantee of God's salvation in the future.

Structural Overview: Paul begins the body of Ephesians with a prayer broken into two sections (Eph. 1:3–14, 15–23). He normally begins his letters with a prayer of thanksgiving for the believers. In Ephesians, he offers a prayer of blessing to God echoing the Old Testament psalms. In the next section (Eph. 1:15–23) Paul gives his normal prayer of thanksgiving on behalf of the believers, a parallel prayer that we might find in his other books.

This psalm of praise is a single sentence—202 words total, which is characteristic of Paul's writing style in Ephesians. He begins giving praise to God because of what he has done for believers who are "in Christ." He repeats the "in Christ" formula, or some variation, eleven times throughout this section (1:3, 4, 6, 7, 9, 10 [2x], 11, 12, 13 [2x]; cf. 1:1d). The phrase underscores the relationship between the believer and Christ. He develops the significance of this relationship further in Ephesians 2.

Paul lists three blessings that God has given to the believer. Each blessing is offset by a refrain: "to the praise of his glory" (1:6, 12, 14). The repeated phrase keeps the focus of praise on God. Each blessing spotlights each member of the Trinity: the Father (vv. 3–6), the Son (vv. 7–12), and the Spirit (vv. 13–14). The first spiritual blessing is that God has predestined believers to be adopted as sons and daughters (1:3–6). This adoption leads believers to be "holy and blameless" (Eph. 1:4). The second spiritual blessing is that believers have received redemption through Christ's sacrifice (1:7–12). Christ's sacrifice is part of God's larger plan, which he develops throughout the book. The third spiritual blessing is that believers have received the Holy Spirit, who serves as a promise of God's future salvation (1:13–14).

Outline:
> God blesses the believer by choosing us before the foundation of the
>> world (vv. 3–6)
>> God chose believers to be holy and blameless (vv. 3–4)
>> God chose believers for adoption based on their relationship with
>>> Christ (vv. 5–6)
>
> God blesses the believer through redemption through the death of
>> Christ (vv. 7–12)
>> God's redemption is a part of his plan (vv. 7–10)
>> God's redemption leads to a rich inheritance (vv. 11–12)
>
> God blesses the believer by giving us the Holy Spirit as a promise for
>> future salvation (vv. 13–14)

Clausal Outline for Ephesians 1:3–14

1:3a Εὐλογητὸς [ἔστιν] ὁ θεὸς καὶ πατὴρ τοῦ κυρίου ἡμῶν Ἰησοῦ Χριστοῦ,
1:3a <u>Blessed</u> [**be**] the God and Father of our Lord Jesus Christ

    1:3b (ὁ εὐλογήσας) ἡμᾶς ἐν πάσῃ εὐλογίᾳ πνευματικῇ ἐν τοῖς
       ἐπουρανίοις ἐν Χριστῷ,
    1:3b (who blesses) us with all spiritual blessing in the heavenly places in Christ,

1:4a **καθὼς ἐξελέξατο** ἡμᾶς ἐν αὐτῷ πρὸ καταβολῆς κόσμου
1:4a **because he chose** us in him before the foundation of the world

    1:4b **εἶναι** ἡμᾶς ἁγίους καὶ ἀμώμους κατενώπιον αὐτοῦ ἐν ἀγάπῃ,
    1:4b **so that** we **should be** holy and blameless before him in love,

    1:5 **προορίσας** ἡμᾶς εἰς υἱοθεσίαν διὰ Ἰησοῦ Χριστοῦ εἰς αὐτόν,
    κατὰ τὴν εὐδοκίαν τοῦ θελήματος αὐτοῦ 1:6a εἰς ἔπαινον δόξης
    τῆς χάριτος αὐτοῦ
    1:5 **while predestining** us for adoption through Jesus Christ to himself
    according to his pleasurable will 1:6a for the praise for his glorious grace,

        1:6b **ἧς ἐχαρίτωσεν** ἡμᾶς ἐν
        (τῷ ἠγαπημένῳ).
        1:6b which **he gave** to us in
        (the beloved).

1:7 ἐν ᾧ **ἔχομεν** τὴν ἀπολύτρωσιν διὰ τοῦ αἵματος αὐτοῦ τὴν ἄφεσιν τῶν
παραπτωμάτων κατὰ τὸ πλοῦτος τῆς χάριτος αὐτοῦ
1:7 In <u>whom</u> **we have** the redemption through his blood the forgiveness of our
trespasses according to his rich grace

    1:8 ἧς **ἐπερίσσευσεν** εἰς ἡμᾶς, ἐν πάσῃ σοφίᾳ καὶ φρονήσει,
    1:8 which **he lavished** on us in all wisdom and insight,

       1:9a **γνωρίσας** ἡμῖν τὸ μυστήριον τοῦ θελήματος αὐτοῦ, κατὰ τὴν
       εὐδοκίαν αὐτοῦ
       1:9a **by making known** to us the mystery of his will, according to his
       pleasure

    1:9b ἣν **προέθετο** ἐν αὐτῷ 1:10a εἰς οἰκονομίαν τοῦ πληρώματος τῶν καιρῶν
    1:9b which **he intended** in him 1:10a for the administration of the fullness of time

[τὸ μυστήριον (v. 9a)]
[the mystery (v. 9a)]

1:10b **ἀνακεφαλαιώσασθαι** τὰ πάντα ἐν τῷ Χριστῷ τὰ ἐπὶ τοῖς
οὐρανοῖς καὶ τὰ ἐπὶ τῆς γῆς ἐν αὐτῷ.
1:10b **namely, to bring** all things **together** in Christ, the things in the heavens
and the things on the earth in him.

[ἐν τῷ Χριστῷ (v. 10b)]
[in Christ (v. 10b)]

1:11a Ἐν ᾧ καὶ **ἐκληρώθημεν**
1:11a In him **we have** also **obtained an inheritance**

1:11b **προορισθέντες** κατὰ πρόθεσιν (τοῦ τὰ πάντα
ἐνεργοῦντος) κατὰ τὴν βουλὴν τοῦ θελήματος αὐτοῦ
1:11b **because we were predestined** according to the plan of (the one
who works all things) according to the will of his desire

1:12 **εἰς τὸ εἶναι** ἡμᾶς εἰς ἔπαινον δόξης αὐτοῦ (τοὺς
προηλπικότας ἐν τῷ Χριστῷ).
1:12 **so that** we (the ones who have already hoped in Christ) **might
be** for the praise for his glory.

[ἐν τῷ Χριστῷ (v. 12)]
[in Christ (v. 12)]

1:13a ἐν ᾧ καὶ ὑμεῖς **ἀκούσαντες** τὸν λόγον τῆς ἀληθείας, τὸ
εὐαγγέλιον τῆς σωτηρίας ὑμῶν,
1:13a In him you **also, when you heard** the word of truth, the gospel
of your salvation,

1:13b ἐν ᾧ καὶ **πιστεύσαντες**
1:13b in whom also, **when you believed**

1:13c **ἐσφραγίσθητε** τῷ πνεύματι τῆς ἐπαγγελίας τῷ ἁγίῳ,
1:13c **you were sealed** with the promised Holy Spirit,

1:14 ὅ **ἐστιν** ἀρραβὼν τῆς κληρονομίας
ἡμῶν, εἰς ἀπολύτρωσιν τῆς
περιποιήσεως, εἰς ἔπαινον τῆς
δόξης αὐτοῦ.
1:14 who **is** the down payment of our inheritance, until the redemption of the
possession, for the praise of his glory.

Syntax Explained for Ephesians 1:3–14

1:3a εὐλογητός: The Greek word εὐλογητός is a masculine nominative singular adjective that means "blessed" or "praised" (BDAG, s.v. "εὐλογητός," p. 408). **Syntactically**, εὐλογητός functions as a predicate adjective modifying "God and Father" (ὁ θεὸς καὶ πατήρ). Either the imperative form of εἰμί (ἔστω; "let God be blessed"), the optative (εἴη; "may God be blessed"), or indicative (ἔστιν; "God is blessed" or εἶ; "you, God, are blessed") can be implied (Bratcher and Nida 1993, 9; Robertson, 396). **Semantically**, the phrase is a noncontingent statement. The article modifies both singular nouns (θεός and πατήρ) separated by the conjunction καί, making this an example of the Granville Sharp construction. Both nouns refer to the same person (W, 270–90). The following genitive phrase τοῦ κυρίου ἡμῶν Ἰησοῦ Χριστοῦ ("of our Lord Jesus Christ") modifies both God and Father (Hoehner, 164). The genitive τοῦ κυρίου defines the relationship between the Father and the Lord Jesus Christ (W, 83–84). The genitive ἡμῶν expresses subordination: "Lord *over* us" (W, 103–4). This formula mimics an early Christian confession: "Jesus is Lord" (Acts 2:36; Rom. 10:9; 14:9; 1 Cor. 12:3; 2 Cor. 4:5; Phil. 2:11; Hoehner, 255). Paul uses a similar construction five times throughout the letter (1:3, 17; 5:20; 6:24, 23).

Theological Nugget: What is the background for the Paul's praise song? The psalm writers use a similar phrase to praise God throughout the Psalter (Pss. 28:6 [LXX 27:6]; 31:21 [LXX 30:22]; 41:13 [LXX 40:14]; 119:12 [LXX 118:12]). Paul introduces a section of praise in 2 Corinthians 1:3 with the exact phrase: "Blessed be the God and Father of our Lord Jesus Christ" (Εὐλογητὸς ὁ θεὸς καὶ πατὴρ τοῦ κυρίου ἡμῶν Ἰησοῦ Χριστοῦ) (cf. 1 Pet. 1:3). Most commentators agree that this introduces a type of psalm known as a *berakah*, coming from the Hebrew term for praise (ברוך/*bārûch*). This entire section (vv. 3–14) is a song of praise to God for the blessing that he has given to the believer (cf. Arnold, 77–78; see Hoehner, 153–61 for the history of interpretation).

1:3b ὁ εὐλογήσας: The Greek word εὐλογήσας is a masculine nominative singular aorist active participle from the verb εὐλογέω that means "provide with benefits" (BDAG, s.v. "εὐλογέω" 3, pp. 407–8). **Syntactically**, ὁ εὐλογήσας is a substantival participle in apposition to ὁ θεός, so the participle could be translated as a relative pronoun: "God … who blesses us" (NRSV, NIV, ESV, NET). **Semantically**, εὐλογήσας is a constative aorist, emphasizing God's blessing without any attention to the beginning or end of that blessing (W, 557–58). The use of the adjective, the participle, and the noun ("*Blessed* be God … who *blesses* … with spiritual *blessing*") emphasizes God's blessing.

Syntactical Nugget: How do the repeated prepositions "in" (ἐν) relate to the context:

ὁ εὐλογήσας ἡμᾶς
  <u>ἐν</u> πάσῃ εὐλογίᾳ πνευματικῇ
  <u>ἐν</u> τοῖς ἐπουρανίοις
  <u>ἐν</u> Χριστῷ

the one who blesses us
  <u>with</u> all spiritual blessing
  <u>in</u> the heavenly places
  <u>in</u> Christ

The repetition of the preposition places a spotlight on the blessing. Some have classified the first dative as a dative of reference: "*with reference* to every spiritual blessing" (Merkle, 19; Larkin, 6); but is best understood as a dative of instrument: "*with* all spiritual blessing" (BDAG, s.v. "ἐν" 5b, pp. 328–29; ESV, RSV, NRSV, NIV, NET, CSB, HCSB, NASB, NKJV, KJV, NLT). The second two prepositional phrases are datives of sphere (W, 153–55), indicating where this blessing takes place—in the heavenly places and in Christ. The last prepositional phrase refers to the believer's relationship to Christ, who is in heaven.

1:4a καθώς: The Greek word καθώς is a conjunction that expresses cause. The conjunction could be rendered "since" or "in so far as" (BDAG, s.v. "καθώς" 3, p. 494). Some English versions translate the conjunction as "even as" (ESV, RSV) or "just as" (NRSV, NASB, NKJV). Due to the length of the sentence in Greek, some English translations begin a new sentence and translate the conjunction as "For" (NET, NIV, CSB). **Syntactically**, καθώς introduces a dependent conjunctive clause "*for* he chose us in him before the foundation of the world" (καθὼς ἐξελέξατο ἡμᾶς ἐν αὐτῷ πρὸ καταβολῆς κόσμου). The clause functions adverbially. **Semantically**, καθώς normally introduces a comparison (cf. ESV, RSV, NRSV, NASB, NKJV), but here it is best understood as introducing the cause of this spiritual blessing (Baugh, 80; cf. NET, NLT). We have received this blessing because he chose us.

ἐξελέξατο: The Greek word ἐξελέξατο is a third-person singular aorist middle (deponent) indicative from the verb ἐκλέγομαι that means "to choose" or "select" (BDAG, s.v. "ἐκλέγομαι" 2cγ, p. 305). **Syntactically**, ἐξελέξατο functions as the verb of the dependent conjunctive clause introduced by καθώς. The subject is implied from the verb: "he," referring to God. The direct object is "us" (ἡμᾶς), referring to believers. **Semantically**, ἐξελέξατο is an ingressive aorist emphasizing God's initial choice (W, 558–59). This verb is an indirect middle voice—God chooses the believer for his own interests (W, 419–21; KMP, 195). God simultaneously blesses and chooses us. This choice was made "in him" (ἐν αὐτῷ), referring to the believer's relationship with Christ, and "before the foundation of the world" (πρὸ καταβολῆς κόσμου), suggesting that this choice was always a part of God's plan.

Theological Nugget: What does the prepositional phrase "in him" (ἐν αὐτῷ) mean? Paul introduces the prepositional phrase in verse 3b. He repeats some variation of this clause eleven times throughout this section (1:3, 4, 6, 7, 9, 10 [2x], 11, 12, 13 [2x]). Paul uses some variation of the clause thirty-nine times throughout the letter (for a catalog of the variation of Paul's usage, see Hoehner, 173–74). In stark contrast, the phrase only occurs three times outside of Paul's letters (1 Pet. 3:16; 5:10, 14; Dunn 1998, 396). The preposition could express instrumentality: "we have been chosen *through* Christ." It can also express sphere, describing the union of the believer with Christ. Since the phrase occurs so often, readers have to be sensitive to the context to understand how it is used (Harris 2012, 122–23; Campbell 2012, 67–73). The emphasis here is on the believer's relationship with Christ. In Ephesians 2, Paul argues that through Christ's work on the cross, the believer has a new relationship with God (2:5–6, 14–16). Paul will describe this relationship between the community of believers and Christ as a building, of which Christ is the cornerstone (2:20–22) or as an organic body, of which Christ is the head (4:15–17). Both images make this incorporation explicit.

1:4b εἶναι: The Greek word εἶναι is a present active infinitive from the verb εἰμί that means "to be" (BDAG, s.v. "εἰμί" 2a, p. 282). **Syntactically**, εἶναι introduces a dependent adverbial infinitive clause modifying the main verb ἐξελέξατο: "He chose us for the purpose that we be holy and blameless." The accusative ἡμᾶς ("us") functions as the subject of the infinitive; "holy" and "blameless" (ἁγίους and ἀμώμους) are the objects of the infinitive (W,192–97). **Semantically**, εἶναι expresses the purpose of the main verb: "he chose us … *so that* we might be holy and blameless." The infinitive functions as a progressive present (W, 518–19). In Ephesians 5, Paul will describe the church as "holy and blameless" (Eph. 5:27; cf. Col. 1:22).

Syntactical Nugget: What is the relationship of "in love" (ἐν ἀγάπῃ) to the context? The prepositional phrase could modify the following participle "predestining" (προορίσας, v. 5). If the phrase modifies the following participle it states the cause of God's predetermination: "In love he predestined us" (NIV, ESV, NASB, HCSB, cf. RSV [v. 5]). This option suggests that Paul has God's love in mind (Arnold, 82; Best, 122–23; Baugh, 82–83). On the other hand, the prepositional phrase could modify the previous adjectives, describing the believers' response to God's choice to make them holy and blameless—love (cf. NRSV, NET, CSB, NKJV, KJV). This option suggests that Paul has human love in view. In Ephesians, Paul writes about human love more often (1:15; 4:2, 15, 16; 5:2; 6:23), but can refer to divine love (2:4; 3:17, 19). Paul predominantly uses the prepositional phrase ἐν ἀγάπῃ to refer to human love (4:2, 15, 16; 5:2; the phrase appears in 3:17 referring to divine love). Finally, in the immediate context (Eph. 1:3–14), Paul usually inserts the prepositional phrases after the element that they modify. For these reasons, the prepositional phase is best understood as modifying the previous adjectives: God chose us to be holy and blameless in love (Hoehner, 183–85; Lincoln, 17).

1:5a προορίσας: The Greek word προορίσας is a masculine nominative singular aorist active participle from the verb προορίζω that means "to predetermine" or "decide beforehand" (BDAG, s.v. "προορίζω," p. 873). Most English translations render the verb as "he predestined" (ESV, NIV, CSB, NASB, NKJV, KJV) or "he destined" (RSV, NRSV). The NLT renders the verb as "God decided in advance." Due to the length of this sentence in Greek, many English versions render the participle as an indicative, making it the main verb of a new sentence in English (RSV, NRSV, NET, CSB, HCSB, NASB, NLT). **Syntactically**, προορίσας introduces a dependent participle clause. It functions adverbially modifying "he chose us" (ἐξελέξατο, v. 4a). The direct object of the participle is "us" (ἡμᾶς). **Semantically**, προορίσας could express cause, giving the reason why he chose us: "*because* he predestined us" (Hoehner, 194). It could express means, indicating how he chose us: "*by* predestining us" (Schreiner 2001, 240). Or it could be temporal, stating when he chose us: "*when* he predestined us" (W, 624–25; Arnold, 81–82). The temporal element seems to be the focus of the phrase, but cause or means could be a secondary sense (W, 624 n. 30). The aorist is an ingressive aorist emphasizing God's decision.

Syntactical Nugget: How do the following prepositions relate to the context (vv. 5b–6a)? Paul inserts five prepositional phrases after the participle προορίσας. Even though there are no structural markers, we have set these off in the structural layout. The first prepositional phrase most likely modifies the participle, while the following phrases modify the initial preposition:

    προορίσας ἡμᾶς
      <u>εἰς</u> υἱοθεσίαν
        <u>διὰ</u> Ἰησοῦ Χριστοῦ
      <u>εἰς</u> αὐτόν
      <u>κατὰ</u> τὴν εὐδοκίαν τοῦ θελήματος αὐτοῦ
      <u>εἰς</u> ἔπαινον δόξης τῆς χάριτος αὐτοῦ

> while predestining us
>> <u>for</u> adoption
>>> <u>through</u> Jesus Christ
>>> <u>to</u> himself
>>> <u>according</u> to his pleasurable will
>>> <u>for</u> the praise of his glorious grace

The first prepositional phrase (εἰς υἱοθεσίαν) describes the purpose of God's predetermination: "*for* adoption" (BDAG, s.v. "εἰς" 4f, p. 290; cf. ESV, RSV, NIV). The second prepositional phrase (διὰ Ἰησοῦ Χριστοῦ) identifies the intermediate agent of this adoption: "*through* Jesus Christ" (W, 433–34). Through the believer's relationship with Christ, they are now in a position to be adopted. The third prepositional phrase (εἰς αὐτόν) describes purpose or interest of the adoption (BDAG, s.v. "εἰς" 4g, p. 290). The pronoun most likely refers to the Father, and could be rendered reflexively: "to himself" (Hoehner, 197–98). The fourth prepositional phrase (κατὰ τὴν εὐδοκίαν τοῦ θελήματος αὐτοῦ) describes the standard, by which this adoption occurs (BDAG, s.v. "κατά" B5aδ, pp. 512–13). The believer's adoption is according to God's will. The genitive τοῦ θελήματος could either be a genitive of source ("pleasure from his will"; Hoehner, 199), but is best rendered as an attributed genitive ("pleasurable will" or "favorable decision"; Larkin, 8; W, 89–91). In sum, the believer's adoption has a basis in our relationship with Christ for the benefit of God and according to his will.

The final prepositional phrase (εἰς ἔπαινον δόξης τῆς χάριτος αὐτοῦ) is a repeated refrain throughout the passage (vv. 6, 12, 14). It marks the conclusion of each section of Paul's blessing. In verses 12 and 14, Paul omits the genitive τῆς χάριτος. In verse 6, God's grace (χάρις) becomes the object of praise. He creates a wordplay in Greek with the following relative clause: "his glorious grace which he gave us" (δόξης τῆς χάριτος αὐτοῦ ἧς ἐχαρίτωσεν ἡμᾶς). The repetition emphasizes God's grace. The preposition εἰς expresses purpose: "*for* praise." The genitive construction δόξης τῆς χάριτος αὐτοῦ has been understood a number of different ways. First, δόξης can be an attributive genitive modifying ἔπαινον and χάριτος an objective genitive: "*glorious praise* of his *grace*" (Bruce, 1984, 258). Second, χάριτος could be construed as an attributive genitive and δόξης as the objective genitive: "*praise* of his *gracious glory*." The strength of this position is that Paul omits χάριτος from the repeated phrase, making δόξης the objective genitive in the later refrains (vv. 12, 14) (Hoehner, 202). Third, δόξης is an attributed genitive modifying χάριτος and χάριτος is the objective genitive modifying ἔπαινον: "*praise* for his *glorious grace*" (ESV, NIV, RSV, NRSV, CSB, HCSB; Arnold, 84). The third option is best because it retains the parallelism in the repeated phrase and accounts for Paul's focus on God's grace in this section (Merkle, 21).

Lexical Nugget: What does Paul mean by "adoption" (υἱοθεσία)? In the New Testament, the Greek term υἱοθεσία ("adoption") only appears in Paul's letters (Rom. 8:15, 23; 9:4; Gal. 4:5; Eph. 1:5). Through adoption, one was released from the authority of their natural father and placed under the authority of a new father. Unlike adoption in the west, in which the adoptee is an infant or young child, generally, in antiquity, adult males were adopted in order to carry on the line of the new family. In the West, adoption is focused on the adoptee; in antiquity, it was focused on the adopter. The adopted child retained all of the rights of a natural born son, specifically in terms of receiving an inheritance (Gal. 4:5–7), but they had to be worthy of the inheritance. Perhaps the most well-known adoption in the Roman world was Augustus's adoption by Julius Caesar. Since Julius Caesar was considered to be divine after his death, Augustus was considered to be the "son of god" (*divi filius*). The adoption legitimized his Roman rule. Paul's message in Ephesians is remarkable in light of this background. In Ephesians 2, he describes the believers as dead in sin, destined for wrath (2:1–3; cf. 4:17–19). The Gentile believers were estranged from God (2:11–12). Despite our significant problems, making us the most unlikely of choices, God decided to adopt us. Paul most likely had the Old Testament in mind as well. The Davidic covenant describes the Davidic heir as God's son (2 Sam. 7:12–14). While the Roman laws help illustrate the adoption process, the Old Testament provides a nice point of departure for Paul. Through their union with Christ, the believer becomes God's child (Rom. 8:16, 17, 21; Eph. 5:1). The believer's adoption comes "through Jesus Christ" (Scott 1993, 15–18; Arnold, 82).

1:6b ἧς: The Greek word ἧς is a feminine singular genitive from the relative pronoun ὅς that means "which" in this context (BDAG, s.v. "ὅς" 1dβ, p. 726). **Syntactically**, ἧς introduces a dependent adjectival relative clause "*which* he gave to us in the beloved" (ἧς ἐχαρίτωσεν ἡμᾶς ἐν τῷ ἠγαπημένῳ). The antecedent of the pronoun is "grace" (τῆς χάριτος; v. 6a). The pronoun functions as the direct object of the verb "gave us" (ἐχαρίτωσεν) and should be accusative, but due to attraction the case of the relative pronoun has shifted to genitive (BDF §294.2).

Text-Critical Nugget: Did Paul insert the preposition "in" (ἐν)? Several Western (D, F, G) and Byzantine (K, L, 𝔐) manuscripts insert the preposition ἐν and replace the genitive form of the relative pronoun with the dative: ἐν ᾗ. The Alexandrian text type stands squarely behind the textual reading (ἧς) (𝔓46, ℵ, B, 33, 81, 1175, 1739, 1881). Even though the reading with the prepositional phrase has better external support with support from both the Western and Byzantine text types, it seems more likely that a scribe would add the prepositional phrase than add the genitive pronoun.

As the direct object of the verb, we would expect to find the accusative. Due to attraction to the antecedent, Paul uses the genitive. This is consistent with Paul's style throughout the book of Ephesians, but it is grammatically harder. It makes more sense that a scribe would alter the text to make it grammatically easier rather than harder (Metzger, 532).

ἐχαρίτωσεν: The Greek word ἐχαρίτωσεν is a third-person singular aorist active indicative from the verb χαριτόω that means "to bestow favor on" or "bless" (BDAG, s.v. "χαριτόω," p. 1081). **Syntactically,** ἐχαρίτωσεν functions as the main verb of the relative clause "which *he gave* to us in the beloved" (ἧς ἐχαρίτωσεν ἡμᾶς ἐν τῷ ἠγαπημένῳ). **Semantically,** ἐχαρίτωσεν functions as an ingressive aorist: "he gave" or "bestowed" (RSV, NRSV, NET, NASB). The CSB translates it "lavished"; the NLT translates it "has poured out." The use of the verb along with the antecedent—literally: "the *grace* with which he *graced* us," emphasizes God's grace. The prepositional phrase (ἐν τῷ ἠγαπημένῳ) expresses the sphere in which this grace was given: in the beloved, referring to Jesus (see Theological Nugget at 1:4a).

τῷ ἠγαπημένῳ: The Greek word ἠγαπημένῳ is a masculine dative singular perfect passive participle from the verb ἀγαπάω that means "to cherish" or "love" (BDAG, s.v. "ἀγαπάω" 1bα, p. 5). **Syntactically,** τῷ ἠγαπημένῳ functions as the object of the preposition ἐν: "in the beloved" (ESV, RSV, NRSV, HCSB, NASB, NKJV, KJV) or "the beloved one" (CSB; cf. NIV). **Semantically,** τῷ ἠγαπημένῳ functions as an extensive perfect, referring to a previous action with ongoing results. The participle describes God's love for the son. The NET renders the participle as "his dearly loved son." Both at Jesus's baptism (Matt. 3:17; Mark 1:11; Luke 3:22) and the transfiguration (Matt. 17:3; Mark 9:7; cf. 2 Pet. 1:17), God refers to Jesus as the "beloved son." In Colossians 1:13, Paul refers to Jesus as the "son of his love," suggesting that this is an abbreviated reference to Jesus's sonship. The Apostolic Fathers use this shortened form to refer to Jesus (Barn. 3:6; 4:3, 8), suggesting that this became a common way to refer to Jesus (Hoehner, 203–4; Barth, 82).

1:7 ᾧ: The Greek word ᾧ is a masculine singular dative from the relative pronoun ὅς that means "whom" (BDAG, s.v. "ὅς" 1a, pp. 725–26). **Syntactically,** ᾧ functions as the object of the preposition ἐν. The relative pronoun introduces a dependent adjectival relative clause "in *whom* we have redemption through his blood" (ἐν ᾧ ἔχομεν τὴν ἀπολύτρωσιν διὰ τοῦ αἵματος αὐτοῦ) (cf. KJV). Many translations begin a new sentence with verse 7, and translate the relative pronoun as a personal pronoun: "In him" (ESV, NRSV, NET, NIV, NASB). The antecedent of the pronoun is "the beloved" (τῷ ἠγαπημένῳ), referring to Christ (v. 6b). **Semantically,** ἐν expresses sphere ("in Christ") (see Theological Nugget at 1:4a). Redemption comes through our relationship with Christ.

ἔχομεν: The Greek word ἔχομεν is a first-person plural present active in-dicative from the verb ἔχω that means to have an experience, or to take ad-vantage of some benefit (BDAG, s.v. "ἔχω" 7aγ, p. 420), in this case: redemp-tion. Most English versions translate this verb as "we have" (cf. ESV, NET, NIV, RSV, CSB, HCSB, NRSV, NASB, NKJV, KJV). **Syntactically**, ἔχομεν functions as the main verb of the relative clause "in whom *we have* redemption through his blood" (ἐν ᾧ ἔχομεν τὴν ἀπολύτρωσιν διὰ τοῦ αἵματος αὐτοῦ). The subject is implied by the verb: "we," referring to believers. The direct object is "redemption" (ἀπολύτρωσιν). This redemption refers to the manumis-sion of captives of slaves (BDAG, s.v. "ἀπολύτρωσις" 2a, p. 117). Implic-itly, the term has an economic connotation, which Paul will develop later in the prayer (v. 14) (Thielman, 58–60). The accusative τὴν ἄφεσιν ("the forgiveness") is in apposition to "redemption." It gives this redemption more definition. **Semantically**, ἔχομεν could either be a progressive present or extending-from-past present emphasizing a past action that continues into the present (W, 519–20). Paul predominantly uses the aorist tense through-out this section, so this present tense verb stands out, placing emphasis on the believer's current status (Merkle, 25).

Syntactical Nugget: How do the two prepositional phrases "through his blood" (διὰ τοῦ αἵματος αὐτοῦ) and "according to his rich grace" (κατὰ τὸ πλοῦτος τῆς χάριτος αὐτοῦ) relate to the context of the sentence? The first prepositional phrase "through his blood" (διὰ τοῦ αἵματος αὐτοῦ) describes the means by which we have received this re-demption (BDAG, s.v. "διά" 3a, p. 224). Paul's reference to Christ's blood is metonymy, representing his sacrificial death (cf. Eph. 2:13). The second prepositional phrase (κατὰ τὸ πλοῦτος τῆς χάριτος αὐτοῦ) expresses a standard: this redemption is "according to the riches of his grace." Both prepositional phrases modify ἔχομεν, creating a parallel with the previ-ous object and prepositional phrase. Paul inserts the phrase "the forgive-ness of trespasses" (τὴν ἄφεσιν τῶν παραπτωμάτων) in apposition to "the redemption:"

τὴν ἀπολύτρωσιν
  <u>διὰ</u> τοῦ αἵματος αὐτοῦ
τὴν ἄφεσιν τῶν παραπτωμάτων
  <u>κατὰ</u> τὸ πλοῦτος τῆς χάριτος αὐτοῦ

the redemption
  <u>through</u> his blood
the forgiveness of trespasses
  <u>according</u> to his rich grace

Theological Nugget: What does it mean to be redeemed? In verse 7, Paul shifts from God's choice of the believer to the believer's salvation. He characterizes this salvation through terms to describe the manumission of a slave. The payment for this redemption is made through Christ's death (διὰ τοῦ αἵματος αὐτοῦ) (cf. 1 Tim. 2:6; Tit. 2:14). Romans 3:21–26 makes this most explicit where Paul states that believers are justified "through the redemption that is in Jesus Christ" (Rom. 3:24). We might press the metaphor too far by asking who received this redemption? Or rather who held the believer captive? But Paul will describe the believer as under the authority of "the ruler of the air, the spirit who is now at work in the sons of disobedience" (Eph. 2:1–3). In Romans, Paul can describe the believer as having been freed from sin in order to be enslaved to God (Rom. 6:18, 22; cf. Gal. 5:1, 13; Schreiner 2001, 230–32) The Old Testament might provide a better context. The Pentateuch describes the exodus in terms of redemption (cf. Exod. 6:6; Deut. 15:15; 24:18; Arnold, 85). The concept of "forgiveness" (ἄφεσις) can also describe the liberation of slaves (BDAG, s.v. "ἄφεσις" 1, p. 155). In Luke 4:18, Jesus quotes Isaiah 61:1 to describe his ministry—"to preach the release of the captives." Even though the two phrases are in apposition, together they fill out the image. Hoehner states: "Redemption is the cause and forgiveness is the effect" (Hoehner, 208; cf. Schreiner 2001, 230–32).

1:8 ἧς: The Greek word ἧς is a feminine singular genitive from the relative pronoun ὅς that means "which" (BDAG, s.v. "ὅς" 1dβ, p. 726). **Syntactically**, ἧς introduces a dependent adjectival relative clause "*which* he lavished on us in all wisdom and insight" (ἧς ἐπερίσσευσεν εἰς ἡμᾶς, ἐν πάσῃ σοφίᾳ καὶ φρονήσει). The antecedent of the pronoun is "grace" (τῆς χάριτος; v. 7b). The pronoun functions as the direct object within the clause; it should be accusative, but due to attraction the case has shifted to genitive (BDF §294.2).

ἐπερίσσευσεν: The Greek word ἐπερίσσευσεν is a third-person singular aorist active indicative from the verb περισσεύω that means "to cause to abound" or "grant something to someone richly" (BDAG, s.v. "περισσεύω" 2a, p. 805). Most translations render the verb as "he lavished" (ESV, NET, NIV, RSV, NRSV, HCSB, NASB). The CSB translates the verb as "richly poured out." **Syntactically**, ἐπερίσσευσεν functions as the main verb of the relative clause "which *he lavished* on us in all wisdom and insight" (ἧς ἐπερίσσευσεν εἰς ἡμᾶς, ἐν πάσῃ σοφίᾳ καὶ φρονήσει). The subject is implied by the verb: "he," referring to God. **Semantically**, ἐπερίσσευσεν is rendered as a constative aorist, with no emphasis on the beginning or end of the action (W, 557–58). The tense simply reports that God lavished his grace on the believer.

Syntactical Nugget: What is the relationship of the prepositional phrase "in all wisdom and insight" (ἐν πάσῃ σοφίᾳ καὶ φρονήσει) to the context? The prepositional phrase can either modify the verb "he lavished" (ἐπερίσσευσεν) or the following participle "making known" (γνωρίσας). The first option expresses the manner in which he lavishes his grace (v. 8) (NET, NKJV; Hoehner, 212–23; Thielman, 62). The second option expresses the manner in which he makes known the mystery of his will (v. 9a) (ESV, NIV, NRSV, RSV, NASB; Arnold, 86). While both options are possible, Paul normally places the prepositional phrase after the verb that it modifies, particularly in this section (Merkle, 26). Because of this, the phrase most likely refers to God lavishing his grace on the believer (v. 8).

Lexical Nugget: What do the terms "wisdom and insight" (σοφίᾳ καὶ φρονήσει) mean? These words are virtual synonyms. Both terms refer to some type of intelligence in practical matters. Σοφία generally describes a skill (GE, s.v. "σοφία," pp. 1940–41). Φρόνησις can refer to good sense or prudence (GE, s.v. "φρόνησις," p. 2308). In Proverbs, the terms are used synonymously to describe the wise (Prov. 3:13, 19; 7:4; 8:1; 10:23; 16:16). Paul uses the terms in the same way, creating a hendiadys, a single concept created by two terms (Lincoln, 29). The following clause implies that this wisdom comes from divine revelation.

1:9a γνωρίσας: The Greek word γνωρίσας is a masculine nominative singular aorist active participle from the verb γνωρίζω that means "to make known" or "reveal" (BDAG, s.v. "γνωρίζω" 1, p. 203). Due to the length of the sentence, several translations begin a new sentence with verse 9 and insert the pronoun: "He made known" (NET, RSV, HCSB, CSB, NASB). **Syntactically**, γνωρίσας introduces a dependent participle clause. It functions adverbially modifying ἐπερίσσευσεν ("which he lavished," v. 8). The direct object of the participle is "mystery" (τὸ μυστήριον). The indirect object is "us" (ἡμῖν). **Semantically**, γνωρίσας could be understood as temporal: "*when he revealed* the mystery to us" (NET; Arnold, 86); or means: "*by revealing* the mystery to us" (Thielman, 63; Hoehner, 214). The second option gives the participle more specificity without losing the temporal element. God lavished grace on the believer by making known this mystery. The preposition κατά expresses the standard (BDAG, s.v. "κατά" B5aδ, pp. 512–13) to which he makes this mystery known: "*according* to his good pleasure."

Theological Nugget: What does Paul mean by "mystery"? Unlike modern mysteries that anyone can solve by arranging the clues, the Old Testament describes mysteries as something that only God can reveal. For example, in Daniel 2, Nebuchadnezzar demands his advisers to interpret a dream—but without telling them the dream itself. His advisers say that no one except the gods can do this (2:10–11). In the meantime, God reveals this "mystery" to

Daniel (2:18–19). When Daniel gives the king his dream and interprets it, he clarifies that this came from God "in heaven who reveals mysteries" (2:28). The story concludes with the king declaring God as the one who "reveals all hidden mysteries" (2:47). In Ephesians 1:9, Paul simply refers to the "mystery of his will." But in Ephesians 3, he specifies that this mystery is the inclusion of Gentiles as God's people as a mystery revealed to him, and that God has given him the task of proclaiming (3:6)—a mystery hidden from previous generations and now revealed "to his apostles and prophets by the Spirit" (3:5).

1:9b ἥν: The Greek word ἥν is a feminine singular accusative from the relative pronoun ὅς that means "which" in this context (BDAG, s.v. "ὅς" 1a, p. 725). **Syntactically**, ἥν introduces a dependent adjectival relative clause "*which* he established in him" (ἣν προέθετο ἐν αὐτῷ). The antecedent of the pronoun is in verse 9a: "pleasure" (τὴν εὐδοκίαν). The pronoun functions as the direct object of the verb προέθετο ("he established").

προέθετο: The Greek word προέθετο is a third-person singular aorist middle indicative from the verb προτίθημι that means "to plan," "propose," or "intend" (BDAG, s.v. "προτίθημι" 3, p. 889). Some translations render this as "set forth" (ESV, NET, RSV, NRSV). **Syntactically**, προέθετο is the main verb of the relative clause "which *he established* in him" (ἣν προέθετο ἐν αὐτῷ). The subject of the verb is implied: "he," referring to God. **Semantically**, προέθετο is an ingressive aorist that stresses the start of the action (W, 558–59). The prepositional phrase "in him" (ἐν αὐτῷ) expresses sphere. The antecedent of the pronoun is Christ (see Theological Nugget at 1:4a).

Semantical Nugget: What does the prepositional phrase "for the administration of the fullness of time" (εἰς οἰκονομίαν τοῦ πληρώματος τῶν καιρῶν) mean? The prepositional phrase modifies the verb "intended" (προέθετο). The preposition εἰς could be temporal since the following phrase has a temporal element: "God intended *at the time of the administration*" (Hoehner, 217). However, it is probably best to understand the preposition as expressing purpose: "for" (BDAG, s.v. "εἰς" 4f, p. 290). The NASB renders the preposition: "with a view to" (cf. HCSB). This decision suggests that the object of the preposition "administration" (οἰκονομίαν) is the actual management of God's plan (BDAG, s.v. "οἰκονομία" 2b, pp. 697–98). Later in Ephesians, Paul will use the word to describe his role as a manager in this plan (Eph. 3:2) or as the plan itself (Eph. 3:9). Here, Paul uses the phrase to describe God's control over the events of this age (Thielman, 64; Best, 138–39). The genitive τῶν καιρῶν is objective: "he administrates the time" (W, 116–19). The genitive τοῦ πληρώματος describes τῶν καιρῶν, referring to a point when time is completed: "the fullness of time" (BDAG, s.v. "πλήρωμα" 5, p. 830; Hoehner, 219; Best, 139; cf. Gal. 4:4).

1:10b ἀνακεφαλαιώσασθαι: The Greek word ἀνακεφαλαιώσασθαι is an aorist middle infinitive from the verb ἀνακεφαλαιόω that means "to sum up" or "recapitulate" (BDAG s.v. "ἀνακεφαλαιόω" 1, p. 65). Most translations render this verb as "to unite all things" (ESV, RSV) or "to bring together" (CSB; cf. NIV, NRSV). Some argue that the word derives from the noun κεφαλή ("head") and translate the phrase as "to head up all things" (NET; Arnold, 88–89). Hoehner argues that both definitions are in view. The immediate context describes God's plan culminating with Christ's return. At that point all things will be subjected to Christ, the head over all things (Eph. 1:22; Hoehner, 220–21). **Syntactically**, ἀνακεφαλαιώσασθαι introduces a dependent substantival infinitive clause in apposition to "the mystery" (τὸ μυστήριον, v. 9a). The infinitive gives more definition to the noun: "by making known the mystery … *namely*, to bring all things together" (W, 606–7). The object of the infinitive is "all things" (τὰ πάντα). **Semantically**, ἀνακεφαλαιώσασθαι is a consummative aorist, emphasizing the time when Christ will unite all things (W, 559–61). Paul indicates that this happens "in Christ" (ἐν τῷ Χριστῷ). He will repeat the preposition at the end of the verse (ἐν αὐτῷ) to add emphasis. Both prepositional phrases express sphere ("in Christ/him") (see Theological Nugget at 1:4a).

> **Grammatical Nugget**: How do the two prepositional phrase "in the heavenly places" and "on earth" relate to the context? The final phrase of verse 10b ("the things in the heavens and the things on the earth in him") is in apposition to τὰ πάντα, describing "all things." The article before the preposition makes these phrases substantival: "the things" (W, 236). The series could be laid out in this manner:
>
> τὰ πάντα ἐν τῷ Χριστῷ
>   τὰ ἐπὶ τοῖς οὐρανοῖς
> καί
>   τὰ ἐπὶ τῆς γῆς ἐν αὐτῷ
>
> all things in Christ
>   the things in the heavenly places
> and
>   the things on the earth in him
>
> The object of the preposition shifts from dative (οὐρανοῖς) to genitive (γῆς). When the object is dative, the preposition ἐπί means "above" (BDAG, s.v. "ἐπί" 1bα, p. 363). When the object is genitive, ἐπί means "on" (BDAG, s.v. "ἐπί" 1a, p. 363). Both phrases have the same basic thrust; the change is due to the orientation of these spaces. The repetition of the preposition emphasizes the scope of Christ's dominion—all things includes all things in heaven and on earth.

^{1:11a} ᾧ: The Greek word ᾧ is a masculine singular dative from the relative pronoun ὅς that means "whom" in this context (BDAG, s.v. "ὅς" 1, p. 725). **Syntactically**, ᾧ introduces a dependent adjectival relative clause "in *whom* we have also obtained an inheritance" (ἐν ᾧ καὶ ἐκληρώθημεν). The antecedent of the pronoun is "Christ" (Χριστῷ; v. 10b). The pronoun functions as the object of the preposition ἐν. This phrase ἐν ᾧ is repeated throughout this section (vv. 7, 13a, 13b). Due to the length of the sentence in Greek, many translations begin a new sentence at this point, translating the relative pronoun as a personal pronoun: "in him" (ESV, NIV, RSV, CSB, NKJV). The NET makes the antecedent explicit: "in Christ." **Semantically**, ἐν expresses sphere ("in whom") (see Theological Nugget at 1:4a). We have been chosen by God because of our relationship with Christ.

καί: The Greek word καί is a conjunction that means "and" (BDAG, s.v. "καί" 1b, p. 494). **Syntactically**, καί introduces a conjunctive clause: "in whom we have *also* obtained an inheritance" ('Εν ᾧ καὶ ἐκληρώθημεν). **Semantically**, καί is a connective conjunction. Several English versions omit the conjunction, but some render the conjunction as "also" (NRSV, NIV, HCSB, CSB, NABS, NKJV, KJV). The NLT renders the conjunction as "furthermore." The conjunction connects the phrase with the parallel statement in verse 7: "in whom we have the redemption" (ἐν ᾧ ἔχομεν τὴν ἀπολύτρωσιν).

ἐκληρώθημεν: The Greek word ἐκληρώθημεν is a first-person plural aorist passive indicative from the verb κληρόω that means "to obtain" or "appoint" (BDAG, s.v. "κληρόω" 2, pp. 548–49). **Syntactically**, ἐκληρώθημεν functions as the main verb of the relative clause "in whom *we have also obtained an inheritance*" (ἐν ᾧ καὶ ἐκληρώθημεν). The subject is implied: "we," referring to the believer. **Semantically**, ἐκληρώθημεν is an ingressive aorist emphasizing the new role of the believer (W, 558–59).

> **Lexical Nugget**: What does the verb "obtain" (κληρόω) mean? The Greek term κληρόω only occurs once in the New Testament. The exact meaning of the term is debated. On the one hand, it could be rendered: "to appoint by lot" (BDAG, s.v. "κληρόω" 1, p. 548). This sense suggests that believers are appointed as God's own inheritance. The NET renders the phrase as "we too have been claimed as God's own possession" (cf. LEB, NIV). The Old Testament establishes this pattern by calling Israel "God's inheritance (Deut. 4:20; 9:29; 32:8–9). First Peter 2:9 makes a similar point: "You are a chosen people, a royal priesthood, a holy nation, *a people for his own possession*" (Hoehner, 226–28; Arnold 201, 89; Osborne, 28–29). The problem with this position is that the focus of the passage describes the benefits that God gives to believers through their relationship with Christ. On the other hand, the verb can be translated as "to obtain by

lot" (BDAG, s.v. "κληρόω" 2, pp. 548–49). This translation implies that the believer has received an inheritance from God. Most English versions translate the verb: "we have obtained an inheritance" (ESV, NRSV, NASB, NKJV, KJV) or "received an inheritance" (CSB, HCSB, NLT). The immediate context describes God's blessing for the believer. The adoption metaphor that Paul introduces in verse 5 focuses on the adoptee's reception of an inheritance (see Lexical Nugget at 1:5b). Ephesians 1:14 characterizes the Holy Spirit as a "down payment of our inheritance" (cf. Col. 1:12; Rom. 8:17) (Thielman, 72–73; Larkin, 13).

1:11b προορισθέντες: The Greek word προορισθέντες is a masculine nominative plural aorist passive participle from the verb προορίζω that means "to predetermine" or "decide beforehand" (BDAG, s.v. "προορίζω," p. 873). Paul uses the same verb in verse 5. **Syntactically**, προορισθέντες introduces a dependent participle clause. It functions adverbially modifying the verb "we have obtained an inheritance" (ἐκληρώθημεν). **Semantically**, προορισθέντες expresses cause: "*because* we were predestined" (CSB, NET; W, 631–32; Hoehner, 228). Since the main verb is also aorist, the action of the participle is simultaneous to the action of the main verb (W, 624–25). The participle is an ingressive aorist emphasizing the point in time when God first chose the believer.

ἐνεργοῦντος: The Greek word ἐνεργοῦντος is a present active participle masculine singular genitive from the verb ἐνεργέω that means "to work," "produce," or "effect" (BDAG, s.v. "ἐνεργέω" 2, p. 335). **Syntactically**, ἐνεργοῦντος functions as a substantival participle. The participle phrase "the one who works all things" (τοῦ τὰ πάντα ἐνεργοῦντος) modifies πρόθεσιν ("plan"), the object of the preposition κατά. **Semantically**, ἐνεργοῦντος is a gnomic present: "works" (ESV, CSB, NASB, NKJV), "works out" (NIV, HCSB), or "accomplishes" (RSV, NRSV, NET). The present tense describes a timeless attribute about God (W, 521–22).

Syntactical Nugget: How do the following prepositional phrase relate to the context? Paul ends verse 11 with two prepositional phrases, both modifying the participle "having been predestined":

προορισθέντες
    <u>κατὰ</u> πρόθεσιν τοῦ τὰ πάντα ἐνεργοῦντος
    <u>κατὰ</u> τὴν βουλὴν τοῦ θελήματος αὐτοῦ

because we were predestined
    <u>according</u> to plan of the one who works all things
    <u>according</u> to the will of his desire

Both prepositions indicate that God's predestination have been "according to" or "in conformity with" a standard (BDAG, s.v. "κατά" B5aδ, pp. 512–13). The first prepositional phrase states that this predestination was "*according to* the plan of the one who works all things," a reference to God's will (vv. 9–10). The substantival participle phrase (τοῦ τὰ πάντα ἐνεργοῦντος) functions as a subjective genitive: "the one who produces all things according to the plan" (W, 113–17). The NLT renders the phrase "he makes everything work out."

The second prepositional phrase states that this predestination is "*according to* the will of his desire." There is a significant overlap between βουλή and θέλημα ("will" and "desire"), to the extent that the NRSV renders the two nouns with a coordinating conjunction: "his counsel and will." Hoehner notes that βουλή describes some type of deliberation (Hoehner, 229–30; cf. BDAG, s.v. "βουλή" 2b, p. 182; LSJ, s.v. "βουλή," p. 325). θέλημα is a broader term, referring to God's will (BDAG, s.v. "θέλημα" 2b, p. 447). The genitive relationship is debated. The genitive τοῦ θελήματος could be an objective genitive, meaning that God's will (θέλημα) comes from his deliberation (βουλή) (Hoehner, 230). It could be a subjective genitive, meaning that his will (θέλημα) gives deliberation (βουλή) (Larkin, 14). Finally, it could be a genitive of source: "deliberation that comes from his will" (Larkin, 14). Since the terms are synonymous a decision is difficult—does God's will come from counsel or does counsel come from his will? Because βουλή is a more specific term, the subjective genitive makes more sense. The synonyms in the passage (πρόθεσις, βουλή, θελήμα) create a rhetorical effect emphasizing God's sovereignty (Arnold, 90; Thielman, 74).

1:12   εἰς τὸ εἶναι: The Greek word εἶναι is a present active infinitive from the verb εἰμί that means "to be" (BDAG, s.v. "εἰμί" 3c, p. 284). **Syntactically**, εἶναι introduces a dependent adverbial infinitive clause modifying the main verb ἐκληρώθημεν ("we have been chosen," v. 11a). The subject of the infinitive is "we" (ἡμᾶς). The substantival participle phrase "the ones who already hoped in Christ" (τοὺς προηλπικότας ἐν τῷ Χριστῷ) is in apposition to the subject (ἡμᾶς). The prepositional phrase "to the praise of his glory" (εἰς ἔπαινον δόξης αὐτοῦ) functions as the object of the infinitive. The entire phrase could be rendered: "so that we, the ones who first hoped in Christ, might be to the praise of his glory." **Semantically**, εἶναι expresses the purpose of the believer receiving an inheritance for God "*so that* we might be to the praise of his glory" (Robertson, 991). The prepositional phrase "to the praise of his glory" (εἰς ἔπαινον δόξης αὐτοῦ) expresses purpose—we were chosen for praise (Thielman, 74). The genitive δόξης is objective and αὐτοῦ is possessive: "praise for his glory." The phrase is a repeated refrain throughout

Paul's statement (cf. vv. 6, 14; see the Syntactical Nugget at 1:6a). The prepositional phrase ἐν τῷ Χριστῷ expresses sphere ("in Christ") (see Theological Nugget at 1:4a).

> **Lexical Nugget**: What does Paul mean by "hope beforehand"? The Greek word προελπίζω only occurs once in the New Testament. The prefixed form of the verb προελπίζω adds a temporal element to the verb describing a prior action (L&N, 25.60; Metzger 1997, 84; cf. BDAG, s.v. "προελπίζω," p. 868). Most English translations render the participle as "first to hope" (ESV, NASB; cf. RSV) or "first to put our hope (NIV; cf. NET, NRSV). Because of this temporal element along with the shift from the first-person plural pronoun ("we") to the second-person plural pronoun ("you") in verse 13, Barth argues that Paul describes Jewish hope. In Ephesians 2:11–12, Paul will make a similar distinction between Jews and Gentiles—"once hopeless and godless in the world" (Barth, 130–33). The NLT brings out this interpretation by translating the phrase: "God's purpose was that we Jews who were the first to trust in Christ would bring praise and glory to God." However, the delineation between Jew and Gentile is not clear in this section. Beginning with verse 3, Paul refers to all believers (Lincoln, 37). The perfect tense of the participle emphasizes their enduring faith (Arnold, 91). In this case, the reference may not be restricted to just Jews, but to Gentiles who have previously put their faith in Christ. The CSB captures this well: "as we who already put our hope in Christ."

1:13a ᾧ: The Greek word ᾧ is a masculine singular dative from the relative pronoun ὅς that means "whom" (BDAG, s.v. "ὅς" 1, p. 725). **Syntactically**, ᾧ introduces a dependent adjectival relative clause "in *whom* also you … have been sealed" (ἐν ᾧ καὶ ὑμεῖς … ἐσφραγίσθητε). The antecedent of the pronoun is "Christ" (τῷ Χριστῷ; v. 12). It functions as the object of the preposition ἐν. This phrase is repeated throughout this section (vv. 7, 11, 13b). Due to the length of the sentence in Greek, many translations begin a new sentence at this point, translating the relative pronoun as a personal pronoun: "In him" (ESV, NIV, RSV, NRSV, CSB, NASB, NKJV, KJV). **Semantically**, the prepositional phrase ἐν ᾧ expresses sphere ("in whom") (see Theological Nugget at 1:4a). We are sealed with the Holy Spirit because of our relationship with Christ.

καί: The Greek word καί is a conjunction that means "and," or in this context "also" (BDAG, s.v. "καί" 1b, p. 494). **Syntactically**, καί introduces an independent conjunctive clause: "in whom *also* you … have been sealed" (Ἐν ᾧ καὶ ἐσφραγίσθητε). **Semantically**, καί is a connective conjunction: "also" (ESV, RSV, NRSV, NIV, CSB, NASB, NKJV, KJV). The phrase is part of a pattern that Paul began in verse 7 and continues in verse 11a. The conjunction connects the main verb "you have been sealed" (ὑμεῖς … ἐσφραγίσθητε) with the previous two clauses: "in whom we have the redemption" (ἐν ᾧ ἔχομεν τὴν ἀπολύτρωσιν) (v. 7) and "in whom we have also obtained an inheritance" (ἐν ᾧ καὶ ἐκληρώθημεν) (v. 11a). The verb in verse 13c is modified by two adverbial participles: ἀκούσαντες and πιστεύσαντες (vv. 13a and 13b).

ἀκούσαντες: The Greek word ἀκούσαντες is a masculine nominative plural aorist active participle from the verb ἀκούω that means "to hear" (BDAG, s.v. "ἀκούω" 1bα, p. 37). **Syntactically**, ἀκούσαντες introduces a dependent participle clause. It functions adverbially modifying the verb "you were sealed" (ἐσφραγίσθητε). The direct object of the participle is "the word" (τὸν λόγον, more specifically a "statement"; BDAG, s.v. "λόγος" 1aβ, pp. 599–600). The second accusative is in apposition to the first and clarifies it: "the word of truth, *that is* the gospel of your salvation." **Semantically**, ἀκούσαντες could be causal: "*because* you heard." However, it is best understood as temporal: "*when* you heard," describing the point of their conversion (Hoehner, 237; ESV, NET, NIV, NRSV, CSB). The NASB renders the participle as antecedent in time to the action of the main verb: "*after* listening" (cf. NKJV, KJV). However since the tense of both the participle and main verb are aorist, the action is simultaneous with the action of the main verb (W, 624–25).

1:13b ᾧ: The Greek word ᾧ is a masculine singular dative from the relative pronoun ὅς that means *whom* (BDAG, s.v. "ὅς" 1, p. 725). **Syntactically**, ᾧ introduces a dependent adjectival relative clause "in *whom* also … you have been sealed" (ἐν ᾧ καὶ ὑμεῖς … ἐσφραγίσθητε). The antecedent of the pronoun is "Christ" (τῷ Χριστῷ; v. 12). It functions as the object of the preposition ἐν. This phrase is repeated throughout this section (vv. 7, 11). The prepositional phrase is in apposition with the previous use of ἐν (v. 13a). **Semantically**, the prepositional phrase ἐν ᾧ expresses sphere ("in whom") (see Theological Nugget at 1:4a).

καί: The Greek word καί is a conjunction that means "and," or in this context "also" (BDAG, s.v. "καί" 1b, p. 494). **Syntactically**, καί introduces an independent conjunctive clause: "in whom *also* you … have been sealed" (ἐν ᾧ καὶ … ἐσφραγίσθητε). **Semantically**, καί is a resumption of the initial clause begun in verse 13a (Hoehner, 237; Merkle, 35). It coordinates the main verb: "you have been sealed" (ὑμεῖς … ἐσφραγίσθητε) with the previous two clauses: "in whom we have the redemption" (ἐν ᾧ ἔχομεν τὴν ἀπολύτρωσιν) (v. 7) and "in whom we have also obtained an inheritance" (ἐν ᾧ καὶ ἐκληρώθημεν) (v. 11a).

πιστεύσαντες: The Greek word πιστεύσαντες is a masculine nominative plural aorist active participle from the verb πιστεύω that means "to believe (in)" or "trust" (BDAG, s.v. "πιστεύω" 2b, pp. 817–18). **Syntactically**, πιστεύσαντες introduces a dependent participle clause. It functions adverbially modifying "you were sealed" (ἐσφραγίσθητε). **Semantically**, πιστεύσαντες could be causal:"*because* you believed." However, like ἀκούσαντες, it is best understood as temporal: "*when* you believed," describing the point in time of their conversion (Hoehner, 237; Arnold, 91). Just like ἀκούσαντες, the aorist tense indicates that the action is simultaneous to the action of the main verb as well as the previous participle (W, 624–25). Hoehner states that "it should be regarded that the hearing was the hearing of faith (Rom. 10:14–17)" (Hoehner, 238).

1:13c ἐσφραγίσθητε: The Greek word ἐσφραγίσθητε is a second-person plural aorist passive indicative from the verb σφραγίζω that means "to mark" or "to seal" (BDAG, s.v. "σφραγίζω" 3, p. 980). **Syntactically**, ἐσφραγίσθητε functions as the main verb of the relative clause begun in verse 13 "in whom also you … *were sealed*" (ἐν ᾧ καὶ ὑμεῖς … ἐσφραγίσθητε). The subject of the verb is the second-person plural pronoun: "you" (ὑμεῖς), referring to the believer (v. 13a). **Semantically**, ἐσφραγίσθητε is an ingressive aorist emphasizing the point at which the state of the believer has changed. It is a divine passive; God is the implied agent. The dative τῷ πνεύματι ("Spirit") expresses the means by which God seals the believer: "*with* the Holy Spirit" (Robertson, 533; W, 162–63; cf. ESV, RSV, CSB, HCSB, NASB, NKJV, KJV). The genitive τῆς ἐπαγγελίας ("promise"; BDAG, s.v. "ἐπαγγελία" 1ba, pp. 355–56) is an attributive genitive (Moule, 176): "the *promised* Holy Spirit."

> **Lexical Nugget**: What does it mean for the believer to be "sealed"? σφραγίζω refers to some means of identification, to "mark" or "seal" (BDAG, s.v. "σφραγίζω" 3, p. 980). Metaphorically, the term describes some form of authentication (cf. John 3:33). In antiquity, legal documents were marked with a seal in order to show their authenticity (GE, s.v. "σφραγίζω," p. 2067; cf. LXX Jer. 39:11). The Old Testament describes royal decrees as having been sealed (LXX Esther 8:8, 10). In these instances, the seal made the decree legally binding. Seals also signified ownership. Slaves or soldiers were marked (Herodotus, *Hist.* 2.113; Fitzer 1971, 939–43). This gloss best fits the context. Paul has just described God having chosen the believer for adoption (vv. 4–5) (Hoehner, 238–39; Arnold, 92–93). In Ephesians 4:30, Paul states that the Spirit seals the believer "for the day of redemption." In Ephesians 1:14, he describes the Spirit as a down payment "for the redemption of possession." Both passages orientate the image toward the future (Thielman, 80–81).

1:14a ὅ: The Greek word ὅ is a neuter singular nominative from the relative pronoun ὅς that means "who" (BDAG, s.v. "ὅς" 1, p. 725). **Syntactically**, ὅ introduces a dependent adjectival relative clause "*which* is the down payment of our inheritance" (ὅ ἐστιν ἀρραβὼν τῆς κληρονομίας ἡμῶν). The antecedent is "the Spirit" (τῷ πνεύματι; v. 13c). The relative pronoun functions as the subject of the verb ἐστίν.

Text-Critical Nugget: Is the relative pronoun masculine or neuter? The NA[25] includes the masculine pronoun (ὅς) (cf. MT; RP[2005]), while the NA[28] includes the neuter pronoun (ὅ) (cf. THGNT; SBL). The split decision in these editions points to the level of difficulty of the problem. Externally, the majority of Byzantine manuscripts (𝔐) along with the significant Alexandrian (ℵ) and Western (D) manuscripts have replaced the neuter relative pronoun with the masculine: ὅς. On the other hand, the neuter pronoun is found in both the Alexandrian (𝔓46, A, B, 1739, 1881) and Western (F, G) text types. On internal grounds both readings are possible. Paul could have initially used the masculine due to attraction to the gender of the predicate nominative ἀρραβών and a scribe shifted it to a neuter pronoun to agree with the gender of the antecedent. Or else he could have used the neuter and a scribe shifted it to a masculine pronoun according to Paul's normal style (Metzger, 533). The internal evidence is split. The distribution of the neuter reading in the Alexandrian and Western text types suggests that it is more original (*contra* Hoehner, 241 n. 1).

ἐστίν: The Greek word ἐστίν is a third-person singular present active indicative from the verb εἰμί that means "to be" (BDAG s.v. "εἰμί" 2cα, p. 284). **Syntactically**, ἐστίν functions as the main verb of the relative clause: "which *is* the down payment of our inheritance" (ὅ ἐστιν ἀρραβὼν τῆς κληρονομίας ἡμῶν). The subject of the verb is the relative pronoun. The predicate nominative is "down payment" (ἀρραβών). **Semantically**, ἐστίν functions as an equative present tense. The genitive τῆς κληρονομίας ("inheritance," referring to our salvation; BDAG, s.v. "κληρονομία" 3, p. 548) is a partitive genitive. The head noun ἀρραβών ("down payment," "pledge," or "deposit"; BDAG, s.v. "ἀρραβών," p. 134) characterizes the Spirit as an initial payment with the full inheritance to come in the future (W, 84–86). Paul makes a similar statement in 2 Corinthians (1:22; 5:5).

Semantical Nugget: What do the final two prepositional phrases ("until the redemption of possession" and "for the praise of his glory") mean? Paul rounds out this section with these two prepositional phrases. Both phrases relate to the main verb "you have been sealed" (ἐσφραγίσθητε) (v. 13c). In the first prepositional phrase, "until the redemption of possession" (εἰς ἀπολύτρωσιν τῆς περιποιήσεως), the preposition εἰς could convey the purpose for being sealed (Larkin, 16; Best, 152), but it most likely expresses a temporal element: "until" (Hoehner, 245; Arnold, 93; ESV, RSV, NIV, NET, CSB, KJV, NKJV). The image of a down payment that Paul introduces looks forward to a time when the inheritance will be paid in full. Ephesians 4:30 makes this temporal concept explicit by describing a "day of redemption." The genitive περιποιήσεως ("possession" or "property"; BDAG, s.v. "περιποίησις" 3, p. 804) could be understood as an objective genitive with God as the implied subject: "until God redeems the possession." This interpretation implies that God will one day take possession of the believer. The NIV brings out this notion: "until the redemption of *those who are God's possession*" (cf. NRSV, NET, NASB, NLT). On the other hand, it could be an epexegetical genitive: "until the redemption, *that is the possession.*" This interpretation looks forward to a time when the believer will take possession of the inheritance that God has for them. This interpretation makes good sense of the thrust of the passage: what God has given to believers, whom he has adopted (Best, 152–53). The ESV captures this idea: "until we acquire possession of it" (cf. RSV).

The second prepositional phrase "for the praise of his glory" (εἰς ἔπαινον τῆς δόξης αὐτοῦ) most likely conveys the notion of purpose explaining why God sealed the believer. Paul ends the eulogy with this repeated refrain (cf. v. 6a, 12; see Syntactical Nugget at v. 6a).

EPHESIANS 1:15–23

Big Greek Idea: Paul prays that through spiritual insight God reveals the hope of the believers' call, the depth of his inheritance, and his immeasurable power available to them; the same power through which God raised Christ from the dead and gives him dominion over all the authorities of the world.

Structural Overview: After giving praise to God for what he has done for the believer (Eph. 1:3–14), Paul shifts to a prayer of thanksgiving for the believer. Paul offers this sort of prayer of thanksgiving at the beginning of his letters (Rom. 1:8; 1 Cor. 1:4–8; Phil. 1:3–6; Col. 1:3–6; 1 Thess. 1:2–5; 2 Thess. 1:3–4; 2 Tim. 1:3–5; Philem. 4–7; O'Brien 1993a, 70–71). Just like the previous section, the prayer is a single sentence, 169 words long.

After a short statement of thanksgiving for the believers' faith in the Lord and their love for other believers (1:15–16), Paul prays that God will give them insight into the power that God has provided them. The central request is found in verse 17 (introduced with ἵνα): that God gives these believers spiritual wisdom and revelation. He amplifies this request with a second, but related request: that with this spiritual insight they might understand the power that God has provided for them. He expands this second request by providing the specific content he hopes that these believers come to understand. He introduces with the interrogative pronoun (τίς): (1) what is the believer's hope (v. 18c); (2) what is their inheritance (v. 18d); and (3) what is the power for the believer (v. 19).

The remainder of the prayer (vv. 20–23) expands on this power at work within the believer. This is the same power at work in Christ when God raised him from the dead, seated him in heaven, and gave him authority over all authorities. Even though Paul does not identify these powers, they appear to be antagonistic to the church. Paul quotes two psalms (Ps. 110:1 in 1:20 and Ps. 8:6 in 1:22)—both psalms describe a conflict. Later in the letter, Paul describes these powers as hostile to God and the church (2:2–3; 6:12).

Outline:
> A prayer of thanksgiving leads to a deeper understanding of the power
> > God has for the believer (vv. 15–19)
> > Faith and love serves as a reason for thanksgiving (vv. 15–16a)
> > First prayer request: Paul prays that God gives the believer spiritual
> > > knowledge (vv. 16b–17)
> > Second prayer request: Paul prays that God helps the believer understand the power he has provided (vv. 18–19)
> > The same power available to the believer is at work in the resurrection
> > > and rule of Christ (vv. 20–23)

CLAUSAL OUTLINE FOR EPHESIANS 1:15–23

^{1:15} <u>Διὰ τοῦτο</u> κἀγὼ **ἀκούσας** τὴν καθ' ὑμᾶς πίστιν ἐν τῷ κυρίῳ Ἰησοῦ καὶ τὴν ἀγάπην τὴν εἰς πάντας τοὺς ἁγίους

^{1:15} <u>For this reason</u>, **after hearing** about your faith in the Lord Jesus and your love for all of the saints

^{1:16a} οὐ **παύομαι**

^{1:16a} **I do** not **cease**

^{1:16b} **εὐχαριστῶν** ὑπὲρ ὑμῶν

^{1:16b} **giving thanks** on your behalf

^{1:16c} μνείαν **ποιούμενος** ἐπὶ τῶν προσευχῶν μου

^{1:16c} **while remembering** you in my prayers,

^{1:17} **ἵνα** ὁ θεὸς τοῦ κυρίου ἡμῶν Ἰησοῦ Χριστοῦ, ὁ πατὴρ τῆς δόξης, **δώῃ** ὑμῖν πνεῦμα σοφίας καὶ ἀποκαλύψεως ἐν ἐπιγνώσει αὐτοῦ,

^{1:17} **that** the God of our Lord Jesus Christ, the glorious Father **might give** to you spiritual wisdom and revelation in knowing him

[δώῃ (v. 17)]
[he might give (v. 17)]

^{1:18a} **πεφωτισμένους** τοὺς ὀφθαλμοὺς τῆς καρδίας ὑμῶν

^{1:18a} <u>since</u> the eyes of your heart **have been enlightened**

^{1:18b} **εἰς τὸ εἰδέναι** ὑμᾶς

^{1:18b} **so that** you **may know**

^{1:18c} <u>τίς</u> **ἐστιν** ἡ ἐλπὶς τῆς κλήσεως αὐτοῦ,

^{1:18c} <u>what</u> **is** the hope of his calling

^{1:18d} <u>τίς</u> [**ἐστιν**] ὁ πλοῦτος τῆς δόξης τῆς κληρονομίας αὐτοῦ ἐν τοῖς ἁγίοις,

^{1:18d} <u>what</u> [**is**] the wealth of the glorious inheritance from him among the saints,

^{1:19} καὶ <u>τί</u> [**ἐστιν**] (τὸ ὑπερβάλλον μέγεθος τῆς δυνάμεως αὐτοῦ) εἰς (ἡμᾶς τοὺς πιστεύοντας) κατὰ τὴν ἐνέργειαν τοῦ κράτους τῆς ἰσχύος αὐτοῦ.

^{1:19} and <u>what</u> [**is**] (his surpassingly great power) for (us who believe) according to the working of his strong might.

[ἐνέργειαν (v. 19a)]
[working (v. 19a)]
    |
  1:20a <u>ἣν</u> **ἐνήργησεν** ἐν τῷ Χριστῷ
  1:20a **He exercised** this power in Christ
      |
    1:20b **ἐγείρας** αὐτὸν ἐκ νεκρῶν
    1:20b **by raising** him from the dead
        |
      1:20c <u>καὶ</u> **καθίσας** ἐν δεξιᾷ αὐτοῦ ἐν τοῖς ἐπουρανίοις 1:21 ὑπεράνω πάσης ἀρχῆς καὶ ἐξουσίας καὶ δυνάμεως καὶ κυριότητος καὶ (παντὸς ὀνόματος ὀνομαζομένου), οὐ μόνον ἐν τῷ αἰῶνι τούτῳ ἀλλὰ καὶ (ἐν τῷ μέλλοντι·)
      1:20c and **by seating** him at his right hand in the heavenly places 1:21 high above every ruler and authority and power and dominion and (every name which is called upon) not only in this age, but also (in the one to come);

[ἐνήργησεν (v. 20a)]
[he exercised (v. 20a)]
  |
1:22a <u>καὶ</u> πάντα **ὑπέταξεν** ὑπὸ τοὺς πόδας αὐτοῦ
1:22a <u>And</u> **he put** all things under his feet
  |
1:22b <u>καὶ</u> αὐτὸν **ἔδωκεν** κεφαλὴν ὑπὲρ πάντα τῇ ἐκκλησίᾳ,
1:22b <u>and</u> **he appointed** him as the head over all things to the church,

        1:23 <u>ἥτις</u> **ἐστὶν** τὸ σῶμα αὐτοῦ, τὸ πλήρωμα (τοῦ τὰ πάντα ἐν πᾶσιν πληρουμένου).
        1:23 <u>which</u> **is** his body, the fullness of (the one who fills all in all).

Syntax Explained for Ephesians 1:15–23

1:15 Διὰ τοῦτο: The Greek word τοῦτο is a neuter singular accusative from the demonstrative pronoun οὗτος. The pronoun with the preposition διά expresses a causal relation to the preceding context (Runge 2010, 48). Most English translations render the phrase "For this reason" (ESV, NET, NIV, RSV, NRSV, NASB; BDAG, s.v. "οὗτος" 1bβ, p. 741; W, 658). The CSB renders the clause as "This is why." **Syntactically**, the phrase points back to the eulogy (1:3–14), which provides the reason for Paul's prayer of thanksgiving, which he begins in verse 16 (Arnold, 102).

ἀκούσας: The Greek word ἀκούσας is an aorist active participle masculine singular nominative from the verb ἀκούω that means "to hear" or "learn about" (BDAG, s.v. "ἀκούω" 3b, p. 38). **Syntactically**, ἀκούσας introduces a dependent participle clause. It functions adverbially modifying "I am not ceasing" (παύομαι, v. 15a). The accusatives "your faith" (τὴν καθ᾽ ὑμᾶς πίστιν) and "your love" (τὴν ἀγάπην) function as direct objects. **Semantically**, ἀκούσας could be causal: "*because* I heard" (ESV, NET, RSV). However, it is most likely temporal: "*after* I heard" (NKJV) or "*since* I heard" (CSB, NIV, NLT). This interpretation makes better sense of the temporal element embedded in the main verb in verse 16a—from the point of Paul's hearing he has continued to give thanks for the Ephesian believers. A parallel text in Colossians 1:9 makes the temporal element explicit (Hoehner, 248; W, 627).

Text-Critical Nugget: Does Paul refer to the believers' love in verse 15? Several key Alexandrian manuscripts omit τὴν ἀγάπην—the second direct object ($\mathfrak{P}^{46}$, ℵ, A, B, 1739, 1881). The omission gives the notion that these believers have faith in the Lord Jesus and are faithful to all the saints: "having heard of your faith in the Lord Jesus and to all of the believers." This reading implies that these believers have faith in Christ as well as other believers. The Western text type inserts ἀγάπην, but omits the second article: τὴν ἀγάπην εἰς πάντας τοὺς ἀγίους (D, F, G). A handful of manuscripts place ἀγάπην at the end of the phrase: τὴν εἰς πάντας τοὺς ἀγίους ἀγάπην (81, 104, 326, 365, 1175). And finally, the majority of Byzantine manuscripts (K, L, 𝔐) include both articles: τὴν ἀγάπην τὴν εἰς πάντας τοὺς ἀγίους. These readings may have risen from the interpretative difficulty of the shorter reading—would Paul have suggested that these believers are the object of faith? Best supports the shorter reading and argues that "faith" should be "faithful" or "loyal" (Best, 160). Equating the faithfulness between believers to faith in Christ might place too much strain on this option. If the omission is original, this is the only occurrence that does not distinguish between a believer's faith in Christ and their faithfulness to one another (Lincoln, 47). Even though the shorter reading is the harder reading, it might be too hard. More likely a scribe accidentally omitted ἀγάπην by allowing their eye to skip from the first article to the second (NET n. 42; Metzger, 533; Thielman, 102–3; Hoehner, 249 n. 5).

Semantical Nugget: How do the prepositional phrases in verse 15 relate to the direct objects "faith" and "love"? The accusative τὴν πίστιν and τὴν ἀγάπην are the objects of the participle, providing the content of the news that Paul received. The embedded prepositional phrase καθ᾽ ὑμᾶς expresses possession (BDAG, s.v. "κατά" B7b, p. 513). Paul shifts the preposition from ἐν to εἰς.

> κἀγὼ ἀκούσας
>> τὴν καθ᾽ ὑμᾶς πίστιν <u>ἐν</u> τῷ κυρίῳ Ἰησοῦ
> καί
>> τὴν ἀγάπην τὴν εἰς πάντας τοὺς ἁγίους
>
> and I, after hearing about
>> your faith <u>in</u> the Lord Jesus
> and
>> the love for all the saints

The first prepositional phrase "in the Lord Jesus" (ἐν τῷ κυρίῳ Ἰησοῦ) expresses sphere, articulating where the believer's faith resides, rather than the object of their faith. The preposition is rarely used to modify πίστις in Paul's writing (see Rom. 3:25; Col. 1:4; 1 Tim. 3:13; 2 Tim. 3:15). Each occurrence is best understood as sphere (Moule, 80–81; Hoehner, 249; Harris 2012, 234–35). The second prepositional phrase "for all the saints" (εἰς πάντας τοὺς ἁγίους) expresses direction. The article before the preposition makes the prepositional phrase adjectival, modifying τὴν ἀγάπην (Larkin, 19), captured with the relative pronoun: "*which* is for all the saints."

1:16a παύομαι: The Greek word παύομαι is a first-person singular present middle indicative from the verb παύω that means "to stop" or "cease" (BDAG, s.v. "παύω" 2, p. 790). **Syntactically**, παύομαι functions as the main verb of the independent prepositional clause introduced by Διὰ τοῦτο (v. 15). The subject of the verb is the first-person singular pronoun: "I" (καγώ), referring to Paul. **Semantically**, παύομαι is a customary present, describing an ongoing habit for Paul. He continually prays for these believers. The verb is a direct middle, adding a reflexive idea: "I have not stopped myself" (W, 416–18).

1:16b εὐχαριστῶν: The Greek word εὐχαριστῶν is a present active participle masculine singular nominative from the verb εὐχαριστέω that means "to give thanks" or "express thanks" (BDAG, s.v. "εὐχαριστέω" 2, p. 415). **Syntactically**, εὐχαριστῶν introduces a dependent participle clause. It functions adverbially modifying the main verb: "I have not ceased" (παύομαι). **Semantically**, εὐχαριστῶν functions as a complementary participle, which completes the idea of the main verb (W, 646; Porter, 193). The prepositional phrase "on your behalf" (ὑπὲρ ὑμῶν) expresses advantage—Paul prayers are for the advantage of the believers (BDAG, s.v. "ὑπέρ" A2, p. 1031).

1:16c ποιούμενος: The Greek word ποιούμενος is a present middle participle masculine singular nominative from the verb ποιέω that means "to make" or "do something for oneself" (BDAG, s.v. "ποιέω" 7a, pp. 841–42). **Syntactically**, ποιούμενος introduces a dependent participle clause. It functions adverbially, modifying the main verb "I have not ceased" (παύομαι). The object of the participle is "mention" (μνείαν; BDAG, s.v. "μνεία" 2, p. 654). The phrase literally means "making mention" (NASB). The phrase is idiomatic meaning "to make mention of something" or "to recall something" (GE, s.v. "μνεία," p. 1354). Paul regularly uses the phrase within the context of prayer (Rom. 1:9; 1 Thess. 1:2; Philem. 4; cf. Phil. 1:3; 1 Thess. 3:6; 2 Tim. 1:3). **Semantically,** ποιούμενος functions as a temporal participle. Since both the participle and the main verb are in the present tense, then the actions are contemporaneous: "*while* making mention" (NASB; cf. NET) or "*as* I remember" (CSB, HCSB, NRSV) (W, 623–27). The prepositional phrase "in the time of my prayers" (ἐπὶ τῶν προσευχῶν μου) is temporal (BDAG, s.v. "ἐπί" 18a, p. 367).

1:17 ἵνα: The Greek word ἵνα is a conjunction that means "that" in this context (BDAG, s.v. "ἵνα" 2aγ, p. 476). Due to the length of the sentence in Greek, several English versions start a new sentence by inserting "I pray" (NET, NRSV, CSB) or "I keep asking" (NIV). **Syntactically,** ἵνα introduces a dependent conjunctive clause "*that* the God of our Lord Jesus Christ, the glorious Father, may give to you spiritual wisdom and revelation" (ὁ θεὸς τοῦ κυρίου ἡμῶν Ἰησοῦ Χριστοῦ, ὁ πατὴρ τῆς δόξης, δώῃ ὑμῖν πνεῦμα σοφίας καὶ ἀποκαλύψεως ἐν ἐπιγνώσει αὐτοῦ). The conjunction functions substantivally as the direct object of the participle "while making mention" (μνείαν ποιούμενος; v. 16c). **Semantically,** ἵνα introduces the content of Paul's prayer for the Ephesian believers (Hoehner, 254; W, 474–75; Moule, 145).

δώῃ: The Greek word δώῃ is a third-person singular aorist active subjunctive from the verb δίδωμι that means "to give," "bestow," or "grant" (BDAG, s.v. "δίδωμι" 17b, p. 243). **Syntactically,** δώῃ functions as the main verb of the dependent conjunctive clause introduced by ἵνα. The subject is "the God of our Lord Jesus Christ"; the phrase "the Father of glory" is in apposition. The direct object is "spiritual wisdom and revelation" (πνεῦμα σοφίας καὶ ἀποκαλύψεως). Paul asks that God grant the Ephesian believers wisdom and revelation, which can only come from the Spirit. The indirect object is "you" (ὑμῖν), referring to the believers. **Semantically,** δώῃ is a constative aorist describing the event as a whole (W, 557–58). Paul's prayer is that God grant this insight to the believers.

Semantical Nugget: How does Paul refer to God throughout Ephesians? Paul refers to God as "Father" regularly throughout the letter (Eph. 1:2, 3, 17; 2:18; 3:14; 4:6; 5:20; 6:23). In every instance (except 2:18 and 3:14) Paul uses the term "God" (θεός) with it. He can either connect the two terms with καί "God and Father" (1:3; 4:6; 5:20) or place them in apposition (1:2, 17; 6:23). On occasion he adds a genitive construction to one of the terms (1:2, 3; 4:6); this is the only occasion that he adds a genitive construction to both terms. The first genitive construction (τοῦ κυρίου ἡμῶν Ἰησοῦ Χριστοῦ) modifies ὁ θεός. τοῦ κυρίου is a genitive of relationship, defining the relationship between the Father and Jesus. ἡμῶν is a genitive of subordination: "Lord over us" (W, 103–4). Ἰησοῦ Χριστοῦ ("Jesus Christ") are genitives in simple apposition to τοῦ κυρίου. Paul uses a similar construction in verse 3. This formula mimics the early Christian confession: "Jesus is Lord" (Acts 2:36; Rom. 10:9; 14:9; 1 Cor. 12:3; 2 Cor. 4:5; Phil. 2:11; Hoehner, 255). In the second genitive construction, Paul uses τῆς δόξης to modify ὁ πατήρ. This genitive functions as an attributive genitive: "glorious Father" (NIV, CSB, LEB).

Theological Nugget: Does Paul use πνεῦμα to refer to a generic spirit (i.e., "a spirit of wisdom") or the Holy Spirit (i.e., "the Spirit of wisdom")? The term can refer to either—context determines the exact meaning. Since Paul has already indicated that believers have received the Spirit (1:13–14), several translations render this "a spirit" (RSV, NRSV, HCSB, NASB). The problem with this interpretation is that Paul prays that the believer receives some sort of divine revelation. Later in the letter, he will say that all revelation (ἀποκάλυψις) comes from God (Eph. 3:3–5). If πνεῦμα refers to the Holy Spirit (ESV, NIV, CSB), then it represents metonymy of cause for effect—rather than praying that they receive the Spirit, Paul prays that the believers realize the wisdom and revelation that comes from the Spirit (W, 90–91; Hoehner, 256–58; Arnold, 104; Thielman, 96). Later in the letter, Paul will state that this revelation comes from God by the Spirit (3:5). In this case, the genitives (σοφίας and ἀποκαλύψεως) could be understood as either genitives of product: "the Spirit *who produces* wisdom and revelation." But it might be best to take it as an attributed genitive: "spiritual wisdom and revelation" (NET, NLT; W, 89–91). Wallace notes that since "wisdom" and "revelation" are qualitative, we should consider "spirit" (an anarthrous head noun with an anarthrous genitive) as qualitative as well (W, 250–54).

1:18a πεφωτισμένους: The Greek word πεφωτισμένους is a perfect passive participle masculine plural accusative from the verb φωτίζω that means "to bring light" or "reveal" (BDAG, s.v. "φωτίζω" 3a, p. 1074). **Syntactically**, πεφωτισμένους can relate to the context in one of three ways. The first option is that πεφωτισμένους could function as the direct object of the verb: "he might give" (δώῃ, v. 17) (Best, 165). This suggests that Paul prays that God grant the believers this enlightenment. The NIV begins a new sentence with the participle: "I pray that the eyes of your heart may be enlightened" (cf. NASB, NLT, CSB). This makes the best sense of the accusative case, but we would anticipate that Paul inserts a coordinating conjunction (καί) and add an article before the participle (Arnold, 105–6). Also, this option fails to make sense of the perfect tense (Hoehner, 261). The second option is that πεφωτισμένους introduces a substantival clause in apposition to ὑμῖν (v. 17), suggesting that the participle describes the current state of the believers. Paul prays that God grant spiritual wisdom to you "who had the eyes of your heart enlightened." This interpretation makes better sense of the perfect tense, but we would expect that Paul would use the dative case to agree with the case of the pronoun, not the accusative. The third option is that πεφωτισμένους introduces a dependent participle clause, adverbially modifying δώη. The case of the participle is accusative because the case of the subject shifts accusative following an infinitive in verse 18b (εἰς τὸ εἰδέναι ὑμᾶς) (Thielman, 97–98). Hoehner argues that this is an accusative absolute looking back to ὑμῖν (v. 17) and toward ὑμᾶς (v. 18b). He offers this translation: "that God may give *you* the Spirit of insight and revelation in the knowledge of him, [*you*] having had the eyes of your heart enlightened, in order that *you* might know" (Hoehner, 262; cf. Porter, 92). Hoehner argues that the participle functions adverbially expressing cause. The NET offsets the phrase with dashes and renders it: "since the eyes of your heart have been enlightened." **Semantically**, πεφωτισμένους is an intensive perfect, which emphasizes the present result of a past action (W, 574–76). The participle expresses cause: "*since* the eyes of your heart have been enlightened" (W, 631 n. 47). Since God has opened the eyes of the believers' hearts, Paul prays that they come to fully understand this revelation.

Text-Critical Nugget: Why does the NA[28] text place brackets around the pronoun ὑμῶν? While the majority of manuscripts contain ὑμῶν following τῆς καρδίας ("your heart"), several early Alexandrian manuscripts omit the pronoun (𝔓46, B, 33, 1739, 1881). On the other hand, the majority of Western (D, F, G, latt) and Byzantine (K, L, 𝔐) manuscripts contain the pronoun. In addition, a number of Alexandrian manuscripts include the pronoun as well (ℵ, A, 81, 104). Internally, the reading without the pronoun is shorter and harder. The omission does not change the meaning of the text—Paul is clearly referring to the eyes of the believer's heart. A scribe could have inserted the pronoun to clarify the text. Even though the reading with the omission is shorter and harder, the reading with the pronoun is found in all three text types and is most likely the superior reading (cf. Hoehner, 260 n. 1).

Lexical Nugget: What does the metaphor "the eyes of my heart" mean? The metaphor is unique to Paul. In the Old Testament, the Psalmist can pray that God might "illuminate my eyes" (Pss. 13:3 [LXX 12:4]; 19:8 [LXX 18:9]). Paul adds "heart" to the metaphor. In antiquity, the heart was the center and course of one's inner life—their thinking, feeling, and volition (BDAG, s.v. "καρδία" 1bβ, pp. 508–9). Paul does not just pray for the illumination of the believers, but that their innermost being is illuminated by God (Conzelmann, 1974, 347). Throughout the letter, Paul develops this image of "light." In Ephesians 3:8–9, Paul's apostolic mandate is "to preach the good news to the nations" and "to give light [φωτίσαι] to everyone what is the plan of mystery hidden from the ages by God who created all things." In Ephesians 5:8–14, he encourages believers to live "as children of light" (τέκνα φωτός).

1:18b εἰς τὸ εἰδέναι: The Greek word εἰδέναι is a perfect active infinitive from the verb οἶδα that means "to understand," "recognize," or "experience" (BDAG, s.v. "οἶδα" 4, p. 694). **Syntactically**, εἰδέναι introduces a dependent adverbial infinitive clause modifying the verb δώῃ. The subject of the infinitive is the second-person plural pronoun: "you" (ὑμᾶς). **Semantically**, the preposition εἰς with the infinitive can express purpose or result (W, 611). This instance expresses purpose: "*so that* you may know" (NET, CSB, NASB). εἰδέναι is an intensive perfect, which emphasizes the present result of a past action (W, 574–76).

1:18c τίς: The Greek word τίς is an indefinite pronoun from the word τις that means "what" or "what sort of" (BDAG, s.v. "τίς" 1aβ‍ב, p. 1007; W, 345–46). **Syntactically**, τίς introduces the first of three clauses that serve as the object of the infinitive εἰδέναι. Paul repeats the pronoun two more times (cf. vv. 18d, 19). The clause expresses the content of what Paul wants believers to know.

ἐστίν: The Greek word ἐστίν is a third-person singular present active indicative from the verb εἰμί that means "to be" (BDAG, s.v. "εἰμί" 2cβ, p. 284). **Syntactically**, ἐστίν is the main verb of the object clause introduced by τίς. The subject is "the hope of his calling" (ἡ ἐλπὶς τῆς κλήσεως αὐτοῦ), giving the first item that Paul wants the believers to know. **Semantically**, ἐστίν functions as an equative present.

Semantical Nugget: What is the relationship between the genitive phrase τῆς κλήσεως αὐτοῦ ("his calling") and the head noun ἡ ἐλπίς ("hope")? The genitive τῆς κλήσεως could express source: "hope *that comes from* a calling." The genitive αὐτοῦ could be subjective: "what is the hope to which *he called you*" (ESV cf. NIV, NRSV, RSV; Merkle, 43; Larkin, 21). However, it might be best to understand τῆς κλήσεως as a subjective genitive and αὐτοῦ as possessive. This interpretation suggests that God's call leads to hope (Hoehner, 265). The CSB renders the phrase: "what is the hope of his calling" (cf. NET, NASB, NKJV, KJV).

1:18d τίς: The Greek word τίς is an indefinite pronoun from the word τις that means "what" or "what sort of" (BDAG, s.v. "τίς" 1aβ‍ב, p. 1007; W, 345–46). **Syntactically**, τίς introduces the second clause that serves as the object of the infinitive εἰδέναι (cf. vv. 18c, 19a). The pronoun introduces the second element that Paul wants the believers to know: "the wealth of his glorious inheritance."

[ἐστίν]: The Greek word ἐστίν is a third-person singular present active indicative from the verb εἰμί that means "to be" (BDAG, s.v. "εἰμί" 2cβ, p. 284). **Syntactically**, The verb is an ellipsis. The elliptical [ἐστίν] functions as the main verb of the object clause introduced by τίς. The subject is "his glorious inheritance" (ἡ ἐλπὶς τῆς κλήσεως αὐτοῦ), giving the second item that Paul wants the believers to know. **Semantically**, [ἐστίν] functions as an equative present. Here he adds the prepositional phrase among the saints (ἐν τοῖς ἁγίοις), expressing sphere. God's inheritance is found among the believers.

> **Semantical Nugget**: What does the genitive construction "the riches of his glorious inheritance" (ὁ πλοῦτος τῆς δόξης τῆς κληρονομίας αὐτοῦ) mean? There are two issues. First, the genitive τῆς δόξης ("glory") could function as an attributive genitive modifying ὁ πλοῦτος: *the glorious wealth* of his inheritance" (HCSB; W, 90). However, it is better understood as an attributive genitive modifying τῆς κληρονομίας: "the wealth of his *glorious inheritance*" (cf. ESV, CSB, NET, NIV, RSV, NRSV) Paul places the emphasis on inheritance throughout this section (Merkle, 43; Hoehner, 266). The second issue is how to understand the genitive αὐτοῦ. It could be possessive: "*his* inheritance." This interpretation—that the inheritance belongs to God—implies that Paul has the believer in mind (see the Lexical Nugget at 1:11a; see Thielman, 99–100; Hoehner, 266–67). But it might be best to understand the genitive as source: an inheritance "*from him*." This suggests that inheritance is from God for believers. Paul's emphasis throughout this section is on the benefit that God gives the believer (Larkin, 22).

1:19 τί: The Greek word τί is an indefinite pronoun from the word τίς that means "what" or "what sort of" (BDAG, s.v. "τίς" 1aβﬧ, p. 1007; W, 345–46). **Syntactically**, τί introduces the third clause that serves as the direct object of the infinitive εἰδέναι (cf. vv. 18c, 18d). The clause expresses the content of the last element that Paul wants believers to know.

[ἐστίν]: The Greek word ἐστίν is a third-person singular present active indicative from the verb εἰμί that means "to be" (BDAG, s.v. "εἰμί" 2cβ, p. 284). **Syntactically**, [ἐστίν] is an ellipsis. The elliptical verb functions as the main verb of the object clause introduced by τί. The subject is "the surpassing greatness of his power" (τὸ ὑπερβάλλον μέγεθος τῆς δυνάμεως αὐτοῦ), giving the final item that Paul wants the believers to know. The Greek word μέγεθος is only used once in the New Testament. It can mean "great," in respect to size, but might be best understood as a quality: "greatness" (BDAG, s.v. "μέγεθος" 2, pp. 624–25). **Semantically**, [ἐστίν] functions as an equative present.

ὑπερβάλλον: The Greek word ὑπερβάλλον is a present active participle neuter singular nominative from the verb ὑπερβάλλω that means "to go beyond" or "surpass" (BDAG, s.v. "ὑπερβάλλω," p. 1032). **Syntactically**, ὑπερβάλλον is an attributive participle modifying "greatness" (μέγεθος). The genitive τῆς δυνάμεως ("power" or "capability"; BDAG, s.v. "δύναμις" 1a, p. 262) is an attributed genitive: "his incomparably great power" (NIV; cf. W, 90; Larkin, 22). The participle phrase ("the surpassing great power") functions as the subject of the elliptical verb ἐστίν. **Semantically**, ὑπερβάλλον is a gnomic present: "surpassing" (NASB), "immeasurable" (ESV, RSV, NRSV, CSB, HCSB), or "incomparable" (NET). The present tense describes a general attribute of God's greatness (W, 523–24).

πιστεύοντας: The Greek word πιστεύοντας is a present active participle masculine plural accusative from the verb πιστεύω that means "to believe in" or "trust" (BDAG, s.v. "πιστεύω" 2b, pp. 817–18). **Syntactically**, πιστεύοντας is a substantival participle in apposition to the pronoun ἡμᾶς, the object of the preposition εἰς: "for us who believe." **Semantically**, πιστεύοντας is a customary present: "believe" (ESV, RSV, NRSV, NIV, NET, CSB, HCSB, NASB, NKJV, KJV, NLT). The present tense describes an ongoing state (W, 521–22).

Semantical Nugget: How do the following two prepositions (εἰς and κατά) describe God's great power? The prepositions could be laid out this way:

τὸ ὑπερβάλλον μέγεθος τῆς δυνάμεως αὐτοῦ
<u>εἰς</u> ἡμᾶς τοὺς πιστεύοντας
<u>κατὰ</u> τὴν ἐνέργειαν τοῦ κράτους τῆς ἰσχύος αὐτοῦ

the surpassing greatness of his power
   <u>for</u> us who believes
   <u>according</u> to the working of his mighty strength

The first preposition (εἰς) expresses advantage rather than direction. This power is for the believer (BDAG, s.v. "εἰς" 4g, p. 290). The NIV renders the preposition: "for us" (cf. NRSV). The substantival participle τοὺς πιστεύοντας ("the believers") is in apposition to ἡμᾶς. The second preposition (κατά) expresses a standard of his great power ("in accordance" or "in conformity with"; BDAG, s.v. "κατά" B5aα, pp. 512–13). The object, τὴν ἐνέργειαν ("working" or operation"), is modified by three genitives. The first genitive, τοῦ κράτους ("might"), most likely functions as a subjunctive genitive modifying τὴν ἐνέργειαν. The second genitive, τῆς ἰσχύος ("strength"), is an attributive genitive modifying τοῦ κράτους ("strong might"; Moule, 175; ESV), rather than an attributed genitive ("mighty strength"; NIV, NET, NRSV, HCSB). God's strong might brings about this working. These terms (ἐνέργεια, κράτος, and ἰσχύς) along with δύναμις are synonymous. Even though each term brings out some individual significance (see, e.g., Hoehner, 269–71), Paul's use of these synonyms slows down the discourse, adding emphasis to this power available to the believer.

1:20a ἥν: The Greek word ἥν is a feminine singular accusative from the relative pronoun ὅς that means "which" (BDAG, s.v. "ὅς" 1a, p. 725). **Syntactically**, ἥν is a dependent adjectival relative clause functioning as the direct object of the verb. The antecedent of the pronoun could be "strength" (τῆς ἰσχύος) but is most likely "working" (τὴν ἐνέργειαν, v. 19b) due to the lexical parallel with the verb in the relative clause (ἐνήργησεν). Due to the length of the sentence in Greek, some translations begin a new sentence and insert the antecedent as the direct object of the verb (cf. NRSV, NET, CSB, HCSB). This power available for the believer (cf. v. 19) is the same power at work in raising Christ from the dead and glorifying him. This is resurrection power.

ἐνήργησεν: The Greek word ἐνήργησεν is a third-person singular aorist active indicative from the verb ἐνεργέω that means "to work," "produce," or "effect" (BDAG, s.v. "ἐνεργέω" 2, p. 335). Several English translations render the verb as "worked" (ESV, NKJV, NRSV) or "brought about" (NASB). The NIV renders the verb as "exerted"; the CSB gives a similar translation: "exercised" (cf. NET). **Syntactically**, ἐνήργησεν is the main verb of the relative clause: "which *he exercised* in Christ" (ἥν ἐνήργησεν ἐν τῷ Χριστῷ). The implied subject is God. The relative clause functions as the direct object. **Semantically**, ἐνήργησεν is a constative aorist, which identifies God's work in Christ as completed with no emphasis on the beginning, end, or continuation of the action (W, 557–58). The preposition "in Christ" (ἐν τῷ Χριστῷ) expresses sphere (Hoehner, 274).

Theological Nugget: How does God demonstrate this power in the life of the believer? The remaining verses (vv. 20–23) give further detail about the power that God has reserved for the believer (v. 19). The following participles (ἐγείρας and καθίσας) show how God made this power public: he raised Christ from the dead and sat him at the right hand. In Ephesians 2, Paul uses the same verbs with a συν- prefix to describe how God treated believers (vv. 5–6).

1:20	2:5–6
ἐνήργησεν	συνεζωοποίησεν
ἐγείρας	συνήγειρεν
καθίσας	συνεκάθισεν

> Just as God demonstrates his might in raising Christ from the dead, he makes the believer alive (συνεζωοποίησεν). And just as he raised Christ from the dead (ἐγείρας) and sat him at the right hand (καθίσας), he "raised" (συνήγειρεν) the believer and "seated" (συνεκάθισεν) the believer in heaven with Christ.

1:20b ἐγείρας: The Greek word ἐγείρας is an aorist active participle masculine nominative singular from the verb ἐγείρω that means "raise up" (BDAG, s.v. "ἐγείρω" 6, pp. 271–72). **Syntactically**, ἐγείρας introduces a dependent participle clause. It functions adverbially modifying the verb "he worked" (ἐνήργησεν). The direct object is "him" (αὐτόν), referring to Christ. **Semantically**, ἐγείρας could function temporally, describing a simultaneous action: *"when* he raised him" (NIV, NET, ESV, RSV, NASB, NKJV, KJV; W, 624–25). It could also intimate the means by which the action of the main verb is accomplished: *"by* raising him" (CSB; W, 630; KMP, 329). Even though the participle could be understood temporally, translating it as means gives more specificity, particularly due to the unique nature of events that Paul describes in the passage. (Hoehner, 274).

1:20c καί: The Greek word καί is a conjunction that means "and" (BDAG, s.v. "καί" 1bα, p. 494). **Syntactically**, καί introduces a dependent conjunctive clause: *"and* by seating him" (καὶ καθίσας). **Semantically**, καί is a coordinating connective: "and" (ESV, RSV, NRSV, NIV, NET, CSB, HCSB, NASB, KJV, NKJV). The conjunction correlates the two participles "by raising him" and "by seating him" (ἐγείρας and καθίσας). Both participles modify the main verb "he worked" (ἐνήργησεν).

καθίσας: The Greek word καθίσας is an aorist active participle masculine nominative singular from the verb καθίζω that means "to seat" or "set" (BDAG, s.v. "καθίζω" 1, pp. 491–92). **Syntactically**, καθίσας introduces a dependent participle clause introduced by καί. It functions adverbially modifying the verb "he worked" (ἐνήργησεν). **Semantically**, καθίσας most likely follows the same pattern of the previous participle (ἐγείρας). Even though it could function temporally, it most likely functions as means (see ἐγείρας above): *"by* seating him at his right hand in the heavens." Paul modifies the participle with three prepositional phrases expressing specifically where God has seated Jesus.

    Καθίσας
        <u>ἐν</u> δεξιᾷ αὐτοῦ
        <u>ἐν</u> τοῖς ἐπουρανίοις
        21a <u>ὑπεράνω</u> πάσης ἀρχῆς καὶ ἐξουσίας καὶ δυνάμεως καὶ
        κυριότητος

    by seating him
        <u>at</u> his right hand

<u>in</u> the heavenly places
²¹ᵃ <u>high above</u> every ruler and authority and power and dominion

The first prepositional phrase places Christ at God's right hand, an allusion to Psalm 110:1 (LXX 109:1). He will quote Psalm 8:6 (LXX 8:7) in verse 22 to describe Christ's subjugation of all things (see Theological Nugget at 1:22a). The second prepositional phrase places Christ in the heavenly places, an important theme that runs throughout the book. It describes where this struggle occurs (see Lexical Nugget at 1:20b). The third prepositional phrase places Christ over these rulers. Paul lists four objects for the preposition. As the letter unfolds we learn that these rulers are hostile (cf. Eph. 2:2; 6:12). Paul derives these labels from the Jewish spiritual world (see Arnold 1989, 52–54 for a survey of Jewish texts that use these terms). The first object is ἀρχῆς ("ruler"); this term refers to an authority figure that initiates an activity (BDAG, s.v. "ἀρχή" 6, p. 138). The second object is ἐξουσίας ("authority"); this term refers to someone who bears ruling authority (BDAG, s.v. "ἐξουσία" 5b, p. 353). The third object is δυνάμεως ("power"); this term refers to a being characterized with remarkable power (BDAG, s.v. "δύναμις" 5, p. 263). The fourth object is κυριότητος ("dominion"); this term refers to a class of angelic powers—"bearers of the ruling power" or "dominions" (BDAG, s.v. "κυριότης" 3, p. 579). All four objects are synonyms. The adjective πᾶς modifies each one to specify everything that belongs in a particular class: "every kind of" (BDAG, s.v. "πᾶς" 5, p. 784). The Jewish background describes God initially establishing these figures to ensure peace on earth; however, these beings rebelled and led the people astray (see, e.g., Jub. 15:31–32; 1 En. 8:1–4); nonetheless, God has subjugated these beings to Christ (Gombis 2010, 35–48).

Text-Critical Nugget: Did Paul use an indicative verb or a participle to describe Christ seating? Several Western (D, F, G) and Byzantine (𝔐) manuscripts replace the participle καθίσας with the indicative form ἐκάθισεν. The majority of Alexandrian manuscripts read the participle (𝔓92, ℵ, A, B, 1175, 1739, 1881). The indicative is found in the MT and RP²⁰⁰⁵, while the participle is found in the NA²⁸, SBL, and THGNT. The decision impacts the structure of the passage. If the indicative is original, the verb should coordinate with ἐνήργησεν (v. 20a)—God worked in Christ … and seated him. However, if the participle is original, the verb should coordinate with the previous participle ἐγείρας (see the clausal outline above). In this case, the two participles describe how God worked in Christ, namely by raising him from the dead (v. 20b) and seating him at the right hand (v. 20c). Even though the reading with the indicative has better external evidence, being found in both the Western and Byzantine text types, the reading with the participle is solidly within the Alexandrian text type. On internal grounds, the reading with the participle makes better sense. God demonstrated his power by raising Christ and seating him at his right hand.

Lexical Nugget: What does Paul mean by the "heavenly places"? Out of the twelve times that Paul uses the word "heavenly places" (ἐπουρανίοις), it appears five times in Ephesians (Eph. 1:3, 20; 2:6; 3:10; 6:12). In addition, he uses the plural form of οὐρανός ("heavens") another four times (Eph. 1:10; 3:15; 4:10; 6:9). In other letters, he uses both the singular and the plural. In Ephesians, these terms only appear in the plural. The plural reflects a Hebrew idea that the heavens are multilayered (Roberts 2016, 23). Not only does God dwell in the heavenly places (Eph. 6:9), but other spiritual beings do as well (Eph. 1:10; 3:10), some of which are evil (Eph. 6:12). As Ephesians unfolds, Paul describes Jesus as victor over these evil spirits as God has vindicated him by raising him from the dead (Eph. 1:20; 4:10). Because of this victory, the believer has received a blessing in the heavens (Eph. 1:3; 2:6). In Ephesians, Paul describes this struggle taking place in the heavenly places. This spiritual reality corresponds to the world of the believer (cf. Eph. 6:12). Even though the victory has been achieved through the resurrection, these powers are still at work in the life of both believers and unbelievers (Eph. 2:1–3; 4:17–19; 6:12).

καί: The Greek word καί is a conjunction that means "and" (BDAG, s.v. "καί" 2a, p. 495). **Syntactically**, καί introduces the last item in a list Paul began in verse 21a: "*and* every name that is named" (καὶ παντὸς ὀνόματος ὀνομαζομένου). **Semantically**, καί is most likely ascensive, since it introduces the last element of a list: "even" (Larkin, 24; Merkle, 46). Most English versions translate it as "and" (ESV, RSV, NRSV, NIV, NET, CSB, HCSB, NASB, NKJV, KJV). The clause concludes Paul's list of powers that God has placed under Christ's dominion; however, this element is modified by a participle (ὀνομαζομένου).

ὀνομαζομένου: The Greek word ὀνομαζομένου is a present passive participle neuter genitive singular from the verb ὀνομάζω that means "to name a name" or "use a name" (BDAG, s.v. "ὀνομάζω" 2, p. 714). Arnold notes that first-century readers would associate "naming a name" with magic. Within a magical context, one could invoke a name to conjure power. Luke describes Jewish exorcists calling on the name of the Lord to drive out demons (Acts 19:13) (Arnold, 114). **Syntactically**, ὀνομαζομένου functions as an attributive participle that modifies ὀνόματος, rendered: "above every name that is named" (ESV, NET, RSV, NRSV, NASB, NKJV, KJV). The NIV seems to take advantage of the background rendering it as: "every name that is invoked" (cf. BDAG, s.v. "ὀνομάζω" 2, p. 714). **Semantically**, ὀνομαζομένου is a customary present, which signals an action that regularly occurs (W, 521–22). The participle clause is the last item of a list: all rulers, authorities, powers, and lordships. However, the shift to the participle makes this a catchall. Because of the move from the series of prepositions to the participle, we have placed this on a separate line in the structural layout.

μέλλοντι: The Greek word μέλλοντι is a present active participle masculine dative singular from the verb μέλλω that means "to come" (BDAG, s.v. "μέλλω" 3, p. 628). **Syntactically**, Larkin gives the possibility that this is a neuter substantival participle referring to the future (Larkin, 24). However, it is best to consider μέλλοντι as an attributive participle modifying an implied masculine noun τῷ αἰῶνι: "the age to come" (NRSV) or "the one to come" (ESV, RSV, NIV, NET, CSB, HCSB, NASB). **Semantically**, μέλλοντι is a gnomic present: "to come" (ESV, RSV, NRSV, NIV, NET, CSB, HCSB, NASB, NKJV, KJV, NLT). The present tense describes a timeless fact (W, 523–24).

> **Syntactical Nugget**: How do the prepositional phrases relate to the context in verse 21? Paul inserts two prepositional phrases "in this age" (ἐν τῷ αἰῶνι τούτῳ) and "in the age to come" (ἐν τῷ μέλλοντι). Both prepositions function temporally describing points in time. The construction οὐ μόνον … ἀλλὰ καί creates a contrast between the two time periods (BDAG, s.v. "μόνος" 2cα, p. 695). Christ's authority extends to both periods. In verse 21b, Paul describes Christ's lordship in physical terms. He is over all angelic rulers. In verse 21c, he describes it temporally—his lordship is over all time. No name now or in the future will rival Jesus's name. Today we might say: "anytime, anywhere."

1:22a καί: The Greek word καί is a conjunction that means "and" (BDAG, s.v. "καί" 1bα, p. 494). **Syntactically**, καί introduces an independent conjunctive clause: "and he put all things under his feet" (καὶ πάντα ὑπέταξεν ὑπὸ τοὺς πόδας αὐτοῦ). **Semantically**, καί is a coordinating connective: "and" (ESV, RSV, NRSV, NIV, NET, CSB, HCSB, NASB, NKJV, KJV). The conjunction connects this phrase to the previous indicative verb in verse 20a: "he worked" (ἐνήργησεν). Paul will add a third indicative to his list in verse 22b: "he gave" (ἔδωκεν).

ὑπέταξεν: The Greek word ὑπέταξεν is a third-person singular aorist active indicative from the verb ὑποτάσσω that means "to subject" or "subordinate" (BDAG, s.v. "ὑποτάσσω" 1a, p. 1042). **Syntactically**, ὑπέταξεν is the main verb of the independent conjunctive clause introduced by καί, parallel with the ἐνήργησεν (v. 20a). The subject is implied by the verb: "he," referring to God. The direct object is "all things" (πάντα). **Semantically**, ὑπέταξεν could be classified as a proleptic aorist (W, 564). In 1 Corinthians, Paul describes this subjugation as a future event (1 Cor. 15:27). If this is the case, the aorist verb describes a future event. However, in 1 Corinthians 15:23–27, Paul describes the events culminating at the end. Here, Paul is discussing Christ's subjugation of demonic powers at the resurrection and exaltation (Hoehner, 284; Arnold, 115). In this case, the aorist is best understood as an ingressive aorist emphasizing the point of time in which all things are subjugated to Christ (W, 558–59).

> **Theological Nugget**: How does Paul apply Psalm 8 to Christ in Ephesians? In Ephesians 1:20 Paul alludes to Psalm 110:1 (LXX 109:1); in verse 22 he quotes Psalm 8:6 (LXX 8:7). Even though Psalm 8 alludes to Adam rather than a messianic figure, other New Testament passages link the two psalms and apply them to Christ (1 Cor. 15:25–27; Heb. 1:13; 2:6–8). Psalm 110 describes the defeat of the Messiah's enemies, while the Messiah sits at the right hand of the Lord. Jesus's resurrection (v. 20) provides proof that he is God's Messiah and implies that he will subjugate his enemies. However, Psalm 110 seems to have earthly rulers in mind. In the same way, Psalm 8 describes Adam's dominion over the created order—livestock, birds, fish (Ps. 8:7–8). In Ephesians, Paul describes Christ's dominion to include all things on the earth, but also all of the powerful elements in the heavenly places (Eph. 1:20–21). Like Adam, Christ has dominion over all things; unlike Adam, his dominion extends over spiritual beings as well.

1:22b καί: The Greek word καί is a conjunction that means "and" (BDAG, s.v. "καί" 1bα, p. 494). **Syntactically**, καί introduces an independent conjunctive clause: "*and* he gave him" (καὶ αὐτὸν ἔδωκεν). **Semantically**, καί is a coordinating connective: "and" (ESV, RSV, NRSV, NIV, NET, CSB, HCSB, NASB, NKJV, KJV). The conjunction introduces the last indicative of the relative clause that Paul began in verse 20a. The indicative is parallel with the two verbs "he worked" (ἐνήργησεν, v. 20a) and "he subjected" (ὑπέταξεν, v. 22a).

ἔδωκεν: The Greek word ἔδωκεν is a third-person singular aorist active indicative from the verb δίδωμι that means "to give," or in this case "to appoint" (BDAG, s.v. "δίδωμι" 7, p. 242). Some English versions render the verb literally: "and gave him" (ESV, NET, NASB, NKJV, KJV), the sense of the verb is that God "appointed" (NIV, CSB, HCSB) or "made" (RSV, NRSV, NLT) Christ as the head. **Syntactically**, ἔδωκεν is the main verb of the independent conjunctive clause introduced by καί. The subject is implied by the verb: "he," referring to God. The direct object is "him" (αὐτόν). The second accusative "head" (κεφαλήν) is the complement in an object-complement double accusative construction (W, 182–89). The indirect object is "church" (τῇ ἐκκλησίᾳ). **Semantically**, ἔδωκεν is an ingressive aorist emphasizing the point at which God appointed Christ as the head over all the church. The prepositional phrase "over all things" (ὑπὲρ πάντα) describes Christ's position over all things (KMP, 410; BDAG, s.v. "ὑπέρ" B, p. 1031). The dative τῇ ἐκκλησίᾳ ("church") could be a dative of advantage: "over everything for the church" (NIV, RSV, NRSV), but is best understood as the indirect object: "he gave him to the church as head over all things" (NET; cf. ESV, NASB, NKJV, KJV).

1:23a ἥτις: The Greek word ἥτις is a feminine singular nominative from the indefinite relative pronoun ὅστις that means "which" in this context (BDAG, s.v. "ὅστις" 2b, pp. 729–30; Zerwick §216). **Syntactically**, ἥτις introduces a dependent adjectival relative clause *"which* is his body" (ἥτις ἐστὶν τὸ σῶμα αὐτοῦ). The antecedent of the pronoun is "the church" (τῇ ἐκκλησίᾳ). The pronoun functions as the subject of the relative clause.

ἐστίν: The Greek word ἐστίν is a third-person singular present active indicative from the verb εἰμί that means "to be" (BDAG, s.v. "εἰμί" 2a, p. 283). **Syntactically**, ἐστίν functions as the main verb of the relative clause. The relative pronoun ἥτις is the subject; the predicate nominative is "his body" (τὸ σῶμα αὐτοῦ). **Semantically**, ἐστίν is an equative present tense: "is" (ESV, NIV, RSV, NRSV, NASB, NKJV, KJV). The relative pronoun emphasizes the organic relationship between Christ and the church, which Paul will develop throughout the book.

> **Theological Nugget**: How does Paul use the "body" metaphor in Ephesians? In other books, Paul uses the metaphor of a body to describe the different roles that believers play in the community of believers (Rom. 12:4–8; 1 Cor. 12:12–31). In Ephesians, he uses the metaphor to emphasize the unity of the believers and their relationship to Christ (1:22, 23; 2:16; 4:4, 12, 15, 16; 5:23, 30). In the current context (Eph. 1:20–23), the image depicts Christ's authority over all things, including the church. Later in the book, he uses the image to convey the notion of Christ's provision for the body (Arnold, 115). Christ's work on the cross brings Jews and Gentiles into one body (2:16; cf. 4:4). He provides for the church so that the body may "grow into him who is the head, Christ" (Eph. 4:15). In Ephesians 5, Paul uses the language to describe the marital relationship (Eph. 5:21–33). As he builds the image, he states that husbands should nourish and cherish their wives as they would their own bodies—"just as also Christ does the church" (5:29).

1:23b πληρουμένου: The Greek word πληρουμένου is a present middle participle masculine genitive singular from the verb πληρόω that means "to fill" (BDAG, s.v. "πληρόω" 1a, p. 828). **Syntactically**, πληρουμένου is a substantival participle. The participle phrase "the one who fills all things in all ways" (τοῦ τὰ πάντα ἐν πᾶσιν πληρουμένου) modifies "fullness" (τὸ πλήρωμα), which is in apposition to τὸ σῶμα. **Semantically**, πληρουμένου is a customary present: "fills" (ESV, RSV, NRSV, NIV, NET, CSB, HCSB, NASB, NKJV, NLT). The verb describes an ongoing action of Christ (W, 521–22).

Grammatical Nugget: What does the phrase "the fullness of the one who fills everything in every way" (τὸ πλήρωμα τοῦ τὰ πάντα ἐν πᾶσιν πληρουμένου) mean? The phrase forms an alliteration in Greek with the "P" sound, giving the passage a rhetorical effect (Thielman, 116), but leaving a few grammatical questions. Each part of the phrase is debated. First, the Greek word πλήρωμα is in apposition to σῶμα, a reference to the church. The term can either have an active meaning: "that which fills" (BDAG, s.v. "πλήρωμα" 1b, p. 829); or it can have a passive meaning: "that which is full of something" (BDAG, s.v. "πλήρωμα" 2, p. 829). The passive meaning is more consistent with Paul's usage throughout the letter. In Ephesians 3:19, believers are filled with the fullness of God; in Ephesians 5:18, they are filled with the Spirit. On the other hand, in Ephesians 4:10, Christ fills all things; believers are growing to his stature (Eph. 4:13). Throughout the letter, Christ is the active agent and the church is passive (Thielman, 114; Hoehner, 299; Barth, 209; Larkin, 26; Lincoln, 75).

The second issue is the voice of the participle πληρουμένου—it could be interpreted with the passive voice: "the one who is being filled." This implies that Christ is being filled by God (Hoehner, 296–300; Best, 184). In Ephesians 4:10, Paul uses the active form of the verb, suggesting that he intends the passive voice here. On the other hand, it might be best to take the participle as a middle because of the accusative τὰ πάντα—the passive voice cannot take a direct object (Larkin, 26; Arnold, 117–18). Most English versions render the participle with an active force: "the one who fills" (ESV, RSV, NRSV, NIV, NET, CSB, HCSB, NASB, NKJV, KJV; cf. BDAG, s.v. "πληρόω" 1a, p. 828; BDF §316.1).

Finally, it is possible that the accusative clause function adverbially: "the one who is being filled *completely*" (Moule, 160). Commentators who understand the participle as passive must interpret the phrase this way; however, it is rare. Elsewhere the phrase appears as the direct object (cf. 1 Cor. 12:6; 15:28). It is used as a direct object in verse 22 (Merkle, 48). This interpretation underscores the fact that the participle has an active meaning. The prepositional phrase ἐν πᾶσιν expresses reference. Christ fills all things "everywhere" (NLT) or "in every way" (NIV, CSB, HCSB, LEB). In short, as Christ fills the church, his body, he fills all things.

Ephesians 2:1–10

Big Greek Idea: Despite once being dead in sins and under satanic control, God demonstrates his mercy to the world by saving believers, making them alive, and giving them a seat in the heavenlies with Christ—an act of grace—so that they might walk in the good works that he has prepared for them.

Structural Overview: The section begins with "And you" (2:1), marking a shift in his discussion from the power at work in Jesus's resurrection and ascension to how this power impacts the believer and their relationship to God. Even though this is a new section, Paul draws from his discussion about power in verse 19. By using similar language, he shifts the spotlight to discuss the believer: because of their relationship to Christ the believer is made alive, raised up, and seated with Christ in the heavenlies (2:5–6; cf. 1:20). The significance of Christ's new position at the right hand of God is that the same power is at work to make the believer alive.

The first part of this section (2:1–7) is a single sentence, which contrasts the believer's former life with God's salvation. The first part of the sentence (2:1–3) is a digression—the main verb does not appear until verse 5. Paul describes the believers as spiritually dead, having conducted their lives under the influence of the evil spirits at work in the current age. Even though he is not explicit, he alludes to Satan by describing a single power who has authority over this world (v. 2). The second part of the sentence establishes the contrast: while we were dead in our sins, through an act of mercy God raised us with Christ (2:4–6). As a result of this act of salvation he demonstrated his grace to the world (2:7).

Paul rounds off the paragraph with a second result (2:8–10): God saved us in order to create a people for good works. He repeats the main idea of the sentence: "you are saved by grace" (2:8a; cf. 2:5c) and works out the implications. Because this salvation comes through grace, no one can boast. Rather than relying on our own works for salvation (ἔργον), Paul states that we are God's work, or literally "creation" (ποίημα). He created us in order to "walk" in the good works that God prepared for us. The verb "to walk" (περιπατέω) forms an *inclusio*. The believer once "walked" in sin (2:2), but now "walks" in these good works. In the second part of the book, Paul will use the same verb to describe specifically how the believer should conduct their lives (4:1, 17; 5:2, 8, 15).

Outline:
    Before salvation, the believer was dead in sin and under the control of satanic powers (vv. 1–3)
    God saves the believer by his grace, and makes us alive in Christ (vv. 4–7)
      God saved the believer because of his mercy (v. 4)

God saved the believer despite their being spiritually dead (vv. 5–6)
God saved the believer to demonstrate his grace (v. 7)
Because God saved the believer through grace, no one can boast (vv. 8–10)
God's salvation is by grace so that no one can boast (vv. 8–9)
God's salvation is by grace leading the believer into good works provided by God (v. 10)

CLAUSAL OUTLINE FOR EPHESIANS 2:1–10

[συνεζωοποίησεν (v. 5b)]
[he made us alive (v. 5b)]

2:1 Καὶ ὑμᾶς **ὄντας** νεκροὺς τοῖς παραπτώμασιν καὶ ταῖς ἁμαρτίαις ὑμῶν,
2:1 And **even though** you **were** dead in your trespasses and sins,

2:2 ἐν αἷς ποτε **περιεπατήσατε** κατὰ τὸν αἰῶνα τοῦ κόσμου τούτου, κατὰ τὸν ἄρχοντα τῆς ἐξουσίας τοῦ ἀέρος, (τοῦ πνεύματος τοῦ νῦν ἐνεργοῦντος ἐν τοῖς υἱοῖς τῆς ἀπειθείας)·
2:2 in which **you** once **walked** according to the age of this world, according to the ruler over the authority of the air, (over the spirit who is now working in the sons of disobedience);

[τοῖς υἱοῖς τῆς ἀπειθείας (v. 2)]
[the sons of disobedience (v. 2)]

2:3a ἐν οἷς καὶ ἡμεῖς πάντες **ἀνεστράφημέν** ποτε ἐν ταῖς ἐπιθυμίαις τῆς σαρκὸς ἡμῶν,
2:3a among whom also we all **behaved** once in the lusts of our flesh,

2:3b **ποιοῦντες** τὰ θελήματα τῆς σαρκὸς καὶ τῶν διανοιῶν,
2:3b **by carrying out** the will of the flesh and mind

[ἀνεστράφημεν (v. 3a)]
[we behaved (v. 3a)]

2:3c καὶ **ἤμεθα** τέκνα φύσει ὀργῆς
2:3c and **we were** children destined for wrath because of our nature

2:3d ὡς καὶ οἱ λοιποὶ [**ἦσαν**]·
2:3d even as the rest [**were**];

2:4a ὁ δὲ θεὸς πλούσιος **ὢν** ἐν ἐλέει, διὰ τὴν πολλὴν ἀγάπην αὐτοῦ
2:4a <u>but</u> God, **because he is** rich in mercy, because of his great love

                        2:4b ἣν **ἠγάπησεν** ἡμᾶς,
                        2:4b <u>with which</u> **he loved** us,

2:5a καὶ **ὄντας** ἡμᾶς νεκροὺς τοῖς παραπτώμασιν
2:5a <u>and</u> **even though** we **were** dead in our trespasses

2:5b **συνεζωοποίησεν** τῷ Χριστῷ
2:5b **he made us alive** with Christ

2:5c —χάριτί **ἐστε σεσωσμένοι**—
2:5c —**you are saved** on the basis of grace—

2:6a καὶ **συνήγειρεν**
2:6a <u>and</u> **he raised us with Him**

2:6b καὶ **συνεκάθισεν** ἐν τοῖς ἐπουρανίοις ἐν Χριστῷ Ἰησοῦ,
2:6b <u>and</u> **he seated us** in the heavenly places in Christ Jesus

    2:7 **ἵνα ἐνδείξηται** (ἐν τοῖς αἰῶσιν τοῖς ἐπερχομένοις) (τὸ ὑπερβάλλον πλοῦτος τῆς χάριτος αὐτοῦ) ἐν χρηστότητι ἐφ᾽ ἡμᾶς ἐν Χριστῷ Ἰησοῦ.
    2:7 **so that he might show** (his surpassing wealth of grace) in kindness toward us in Christ Jesus (in the coming age).

2:8a τῇ γὰρ χάριτί **ἐστε σεσωσμένοι** διὰ πίστεως·
2:8a <u>For</u> **you are saved** on the basis of grace through faith;

2:8b καὶ τοῦτο [**ἐστίν**] οὐκ ἐξ ὑμῶν,
2:8b <u>and</u> this [**is**] not from yourselves,

2:8c θεοῦ τὸ δῶρον [**ἐστίν**]·
2:8c it [**is**] a gift from God

2:9a οὐκ ἐξ ἔργων [**ἐστίν**],
2:9a it [**is**] not from works

    2:9b **ἵνα** μή τις **καυχήσηται**.
    2:9b **so that** no one **can boast**.

²:¹⁰ᵃ αὐτοῦ γάρ **ἐσμεν** ποίημα,
²:¹⁰ᵃ <u>For **we are**</u> his workmanship

      ²:¹⁰ᵇ **κτισθέντες** ἐν Χριστῷ Ἰησοῦ ἐπὶ ἔργοις ἀγαθοῖς
      ²:¹⁰ᵇ <u>**because we have been created**</u> in Christ Jesus for good works,

    ²:¹⁰ᶜ <u>οἷς</u> **προητοίμασεν** ὁ θεὸς
    ²:¹⁰ᶜ <u>which</u> God **prepared beforehand**

      ²:¹⁰ᵈ **ἵνα** ἐν αὐτοῖς **περιπατήσωμεν**.
      ²:¹⁰ᵈ <u>**so that we might walk**</u> in them.

SYNTAX EXPLAINED FOR EPHESIANS 2:1–10

²:¹ καί: The Greek word καί is a conjunction that means "and" (BDAG, s.v. "καί" 1e, p. 495). **Syntactically**, καί introduces an independent conjunctive clause: "*and* you being dead" (Καὶ ὑμᾶς ὄντας νεκρούς). **Semantically**, καί is a co-ordinating connective: "and" (ESV, RSV, NET, CSB, HCSB, NASB, NKJV, KJV). The conjunction introduces a new section by linking it to the previous discussion of God's power at work in the Christ. The conjunction marks a shift in focus to discuss the believer (Hoehner, 307). The NIV brings out this sense by rendering the phrase as "As for you."

ὄντας: The Greek word ὄντας is a present active participle masculine plural accusative from the verb εἰμί that means "to be" (BDAG, s.v. "εἰμί" 2a, p. 283). Due to the fact that Paul does not provide the main verb until verse 5, many translations render the participle as the main verb of the sentence—"you were" (ESV, NRSV, NIV, HCSB, NASB). **Syntactically**, ὄντας introduces a dependent participle clause, modifying the main verb in verse 5: "he made us alive" (συνεζωοποίησεν). The direct object of the main verb is the second-person personal pronoun "you" (ὑμᾶς). The accusative νεκρούς is the predicate of the participle. The participle phrase describes the believers' state before God "made them alive" (v. 5). **Semantically**, ὄντας functions as concessive: "*although* you were dead" (NET, LEB). The participle of concession establishes a contrast between the participle and the main verb (W, 634). Despite the fact that these believers were once dead in their sin, God has made them alive.

Semantical Nugget: What does the dative phrase τοῖς παραπτώμασιν καὶ ταῖς ἁμαρτίαις mean? The phrase "in your trespasses and sins" (τοῖς παραπτώμασιν καὶ ταῖς ἁμαρτίαις) forms a hendiadys—two words brought together to make a single concept. The datives could express cause: you were dead "*because* of your trespasses and sins" (Arnold, 130). However, they express sphere; they describe the state of the believer prior to their relationship with Christ (W, 154). In Colossians, Paul uses a similar phrase with the preposition ἐν, making the idea of sphere more explicit (2:13).

Grammatical Nugget: Who is actually dead? We do not encounter the main verb of the sentence until verse 5: "he made us alive" (συνεζωοποίησεν). Due to the length of the sentence, Paul repeats the participle clause from verse 1 in verse 5 to pick up the argument that he begins in Chapter 2. However, when he repeats the clause, he changes the pronoun form second-person to first-person:

> v. 1: καὶ ὑμᾶς ὄντας νεκρούς ("and you being dead")
> v. 5: καὶ ὄντας ἡμᾶς νεκρούς ("and us being dead")

The use of the second person in verse 1 might suggest that Paul only has Gentile believers in mind; however, the change to the first person suggests that he has all believers in mind. The repetition suggests that he digresses from his main argument to describe the level of depravity of the believer's former position. The extensive discussion sharpens the contrast between the sin of those believers and the rich mercy and the great love of God (2:4). Paul gives a similar description of the believer's former position later in the letter (Eph. 4:17–19).

2:2a αἷς: The Greek word αἷς is a feminine plural dative from the relative pronoun ὅς that means "which" in this context (BDAG, s.v. "ὅς" 1a, p. 725). **Syntactically**, αἷς introduces a dependent adjectival relative clause "in *which* you once walked" (ἐν αἷς ποτε περιεπατήσατε). The antecedent of the pronoun is both "your trespasses and sin" (τοῖς παραπτώμασιν and ταῖς ἁμαρτίαις). The relative pronoun is feminine, in agreement with the closest referent (ταῖς ἁμαρτίαις). The pronoun functions as the object of the preposition "in" (ἐν), describing the sphere in which the believers once walked.

περιεπατήσατε: The Greek word περιεπατήσατε is a second-person plural aorist active indicative from the verb περιπατέω that means "to behave" or "live" (BDAG, s.v. "περιπατέω" 2aδ, p. 803). Many English versions render the verb literally: "you once walked" (ESV, RSV, HCSB, NASB, NKJV, KJV); others opt to treat the verb metaphorically: "you once lived" (NIV, NRSV, CSB, NET). This is a common Jewish metaphor to describe how one behaves. In verse 10, Paul will say that God has prepared good works in which the believer "walks," creating a contrast. Verse 2 describes their former behavior; verse 10 describes their behavior in light of God's salvation. In the second half of the letter, Paul uses the verb to describe a believer's conduct in fuller detail (4:1, 17; 5:2, 8, 15). **Syntactically**, περιεπατήσατε functions as the main verb of the relative clause. The subject of the verb is implied:

"you," referring to the Ephesian believers. **Semantically**, περιεπατήσατε is rendered as a constative aorist, with no emphasis on the beginning or end of the action (W, 557–58). The verb describes their former behavior.

Theological Nugget: When did these believers follow this behavior? Paul uses the adverb ποτε to mark this former behavior. English translations render the adverb as either "once" (ESV, RSV, NRSV, NKJV), "formerly" (NET, NASB), or "previously" (CSB, HCSB) (BDAG, s.v. "ποτέ" 1, p. 856). The adverb highlights the temporal contrast between the former life of the Ephesian believers and their current life in Christ. Paul will repeat the adverb in verse 3 creating a contrast between this state and God's salvation described in verses 5b–6. The temporal contrast draws out the soteriological implications for the Ephesian believers. Because of God's grace, they have a different relationship with those powers at work in the world (cf. Rom. 6:6–11). Paul will use a similar technique throughout the letter. He contrasts the Gentiles' former position prior to Christ's death (Eph. 2:11–13). He makes a similar contrast with the believers' conduct as "children of darkness" before "walking as children of light" (Eph. 5:8).

Semantical Nugget: How do the following prepositional phrases relate to the context and what do they mean? Paul repeats the preposition κατά, both modifying περιεπατήσατε.

> περιεπατήσατε
>> <u>κατὰ</u> τὸν αἰῶνα τοῦ κόσμου τούτου
>> <u>κατὰ</u> τὸν ἄρχοντα τῆς ἐξουσίας τοῦ ἀέρος

> you once walked
>> <u>according to</u> the age of this world
>> <u>according to</u> the authority of the air

The preposition κατά normally expresses a standard; however, in this context, it most likely indicates some level of control (Best, 202; BDAG, s.v. "κατά" B5aα, p. 512). Some English versions render the preposition "following" (ESV, RSV, NRSV; cf. NIV). The object of the first preposition (αἰών) can refer to an evil, or demonic power (BDAG, s.v. "αἰών" 4, p. 33; Barth, 214). However, the wider context suggests that this is a temporal element, which is consistent with his usage in the wider context (1:21; 2:7; 3:9, 11, 21; cf. Gal. 1:4; Thielman, 123; Arnold, 131). The genitive τοῦ κόσμου ("world") is most likely an attributive genitive: "this worldly age"; or as a descriptive genitive: "age of this world" in contrast to the world to come (Hoehner, 310). Most English versions render the phrase: "the course of this world" (ESV, RSV, NRSV, NASB, NKJV, KJV) or "the ways of this world" (NIV, HCSB).

The object of the second preposition "ruler" (τὸν ἄρχοντα) is modified by the genitive τῆς ἐξουσίας ("authority"). English translations have rendered τῆς ἐξουσίας as "power" (ESV, RSV, NRSV, NASB) or "kingdom" (NET, NIV); the HCSB renders the phrase: "the ruler who exercises authority over." BDAG states that the usage here describes "the sphere in which power is exercised" or "domain" (BDAG, s.v. "ἐξουσία" 6, p. 353). The genitive τῆς ἐξουσίας could either be an attributive ("powerful ruler"), but is best understood as a genitive of subordination "ruler over authority"). The genitive τοῦ ἀέρος is in apposition modifying τῆς ἐξουσίας, defining the domain of this authority. "Air" refers to the space above the earth—the sky (BDAG, s.v. "ἀήρ" 2b, p. 23). This ruler exercises authority in the world (Larkin, 28). The HCSB renders the clause as "the ruler who exercises authority over the lower heavens."

ἐνεργοῦντος: The Greek word ἐνεργοῦντος is a present active participle neuter singular genitive from the verb ἐνεργέω that means "to work" or "operate" (BDAG, s.v. "ἐνεργέω" 1a, p. 335). Most English versions translate the verb as "working"; the NET translates the participle as "energizing." Paul uses the same verb to describe the power at work in Christ when God raised him from the dead (Eph. 1:20). At the resurrection, God was at work in Christ. And subsequently, he is at work in the life of the believer. However, before salvation, this ruling authority is at work in the life of the unbeliever. **Syntactically**, ἐνεργοῦντος is an attributive participle in the genitive position modifying τοῦ πνεύματος ("spirit"). **Semantically**, the present tense functions as a customary or gnomic present describing how this spirit influences nonbelievers. The prepositional phrase "in the sons of disobedience" expresses sphere. This spirit is working in the midst of these people. The phrase "sons of disobedience" (τοῖς υἱοῖς τῆς ἀπειθείας) is a Hebrew idiom. The genitive is attributive ("disobedient sons), showing a characteristic of these people (Moule, 174–75; Robertson, 651–52).

Syntactical Nugget: What is the relationship between the participle phrase "the spirit who is now working" (τοῦ πνεύματος τοῦ νῦν ἐνεργοῦντος) and the head noun "the ruler" (τὸν ἄρχοντα)? It is possible that τοῦ πνεύματος is in apposition to ἄρχοντα, referring to Satan (Best, 205; Larkin, 28). Most English translations follow this reading by inserting a comma before the genitive: "the prince of the power of the air, *the spirit that is now at work*" (ESV; cf. RSV, NRSV, NIV, CSB, HCSB, NASB, NKJV, KJV). The problem with this view is that the case is not the same. If this were true, we would anticipate that the case of τοῦ πνεύματος be accusative, not genitive (W, 94–100, 104). A better interpretation is to view the genitive τοῦ πνεύματος as parallel to previous genitive τῆς ἐξουσίας, functioning as a genitive of subordination: "the ruler *over* the domain of the air *and over* the spirit who is now working") (W, 104; Hoehner, 314–15). The NET brings out this interpretation by repeating ruler: "the ruler of the kingdom of the air, *the ruler of the spirit*."

2:3a οἷς: The Greek word οἷς is a masculine plural dative from the relative pronoun ὅς that means "in whom" in the context (BDAG, s.v. "ὅς" 1bα, pp. 725–26). Due to the length of the sentence in Greek, several English translations begin a new sentence here and render the relative pronoun as a pronoun: "Among them" (RSV; cf. NIV, NRSV, CSB, HCSB, NASB, NLT). **Syntactically**, οἷς introduces a dependent substantival relative clause "in *whom* also we all behaved once" (ἐν οἷς καὶ ἡμεῖς πάντες ἀνεστράφημέν ποτε). The antecedent of the pronoun could be "trespasses" (τοῖς παραπτώμασιν) (cf. RSV), but more likely it is "the sons" (τοῖς υἱοῖς, v. 2b) since it is nearer. The relative clause functions as the object of the preposition ἐν, expressing sphere of this former behavior. Because of the referent, we can render the prepositional phrase as "among *whom*."

καί: The Greek word καί is a conjunction that means "and" (BDAG, s.v. "καί" 2a, p. 495). **Syntactically**, καί introduces an independent conjunctive clause: "*also* we all behaved" (καὶ ἡμεῖς πάντες ἀνεστράφημέν). **Semantically**, καί is a coordinating connective: we "also" (NIV, NET, NKJV, KJV) or we "too" (CSB, HCSB, NASB). Several versions simply omit the conjunction (ESV, RSV, NRSV). The conjunction links the clause to verse 1: "And you" (Καὶ ὑμᾶς). Paul begins by describing the former behavior of some people, but then widens the scope and applies this to all people.

ἀνεστράφημεν: The Greek word ἀνεστράφημεν is a first-person plural aorist passive indicative from the verb ἀναστρέφω that means "to behave" or "act" (BDAG, s.v. "ἀναστρέφω" 3b, p. 73). **Syntactically**, ἀνεστράφημεν functions as the main verb of the relative clause. The subject of the verb is the first-person plural pronoun: "we" (ἡμεῖς), which includes Paul along with the readers. Paul shifts the person of the verb from second-person ("you once walked" v. 2) to first-person. The adjective πάντες emphasizes the shift: "we all" (BDAG, s.v. "πᾶς" 1cα, p. 783). **Semantically**, ἀνεστράφημεν functions as a constative aorist with no emphasis on the beginning or end of the action (W, 557–58). The verb is synonymous with the main verb in verse 2: "you walked" (περιεπατήσατε). The focus of both verbs is on how believers acted prior to salvation. By using the adverb "once" (ποτε), Paul strengthens the correlation. The following prepositional phrase "in the desires of our flesh" (ἐν ταῖς ἐπιθυμίαις τῆς σαρκὸς ἡμῶν) expresses sphere. The genitive τῆς σαρκός could be an attributive: "fleshly desires" (CSB, HCSB; cf. NLT), but is most likely a subjective genitive: "flesh that *produces* desires" (Hoehner, 320). ἡμῶν is possessive.

Grammatical Nugget: Why does Paul shift the subject from the second-person plural pronoun to the first-person plural form ἡμεῖς? Later in the chapter, Paul distinguishes his audience ("you all") as Gentiles (cf. 2:11–12) from Jews ("we"). It is possible that Paul had Gentiles in mind as he began the chapter, and changes the person to include Jews (Abbott,

1909, 43). The problem with this view is that Paul does not introduce an ethnic division until Ephesians 2:11 (Thielman, 125). His use of πάντες suggests that this is a universal problem (Hoehner, 317). Regardless, the shift in person makes a significant point: all believers once lived under the influence of the flesh and its desires—Paul included.

2:3b ποιοῦντες: The Greek word ποιοῦντες is a present active participle masculine nominative plural from the verb ποιέω that means " to do" or "to carry out" (BDAG, s.v. "ποιέω" 3a, p. 840). English translations render the participle a number of ways: "carrying out" (ESV, HCSB), "following (NIV, RSV, NRSV), "indulging" (NET, NASB), or "fulfilling" (KJV, NKJV). **Syntactically**, ποιοῦντες introduces a dependent participle clause. It functions adverbially modifying the verb "we behave" (ἀνεστράφημεν). The direct object is "the will" (τὰ θελήματα). **Semantically**, ποιοῦντες functions as a participle of manner. It describes how the believers were formerly conducting their lives: "*by* carrying out the will of the flesh and the mind."

Theological Nugget: What does "flesh" mean in Ephesians? The genitive τῆς σαρκός ("flesh") is a subjective genitive modifying the head noun τὰ θελήματα ("the will") and should be rendered: "what the flesh desires." Throughout Ephesians, Paul uses σάρξ in a neutral manner referring to the physical world (cf. Eph. 2:11, 14; 5:29, 31; 6:5, 12). Here, σάρξ describes an element at work within the unbeliever and at odds with the Spirit. Paul develops this image in both Romans and Galatians (Rom. 8:5–8; Gal. 5:17–26; Dunn 1998, 62–70). In both books, Paul can talk about flesh along with its desires (ἐπιθυμία) (Rom. 13:14; Gal. 16, 24). In this section, Paul describes two elements that influence unbelievers: the ruler of the authority of the air (v. 2) and the desires of the flesh (v. 3). Not only is the unbeliever effected by an external force—spiritual rulers—they have an internal problem—the flesh.

2:3c καί: The Greek word καί is a conjunction that means "and" (BDAG, s.v. "καί" 2c, p. 495). **Syntactically**, καί introduces a dependent conjunctive clause: "*and* we were children by nature of wrath" (καὶ ἤμεθα τέκνα φύσει ὀργῆς). **Semantically**, καί is a coordinating connective: "and" (ESV, NRSV, NET, CSB, HCSB, NASB, NKJV, KJV). The conjunction makes this parallel with the first half of the verse: "among whom also we all behaved" (Hoehner, 322).

ἤμεθα: The Greek word ἤμεθα is a first-person plural imperfect middle indicative from the verb εἰμί that means "to be" (BDAG, s.v. "εἰμί" 2a, p. 283). **Syntactically**, ἤμεθα functions as the main verb of the dependent conjunctive clause introduced by καί. The clause coordinates with verb ἀνεστράφημεν ("we behaved … and we were"). **Semantically**, ἤμεθα is a customary imperfect describing an ongoing state in the past time (W, 548).

Semantical Nugget: What does Paul mean by "children of wrath by nature" (τέκνα φύσει ὀργῆς)? The phrase is a Hebrew idiom similar to the one that Paul uses in verse 2b: "sons of disobedience" (τοῖς υἱοῖς τῆς ἀπειθείας) (Moule, 175). The idiom conveys the notion that this is characteristic of this group (BDAG, s.v. "τέκνον" 6, p. 995). However, here the genitive is best understood as describing destination: "children *destined for* wrath" (W, 101). Paul clearly refers to God's wrath (Rom. 1:18; Eph. 5:6; Col. 3:6; 1 Thess. 1:10). The Greek term φύσις refers to a condition determined by birth: "by nature" (BDAG, s.v. "φύσις" 1, p. 1069). The dative could either express means: "*by the means* of our nature"; or cause: "*because of* our nature." Here cause makes more sense—we were destined for wrath because of the condition we inherited from Adam (cf. Rom. 5:12–21) (Hoehner, 323).

ὡς καί: The Greek word ὡς is a conjunction that means "as" in this context (BDAG, s.v. "ὡς" 1bα, pp. 1103–4). The Greek word καί is a conjunction that means "also" in this context (BDAG, s.v. "καί" 2c, pp. 495–96). **Syntactically**, ὡς καί introduces a dependent conjunctive clause "*even as* the rest" (ὡς καὶ οἱ λοιποί). The entire clause functions adverbially modifying the verb "we were" (ἤμεθα). **Syntactically**, ὡς expresses a comparison, while καί is adjunctive: "even as the rest" (NASB, NET, NKJV, KJV) or "as the others were also" (CSB, HCSB). Other versions omit καί but retain ὡς (ESV, RSV, NRSV, NIV). The clause emphasizes the fact that all of humanity faced this situation.

[ἦσαν]: The Greek word ἦσαν is a third-person plural imperfect active indicative from the verb εἰμί that means "to be" (BDAG, s.v. "εἰμί" 2a, p. 283). **Syntactically**, the ellipsis [ἦσαν] is the main verb of the dependent conjunctive clause introduced by ὡς καί. The subject is the "rest" (οἱ λοιποί): "as also the rest were." Several English versions simply omit the ellipsis: "like the rest" (NIV; cf. ESV, RSV, NRSV, NASB, NKJV, KJV).

2:4a δέ: The Greek word δέ is a conjunction that means "but" (BDAG, s.v. "δέ" 4a, p. 213). **Syntactically**, δέ is in the postpositive position introducing an independent conjunctive clause: "*But* God, being rich in his mercy" (ὁ δὲ θεὸς πλούσιος ὢν ἐν ἐλέει). **Semantically**, δέ is adversative: "but" (ESV, RSV, NRSV, NIV, NET, CSB, HCSB, NASB, NKJV, KJV, NLT). The phrase contrasts Paul's negative description of unbelievers by characterizing God's mercy. Paul ends the description by alluding to God's wrath—now he describes God's mercy.

ὤν: The Greek word ὤν is a present active participle masculine nominative singular from the verb εἰμί that means "to be" (BDAG, s.v. "εἰμί" 2a, p. 283). **Syntactically**, ὤν introduces a dependent participle clause. Several translations treat the verb as an attributive participle: "who is rich in mercy" (NIV, RSV, NRSV, CSB, HCSB, NKJV, KJV); however, since there is no article, it is best understood as an adverbial participle modifying the main verb in verse 5: "he made alive" (συνεζωοποίησεν). "God" (ὁ θεός) is the subject of the main verb, and so the subject of the participle. The predicate nominative is the adjective "rich" (πλούσιος). **Semantically**, ὤν functions as a participle of cause: "*because* of his great mercy." God's extensive mercy serves as the basis for his salvation, which he clarifies in verse 5.

> **Semantical Nugget**: What does the prepositional phrase "because of his great love" (διὰ τὴν πολλὴν ἀγάπην αὐτοῦ) mean? The phrase modifies the main verb of the sentence: "he made alive" (συνεζωοποίησεν) (Larkin, 30). The preposition best conveys the idea of cause (Robertson, 584; BDAG, s.v. "διά" B2a, p. 225). Most English translations render the prepositional phrase: "because of his great love" (ESV, NET, NIV, HCSB, NASB, NKJV). The genitive αὐτοῦ could be possessive: "God's love" (cf. NIV, CSB, HCSB, NASB), but the following relative clause suggests that this is a subjective genitive: God's love directed toward the believer. The prepositional phrase gives the second reason for God's salvation: because of his love. Hoehner states: "It is given irrespective of merit and to those who are undeserving" (Hoehner, 327).

2:4b ἥν: The Greek word ἥν is a feminine singular accusative from the relative pronoun ὅς that means "which" in this context (BDAG, s.v. "ὅς" 1dδ, p. 726). **Syntactically**, ἥν introduces a dependent adjectival relative clause "with *which* he loved us" (ἣν ἠγάπησεν ἡμᾶς). The antecedent of the pronoun is "love" (ἀγάπην, v. 4b). It functions as the instrument of the verb, which would make the pronoun dative. Due to attraction, it agrees with the case of the antecedent.

ἠγάπησεν: The Greek word ἠγάπησεν is a third-person singular aorist active indicative from the verb ἀγαπάω that means "to love" or "cherish" (BDAG, s.v. "ἀγαπάω" 2, pp. 5–6). **Syntactically**, ἠγάπησεν functions as the main verb of the relative clause. The subject is implied by the verb: "he," referring to God. The direct object is the first-person plural pronoun: "us" (ἡμᾶς). The redundant use of the verb in the relative clause modifying the related noun (ἀγάπη) emphasizes God's love (BDF §156; Arnold, 135). **Semantically**, ἠγάπησεν is a constative aorist, with no emphasis on the beginning or end of the action (W, 557–58). The aorist is used to describe the totality of God's love. In the following verses, Paul explains how he shows this love to the believer—by making us alive and raising us with Christ (vv. 5–6).

2:5a καί: The Greek word καί is a conjunction that means "and" (BDAG, s.v. "καί" 1e, p. 495). **Syntactically**, καί introduces an independent conjunctive clause: "*and* even though we were dead in our trespasses" (καὶ ὄντας ἡμᾶς νεκροὺς τοῖς παραπτώμασιν). **Semantically**, καί could be resumptive, picking up the argument that Paul began in verse 1 (Larkin, 30), but it is most likely ascensive, underscoring the contrast between the state of the unbeliever and God's mercy (Hoehner, 329; Barth, 219): "*even* when we were dead" (ESV, RSV, NRSV, CSB, HCSB, NASB, NKJV, KJV, NET).

ὄντας: The Greek word ὄντας is a present active participle masculine plural accusative from the verb εἰμί that means "to be" (BDAG, s.v. "εἰμί" 2a, p. 283). **Syntactically**, ὄντας introduces a dependent participle clause. It functions adverbially modifying the main verb in verse 5: "he made alive" (συνεζωοποίησεν). The direct object of the main verb is the first-person personal pronoun "us" (ἡμᾶς). In verse 1, Paul writes a similar phrase, but uses the second-person personal pronoun: "you"; in verse 5 he shifts the person (see the Grammatical Nugget at 2:1). **Semantically**, ὄντας is present tense indicating that this was simultaneous with the action of the main verb. Most English translations render it temporally: "*when* we were dead" (ESV, NRSV, RSV, NIV, NASB, NKJV, KJV). The participle phrase describes the position of the believer prior to coming into new life. When they were dead God himself stepped in and saved these believers (cf. Rom. 5:6, 8, 10) (Thielman, 133). On the other hand, the participle is repeated from verse 1, which expresses concession. The participle of concession expresses a contrast between the believers' previous situation and their new position in light of God's salvation: "*even though* you were dead in your trespasses" (NET, CSB, HCSB, NLT) (W, 634). The dative "trespasses" (τοῖς παραπτώμασιν) can express cause: "we were dead *because of* our sins" (NLT), but it most likely describes sphere: "being dead *in* our trespasses" (ESV, NIV, CSB, HCSB, NET, NKJV, KJV). In verse 1, Paul uses a hendiadys "trespasses and sins" to express the state of the believer prior to their relationship with Christ (see Semantical Nugget at 2:1); here he abbreviates it to "trespasses."

Text-Critical Nugget: How should the dative be read in verse 5? There are a number of different readings for the dative in verse 5a. First, 𝔓46 replaces the dative τοῖς παραπτώμασιν with τοῖς σώμασιν: "we were dead in our *bodies*." Codex D replaces it with ταῖς ἁμαρτίαις: "we were dead in *sins*" (F and G give the singular form). A number of manuscripts insert καὶ ταῖς ἁμαρτίαις after τοῖς παραπτώμασιν (Ψ), a conflation with verse 1. B inserts καὶ ταῖς ἐπιθυμίαις after τοῖς παραπτώμασιν, a conflation with verse 1 in B only, which replaces ἁμαρτίαις with ἐπιθυμίαις. Finally, the majority of Alexandrian (ℵ, A, 33, 81, 104, 1175, 1739, 1881) and Byzantine manuscripts (K, L, 𝔐) contain the reading found in the NA²⁸: τοῖς παραπτώμασιν ("we were dead in our *trespasses*"). This reading has the best external support. Internally, a scribe would be more likely to add ταῖς ἁμαρτίαις to agree with verse 1 than to omit it.

2:5b συνεζωοποίησεν: The Greek word συνεζωοποίησεν is a third-person singular aorist active indicative from the verb συζωοποιέω that means "to make alive together" (BDAG, s.v. "συζωοποιέω," pp. 954–55). Most English translations render the verb: "made us alive together with" (ESV, RSV, NRSV, NET). The NIV and HCSB give an abbreviated translation "made us alive." **Syntactically**, συνεζωοποίησεν functions as the main verb of the independent conjunctive clause introduced by δέ in verse 4a. The subject of the verb is "God" (ὁ θεός). The direct object is "us" (ἡμᾶς), referring to the believer. Paul will use two more verbs with a συν- prefix in verse 6 (συνήγειρεν and συνεκάθισεν) in parallel to συνεζωοποίησεν. **Semantically**, συνεζωοποίησεν is rendered as an ingressive aorist (W, 558–59), highlighting the contrast between the old state of the believer and the entrance into a new state. The dative *"with* Christ" (τῷ Χριστῷ) is a dative of association following a verb with a συν- prefix (W, 159–61; cf. ESV, RSV, NRSV, NIV, CSB, HCSB, NET, NKJV, KJV).

> **Text-Critical Nugget**: Does Paul insert the preposition ἐν before the dative τῷ Χριστῷ? A few manuscripts (𝔓⁴⁶, B, 33) add the preposition ἐν before the dative τῷ Χριστῷ: "he made us alive *in* Christ." 𝔓⁴⁶ and B are two of our more significant manuscripts for Ephesians; however, the reading without the preposition is by far superior. First, we should anticipate the simple dative following a verb with a συν- prefix (Baugh, 144). Second, the insertion of the preposition is an assimilation with verse 6 (Metzger, 533).

2:5c ἐστε σεσῳσμένοι: The Greek word ἐστέ is a second-person plural present active indicative from the verb εἰμί that means "to be" (BDAG, s.v. "εἰμί" 11a, p. 285). The Greek word σεσῳσμένοι is a perfect passive participle masculine plural nominative from the verb σῴζω that means "to save" (BDAG, s.v. "σῴζω" 2b, p. 983). **Syntactically**, the periphrastic ἐστε σεσῳσμένοι is the main verb of an asyndeton clause. The subject of the verb is implied: "you," referring to the believer. The change from the third person (v. 5b) to the second person suggests that the phrase is a parenthetical comment to clarify the main verb. The phrase looks forward to Paul's explanation of this salvation in verse 8. Most English versions place dashes or parentheses around the phrase (NET, NIV, NASB, NRSV, RSV, NKJV, KJV). The CSB and HCSB render the phrase as a distinct sentence. **Semantically**, ἐστε σεσῳσμένοι is a perfect periphrastic, functioning as an intensive perfect. This emphasizes the present situation of the believer (W, 574–75, 649). The surrounding aorist verbs in verses 5 and 6 (συνεζωοποίησεν, συνήγειρεν, and συνεκάθισεν) creates a contrast with the continuous idea from the present tense verb. The passive participle is a divine passive. Even though the voice obscures the actor, God is the subject (Hoehner, 333).

Semantical Nugget: What does the dative χάριτί ("grace") mean? The dative can express means: "*by* grace you have been saved" (ESV, RSV, NRSV, NIV, CSB, HCSB, NASB, NKJV, KJV, NLT) (Porter, 99; Robertson, 533). On the other hand, it is better understood as a dative of cause: "*on the basis of* grace you have been saved" (Hoehner, 149). Up to this point in his argument, Paul specifies that God's salvation is based on his mercy and love (2:4); he saves us despite our helpless situation (2:1–3, 5a). In the conclusion, he highlights that this is a gift from God, not from ourselves nor from any work that we can do (2:8–9). This is unmerited favor from God (cf. Rom. 3:23–24).

2:6a καί: The Greek word καί is a conjunction that means "and" (BDAG, s.v. "καί" 1aα, p. 494). **Syntactically**, καί introduces an independent conjunctive clause: "*and* he has raised you" (καὶ συνήγειρεν). **Semantically**, καί is a coordinating connective: "and" (ESV, RSV, NRSV, NIV, NASB, NKJV, KJV). The CSB begins a new sentence with the conjunction and translates it as "also" (cf. HCSB). Larkin points out that the verb "he raised us with" (συνήγειρεν) is an elaboration of what it means to be "made alive" (v. 5b) and labels this epexegetical (Larkin, 31; Best, 217).

συνήγειρεν: The Greek word συνήγειρεν is a third-person singular aorist active indicative from the verb συνεγείρω that means "to raise with" (BDAG, s.v. "συνεγείρω" 2b, p. 967). **Syntactically**, συνήγειρεν functions as the main verb of the independent conjunctive clause introduced by καί. The subject is implied by the verb: "he," referring to God (cf. v. 4). The direct object is implied from verse 5a: "us" (ἡμᾶς). This is the second of three verbs with a συν- prefix (συνεζωοποίησεν and συνεκάθισεν). **Semantically**, συνήγειρεν is rendered as an ingressive aorist (W, 558–59), highlighting the change of the believers' status.

Theological Nugget: Why does Paul use verbs with the συν- prefix? The verbs in 2:6 recall how God treated Christ in 1:20. There Paul states that God raised (ἐγείρας) Christ from the dead and seated (καθίσας) him in the heavenly places. In the present context, God raised (συνήγειρεν) the believers and seated (συνεκάθισεν) them in the heavenlies with Christ. The repetition of the verbs underscores the believers' participation in Christ's death and resurrection (Rom. 6:3–5). Besides the addition of the συν prefix, Paul notes that Jesus sits "at the right hand" (ἐν δεξιᾷ αὐτοῦ); he states that the believers sit "in Christ Jesus" (ἐν Χριστῷ Ἰησοῦ). The believers' relationship is established by Christ's own unique position in the heavenlies (Best, 219). Despite the victory that believers experience through Christ, we still live in a world of conflict. The point of the letter is to instruct believers on how they should live in a world faced with the ongoing conflict with these powers (Lincoln, 109).

2:6b καί: The Greek word καί is a conjunction that means "and" (BDAG, s.v. "καί" 1ba, p. 494). **Syntactically,** καί introduces an independent conjunctive clause: "*and* he seated us in the heavenly places in Christ Jesus" (καὶ συνεκάθισεν ἐν τοῖς ἐπουρανίοις ἐν Χριστῷ Ἰησοῦ). **Semantically,** καί is a coordinating connective: "and" (ESV, RSV, NRSV, NET, CSB, HCSB, NASB, NKJV, KJV).

συνεκάθισεν: The Greek word συνεκάθισεν is a third-person singular aorist active indicative from the verb συγκαθίζω that means "to sit down with" (BDAG, s.v. "συγκαθίζω" 1, p. 951). **Syntactically,** συνεκάθισεν functions as the main verb of the independent conjunctive clause introduced by καί. The subject is implied by the verb: "he," referring to God. This is the third verb with συν- prefix (συνεζωοποίησεν and συνήγειρεν). **Semantically,** συνεκάθισεν could be rendered as a proleptic aorist, looking forward to a future state for the believer (W, 563). However, the verb probably refers to the believers' current state. Elsewhere, Paul can state that believers have some participation in the heavenlies (Phil. 3:20; Col. 3:1–2) and in the resurrection (Rom. 6:4) (Arnold, 137; Osborne, 53). Because of this, the verb is most likely rendered as an ingressive aorist. Just like the other parallel verbs, συνεκάθισεν highlights the change in the believers' status. The verb is modified by two prepositional phrases. Paul uses the identical phrase in Ephesians 1:3: God blessed us with all spiritual blessing "in the heavenly places in Christ" (ἐν τοῖς ἐπουρανίοις ἐν Χριστῷ). Both prepositional phrases "in the heavenly places" and "in Christ Jesus" (ἐν τοῖς ἐπουρανίοις ἐν Χριστῷ Ἰησοῦ) express sphere, which might appear redundant with the συν- verb (συνεκάθισεν). Most English versions translate the phrase by inserting an object along with the prepositional phrase, like the ESV: "and seated us *with him* in the heavenly places *in Christ Jesus*" (cf. RSV, NRSV, NIV, NET, CSB, NASB). The HCSB omits the repeated object: "Together *with Christ* he also raised us up and seated us in the heavens" (cf. NKJV, KJV). On the other hand, there is no object in Greek. Campbell suggests this translation: "He also co-raised us and co-seated us in the heavens with Christ Jesus" (Campbell, 2012, 85). The NLT gives a similar gloss: "For he … seated us with him in the heavenly realms because we are *united with Christ Jesus*." We are raised because of our relationship with Christ. Hoehner states: "it underscores the reason we are seated in the heavenlies with Christ, namely, because we are in him. It is our union with Christ that gives us the right to be in the heavenly places" (Hoehner, 334–35).

2:7 ἵνα: The Greek word ἵνα is a conjunction that means "so that" in this context (BDAG, s.v. "ἵνα" 3, p. 477). Some English translations render the conjunction as "in order that" (NIV) or "so that" (ESV, NRSV, CSB, HCSB, NASB). **Syntactically,** ἵνα introduces a dependent conjunctive clause "*so that* he might show his surpassing wealth of grace in kindness to us in Christ Jesus in the coming age" (ἵνα ἐνδείξηται ἐν τοῖς αἰῶσιν τοῖς ἐπερχομένοις τὸ ὑπερβάλλον πλοῦτος τῆς χάριτος αὐτοῦ ἐν χρηστότητι ἐφ᾽ ἡμᾶς ἐν Χριστῷ Ἰησοῦ). The clause functions adverbially modifying the main verbs "made alive," "raised together," and "seated" with Christ (συνεζωοποίησεν … συνήγειρεν … συνεκάθισεν). **Semantically,** ἵνα is purpose-result, providing both the intention and results of the action of the main verbs (W, 473–74). God's purpose behind his act of salvation is to "prove the surpassing wealth of his grace" (Lincoln, 109).

ἐνδείξηται: The Greek word ἐνδείξηται is a third-person singular aorist middle subjunctive from the verb ἐνδείκνυμι that means "to show" or "demonstrate" (BDAG, s.v. "ἐνδείκνυμι" 1, p. 331). The csb renders the verb as "he might display" (cf. hcsb). Abbott suggests that it be rendered "exhibit" (Abbott, 1909, 50; cf. 2 Tim. 4:14). **Syntactically,** ἐνδείξηται functions as the main verb of the dependent conjunctive clause introduced by ἵνα. The subject is implied by the verb: "he," referring to God. The direct object is "wealth" (πλοῦτος), which is modified by a participle phrase: "his surpassing wealth of grace." **Semantically,** ἐνδείξηται is rendered as a constative aorist, with no emphasis on the beginning or end of the action (W, 557–58; cf. Carson, 1996, 69). By saving these unbelievers, God puts his grace on display (cf. Rom. 3:26).

ἐπερχομένοις: The Greek word ἐπερχομένοις is a present middle participle masculine plural dative from the verb ἐπέρχομαι that means "to come about" or "happen" (BDAG, s.v. "ἐπέρχομαι" 2a, p. 361). Most English versions render the phrase as "the coming ages" (esv, net, niv, rsv, csb, hcsb) or "the ages to come" (nrsv, nasb, nkjv, kjv). **Syntactically,** ἐπερχομένοις functions as an attributive participle modifying "age" (αἰῶσιν). The phrase τοῖς αἰῶσιν τοῖς ἐπερχομένοις is the object of the preposition ἐν. **Semantically,** ἐπερχομένοις functions as a futuristic present, which describes the immediacy and certainty of a future event (W, 535–36). Barth argues that τοῖς αἰῶσιν refers to hostile spiritual powers (Barth, 223). In this case, ἐν would express location ("God displays his surpassing wealth before these powers"). However, the wider context suggests that τοῖς αἰῶσιν is temporal: "ages" (cf. 1:21; 2:2; BDAG, s.v. "αἰών" 2b, pp. 32–33). In this case, ἐν would function temporally. Paul makes a similar statement about the extent of Christ's rule (Eph. 1:21).

Text-Critical Nugget: Does Paul use the masculine or neuter form of πλοῦτος? The majority of Byzantine manuscripts use the masculine form of πλοῦτος: τὸν ὑπερβάλλοντα πλοῦτον ("surpassing wealth") (see MT; RP2005). The neuter form (τὸ ὑπερβάλλον πλοῦτος) appears in the majority of Alexandrian (𝔓⁴⁶, A, B, 33, 81, 1175, 1739, 1881) and Western manuscripts (D, F, G) (see NA²⁸; SBL; THGNT). There is no difference in meaning. The difference is in spelling. Paul uses both the masculine and neuter throughout his letters (see BDAG, s.v. "πλοῦτος," p. 832; BDF §51.2). In Ephesians he uses the neuter form in 1:7; 3:8, 16, but the masculine form in 1:18. Based on the external evidence, the neuter form is most likely original.

ὑπερβάλλον: The Greek word ὑπερβάλλον is a present active participle neuter singular accusative from the verb ὑπερβάλλω that means "to go beyond" or "surpass" (BDAG, s.v. "ὑπερβάλλω," p. 1032). Some English versions render the participle as "immeasurable" (ESV, RSV, NRSV, CSB, HCSB), "incomparable" (NIV), or "exceeding" (NKJV, KJV). **Syntactically**, ὑπερβάλλον functions as an attributive participle, in the first attributive position. It modifies "riches" (πλοῦτος). In the sentence, the phrase τὸ ὑπερβάλλον πλοῦτος ("surpassing riches") functions as the direct object of the verb ἐνδείξηται ("he might show"). **Semantically**, ὑπερβάλλον functions as a customary present, describing an ongoing state (W, 521–22). The genitive τῆς χάριτος could either be an epexegetical genitive ("according to the wealth, namely his grace"), but it is probably best to understand this as an attributed genitive ("according to his rich grace"). Because of the attributive participle, we have rendered the phrase: "his surpassing wealth of grace." Paul uses a similar genitive construction in Ephesians 1:7.

Semantical Nugget: How do the three prepositional phrases in verse 7 relate to the context? Paul uses the preposition ἐν three times in verse 7, each instance modifies the main verb (ἐνδείξηται) in verse 7:

ἐνδείξηται ... τὸ ὑπερβάλλον πλοῦτος τῆς χάριτος αὐτοῦ
    ... <u>ἐν</u> τοῖς αἰῶσιν τοῖς ἐπερχομένοις ...
<u>ἐν</u> χρηστότητι ἐφ' ἡμᾶς
<u>ἐν</u> Χριστῷ Ἰησοῦ

that he might show ... his surpassing wealth of grace
    ... <u>in</u> the coming age ...
<u>in</u> kindness toward us
<u>in</u> Christ Jesus

The first prepositional phrase "in the coming age" (ἐν τοῖς αἰῶσιν τοῖς ἐπερχομένοις) is temporal. Even though God's salvation impacts the believer now, the implications of this salvation will continue to be felt throughout time. The second phrase "in kindness toward us" (ἐν χρηστότητι ἐφ' ἡμᾶς) expresses the means of this demonstration. Through salvation, believers become the object of God's kindness (BDAG, s.v. "χρηστότης" 2b, p. 1090). The concept of kindness accentuates God's grace that Paul introduces in verse 5 and weaves through the passage (vv. 7, 8–9). The final phrase (ἐν Χριστῷ Ἰησοῦ) expresses sphere. Just as it did in verse 6, the phrase emphasizes the believers' relationship with Jesus.

2:8a γάρ: The Greek word γάρ is a conjunction that means "for" or "therefore" (BDAG, s.v. "γάρ" 1a, p. 189). Most English versions translate the conjunction as "for" (ESV, RSV, NRSV, NIV, NET, CSB, HCSB, NASB, NKJV, KJV). **Syntactically**, γάρ is in a postpositive position, introducing the clause as an independent conjunctive clause: "*For* you are saved by grace through faith" (τῇ γὰρ χάριτί ἐστε σεσῳσμένοι διὰ πίστεως). **Semantically**, γάρ explains that this salvation is based on God's grace, which Paul presented in verse 7.

ἐστε σεσῳσμένοι: The Greek word ἐστέ is a second-person plural present active indicative from the verb εἰμί that means "to be" (BDAG, s.v. "εἰμί" 11a, p. 285). The Greek word σεσῳσμένοι is a perfect passive participle masculine plural nominative from the verb σῴζω that means "to save" (BDAG, s.v. "σῴζω" 2b, p. 983). **Syntactically**, ἐστε σεσῳσμένοι is the main verb of the independent conjunctive clause introduced by γάρ. Paul essentially repeats the phrase from verse 5, where he uses it as a parenthetical idea. **Semantically**, like verse 5, ἐστε σεσῳσμένοι is a perfect periphrastic, which is most likely intensive, emphasizing the present situation of the believer (W, 574–75, 649). To emphasize the continuous results, the NET translates this "you are saved." The passive participle is a divine passive. Even though the voice obscures the actor, God is the subject (Hoehner, 333). Paul makes three changes to the repeated phrase in verse 5. First, he adds the explanatory γάρ. Second, he adds an article to χάριτι: τῇ χάριτι. Similar to verse 5c, the dative expresses cause (W, 167–68). The article is anaphoric, referring to verse 5 (W, 250). Finally, in verse 8, he adds the prepositional phrase "through faith" (διὰ πίστεως). The preposition conveys the notion of means (W, 167–68). He regularly uses the phrase to express the means through which believers are saved (Rom. 3:22; Gal. 2:16; Phil. 3:9; 2 Tim. 3:15). God's gift of salvation is given freely, but Paul clearly states that this is "through faith." Hoehner observes that God's grace is the objective basis of God's salvation, but faith is the subjective means by which the believer is saved (Hoehner, 340–41).

2:8b καί: The Greek word καί is a conjunction that means "and" (BDAG, s.v. "καί" 1c, p. 495; BDF §442.9). **Syntactically**, καί introduces an independent conjunctive clause "and this is not from you" (καὶ τοῦτο οὐκ ἐξ ὑμῶν). **Semantically**, καί is explanatory, providing more information about the believers' salvation.

[ἐστίν]: The Greek word ἐστίν is a third-person singular present active indicative from the verb εἰμί that means "is" (BDAG, s.v. "εἰμί" 2a, p. 283). Most English versions include the ellipsis: "and this *is* not from yourself" (ESV, RSV, NRSV, NIV, NET, CSB, HCSB; cf. NASB, NKJV, KJV). **Syntactically**, the ellipsis [ἐστίν] is the main verb of the independent conjunctive clause introduced by καί. The subject is the demonstrative: "this" (τοῦτο). τοῦτο is neuter, but the nearest nouns are feminine, so the antecedent is not clear. Paul most likely uses the neuter to refer to the entire concept of God's salvation, which he begins discussing in verse 5b (Robertson, 704; W, 334–35). Paul uses the phrase in a similar manner elsewhere in Ephesians: in 1:15 the pronoun refers to 1:3–14; in 3:1 the pronoun refers to 2:11–22; in 3:14 the pronoun refers to 3:1–13 (Hoehner, 343). The prepositional phrase "from you" (ἐξ ὑμῶν) functions as the predicate nominative. The preposition expresses source. **Semantically**, [ἐστίν] is an equative present underscoring the fact that this salvation does not come from any human effort.

2:8c [ἐστίν]: The Greek word ἐστίν is a third-person singular present active indicative from the verb εἰμί that means "is" (BDAG, s.v. "εἰμί" 2a, p. 283). Most English versions include the ellipsis: "*it is* a gift of God" (cf. ESV, RSV, NRSV, NIV, NET, CSB, HCSB, NASB, NKJV, KJV). **Syntactically**, the ellipsis [ἐστίν] is the main verb in the asyndeton clause. The predicate nominative is "gift" (τὸ δῶρον). **Semantically**, [ἐστίν] is an equative present, emphasizing the fact that this salvation that comes from God is a free gift. The genitive ("of God") is best understood as a genitive of source in contrast with the previous preposition: "this is not *from* you—it is a gift *from* God" (cf. NLT).

> **Syntactical Nugget**: What is the structure of Paul's argument in verse 8? Paul shifts from a long sentence with subordinating clauses in verses 1–5 and 6–7, to short or verbless independent clauses in verses 8–9. After claiming salvation for the believer (v. 8a), he develops this through three short statements (vv. 8b, 8c, 9a). The last two clauses are asyndetons.
>
> 8b καὶ τοῦτο οὐκ ἐξ ὑμῶν,
> 8c θεοῦ τὸ δῶρον·
> 9a οὐκ ἐξ ἔργων,
>
> 8b and this is not from yourselves,
> 8c it is a gift from God
> 9a not from works
>
> The first and last clause (vv. 8b and 9a) are negative statements that contrast the positive statement in verse 8c. Paul repeats the preposition ἐκ in the negative statements, expressing "source." He omits the preposition in the positive statement, but uses the genitive θεοῦ. The genitive clearly conveys the notion of source as well: "it is a gift *from* God." The negative statements underscore this positive statement creating a chiastic structure (Barth, 225–26; Larkin, 33). By placing the genitive before the head noun, Paul highlights that God is the source of this salvation (Hoehner, 343–44).

2:9a [ἐστίν]: The word ἐστίν is a third-person singular present active indicative from the verb εἰμί that means "to be" (BDAG, s.v. "εἰμί" 2a, p. 283). Most English versions omit the ellipsis, except for the NET: "*it is* not from works." **Syntactically**, the ellipsis [ἐστίν] is the main verb in the asyndeton clause. The prepositional phrase "from works" (ἐξ ἔργων) functions as the predicate nominative. **Semantically**, [ἐστίν] is an equative present, repeating the contrasting statement from verse 8b.

^{2:9b} ἵνα: The Greek word ἵνα is a conjunction that means "so that" in this context (BDAG, s.v. "ἵνα" 3, p. 477). Most English translations render the conjunction as "so that" (ESV, NRSV, HCSB, NIV, HCSB, NASB). **Syntactically**, the conjunction ἵνα introduces a dependent conjunctive clause "*so that* no one might boast" (ἵνα μή τις καυχήσηται). The clause functions adverbially modifying the verbless phrases in verses 8b, 8c, and 9a "and this is not from you; it is a gift from God; it is not from works" (καὶ τοῦτο οὐκ ἐξ ὑμῶν, θεοῦ τὸ δῶρον οὐκ ἐξ ἔργων). **Semantically**, the ἵνα is purpose-result, providing both the intention and results of the action of the main verbs (W, 473–74). God gives this salvation as a gift so that no one can boast (cf. Rom. 3:27–4:8).

καυχήσηται: The Greek word καυχήσηται is a third-person singular aorist middle (deponent) subjunctive from the verb καυχάομαι that means "to boast," "glory," or "pride oneself" (BDAG, s.v. "καυχάομαι" 1, p. 536). **Syntactically**, καυχήσηται functions as the main verb dependent conjunctive clause introduced by ἵνα. The subject of the verb is the indefinite pronoun "anyone" (τις). With the negating adverb μή, most translations render the subject as "no one" (ESV, NRSV, NIV, NET, CSB, HCSB, NASB). **Semantically**, καυχήσηται is a constative aorist: "boast" (ESV, RSV, NRSV, NIV, NET, CSB, HCSB, NASB, NKJV, KJV, NLT). There is no emphasis on the beginning or end of the action (W, 557–58). This gift is given freely so that no one is able to boast.

> **Lexical Nugget**: What does Paul mean by "boasting"? Throughout his letters, Paul uses the verb καυχάομαι to contrast God's salvation with human effort, particularly in regard to following the law. In Romans, he criticizes the Jew for "boasting in the law" (Rom. 2:17) even though he breaks the law. In contrast, God justifies the believer through faith so that no one can boast (Rom. 3:27–31). He puts forward both Abraham and David as examples of those who have been justified by faith (Rom. 4:1–8). He makes a similar point in Galatians (Gal. 6:13–14) and Philippians (Phil. 3:3). In this context, the Jewish polemic is not as pronounced; the term most likely refers to a general confidence in oneself. This accounts for Paul's abbreviated use of "works" (v. 9a) instead of "works of the law."

^{2:10a} γάρ: The Greek word γάρ is a conjunction that means "for" or "therefore" (BDAG, s.v. "γάρ" 1a, p. 189). Most English versions translate the conjunction as "for" (ESV, RSV, NRSV, NIV, NET, CSB, HCSB, NASB, NKJV, KJV). **Syntactically**, γάρ is in a postpositive position, introducing the clause as an independent conjunctive clause: "*For* we are his workmanship" (αὐτοῦ γάρ ἐσμεν ποίημα). **Semantically**, γάρ explains the previous phrase (Hoehner, 346; Thielman, 144–45). Even though God's salvation does not come to us out of our own works, God provides works for the believer.

ἐσμέν: The Greek word ἐσμέν is a first-person plural present active indicative from the verb εἰμί that means "to be" (BDAG, s.v. "εἰμί" 2a, p. 283). **Syntactically,** ἐσμέν is the main verb of the independent conjunctive clause introduced by γάρ. The subject is implied by the verb: "we," referring to all believers. The predicate nominative is "workmanship" (ποίημα). **Semantically,** ἐσμέν is an equative present—because of God's salvation, the believer is now God's handiwork.

> **Lexical Nugget:** What does the term "workmanship" mean? Most English versions render the Greek term ποίημα as "workmanship" (ESV, NET, NASB, RSV, NKJV, KJV) or "handiwork" (NIV). The term generally refers to some type of divine creation (BDAG, s.v. "ποίημα," p. 842; cf. Rom. 1:20). Because of this background, the HCSB might be more accurate with the translation "creation" (cf. LEB). The following participle (κτισθέντες, "having been created") underscores this creation theme. The believer as a divine creation stands in contrast to human works, which Paul calls ἔργον (v. 9). Salvation does not come from work that believers can do, but as a result of God's salvation we are his creation. The rest of verse 10 explains that we are created for good works—but that God prepared them beforehand. Paul inserts the genitive αὐτοῦ before the head noun (ποίημα), giving the pronoun emphasis (Robertson, 681). The genitive could be possessive (ESV: "we are his creation" [cf. NIV]) or subjective (NRSV: "we are what he has made us" [cf. GNT]).

2:10b κτισθέντες: The Greek word κτισθέντες is an aorist passive participle masculine nominative plural from the verb κτίζω that means "to create" (BDAG, s.v. "κτίζω," p. 572). **Syntactically,** κτισθέντες introduces a dependent participle clause. It functions adverbially modifying the main verb: "we are" (ἐσμέν). **Semantically,** κτισθέντες conveys the notion of cause: "*because we have been created*" (Hoehner, 347; Arnold, 140). Since κτισθέντες is aorist, the action of the participle is subsequent to the action of the main verb. The participle is a divine passive—God is the one who creates the believer into this new creation. Two prepositional phrases modify the participle:

κτισθέντες
   <u>ἐν</u> Χριστῷ Ἰησοῦ
   <u>ἐπὶ</u> ἔργοις ἀγαθοῖς

Because we have been created
   <u>in</u> Christ Jesus
   <u>for</u> good works

The first prepositional phrase "in Christ Jesus" (ἐν Χριστῷ Ἰησοῦ) expresses sphere. The idea alludes to verse 6—the believer was raised and seated in the heavenlies "in Christ." The union between the believer and Christ serves as the basis for their new creation (Hoehner, 348). The second prepositional phrase "for good works" (ἐπὶ ἔργοις ἀγαθοῖς) expresses purpose (Robertson, 605; BDF §235.4; Zerwick §129). This creates a contrast between verses 8 and 9—salvation does not come from works (ἐξ ἔργων), but salvation should lead to good works (ἐπὶ ἔργοις ἀγαθοῖς) (cf. Rom. 6:19, 22; 1 Thess. 1:3). Unlike the works in verse 8 that have human origin, the next clause states that God has prepared these works for the believer.

2:10c οἷς: The Greek word οἷς is a neuter plural dative from the relative pronoun ὅς that means "which" in this context (BDAG, s.v. "ὅς" 1da, p. 726). **Syntactically**, οἷς introduces a dependent adjectival relative clause "*which* God prepared beforehand" (οἷς προητοίμασεν ὁ θεός). The antecedent of the pronoun is ἔργοις ἀγαθοῖς (v. 10b). The pronoun functions as the direct object of the verb προητοίμασεν, which would make the pronoun accusative. Due to attraction, it agrees with the case of the antecedent.

προητοίμασεν: The Greek word προητοίμασεν is a third-person singular aorist active indicative from the verb προετοιμάζω that means "to prepare beforehand" (BDAG, s.v. "προετοιμάζω," p. 869). **Syntactically**, προητοίμασεν functions as the main verb of the relative clause. The subject of the verb is "God" (ὁ θεός). **Semantically**, προητοίμασεν is rendered as a constative aorist, with no emphasis on the beginning or end of the action (W, 557–58). Paul uses the same word in Romans 9:23, where God is the subject of the verb. The prefix προ- suggests that God prepared these good works before the creation of the believer (cf. Eph. 1:4) (Hoehner, 348–49).

2:10d ἵνα: The Greek word ἵνα is a conjunction that means "that" in this context (BDAG, s.v. "ἵνα" 3, p. 477). Some English translations render the conjunction as "that" (ESV, RSV, NKJV, KJV) or "so that" (HCSB, NASB). **Syntactically**, ἵνα introduces the clause as a dependent conjunctive clause. The clause "so that we might walk in them" (ἵνα ἐν αὐτοῖς περιπατήσωμεν) functions adverbially modifying the verb "God prepared beforehand" (οἷς προητοίμασεν ὁ θεός). **Semantically**, ἵνα expresses purpose, providing both the intention and results of the action of the main verbs (W, 472)—God prepared these good works for the believer to walk in them.

περιπατήσωμεν: The Greek word περιπατήσωμεν is a first-person plural aorist active subjunctive from the verb περιπατέω that means "to live" or "go about" (BDAG, s.v. "περιπατέω" 2aδ, p. 803). Several English translations render the verb "walk" (ESV, RSV, HCSB, NASB, NKJV, KJV). Some translations make the metaphor more explicit: "for us to do" (NIV, CSB) or "to be our way of life" (NRSV). **Syntactically**, περιπατήσωμεν functions as the main verb of the dependent conjunctive clause introduced by ἵνα. The subject is implied by the verb: "we," referring to believers. **Semantically**, περιπατήσωμεν is rendered as a constative aorist, with no emphasis on the beginning or end of the action (W, 557–58). The preposition "in them" (ἐν αὐτοῖς) expresses sphere. The antecedent of the pronoun is "good works" (v. 10b). Believers should characterize their lives by doing these good works that God has placed before them.

Theological Nugget: What does it mean to "walk" in good works? Paul uses περιπατέω in verses 2 and 10 creating an *inclusio*. The use of the two verbs frames this entire section. The term is a common Jewish metaphor to describe how one conducts their life (see our comments at 2:2a). In Ephesians 2:2, Paul uses the term to describe the believers' former life—a time in which they walked "according to the age of the world, according to the ruler of the authority." Now these believers walk in good works but works that God has prepared beforehand. Paul uses the term to organize the second part of the letter (4:1, 17; 5:2, 8, 15). In the second half of Ephesians, he clearly delineates what it looks like for a believer to "walk in these good works." Besides initiating a theme that he will develop in the second part of the book, the verb serves a second purpose: Paul uses it to carefully delineate the works to achieve salvation from those works that God has prepared beforehand. There is no work that believers can do to merit salvation; however, God creates these good works for the believer. God provides these works for believers—not to do them, but more specifically that they may "walk in them."

EPHESIANS 2:11–22

Big Greek Idea: Even though Gentiles were once without hope and alienated from the covenantal promises that God gave to Israel, Christ destroyed the hostility between the two groups through his death by nullifying the law and granting peace and access to God for both groups. As a result he created a new people group out of the two, the church, founded on Christ, and in which the Spirit of God dwells.

Structural Overview: After explaining how God brought about his salvation for all people (2:1–10), Paul explains how these individuals are incorporated into the people of God. More specifically, how God has made a new people group out of Jews and Gentiles. The paragraph has three major sections. The first section (2:11–13) presents a temporal contrast, as he did in the previous paragraph (2:1–3). He uses the temporal markers "once" (ποτέ) and "now" (νυνί) to contrast the Gentile's previous situation with their current one as believers. Since they were alienated from the nation of Israel, they were unable to enjoy the benefits that came to the nation. As a result, they were in a hopeless situation. However, they are presently unified with the people of God through Jesus's sacrificial death (2:13).

The next section (2:14–18) explains how this change in status occurred—specifically through the death of Christ. By nullifying the law, Christ destroyed the enmity between Jews and Gentiles, and as a result, he made them one. The unification creates an interesting paradox: through the destruction of the enmity, which divided Jews and Gentiles, Christ created one new people. Throughout this section, he refers to both groups as "both" (vv. 14, 16, 18) or "the two" (v. 17) and emphasizes the unity by calling them "one" (v. 14) or "one new person" (v. 15). Not only do these two groups have peace with one another, they also have peace with God having been reconciled in "one body" to God and have access to him through "one Spirit" (v. 18).

The final section describes the benefits that these Gentiles now enjoy. They are no longer strangers, but cocitizens (2:19). Paul describes this new humanity in spatial terms. Both Jews and Gentiles make up a temple, in which God dwells (2:20–22). As he did in Ephesians 2:5–6, Paul uses a series of compound words with the συν- prefix. Jews and Gentiles are "fellow citizens" (συμπολίτης, v. 19b), they have been "joined together" (συναρμολογέω, v. 21a) and "built together" (συνοικοδομέω, v. 22). In Ephesians 2:5–6, the prefixed verbs highlight the unity between the believer and Christ; in Ephesians 2:19–22, these verbs emphasize the unity between Jews and Gentiles.

Outline:

> The Gentiles, once separated from Jews, have been united through the
> death of Christ (vv. 11–13)
> Through his death, Christ breaks the division between Jews and Gen-
> tiles, giving them peace (vv. 14–18)
> Because they have been united, Jews and Gentiles have peace (vv.
> 14–16)
> As a result, Jews and Gentiles have peace with God and access to him
> (vv. 17–18)
> Jews and Gentiles are now a part of a new community, the people of
> God, in whom the Spirit dwells (vv. 19–22)

CLAUSAL OUTLINE FOR EPHESIANS 2:11–22

2:11a Διὸ **μνημονεύετε**
2:11a Therefore, **remember**

2:11b **ὅτι** ποτὲ ὑμεῖς τὰ ἔθνη ἐν σαρκί, (οἱ λεγόμενοι ἀκροβυστία) ὑπὸ
(τῆς λεγομένης περιτομῆς) ἐν σαρκὶ χειροποιήτου,
2:11b **that** once you—Gentiles in flesh, (the ones called 'uncircumcised') by
(the so-called 'circumcised') done by hand in the flesh—

2:12a **ὅτι ἦτε** τῷ καιρῷ ἐκείνῳ χωρὶς Χριστοῦ,
2:12a **that you were** at that time without the Messiah,

2:12b **ἀπηλλοτριωμένοι** τῆς πολιτείας τοῦ Ἰσραὴλ
2:12b **by being alienated** from the citizenship of Israel

2:12c καὶ ξένοι τῶν διαθηκῶν τῆς ἐπαγγελίας,
2:12c and strangers of the covenants of promise

2:12d ἐλπίδα μὴ **ἔχοντες**
2:12d by **having** no hope

2:12e καὶ ἄθεοι ἐν τῷ κόσμῳ.
2:12e and godless in the world

2:13 νυνὶ δὲ ἐν Χριστῷ Ἰησοῦ ὑμεῖς (οἵ ποτε ὄντες μακρὰν) **ἐγενήθητε**
ἐγγὺς ἐν τῷ αἵματι τοῦ Χριστοῦ.
2:13 But now in Christ Jesus you, (who were once far off) **have been brought** near
by the blood of Christ.

2:14a Αὐτὸς γάρ **ἐστιν** ἡ εἰρήνη ἡμῶν,
2:14a <u>For</u> he **is** our peace,

2:14b (ὁ ποιήσας τὰ ἀμφότερα ἓν) καὶ (τὸ μεσότοιχον τοῦ φραγμοῦ
λύσας), τὴν ἔχθραν, ἐν τῇ σαρκὶ αὐτοῦ
2:14b (the one who made both groups into one) and (destroyed the dividing
wall, the partition,) which is the hostility, in his flesh,

2:15a τὸν νόμον τῶν ἐντολῶν ἐν δόγμασιν **καταργήσας**,
2:15a **by making** the law of commandments in ordinances **powerless**,

2:15b **ἵνα** τοὺς δύο **κτίσῃ** ἐν αὐτῷ εἰς ἕνα καινὸν ἄνθρωπον
2:15b **so that** **he might create** in him one new person from the two

2:15c **ποιῶν** εἰρήνην,
2:15c as a result **making** peace,

[ἵνα (v. 15b)]
[so that (v. 15b)]

2:16a καὶ **ἀποκαταλλάξῃ** τοὺς ἀμφοτέρους ἐν ἑνὶ σώματι τῷ θεῷ
διὰ τοῦ σταυροῦ,
2:16a <u>and</u> so that **he might reconcile** both in one body to God through
the cross,

2:16b **ἀποκτείνας** τὴν ἔχθραν ἐν αὐτῷ.
2:16b **by killing** the enmity in it.

2:17a καὶ **ἐλθὼν**
2:17a <u>and</u> **when he came**,

2:17b **εὐηγγελίσατο** εἰρήνην ὑμῖν τοῖς μακρὰν καὶ εἰρήνην τοῖς ἐγγύς·
2:17b **he proclaimed the good news** of peace to you who were far off and peace to
those who were near,

2:18 **ὅτι** δι' αὐτοῦ **ἔχομεν** τὴν προσαγωγὴν οἱ ἀμφότεροι ἐν ἑνὶ
πνεύματι πρὸς τὸν πατέρα.
2:18 **for** through him **we both have** access in one Spirit to the Father.

2:19a ἄρα οὖν οὐκέτι **ἐστὲ** ξένοι καὶ πάροικοι,
2:19a <u>So then</u>, **you are** no longer strangers and aliens

> 2:19b ἀλλ᾽ **ἐστὲ** συμπολῖται τῶν ἁγίων καὶ οἰκεῖοι τοῦ θεοῦ
> 2:19b <u>but</u> **you are** fellow citizens with the saints and members of the
> house of God,

>> 2:20a **ἐποικοδομηθέντες** ἐπὶ τῷ θεμελίῳ τῶν ἀποστόλων καὶ
>> προφητῶν,
>> 2:20a **because you have been built** on the foundation, namely the
>> apostles and prophets,

[2:20b **ὄντος** ἀκρογωνιαίου αὐτοῦ Χριστοῦ Ἰησοῦ,]
[2:20b Christ Jesus himself **being** the cornerstone,]

2:21a ἐν ᾧ πᾶσα οἰκοδομὴ **συναρμολογουμένη**
2:21a in <u>whom</u> the whole building, **by being joined together**,

2:21b **αὔξει** εἰς ναὸν ἅγιον ἐν κυρίῳ,
2:21b **grows** into a holy temple in the Lord,

[Χριστοῦ Ἰησοῦ (2:20)]

2:22 ἐν ᾧ καὶ ὑμεῖς **συνοικοδομεῖσθε** εἰς κατοικητήριον τοῦ θεοῦ ἐν πνεύματι.
2:22 in <u>whom</u> also **you are being built together** into a dwelling place for God by
the Spirit.

SYNTAX EXPLAINED FOR EPHESIANS 2:11–22

2:11a διό: The Greek word διό is a conjunction that means "therefore" (BDAG, s.v.
"διό," p. 250; cf. ESV, RSV, NIV, NET, NASB, NKJV). The CSB renders the conjunction as "so then" (cf. HCSB, NRSV). **Syntactically**, διό introduces an independent conjunctive clause: "Therefore remember" (διὸ μνημονεύετε). **Semantically**, διό is inferential (W, 673). With the use of the conjunction, Paul
draws a number of implications based on his previous section, namely that
the Gentile believers "remember" their old position in light of the salvation
described in the previous section. The command to remember sets the foundation for Paul's discussion on how this salvation impacts the relationship
between Jews and Gentiles and their relationship with God.

μνημονεύετε: The Greek word μνημονεύετε is a second-person plural
present active imperative from the verb μνημονεύω that means "to remember" or "keep in mind" (BDAG, s.v. "μνημονεύω" 3c, p. 656). Most English

versions render the verb as "remember" (ESV, RSV, NRSV, NIV, NET, CSB, HCSB, NASB, NKJV, KJV). The NLT draws out the imperative idea by translating the verb: "Don't forget." **Syntactically**, μνημονεύετε functions as the main verb of the independent conjunctive clause introduced by διό. The subject is implied by the verb: "you," referring to the Gentile believers. **Semantically**, the present tense functions as a customary present. The present imperative communicates a general precept (W, 722). The command instructs these Gentile believers to live their lives in light of their previous state.

2:11b ὅτι: The Greek word ὅτι is a conjunction that means "that" in this context (BDAG, s.v. "ὅτι" 1c, p. 732). **Syntactically**, the conjunction ὅτι introduces a dependent conjunctive clause "*that* once you" (ὅτι ποτὲ ὑμεῖς). The entire clause functions substantively as the direct object of the main verb "remember" (μνημονεύετε). The nominative ὑμεῖς functions as the subject of the verb "you were" (ἦτε) in verse 12a. **Semantically**, ὅτι marks the clause as indirect discourse (W, 456–58). The clause provides the content of what these Gentiles should remember—what they once were.

> **Theological Nugget**: What do the temporal markers in verse 11b mean? Just as he did in verses 2–3, Paul uses a temporal marker to show a contrast between the former state of the Gentile believers (vv. 11–12) and their present condition (v. 13). By using the dative "in that time" (τῷ καιρῷ ἐκείνῳ) and the adverb "but now" (νυνὶ δέ) he makes the contrast starker. The significant difference between 2:1–4 and 2:11–13 is that in Ephesians 2:1–10 he does not distinguish Jewish or Gentile believers—both groups find themselves hopeless before God's salvation. In Ephesians 2:11–13, he describes the Gentiles in particular, that they are separated from the Old Testament promises that God made to the Jewish people, and as a result, they were without hope and godless. In Romans, Paul notes that the position of the Jewish people gives them an advantage (Rom. 3:3; 9:3–5).

λεγόμενοι: The Greek word λεγόμενοι is a present passive participle masculine plural nominative from the verb λέγω that means "to call" or "name" (BDAG, s.v. "λέγω" 4, p. 590). **Syntactically**, the participle phrase, along with the phrase "Gentiles in the flesh" (τὰ ἔθνη ἐν σαρκί), is in apposition to the pronoun "you" (ὑμεῖς) (Merkle, 67; Hoehner, 353). The CSB translates the phrase with an implied verb ἦτε: "you were Gentiles" (cf. HCSB, NIV, KJV; Larkin, 37). However, since Paul includes the verb in verse 12, but omits it in this clause, it is best to understand the phrase in apposition. Most English translations simply insert a comma (ESV, RSV, NRSV, NASB) or a dash (NET, CSB, HCSB, NKJV) to show the relationship. **Semantically**, λεγόμενοι is a customary present: "called" (ESV, RSV, NRSV, NIV, NET, CSB, HCSB, NASB, NKJV, KJV, NLT). The present tense describes an ongoing state (W, 521–22).

λεγομένης: The Greek word λεγομένης is a present passive participle feminine singular genitive from the verb λέγω that means "to call" or "name" (BDAG, s.v. "λέγω" 4, p. 590). **Syntactically**, λεγομένης is an attributive participle, modifying περιτομῆς: "the ones called 'circumcision.'" The participle phrase functions as the object of the preposition ὑπό expressing agency: Jews—"the circumcised"—call the Gentiles "uncircumcised." **Semantically**, λεγομένης is a customary present: "called" (ESV, RSV, NRSV, CSB, HCSB, NKJV) or "so-called" (NASB, NET; cf. BDAG, s.v. "λέγω" 4, p. 590). The action of the verb describes an ongoing action (W, 521–22). The participle makes the point that these are Jewish delineations. Paul repeats the phrase "in the flesh" (ἐν σαρκί). The prepositional phrase expresses reference—Jews and Gentiles are marked in the flesh (Hoehner, 353–54). The repetition creates a chiastic structure:

> A τὰ ἔθνη <u>ἐν σαρκί</u>
>> B <u>οἱ λεγόμενοι</u> ἀκροβυστία
>> B' ὑπὸ <u>τῆς λεγομένης</u> περιτομῆς
> A' <u>ἐν σαρκὶ</u> χειροποιήτου

> A Gentiles <u>in the flesh</u>
>> B <u>who are called</u> uncircumcised
>> B' by <u>the so-called</u> circumcised
> A' <u>in the flesh</u> done by hand

Theological Nugget: What does Paul mean by circumcision "done in the flesh, by hands"? In Galatians and 1 Corinthians, Paul argues that neither circumcision nor uncircumcision counts before God (1 Cor. 7:19; Gal. 5:6; 6:15). On the other hand, Paul describes believers as having a circumcised heart (Rom. 2:29; cf. Col. 2:11; Phil. 3:3). This circumcision of the heart alludes to the new covenant. In Deuteronomy, Moses looked forward to a time when God would circumcise the hearts of his people (Deut. 30:6). Jeremiah promised a time would come when God would write his law on the hearts of his people (Jer. 31:33; cf. Ezek. 36:26–27). For Paul physical circumcision meant nothing, but the circumcision of the heart represented a significant shift—God has inaugurated the new covenant (Dunn 1998, 643–44). He notes that the Jewish circumcision is "done by hand" (χειροποιήτου). In Colossians, he describes the inverse—believers have received a circumcision "done without hands" (ἀχειροποίητος). Other New Testament writers use the word to refer to the temple built by man opposed to what God has done (Mark 14:58; Acts 7:48; 17:24; Heb. 9:11, 24). The Old Testament uses the adjective substantivally to refer to idols, literally: "handmades" (Lev. 26:1; Isa. 2:18; 10:11; 16:12; 19:1; 21:9; 46:6; cf. Dan. 5:4, 23; 6:28). By calling the circumcision "done by hand," Paul insinuates that the circumcision—the Jewish mark of the covenant—has itself become idolatrous.

^{2:12a} ὅτι: The Greek word ὅτι is a conjunction that means "that" in this context (BDAG, s.v. "ὅτι" 1c, p. 732). **Syntactically**, ὅτι is resumptive, parallel to the ὅτι clause in 2:11b. The conjunction introduces a dependent conjunctive clause "*that* you were once in that time without the Messiah" (ὅτι ἦτε τῷ καιρῷ ἐκείνῳ χωρὶς Χριστοῦ). The clause functions substantively as the direct object of the main verb in verse 11: "remember" (μνημονεύετε). The second ὅτι clause introduces a list of five disadvantages that faced the Gentiles: (1) they were separated from the Messiah; (2) they were estranged from the citizenship of Israel; (3) they were strangers of the covenants of promise; (4) they were without hope; (5) and they were godless. **Semantically**, the ὅτι marks the clause as indirect discourse continuing the content of what the Ephesians should remember (W, 456–58).

ἦτε: The Greek word ἦτε is a second-person plural imperfect active indicative from the verb εἰμί that means "to be" (BDAG, s.v. "εἰμί" 2a, p. 283). **Syntactically**, ἦτε functions as the main verb of the dependent conjunctive clause introduced by ὅτι. The prepositional phrase "without the Messiah" (χωρὶς Χριστοῦ) functions as the predicate of the verb: "you were without the Messiah." **Semantically**, the imperfect tense is rendered as an imperfect retained in indirect discourse and should be translated as a past perfect: "you had been, at that time without the Messiah" (W, 552–54).

> **Lexical Nugget**: What is the difference between "Christ" and "Messiah"? Most English translations render χωρὶς Χριστοῦ as "apart from Christ" (ESV, LEB, NIV, RSV, NRSV, NASB, NKJV, KJV, CSB). However, a few translations render the word "Messiah" (HCSB, NET, CJB). Χριστός can mean either "Christ" or "Messiah." The term χριστός can refer to a more general promise that God will send his promised messiah to Israel (BDAG, s.v. "Χριστός" 1, p. 1091). On the other hand, by the time Paul had written Ephesians, it had come to be a name for Jesus: "Jesus Christ" (BDAG, s.v. "Χριστός" 2, p. 1091). Since this section describes the time that these Gentiles were excluded from God's promises, Paul most likely has the more general title in mind. The use of the messianic title is a metonymy, a substitution for the concept of "messianic hope" (Larkin, 37; Best, 241).

^{2:12b} ἀπηλλοτριωμένοι: The Greek word ἀπηλλοτριωμένοι is a perfect passive participle masculine plural nominative from the verb ἀπαλλοτριόω that means "to estrange" or "alienate" (BDAG, s.v. "ἀπαλλοτριόω," p. 96). **Syntactically**, ἀπηλλοτριωμένοι introduces a dependent participle clause. It functions adverbially modifying "you were" (ἦτε). **Semantically**, ἀπηλλοτριωμένοι functions as manner describing the previous state of the believers: "*by being estranged* from the citizenship of Israel." Even though they were excluded, Paul will argue that through Christ, both Jews and Gentiles

have access to the Father (v. 18). The genitive τῆς πολιτείας ("citizenship") expresses separation: "*from* the citizenship of Israel."

> **Lexical Nugget**: What does it mean to be a "citizen" (πολιτεία)? The Greek term πολιτεία is a sociopolitical term referring to an individual member of a particular group, a "citizen." In the current context, it most likely refers to the group made up by these members (BDAG, s.v. "πολιτεία" 2, p. 845). Even though Paul presents the spiritual condition of these Gentile believers before coming to Christ, he does it with political terms. By the end of the passage, he will come full circle. While the Gentiles are alienated from the "citizenship of Israel" (τῆς πολιτείας τοῦ Ἰσραήλ) (v. 12), he states in verse 19 that they are "fellow citizens with the saints" (συμπολῖται τῶν ἁγίων). While they are "strangers of the covenants of promise" (ξένοι τῶν διαθηκῶν τῆς ἐπαγγελίας), he states in verse 19 that they are no longer "strangers and foreigners" (ξένοι καὶ πάροικοι). Verse 13 draws out the contrast with spatial terms: "those who were once *far off* have been brought *near*." The progression of Paul's argument is subtle. Hoehner summarizes it nicely: "Paul demonstrates that believing Jews and Gentiles become the church (Eph. 3:13–22) but that unbelieving Jews and Gentiles still remain as two separate entities distinct from the church (1 Cor. 10:32)" (Hoehner, 361).

2:12c καί: The Greek word καί is a conjunction that means "and" (BDAG, s.v. "καί" 1b, p. 494). **Syntactically**, καί introduces a dependent conjunctive clause: "*and* strangers of the covenants of promise" (καὶ ξένοι τῶν διαθηκῶν τῆς ἐπαγγελίας). **Semantically**, καί is explanatory (Larkin, 38; Arnold, 155). The phrase explains specifically that these Gentiles are strangers of the covenants of promise. There is some debate about the specific identity of the covenants here. Hoehner argues that Paul has the series of unconditional promises in mind: the Abrahamic, Davidic, and new covenant (Hoehner, 359). Thielman follows Hoehner but excludes the Davidic covenant since Paul does not mention it in the letter (Thielman, 156). However, Arnold persuasively argues that since Paul uses the plural form, this refers to the broadest sense of the term, including the Mosaic covenant, which includes God's future blessing for his people (Arnold, 155).

2:12d ἔχοντες: The Greek word ἔχοντες is a present active participle masculine plural nominative from the verb ἔχω that means "to have," or in this instance "experience" (BDAG, s.v. "ἔχω" 7aβ, p. 421). **Syntactically**, ἔχοντες introduces a dependent participle clause. It functions adverbially modifying the main verb: "you were" (ἦτε). **Semantically**, the participle functions as manner, describing their position without Christ: "*by not having* hope." Even though the participle is present tense, it describes a former time (Thielman,

157). Most versions render the participle as "without hope" (NIV, CSB, HCSB) or "having no hope" (ESV, RSV, NRSV, NASB, NKJV, KJV).

2:12e καί: The Greek word καί is a conjunction that means "and" (BDAG, s.v. "καί" 1b, p. 494). **Syntactically**, καί introduces an independent conjunctive clause: "*and* godless in the world" (καὶ ἄθεοι ἐν τῷ κόσμῳ). **Semantically**, καί is explanatory (Larkin, 38). The phrase gives a specific reason why these Gentiles were hopeless (v. 12d)—they were "godless in the world" (ἄθεοι ἐν τῷ κόσμῳ). The Greek word ἄθεος is a *hapax legomenon*; the English word "atheist" comes from this Greek word (ἄθεος). Of course, all Gentiles were polytheistic, worshiping many gods. In fact, many Christians were called atheists because of their insistance on worshiping one God (Mart. Pol. 3:2; 9:2). Paul writes the list from the Jewish perspective. Despite their extreme religiosity, most Jews would have viewed the Gentiles as living apart from the one, true God.

2:13 δέ: The Greek word δέ is a conjunction that means "but" (BDAG, s.v. "δέ" 2, p. 213). **Syntactically**, δέ introduces an independent conjunctive clause: "*but* now in Christ Jesus you … have been brought near " (νυνὶ δὲ ἐν Χριστῷ Ἰησοῦ ὑμεῖς … ἐγενήθητε). **Semantically**, δέ is a contrastive conjunction. With the temporal adverb "now" (νυνί), Paul uses the conjunction to contrast the Gentiles previous state with their present state as a result of their relationship with Jesus: "But now" (ESV, RSV, NRSV, NIV, NET, CSB, HCSB, NASB, NKJV, KJV).

ὄντες: The Greek word ὄντες is a present active participle masculine plural nominative from the verb εἰμί that means "to be" (BDAG, s.v. "εἰμί" 3a, p. 284). **Syntactically**, ὄντες functions as a substantival participle. The participle phrase "the ones who were once far" (οἵ ποτε ὄντες μακράν) is in apposition to ὑμεῖς, the subject of the sentence. Most English versions render the participle phrase as a relative clause. **Semantically**, the present tense is rendered as a customary present. Present tense participles generally represent an action that is contemporaneous to the action of the main verb, but in this instance, due to the force of the adverb ποτε, the participle is antecedent to the main verb (W, 625–26). The repeated adverb ποτε draws the reader's attention back to Paul's list of disadvantages facing Gentiles (vv. 11–12).

Theological Nugget: What is the reference to "near" and "far" in verse 13? Paul changes his temporal metaphor to a spatial one. These Gentiles who were once far off have now been brought near. In verse 17, Paul will allude to Isaiah 57:19: "Peace upon peace to those who are far and to those who are near." Paul draws this near/far language (μακράν/ἐγγύς) from Isaiah and uses it to point forward to verse 17. In the context of Isaiah, "those who were near" refer to Jews living in Israel and "those who were far off" refer to those Jews living in exile. Paul applies the language to Gentiles by

> describing them as far off but having been brought near (cf. v. 13b). Even Isaiah looked forward to a time when the nations would come and worship the one true God of Israel (Isa. 56:6–8).

ἐγενήθητε: The Greek word ἐγενήθητε is a second-person plural aorist passive indicative from the verb γίνομαι that means "to become," or in this instance "to move" or "come" (BDAG, s.v. "γίνομαι" 6g, p. 199). **Syntactically**, ἐγενήθητε functions as the main verb of the independent conjunctive clause introduced by δέ. The subject of the verb is the second-person personal pronoun: "you" (ὑμεῖς), referring to the Gentile believers. **Semantically**, the aorist tense is rendered as an ingressive aorist emphasizing the point when these Gentiles have been brought near (W, 558–59). Paul will argue that through his work on the cross, Christ created one new people out of Jews and Gentiles and reconciled them to God; they now have access to God (Eph. 2:16, 18). The passive voice is a divine passive. Even though it is not stated, God is the one who brings these Gentiles near.

> **Lexical Nugget**: What does Paul's reference to Christ's blood mean? The prepositional phrase "by his blood" to express the means by which the Gentiles are brought near. In this context, the reference to Christ's blood (αἷμα) is metonymy, figuratively referring to Christ's sacrificial death (BDAG, s.v. "αἷμα" 2b, pp. 26–27). In Romans, Paul presents the death of Christ as propitiation—satisfying God's demand for holiness (Rom. 3:25; 5:9; cf. Mark 14:24; Exod. 24:8). In Ephesians, he seems to emphasize a different picture of Christ as one ascending high above, subjugating his enemies (cf. Eph. 1:20–23). However, Paul does touch on this theme throughout the letter. Earlier, he states that Christ's blood forms the means for God's redemption (Eph. 1:7). In Ephesians 5, he states that Christ's death becomes an example of how we should love one another (Eph. 5:2, 25–30).

2:14a γάρ: The Greek word γάρ is a conjunction that means "for" or "therefore" (BDAG, s.v. "γάρ" 1a, p. 189). Most English versions translate the conjunction as "for" (ESV, RSV, NRSV, NIV, NET, CSB, HCSB, NASB, NKJV, KJV). **Syntactically**, γάρ introduces the clause as an independent conjunctive clause: "*For he is our peace*" (Αὐτὸς γάρ ἐστιν ἡ εἰρήνη ἡμῶν). **Semantically**, γάρ is explanatory. This new section (vv. 14–16) provides the specifics of Paul's declaration in verse 13—that Gentiles have been brought near (Thielman, 163).

ἐστίν: The Greek word ἐστίν is a third-person singular present active indicative from the verb εἰμί that means "to be" (BDAG, s.v. "εἰμί" 2a, p. 283). **Syntactically**, ἐστίν functions as the main verb of the independent conjunctive clause introduced by γάρ. The subject is the third-person personal pronoun: "he" (αὐτός). The inclusion of the pronoun at the beginning of the clause adds emphasis. The predicate nominative is "our peace" (ἡ εἰρήνη ἡμῶν). **Semantically**, the present tense is rendered as a customary present. The present tense describes an ongoing relationship between Christ and the believer (W, 521–22).

> **Lexical Nugget**: How does Paul use the term "peace" in this section? Throughout this section, he repeats the word "peace" (εἰρήνη) several times. Hoehner points out that half of the eight occurrences of the word in Ephesians appear in this section (vv. 14, 15, 17 [2x]) (Hoehner, 367). Paul uses the word as a part of his salutations (cf. Eph. 1:2; 6:23). Later he will allude to this section by calling his preaching the "gospel of peace" (Eph. 6:15). This concept of peace comes from Isaiah. He has already alluded to Isaiah 57:19 in verse 13. He will allude to the text again in verse 17 (see Theological Nugget at 2:13). In the Old Testament, peace ("shalom"; שָׁלוֹם) is more than the cessation of hostility, but harmony between people or groups. Ultimately, this peace comes from God (Num. 6:24–27). Isaiah looked forward to a time characterized by peace (Isa. 48:18; 52:7; 54:13; 57:19; 66:12), specifically between God and his people. By drawing his language from Isaiah, Paul suggests that this peace not only exists between two people groups but between humanity and God.

2:14b ποιήσας: The Greek word ποιήσας is an aorist active participle masculine singular nominative from the verb ποιέω that means "to bring about" or "accomplish" (BDAG, s.v. "ποιέω" 2hβ, pp. 839–40). **Syntactically**, ποιήσας introduces a substantival clause "the one who made both groups one" (ὁ ποιήσας τὰ ἀμφότερα ἕν). The participle phrase is in apposition to αὐτός, the subject of the sentence. The direct object of the participle is "both" (τὰ ἀμφότερα); the object complement is "one" (ἕν) (W, 182–89). In the clausal outline, we have offset the participle phrase to help show the relationship between the clause and the subject. **Semantically**, the aorist tense is rendered as a constative aorist: "made" (CSB, HCSB, NASB, NET) or "has made" (ESV, RSV, NRSV, NKJV). It describes the action as a whole (W, 557–58). These two groups which were at one time at odds, one of which faced significant disadvantages, have been made into a single group.

λύσας: The Greek word λύσας is an aorist active participle masculine singular nominative from the verb λύω that means "to destroy" (BDAG, s.v. "λύω" 3, p. 607). **Syntactically**, λύσας functions as a substantival participle. The direct object is "the dividing wall" (τὸ μεσότοιχον). Just like ποιήσας, the participle phrase "the one who destroys the dividing wall of partition" (τὸ μεσότοιχον τοῦ φραγμοῦ λύσας) is in apposition to the subject of the sentence "he" (αὐτός), referring to Christ. It is the second participle in a Granville Sharp construction ("the one who makes … and destroys"). The single article modifies both participles separated by καί to describe the same person (W, 271–72).

ὁ <u>ποιήσας</u> τὰ ἀμφότερα ἓν
καὶ
    τὸ μεσότοιχον τοῦ φραγμοῦ <u>λύσας</u>

The one who <u>makes</u> both groups into one
and
    <u>destroyed</u> the dividing wall

Semantically, the aorist tense is a constative aorist: "tore down" (CSB, HCSB) or "destroyed" (NET). It describes the action of the verb as a whole (W, 557–58). The two participles are parallel. Christ brought these two groups together by destroying the wall that kept them apart. The Greek term μεσότοιχον ("dividing wall") is a *hapax legomenon*. The genitive τοῦ φραγμοῦ ("the wall") is most likely a genitive of apposition: "the wall, *namely* the dividing wall" (Hoehner, 368; Larkin, 40; Lincoln, 141).

> **Syntactical Nugget**: What is the relationship of the final two clauses ("the hostility" and "in his flesh") to the context? There are three options. The first option is that both phrases could modify the following participle in verse 15: "to make powerless" (καταργήσας) (Lincoln, 142). The NASB follows this syntax: "who … broke down the barrier of the dividing wall, by abolishing *in His flesh, the enmity*, which is the Law of commandments" (cf. NKJV KJV). The significant problem with this position is that it is doubtful that Paul would refer to the law as hostile. In Romans 7, he refers to it as ineffective, but holy (Rom. 7:12). The second option is that "hostility" (τὴν ἔχθραν) stands in apposition to "the dividing wall" (τὸ μεσότοιχον) and the prepositional phrase "in his flesh" (ἐν τῇ σαρκὶ αὐτοῦ) modifies the following participle (καταργήσας) (Hoehner, 371–73; Merkle, 73). The NIV follows this syntax: "who … has destroyed the barrier, the dividing wall *of hostility*, by setting aside *in his flesh*…" (cf. CSB, HCSB, RSV, NET). Finally, the third option is that both phrases modify the participle "destroyed" (λύσας) (Thielman, 168; Arnold, 159). The ESV follows this syntax: "who … has broken down *in his flesh* the dividing wall of *hostility*" (cf. NRSV, NLT). The second and third options are more attractive than the first, but the latter is preferable. Paul uses a similar phrase in verse 16: "the enmity in him" (τὴν ἔχθραν ἐν αὐτῷ), which suggests that the prepositional phrase modifies the preceding phrase rather than the following one. The syntax in verse 14 is difficult, presenting interpreters with a number of options. But by stacking up these phrases, he gives a rhetorical effect. He slows down his argument to make a point: Christ has removed all division between Jews and Gentiles to make peace between the two.

Lexical Nugget: What is the reference to this dividing wall (τὸ μεσότοιχον τοῦ φραγμοῦ)? Out of the significant list of options that commentators have presented, two possibilities stand out: it can either refer to a literal wall or a metaphorical one. First, there is a physical wall in the temple, specifically to divide the Court of the Gentiles from the inner courts in the temple (Abbott 1909, 61; Arnold, 159–60). Temple authorities threatened death for Gentiles coming into this part of the temple (cf. Josephus, *Ant.* 15.11.5 §417; *J.W.* 5.5.2 §193–94). In Acts, Paul was accused of taking Gentiles into the temple. The fact that these men were from Ephesus makes this view tantalizing (cf. Acts 21:28–29). And later in the chapter, Paul will describe the church, made up of both Jews and Gentiles, as a temple (vv. 20–22). Second, many have argued that this wall refers to the Jewish law, which was described as a fence around the Jewish people (cf. Let. Aris. 139; m. 'Abot 1:1) (Hoehner, 370–71; Thielman, 166–67). There is no explicit reference to the temple in the immediate context. And since Paul is writing before the destruction of the temple, an allusion to the destruction of a physical structure would not have been apparent to the audience. Paul's emphasis on the law, which he addresses specifically in the following clause, makes the metaphorical view a better option.

2:15a καταργήσας: The Greek word καταργήσας is an aorist active participle masculine singular nominative from the verb καταργέω that means "to make powerless" or "invalidate" (BDAG, s.v. "καταργέω" 2, p. 525). **Syntactically**, καταργήσας introduces a dependent participle clause. It functions adverbially modifying "destroyed" (λύσας). The direct object of the participle is "the law" (τὸν νόμον) (Rosner, 2013, 77). **Semantically**, the action of the participle is simultaneous with the action of the main verb since both are aorist tense (W, 624–25). The NET renders the participle temporally: "*when* he nullified." However, it might be best treated as a participle of means describing how Christ destroyed the dividing wall: "*by* abolishing" (ESV, RSV, NIV, NASB, NLT; Hoehner, 375; Thielman, 168; Merkle, 73; Larkin, 40; W, 629–30).

Lexical Nugget: What does it mean to "make the law powerless" (καταργέω)? Even though the previous participle (λύσας) points toward destruction, καταργέω has a softer meaning. When Paul refers to the law, the verb generally carries the meaning of "invalidating" or "rendering inoperable" (BDAG, s.v. "καταργέω" 2, p. 525). In Romans 7, Paul uses the same verb to describe how those who have died to the law have been released (κατηργήθημεν) from it (Rom. 7:2, 6; cf. 2 Cor. 3:7, 11–14). In Romans, Paul states that Jesus is the "end of the law" (Rom. 10:4), meaning that everything in the law led up to and pointed toward Christ. The NIV translates Romans 10:4: "Christ is the culmination of the law." Jesus makes a similar point in the Sermon on the Mount: he did not come "to destroy [καταλύω] the law, but to fulfill it" (Matt. 5:17). According to Paul, the law has become ineffective, but it still serves a role for the believer (Rom. 2:14; 3:31). Even in Ephesians, Paul will appeal to the law for instruction (Eph. 6:2–3, citing Exod. 20:12; Deut. 5:16) (Delling, 1964, 453–54; Thielman, 169–70). Rosner states that the law as a covenant, particularly the commandment-keeping aspect of the law, has been abolished by being replaced by the new covenant (Rosner, 2013, 78).

2:15b ἵνα: The Greek word ἵνα is a conjunction that means "that" to denote purpose (BDAG, s.v. "ἵνα" 1aε, p. 475). **Syntactically**, ἵνα introduces a dependent conjunctive clause "*that* he might create in him one new person" (τοὺς δύο κτίσῃ ἐν αὐτῷ εἰς ἕνα καινὸν ἄνθρωπον). The entire clause functions adverbially modifying the participle "make powerless" (καταργήσας). The conjunction governs the clause in verse 16a as well: "that he might reconcile both into one body to God through the cross." **Semantically**, the ἵνα expresses the purpose of Christ nullifying the law: "*so that* he might create" (CSB, HCSB, NASB) or "*that*" (ESV, RSV, NRSV). The NIV begins a new sentence at this point and translates the conjunction: "His purpose was to create."

κτίσῃ: The Greek word κτίσῃ is a third-person singular aorist active subjunctive from the verb κτίζω that means "to create" (BDAG, s.v. "κτίζω," p. 572). **Syntactically**, κτίσῃ functions as the main verb of the dependent conjunctive clause introduced by ἵνα. The subject is implied: "he," referring to Christ (v. 13). The direct object is "the two" (τοὺς δύο), referring to the two groups delineated in verses 11–12, corresponding to "both" (τὰ ἀμφότερα; v. 14). **Semantically**, the aorist tense functions as a constative aorist: "he might create" (ESV, RSV, NRSV, CSB, HCSB; cf. NIV, NET). It describes the action of the verb as a whole (W, 557–58), emphasizing the new reality facing Jews and Gentiles in their relationship with Christ. Christ nullified the law for the purpose of creating one new group of people out of the two groups delineated in verses 11–12. The prepositional phrase "into one new person" (εἰς ἕνα καινὸν ἄνθρωπον) describes the result of this creation. The prepositional phrase "in him" (ἐν αὐτῷ) expresses sphere—this all occurs in relationship with Christ.

Theological Nugget: What does it mean to "create one new person" in Ephesians? Ultimately, God is the creator of all things (Rom. 1:25; Eph. 3:9). In the previous section, Paul states that the believer is God's "handiwork, having been created [κτισθέντες] in Christ Jesus" (2:10). In this section, he states that he created this new person—or humanity—from Jews and Gentiles. Their relationship in Christ holds them together. Later in the letter, Paul will encourage believers "to put on the new self who was created (κτισθέντα) according to God" (4:24), an allusion to Ephesians 2:15. Paul emphasizes this unity by contrasting "the two" with "the one" throughout this passage. First, Christ makes both groups into one (v. 14b). Second, he makes the two into one new person (v. 15b). Third, he reconciles them both into one body (v. 16a). Finally, through "one spirit," they both have access to the Father. Despite everything that separated these two groups, the two have been brought together and through this new relationship can come before God.

2:15c ποιῶν: The Greek word ποιῶν is a present active participle masculine singular nominative from the verb ποιέω that means "to bring about" or "accomplish" (BDAG, s.v. "ποιέω" 2c, p. 839). **Syntactically**, ποιῶν introduces a dependent participle clause. It functions adverbially modifying "he might create" (κτίσῃ). The direct object is "peace" (εἰρήνην), a repeated theme throughout this section (see Lexical Nugget at 2:14a). **Semantically**, the present tense indicates that the action of the participle is simultaneous with the action of κτίσῃ (W, 625–26). The participle expresses the result of Christ creating one new person: "*so* making peace" (ESV, RSV, KJV) or "*thus* making peace" (NRSV, NIV, NET, NASB, NKJV). The CSB highlights this by translating the participle "*resulting* in peace" (cf. HCSB). The NLT makes the participle the main verb: "He made peace between Jews and Gentiles by creating in himself one new people."

2:16a καί: The Greek word καί is a conjunction that means "and" (BDAG, s.v. "καί" 1b, p. 494). **Syntactically**, καί introduces a dependent conjunctive clause: "*and* he might reconcile both in one body to God through the cross" (καὶ ἀποκαταλλάξῃ τοὺς ἀμφοτέρους ἐν ἑνὶ σώματι τῷ θεῷ διὰ τοῦ σταυροῦ). **Semantically**, καί is a coordinating connective: "and" (ESV, RSV, NRSV, NIV, NET, NASB, NKJV, KJV). The clause is parallel to the previous subjunctive verb in verse 15b: "he might create" (κτίσῃ), giving a second purpose for nullifying the law: God reconciles these groups together.

ἀποκαταλλάξῃ : The Greek word ἀποκαταλλάξῃ is a third-person singular aorist active subjunctive from the verb ἀποκαταλλάσσω that means "to reconcile" (BDAG, s.v. "ἀποκαταλλάσσω," p. 12). **Syntactically**, ἀποκαταλλάξῃ functions as the main verb of the dependent conjunctive clause introduced by ἵνα in verse 15b. The subject is implied by the verb: "he," referring to Christ (v. 13). The direct object is "both" (τοὺς ἀμφοτέρους); the indirect object is "God" (τῷ θεῷ)—Christ reconciles both groups to God. **Semantically**, the aorist tense functions as a constative aorist: "might reconcile" (ESV, RSV, NRSV, NIV, CSB, HCSB, NASB, NKJV, KJV). It describes the action of the verb as a whole (W, 557–58). God created this new group of people by reconciling the two groups together. The prepositional phrase "in one body" (ἐν ἑνὶ σώματι) expresses the goal for reconciliation: "into" (BDAG, s.v. "ἐν" 3, p. 327). The prepositional phrase "through the cross" (διὰ τοῦ σταυροῦ) expresses the means by which this reconciliation occurs (BDAG, s.v. "διά" 3a, p. 224).

2:16b ἀποκτείνας: The Greek word ἀποκτείνας is an aorist active participle masculine singular nominative from the verb ἀποκτείνω that means "to put to death" or "eliminate" (BDAG, s.v. "ἀποκτείνω" 2, p. 114). **Syntactically**, ἀποκτείνας introduces a dependent participle clause. It functions adverbially modifying the verb "he might reconcile" (ἀποκαταλλάξῃ). The direct object is "enmity" (τὴν ἔχθραν). **Semantically**, ἀποκτείνας could express result: "*thereby* putting to death" (ESV, RSV, NRSV, NKJV; Larkin, 42); however, it probably best expresses the means by which this reconciliation occurs: "*by means* of killing the enmity" (Arnold, 166; Hoehner, 384). Arnold notes the irony: "It is by Jesus' being killed on the cross that he is able to kill the enmity separating people from God and from one another" (Arnold, 166). He cites Robinson, who poetically states: "the slain was a slayer too" (Robinson, 1907, 65).

> **Syntactical Nugget**: What is the referent to the pronoun αὐτῷ in verse 16? On the one hand, Paul regularly refers to the believer's relationship to Christ throughout this section (cf. Eph. 2:13, 21, 22), leading some to conclude that the pronoun refers to Christ (Lincoln, 146; Arnold, 166). On the other hand, the nearest referent is "the cross." Paul's emphasis in the most immediate section is on Christ's death (Eph. 2:13, 14). Even though Paul favors this formula to refer to the union between Christ and the believer, the most likely referent is the cross (Hoehner, 384; Thielman, 172–73).

2:17a καί: The Greek word καί is a conjunction that means "and" (BDAG, s.v. "καί" 1e, p. 494). **Syntactically**, καί introduces an independent conjunctive clause: "*and* when he came he proclaimed the good news of peace to you" (καὶ ἐλθὼν εὐηγγελίσατο εἰρήνην ὑμῖν). **Semantically**, καί is a coordinating connective: "and" (ESV, RSV, NET, NASB, NKJV, KJV). The conjunction could connect this clause to verse 16, but most likely introduces a clause parallel to verse 14 (Hoehner, 384; Merkle, 75).

ἐλθών: The Greek word ἐλθών is an aorist active participle masculine singular nominative from the verb ἔρχομαι that means "to come" or "appear" (BDAG, s.v. "ἔρχομαι" 1bα, p. 394). **Syntactically**, ἐλθών introduces a dependent participle clause. It functions adverbially, modifying the following verb: "he proclaimed the good news" (εὐηγγελίσατο). **Semantically**, the action of the participle is simultaneous with the action of the main verb since both are aorist tense (W, 624–25). Some translations render the participle as attendant circumstance: "he came and preached" (ESV, NET, NIV, RSV, NRSV, NASB, CSB; cf. W, 640–45). However, it is best to understand the participle as temporal: "*while* coming" (Hoehner, 285; cf. HCSB). The temporal participle marks the point in time when Jesus preached this good news—when he came.

Theological Nugget: When did Christ come preaching peace? The reference possibly refers to Christ's incarnation or perhaps his own preaching ministry (Best, 271–73). The strength of this position is that the verbs are aorist and the Gospels describe Jesus having an active preaching ministry. The real problem with this position is that Jesus predominantly worked with Jews, not Gentiles. And Paul's emphasis throughout this section is on how Christ's death affects the Gentile believers. Another option is that it refers specifically to Jesus's death on the cross—his death proclaimed peace (Lincoln, 148–49). Paul emphasizes Christ's death throughout this section (vv. 14–16), but the verb εὐαγγελίζω refers to an oral pronouncement, not a metaphorical statement. Finally, most argue that this refers to Christ's proclamation through his apostles and prophets. Later in the passage, Paul describes the church being built upon a foundation of the apostles and prophets—Christ himself as the cornerstone (v. 20). In Ephesians 3, Paul states that God revealed that Gentiles partake in the promise of God along with the Jews to his apostles and prophets (3:5–6). He describes his ministry as proclaiming this message (3:8–10) (Hoehner, 385; Arnold, 166). The last view makes the most sense of the context of Paul's argument.

[2:17b] εὐηγγελίσατο: The Greek word εὐηγγελίσατο is third-person singular aorist middle indicative from the verb εὐαγγελίζω that means "to proclaim the gospel" (BDAG, s.v. "εὐαγγελίζω" 2aα, p. 402). **Syntactically**, εὐηγγελίσατο functions as the main verb of the independent conjunctive clause introduced by καί. The subject is implied by the verb: "he," referring to Christ. The direct object is "peace" (εἰρήνην). The indirect object is the second-person personal pronoun "you" (ὑμῖν). The adjectives "far" (τοῖς μακράν) and "near" (τοῖς ἐγγύς) are in apposition to ὑμῖν. Both adjectives function substantivally: "those far off," corresponding to Gentile believers; "those near," corresponding to Jewish believers (cf. vv. 11–12). **Semantically**, the aorist tense functions as a constative aorist: "he preached" (ESV, RSV, NIV, NET, NASB, NKJV, KJV) or "proclaimed" (CSB, HCSB, NRSV). It describes the action of the verb as a whole (W, 557–58). Christ proclaimed this gospel message to both Jews and Gentiles.

Theological Nugget: What is the significance of Paul's use of Isaiah 57:19 in the text? Even though it is not clear, Paul seems to have Isaiah 57:19 in mind. The prophet writes: "peace, peace, to the far and to the near" (ESV). The LXX reads εἰρήνην ἐπ᾽ εἰρήνην τοῖς μακρὰν καὶ τοῖς ἐγγὺς οὖσιν ("peace upon peace to the ones who are far off and to the ones who are near"). Paul does not explicitly quote from the text, but he derives the "peace" language from Isaiah. The repetition of "peace" here, along with the spatial imagery, suggests that he is alluding to Isaiah 57:19. Beginning in verse 13, he has used the near/far language to describe Jews and Gentiles. Isaiah used the image to refer to Jews in the promised land (near) and those in the diaspora (far). Due to his use of Isaiah in the text, the image of "preaching the good news" may also come from Isaiah (cf. Isa. 40:9; 52:7; 61:1). Paul actually quotes Isaiah 52:7 in Romans 10:15. Later in Ephesians, he will refer to the gospel as the "gospel of peace" (Eph. 6:15). The verb εὐαγγελίζω could be political, referring to reporting military victories. Old Testament writers use this verb to describe God's victories (2 Sam. 4:10; 18:19–31). Isaiah gave the term more of a theological nuance. For the prophet, the gospel message is an announcement of God's coming reign and the end of the exile for the nation (Isa. 40:3, 9; 52:7), a time when freedom would come to those who are enslaved (Isa. 61:1). By alluding to Isaiah, Paul points to the inauguration of God's kingdom that Isaiah anticipated, and the implications that this inauguration has for both Jews and Gentiles.

Text-Critical Nugget: Does Paul write "peace" once or twice in verse 17? Several Byzantine manuscripts (K, L, 𝔐) omit the second occurrence of the word "peace" (εἰρήνην): "He preached the good news of peace to you who were far off and to who were near" (cf. MT and RP²⁰⁰⁵). However, the majority of Alexandrian (𝔓46, ℵ, A, B, 33, 1739, 1881) and Western (D, F, G) manuscripts include εἰρήνην before τοῖς ἐγγύς: "peace to you who were far of and *peace* to you who were near" (NA²⁸, SBL, and THGNT). The omission does not alter the meaning significantly, but the repetition underscores Paul's allusion to Isaiah 57:19. We could argue that a scribe inserted the word to cohere with Isaiah 57:19, but Ephesians 2:17 is still somewhat distinct from the text in Isaiah. And while the Byzantine reading is shorter and harder, the overwhelming external support in favor of the inclusion suggests that it is original.

²:¹⁸ ὅτι: The Greek word ὅτι is a conjunction that means "because" or "for" in this context (BDAG, s.v. "ὅτι" 4a, p. 732). **Syntactically**, the conjunction ὅτι introduces a dependent conjunctive clause: "that through him we both have access" (δι᾽ αὐτοῦ ἔχομεν τὴν προσαγωγὴν οἱ ἀμφότεροι). The entire clause functions adverbially modifying the main verb "he proclaimed the gospel" (εὐηγγελίσατο). **Semantically**, ὅτι expresses cause, providing the reason for Christ's proclamation: "*for* through him we both have access" (ESV, NIV, CSB, HCSB, NASB, RSV, NRSV, NKJV, KJV; Arnold, 167; Hoehner, 388).

ἔχομεν: The Greek word ἔχομεν is a first-person plural present active indicative from the verb ἔχω that means "to have" or in this instance "to be able to" (BDAG, s.v. "ἔχω" 5, p. 421). **Syntactically**, ἔχομεν functions as the main verb of the dependent conjunctive clause introduced by ὅτι. The subject is implied by the verb: "we." The adjective "both" (οἱ ἀμφότεροι) functions substantivally in apposition to the implied subject, referring to Jews and Gentiles (cf. vv. 11–12, 14, 15, 16; Larkin, 43). The direct object is "access" (τὴν προσαγωγήν).

Semantically, ἔχομεν is a customary present: "we both have." The present tense describes the ongoing access that the believer has because of what Christ has done (W, 521–22). The verb is modified by three prepositional phrases. The first prepositional phrase "through him" (δι᾽ αὐτοῦ) identifies the intermediate agent. This access was granted "through him," a reference to Christ. The second prepositional phrase "in one Spirit" (ἐν ἑνὶ πνεύματι) can either express means: "*by* one Spirit" (NIV, HCSB, NKJV, KJV; Larkin, 43; Best, 274). But it best expresses sphere: "*in* one Spirit" (ESV, NET, RSV, NRSV, NASB, CSB). Throughout the immediate context, Paul describes Christ's death as the means through which the believer has access (Hoehner, 389; Thielman, 175). Finally, this access is granted "to the Father" (πρὸς τὸν πατέρα). The structure of the prepositional phrases gives a trinitarian formula (Merkle, 76).

> **Lexical Nugget**: What does the term "access" (προσαγωγή) mean? Paul is the only New Testament writer to use the term προσαγωγή ("access") (Rom. 5:2; Eph. 2:18; 3:12). In the Old Testament, the term has a cultic meaning. Worshipers approached God with their sacrifices (Lev. 1:3; 3:3; 4:14; Lincoln, 149). This nuance fits the context. Up to this point, Paul's focus has been on Christ's death (vv. 13–16); the remainder of the section describes the church as a temple, in which dwells the Holy Spirit (vv. 19–22). Rather than coming to God through sacrifices, the believer comes to God through faith (Rom. 5:2; Eph. 3:12) (Schreiner, 2001, 343).

2:19a ἄρα οὖν: The phrase ἄρα οὖν functions as a conjunction that means "so then" (BDAG, s.v. "ἄρα" 2b, p. 127). The phrase is unique to Paul (Porter, 207). Most English versions translate the phrase as "so then" (ESV, RSV, NRSV, CSB, HCSB, NASB, NET). The NIV translates the phrase as "consequently." **Syntactically**, ἄρα οὖν introduces an independent conjunctive clause: "So then, you are no longer strangers and aliens" (ἄρα οὖν οὐκέτι ἐστὲ ξένοι καὶ πάροικοι). **Syntactically**, both conjunctions are inferential. The combination provides emphasis (BDF §451.2). The conjunction introduces the final section of this larger paragraph providing the detail of what it means to be brought "near" (cf. v. 17).

ἐστέ: The Greek word ἐστέ is a second-person plural present active indicative from the verb εἰμί that means "to be" (BDAG, s.v. "εἰμί" 9, p. 285). **Syntactically**, ἐστέ functions as the main verb of the independent conjunctive clause introduced by ἄρα οὖν. The subject is implied by the verb: "you," referring to Gentile believers. The nominatives "strangers" (ξένοι) and "aliens" (πάροικοι) function as the predicate nominatives. **Semantically**, ἐστέ is a customary present: "you are" (ESV, RSV, NRSV, NIV, NET, CSB, HCSB, NASB, NKJV, KJV). The action of the verb describes an ongoing state of the believer as a result of their new relationship with Christ (W, 521–22).

Lexical Nugget: What does it mean for Paul to refer to these Gentile believers as "strangers and aliens"? In verse 12, Paul refers to the Gentiles as "strangers of the covenants of promise" (ξένοι τῶν διαθηκῶν τῆς ἐπαγγελίας). The Greek word ξένος refers to an "alien," a "foreigner" (BDAG, s.v. "ξένος" 2a, p. 684.2). Old Testament writers use the term to refer to Gentiles living in the Promised Land (Ruth 2:10; 2 Sam. 12:4; 15:19). The Greek word πάροικος has a similar meaning, referring specifically to a resident foreigner living in a place that is not one's home, an "expatriate" (BDAG, s.v. "πάροικος" 2, p. 779). The Old Testament uses the term synonymously with ξένος (Gen. 15:13; 23:4; Lev. 22:10; 25:6, 23, 35, 40, 45, 47; Num. 35:15; Deut. 14:21; 23:8). Despite living in the land, these non-Jews had limited rights within the Jewish community. Paul uses these sociopolitical terms to describe their previous spiritual reality and contrast it with their current reality. Now they are "fellow citizens with the saints" and "members of the household of God" (v. 19b). These Gentile believers—once outsiders—are now insiders.

2:19b ἀλλ': The Greek word ἀλλά is a conjunction that means "but" (BDAG, s.v. "ἀλλά" 1a, pp. 44–45). **Syntactically**, ἀλλά introduces an independent conjunctive clause: "*but* you are fellow citizens with the saints and members of the house of God" (ἀλλ' ἐστὲ συμπολῖται τῶν ἁγίων καὶ οἰκεῖοι τοῦ θεοῦ). **Semantically**, ἀλλά is a contrastive connective: "but" (ESV, RSV, NRSV, NIV, NET, CSB, HCSB, NASB, NKJV, KJV).

Syntactical Nugget: What is the structure between the two clauses in verse 19? Paul presents parallel statements in both halves of verse 19:

Ἄρα οὖν	οὐκέτι ἐστὲ	ξένοι καὶ πάροικοι
ἀλλ'	ἐστὲ	συμπολῖται τῶν ἁγίων καὶ οἰκεῖοι τοῦ θεοῦ
So then	you are no longer	strangers and aliens
but	you are	fellow citizens with the saints and members of the house of God

Paul repeats the verb (ἐστέ); both clauses have two predicates. The first clause is negative; the second clause introduces a positive connotation with the conjunction "but" (ἀλλά). Both predicates in the second clause are modified with genitives. The first genitive is a genitive of association (W, 128–30): "fellow citizens with the saints." The second genitive is possessive (W, 81–83): these Gentile believers are "members of God's household" (BDAG, s.v. "οἰκεῖος" b, p. 694).

ἐστέ: The Greek word ἐστέ is a second-person plural present active indicative from the verb εἰμί that means "to be" (BDAG, s.v. "εἰμί" 9, p. 285). **Syntactically**, ἐστέ functions as the main verb the independent conjunctive clause introduced by ἀλλά. The subject is implied by the verb: "you," referring to the Gentile believers. The nominatives "fellow citizen" (συμπολῖται) and "household member" (οἰκεῖοι) function as the predicate nominatives. The Greek term συμπολίτης is a *hapax legomenon*. **Semantically**, ἐστέ is a customary present: "you are" (ESV, RSV, NRSV, NASB, NET). The action of the verb describes an ongoing state of the believer as a result of their new relationship with Christ (W, 521–22). Due to the repetition of the verb several English versions omit it (NIV, CSB, HCSB, NKJV, KJV).

> **Lexical Nugget**: Who are the saints (ἁγίων) to whom Paul refers in verse 19b? Since Paul is addressing Gentiles Christians it is possible that he has Jewish believers or the nation Israel in mind (Barth, 269). The problem with this approach is that he uses the term throughout the letter without ethnic distinction (1:1, 15, 18; 3:8; 4:12; 5:3; 6:18). This implies that he is referring to all believers, both Jews and Gentiles. The remainder of the section goes on to describe these saints as a building founded on the apostles and prophets, suggesting that Paul uses the term inclusively. Arnold states: "Paul has been careful not to teach that the Gentiles have been added to Israel, but that they together now form a new entity—'one new man' (2:15) or 'one body' (2:16), which he now terms the 'household of God' (οἰκεῖοι τοῦ θεοῦ)" (Arnold, 168; cf. Hoehner, 395–96; Thielman, 179).

2:20a ἐποικοδομηθέντες: The Greek word ἐποικοδομηθέντες is an aorist passive participle masculine plural nominative from the verb ἐποικοδομέω that means "to build on to" (BDAG, s.v. "ἐποικοδομέω" 1b, p. 387). **Syntactically**, ἐποικοδομηθέντες introduces a dependent participle clause. It functions adverbially modifying the main verb "you are" (ἐστέ). **Semantically**, ἐποικοδομηθέντες could be temporal. As an aorist participle, the action of the participle is antecedent of the main verb: "*after* having being built" (cf. NASB, NKJV). However, it is best understood as a participle of cause: "*because* you have been built" (NET). The participle provides the reason that these believers have become citizens with the saints and members of God's household (Hoehner, 397; Thielman, 179; Best, 279). This is a divine passive—God is the one who does the building. All of the verbs in this section (vv. 19–22) are present tense. Paul shifts to the aorist to describe a completed action that forms the basis of God's ongoing activity with the believer. The verb signals a shift in Paul's imagery from a citizenship to a building structure. He initiates this theme in verse 14 by describing the destruction of the dividing wall. These people are being built up into a temple in which the Spirit will indwell (cf. 5:18).

Semantical Nugget: What does the phrase "apostles and prophets" mean? The prepositional phrase "on the foundation" (ἐπὶ τῷ θεμελίῳ) modifies the participle ἐποικοδομηθέντες, conveying the location of this building on the foundation. The following genitives τῶν ἀποστόλων καὶ προφητῶν are genitives of apposition, clarifying the foundation: "on the foundation, *namely* the apostles and prophets." The genitive phrase is a Granville Sharp construction: both nouns are governed by one article and joined together with καί (W, 270–71). Since both nouns are plural the groups are either distinct or somewhat overlapping (i.e., apostles, prophets, and some who are both), which is the likely case (W, 284–86). The importance of the structure shows that both groups are united in purpose (Robertson, 787). Even though it is possible that Paul has Old Testament prophets in mind here, he most likely describes New Testament prophets. First, the word order, by placing "apostles" before "prophets," suggests that he envisions New Testament prophets. Second, Ephesians 3:5 uses a similar phrase ("his holy apostles and prophets"; τοῖς ἁγίοις ἀποστόλοις αὐτοῦ καὶ προφήταις) to describe those to whom God revealed the mystery of the gospel. Finally, Ephesians 4:11 describes a prophet as an office gifted by the Holy Spirit (cf. 1 Cor. 12:28; Rom. 12:6) (Hoehner, 399–400; Thielman, 180; Arnold, 169).

2:20b ὄντος: The Greek word ὄντος is a present active participle masculine singular genitive from the verb εἰμί that means "to be" (BDAG, s.v. "εἰμί" 2b, p. 283). **Syntactically**, ὄντος functions as the main verb of the genitive absolute phrase. The subject of the participle is the genitive phrase "Christ Jesus himself" (αὐτοῦ Χριστοῦ Ἰησοῦ). The predicate is the genitive "cornerstone" (ἀκρογωνιαίου). Grammatically, the genitive absolute is unconnected to the remainder of the sentence (W, 654–55). Several English translations insert the preposition "with" to create a grammatical link in English and omit the verb: "*with* Christ Jesus himself *as* the chief cornerstone" (NIV, NRSV, NET, HCSB, CSB) or offset the clause with commas (ESV, RSV, NASB, NKJV, KJV). **Semantically**, ὄντος functions as an equative present: "being" (ESV, RSV, NASB, NKJV, KJV). Even though the clause is grammatically unconnected from the sentence, logically, the phrase provides further information about the foundation: Christ is the cornerstone (Hoehner, 404).

Lexical Nugget: What does the term "cornerstone" (ἀκρογωνιαῖος) mean? A number of scholars have argued that the term refers to a capstone, the stone at the top of a building holding it together—a keystone (Jeremias, 1964, 792; Lincoln, 154–56; Barth, 317–19). The strength of this position is that Paul describes Christ as the head of the church throughout the letter (Eph. 1:22–23; 4:15–16). The primacy of Christ fits well with the image as the higher cornerstone or pinnacle of the temple. On the other hand, the clause alludes to Isaiah 28:16. In Isaiah, this stone is on the foundation, the cornerstone (cf. 1 Pet. 2:6). While Paul surely refers to Christ as the head of the church throughout Ephesians, he uses a different metaphor at this point. In fact, the immediate context describes the foundation of a building that is growing and incomplete. For this reason, he most likely did not have a keystone in mind. Finally, the previous section envisions Christ as the beginning point of the church. This fits better with a cornerstone image (Hoehner, 404–7; Thielman, 181–83; Arnold, 170–71). The cornerstone image complements Paul's description of Christ's supremacy throughout the letter. With this image in mind, the weight of the entire building rests on this stone. It may sit at the bottom of the building, but it is the most important, structurally bearing the weight of the entire structure.

2:21a ᾧ: The Greek word ᾧ is a masculine singular dative from the relative pronoun ὅς that means "whom" in this context (BDAG, s.v. "ὅς" 1a, p. 725). **Syntactically**, ᾧ introduces a dependent adjectival relative clause "in *whom* the whole building fits together" (ἐν ᾧ πᾶσα οἰκοδομὴ συναρμολογουμένη). The antecedent of the pronoun is "Christ Jesus" (Χριστοῦ Ἰησοῦ). The relative pronoun functions as the object of the preposition ἐν, which expresses sphere. The prepositional phrase refers to the believers' union with Christ.

Text-Critical Nugget: Does Paul omit the article after πᾶσα? Some Alexandrian manuscripts (A, C, 81, 326, 1881) and some other manuscripts (P and 6). A corrector for ℵ and 1739, two significant Alexandrian manuscripts also insert the article. On the other hand, the majority of Western (D, F, G) and Byzantine (𝔐, K, L) manuscripts omit the article. Several significant Alexandrian manuscripts also omit the article (B, 33, 104, 1175). The original scribe for ℵ and 1739 also omitted the article. The articular form suggests that Paul is talking about the "whole building," which fits best within the context of Paul's image of the church being built up into a holy temple. Without the article, the adjective πᾶς can have a distributive effect: "every building" (Turner[1], 199–200; Robertson, 772). However, Turner notes that because of Hebraic influence, the anarthrous form can also describe a class as a whole, but that "it is more likely, however, that πᾶς with this meaning will have the article" (Turner[1], 199–200; cf. W, 253). It is possible that a scribe accidentally dropped the article due to the convergence of the "α" at the end of πᾶσα and the diphthong "οι" at the beginning of οἰκοδομή—a case of itacism (Metzger, 534). But it is more likely that a scribe inserted the article to clarify the meaning of πᾶσα (Metzger, 534; Hoehner, 407 n. 3).

συναρμολογουμένη: The Greek word συναρμολογουμένη is a present passive participle feminine singular nominative from the verb συναρμολογέω, that means "to fit" or "to join together" (BDAG, s.v. "συναρμολογέω," p. 966). It appears that Paul coined the term since it shows up in no literature except

Ephesians (2:21; 4:16) before the second century. Later in the letter, Paul will use the term to describe the church growing as a body, Christ himself as the head (Eph. 4:15–16). This usage suggests that the building described in Ephesians 2 grows organically as well (Lincoln, 157). **Syntactically**, συναρμολογουμένη introduces a dependent participle clause. It functions adverbially modifying the verb in the following clause: "grows" (αὔξει). **Semantically**, the present tense indicates that the action of the participle is simultaneous with the action of the main verb (W, 625–26). The NIV translates the participle as attendant circumstance: "the whole building is joined together and grows" (cf. RSV, NRSV, HCSB). Both Larkin and Merkle identify this as an attributive participle modifying οἰκοδομή (Larkin, 46; Merkle, 82). However, since it is anarthrous it is best to consider it adverbial expressing means or manner (Hoehner, 409): "*by being joined together.*" This is a divine passive. God is the implied agent. This building grows as God joins it together.

> **Semantical Nugget**: What does the prefix συν- mean? Beginning in verse 19, Paul uses three terms with the συν- prefix: συμπολίτης ("fellow citizens," v. 19b), συναρμολογέω ("to fit together," v. 21a), and συνοικοδομέω ("to build up," v. 22). He used a similar technique in Ephesians 2:5–6 to emphasize the believers' union with Jesus Christ (see Theological Nugget at 2:6a). In the current context, the verbs emphasize the unity between Jews and Gentiles. The first term is a *hapax legomenon*, meaning "fellow-citizen" (BDAG, s.v. "συμπολίτης," p. 959). Paul uses the term to contrast the status of the Gentiles, who are no longer foreigners (cf. Eph. 2:11–12, 19a). The first term is a sociopolitical term, the last two are engineering terms: συναρμολογέω means "to fit together" (BDAG, s.v. "συναρμολογέω," p. 966) and συνοικοδομέω means "to build up" (BDAG, s.v. "συνοικοδομέω" 1, p. 974). The two terms are similar. The first term conveys the idea of being "combined" (GE, s.v. "συναρμολογέω," p. 2026). The second term suggests the idea of being built together with other materials (GE, s.v. "συνοικοδομέω," p. 2048). Jews and Gentiles are the materials that God uses to build this building (Hoehner, 412–13).

2:21b αὔξει: The Greek word αὔξει is a third-person singular present active indicative from the verb αὐξάνω that means "to grow" or "increase" (BDAG, s.v. "αὐξάνω" 2b, p. 151). Most English versions translate the verb as "grows" (ESV, RSV, NRSV, NET, CSB, HCSB, NKJV); the NIV translates it "rises." **Syntactically**, αὔξει functions as the main verb of the relative clause. The subject is "the whole building" (πᾶσα οἰκοδομή). **Semantically**, αὔξει is a customary present: "is growing" (NASB). The present tense describes an ongoing process. This structure continues to grow (W, 521–22). The prepositional phrase "into a holy temple" (εἰς ναὸν ἅγιον) conveys the idea of goal (BDAG, s.v. "εἰς" 1aβ, p. 288). The prepositional phrase "in the Lord" (ἐν κυρίῳ) most likely modifies the previous prepositional phrase, not the main verb αὔξει, since the clause began with a similar prepositional phrase (ἐν ᾧ) (Merkle, 82; Larkin, 46).

2:22 ᾧ: The Greek word ᾧ is a masculine singular dative from the relative pronoun ὅς that means "whom" in this context (BDAG, s.v. "ὅς" 1a, p. 725). **Syntactically**, ᾧ introduces a dependent adjectival relative clause "in *whom* also you are being built together into a place of dwelling for God in the Spirit" (ἐν ᾧ καὶ ὑμεῖς συνοικοδομεῖσθε εἰς κατοικητήριον τοῦ θεοῦ ἐν πνεύματι). The antecedent of the pronoun could be "temple" (ναόν), but due to the parallelism between verses 21 and 22, it is most likely Χριστοῦ Ἰησοῦ ("Christ Jesus," v. 20b). The relative pronoun functions as the object of the preposition ἐν, which expresses sphere. The prepositional phrase refers to the believer's union with Christ.

καί: The Greek word καί is a conjunction that means "also" (BDAG, s.v. "καί" 1b, p. 494). **Syntactically**, καί introduces a dependent conjunctive clause: "in whom *also* you are being built together" (ἐν ᾧ καὶ ὑμεῖς συνοικοδομεῖσθε). **Semantically**, καί is an ascensive connective: "also" (ESV, RSV, NRSV, NET, CSB, HCSB, NASB, NKJV, KJV). The conjunction links this clause to the previous prepositional phrase. The two clauses are parallel to one another (cf. Merkle, 82):

21:     <u>ἐν ᾧ</u> πᾶσα οἰκοδομὴ <u>συναρμολογουμένη</u> αὔξει <u>εἰς</u> ναὸν ἅγιον <u>ἐν</u> κυρίῳ

22:     <u>ἐν ᾧ</u> καὶ ὑμεῖς <u>συνοικοδομεῖσθε</u> <u>εἰς</u> κατοικητήριον τοῦ θεοῦ <u>ἐν</u> πνεύματι

21:     <u>in whom</u> the whole building, <u>being fitted together</u> grows <u>into</u> a holy temple <u>in</u> the Lord

22:     <u>in whom</u> also you are <u>being built together into</u> a dwelling for God <u>in</u> the Spirit.

συνοικοδομεῖσθε: The Greek word συνοικοδομεῖσθε is a second-person plural present passive indicative from the verb συνοικοδομέω that means "to build up" (BDAG, s.v. "συνοικοδομέω" 1, p. 974). **Syntactically**, συνοικοδομεῖσθε functions as the main verb of the relative clause. The subject is the second-person personal pronoun: "you" (ὑμεῖς). **Semantically**, συνοικοδομεῖσθε is a customary present: "you are being built together" (ESV, NIV, NET, CSB, HCSB, NASB, NKJV). The present tense describes this building process as an ongoing action (W, 521–22). The voice of the verb is passive. God, who is building up the church, is the implied agent. Paul ends the paragraph with the same set of prepositions that he used at the end of verse 21, creating a parallel. The prepositional phrase "into a dwelling for God" (εἰς κατοικητήριον τοῦ θεοῦ) expresses the goal of the building project.

The genitive τοῦ θεοῦ is best understood as a subjective genitive: "a house in which God dwells" (cf. ESV, NRSV, NIV, NLT). Paul brings the building image back to where he began. In verse 19, he calls the Gentiles "members of the house of God" (οἰκεῖοι τοῦ θεοῦ), but in verse 22, they make up the building in which God himself dwells (Thielman, 185). This is all accomplished by the means of the Spirit (ἐν πνεύματι).

EPHESIANS 3:1–13

Big Greek Idea: According to his plan, God reveals the mystery of Christ to Paul, along with the apostles and prophets, in order to proclaim this mystery to the rulers and authorities of this world, namely that Gentiles have become fellow heirs and fellow partakers of the promise of Christ with the Jews.

Structural Overview: Paul begins Chapter 3 with a prayer. In verse 1, he explains that his current imprisonment is a result of his ministry on behalf of the Gentiles (3:1, 13). In verse 2, he interrupts the prayer to describe his ministry and resumes in the following section (vv. 14–21). He begins verse 2 with a first class conditional statement, but does not give the conclusion until verse 13: "*If* you have heard of the administration given to me, *then* I ask that you not lose heart." Because of this, many have labeled this section as a digression, but this does not mean that Paul is unintentional. The significant portion of the passage (vv. 3–12) describes Paul's ministry, providing the basis of the conditional sentence. This description gives way to the praise section that ends the chapter.

The section has two major parts. The first part (vv. 1–7) describes God's revelation to Paul of how he unifies Jews and Gentiles—what he calls the mystery (v. 6). Paul already described this unification in 2:11–22, which he points out in verse 3. This section focuses on the fact that that this came to Paul through divine insight, by contrasting the idea of revelation with the concept of mystery (3:3, 4, 9, cf. 1:9; 5:32; 6:19). Here the concept of mystery suggests that this was intentionally hidden from previous ages (cf. 3:5, 9). However, God revealed the mystery to his apostles and prophets by the Spirit (3:5).

Having articulated the content of this divine mystery, the second part of the section describes the purpose of Paul's ministry: to make the truth of this mystery known (v. 9). By doing this, God reveals this to all of the cosmic authorities of the current age (3:10; cf. 2:2–3; 6:12) through the creation of the church. All this was part of his plan (v. 11; cf. 1:9–11). And even though believers live in an age controlled by these demonic figures, we have access to God through faith (v. 12).

Paul rounds off this section by completing the first class conditional statement in verse 13. By describing his ministry from this divine perspective, Paul shows that God intended this to occur all along. He proclaimed this mystery as a service to God. Even though this led to his imprisonment, it led to the eternal salvation for the Gentile believers.

Outline:

> God has revealed his plan of making Gentiles fellow heirs to the promise
> > (vv. 1–7)
> > The reconciliation of Jews and Gentiles to God gives cause for
> > > praise (v. 1)
> > This reconciliation of Jews and Gentiles was revealed to Paul, of
> > > which he has become an evangelist (vv. 2–4)
> > The mystery of this reconciliation was not previously known, but
> > > revealed through the Spirit (v. 5–6)
> > This mystery is the basis for Paul's ministry (v. 7)
>
> God proclaims the message of this gospel to the present powers in the
> > world through the church (vv. 8–13)
> > The message was given to Paul for the purpose of proclaiming the
> > > message (vv. 8–9)
> > The message was given to the church to make it known to the powers
> > > in the world (vv. 10–12)
> > Because of the ministry of the gospel, believers should not lose heart
> > > over Paul's situation (v. 13)

Clausal Outline for Ephesians 3:1–13

3:1 <u>Τούτου χάριν</u> ἐγὼ Παῦλος ὁ δέσμιος τοῦ Χριστοῦ Ἰησοῦ ὑπὲρ ὑμῶν τῶν ἐθνῶν

3:1 <u>For this reason</u>, I Paul, a prisoner of Christ Jesus on behalf of you, the Gentiles

3:2 εἴ γε **ἠκούσατε** τὴν οἰκονομίαν (τῆς χάριτος τοῦ θεοῦ τῆς δοθείσης μοι) εἰς ὑμᾶς,

3:2 <u>if indeed **you have heard**</u> of the administration of (God's grace, which was given to me) for you,

3:3a **ὅτι** κατὰ ἀποκάλυψιν **ἐγνωρίσθη** μοι τὸ μυστήριον,

3:3a **that** the mystery **has been made known** to me according to revelation,

3:3b **καθὼς προέγραψα** ἐν ὀλίγῳ,

3:3b **just as I previously wrote** in short,

[Τὸ μυστήριον (v. 3a)]
[the mystery (v. 3a)]
                   |
    ^{3:4}πρὸς <u>ὃ</u> **δύνασθε … νοῆσαι** τὴν σύνεσίν μου ἐν τῷ μυστηρίῳ τοῦ Χριστοῦ,
    ^{3:4} according to which **you are able to understand** my insight in the mystery
    of Christ,
                     |
                ^{3:4b} **ἀναγινώσκοντες**
                ^{3:4b} **when you read**

    ^{3:5a}<u>ὃ</u> ἑτέραις γενεαῖς οὐκ **ἐγνωρίσθη** τοῖς υἱοῖς τῶν ἀνθρώπων
    ^{3:5a} <u>which</u> was not **made known** to the sons of men in other generations

         ^{3:5b}<u>ὡς</u> νῦν **ἀπεκαλύφθη** τοῖς ἁγίοις ἀποστόλοις αὐτοῦ καὶ
             προφήταις ἐν πνεύματι,
         ^{3:5b} as it **has** now **been revealed** to his holy apostles and prophets
             by the Spirit,

    ^{3:6}**εἶναι** τὰ ἔθνη συγκληρονόμα καὶ σύσσωμα καὶ συμμέτοχα τῆς
       ἐπαγγελίας ἐν Χριστῷ Ἰησοῦ διὰ τοῦ εὐαγγελίου,
    ^{3:6} that the Gentiles **are** fellow heirs, fellow members of the body, and
       fellow partakers of the promise in Christ Jesus through the gospel

[τοῦ εὐαγγελίου (v. 6)]
[the gospel (v. 6)]
    |
    ^{3:7}<u>οὗ</u> **ἐγενήθην** διάκονος κατὰ τὴν δωρεὰν (τῆς χάριτος τοῦ θεοῦ τῆς
       δοθείσης μοι) κατὰ τὴν ἐνέργειαν τῆς δυνάμεως αὐτοῦ.
    ^{3:7} <u>of which</u> **I became** a servant according to the gift, namely (God's grace
       which was given to me) according to the working of his power.

^{3:8a}ἐμοὶ τῷ ἐλαχιστοτέρῳ πάντων ἁγίων **ἐδόθη** ἡ χάρις αὕτη,
^{3:8a} This grace **was given** to me, the very least of all of the saints,

   ^{3:8b}τοῖς ἔθνεσιν **εὐαγγελίσασθαι** τὸ ἀνεξιχνίαστον πλοῦτος τοῦ Χριστοῦ,
   ^{3:8b} **to proclaim the good news** of the unfathomable wealth of Christ to the Gentiles,

      ^{3:9a}<u>καὶ</u> **φωτίσαι** πάντας
      ^{3:9a} <u>and</u> **to enlighten** all people
          |
         ^{3:9b}<u>τίς</u> [**ἐστιν**] ἡ οἰκονομία (τοῦ μυστηρίου τοῦ ἀποκεκρυμμένου)
            ἀπὸ τῶν αἰώνων ἐν (τῷ θεῷ τῷ τὰ πάντα κτίσαντι),
         ^{3:9b} <u>what</u> [**is**] the administration of (the mystery which was hidden)
            for ages in (God who created all things),

[εὐαγγελίσασθαι . . . καὶ φωτίσαι (vv. 8–9)]
[to proclaim the gospel . . . and enlighten (vv. 8–9)]
                    |
    3:10 **ἵνα γνωρισθῇ** νῦν ταῖς ἀρχαῖς καὶ ταῖς ἐξουσίαις ἐν τοῖς
          ἐπουρανίοις διὰ τῆς ἐκκλησίας ἡ πολυποίκιλος σοφία τοῦ
          θεοῦ, 11a κατὰ πρόθεσιν τῶν αἰώνων
    3:10 **so that** the multifaceted wisdom of God **might** now **be made
          known** to the rulers and authorities in the heavenly places through
          the church, 3:11a according to his eternal purpose,

[πρόθεσιν (v. 11a)]
[purpose (v. 11a)]
          |
3:11b ἣν **ἐποίησεν** ἐν τῷ Χριστῷ Ἰησοῦ τῷ κυρίῳ ἡμῶν,
3:11b which **he accomplished** in Christ Jesus our Lord,

    3:12 ἐν ᾧ **ἔχομεν** τὴν παρρησίαν καὶ προσαγωγὴν ἐν πεποιθήσει διὰ
          τῆς πίστεως αὐτοῦ.
    3:12 in whom **we have** boldness and access with confidence through faith in
          him.

3:13a διὸ **αἰτοῦμαι**
3:13a Therefore, **I ask**

    3:13b μὴ **ἐγκακεῖν** ἐν ταῖς θλίψεσίν μου ὑπὲρ ὑμῶν,
    3:13b that you not **be discouraged** because of my suffering on your behalf,

          3:13c ἥτις **ἐστὶν** δόξα ὑμῶν.
          3:13c which **is** your glory.

Syntax Explained for Ephesians 3:1–13

3:1 τούτου χάριν: The Greek word τούτου is a neuter genitive singular demonstrative pronoun that means "this" in this context. The neuter form refers to
the preceding context (BDAG, s.v. "οὗτος" 1bα, p. 741). The Greek word
χάριν functions as a preposition that means "for the sake of" or "on behalf
of" (BDAG, s.v. "χάριν" b, pp. 1078–79). Most English versions translate the
phrase: "For this reason" (ESV, NET, NIV, RSV, HCSB, CSB, NASB, NKJV). The NRSV
gives a similar translation: "This is the reason that." Paul is the only New Testament writer to use this phrase (Eph. 3:1, 14; 1 Tim. 5:14). **Syntactically**,
τούτου χάριν introduces Paul's prayer. He does not initially complete the
thought. In verse 2 he breaks off the prayer, which he resumes in the following section (3:14–21). At this point, he shifts the attention to describe his

apostolic ministry—the reason for his imprisonment. Verse 13 comes back to the topic of imprisonment. The Gentiles should not be grieved because his arrest has come as a result of the ministry that God has given him. Many commentators classify this as a digression, but this does not mean that it is pointless (Arnold, 179). Before he begins his prayer in verse 14, he offers a divine perspective of his current situation. On the surface, his situation looks bleak, but he has successfully proclaimed the good news of the gospel, that God's promises have extended to the Gentiles. By looking at his situation from God's perspective, Paul can refer to his imprisonment as God's grace (vv. 2, 7, 8). He returns to his prayer in verse 14 by repeating the phrase "For this reason" (τούτου χάριν). **Semantically**, the phrase conveys the reason for Paul's prayer, which he picks up in verse 14. Since the focus is on the fact that the Gentiles are fellow partners of the promises of God (v. 6), he most likely offers his prayer of thanksgiving with Ephesians 2:11–22 in mind rather than the whole chapter (Best, 294).

> **Grammatical Nugget**: How do the nominatives in verse 1 function? Paul begins his prayer in verse 1 with three nominatives referring to himself: "I, Paul, a prisoner of Christ Jesus on behalf of you Gentiles." (ἐγὼ Παῦλος ὁ δέσμιος τοῦ Χριστοῦ Ἰησοῦ), but there is no verb. In verse 2, he breaks off the prayer, which he resumes in the following section (3:14–21). In verse 14, he uses the first-person verb κάμπτω without a nominative. The first-person personal pronoun serves as the subject of the verb in verse 14. The nominative Παῦλος is in apposition to ἐγώ and ὁ δέσμιος is in apposition to Παῦλος. The genitive τοῦ Χριστοῦ Ἰησοῦ is possessive: Paul is the prisoner of Christ Jesus.

> **Text-Critical Nugget**: Does Paul refer only to "Christ" or "Christ Jesus" in verse 1? The majority of Byzantine (𝔐, K, L) and Alexandrian manuscripts (𝔓⁴⁶, ℵ¹, A, B, 1739) include Ἰησοῦ, but the key Western manuscripts (D, F, G) and one important Alexandrian manuscript (ℵ) omit it. Even though the majority of key manuscripts insert Jesus, the fact that the Western manuscript tradition tends to add to the text, but here omits the name, raises some question about the reading "Christ Jesus." It is possible that later scribes added "Jesus," having been influenced by Philemon 1 and 9 (Thielman, 208). However, the strength of the external evidence suggests that the longer reading is authentic. The majority of Byzantine and Alexandrian readings refer to Paul as "a prisoner of Christ Jesus."

³:² εἴ γε: The Greek word εἰ is an adverbial conjunction that means "if" in this context (BDAG, s.v. "εἰ" 6b, p. 278). The Greek word γέ is a particle that adds emphasis: "if indeed" (BDAG, s.v. "γέ" bα, p. 190; cf. NET, NASB, NKJV, KJV). **Syntactically**, εἰ introduces a dependent conjunctive clause: "*if indeed* you heard of the stewardship of God's grace" (εἴ γε ἠκούσατε τὴν οἰκονομίαν

τῆς χάριτος τοῦ θεοῦ). The entire clause functions adverbially. Paul does not introduce the apodosis of the conditional statement until verse 13: "Therefore, I ask you not be discouraged because of my suffering." **Semantically**, εἰ introduces a first class conditional clause: "if" (NET, NASB, NKJV, KJV). The first class condition puts forward a statement of truth for the sake of an argument (W, 690–94). The NIV translates the conjunction as "*surely* you have heard" (cf. NRSV); the ESV translates it as "*assuming* that you have heard" (cf. RSV). The CSB simply omits the conjunction: "you have heard, *haven't you.*" Paul assumes that the Ephesians have indeed heard about his present situation—if they indeed understand it, then they should not lose heart over Paul's situation.

ἠκούσατε: The Greek word ἠκούσατε is a second-person plural aorist active indicative from the verb ἀκούω that means "learn about" (BDAG, s.v. "ἀκούω" 3b, p. 38). **Syntactically**, ἠκούσατε functions as the main verb of the dependent conjunctive clause introduced by εἴ γε. The subject is implied by the verb: "you," referring to the Ephesian believers. The direct object is "stewardship" (τὴν οἰκονομίαν). **Semantically**, ἠκούσατε is a constative aorist: "you have heard" (ESV, RSV, NRSV, NIV, NET, CSB, HCSB, NASB, NKJV, KJV). The tense describes the action of the verb in summary fashion (W, 557–58). The statement most likely refers to the first part of the letter, where Paul explains how God has created one new humanity out of Jews and Gentiles—a point that he reiterates in verse 6. Having read the first part of the letter, the Ephesians will have understood this ministry.

> **Lexical Nugget**: What does "stewardship" mean? English versions translate the Greek term οἰκονομία a number of different ways. The ESV renders it as "stewardship" (cf. RSV, NET, NASB); the NIV renders it "administration" (cf. CSB, HCSB); the NRSV renders it "commission"; and the NLT renders it "the special responsibility." In Greek, the term οἰκονομία can refer either to an official office, such as a household manager (LSJ, s.v. "οἰκονομία," p. 1204; cf. Luke 16:2–9) or the act of administration. Earlier in the book, Paul uses the term to refer to God's plan to unite all things together in Christ (Eph. 1:10). Later in the passage, Paul uses the term to describe how this mystery is made known to the present age (Eph. 3:9). Even though there is a significant overlap between the meanings—administrators do administrate—the current context emphasizes Paul's role in God's plan (Michel 1967, 151–53). The following genitive τῆς χάριτος ("grace," BDAG, s.v. "χάρις" 4, p. 1080) is most likely an objective genitive: "he *administers* God's grace," a reference to God's plan of salvation. The genitive τοῦ θεοῦ is possessive: "God's grace."

δοθείσης: The Greek word δοθείσης is a feminine genitive singular aorist passive participle from the verb δίδωμι that means "to give," or in this context "to appoint" (BDAG, s.v. "δίδωμι" 7, p. 242). **Syntactically,** δοθείσης functions as an attributive participle modifying "stewardship of God's grace" (τὴν οἰκονομίαν τῆς χάριτος τοῦ θεοῦ). Most English versions translate the participle with a relative pronoun: "which was given to me" (NET, NASB, NKJV, KJV) or "that was given to me" (ESV, RSV, NRSV, NIV, CSB, HCSB). **Semantically,** δοθείσης is a constative aorist: "was given" (ESV, NRSV, RSV, NIV, NASB, NKJV). The tense describes the action of the verb in summary fashion (W, 557–58). The participle is a divine passive—even though it is not stated, God is the implied agent. The CSB brings this out by rendering it with the pronoun: "that he gave to me." The prepositional phrase "for you" (εἰς ὑμᾶς) expresses advantage. This grace was given to Paul *for the benefit* of these Gentiles.

^{3:3a} ὅτι: The Greek word ὅτι is a conjunction that means "that" in this context (BDAG, s.v. "ὅτι" 2a, p. 732). **Syntactically,** the conjunction ὅτι introduces a dependent conjunctive clause "*that* the mystery has been made known to me according to the revelation" (ὅτι κατὰ ἀποκάλυψιν ἐγνωρίσθη μοι τὸ μυστήριον). The entire clause functions substantively as the direct object of the main verb "you have heard" (ἠκούσατε) in apposition to the previous accusative τὴν οἰκονομίαν. **Semantically,** ὅτι marks the clause as a direct object of the main verb, indicating indirect discourse: "that" (NET, NASB, NKJV). The conjunction introduces the content of what the Ephesians have heard. Because of this, the clause is in apposition to the previous phrase. The NIV translates the clause "that is" (Hoehner, 425–26).

> **Text-Critical Nugget:** Why are there brackets around ὅτι? A number of Western (F and G) and Alexandrian (𝔓⁴⁶ and B) manuscripts omit the conjunction, while several manuscripts include it (א, A, C, D, 1739, and 𝔐). The external evidence is slightly in favor of including the conjunction: the Byzantine text type solidly stands behind the conjunction, while both readings appear in the Alexandrian and Western manuscripts. Internally, the inclusion of the conjunction makes better sense. The conjunction provides the content of what the readers have heard (v. 2) continuing the conditional statement. If the conjunction is omitted, verse 3 begins a new sentence, which would not fit the literary character of the letter with long sentences (Thielman, 208; Larkin, 49–50).

ἐγνωρίσθη: The Greek word ἐγνωρίσθη is a third-person singular aorist passive indicative from the verb γνωρίζω that means "to make known" or "reveal" (BDAG, s.v. "γνωρίζω" 1, p. 203). **Syntactically,** ἐγνωρίσθη functions as the main verb of the dependent conjunctive clause introduced by ὅτι. The subject is "mystery" (τὸ μυστήριον). The indirect object is "me" (μοί). **Semantically,** ἐγνωρίσθη is a constative aorist: "was made known" (ESV, RSV, NRSV, CSB, HCSB, NASB). The tense describes the action of the verb in summary fashion

(W, 557–58). The verb is a divine passive—Paul does not state the agent, but God is the one who makes this mystery known to Paul (Hoehner, 426).

> **Theological Nugget**: What does "mystery" mean in the context of Ephesians? In the Old Testament a mystery is something that can only be known through divine revelation (see the Theological Nugget at 1:9a). Paul uses the word in a similar way throughout Ephesians (cf. Eph. 1:9; 3:3, 4, 9; 5:32; 6:19). This mystery has been made known "according to revelation" "by the Spirit" (v. 3, 5). Paul brings the theme to a climax in Ephesians 3 by making the content of the mystery clear: "Gentiles are fellow heirs, fellow members of the body, fellow partakers of the promises through Christ Jesus" (v. 6). Paul comes back to the theme in Ephesians 5. After comparing the marriage relationship to Christ's relationship with the church, he states that this is a "great mystery" (Eph. 5:32). The administration that Paul received from God is to make this mystery known to the present age.

3:3b καθώς: The Greek word καθώς is a conjunction that means "as" or "just as" (BDAG, s.v. "καθώς" 1, p. 493). **Syntactically**, the conjunction καθώς introduces a dependent conjunctive clause: "*just as* I have written in short" (καθὼς προέγραψα ἐν ὀλίγῳ). The clause functions substantively as the direct object of the main verb "have made known" (ἐγνωρίσθη). **Semantically**, καθώς introduces a comparison. Just as God has revealed this mystery to Paul, he has written it to these believers.

προέγραψα: The Greek word προέγραψα is a first-person singular aorist active indicative from the verb προγράφω that means "to write beforehand" (BDAG, s.v. "προγράφω" 1a, p. 867). Most English versions translate the verb as "I have written before" (NASB NET) or "I have already written" (NIV). The CSB translates it as "I have written above" making the reference to an earlier section of Ephesians explicit. **Syntactically**, προέγραψα functions as the main verb of the dependent conjunctive clause introduced by καθώς. The subject is implied by the verb: "I," referring to Paul. **Semantically**, προέγραψα is an immediate past aorist: "I have written" (ESV, RSV, NIV, CSB, HCSB, NKJV) or "I wrote" (NRSV, NET, NASB, KJV). The tense describes the action of the verb as having occurred recently (W, 564–65). It is possible that Paul is referring to a previous letter, but he most likely refers to the earlier part of the letter, specifically Ephesians 2:11–22 (Best, 302–3). Since he just described this mystery, the aorist gives a dramatic effect. The prepositional phrase "in short" (ἐν ὀλίγῳ) expresses manner: Paul has written in brief (BDAG, s.v. "ὀλίγος" 3, p. 703).

3:4a ὅ: The Greek word ὅ is a neuter singular accusative from the relative pronoun ὅς that means "which" in this context (BDAG, s.v. "ὅς" 1a, p. 725). **Syntactically**, ὅ introduces a dependent adjectival relative clause: "with reference to *which* you are able to understand my insight into the mystery of Christ" (πρὸς ὃ δύνασθε ἀναγινώσκοντες νοῆσαι τὴν σύνεσίν μου ἐν τῷ μυστηρίῳ τοῦ Χριστοῦ). The antecedent of the relative pronoun is "the mystery" (τὸ μυστήριον). The relative pronoun functions as the object of the preposition πρός, which expresses reference: "according to which" his readers are able to understand (BDAG, s.v. "πρός" 3eδ, p. 875; Thielman, 195).

δύνασθε: The Greek word δύνασθε is a second-person plural present middle (deponent) indicative from the verb δύναμαι that means "to be able" (BDAG, s.v. "δύναμαι" aβ, pp. 261–62). **Syntactically**, δύνασθε functions as the main verb of the relative clause. **Semantically**, δύνασθε functions as a progressive present: "you are able" (NET, NIV, CSB, HCSB) or "you can" (ESV, RSV, NASB). The tense describes the action as continuous (W, 518–19). The present tense contrasts with the four aorist tense verbs in verses 3 and 4 (ἠκούσατε, δοθείσης, ἐγνωρίσθη, προέγραψα). The aorist verbs provide background information. The Ephesians are able to understand this mystery because God revealed it to Paul and he has clearly communicated it to them.

νοῆσαι: The Greek word νοῆσαι is an aorist active infinitive from the verb νοέω that means "to perceive," "apprehend," or "understand" (BDAG, s.v. "νοέω" 1a, p. 674). **Syntactically**, νοῆσαι introduces a dependent adverbial infinitive clause functioning as the direct object of the main verb "you are able" (δύνασθε). The phrase "my insight in the mystery of Christ" (τὴν σύνεσίν μου ἐν τῷ μυστηρίῳ τοῦ Χριστοῦ) functions as the direct object of the infinitive. **Semantically**, νοῆσαι is a complementary infinitive, completing the idea that the main verb begins: "you are able *to understand*" (CSB, HCSB; cf. NASB, ESV, RSV, NRSV; W, 598–99). This is a constative aorist, which focuses on the action of the verb as a whole (W, 557–58). The genitive τοῦ Χριστοῦ could be considered a genitive of apposition: "the mystery, *that is* Christ" (Arnold, 188). This considers that Christ is the mystery (cf. Col. 2:2; 4:3). However, in Ephesians, the unity between Jews and Gentiles is the mystery (Best, 304). It might be best considered as an objective genitive: this is a mystery *about Christ* (Hoehner, 436; Abbott 1909, 80).

3:4b ἀναγινώσκοντες: The Greek word ἀναγινώσκοντες is a masculine nominative plural present active participle from the verb ἀναγινώσκω that means "to read" (BDAG, s.v. "ἀναγιγνώσκω" a, p. 60). **Syntactically**, ἀναγινώσκοντες introduces a dependent participle clause. It functions adverbially modifying the verb "you are able" (δύνασθε; v. 4a). **Semantically**, the present tense indicates that the action of the participle is simultaneous with the action of the main verb. The participle could express means: "*by* reading" (HCSB, CSB; cf. NIV; Barth, 330), but it is most likely conveys a temporal meaning: "*when* reading" (NET; cf. ESV, NASB, NKJV, KJV, RSV, NLT; Hoehner, 434).

> **Lexical Nugget**: What does it mean to read in antiquity? Paul most likely envisioned a public reading of the letter, not a private reading. Unlike modern readers who might silently flip a few pages to the section before, ancient readers were dependent on the Christian community to hear Paul's letters read aloud. Literacy rates were extremely low, anywhere between 3 and 10 percent (Keith, 2001, 72–75). And the community would have had limited access to the documents. Their only access to the literature would have been through public readings. Elsewhere, Paul instructs that his letters be read out loud (1 Thess. 5:27; Col. 4:16; Arnold, 188; Thielman, 195).

3:5a ὅ: The Greek word ὅ is a neuter singular nominative from the relative pronoun ὅς that means "which" in this context (BDAG, s.v. "ὅς" 1a, p. 725). **Syntactically**, ὅ introduces a dependent adjectival relative clause: "*which* was not made known to the sons of men in other generations" (ὃ ἑτέραις γενεαῖς οὐκ ἐγνωρίσθη τοῖς υἱοῖς τῶν ἀνθρώπων). The antecedent of the relative pronoun is "the mystery" (τὸ μυστήριον; v. 3a). The relative pronoun functions as the subject of the relative clause.

ἐγνωρίσθη: The Greek word ἐγνωρίσθη is a third-person singular aorist passive indicative from the verb γνωρίζω that means "to make known" or "reveal" (BDAG, s.v. "γνωρίζω" 1, p. 203). **Syntactically**, ἐγνωρίσθη functions as the main verb of the relative clause. The subject of the verb is the relative pronoun, a reference to the mystery (v. 3a). The indirect object is "the sons of men" (τοῖς υἱοῖς τῶν ἀνθρώπων), a reference to a larger group—humanity (BDAG, s.v. "υἱός" 2b, p. 1024). The NIV translates the direct object as "people" (cf. CSB, HCSB, NET); the NRSV translates it as "humankind." **Semantically**, ἐγνωρίσθη is a constative aorist: "was not made known" (ESV, RSV, NRSV, NIV, CSB, HCSB, NASB, NKJV, KJV) or "disclosed" (NET). It describes the action of the verb as a whole (W, 557–58). This is a divine passive—God is the implied agent. The verb refers back to verse 3. While God kept this mystery hidden, he revealed it to Paul. The dative phrase "in other generations" (ἑτέραις γενεαῖς) is a dative of time, specifying the time when this mystery was unknowable. BDAG renders the phrase as "at other times" (BDAG, s.v. "γενεά" 3b, p. 192).

> **Grammatical Nugget**: How do the datives function in verse 5? Paul establishes a contrast with the two clauses in verse 5. The structure of each clause is similar:
>
> | | | |
> |---|---|---|
> | ἑτέραις γενεαῖς | οὐκ ἐγνωρίσθη | τοῖς υἱοῖς τῶν ἀνθρώπων |
> | ὡς νῦν | ἀπεκαλύφθη | τοῖς ἁγίοις ἀποστόλοις |
> | | | αὐτοῦ καὶ προφήταις |

| in other generations | was not made known | to the sons of men |
| as now | it has been revealed | to his holy apostles and prophets |

Both clauses have a temporal element. The first dative ἑτέραις γενεαῖς is a dative of time (W, 155–56). The second clause begins with the temporal marker: "as now," making a contrast in time. Both verbs allude to the revelation of the mystery that he begins discussing in verse 3. Paul concludes both clauses with datives functioning as direct objects. In the first clause, he states that this mystery was unknown to the "sons of men," a merism, referring to humanity. In the second clause, he states that this mystery has been revealed to his apostles and prophets. In the following section (vv. 8–13), he will describe his own role in God's plan. As God has revealed this mystery to his apostles and prophets, they in turn proclaim it to the world.

3:5b ὡς: The Greek word ὡς is a conjunction that means "as" in this context (BDAG, s.v. "ὡς" 1a, p. 1103). **Syntactically**, ὡς introduces a dependent conjunctive clause "*as* now revealed to his holy apostles and prophets" (ὡς νῦν ἀπεκαλύφθη τοῖς ἁγίοις ἀποστόλοις αὐτοῦ καὶ προφήταις). The clause functions adverbially modifying the verb "was not made known" (οὐκ ἐγνωρίσθη; v. 5a). **Semantically**, ὡς expresses comparison: "as" (ESV, RSV, NRSV, NIV, NET, CSB, HCSB, NASB, NKJV, KJV). The conjunction could express a comparison of degree—the mystery was not revealed in the other generations as God reveals it now, implying that God revealed the mystery in the past but to a lesser degree. However, the contrast between the two clauses suggests that Paul uses the conjunction to express a comparison of kind. God did not reveal this mystery to previous generations the way that he reveals it to his apostles and prophets. This suggests that these previous generations did not receive this revelation. Later in the passage, Paul states that this mystery has been hidden to previous generations and that it has now been made known (vv. 9–10) (Hoehner, 439–40; Arnold, 189–90; Thielman, 198).

ἀπεκαλύφθη: The Greek word ἀπεκαλύφθη is a third-person singular aorist passive indicative from the verb ἀποκαλύπτω that means "to make fully known" or "to bring to light" especially pertaining to divine revelation (BDAG, s.v. "ἀποκαλύπτω" b, p. 112). **Syntactically**, ἀπεκαλύφθη functions as the main verb of the dependent conjunctive clause introduced by ὡς. The subject is implied by the verb: "it," referring to the mystery. The indirect objects are "his holy apostles and prophets" (τοῖς ἁγίοις ἀποστόλοις αὐτοῦ καὶ προφήταις). **Semantically**, ἀπεκαλύφθη is a constative aorist: "has been revealed" (ESV, RSV, NRSV, NIV, NET, NASB, NKJV). It describes the action of the verb as a whole (W, 557–58). The passive voice functions as a divine passive. Without stating the agent, God is the one who reveals this mystery to the holy apostles and prophets. Paul makes a similar statement in verse 3a, but God did not reveal this mystery just to him. He revealed it to all of the apostles and prophets. By referring to the gospel, he most likely describes New Testament prophets (see the Syntactical Nugget at 2:20a).

3:6 εἶναι: The Greek word εἶναι is a present active infinitive from the verb εἰμί that means "to be" (BDAG, s.v. "εἰμί" 2b, p. 283). **Syntactically**, εἶναι introduces a dependent adjectival infinitive clause related to τὸ μυστήριον ("the mystery," v. 3a). The subject of the infinitive is the accusative "Gentiles" (τὰ ἔθνη). The phrase "fellow heirs, fellow members, and fellow partakers of the promise" (συγκληρονόμα καὶ σύσσωμα καὶ συμμέτοχα τῆς ἐπαγγελίας) functions as the accusative predicate (W, 190–91). **Semantically**, εἶναι is an epexegetical infinitive, providing the content of the mystery (W, 607; Robertson, 1078). Some English versions translate the clause "namely, that" (NET), "to be specific" (NASB), or "that is" (RSV, NRSV). Due to the length of the sentence in Greek, some English versions restate the subject with an equative verb: *"The mystery is* that" before the clause (ESV, NIV; cf. NLT). The verb is an equative present. These Gentiles have become heirs to the promise. The following prepositional phrases provide the basis for this new relationship. The first prepositional phrase "in Christ Jesus" (ἐν Χριστῷ Ἰησοῦ) expresses sphere. The second prepositional phrase "through the gospel" (διὰ τοῦ εὐαγγελίου) expresses means.

Lexical Nugget: What does it mean for Gentiles to be "fellow heirs" (συγκληρονόμα), "fellow members of the body" (σύσσωμα), and "fellow partakers" (συμμέτοχα)? All three of these words are rare. The Greek term συγκληρονόμος is used four times in the New Testament (Rom. 8:7; Eph. 3:6; Heb. 11:9; 1 Pet. 3:7). The word describes a relationship between two heirs, who receive an inheritance—to inherit together (BDAG, s.v. "συγκληρονόμος," p. 952). The Greek term σύσσωμος is a *hapax legomenon*, occurring only in Ephesians 3:6. It describes a person who belongs to the same group: "united in one body" (BDAG, s.v. "σύσσωμος," p. 978; LSJ, s.v. "σύσσωμος," p. 1734). Finally, the Greek term συμμέτοχα occurs only in Ephesians (3:6; 5:7). The word insinuates possession: to share something together with another (BDAG, s.v. "συμμέτοχος," p. 958). In Ephesians 2, Paul uses similar expressions by creating compound words with the preposition σύν. In Ephesians 2:5–6, believers are made alive with Christ, having been raised and seated with Christ (συνεζωοποίησεν, συνήγειρεν, συνεκάθισεν). In Ephesians 2:19–22, he describes Gentiles as fellow citizens, being joined together, and built together (συμπολῖται, συναρμολογουμένη, συνοικοδομεῖσθε). The first instance stresses the believer's relationship with Christ. In Ephesians 2:19–22 and 3:6, Paul emphasizes the unity between Jews and Gentiles.

3:7 οὗ: The Greek word οὗ is a neuter singular genitive from the relative pronoun ὅς that means "of which" in this context (BDAG, s.v. "ὅς" 1a, p. 725). **Syntactically**, οὗ introduces a dependent adjectival relative clause "of which I became a servant according to the gift of the grace of God" (οὗ ἐγενήθην διάκονος κατὰ τὴν δωρεὰν τῆς χάριτος τοῦ θεοῦ). The antecedent of the relative pronoun is "the gospel" (τοῦ εὐαγγελίου; v. 6). Due to the length of the sentence, some English versions convert the relative clause into an independent sentence: "I became a servant of this gospel" (NIV, NET; cf. ESV, RSV, NRSV, CSB, HCSB). The relative pronoun modifies the head noun "servant" (διάκονος). It functions as an objective genitive (W, 116–19). As a servant, Paul serves, or ministers, the gospel (Merkle, 91).

Lexical Nugget: What does it mean for Paul to refer to himself as a "servant" (διάκονος)? Generally, the term διάκονος refers to an assistant or a servant—an attendant. It implies that one works on behalf of another (BDAG, s.v. "διάκονος" 1, p. 230; LSJ, s.v. "διάκονος," p.398). The term implies some level of humility offering service to another. He regularly refers to himself as a servant (1 Cor. 3:5; 2 Cor. 11:23; Phil. 1:1; Col. 1:23, 25). He can refer to his coworkers as "servants of God" or "servants of Christ" (2 Cor. 6:4; Col. 1:7). In Ephesians 6:21, he calls Tychicus a "faithful servant in the Lord" (πιστὸς διάκονος ἐν κυρίῳ). He can even refer to the emperor as the "servant of God" (Rom. 13:4) (Kruse, 1993, 869–71).

ἐγενήθην: The Greek word ἐγενήθην is a first-person singular aorist passive indicative from the verb γίνομαι that means "to become" (BDAG, s.v. "γίνομαι" 5a, p. 198). **Syntactically**, ἐγενήθην functions as the main verb of the relative clause. The subject is implied by the verb: "I," referring to Paul. The predicate nominative is "servant " (διάκονος). **Semantically**, ἐγενήθην functions as an ingressive aorist: "I became" (NIV, NET, NKJV; cf. NRSV) or "I was made" (ESV, RSV, CSB, HCSB, NASB, KJV). The tense focuses on the point when Paul became a servant of the gospel (W, 558–59). The verb is a divine passive. Without stating the agent, God is the one who made Paul a servant. The statement refers to Paul's Damascus road experience (Acts 9:1–19; 22:1–21; 26:1–32; Arnold, 192).

δοθείσης: The Greek word δοθείσης is a feminine genitive singular aorist passive participle from the verb δίδωμι that means "to give," or in this context "to appoint" (BDAG, s.v. "δίδωμι" 7, p. 242). **Syntactically**, δοθείσης functions as an attributive participle modifying "grace" (τῆς χάριτος). Most English versions translate the participle with a relative pronoun: "which was given to me" (ESV, NRSV, NASB) or "that was given to me" (NRSV, NET, CSB, HCSB). **Semantically**, δοθείσης is a constative aorist: "was given." The tense describes the action of the verb in summary fashion (W, 557–58). The participle is a divine passive—even though it is not stated, God is the implied agent. The attributive participle creates a link to verse 2 ("the grace of God given to me"), forming an *inclusio* (Arnold, 192). The verse also serves as a hinge between verses 2–6 and 8–13. In verses 2–6, Paul focuses on God's revelation of the mystery to his apostles, specifically Paul. In verses 8–13, he shifts the discussion to his response to this revelation—actually proclaiming this mystery to the powers and authorities in the world today (Best, 313).

Text-Critical Nugget: Is the participle genitive or accusative? A few manuscripts have the accusative form of the participle (τὴν δοθεῖσαν) instead of the genitive form—predominantly from the Byzantine text type (K, L, 𝔐), but also a few Alexandrian manuscripts (1739, 1881). This reading suggests that the participle modifies the accusative τὴν δωρεάν instead of the genitive τῆς χάριτος. There is little difference between the two since the genitive is in apposition—the gift and grace are one and the same, they both come from God. The genitive form is found in both the Alexandrian (𝔓46, ℵ, A, B, C, 33, 81, 104, 326, 1175) and Western manuscripts (D, F, G). Based on the external evidence, the genitive form is most likely the original.

Syntactical Nugget: What is the relationship between the prepositional phrase "according to the gift of God's grace" and the prepositional phrase "according to the working of his power"? The first prepositional phrase "according to the gift of God's grace" (κατὰ τὴν δωρεὰν τῆς χάριτος τοῦ θεοῦ) modifies the main verb ἐγενήθην. The preposition κατά expresses the idea of standard. Paul's ministry is according to the "gift of God's grace." The genitive τῆς χάριτος is in apposition. The genitive τοῦ θεοῦ could express the idea of source: "grace *from God*"; or possession; "*God's* grace." Paul will make a similar statement in Ephesians 4, referring to grace given to each believer "according to the measure of the gift of Christ" (κατὰ τὸ μέτρον τῆς δωρεᾶς τοῦ Χριστοῦ). In the current context, he is referring to the gift given to him specifically. The second prepositional phrase "according to the working of his power" (κατὰ τὴν ἐνέργειαν τῆς δυνάμεως αὐτοῦ) most likely modifies the participle δοθείσης (Hoehner, 451; Larkin, 52; Merkle, 91). Like the first preposition, κατά expresses the idea of standard: this gift was given to Paul according to the "working of his power." The Greek terms ἐνέργεια and δύναμις are synonymous. Paul used both terms in Ephesians 1:19 to refer to God's power at work in Christ's resurrection (1:20). The genitive τῆς δυνάμεως is most likely subjective: God's power is at work (Hoehner, 451).

3:8a ἐδόθη: The Greek word ἐδόθη is a third-person singular aorist passive indicative from the verb δίδωμι that means "to give" or "appoint" (BDAG, s.v. "δίδωμι" 7, p. 242). **Syntactically**, ἐδόθη functions as the main verb of the asyndeton. The subject is "this grace" (ἡ χάρις αὕτη), a reference to his ministry. The indirect object is "me" (ἐμοί). The substantival adjective τῷ ἐλαχιστοτέρῳ ("the least") is in apposition to the pronoun. This is the comparative with the sense of the superlative. Wallace suggests that a literal translation might be: "leaster" (W, 302; cf. BDAG, s.v. "ἐλάχιστος" 1, p. 314). The genitive ἁγίων ("saints") is a partitive genitive: "the least of all the saints" (cf. 1 Cor. 15:8–9; 1 Tim. 1:15). **Semantically**, ἐδόθη is a constative aorist: "was given" (ESV, RSV, NRSV, NIV, NET, CSB, HCSB, NASB, NKJV). It describes the action of the verb as a whole (W, 557–58). The passive voice is a divine passive. Without stating the agent, God is the one who gives this grace. Paul makes a similar statement in verse 2, referring to his own role in God's plan of salvation and repeats it in verse 7. He envisions his work, and consequently his imprisonment, as a gift of grace given to him by God.

3:8b εὐαγγελίσασθαι: The Greek word εὐαγγελίσασθαι is an aorist middle infinitive from the verb εὐαγγελίζω that means "to proclaim the gospel" (BDAG, s.v. "εὐαγγελίζω" 2aα, p. 402). **Syntactically**, εὐαγγελίσασθαι could introduce a dependent adverbial infinitive clause stating the purpose of the main verb "was given" (ἐδόθη), but it might be better understood as introducing a dependent adjectival infinitive clause related to the subject "this grace" (ἡ χάρις αὕτη). Paul normally uses this verb without expressing the object; however, the direct object is "the unfathomable riches of Christ" (τὸ ἀνεξιχνίαστον πλοῦτος τοῦ Χριστοῦ). The accusative describes the content of his preaching. The indirect object is "the Gentiles" (τοῖς ἔθνεσιν). **Semantically**, the infinitive is epexegetical (W, 607), giving more detail about the grace that God has given to Paul (Thielman, 212–13; Lincoln, 182; Larkin, 53). The verb is a constative aorist: "to preach" (ESV, RSV, NIV, NASB) or "to proclaim" (CSB, HCSB, NET). It describes the action of the verb as a whole (W, 557–58).

Lexical Nugget: What does "unfathomable" mean? The Greek word ἀνεξιχνίαστος means "inscrutable" or "incomprehensible" (BDAG, s.v. "ἀνεξιχνίαστος," p. 77). The word is used in the New Testament only by Paul (2x). Paul possibly borrowed the word from Job (Job 5:9; 9:10; 34:24; MM, s.v. "ἀνεξιχνίαστος," p. 41). The term derives from the verbal idea: ἐξιχνεύω, which means "I track," referring to a hunter or tracker—one following the footprints (ἴχνος) of another. The term could be metaphorical: to search for the truth (LSJ, s.v. "ἀνεξιχνίαστος," p. 595). In Romans, Paul states that God's ways are unsearchable, or literally, untraceable (Rom. 11:33). In the current context, he states that Christ's wealth is unsearchable (cf. Col. 2:2–3; Arnold, 194). In Ephesians, Paul can use the term "wealth" in regard to God's grace (Eph. 1:7; 2:7) or God's glory (Eph. 1:18; 3:16). Even though Paul is not specific in verse 8, the concept of God's grace has dominated the attention of the text.

3:9a καί: The Greek word καί is a conjunction that means "and" (BDAG, s.v. "καί" 1b, p. 494). **Syntactically**, καί introduces a dependent conjunctive clause: "*and* to enlighten all people" (καὶ φωτίσαι πάντας). **Semantically**, καί is a coordinating connective: "and" (ESV, RSV, NRSV, NIV, NET, CSB, HCSB, NASB, NKJV, KJV). The clause is parallel to the previous infinitive clause explaining what this grace is (Hoehner, 455; Arnold, 195).

φωτίσαι: The Greek word φωτίσαι is an aorist active infinitive from the verb φωτίζω that means "to enlighten" or "shed light upon" in reference to transcendent matters (BDAG, s.v. "φωτίζω" 3a, p. 1074). Most English versions retain the metaphor by translating the infinitive as "to bring light" (ESV, NASB), "to enlighten" (NET), or "to shed light" (HCSB, CSB). Other versions translate it "to make plain" (NIV), "to make everyone see" (NRSV, cf. RSV), or "to explain" (NLT). Paul uses the same verb in Ephesians 1:18. **Syntactically**, φωτίσαι introduces a dependent adjectival infinitive clause, parallel to the previous infinitive "to proclaim the gospel" (εὐαγγελίσασθαι; v. 8b). Just like εὐαγγελίσασθαι, the clause is related to "this grace" (ἡ χάρις αὕτη). The accusative "all people" (πάντας) functions as the "person" in a double accusative construction. The following clause introduced by τίς ("what is the stewardship of the mystery") functions as the "thing" in a double accusative construction (W, 181–82; Larkin, 54). **Semantically**, just like the previous clause, the infinitive is epexegetical (W, 607). The aorist tense functions as a constative aorist presenting the action of the verb in summary (W, 557–58). Even though the two clauses are closely related, they are distinct actions. On the one hand, Paul is called to preach the good news to Gentiles (v. 8b). On the other hand, he is called to enlighten all people to God's plan (Thielman, 213–14).

> **Text-Critical Nugget**: Why is the accusative πάντας set in brackets? A few Alexandrian manuscripts omit πάντας (ℵ, A, 1739, 1881), which is the shorter, harder reading. While it is possible that πάντας may have been accidentally omitted, New Testament writers usually include an accusative after the verb φωτίζω, suggesting that a scribe inserted the accusative at this point. On the other hand, the reading with πάντας is found in the majority of Western manuscripts (D, F, G) and Byzantine manuscripts (𝔐), as well as solid Alexandrians manuscripts (𝔓⁴⁶, B). A scribe could have intentionally omitted the accusative since it does not agree with the gender of τοῖς ἔθνεσιν (Thielman, 223). The grammatical problem with the gender along with the external evidence suggests that πάντας is the original reading. And if a scribe felt compelled to insert an accusative, we would anticipate other accusatives (such as αὐτούς) to appear in the transmission (Metzger, 534).

3:9b τίς: The Greek word τίς is an indefinite pronoun from the word τίς that means "what" or "what sort of" (BDAG, s.v. "τίς" 1aβ ב, p. 1007; W, 345–46).

Syntactically, τίς introduces a dependent clause functioning as the direct object of the infinitive "to enlighten" (φωτίσαι). The clause introduces what Paul makes known to all of humanity. The pronoun functions as the predicate nominative of an implied equative verb: ἐστίν.

[ἐστίν]: The Greek word ἐστίν is a third-person singular present active indicative from the verb εἰμί that means "to be" (BDAG, s.v. "εἰμί" 2cβ, p. 284). **Syntactically**, [ἐστίν] is an ellipsis. The elliptical verb is the main verb of the object clause introduced by τίς. The subject is "the stewardship of the mystery" (ἡ οἰκονομία τοῦ μυστηρίου). **Semantically**, [ἐστίν] functions as an equative present: "is" (ESV, RSV, NRSV, NASB, NKJV, KJV). Some versions substitute the indefinite pronoun and the implied verb with the preposition "about" (NET, CSB, HCSB). Paul uses the Greek term οἰκονομία in verse 2. The term can refer to either an official office or some type of administration (see the Lexical Nugget at 3:2). In Ephesians 3:2, Paul seems to be describing his own role in God's plan; however, in the current context, the word seems to mean "the act of administration" (BDAG, s.v. "οἰκονομία" 2b, pp. 697–98; cf. Fowl, 2012, 111). He uses the term in the same way in Ephesians 1:10. The genitive τοῦ μυστηρίου ("the mystery") is in apposition to the head noun, ἡ οἰκονομία: "the stewardship, *namely* the mystery" (W, 95–100; Merkle, 95).

ἀποκεκρυμμένου: The Greek word ἀποκεκρυμμένου is a neuter genitive singular perfect passive participle from the verb ἀποκρύπτω that means "to keep secret" (BDAG, s.v. "ἀποκρύπτω" 2, p. 114). **Syntactically**, ἀποκεκρυμμένου functions as an attributive participle modifying "mystery" (τοῦ μυστηρίου). Some English versions translate the participle with the relative pronoun: "which has been hidden" (NASB, NKJV, KJV; cf. NIV) or "the mystery hidden" (ESV, NRSV, RSV, CSB, HCSB). **Semantically**, ἀποκεκρυμμένου is an extensive perfect (W, 577). The tense describes a completed action, but with ongoing results, namely that this mystery had been kept hidden for a specific set of time. The passive voice is a divine passive. Without stating the agent, God is the one who keeps this mystery hidden. Paul uses two prepositional phrases to modify the participle. The first prepositional phrase "from eternity" (ἀπὸ τῶν αἰώνων) is temporal, marking the time when this mystery was hidden: "from eternity" (BDAG, s.v. "ἀπό" 2bα, p. 105). Several English versions translate the phrase: "for ages" (ESV, NET, NIV, NRSV, RSV, HCSB, CSB, NASB). The NLT renders the phrase as "from the beginning" (cf. NKJV, KJV). The second prepositional phrase "in God" (ἐν τῷ θεῷ) could express agency: God is the one who hides this mystery (Best, 321; cf. LEB). The NLT omits the prepositional phrase and makes "God" the subject of the participle: "that God, the Creator of all things, had kept secret from the beginning." However, it best expresses sphere—this mystery is hidden "*in* God" (cf. ESV, NET, NIV, RSV, NRSV, HCSB, CSB, NASB). This use of the preposition highlights both the inscrutability of the mystery but also the certainty of its realization (cf. Col. 3:3) (Lincoln, 185).

κτίσαντι: The Greek word κτίσαντι is a masculine dative singular aorist active participle from the verb κτίζω that means "to create" (BDAG, s.v. "κτίζω," p. 572). **Syntactically**, κτίσαντι functions as an attributive participle modifying "God" (τῷ θεῷ). Most English versions translate the participle with a relative clause: "*who* created all things" (ESV, RSV, NRSV, NIV, CSB, HCSB, NASB, NKJV, KJV). **Semantically**, κτίσαντι is a constative aorist: "created" (ESV, RSV, NRSV, NIV, CSB, HCSB, NASB, NKJV, KJV). It describes the action of the verb as a whole (W, 557–58). The participle phrase highlights God's omnipotence. Even though this is the only reference in Ephesians to God's act of creation, the phrase reminds the reader that God has created a new humanity (Eph. 2:15; 4:24).

Text-Critical Nugget: Did Paul include the prepositional phrase "through Jesus Christ" (διὰ Ἰησοῦ Χριστοῦ) after the participle? Both the MT and RP2005 insert the prepositional phrase διὰ Ἰησοῦ Χριστοῦ after the participle, expressing the means by which God created all things: "through Jesus Christ." Both the THGNT and SBL follow the NA28, omitting the preposition. The reading with the phrase is found primarily in the Byzantine text type (𝔐, K, L) and two secondary Alexandrian manuscripts (104, 1881). The omission is found in the bulk of Alexandrian (𝔓46, ℵ, A, B, C, 33, 81, 1175, 1739) and Western (D, F, G, latt) manuscripts. Based on the geographical distribution and solid Alexandrian and Western text types, the reading with the omission is most likely original.

3:10 ἵνα: The Greek word ἵνα is a conjunction that means "so that" in this context (BDAG, s.v. "ἵνα" 3, p. 477). Due to the length of the sentence in Greek, some English versions begin a new sentence by inserting a demonstrative adjective expressing purpose: "The purpose of this enlightenment is" (NET), "His intent was that" (NIV), or "This is so" (CSB, HCSB). **Syntactically**, ἵνα introduces a dependent conjunctive clause "*so that* the many-sided wisdom of God might now be made known" (ἵνα γνωρισθῇ νῦν ... ἡ πολυποίκιλος σοφία τοῦ θεοῦ). The entire clause functions adverbially modifying the infinitives "to proclaim the good news" (εὐαγγελίσασθαι) and "to enlighten" (φωτίσαι) (vv. 8–9). **Semantically**, ἵνα expresses the purpose: "so that" (ESV, NASB) (W, 472). Paul proclaims this mystery so that God's manifold wisdom might be made known to the rulers and authorities (Hoehner, 458–59).

γνωρισθῇ: The Greek word γνωρισθῇ is a third-person singular aorist passive subjunctive from the verb γνωρίζω that means "to make known" or "reveal" (BDAG, s.v. "γνωρίζω" 1, p. 203). The NET translates the verb as "disclosed." **Syntactically**, γνωρισθῇ functions as the main verb of the dependent conjunctive clause introduced by ἵνα. The subject is "the multifaceted wisdom of God" (ἡ πολυποίκιλος σοφία τοῦ θεοῦ). The indirect object is "the rulers and authorities" (ταῖς ἀρχαῖς καὶ ταῖς ἐξουσίαις). **Semantically,** γνωρισθῇ is a constative aorist: "might be made known" (ESV, RSV, NRSV, CSB, HCSB, NASB, NKJV) or "should be known" (NIV; cf. NET). It describes the action of the verb as a whole (W, 557–58). The passive voice is a divine passive. Even though Paul preaches this gospel message, God makes this wisdom known to these rulers through the church. The clause is modified by three prepositional phrases. The first prepositional phrase is "in the heavenly places" (ἐν τοῖς ἐπουρανίοις). The preposition ἐν states where this revelation takes place. Paul uses the term ἐπουράνιος throughout Ephesians to describe the place of conflict between Christ and the authorities (cf. 6:12; see Lexical Nugget at 1:20c). The second prepositional phrase is "through the church" (διὰ τῆς ἐκκλησίας). The preposition διά expresses agency. God makes this wisdom known through the church. The final prepositional phrase is "according to the eternal purpose" (κατὰ πρόθεσιν τῶν αἰώνων, v. 11a). The preposition κατά expresses the standard by which God makes his wisdom known—this was a part of his eternal plan (cf. Eph. 1:11). The genitive τῶν αἰώνων ("ages" or "eternal") is an attributive genitive: "eternal plan" or "eternal purpose" (BDAG, s.v. "αἰών" 1b, p. 32; cf. ESV, NRSV, RSV, NIV, NET, CSB, HCSB, NASB, NKJV, KJV, NLT).

Lexical Nugget: What does "multifaceted" (πολυποίκιλος) mean? The term is a *hapax legomenon*, occurring only here in the New Testament. English translations render it a number of different ways: "manifold" (ESV, RSV, NIV, NASB, NKJV, KJV); "multifaceted" (NET, CSB, HCSB); or "in its rich variety" (NRSV, NLT). It literally means "many-sided," referring to diversity (BDAG, s.v. "πολυποίκιλος," p. 847; cf. LEB). The word is a compound word with πολύς ("many") and ποικίλος ("manifold" or "variegated"). The former term refers to objects that have many different colors. In the LXX, it refers to Joseph's "coat of many colors" (Gen. 37:3, 23, 32). The prefixed word (πολύς) heightens the meaning—as God's wisdom is very complex. Earlier, he stated that Christ's wealth is "unsearchable" (v. 8), here God's wisdom is many-sided. To bring out the nuance of the word, Thielmann suggests this translation: "the beautifully complex wisdom of God" (Thielman, 215). The prepositional phrase "through the church" (διὰ τῆς ἐκκλησίας) expresses means (BDAG, s.v. "διά" A3d, pp. 224–25). God makes this wisdom known through his church. This does not necessarily mean that the church actively proclaims this wisdom, rather God puts his wisdom on display in the heavenly places through his creation of the church (cf. 2:15). Gombis states: "The powers have ordered the present evil age in such a way as to exacerbate the divisions within humanity (Eph. 2:11–12). God confounds them by creating in Christ one unified, multiracial body consisting of formerly divided groups of people. And it is the existence of the church as such a body set within the hostile environment of the present evil age that proclaims to them the wisdom of God" (Gombis, 2010, 117).

> **Theological Nugget**: What does the adverb νῦν ("now") specify? The adverb νῦν is a temporal marker, contrasting between two eras. In verse 9, Paul states that the administration of the mystery was hidden for ages, but now God has made it known. Paul makes a similar contrast in verse 5— this mystery was hidden from humanity but revealed to the holy apostles and prophets. In the current context, this wisdom is made known to the rulers and authorities in the heavenly places. Paul most likely envisions spiritual beings hostile to the church—demons (see "καθίσας" at 1:20c). At the end of the book, Paul describes these rulers as waging war against the believer (Eph. 6:11–12; cf. 2:2). Nonetheless, God has placed all of these powers under Christ's feet at his resurrection (1:20–22), a victory in which believers partake (2:6). This background suggests that Paul's preaching is good news to the believer but on the other hand a taunt to those powers at work in the world today (cf. 2 Cor. 2:25–26).

3:11b ἥν: The Greek word ἥν is a feminine singular accusative from the relative pronoun ὅς that means "which" in this context (BDAG, s.v. "ὅς" 1a, p. 725). **Syntactically**, ἥν introduces a dependent adjectival relative clause "*which* he accomplished in Christ Jesus our Lord" (ἥν ἐποίησεν ἐν τῷ Χριστῷ Ἰησοῦ τῷ κυρίῳ ἡμῶν). The antecedent of the relative pronoun is "purpose" (πρόθεσιν). The relative pronoun functions as the direct object of the main verb of the clause ἐποίησεν—he brought about this purpose.

ἐποίησεν: The Greek word ἐποίησεν is a third-person singular aorist active indicative from the verb ποιέω that means "to do" or "bring about" (BDAG, s.v. "ποιέω" 2d, pp. 839–40). The immediate context suggests that God has achieved his plan, not that he has simply purposed it, or thought it up (*contra* KJV; Arnold, 198). Most English versions translate the verb as "realized" (ESV, RSV), "accomplished" (CSB, HCSB, NET, NIV, NKJV), or "carried out" (NRSV, NASB). **Syntactically**, ἐποίησεν functions as the main verb of the relative clause. God is the implied subject of the verb. **Semantically**, ἐποίησεν is a constative aorist: "he accomplished" (NIV, CSB, HCSB, NKJV). It describes the action of the verb as a whole (W, 557–58). The prepositional phrase "in Christ Jesus our Lord" (ἐν τῷ Χριστῷ Ἰησοῦ τῷ κυρίῳ ἡμῶν) expresses sphere— God brings about this plan in Christ.

3:12 ᾧ: The Greek word ᾧ is a masculine singular dative from the relative pronoun ὅς that means "whom" in this context (BDAG, s.v. "ὅς" 1a, p. 725). **Syntactically**, ᾧ introduces a dependent adjectival relative clause "in *whom* we have boldness and access in confidence through faith in him" (ἐν ᾧ ἔχομεν τὴν παρρησίαν καὶ προσαγωγὴν ἐν πεποιθήσει διὰ τῆς πίστεως αὐτοῦ). The antecedent of the relative pronoun is "Christ Jesus our Lord" (τῷ Χριστῷ Ἰησοῦ τῷ κυρίῳ ἡμῶν). The relative pronoun functions as the object of the preposition ἐν ("in *whom*"). Paul uses the same preposition in verse 11b: God accomplishes his purpose in Christ Jesus. In verse 12, the preposition emphasizes the believer's relationship with Christ and the benefits that come with it, namely access to the Father (cf. Eph. 2:18).

ἔχομεν: The Greek word ἔχομεν is a first-person plural present active indicative from the verb ἔχω that means "to have." In this instance, the verb carries the notion of being in "a position to do something" (BDAG, s.v. "ἔχω" 5, p. 421). The NIV translates the verb as "*we may* approach God" (cf. NLT). **Syntactically**, ἔχομεν functions as the main verb of the relative clause. The subject is implied by the verb: "we," referring to believers. The direct object is "boldness and access" (τὴν παρρησίαν καὶ προσαγωγήν). The phrase functions as a hendiadys—two words that communicate a single idea (Arnold, 198). Even though it is not explicit in the Greek text, the phrase probably means that the believer has access *to the Father* (cf. Eph. 2:18). Several English versions insert "God" as the indirect object to make this clear (cf. NET, NIV, NRSV, NLT). **Semantically**, ἔχομεν is a customary present: "we have" (ESV, RSV, NRSV, NET, CSB, HCSB, NASB, NKJV, KJV). The present tense describes the ongoing relationship between the believer and God (W, 521–22). The prepositional phrase "with confidence" (ἐν πεποιθήσει) expresses the manner in which the believer can take advantage of this access. The prepositional phrase "through faith in him" (διὰ τῆς πίστεως αὐτοῦ) expresses the means by which the believer has this access.

Semantical Nugget: How should the genitive αὐτοῦ be classified? The genitive construction τῆς πίστεως αὐτοῦ is debated. The genitive αὐτοῦ could either be subjective referring to Christ's faithfulness (NET, CJB) or objective referring to the believer's faith in Christ (ESV, NIV, RSV, NRSV, HCSB, CSB, NASB, NKJV). Either option is possible. In favor of the subjective genitive, Paul has already stated that the believer's access is based on their relationship with Christ ("in whom") making the objective genitive redundant (Best, 330). However, the wider context of Ephesians makes the objective genitive a better option. Throughout the letter, Paul seems to refer to the believer's faith when he uses the preposition διά (Eph. 2:8; 3:17) (Arnold, 199; Hoehner, 466–67; Lincoln, 190–91; Thielman, 219).

3:13a διό: The Greek word διό is a conjunction that means "therefore" (BDAG, s.v. "διό," p. 250). **Syntactically**, διό introduces an independent conjunctive clause: "Therefore, I ask" (διὸ αἰτοῦμαι). **Semantically**, διό is inferential (W, 673). The conjunction draws this section to a conclusion. Most English versions translate the conjunction as "therefore" (NIV, NRSV, NASB, NKJV) or "so then" (CSB, HCSB; cf. ESV, RSV, NLT). The NET translates the conjunction as "for this reason." Up to this point, Paul has explained his situation from a divine perspective. Even though Paul's situation looks dire, from this point of view, his experience is all a part of God's plan. Because of this, Paul asks that the Ephesian believers not lose heart over his situation.

αἰτοῦμαι: The Greek word αἰτοῦμαι is a first-person singular present middle indicative from the verb αἰτέω that means "to ask" with no real difference between the active and middle forms (BDAG, s.v. "αἰτέω," p. 30). **Syntactically**, αἰτοῦμαι functions as the main verb of the independent conjunctive clause introduced by διό. The subject is implied by the verb: "I," referring to Paul. The infinitive clause "that you not lose heat" (μὴ ἐγκακεῖν) serves as the direct object. **Semantically**, αἰτοῦμαι is an instantaneous present: "I ask" (ESV, RSV, NET, CSB, HCSB, NASB, NKJV). The present tense describes the action of the verb completed at the point when Paul made the request (W, 517–18). Most of the verbs in this section (vv. 2–11) are aorist tense, which describes how God reveals the mystery of his message to the world through Paul. In the conclusion (vv. 11–12), which describes the implications for both Paul and the believers, he shifts to the present tense (vv. 12–13).

> **Grammatical Nugget**: How does verse 13 relate to the context? In verse 2, Paul gives the protasis of a first class conditional statement, but never gives the apodosis. Finally, in verse 13, we get the second part of the clause: if the Ephesians understood his ministry, then they would not lose heart over his situation. The significant part of the passage (vv. 3–12) defines Paul's ministry and gives it purpose—his suffering is a part of God's larger plan. Paul's request may seem cryptic without this wider perspective. His ministry to the Gentiles led to his imprisonment, but it has also led to salvation for the Gentiles. And all of this is part of God's plan. This verse sets up Paul's prayer in the following section (vv. 14–21). With this divine perspective, he is able to give God praise despite his imprisonment (cf. 2 Tim. 2:8–10).

3:13b ἐγκακεῖν: The Greek word ἐγκακεῖν is a present active infinitive from the verb ἐγκακέω that means "to lose enthusiasm" or "be discouraged" (BDAG, s.v. "ἐγκακέω" 1, p. 272). Several English versions translate the verb as "lose heart" (ESV, NET, RSV, NRSV, NASB, NKJV, KJV). **Syntactically**, ἐγκακεῖν introduces a dependent substantival clause functioning as the direct object of the verb "I ask" (αἰτοῦμαι). **Semantically**, ἐγκακεῖν is a customary present: "lose heart" (ESV, RSV, NRSV, NET, NKJV). The tense describes an ongoing activity (W, 521–22). The prepositional phrase "because of my suffering" (ἐν ταῖς θλίψεσίν μου) expresses cause (BDAG, s.v. "ἐν" 9a, p. 329.9.a), stating the basis for this possible discouragement (Lincoln, 191). The second prepositional phrase (ὑπὲρ ὑμῶν) expresses advantage. Paul's suffering is for the Ephesian believers. Most English versions translate the prepositional phrase as either *"on your behalf"* (HSCB, CSB, NASB) or simply *"for* you" (ESV, NIV, NET, RSV, NRSV, NKJV, KJV) (cf. v. 1).

> **Syntactical Nugget**: Who is the subject of the infinitive ἐγκακεῖν? Paul does not specify the subject of the infinitive: he could refer to either the Ephesians or himself. If he has the Ephesians in mind, then he is asking that they not lose heart about his situation. If he has himself in mind, then he could be asking God, or the Ephesians to pray on his behalf, that he does not lose heart. The first option makes better sense of the context. The first part of the conditional statement: "if you have heard" (v. 2) implies that he has the Ephesians in mind. At the end of the verse, he states that he suffers on their behalf (ὑπὲρ ὑμῶν) and for their glory (δόξα ὑμῶν). The second-person pronouns suggests that he has the Ephesians in mind (Larkin, 57; Hoehner, 468–69).

3:13c ἥτις: The Greek word ἥτις is a feminine singular nominative from the indefinite relative pronoun ὅστις. In this context it functions as the relative clause meaning "which" (BDAG, s.v. "ὅστις" 3, p. 730). **Syntactically**, ἥτις introduces a dependent adjectival relative clause "which is your glory" (ἥτις ἐστὶν δόξα ὑμῶν). The antecedent of the relative pronoun is "my suffering" (ταῖς θλίψεσίν μου). The relative pronoun functions as the subject of the relative clause.

ἐστίν: The Greek word ἐστίν is a third-person singular present active indicative from the verb ἐστίν that means "to be" (BDAG, s.v. "εἰμί" 2b, p. 283). **Syntactically**, ἐστίν functions as the main verb of the relative clause. The subject is the relative pronoun (ἥτις). The predicate nominative is "your glory" (δόξα ὑμῶν). **Semantically**, the present tense functions as a customary present expressing an ongoing state (W, 521–22). Paul's present tribulation is in fact a glory for the Ephesian believers.

EPHESIANS 3:14–21

Big Greek Idea: God, who is able to do more than anyone can imagine, deserves all glory for strengthening the believers and for allowing them to grow in ways that are inconceivable, since they have a firm foundation.

Structural Overview: Paul ends the first major section of Ephesians with a prayer of benediction. The previous section forms the basis of prayer—his ministry to proclaim the mystery of God, the inclusion of the Gentiles into the people of God (3:1–13). Paul begins the prayer in verse 1, but interrupts himself to describe his ministry, the reason for his imprisonment. In verse 14, he resumes the prayer by describing the posture of prayer, bowing his knees. The prayer has two parts. The first part consists of three requests marked by ἵνα (vv. 16a, 18a, and 19b). All three requests focus on strength for the believer so that they might be unified. The first request is that the believers be strengthened by the Spirit with the result that they established by Christ (3:16–17). The second request is that the believers might be strong enough to understand the depth of the love of Christ (vv. 18–19a). The third request is that the believers might be filled with the fullness of God (v. 19b).

Paul closes the prayer, and the first part of the letter, with a formal benediction (vv. 20–21). The benediction focuses on God's power, a theme that Paul begins in verse 15, where he describes the scope of God's dominion. Every name comes from God. The right to give names underscores God's authority. The benediction picks up this authority. Paul begins the benediction with a substantival participle: "To the one who is able." The participle phrase focuses on God's ability to work in the believer's life. Paul's description of God's power in the life of the believer alludes to the power at work in Christ's resurrection (1:19–20). Because of this power, all glory should be given to God.

Outline:

> Because of his ministry, Paul prays that the believers will be strength-
> ened (vv. 14–19)
>> The first request is that God grant believers strength (vv. 14–17a)
>> The second request is that the believer come to know the depth of
>> God's love (vv. 17b–19)
> Because of all that he has done, even more than we could imagine, God
> deserves glory (vv. 20–21)

CLAUSAL OUTLINE FOR EPHESIANS 3:14–21

3:14 Τούτου χάριν **κάμπτω** τὰ γόνατά μου πρὸς τὸν πατέρα,
3:14 For this reason, **I bow** my knees before the Father,

> 3:15 ἐξ οὗ πᾶσα πατριὰ ἐν οὐρανοῖς καὶ ἐπὶ γῆς **ὀνομάζεται**,
> 3:15 from whom every family in the heavens and on earth **receives its name**

[κάμπτω, v. 14]
[I bow (v. 14)]

3:16a **ἵνα δῷ** ὑμῖν κατὰ τὸ πλοῦτος τῆς δόξης αὐτοῦ
3:16a **that he grant** you, according to his glorious wealth,

> 3:16b δυνάμει **κραταιωθῆναι** διὰ τοῦ πνεύματος αὐτοῦ εἰς τὸν ἔσω ἄνθρωπον,
> 3:16b **to be strengthened** with power through his Spirit in your inner being,

>> 3:17a **κατοικῆσαι** τὸν Χριστὸν διὰ τῆς πίστεως ἐν ταῖς καρδίαις ὑμῶν,
>> 3:17a that Christ **might dwell** through faith in your hearts,

> 3:17b ἐν ἀγάπῃ **ἐρριζωμένοι**
> 3:17b because **you have been rooted**

> 3:17c καὶ **τεθεμελιωμένοι**,
> 3:17c and **established** in love

3:18a **ἵνα ἐξισχύσητε**
3:18a **that you may be able**

> 3:18b **καταλαβέσθαι** σὺν πᾶσιν τοῖς ἁγίοις
> 3:18b **to comprehend** with all of the saints

>> 3:18c τί [**ἐστιν**] τὸ πλάτος καὶ μῆκος καὶ ὕψος καὶ βάθος,
>> 3:18c what [**is**] the width and length and height and depth,

> 3:19a **γνῶναί** τε (τὴν ὑπερβάλλουσαν τῆς γνώσεως ἀγάπην τοῦ Χριστοῦ),
> 3:19a and **to know** (Christ's love for you, which surpasses knowledge),

3:19b **ἵνα πληρωθῆτε** εἰς πᾶν τὸ πλήρωμα τοῦ θεοῦ.
3:19b **that you might be filled** to all of the fullness of God.

3:20a (Τῷ δὲ δυναμένῳ) ὑπὲρ πάντα **ποιῆσαι** ὑπερεκπερισσοῦ
3:20a <u>Now</u> (to the one who is able) **to do** above all infinitely more than

> 3:20b ὧν **αἰτούμεθα**
> 3:20b what **we ask**
>
> 3:20c ἣ **νοοῦμεν** κατὰ (τὴν δύναμιν τὴν
> ἐνεργουμένην) ἐν ἡμῖν,
> 3:20c <u>or **think**</u> according to (the power that works)
> in us,

[Τῷ δυναμένῳ (v. 20)]
[to the one who is able (v. 20)]

> 3:21 αὐτῷ [**ἐστιν**] ἡ δόξα ἐν τῇ ἐκκλησίᾳ καὶ ἐν Χριστῷ Ἰησοῦ εἰς
> πάσας τὰς γενεὰς τοῦ αἰῶνος τῶν αἰώνων· ἀμήν.
> 3:21 to him [**be**] the glory in the church and in Christ Jesus in all of the gener-
> ations for ever and ever, amen

SYNTAX EXPLAINED FOR EPHESIANS 3:14–21

3:14 τούτου χάριν: The Greek word τούτου is a neuter genitive singular demonstrative pronoun that means "this" in this context. The neuter form refers to
the preceding context (BDAG, s.v. "οὗτος" 1bα, p. 741). The Greek word
χάριν functions as a preposition that means "for the sake of" or "on behalf
of" (BDAG, s.v. "χάριν" b, pp. 1078–79). Most English versions translate the
phrase: "For this reason" (ESV, NET, NIV, RSV, NRSV, HCSB, CSB, NASB, NKJV,
KJV; KMP, 398). **Syntactically**, τούτου χάριν conveys the reason for Paul's
prayer. He uses the same phrase in verse 1, where he began the prayer, but
digressed to discuss his apostolic calling (vv. 2–13). At this point, he comes
back to the prayer. As in verse 1, Paul most likely has Ephesians 2:11–22 in
mind. His digression revisited the dominant theme: Jews and Gentiles have
been reconciled. This theme forms the basis of his prayer.

κάμπτω: The Greek word κάμπτω is a first-person singular present active indicative from the verb κάμπτω that means "to bow" or "bend" generally as a
sign of devotion (BDAG, s.v. "κάμπτω" 1, p. 507). Some translations render
this as "kneel" (NET, NIV, HCSB). **Syntactically**, κάμπτω functions as the main
verb of the dependent conjunctive clause introduced by τούτου χάριν. The
subject is Paul, which he makes explicit in verse 1: "I, Paul, a prisoner of Christ
Jesus on behalf of you Gentiles." The phrase "my knees" (τὰ γόνατά μου) is the
direct object. Paul's prayer is made up of three requests that he introduces with
ἵνα (vv. 16, 18, 19b). **Semantically**, κάμπτω functions as an iterative present,

suggesting that Paul offers a similar prayer in regular intervals (W, 520–21). The verb is a metonymy, substituting his posture for any mention of the word "prayer" (W, 475). Paul uses this image to describe worship elsewhere (Rom. 11:4; 14:11; Phil. 2:10). Even though prayer was regularly done standing up (cf. Mark 11:25), it was common to prostrate oneself for prayer, particularly if they were emotionally charged (Luke 5:8; 22:41; Acts 7:60; 20:36; 21:5) (Thielman, 227). The prepositional phrase πρὸς τὸν πατέρα ("before the Father") modifies the main verb κάμπτω ("I bend"). It can either express direction ("to the Father"; NLT, NKJV, KJV; Abbott, 1909, 93) or relationship ("before the Father"; ESV, NET, NIV, RSV, NRSV, HCSB, NASB). Since he characterizes his prayer with a posture of kneeling, the preposition best describes relationship (Hoehner, 473).

Text-Critical Nugget: Does Paul insert the genitive phrase "of our Lord Jesus Christ" at the end of verse 14? Both the MT and RP[2005] insert the genitive construction τοῦ κυρίου ἡμῶν Ἰησοῦ χριστοῦ suggesting that Paul prays to the Father "of our Lord Jesus Christ." Several Western (D, F, G) and Byzantine (K, L, 𝔐) manuscripts include the phrase, but most Alexandrian manuscripts omit it (𝔓[46], ℵ, A, B, C, P, 33, 81, 365, 1175, 1739). Hoehner accepts the reading on external grounds (Hoehner, 473 n. 1). The internal evidence suggests that the insertion is secondary. First, it is the shorter reading. Scribes had a tendency to expand. There is a better chance that a scribe would have added the phrase rather than omit it. Second, it is possible that a scribe added the gloss from the familiar phrase in Ephesians 1:3 (Metzger, 535). Finally, the insertion ruins the wordplay between πατέρα and πᾶσα πατριά in the following verse (Best, 377). Even though the longer reading is found in both the Western and Byzantine text types, internal evidence suggests that it is secondary.

3:15 οὗ: The Greek word οὗ is a masculine singular genitive from the relative pronoun ὅς that means "whom" in this context (BDAG, s.v. "ὅς" 1a, p. 725). **Syntactically**, οὗ introduces a dependent adjectival relative clause "from *whom* every family in heaven and on earth is named" (ἐξ οὗ πᾶσα πατριὰ ἐν οὐρανοῖς καὶ ἐπὶ γῆς ὀνομάζεται). The antecedent of the pronoun is "the Father" (τὸν πατέρα). It functions as the object of the preposition ἐκ. The preposition expresses the source or derivation of the names of all of the families (BDAG, s.v. "ἐκ" 3c, p. 296).

ὀνομάζεται: The Greek word ὀνομάζεται is a third-person singular present passive indicative from the verb ὀνομάζω that means "to call" or "name." The passive voice can be rendered "receive its name" (BDAG, s.v. "ὀνομάζω" 1, p. 714). Most English versions translate the verb as "is named" (ESV, NET, RSV, CSB, HCSB, NKJV, KJV). The NIV and NASB render it "derives its name," and the NRSV renders it "takes its name." **Syntactically**, ὀνομάζεται functions as the main verb of the relative clause. The subject is "every family" (πᾶσα πατριά; BDAG, s.v. "πατριά" 3, p. 78; s.v. "πᾶς" 1aα, p. 782; cf. ESV, NET, NIV, RSV, NRSV, HCSB, NASB). **Semantically**, ὀνομάζεται functions as an extending-from-past present, emphasizing an event that has begun in the past and continues into the present (W, 519–20). The right to name indicates authority (cf. Isa. 40:26). God gave Adam the right to name the animals in Eden (Gen. 2:19–20). Earlier in the letter, Paul indicates that God will seat Christ at his right hand far above "every name that is named" (1:21).

> **Semantical Nugget**: How do the prepositional phrases "in the heavens" (ἐν οὐρανοῖς) and "on earth" (ἐπὶ γῆς) function? Both prepositional phrases express location, creating a contrast that describes the extent of God's authority—spanning from heaven to earth (cf. 1 Cor. 8:5; Eph. 1:10; Col. 1:16, 20). The prepositions, particularly referring to those families "in the heavens," raise the question about the identity of these families. Paul most likely has in mind those rulers, authorities, and powers that he has referenced throughout the letter (Eph. 1:23; 3:10; 6:12; Thielman, 227). The Greek term for "family" (πατριά) creates an alliteration with "Father" (πατέρα): πατέρα ἐξ οὗ πᾶσα πατριά.

3:16a ἵνα: The Greek word ἵνα is a conjunction that means "that" in this context (BDAG, s.v. "ἵνα" 2aγ, p. 476). **Syntactically**, ἵνα introduces a dependent conjunctive clause "that he might give to you power" (ἵνα δῷ ὑμῖν … δυνάμει). The entire clause functions substantively as the direct object of the main verb "I bow" (κάμπτω). In the context of prayer, the ἵνα marks the content of the prayer (W, 475). Due to the length of the sentence in Greek, several English versions begin a new sentence at verse 16a by repeating the main verb: "*I pray* that" (NET, NIV, NRSV, HCSB, NLT, GNB, CSB). This is the first of three requests that Paul makes in his prayer; he uses the same conjunction in verses 18a and 19b to introduce the other two requests. **Semantically**, ἵνα introduces the content of Paul's prayer (W, 474–75; Moule, 145).

δῷ: The Greek word δῷ is a third-person singular aorist active subjunctive from the verb δίδωμι that means "to give" or "grant" (BDAG, s.v. "δίδωμι" 2, p. 242). **Syntactically**, δῷ functions as the main verb of the dependent conjunctive clause introduced by ἵνα. The subject is implied by the verb: "he," referring to the Father, to whom Paul is directing his prayer. The indirect object is "you" (ὑμῖν). **Semantically**, δῷ functions as an ingressive aorist focusing on the entrance of a new state (W, 558–59). The subjunctive following ἵνα can express purpose or result. In this case, it expresses the main content of Paul's prayer.

> **Semantical Nugget**: What does the prepositional phrase "according to his rich glory" mean? The preposition κατά gives the standard by which Paul

asks God to give (BDAG, s.v. "κατά" B5aγ, p. 512). Most English versions translate the preposition "according to" (ESV, NET, NRSV, RSV, HCSB, NASB, KJV, NKJV). The genitive τῆς δόξης could be rendered as an attributed genitive: "rich *glory*" (Merkle, 104); or as an attributive genitive: "*glorious* riches" (NIV). Larkin argues that it is an epexegetical genitive: "wealth, *that is his glory*" (Larkin, 61; Best, 339). The first option is preferable. Paul has used the Greek term πλοῦτος throughout the letter. In Ephesians 1:18, he uses the term to refer to the believers' inheritance—"the wealth of his glorious inheritance" (see the Semantical Nugget at 1:18d).

3:16b κραταιωθῆναι: The Greek word κραταιωθῆναι is an aorist passive infinitive from the verb κραταιόω that means "to become strong" (BDAG, s.v. "κραταιόω," p. 564). **Syntactically**, κραταιωθῆναι introduces a dependent substantival infinitive clause functioning as the direct object of the main verb "he might give" (δῷ) (W, 601–3). **Semantically**, κραταιωθῆναι as an ingressive aorist, which focuses on the entrance of a new state (W, 558–59). The voice is a divine passive. Without stating the agent, God is the one who strengthens the believer. The NIV converts the passive voice into active "he may strengthen you," but most translations retain the passive voice: "to be strengthened" (ESV, NET). δυνάμει is best understood as a dative of means, expressing how God might strengthen the believer: "with power." The prepositional phrase "through his Spirit" (διὰ τοῦ πνεύματος αὐτοῦ) expresses agency. In this case, the Spirit is an intermediate agent through whom God will strengthen the believer (W, 433–34). The prepositional phrase "in the inner person" (εἰς τὸν ἔσω ἄνθρωπον) expresses sphere (BDF §205). The phrase is most likely parallel to the phrase ἐν ταῖς καρδίαις ὑμῶν in the following clause (v. 17b). Most English versions translate the phrase "in the inner man" (RSV, HCSB, NASB, NKJV, KJV) or "in your inner being" (ESV, NRSV, NIV, CSB). The phrase refers to the mental and emotional capacity of a person (cf. Rom. 7:22; 2 Cor. 4:16; BDAG, s.v. "ἄνθρωπος" 5a, p. 82; Hoehner, 479).

3:17a κατοικῆσαι: The Greek word κατοικῆσαι is an aorist active infinitive from the verb κατοικέω that means "to live" or "dwell" with a specific focus on the relationship between God and humans (BDAG, s.v. "κατοικέω" 1b, p. 534). Most English versions translate the verb as "dwell" (ESV, NET, NIV, RSV, NRSV, HCSB), but the NLT translates it: "will make his home." **Syntactically**, κατοικῆσαι introduces a dependent substantival infinitive clause. It could either modify the previous infinitive "to be strengthened" (κραταιωθῆναι; v. 16b) or the main verb "he might give" (δῷ; v. 16a). If it modifies κραταιωθῆναι it would express the result of the believer being strengthened: "*so that* Christ may dwell in your heart" (ESV, NASB, NIV; Hoehner, 481). However, the parallelism between this clause and the previous clause (v. 16b) suggests that the infinitive modifies the main verb δῷ instead. Several English versions render the phrase as a second request by inserting "and" (RSV, NRSV, HCSB, CSB). The problem is that there is no coordinating conjunction in the Greek text. Finally, since there is no coordinating conjunction and the statements overlap, the clause is best understood as epexegetical (Larkin, 62; Barth, 369–70; Best, 341; Arnold, 210–11). The infinitive offers a further explanation of the previous infinitive clause. The subject of the infinitive is the accusative "Christ" (τὸν Χριστόν). **Semantically**, κατοικῆσαι functions as an ingressive aorist, which focuses on the entrance of a new state (W, 558–59). Just like the previous infinitive clause, the infinitive is modified by two prepositional phrases. The first prepositional phrase "through faith" (διὰ τῆς πίστεως) expresses means (BDAG, s.v. "διά" A3d, p. 224). Christ dwells in the heart of the believer through their act of believing (cf. 1:15; 2:8; 3:12). The second prepositional phrase "in your hearts" (ἐν ταῖς καρδίαις ὑμῶν) expresses sphere. This indwelling of Christ is "*in* your hearts."

> **Syntactical Nugget**: What is the relationship between the prepositional phrase "in love" (ἐν ἀγάπῃ) and the rest of the context? It is possible that the prepositional phrase modifies the previous infinitive clause: "that Christ might dwell through faith in your hearts *in love.*" The problem with this is that it breaks the parallelism of the previous infinitive clause and it leaves the participles suspended. On the other hand, it could modify the following two participles (ἐρριζωμένοι and τεθεμελιωμένοι) "*in love* having been rooted and established." This position balances Paul's use of the prepositions. In this case, the preposition is in the first position for emphasis (Baugh, 273–74). The preposition expresses sphere in which the believer is rooted and grounded (Thielman, 231; Larkin, 62; ESV, RSV, NRSV, NIV, CSB, HCSB, NASB, NKJV, KJV). In Ephesians, Paul can talk about the believer's love for one another (1:15; 4:2, 15–16; 5:2) or God's love for the believer (1:4; 2:4; 5:2). Paul most likely has God's love in view here since the following focuses on the depth of Christ's love (Thielman, 233; Arnold, 213; Best, 343). The NLT translates the phrase as "Your roots will grow down into God's love and keep you strong."

3:17b ἐρριζωμένοι: The Greek word ἐρριζωμένοι is a masculine nominative plural perfect middle participle from the verb ῥιζόω that means "to be firmly rooted" or "fixed" (BDAG, s.v. "ῥιζόω," p. 906). **Syntactically**, the relationship of both ἐρριζωμένοι and the parallel participle τεθεμελιωμένοι (v. 17c) to the rest of the context have been interpreted a number of different ways (see Grammatical Nugget below). It is best to understand them as modifying the following subjunctive in verse 18: "that you might be able" (ἐξισχύσητε). **Semantically**, the perfect tense indicates that the action of the participle is antecedent with the action of the main verb. The participle functions as the cause of the main verb (W, 631–32): "*because* you have been rooted and grounded in love" (NET). Because believers are rooted and grounded in love, they might be able to understand the love of Christ (cf. vv. 18–19a).

Grammatical Nugget: How do the participles in verse 17 function in the sentence? There are a number of ways to interpret the participles ἐρριζωμένοι ("being rooted) and τεθεμελιωμένοι ("being founded") each one has significant problems. First, they could be loosely connected to the surrounding context as independent verbal participles (Barth, 371–72) or as "independent parenthetical interjections." In this case, the participles could be translated as indicative verbs in a parenthetical clause: "you are rooted and founded in love" (Thielman, 232; BDF §468; cf. LEB, NLT). The problem with this view is that this category is rare (W, 650–52). Also, the case of the participles makes this difficult. The grammatical subject is God, if the subject shifted to the believer then the participles would most likely be dative to agree with the indirect object in verse 16: ὑμῖν. Second, they could represent a new request related to the previous infinitives (Arnold, 212–13; Lincoln, 197). Again, the forms of the participles create some difficulty with this position. Third, it is possible that the participles modify κατοικῆσαι (v. 17a) expressing the result of the infinitive (Abbott 1909, 97; cf. NRSV). The difficulty with this position is that the participles are perfect tense—the believers have already been rooted and established. Finally, the participles possibly modify the following verb ἐξισχύσητε ("that you might be strong enough," v. 18a) (Hoehner, 483; Larkin, 62–63). Several English versions translate the participles this way by beginning a new sentence at verse 17b: "I pray that you, *being rooted* and *firmly established* in love may be able to comprehend" (NIV, HCSB, CSB, cf. ESV, NASB, RSV, NET). In this case, the participles would express the grounds for the following request. The significant problem with this view is that we would expect the participles to follow the ἵνα. In fact, if these participles modify the following subjunctive, this is the only occurrence where the participles come before the conjunction in the New Testament (Arnold, 212; Moule, 31). Grammatical problems face each view, but the last view makes the most sense of the tense and case of the participles. Regardless, the participles create a nice link between the first two requests. As the believers are strengthened, Paul prays that they are able to comprehend God's plan.

3:17c τεθεμελιωμένοι: The Greek word τεθεμελιωμένοι is a masculine nominative plural perfect passive participle from the verb θεμελιόω that means "to establish" or "strengthen" (BDAG, s.v. "θεμελιόω" 2a, p. 449). Several English versions render the verb as "grounded" (ESV, NET, RSV, NRSV, NASB) or "established" (NIV, HCSB, CSB). **Syntactically**, τεθεμελιωμένοι introduces a dependent participle clause. It functions adverbially modifying "that you might be strong enough" (ἐξισχύσητε; v. 18) (see Grammatical Nugget at 3:17b). **Semantically**, just like the coordinating participle ἐρριζωμένοι, the action of the participle is antecedent with the action of the main verb and functions as a causal participle.

3:18a ἵνα: The Greek word ἵνα is a conjunction that means "that" in this context (BDAG, s.v. "ἵνα" 2aγ, pp. 476). **Syntactically**, ἵνα introduces a dependent conjunctive clause "*that* you might be strong enough" (ἵνα ἐξισχύσητε). The entire clause functions substantively as the direct object of the main verb "I bow" (κάμπτω). In the context of prayer, the ἵνα marks the content of the prayer (W, 475). This is Paul's second request (cf. vv. 16a, 19b). Due to the length of the sentence in Greek, a number of versions begin a new sentence by repeating the verb "I pray that" either at verse 18a (NRSV) or before the previous participles in verse 17 (CSB, HCSB, NIV). Since there is no coordinating conjunction, Hoehner argues that the ἵνα clause is best understood as modifying κατοικῆσαι ("that Christ might dwell," v. 17), expressing the purpose of Christ dwelling in their hearts (Hoehner, 485; cf. Thielman, 233). This is possible, but it ignores how Paul uses the ἵνα to lay out his prayer requests.

ἐξισχύσητε: The Greek word ἐξισχύσητε is a second-person plural aorist active subjunctive from the verb ἐξισχύω that means "to be able," "to be strong enough," or "to be in a position" (BDAG, s.v. "ἐξισχύω," p. 350). The word is a *hapax legomenon*, occurring only once in the New Testament. Some versions render the verb as "you may have the power" (NIV, RSV, NRSV, NLT), while other versions translate the verb as "that you may be able" (NET, HCSB, CSB, NASB, NKJV, KJV). **Syntactically**, ἐξισχύσητε functions as the main verb of the dependent conjunctive clause introduced by ἵνα. The subject is implied by the verb: "you," referring to the believers. **Semantically**, ἐξισχύσητε functions as an ingressive aorist, which focuses on the entrance into a new state (W, 558–59). Paul's second request is that these believers begin to understand the depth of Christ's love.

3:18b καταλαβέσθαι: The Greek word καταλαβέσθαι is an aorist middle infinitive from the verb καταλαμβάνω that means "to grasp" or "understand" (BDAG, s.v. "καταλαμβάνω" 4a, p. 520). **Syntactically**, καταλαβέσθαι introduces a dependent adverbial infinitive clause functioning as the direct object of the main verb "you may be able" (ἐξισχύσητε). **Semantically**, καταλαβέσθαι functions as a complementary infinitive completing the idea of the main verb: "that you may be able *to comprehend*" (NET, CSB, HCSB, NASB, NKJV, KJV; W, 598–99). The aorist tense functions as an ingressive aorist emphasizing the entrance into a state (W, 558–59). The preposition σύν ("with") expresses association: "*with* all the saints." Paul's prayer is that the Ephesian believers are able to comprehend the extent of Christ's love with all of the believers.

3:18c τί: The Greek word τί is an indefinite pronoun from the word τίς that means "what" or "what sort of" (BDAG, s.v. "τίς" 1aβ⊐, p. 1007; W, 345–46). **Syntactically**, τί introduces a clause that serves as the direct object of the infinitive in verse 18: καταλαβέσθαι ("to comprehend"). τί functions as the predicate nominative of the implied verb ἐστίν: "what is."

[ἐστίν]: The Greek word ἐστίν is a third-person singular present active indicative from the verb εἰμί that means "to be" (BDAG, s.v. "εἰμί" 2cβ, p. 282). **Syntactically**, [ἐστίν] is the main verb of the object clause introduced by τί. The clause serves as the object of the infinitive "to comprehend" (καταλαβέσθαι). The subject is the phrase "the width and length and height and depth" (τὸ πλάτος καὶ μῆκος καὶ ὕψος καὶ βάθος). The predicate nominative is the pronoun "what" (τί).

> **Syntactical Nugget**: What is the referent of the description "the width and length and height and depth" (τὸ πλάτος καὶ μῆκος καὶ ὕψος καὶ βάθος)? All four nouns are governed by a single article, creating a TSKS (or Granville Sharp) construction. Each dimension describes a distinct aspect of a single area (W, 286; Porter, 110). The problem is that the referent is not clear. Throughout history, a number of possibilities have been put forward (for a list of options see Arnold, 215–16). Arnold makes a strong case that Paul wants the believer to comprehend God's power. In magical texts, these terms refer to power, and God's power plays a significant role in the book of Ephesians (1:19–22) (Arnold, 216–17). The problem with Arnold's interpretation is that nothing in the immediate context suggests that Paul is making this reference. Another option is that this refers to the expansive plan of God, the stewardship of the mystery (cf. Eph. 3:3–6, 9–10). While this position takes advantage of the wider context, the focus of Paul's discussion has shifted since he began his prayer in verse 14. Perhaps the best option is that these terms describe Christ's love, which becomes the subject of Paul's prayer in verse 19a. Paul uses similar language to describe God's love in Romans 8:39 (Hoehner, 488; Lincoln, 213; Best, 346). Several English versions make the object clear by inserting "the love of Christ" (NIV) or "God's love" (CSB, HCSB; cf. NLT).

3:19a τέ: The Greek word τέ functions as a conjunction that means "and" in this context (BDAG, s.v. "τέ" 2a, p. 993). **Syntactically**, τέ is in the postpositive position introducing a dependent conjunctive clause "*and* to know the love of Christ, which surpasses knowledge" (γνῶναί τε τὴν ὑπερβάλλουσαν τῆς γνώσεως ἀγάπην τοῦ Χριστοῦ). **Semantically**, τέ is a coordinating connective: "and" (ESV, RSV, NRSV, NIV, NET, CSB, HCSB, NASB, KJV). The conjunction introduces a second complementary infinitive.

γνῶναί: The Greek word γνῶναί is an aorist active infinitive from the verb γινώσκω that means to grasp the significance of something, "to understand" or "comprehend" (BDAG, s.v. "γινώσκω" 3a, p. 200). Most English versions translate the verb as "know"; the NLT translates it as "May you experience." **Syntactically**, γνῶναί introduces a dependent adverbial infinitive clause. It is parallel to the previous infinitive καταλαβέσθαι ("to comprehend"). It functions as the direct object of the main verb ἐξισχύσητε ("to be able"). The phrase "the love of Christ which surpasses knowledge" (τὴν ὑπερβάλλουσαν τῆς γνώσεως ἀγάπην τοῦ Χριστοῦ) functions as the direct object of the infinitive. **Semantically**, γνῶναί functions as a second complementary infinitive completing the idea of the verb it modifies ("that you might be able to comprehend … and *to know*") (NIV, ESV, RSV, NRSV, CSB, HCSB, NASB, NKJV, KJV; W, 598–99). The aorist tense functions as an ingressive aorist emphasizing the entrance into a state (W, 558–59).

ὑπερβάλλουσαν: The Greek word ὑπερβάλλουσαν is a feminine accusative singular present active participle from the verb ὑπερβάλλω that means "to surpass," "go beyond," or "outdo" (BDAG, s.v. "ὑπερβάλλω," p. 1032). **Syntactically**, ὑπερβάλλουσαν functions as an attributive participle modifying "love" (ἀγάπην), the direct object of the infinitive "to know" (γνῶναί). **Semantically**, ὑπερβάλλουσαν is a customary present expressing an ongoing state (W, 521–22). The genitive τοῦ Χριστοῦ could either be possessive: "*Christ's* love"; or subjective: "*Christ's* love for the believer." The genitive τῆς γνώσεως is a genitive of comparison (cf. BDAG, s.v. "ὑπερβάλλω," p. 1032; BDF §177; Robertson, 519; W, 110–12)—this love surpasses knowledge. The phrase creates a paradox—Paul hopes that the believer comes to know Christ's love, which he describes as unknowable (Arnold, 217–18). The GNT highlights this tension: "Yes, may you come to know his love—although it can never be fully known."

3:19b ἵνα: The Greek word ἵνα is a conjunction that means "that" in this context (BDAG, s.v. "ἵνα" 2aγ, p. 476). **Syntactically**, ἵνα introduces a dependent conjunctive clause "*that* you might be filled" (ἵνα πληρωθῆτε εἰς πᾶν τὸ πλήρωμα τοῦ θεοῦ). The entire clause functions substantively as the direct object of the main verb "I bow" (κάμπτω). In the context of prayer, the ἵνα marks the content of the prayer (W, 475). This is Paul's final request (cf. vv. 16a, 18a). The request is short and might be seen as a summary of the previous requests. Since there is no coordinating conjunction, Hoehner argues that the ἵνα clause modifies γνῶναι (v. 19a) expressing the purpose of the infinitive (Hoehner, 490; Thielman, 237–38). However, this ignores how Paul uses the ἵνα to lay out his prayer requests.

πληρωθῆτε: The Greek word πληρωθῆτε is a second-person plural aorist passive subjunctive from the verb πληρόω that means "to fill" (BDAG, s.v. "πληρόω" 1b, p. 828). **Syntactically,** πληρωθῆτε functions as the dependent conjunctive clause introduced by ἵνα. The subject is implied by the verb: "you," referring to the believers. **Semantically,** πληρωθῆτε is an ingressive aorist: "that you may be filled" (ESV, RSV, NRSV, NIV, CSB, HCSB, NASB, NKJV, KJV). It describes the entrance into a new state (W, 558–59). The passive voice functions as a divine passive. Without stating the agent, God, or more likely Christ, is the one who fills the believer. The preposition εἰς expresses goal, marking the result of the action (BDAG, s.v. "εἰς" 4e, p. 290). Many translations render the preposition as expressing content "filled up *with* all the fullness of God" (ESV, RSV, NRSV, HCSB, CSB, NKJV, KJV; W, 375). However, the preposition best expresses extent: "filled up *to* all the fullness of God" (NET, NIV, NASB, LEB; cf. Hoehner, 490; Best, 347–48). Paul uses a similar phrase in Ephesians 1:23 (cf. Col. 1:19; 2:9). Later in Ephesians, he looks forward to a time when the saints will grow "into a complete person, into a measure of maturity, *the fullness of Christ*" (4:13; cf. 5:18). The prayer echoes the same desire for the believer's maturity (Hoehner, 490–91; Thielman, 238).

Text-Critical Nugget: Is the verb πληρόω second-person or third-person? Two significant Alexandrian manuscripts ($\mathfrak{P}^{46}$ and B; also 0278, 33, 1175) replace the second-person plural verb with the third-person singular verb and omit the preposition εἰς: πληρωθῇ πᾶν τὸ πλήρωμα τοῦ θεοῦ ("that all the fullness of God may be filled up"). The change most likely came about due to the difficulty with εἰς, which more commonly means "into," not "up to" (Thielman, 238–39). The NA²⁸ text is found in the Alexandrian (א, A, C, 104, 1739, 1881), Western (D, F, G), and the Byzantine (K, L, 𝔐) text types. Besides having superior external support, it is the more difficult reading that explains the rise of the other and is most likely the original.

3:20a δέ: The Greek word δέ is a conjunction that means "now" (BDAG, s.v. "δέ" 2, p. 213). **Syntactically,** δέ is in the postpositive position introducing an independent conjunctive clause, "*Now* … to him be the glory" (δὲ … αὐτῷ ἡ δόξα). The main verb is implied. **Semantically,** δέ links the previous prayer (vv. 14–19) to the benediction (vv. 20–21). Most English versions render the conjunction as "now" (ESV, RSV, NRSV, NIV, NET, CSB, HCSB, NASB, NKJV, KJV, NLT).

τῷ δυναμένῳ: The Greek word δυναμένῳ is a masculine dative singular present middle (deponent) participle from the verb δύναμαι that means "able" or "capable" (BDAG, s.v. "δύναμαι" aβ, p. 262). **Syntactically,** τῷ δυναμένῳ is a substantival participle. The participle phrase is in apposition to αὐτῷ in verse 21, the indirect object of the implied verb ἐστίν. The subject is "glory" (ἡ δόξα; v. 21a): "Glory be to him." By omitting the main verb and moving the dative to the front of the sentence, Paul places emphasis on God—specifically what he is able to do. Since God is the nearest referent (v. 19) and Christ is mentioned in the following verse, God the Father is antecedent. The NLT renders the clause: "Now all glory to God, who is able." **Semantically**, δυναμένῳ functions as a customary present. The present tense describes an ongoing state (W, 521–22).

ποιῆσαι: The Greek word ποιῆσαι is an aorist active infinitive from the verb ποιέω that means "to do" or "bring about" (BDAG, s.v. "ποιέω" 2e, p. 840). Most English versions translate the verb "to do," except the NRSV, which translates it as "to accomplish" (cf. NLT). **Syntactically**, ποιῆσαι introduces a dependent adverbial infinitive clause functioning as the direct object of the substantival participle τῷ δυναμένῳ ("to the one who is able"). **Semantically**, ποιῆσαι is a complementary infinitive, completing the idea of the participle δυναμένῳ: "to him who is able *to do*" (ESV, NIV, CSB, HCSB, NASB, NKJV; cf. NET, KJV; W, 598–99). The infinitive is a constative aorist describing the action of the verb as a whole (W, 557–58). The prepositional phrase ὑπὲρ πάντα expresses the idea of "over and above" or "beyond" (BDAG, s.v. "ὑπέρ" B, p. 1031). Most English versions translate the phrase as "above all" (CSB, HCSB, NKJV, KJV) or "beyond all" (NASB, NET). God is able to do more than what we could ever ask.

> **Lexical Nugget**: What does the term "infinitely more" (ὑπερεκπερισσοῦ) mean? The adverb ὑπερεκπερισσοῦ occurs only once in Ephesians and twice in 1 Thessalonians (3:10; 5:13). The word has two prepositional prefixes (ὑπέρ and ἐκ), which intensifies the meaning of the word. BDAG states that this is the "highest form of comparison imaginable" and renders it "quite beyond all measure" (BDAG, s.v. "ὑπερεκπερισσοῦ," p. 1033). Most English versions translate the adverb as "far more abundantly" (ESV, RSV, NASB, cf. NRSV), "immeasurably more" (NIV), "exceedingly abundantly" (KJV, NKJV), "far beyond all" (NET), or "above and beyond all" (HCSB, CSB). The word is parallel to the previous prepositional phrase, qualifying what it means to do "above all" (ὑπὲρ πάντα) (Larkin, 65). Not only is God able to do above all, he is able to do infinitely more than what these believers could either ask or dream about (Thielman, 242).

3:20b ὧν: The Greek word ὧν is a neuter plural genitive from the relative pronoun ὅς that means "what" or "which" (BDAG, s.v. "ὅς" 1da, p. 726). **Syntactically**, ὧν introduces a dependent adjectival relative clause "*what* we ask or think" (ὧν αἰτούμεθα ἢ νοοῦμεν). The antecedent is an unexpressed object of the preposition ὑπερεκπερισσοῦ: "infinitely more than *this*" (BDAG, s.v. "ὑπερεκπερισσοῦ," p. 1033; BDF §185.1). The pronoun functions as an accusative in the clause, but due to attraction the case has shifted to genitive (see

BDF §294.2). It functions as the direct object of αἰτούμεθα and νοοῦμεν ("we ask or think").

αἰτούμεθα: The Greek word αἰτούμεθα is a first-person plural present middle indicative from the verb αἰτέω that means "to ask" (BDAG, s.v. "αἰτέω," p. 30). **Syntactically**, αἰτούμεθα functions as the main verb of the relative clause. The subject is implied with the verb: "we," referring to both Paul and his readers. The direct object is the relative pronoun. The verb marks a shift from the second person in verses 16–19, where Paul is praying for the Ephesians, to the first person in the benediction (vv. 20–21) (Merkle, 109). **Semantically**, αἰτούμεθα functions as an iterative present describing a repeated event (W, 520–21). No matter what these believers might ask God, he is able to do it.

3:20c ἤ: The Greek word ἤ is a conjunction that means "or" (BDAG, s.v. "ἤ" 1aβ, p. 432). **Syntactically**, ἤ introduces a dependent conjunctive clause: "*or* think according to the power that works in us" (ἢ νοοῦμεν κατὰ τὴν δύναμιν τὴν ἐνεργουμένην ἐν ἡμῖν). **Semantically**, ἤ is a disjunctive connective: "or" (ESV RSV NRSV NIV CSB NASB NKJV KJV). God is able to do even more than we could either ask or even imagine.

νοοῦμεν: The Greek word νοοῦμεν is a first-person plural present active indicative from the verb νοέω that means "to think" or "imagine" (BDAG, s.v. "νοέω" 3, p. 675). **Syntactically**, νοοῦμεν functions as the main verb of the relative clause along with αἰτούμεθα. **Semantically**, νοοῦμεν functions as a customary present, focusing on regularly occurring or ongoing action (W, 521–22). God is able to do more than what these believers could even imagine. The verb alludes to Paul's description of God's plan that he describes in Ephesians 3 (vv. 2–13). This plan is something that no one would have been able to conceive.

ἐνεργουμένην: The Greek word ἐνεργουμένην is a feminine accusative singular present middle participle from the verb ἐνεργέω that means "to be at work" (BDAG, s.v. "ἐνεργέω" 1b, p. 335). **Syntactically**, ἐνεργουμένην functions as an attributive participle modifying "power" (τὴν δύναμιν), the object of the preposition κατά. "Power" (δύναμιν), creates a wordplay with the dative participle (δυναμένῳ v. 20a) that is lost in English: "But to the one who is *able* ... according to his *ability*" (Thielman, 243). **Semantically**, ἐνεργουμένην is a customary present: "that is working" (NET) or "at work" (ESV, RSV, NRSV). The present tense marks the action of the verb as ongoing (W, 521–22). The phrase ties together a number of important theological themes. First, the preposition κατά communicates standard: God's ability to do all things in conformity with this power. Second, this power is the same power working within us. Earlier in

Ephesians, Paul states that this power at work within the believer is the same power at work in Christ's resurrection (1:19–22).

3:21   [ἐστίν]: The Greek word ἐστίν is a third-person singular present active indicative from the verb εἰμί that means "is" (BDAG, s.v. "εἰμί" 9, p. 285). **Syntactically,** the ellipsis [ἐστίν] is the main verb of the independent conjunctive clause introduced by δέ (v. 20a). The subject of the verb is "glory" (ἡ δόξα). The indirect object is the third-person personal pronoun: "to him" (αὐτῷ). The pronoun is resumptive of the earlier participle "to the one who is able" (τῷ δυναμένῳ). By inserting the pronoun, Paul draws the spotlight of the benediction from God's immense power (v. 20) back to his glory. Most English versions place the dative first: "to him be the glory" (ESV, RSV, NRSV, NIV, NET, CSB, HCSB, NASB, NKJV). The NLT omits the ellipsis: "Glory to him." **Semantically,** the ellipsis [ἐστίν] is a gnomic present, describing a general statement (W, 523–25). All glory belongs to God. The clause ends with three prepositional phrases. The first two prepositional phrases (ἐν τῇ ἐκκλησίᾳ and ἐν Χριστῷ Ἰησοῦ) expresses sphere: "in the church" and "in Christ." The repetition of the preposition highlights the relationship between Christ and the church (cf. 5:32). Christ is the head of the church; the church is his body (Eph. 1:22–23; cf. 2:20–22; 4:15–16). The final prepositional phrase (εἰς πάσας τὰς γενεὰς τοῦ αἰῶνος τῶν αἰώνων) expresses a temporal element. The object of the preposition "generations" (γενεάς) can refer to an undefined period of time (BDAG, s.v. "γενεά" 3b, p. 192). Some English versions translate the preposition *"throughout* all generations" (ESV, NIV, KJV), however most translate it *"to* all generations" (NET, RSV, NRSV, HCSB, NASB, NKJV). Paul regularly ends his prayers with an idiomatic phrase referring to eternity (τοῦ αἰῶνος τῶν αἰώνων) (cf. Gal. 1:5; Phil. 4:20; 1 Tim. 1:17; 2 Tim. 4:18). Paul ends the prayer with ἀμήν ("amen") a strong affirmation of what was just stated (BDAG, s.v. "ἀμήν" 1a, p. 53).

EPHESIANS 4:1–16

Big Greek Idea: Believers should walk in a manner worthy of their Christian faith by keeping the unity of the community, which God made possible by appointing Christian leaders to train the body, and which is essential for the growth of the body to withstand attacks of the evil one.

Structural Overview: Paul begins the second half of the book with a call for believers to live a life in a manner worthy of their calling. His exhortation to "walk" links the second half of the book to Ephesians 2:1–10. Believers once walked in trespasses (Eph. 2:1), but now walk in the good works that God has prepared for them (Eph. 2:10). Throughout the second half of the book, he gives specific examples of what this means for the believer, making the command to walk a structural element. This first major section of the second half of the book emphasizes the unity within the community in order to promote maturity. For Paul, this growth of the body is essential to withstand the evil at work within the world.

This section has two parts. Paul begins the first part (vv. 1–6) with an exhortation to walk in a manner worthy of the Christian call, an allusion to the first section of the letter. For the believer this means continually putting the needs of others ahead of their own—humbling themselves, bearing one another in love, keeping unity (vv. 1–3). Paul ends this first part with a series of seven statements emphasizing the unity of the Christian body: one body, one Spirit, one hope, one Lord, one faith, one baptism, and one God and Father (vv. 4–6). The connection between verses 3 and 4 is not clear, but the list suggests that because there is unity in the Christian faith, believers should live the same way.

After emphasizing the unity of the community, the second part discusses the diversity. Paul uses Psalm 68:19 (LXX 67:19) to describe the diverse gifts that God gives the believers. He applies the psalm to Christ's incarnation and ascension, and subsequent distribution of the Spirit (vv. 7–10). The rest of this section (vv. 11–16) consists of a long sentence describing the reason he gave these gifts—for the maturity of the church. As a result, he appointed apostles, prophets, evangelists, pastors, and teachers to equip the body for growth (vv. 11–13). This growth is important to withstand satanic attacks (cf. 6:10–12). Paul uses two images to emphasize the importance. The first image is a boat being tossed around by waves and wind. This maturity should establish stability. The second, and more dominant, image is of a growing child. Like a child, the body should grow into Christlikeness. He uses a similar image in 1 Corinthians 12:1–31—each member uses their own gifts to sustain the body. In this way they are interrelated. However, Paul's emphasis in Ephesians 4:11–16 is on the community becoming like Christ.

Outline:

> Believers should walk in unity as a reflection of their call and the Christian faith (vv. 1–6)
>> Believers should walk in a manner worthy of their calling by seeking unity within the community (vv. 1–3)
>> Believers should walk in unity because it reflects their Christian faith (vv. 4–6)
> God gives diverse gifts so that the body will grow in love (vv. 7–17)
>> God distributes gifts to believers (vv. 7–10)
>> God appoints Christian leaders to build up the Christian body in Christlikeness to withstand attacks from the evil in the world (vv. 11–16)

Clausal Outline for Ephesians 4:1–16

4:1a **Παρακαλῶ** οὖν ὑμᾶς ἐγὼ ὁ δέσμιος ἐν κυρίῳ ἀξίως περιπατῆσαι τῆς κλήσεως

4:1a Therefore, I, a prisoner in the Lord, **urge** you to walk worthy of the calling

4:1b ἧς **ἐκλήθητε**, 2a μετὰ πάσης ταπεινοφροσύνης καὶ πραΰτητος, μετὰ μακροθυμίας,

4:1b by which **you were called** 2a with all humility and gentleness, with patience

[περιπατῆσαι (v. 1b)]
[to walk (v. 1b)]

4:2b **ἀνεχόμενοι** ἀλλήλων ἐν ἀγάπῃ,

4:2b **by bearing** one another with love,

4:3a **σπουδάζοντες** τηρεῖν τὴν ἑνότητα τοῦ πνεύματος ἐν τῷ συνδέσμῳ τῆς εἰρήνης·

4:3a **by making every effort** to keep the unity of the Spirit in the uniting bonds of peace.

4:4a [**ἔστιν**] ἓν σῶμα

4:4a There [**is**] one body

4:4b καὶ [**ἔστιν**] ἓν πνεῦμα,

4:4b and there [**is**] one Spirit

4:4c **καθὼς** καὶ **ἐκλήθητε** ἐν μιᾷ ἐλπίδι τῆς κλήσεως ὑμῶν·

4:4c **just as you have** also **been called** in one hope of your calling;

^{4:5a} [**ἔστιν**] εἷς κύριος,
^{4:5a} there [**is**] one Lord;

^{4:5b} [**ἔστιν**] μία πίστις,
^{4:5b} there [**is**] one faith;

^{4:5c} [**ἔστιν**] ἓν βάπτισμα·
^{4:5c} there [**is**] one baptism;

^{4:6} [**ἔστιν**] εἷς θεὸς καὶ πατὴρ πάντων, (<u>ὁ</u> ἐπὶ πάντων καὶ διὰ πάντων καὶ ἐν πᾶσιν).
^{4:6} there [**is**] one God and Father of all (<u>who is</u> over all and through all and in all).

^{4:7} Ἑνὶ <u>δὲ</u> ἑκάστῳ ἡμῶν **ἐδόθη** ἡ χάρις κατὰ τὸ μέτρον τῆς δωρεᾶς τοῦ Χριστοῦ.
^{4:7} <u>But</u> grace **was given** to each one of us according to the measure of the gift of Christ.

^{4:8a} <u>διὸ</u> **λέγει**,
^{4:8a} <u>Therefore</u> **it says**,

> ^{4:8b} **Ἀναβὰς** εἰς ὕψος
> ^{4:8b} **While ascending** on high,

^{4:8c} **ἠχμαλώτευσεν** αἰχμαλωσίαν;
^{4:8c} **he took** prisoners **captive**,

^{4:8d} **ἔδωκεν** δόματα τοῖς ἀνθρώποις.
^{4:8d} **he gave** gifts to people.

^{4:9a} τὸ δὲ Ἀνέβη τί **ἐστιν**
^{4:9a} <u>Now</u> what **does** "he ascended" **mean**

> ^{4:9b} <u>εἰ μὴ</u> **ὅτι** καὶ <u>κατέβη</u> εἰς τὰ κατώτερα μέρη τῆς γῆς;
> ^{4:9b} <u>except</u> **that he** also **descended** to the lower parts, namely the earth.

^{4:10a} (ὁ καταβὰς αὐτός) **ἐστιν** καὶ (ὁ ἀναβὰς) ὑπεράνω πάντων τῶν οὐρανῶν,
^{4:10a} (The very one who descended) **is** also (the one who ascended) above all of the heavens

> ^{4:10b} **ἵνα πληρώσῃ** τὰ πάντα.
> ^{4:10b} **so that he might fill** all things.

⁴:¹¹ καὶ αὐτὸς **ἔδωκεν** τοὺς μὲν ἀποστόλους, τοὺς δὲ προφήτας, τοὺς δὲ εὐαγγελιστάς, τοὺς δὲ ποιμένας καὶ διδασκάλους, ¹²πρὸς τὸν καταρτισμὸν τῶν ἁγίων εἰς ἔργον διακονίας, εἰς οἰκοδομὴν τοῦ σώματος τοῦ Χριστοῦ,

⁴:¹¹ <u>And</u> he **gave** some as apostles, some as prophets, some as evangelists, and some as shepherds and other teachers ¹²for the equipping of the saints for the work, that is, the ministry for the building up of the body of Christ,

⁴:¹³ **μέχρι καταντήσωμεν** οἱ πάντες εἰς τὴν ἑνότητα τῆς πίστεως καὶ τῆς ἐπιγνώσεως τοῦ υἱοῦ τοῦ θεοῦ, εἰς ἄνδρα τέλειον, εἰς μέτρον ἡλικίας τοῦ πληρώματος τοῦ Χριστοῦ,

⁴:¹³ **until** <u>we</u> all **attain** to the unity of faith and the knowledge of the Son of God, to the complete person, to the measure that is Christ's full stature

⁴:¹⁴ **ἵνα** μηκέτι **ὦμεν** (νήπιοι, κλυδωνιζόμενοι καὶ περιφερόμενοι) παντὶ ἀνέμῳ τῆς διδασκαλίας ἐν τῇ κυβείᾳ τῶν ἀνθρώπων ἐν πανουργίᾳ πρὸς τὴν μεθοδείαν τῆς πλάνης,

⁴:¹⁴ **so that** <u>we are</u> no longer (infants being tossed by the waves and being carried about) by every wind of doctrine, by craftiness of man, by trickery in deceitful schemes

[ἵνα μηκέτι ὦμεν νήπιοι (v. 14)]
[so that we are no longer infants (v. 14)]

⁴:¹⁵ᵃ **ἀληθεύοντες** δὲ ἐν ἀγάπῃ
⁴:¹⁵ᵃ <u>but</u> by **practicing the truth** in love

⁴:¹⁵ᵇ **αὐξήσωμεν** εἰς αὐτὸν τὰ πάντα,
⁴:¹⁵ᵇ that <u>we may grow</u> into him in all things

⁴:¹⁵ᶜ **ὅς ἐστιν** ἡ κεφαλή, Χριστός,
⁴:¹⁵ᶜ <u>who</u> **is** the head, Christ,

⁴:¹⁶ ἐξ **οὗ** πᾶν (τὸ σῶμα συναρμολογούμενον καὶ συμβιβαζόμενον) διὰ πάσης ἁφῆς τῆς ἐπιχορηγίας κατ' ἐνέργειαν ἐν μέτρῳ ἑνὸς ἑκάστου μέρους τὴν αὔξησιν τοῦ σώματος **ποιεῖται** εἰς οἰκοδομὴν ἑαυτοῦ ἐν ἀγάπῃ.

⁴:¹⁶ from <u>whom</u> the whole (body, joined and held together) by every supporting ligament according to the working capacity of each individual part, **makes** the body grow so that it builds itself up in love.

Syntax Explained for Ephesians 4:1–16

[4:1a] οὖν: The Greek word οὖν is a conjunction that means "therefore" or "consequently" (BDAG, s.v. "οὖν" 1a, p. 736). **Syntactically**, οὖν introduces an independent conjunctive clause "*Therefore*, I, a prisoner in the Lord, urge you" (παρακαλῶ οὖν ὑμᾶς ἐγὼ ὁ δέσμιος ἐν κυρίῳ). **Semantically**, οὖν is an inferential conjunction, drawing an inference: "therefore" (CSB, HCSB, KJV, NKJV) or "So" (NET, NIV). The ESV translates it as "Now" (cf. RSV, NRSV). The conjunction refers to the first half of the book (Eph. 1–3). At this point, Paul shifts his attention from a doctrinal discussion about the status of the Gentiles in relationship to God and the Jews to discuss ethical commands that take up the remainder of the book.

παρακαλῶ: The Greek word παρακαλῶ is a first-person singular present active indicative from the verb παρακαλέω that means "to appeal to" or "exhort" (BDAG, s.v. "παρακαλέω" 2, p. 765). **Syntactically**, παρακαλῶ functions as the main verb of the independent conjunctive clause introduced by οὖν. The subject of the verb is "I" (ἐγώ), referring to Paul. The inclusion of ἐγώ is emphatic (1:15; 3:1; Merkle, 112); the nominative phrase "a prisoner in the Lord" (ὁ δέσμιος ἐν κυρίῳ) is in apposition (Turner[1], 37). Paul introduces his prayer in Ephesians 3:1 in a similar manner: "For this reason, I, Paul, a prisoner of Christ Jesus on behalf of you, the Gentiles." The direct object is "you" (ὑμᾶς), referring to the readers. **Semantically**, παρακαλῶ is a progressive present: "I urge" (ESV, NIV, NET, CSB, HCSB) or "I beg" (RSV, NRSV, NLT). The present tense describes the action in progress (W, 518–19). Paul often uses this verb with the infinitive to express a command (Rom. 12:1; 15:30; Col. 3:1; 1 Thess. 2:12; W, 652; BDF §337.1)—in this case "to walk" (περιπατῆσαι). Later, Paul will use the imperatival form of the verb (5:2, 8, 15; Merkle, 112).

Semantical Nugget: How should the prepositional phrase "in the Lord" (ἐν κυρίῳ) be treated? Paul calls himself "a prisoner in the Lord" (ὁ δέσμιος ἐν κυρίῳ)? Several translations render the phrase: "prisoner *for the Lord*" (ESV, NET, NIV, RSV, HCSB). The NLT renders the phrase: "a prisoner *for serving the Lord*," suggesting that the phrase gives the reason for Paul's imprisonment. Barth states that the phrase points to "the price he is paying—that is, perhaps, his specific right to be heard and heeded" (Barth, 426). Other translations render it: "prisoner *of the Lord*" (NASB, KJV, NKJV); or "prisoner *in the Lord*" (NRSV, CSB). Earlier, Paul refers to himself as a "prisoner of Christ Jesus on behalf of you, the Gentiles" (ὁ δέσμιος τοῦ Χριστοῦ Ἰησοῦ ὑπὲρ ὑμῶν τῶν ἐθνῶν; 3:1), so he is most likely referring to Jesus at this point, not the Father. Because of this, the preposition best expresses sphere ("in the Lord"), emphasizing Paul's union with Christ—even in prison, Paul defines himself in relation to Christ (Arnold, 229; Lincoln, 234; Hoehner, 504).

περιπατῆσαι: The Greek word περιπατῆσαι is an aorist active infinitive from the verb περιπατέω that means "to behave" or "live"; the idea is a habit of conduct (BDAG, s.v. "περιπατέω" 2aα, p. 803). Some English versions translate the verb literally: "to walk" (ESV, HCSB, NASB, KJV, NKJV); others present the metaphorical idea: "to live" (NET, CSB), "to live a life" (NIV), or "to lead a life" (RSV, NRSV, NLT). **Syntactically**, περιπατῆσαι introduces a dependent adverbial infinitive clause functioning as the direct object of the main verb "I urge" (παρακαλῶ). **Semantically**, περιπατῆσαι functions as a complementary infinitive, completing the action of the main verb παρακαλῶ: "I urge you *to walk*" (ESV, CSB, HCSB, NASB, NIV, RSV, NRSV, NET, NKJV, KJV, NLT) cf. W, 598–99). The verb is a constative aorist, describing the action of the verb as a whole (W, 557–58). The adverb ἀξίως modifies περιπατῆσαι, adverbially expressing the manner in which the Ephesians should walk (BDAG, s.v. "ἀξίως," p. 94), namely, worthy of their calling.

> **Theological Nugget**: Why does Paul use the verb "to walk" (περιπατέω) to refer to the believer's conduct? The verb περιπατέω begins a theme that runs throughout the remainder of the book. He uses the verb in Ephesians 4–6 to give his argument structure. He repeats the verb six times throughout the second part: believers should walk according to their calling (Eph. 4:1), with a renewed mind (Eph. 4:17 [2x]), in love (Eph. 5:2), in light (Eph. 5:8), and in wisdom (Eph. 5:15). Each occurrence marks a new section. In Ephesians 2, he uses the verb to describe a change in the life of the Ephesian believers: they once walked in sin (Eph. 2:2), but because of God's salvation, they are able to walk through the good works that God has prepared beforehand (Eph. 2:10) (see Theological Nugget at 2:10d). He uses the verb in the second part of the book with specific instructions, giving concrete examples of what it means to "walk in good works" (Eph. 2:10).

4:1b ἧς: The Greek word ἧς is a feminine singular genitive from the relative pronoun ὅς that means "which" in this context (BDAG, s.v. "ὅς" 1dβ, p. 726). **Syntactically**, ἧς introduces a dependent adjectival relative clause "*which you were called*" (ἧς ἐκλήθητε). The antecedent of the pronoun is "the calling" (τῆς κλήσεως). The pronoun functions as the direct object of the verb "you were called" and should be in the accusative case, but due to attraction it agrees with the case of the antecedent: "to which" (ESV, RSV, NRSV) (BDF §294.2; Robertson, 478, 716). Some English versions treat the relative pronoun as a dative of means: "with which" (NET, NASB, NKJV; cf. Larkin, 68).

ἐκλήθητε: The Greek word ἐκλήθητε is a second-person plural aorist passive indicative from the verb καλέω that means "to call," in the sense of "receiving a special benefit or experience" (BDAG, s.v. "καλέω" 4, pp. 503–4). **Syntactically**, ἐκλήθητε functions as the main verb of the relative clause "which *you were* *called*" (ἧς ἐκλήθητε). The redundant use of the verb in the relative clause modifying the related noun (κλῆσις) places emphasis on the believer's calling. **Semantically**, ἐκλήθητε functions as an ingressive aorist (W, 558–59). The action of the tense emphasizes the entry of the believer into this calling. The passive verb is a divine passive. Even though the voice obscures the actor, God is the subject (Lincoln, 235). The relative phrase refers to the believer's new identity in Christ, which Paul described in the first half of the letter.

> **Syntactical Nugget**: What does the prepositional phrases "with all humility and gentleness" (μετὰ πάσης ταπεινοφροσύνης καὶ πραΰτητος) and "with patience" (μετὰ μακροθυμίας) modify? It is possible that the prepositional phrases modify the following participle in verse 2. The NIV renders the verse: "Be completely humble and gentle; be patient, bearing with one another in love." However, these prepositional phrases are best understood modifying the infinitive περιπατῆσαι (v. 1b), expressing manner (BDAG, s.v. "μετά" A2f, p. 637). The prepositional phrases describe how believers should conduct their lives. First, a prepositional phrase follows the first participle ("bearing one another *in love*," v. 2b), suggesting that these prepositions modify the infinitive (Hoehner, 505). Second, these prepositional phrases are semantically parallel to the participles that follow (Best, 361–62; Arnold, 231; Hoehner, 505; Thielman, 253). Even though there are two prepositions, Paul lists three qualities: humility, gentleness, and patience. The first term ταπεινοφροσύνη ("humility") describes the action of putting the needs of others ahead of your own (cf. Phil. 2:3; BDAG, s.v. "ταπεινοφροσύνη," p. 989). The second term πραΰτης ("gentleness") refers to the lack of self-importance (BDAG, s.v. "πραΰτης," p. 861). The final term μακροθυμία ("patience") has the idea of "long-suffering," particularly within the context of provocation (BDAG, s.v. "μακροθυμία" 2a, pp. 612–13). The Old Testament uses this word to describe God's gracious patience toward sinners (Exod. 34:6; Arnold, 230).

4:2b ἀνεχόμενοι: The Greek word ἀνεχόμενοι is a masculine nominative plural present middle participle from the verb ἀνέχω that means "to endure" or "put up with" (BDAG, s.v. "ἀνέχω" 1a, p. 78). L&N suggests the gloss: "to be patient with" (L&N, 25.171). Best notes that the presence of ἀλλήλων implies reciprocity indicating a "dynamic attitude of love," rather than "an attitude of resignation to suffering, or a willingness to tolerate what others are doing" (Best, 364). In this case, "accepting one another" (HCSB), or "making allowance for each other's faults" (NLT), might be better than "putting up with" (LEB) or "bearing with one another" (NET, NIV, ESV, NRSV, CSB, NKJV; cf. RSV, CSB). **Syntactically**, ἀνεχόμενοι introduces a dependent participle clause. It functions adverbially modifying "to walk" (περιπατῆσαι, v. 1b). The genitive ἀλλήλων is the direct object of the participle ἀνεχόμενοι (BDF §176.1). **Semantically**, ἀνεχόμενοι functions as means: "*by the means of* putting up with one another in love" (W, 652). The prepositional phrase "in love" (ἐν ἀγάπῃ) modifies the participle. It could be rendered adverbially "lovingly" (Larkin, 69), but it might be best taken to express means describing how believers should bear one another (Lincoln, 236; Hoehner, 510). Believers walk worthy of their calling by bearing up one another with love. Most English translations render the preposition as "in" (ESV, RSV, NRSV, NIV, NET, CSB, HCSB, NASB, NKJV, KJV); the NLT translates it causal: "because of your love."

> **Grammatical Nugget**: How do the participles ἀνεχόμενοι and σπουδάζοντες function? Some commentators argue that the participles ἀνεχόμενοι and σπουδάζοντες (v. 3a) are imperative participles since they are nominative while the subject of the infinitive is accusative (ὑμᾶς) (Lincoln, 235; Barth, 427; BDF §468.2; Moule, 105; Robertson, 946; cf. NIV, NLT, GNT). Wallace argues that these should be considered adverbial, citing Robertson on the issue: a participle that can be connected to a finite verb should not be considered imperatival (W, 650; cf. Robertson, 1134). The difficulty with taking these participles as adverbial is the case—we would expect them to be in the accusative case to agree with ὑμᾶς, the subject of the infinitive (v. 1a). Wallace argues that we find the nominative at this point as a *construction ad sensum* (construction according to sense). Rather than following the strict grammar rules, the nominative participles modify complete verbal idea expressed with both the indicative and infinitive along with the implied nominative subject (W, 652; cf. Hoehner, 510; Arnold, 230–31).

4:3a σπουδάζοντες: The Greek word σπουδάζοντες is a masculine nominative plural present active participle from the verb σπουδάζω that means "to be zealous," "take pains," or "make every effort" (BDAG, s.v. "σπουδάζω" 3, p. 939). **Syntactically**, σπουδάζοντες introduces a dependent participle clause. It functions adverbially modifying the infinitive in verse 1 "to walk" (περιπατῆσαι). **Semantically**, σπουδάζοντες functions as means: "*by the means of making every effort* to keep the unity*." Modern translations render the phrase as "eager to keep the unity" (ESV, RSV) or "making every effort" (NRSV, NET, CSB). The NIV and NLT render the participle as an imperative, though it is best understood adverbially (see Grammatical Nugget at 4:2b).

τηρεῖν: The Greek word τηρεῖν is a present active infinitive from the verb τηρέω that means "to keep" or "hold," that is, to hold something so as not lose it (BDAG, s.v. "τηρέω" 2c, p. 1002). Most English versions translate the infinitive as "to keep"; the ESV translates it as "to maintain" (cf. RSV, NRSV). Perhaps the NASB renders it best: "to preserve" (cf. GNT). **Syntactically**, τηρεῖν introduces a dependent adverbial infinitive clause functioning as the direct object of the participle "being eager" (σπουδάζοντες). The phrase "the unity of the Spirit" (τὴν ἑνότητα τοῦ πνεύματος) functions as the direct object of the infinitive. **Semantically**, τηρεῖν functions as a complementary infinitive, completing the idea of the participle σπουδάζοντες: "being eager *to keep*" (cf. CSB, NIV, NET, NLT, NKJV, KJV) or "*to maintain*" (ESV, NRSV, RSV; W, 598–99). The present tense is a customary present describing an ongoing state (W, 521–22). Paul wants this attitude to be habitual within the community. The prepositional phrase "in the bonds of peace" (ἐν τῷ συνδέσμῳ τῆς εἰρήνης) could express means: "*through* the bond of peace" (NIV, CSB; cf. HCSB). However, since the Spirit creates this unity, the phrase best expresses sphere: "*in* the bonds of peace" (Hoehner, 512). The genitive τοῦ πνεύματος ("the Spirit") could be subjective: "unity that the Spirit gives" (Thielman, 255) or production: "unity *produced* by the Spirit" (W, 105). Regardless, this unity comes from the Spirit.

4:4a [ἐστίν]: The Greek word ἐστίν is third-person singular present active indicative from the verb εἰμί that means "is" (BDAG, s.v. "εἰμί" 1, pp. 282–83). Most English versions translate the verb: "There is" (ESV, NET, NIV, RSV, NRSV, HCSB, NASB, KJV, NKJV; BDF §127.5). **Syntactically**, the ellipsis [ἐστίν] is the main verb of the independent asyndeton clause. The subject is implied. The predicate nominative is "one body" (ἓν σῶμα). **Semantically**, the ellipsis [ἐστίν] simply makes an assertion: "there is one body." The Greek word σῶμα ("body") refers to a united group of people (BDAG, s.v. "σῶμα" 5, p. 984), in this instance the church (Eph. 1:23; 2:16; 5:30). The ellipsis along with the assertion emphasizes the unity of the group.

> **Syntactical Nugget:** How does this section (4:4–6) relate to the wider context? The significant problem with verses 4–6 is that no conjunction connects it to the wider context. In this section, Paul lists seven clauses: six of them are verbless and five are asyndetic. The repetition of the adjective εἷς along with the omission of the verb emphasizes the unity of the church. Most commentators argue that this section loosely serves as the basis of Paul's exhortation for unity that he gives in verses 1–3 and looks forward to the next section where he discusses the diversity of gifts (vv. 7–11) (Best, 366–67; Arnold, 232; Lincoln, 238; Fee, 2007, 354–56).

4:4b καί: The Greek word καί is a conjunction that means "and" (BDAG, s.v. "καί" 1bα, p. 494). **Syntactically**, καί introduces an independent conjunctive clause: "*and* there is one Spirit" (καὶ ἓν πνεῦμα). **Semantically**, καί is a coordinating connective: "and" (ESV, NET, NIV, RSV, NRSV, HCSB, CSB, NKJV, KJV, NASB). The clause gives a second item of the list Paul began in verse 4a; there one body and there is also one Spirit.

[ἐστίν]: The Greek word ἐστίν is third-person singular present active indicative from the verb εἰμί that means "is" (BDAG, s.v. "εἰμί" 1, pp. 282–83).

Most English versions omit the ellipsis at this point and treat the clause as
a compound predicate nominative: "There is one body *and one Spirit*" (ESV,
NET, NIV, RSV, NRSV, HCSB, CSB, NASB, NKJV, KJV). **Syntactically**, the ellipsis
[ἐστίν] is the main verb of the independent conjunctive clause introduced by
καί: "and there is one Spirit" (καὶ ἓν πνεῦμα). The predicate nominative is
"one Spirit" (ἓν πνεῦμα). **Semantically**, the ellipsis [ἐστίν] simply makes an
assertion: "there is one Spirit" (BDF §127.5) The Greek word πνεῦμα ("Spirit") refers to the Holy Spirit (BDAG, s.v. "πνεῦμα" 5dβ, p. 835). Throughout
Ephesians, Paul describes a relationship between the Spirit and the body. In
Ephesians 1, he states that the Spirit is the down payment for our promised
inheritance (Eph. 1:13–14). In Ephesians 2, he describes the church as a dwelling place for God—a temple—held together by the Spirit (Eph. 2:22). In the
immediate context, Paul describes the Spirit as the source for the unity within
the church (Eph. 4:3).

4:4c καθώς: The Greek word καθώς is a conjunction that means "as" or "just as" in
this context (BDAG, s.v. "καθώς" 1, p. 493). **Syntactically**, καθώς introduces
a dependent conjunctive clause: "*just as* you have also been called into one
hope of your calling" (καθὼς καὶ ἐκλήθητε ἐν μιᾷ ἐλπίδι τῆς κλήσεως
ὑμῶν). The clause functions adverbially modifying the implied verb ἐστίν
(v. 4b). **Semantically**, καθώς can express cause, but most likely functions as a
comparative conjunction: "just as" (ESV, NET, NIV, NRSV, RSV, HCSB, CSB, NASB,
NKJV). The believer is called into one hope the same way they were called into
one body and one Spirit (Best, 367; Arnold, 233). By inserting the conjunctive
καθώς, Paul breaks the repetition that runs through verses 4–6. By inserting
the prepositional phrase, Paul places emphasis on this clause.

ἐκλήθητε: The Greek word ἐκλήθητε is a second-person plural aorist passive
indicative from the verb καλέω that means "to call" in the sense of receiving a
special benefit or experience (BDAG, s.v. "καλέω" 4, pp. 503–4). **Syntactically**, ἐκλήθητε functions as the main verb of the dependent conjunctive clause
introduced by καθώς. The subject of the verb is implied: "you," referring to
the readers. **Semantically**, ἐκλήθητε is a constative aorist: "you were called"
(ESV, RSV, NRSV, NIV, CSB, HCSB, NASB, NKJV, KJV). It describes the action of the
verb as a whole (W, 557–58). The passive verb is a divine passive. Even though
the voice obscures the actor, God is the one who called the believer. The prepositional phrase "in one hope of your calling" (ἐν μιᾷ ἐλπίδι τῆς κλήσεως
ὑμῶν) modifies the verb "you were called." The verb along with the cognate
noun alludes to verse 1b. The preposition expresses sphere (Turner[1], 262–63).
Due to the verb, most English versions translate the prepositional phrase as
"you were called *to* one hope" (ESV, NET, NIV, RSV, NRSV, HCSB, CSB). The genitive τῆς κλήσεως is best understood as subjective: "*your calling gives* hope"
(Arnold, 233; Hoehner, 516). There is an eschatological element to this hope.

Before coming to Christ, these Gentile believers were without hope (Eph. 2:12). In Ephesians 1:18, Paul prays that they come to know the hope of God's call. This call looks forward to God bringing all things under the authority of Christ (Eph. 1:9–10) and ultimately inheriting the kingdom (Eph. 5:5) (Hoehner, 516; Lincoln, 239; Arnold, 233–34).

4:5a [ἐστίν]: The Greek word ἐστίν is third-person singular present active indicative from the verb εἰμί that means "is" (BDAG, s.v. "εἰμί" 1, pp. 282–83). Most English versions omit the ellipsis at this point, alluding to the verbal idea from verse 4a and translate the phrase simply as "one Lord" (ESV, NIV, NET, RSV, NRSV, KJV, NKJV, NASB, HCSB). The NLT begins a new sentence with verse 5 and includes the assumed verb: "There is one Lord" (cf. GNT). This is the fourth clause in the series focusing on the unity of the body. This is the first of three asyndeton clauses in verse 5. **Syntactically**, the ellipsis [ἐστίν] is the main verb of the independent asyndeton clause. The subject is implied. The predicate nominative is "one Lord" (εἷς κύριος). **Semantically**, the ellipsis [ἐστίν] simply makes an assertion: "there is one Lord" (BDF, §127.5). The passage alludes to Deuteronomy 6:4: "Hear Israel, The Lord, our God, the Lord is one" (ἄκουε, Ισραηλ, κύριος ὁ θεὸς ἡμῶν κύριος εἷς ἐστιν). Deuteronomy 6:4 refers to the Father. The text was an important confession emphasizing the monotheism of the Jewish people; however, Paul seems to refer to Christ (cf. 4:1). In verse 6, he will point to the Father. By applying this classic Jewish text to Christ, Paul makes a significant christological point (cf. 1 Cor. 8:6; Fee, 2018, 29–32).

4:5b [ἐστίν]: The Greek word ἐστίν is third-person singular present active indicative from the verb εἰμί that means "is" (BDAG, s.v. "εἰμί" 1, pp. 282–83). Most English versions omit the ellipsis, alluding to the verbal idea from verse 4a and translate the phrase as "one faith" (ESV, NIV, NET, RSV, NRSV, KJV, NKJV, NASB, HCSB). This is the fifth clause in the series. This is the second of three asyndeton clauses in verse 5. **Syntactically**, the ellipsis [ἐστίν] is the main verb of the independent asyndeton clause. The subject is implied. The predicate nominative is "one faith" (μία πίστις). **Semantically**, the ellipsis [ἐστίν] simply makes an assertion: "there is one faith" (BDF §127.5). The referent is the Christian faith—the content of belief, not one's personal trust. This is a common use of the word. Paul will use the term similarly in Ephesians 4:13. In his other letters, he can talk about preaching the faith (Rom. 1:5; 10:8; Gal. 1:28). Paul's statement implies that there is a common set of convictions that believers shared (Arnold, 235; Best, 368–69).

4:5c [ἐστίν]: The Greek word ἐστίν is third-person singular present active indicative from the verb εἰμί that means "is" (BDAG, s.v. "εἰμί" 1, pp. 282–83). Most English versions omit the ellipsis, alluding to the verbal idea from verse

4a and translate the phrase as "one baptism" (ESV, NIV, NET, NRSV, KJV, NKJV, NASB, HCSB). This is the sixth clause in this series and the third of three asyndeton clauses in verse 5. **Syntactically**, the ellipsis [ἐστίν] is the main verb of the independent asyndeton clause. The subject is implied. The predicate nominative is "one baptism" (ἓν βάπτισμα). **Semantically**, the ellipsis [ἐστίν] simply makes an assertion: "there is one baptism" (BDF §127.5). Paul most likely has water baptism in mind—the Christian rite of initiation. The references point to the singular event that every believer has in common (Lincoln, 240). He probably envisions a baptism by the Spirit as well (cf. 1 Cor. 12:13). In 1 Corinthians 12, Paul describes each member of the Christian community as having different functions but unified in its goal (1 Cor. 12:14–31). He makes a similar argument in the next section. After this statement of unity, he will discuss the diverse roles that individual members play in order to build up the church (Eph. 4:7–13). In verse 5, he uses three nouns with different genders, requiring him to use different forms of εἷς. The change gives a rhetorical effect on this section of the confession.

4:6 [ἐστίν]: The Greek word ἐστίν is third-person singular present active indicative from the verb εἰμί that means "is" (BDAG, s.v. "εἰμί" 1, pp. 282–83). Most English versions omit the ellipsis, alluding to the verbal idea from verse 4a and translate the phrase as "one God and Father of all" (ESV, NIV, NET, RSV, NRSV, KJV, NKJV, NASB, HCSB). This is the final clause of the series. **Syntactically**, the ellipsis [ἐστίν] is the main verb of the independent asyndeton clause. The subject is implied. The predicate nominative is the phrase "one God and Father of all" (εἷς θεὸς καὶ πατὴρ πάντων). **Semantically**, the ellipsis [ἐστίν] simply makes an assertion: "there is one God and Father of all" (BDF §127.5). Paul shifts his normal pattern by adding καὶ πατήρ to the predicate nominative θεός: "God and Father." Paul refers to each member of the Trinity throughout this section: the Holy Spirit (v. 4b), Christ (v. 5a), and now the Father (v. 6a). In Ephesians, he refers to God as "God the Father" (Eph. 1:2; 6:23), simply as "Father" (Eph. 1:17; 2:18; 3:14), or as, as he does here, "God and Father" (Eph. 1:3; 4:6; 5:20). The genitive πάντων is a genitive of subordination: "Father *over* all" (W, 103–4). Most English versions translate it as "*of* all" to avoid the redundancy with the following prepositional phrase (v. 6b).

Grammatical Nugget: How does the article function in verse 6? Paul inserts the article before three prepositional phrases: ὁ ἐπὶ πάντων καὶ διὰ πάντων καὶ ἐν πᾶσιν. With the article, the prepositions function substantively (BDAG, s.v. "ὁ" 2e, p. 688; W, 236). Most English versions render the article as a relative pronoun: "who is" (ESV, NET, NIV, RSV, NRSV, HCSB, NASB, NKJV, KJV, CSB). The entire phrase is in apposition to θεός ("God"). The following prepositions give a further description of God's position. The first prepositional phrase, "over all" (ἐπὶ πάντων), signifies control (BDAG, s.v. "ἐπί" 9a, p. 365). The prepositional phrase describes God's omnipotence; his control extends over all things. The second prepositional phrase, "through all things" (διὰ πάντων), expresses agency (BDAG, s.v. "διά" A4bβ, p. 225). The preposition emphasizes origination. All things came about through him (cf. Eph. 3:9, 14–15). The final prepositional phrase, "in all" (ἐν πᾶσιν) expresses the idea of sphere, describing the unique relationship that God has with his creation.

Text-Critical Nugget: Does Paul end verse 6 with the pronoun ἡμῖν? A number of Western (D, F, G, latt) and Byzantine texts (K, L, 𝔐) insert the pronoun ἡμῖν at the end of the clause giving the sense that God is "in us all" (cf. MT; RP[2005]). If the insertion is original, then the adjective πᾶς surely refers to people (see Syntactical Nugget below). The Alexandrian text type solidly represents the omission (𝔓[46], ℵ, A, B, C, 33, 81, 104, 1739, 1881). Hoehner supports the insertion, arguing that the reading has geographical distribution (Hoehner, 519 n. 2). On internal grounds, the omission has better evidence. Besides being the harder, shorter reading, a scribe could have inserted the pronoun to limit the fatherhood of God. Without the pronoun, God could be construed as the Father of all, not just believers. Despite the geographical distribution of the reading with the pronoun, the omission is most likely original (Thielman, 261).

Syntactical Nugget: What does Paul refer to when he writes "all" in verse 6? Paul repeats the adjective πᾶς four times in verse 6: he uses the genitive form three times and the dative form once. All four occurrences could either be neuter or masculine. If they are masculine, Paul might be referring to "all people," particularly believers. If they are neuter, then Paul is referring to "all things," a reference to the created order. Hoehner argues for these adjectives as masculine and that Paul alludes to believers since he has already described God as the Father of the believers through adoption (Eph. 1:5; cf. 2:18, 22; Rom. 8:15; Gal. 4:6; Col. 1:2). This image coheres well with his statement that God rules over the church through Christ, the head (Eph. 1:20–23) (Hoehner, 519–20). On the other hand, throughout the letter, Paul has argued that God maintains control over all things (Eph. 1:10, 11, 22; 3:9, 15). Understanding πᾶς in this way seems to be more natural, particularly due to the syntactical force of the prepositions (Thielman, 259–60; Arnold, 236–37; see Grammatical Nugget at 4:6). This implies that God is over all things, through him all things came into being, and he is in all things. He works all things together to accomplish his will (Eph. 1:11).

4:7 δέ: The Greek word δέ is a conjunction that means "but" (BDAG, s.v. "δέ" 4a, p. 213). **Syntactically**, δέ is in the postpositive position introducing an independent conjunctive clause "*But* grace was given to each one of us according to the measure of the gift of Christ" ('Ενὶ δὲ ἑκάστῳ ἡμῶν ἐδόθη ἡ χάρις κατὰ τὸ μέτρον τῆς δωρεᾶς τοῦ Χριστοῦ). **Semantically**, δέ is a marker of contrast: "but" (ESV, NET, NIV, RSV, NRSV, NASB, NKJV, KJV). The HCSB translates the conjunction as "now" indicating a logical progression in Paul's argument; however, the conjunction marks a contrast between Paul's focus on the unity of the church on the one hand (vv. 1–6) and the diversity of gifts on the other (vv. 7–11).

ἐδόθη: The Greek word ἐδόθη is a third-person singular aorist passive indicative from the verb δίδωμι that means "to give" or "bestow" (BDAG, s.v. "δίδωμι" 17b, p. 243). **Syntactically**, ἐδόθη functions as the main verb of the independent conjunctive clause introduced by δέ. The subject is "grace" (ἡ χάρις). The indirect object is "to each one of us" ('Ενὶ δὲ ἑκάστῳ ἡμῶν), referring to believers. **Semantically**, Hoehner labels this as a gnomic aorist, describing the individual reception of the gift from God (Hoehner, 522; cf. Arnold, 246). However, the gnomic aorist refers to a generic event, not a specific event. Wallace notes that this usage is quite rare in the New Testament (W, 562). ἐδόθη is better understood as a constative aorist: "was given" (ESV, RSV, NRSV, CSB, HCSB, NET, NASB, NKJV), describing the action of the verb as a whole (W, 557–58). The verb is a divine passive, but the context indicates that Christ is the one who gives these gifts (cf. v. 11). The prepositional phrase "according to the measure of the gift of Christ" (κατὰ τὸ μέτρον τῆς δωρεᾶς τοῦ Χριστοῦ) modifies the verb. The preposition κατά expresses a standard (BDAG, s.v. "κατά" B5aγ, p. 512)—Christ gives this grace according to the measure (τὸ μέτρον). The genitive τῆς δωρεᾶς is best understood as a subjective genitive: "*the gift* establishes the measure" (Hoehner, 523). Finally, the genitive τοῦ Χριστοῦ expresses source: "the gift *from Christ*" (Hoehner, 523; Arnold, 246). Thielman states that "the phrase τῆς δωρεᾶς describes what is measured, and the phrase τοῦ Χριστοῦ explains who measures it: Christ gives 'grace' to each believer, and he does so in proportions appropriate to each gift" (Thielman, 264). Just as Paul received grace from God to proclaim the gospel (Eph. 3:2, 7, 8), the believer receives a similar gift.

4:8a δίο: The Greek word δίο is a conjunction that means "therefore" (BDAG, s.v. "δίο," p. 250). Most English versions translate the conjunction as "therefore" (ESV, NET, RSV, NRSV, NASB, NKJV). **Syntactically**, δίο introduces an independent conjunctive clause: "*therefore* it says" (δίο λέγει) **Semantically**, δίο is inferential (W, 673). The conjunctive clause introduces an Old Testament quotation that serves as the grounds for Paul's statement in verse 7. The NIV translates the clause: "This is why it says" (cf. NLT).

λέγει: The Greek word λέγει is a third-person singular present active indicative from the verb λέγω that means "to say" (BDAG, s.v. "λέγω" 1bη,

p. 589). **Syntactically**, λέγει functions as the main verb of the independent conjunctive clause introduced by διό. The subject is implied in the verb, literally: "it says" or "he says." Paul could have either Scripture in mind (cf. NLT; Hoehner, 524), or else God as the author of Scripture (cf. NKJV, KJV; W, 533). **Semantically**, λέγει functions as a perfective present. The force of the tense is that even though these Scriptures were communicated in the past, there are ongoing implications for the present hearers (W, 532–33).

Theological Nugget: Why does Paul change the text of Psalm 68:18 in verse 8? Paul cites Psalm 68:18 [LXX 67:19] to support his claim that believers have received grace from God. The passage provides the language for Paul's explanation of the gifts that God gives believers to do the work of the church (vv. 11–12). Paul cites the text with a number of differences. The first major change is the person of the verbs. The psalmist uses second-person verbs referring to God: "you ascended [ἀνέβης, עלית] … you captured [ᾐχμαλώτευσας, שבית] … you received [ἔλαβες, לקחת]. Paul begins the citation with a participle and uses third-person verbs: "ascending [ἀναβάς] … he captured [ᾐχμαλώτευσεν] … he gave [ἔδωκεν]." The subject is implied by the verb, but the context of Ephesians implies that Christ is the one who gives these gifts. The second change is that he shifts the singular dative ἀνθρώπῳ to the plural dative ἀνθρώποις and omits the preposition ἐν. The third major change is that Paul uses the verb "he gave" (ἔδωκεν) instead of the verb "you received" (ἔλαβες). Instead of humanity giving gifts to God, Christ gives gifts to human beings. We have marked the differences below:

Psalm 67:19:   ἀνέβης εἰς ὕψος,
                      <u>ᾐχμαλώτευσας</u> αἰχμαλωσίαν,
                      ἔλαβες δόματα <u>ἐν ἀνθρώπῳ</u>

Psalm 67:19:   having gone up into the heights,
                      <u>you took</u> prisoners into captivity,
                      you received gifts <u>among a man</u>

Ephesians 4:8:   ἀναβὰς εἰς ὕψος
                      <u>ᾐχμαλώτευσεν</u> αἰχμαλωσίαν,
                      <u>ἔδωκεν</u> δόματα <u>τοῖς ἀνθρώποις</u>.

                      Ephesians 4:8: having gone up into the heights,
                      <u>he took</u> prisoners into captivity,
                      he gave gives <u>to men</u>

Out of the options presented that might account for these changes, two seem to be the most dominant (see Taylor, 1991, 324–29 for a catalog of options).

The first possibility is that Paul relies on the Targum, an Aramaic translation of the psalm, that reads "you distribute gifts" instead of "you receive gifts." Even though the Targum is late it may rely on early Jewish interpretation. Jewish interpreters unanimously understood Moses as the one ascending to heaven, taking captive the torah, and having received it, gave it to humanity. If this is the case, then Paul might present Jesus's ascent and the distribution of the Spirit at Pentecost as a type of Moses (Lincoln, 243–44). The significant problem with this position is that besides the Targum, dated between the fourth and sixth century CE, there is no evidence of the change in verb (Thielman, 267). Second, there is no evidence that links Psalm 68 with Acts 2 or Pentecost. Third, there is no sharp polemic against Moses in Ephesians calling into question the typology (Gombis, 2005, 369–70). The second possibility is that Paul himself made the change. Paul takes advantage of the psalm's theme that God subjugated the enemies and develops the psalm's meaning to fit the context of Ephesians 4. Paul teases out the subjugation theme with the citation: "he took captives." He develops this theme in his interpretation when he refers to Christ "ascending above all the heavens, in order to fill all things," an allusion to Ephesians 1:20–23. Paul develops the theme of giving gifts with the repetition of the verb δίδωμι (vv. 7, 8, 11). Even though Paul may appear to contradict the original text of the psalm by changing the verb from "take" to "give," the thrust of the citation is consistent with the psalm's description of God's triumph over Israel's enemies and the blessings that come as a result (Thielman, 2007, 819–25; Thielman, 267–68; Arnold, 251–52).

4:8b ἀναβάς: The Greek word ἀναβάς is a masculine nominative singular aorist active participle from the verb ἀναβαίνω that means "to go up" or "ascend" (BDAG, s.v. "ἀναβαίνω" 1aβ, p. 58). **Syntactically**, ἀναβάς introduces a dependent participle clause. The participle clause "ascending to the heights" (Ἀναβὰς εἰς ὕψος) functions adverbially modifying the main verbs: "he captured" (ἠχμαλώτευσεν) and "he gave" (ἔδωκεν). **Semantically**, ἀναβάς functions as a temporal participle. Since both the participle and verb it modifies are aorist tense, the action is simultaneous: *"while ascending* on high" (W, 623–27). Most English translations render the participle as an indicative verb ("When he ascended," ESV, NET, NIV, RSV, NRSV, HCSB, NASB, NKJV, KJV). The preposition εἰς expresses location or movement toward a location: "ascending *to* the heights" (BDAG, s.v. "εἰς" 1aα, p. 289). The Greek word ὕψος ("height") is a euphemism for heaven (Luke 1:78; 24:49) (BDAG, s.v. "ὕψος" 1b, p. 1045). The Old Testament uses the term in the same way to refer to heaven (Pss. 17:17 [MT 18:17]; 101:20 [MT 102:20]).

4:8c ἠχμαλώτευσεν: The Greek word ἠχμαλώτευσεν is a third-person singular aorist active indicative from the verb αἰχμαλωτεύω that means "to capture" or "captive" in reference to warfare (BDAG, s.v. "αἰχμαλωτεύω," p. 31). The Greek term αἰχμαλωτεύω is a *hapax legomenon*. **Syntactically**, ἠχμαλώτευσεν is the main verb of the independent asyndeton clause: "he took captives" (ἠχμαλώτευσεν αἰχμαλωσίαν). The subject is implied in the verb: "he." The direct object is "captives" (αἰχμαλωσίαν). In the original context of the psalm, God captures the enemies of Israel; in this context, the subject refers to Jesus taking captive the evil forces at work in the world today—those described as the enemies of Christ in Ephesians (cf. Eph. 1:20–22; 2:2; 6:11–12) (Arnold, 251; Thielman, 268; Lincoln, 242). The direct object is "captives" (αἰχμαλωσίαν). **Semantically**, ἠχμαλώτευσεν is a constative aorist: "he took captives." The tense describes the action of the verb as a whole (W, 557–58). The accusative αἰχμαλωσίαν ("prisoners of war" or "captive," BDAG, s.v. "αἰχμαλωσία" 2, p. 31) functions as a cognate accusative emphasizing the result (Robertson, 477–79; W, 189–90). Literally, the phrase is: "he captured captives." Several English versions avoid the redundancy with a different translation of the verb: "he led a host of captives" (ESV, RSV; cf. NLT) or "he took many captives (NIV; cf. GNT).

4:8d ἔδωκεν: The Greek word ἔδωκεν is a third-person singular aorist active indicative from the verb δίδωμι that means "to give" or "bestow" (BDAG, s.v. "δίδωμι" 17b, p. 243). **Syntactically**, ἔδωκεν is the main verb of the independent asyndeton clause: "he gave gifts to men" (ἔδωκεν δόματα τοῖς ἀνθρώποις). This clause is parallel to the previous asyndeton clause. The subject is implied in the verb: "he." The direct object is "gifts" (δόματα). The indirect object is "men" (τοῖς ἀνθρώποις), a reference to humanity (BDAG, s.v. "ἄνθρωπος" 1c, p. 31.1.c): "to *people*" (CSB, HCSB). The psalmist had the nation of Israel in mind. In the original context of the psalm, God is the subject of the verb; the gifts refer to the tribute that comes from Israel's enemies. In this context, the subject is Jesus giving spiritual gifts to the church, which Paul specifies in verse 11. Some English versions translate the indirect object as "to *his people*" (NRSV, NIV, NLT). **Semantically**, ἔδωκεν functions as a constative aorist. The action of the verb is reported as a summary (W, 557–58). As in verse 8c, the accusative δόματα functions as a cognate accusative: "he gave gifts" (Larkin, 75).

4:9a δέ: The Greek word δέ is a conjunction that means "but" (BDAG, s.v. "δέ" 2, p. 213). **Syntactically**, δέ is in the postpositive position introducing an independent conjunctive clause "Now what does 'he ascended' mean" (τὸ δὲ ἀνέβη τί ἐστιν). **Semantically**, δέ is explanatory. The conjunction introduces Paul's exposition of the Old Testament text (W, 238). Several English versions translate the conjunction as "now" (NET, LEB, NASB, NKJV, KJV, GNT) or "but" (CSB, HCSB). Some English versions give a more dynamic translation: "In saying" (ESV, RSV), "When it says" (NRSV), or "Notice that" (NLT).

ἐστίν: The Greek word ἐστίν is a third-person singular present active indicative from the verb εἰμί that means "to be"; the verb is commonly used with explanations: "that means" or in a question: "what does it mean?" (BDAG, s.v. "εἰμί" 2cα, p. 284). Most English versions translate the phrase as "what does it mean"; the KJV renders the phrase as "what is it?" **Syntactically,** ἐστίν is the main verb of the independent conjunctive clause introduced by δέ. The interrogative pronoun "what" (τί) functions as the predicate nominative. Due to the article, the verb "he ascended" (τὸ ἀνέβη) functions as a substantive (BDF §267; W, 237–38); in this case, it functions as the subject of the sentence. Most English versions render the construction as an indicative verb in quotation marks: "In saying, 'He ascended,' what does it mean" (ESV; cf. RSV, NRSV, NASB) or "What does 'he ascended' mean" (NIV, CSB, HCSB; cf. NET). Paul shifts from the participle (ἀναβάς, v. 8b) to the indicative to correspond with the indicative verb in verse 9b: "he descended" (κατέβη). He could use the phrase to refer to the first part of the quotation (v. 8b) (Arnold, 252), but he most likely refers to the entire quotation (W, 238). **Semantically,** ἐστίν is an equative verb. It is a gnomic present describing a timeless fact. The verb introduces Paul's explanation of the psalm.

4:9b εἰ μή: The construction εἰ μή expresses a contrast or an exception (BDAG, s.v. "εἰ" 6iβ, p. 278; L&N, 89.131). Most English versions render the construction as "but" (ESV, RSV, NRSV, NKJV, KJV) or "except" (NET, NIV, HCSB, CSB, NASB). **Syntactically,** εἰ μή introduces a dependent conjunctive clause. **Semantically,** εἰ μή introduces an exception. The clause introduces Paul's interpretation of the psalm by responding to the question that he raises in verse 9a. Following an interrogative (v. 9a), the exceptive clause is emphasized (Runge, 2010, 85).

ὅτι: The Greek word ὅτι is a conjunction that means "that" in this context (BDAG, s.v. "ὅτι" 2b, p. 732). **Syntactically,** ὅτι introduces a dependent conjunctive clause "*that* also he descended to the lower parts, namely the earth" (καὶ κατέβη εἰς τὰ κατώτερα μέρη τῆς γῆς). The entire clause functions as the subject of an implied equative verb (ἐστίν) in the clause introduced by εἰ μή (Larkin, 76). **Semantically,** ὅτι functions as a substantival clause (W, 453–54).

κατέβη: The Greek word κατέβη is a third-person singular aorist active indicative from the verb καταβαίνω that means "to come down" (BDAG, s.v. "καταβαίνω" 1αδ, p. 514). **Syntactically,** κατέβη functions as the main verb of the dependent conjunctive clause introduced by ὅτι. The subject is implied by the verb: "he," referring to Christ. **Semantically,** κατέβη is a constative aorist: "he descended" (NIV, NET, HCSB, CSB, NKJV, KJV). It describes the action of the verb as a whole (W, 557–58). The action of the verb is reported in summary fashion with no interest in the beginning or end of the action. The prepositional phrase "to the lower parts, namely the earth" (εἰς τὰ κατώτερα μέρη τῆς γῆς) describes the movement toward a location (BDAG, s.v. "εἰς" 1αα, p. 289). The prepositional phrase alludes to the Old Testament quotation in verse 8b, where the psalmist uses the preposition in the same way: "while ascending *on high*" (εἰς ὕψος). Instead of ascending to heaven, Paul states that Christ descended to the lower parts.

Text-Critical Nugget: Why does the MT insert πρῶτον after κατέβη? The majority of Byzantine manuscripts (K, L, 𝔐) insert πρῶτον after κατέβη. The reading clarifies the order of events since verse 9 refers to both the ascent and descent of Christ. If this reading is correct, then the descent came first. This reading is supported by some significant Alexandrian manuscripts (B, 104, 1175). The reading with the omission is found in significant Western (D, F, G) and Alexandrian (𝔓⁴⁶, ℵ, A, C, 33, 81, 1739, 1881) manuscripts. Besides having better external evidence, the reading with the omission is superior on internal grounds as well. It is doubtful that a scribe would have omitted the word making the text ambiguous.

Semantical Nugget: What is the relationship of the genitive τῆς γῆς to the head noun τὰ κατώτερα μέρη ("the lower parts of the earth")? There are two options for understanding the genitive construction—both giving different interpretations. The first option is that the genitive could be understood as a genitive of comparison: "regions lower *than the earth*" (Turner, 1965, 171). This interpretation suggests that Paul describes Christ's descent to Hades. Proponents for this view argue that this is the clearest way to understand the genitive construction. Paul's ancient audience would have had a category for journeys down to Hades. In fact, the earliest interpreters understood this to refer to Christ's descent to hell (Thielman, 270–72; Arnold, 253–54). The second option is that the genitive is in apposition (or epexegetical) giving an explanation of the head noun (Zerwick §45; BDF §167; W, 99–100): "into the lower regions, *namely* the earth" (cf. ESV, NET, NIV, NLT). If this is the case, it could refer to Christ's decent at Pentecost, through the distribution of the Spirit (Lincoln, 244–47; Harris, 1994, 198–214; Gombis, 2005, 367–80). The strength of this position is that the wider context focuses on spiritual gifts (v. 11). The problem with this position is the order of events in verse 10. The descent seems to come before the ascent. If the descent refers to Pentecost, we would anticipate Paul to invert the events in verse 10 since Pentecost came as a result of the ascension. Verse 10 also specifies that Jesus himself was the one who descended (ὁ καταβὰς αὐτός), not the Spirit. The third option is that the genitive could be understood as a genitive in apposition (similar to the second position). This reading points to Christ's descent to earth, namely his incarnation (Hoehner, 535–36; Barth, 433–34). The strength of this position is the order of the verbs. Paul states that he first descended and then ascended, suggesting that this refers to Christ's the incarnation, prior to his ascension. This also fits nicely with the theme of Christ's defeat of his enemies in the "heavenly places" (Eph. 1:10; 3:15; 4:10).

4:10a καταβάς: The Greek word καταβάς is a masculine nominative singular aorist active participle from the verb καταβαίνω that means "to come down," specifically to come down from heaven (BDAG, s.v. "καταβαίνω" 1aγ, p. 514). **Syntactically,** καταβάς is a substantival participle functioning as the subject of the main verb ἐστίν ("*He who descended* is"). Paul adds αὐτός to emphasize the subject (BDAG, s.v. "αὐτός" 1aα, p. 152). Some English translations render the phrase: "he who descended" (ESV, NIV) or render it as a predicate: "He who descended is he who also" (RSV; cf. NRSV, NASB, KJV). The NET translates the phrase: "he, the very one who descended." **Semantically,** καταβάς is a constative aorist: "descended" (ESV, RSV, NRSV, NIV, NET, CSB, HCSB, NASB, NKJV, KJV). It describes the action of the verb as a whole (W, 557–58).

ἐστίν: The Greek word ἐστίν is a third-person singular present active indicative from the verb εἰμί that means "to be" (BDAG, s.v. "εἰμί" 2cα, p. 284). **Syntactically,** ἐστίν functions as the main verb of the independent asyndeton clause. The subject is the substantival participle "the one who descended" (ὁ καταβάς). The predicate nominative is the following substantival participle "the one who ascended" (ὁ ἀναβάς). **Semantically,** ἐστίν is an equative. The one who descended is identical to the one who ascended.

ἀναβάς: The Greek word ἀναβάς is a masculine nominative singular aorist active participle from the verb ἀναβαίνω that means "to go up" or "ascend" (BDAG, s.v. "ἀναβαίνω" 1aβ, p. 58). **Syntactically,** ἀναβάς is a substantival participle functioning as the predicate nominative of the main verb "He who descended is" (ὁ καταβὰς αὐτός ἐστιν). The conjunction καί is most likely ascensive (W, 670–71). Most English versions translate it "also" (ESV, NET, RSV, HCSB, NASB, KJV, NKJV, CSB). **Semantically,** ἀναβάς is a constative aorist: "ascended" (ESV, RSV, NRSV, NIV, NET, CSB, HCSB, NASB, NKJV, KJV, NLT). It describes the action of the verb as a whole (W, 557–58). Paul's use of καταβαίνω and ἀναβαίνω create a chiastic structure (Larkin, 127): ἀνέβη (v. 9a), κατέβη (v. 9b), καταβάς (v. 10a), ἀναβάς (v. 10a). The preposition ὑπεράνω is an improper preposition (BDF §116.3) expressing location (BDF §215.2): "he ascended *high above* all of the heavens" (BDAG, s.v. "ὑπεράνω," p. 1032). Paul makes a similar statement in Ephesians 1 describing Christ seated in the heavenly places "high above [ὑπεράνω] all rulers, authorities, powers, and lords" (Eph. 1:21). Christ's placement alludes to the authority that God has given to Christ (Arnold, 255).

4:10b ἵνα: The Greek word ἵνα is a conjunction that means "that" in this context (BDAG, s.v. "ἵνα" 1aε, p. 475). **Syntactically,** ἵνα introduces a dependent conjunctive clause "*so that* he might fill all things" (ἵνα πληρώσῃ τὰ πάντα). The entire clause functions adverbially modifying the participle phrase "he who ascended" (ὁ ἀναβάς). **Semantically,** ἵνα expresses the purpose of the ascension (W, 472). Several English versions translate the conjunction as "in order to" (NET, NIV) or "so that" (NRSV, NASB, NLT).

πληρώσῃ: The Greek word πληρώσῃ is a third-person singular aorist active subjunctive from the verb πληρόω that means "to make full" or "fill" (BDAG, s.v. "πληρόω" 1a, p. 828). **Syntactically**, πληρώσῃ functions as the main verb of the dependent conjunctive clause introduced by ἵνα. The subject is implied by the verb: "he," referring to Christ. The indirect object is "all things" (τὰ πάντα), an allusion to Ephesians 1:23. **Semantically**, πληρώσῃ is a constative aorist: "might fill" (ESV, RSV, NRSV, HCSB, NASB, NKJV, KJV). The tense describes the action of the verb as a whole (W, 557–58).

4:11 καί: The Greek word καί is a conjunction that means "and" (BDAG, s.v. "καί" 1e, p. 494). **Syntactically**, καί introduces an independent conjunctive clause: "*and* he gave some to be apostles, and prophets, and evangelists, and shepherds and teachers" (καὶ αὐτὸς ἔδωκεν τοὺς μὲν ἀποστόλους, τοὺς δὲ προφήτας, τοὺς δὲ εὐαγγελιστάς, τοὺς δὲ ποιμένας καὶ διδασκάλους). The conjunction possibly connects the sentence to the main idea that Paul begins in verse 7: "Grace was given to each of us." A more likely possibility is that Paul connects the sentence to the second part of the quotation of Psalm 68:18 by repeating the verb "he gave" from verse 8 (ἔδωκεν). Both possibilities give further explanation of what Christ gave and ultimately go back to the concept of "Christ's gift" in verse 7. **Semantically**, Hoehner argues that the conjunction is explicative and suggests rendering it as "namely" (Hoehner, 540). However, it is probably best viewed as coordinating, continuing Paul's exposition (vv. 9–10) (Larkin, 77; Merkle, 127). Most English versions translate it as "and" (ESV, RSV, CSB, HCSB, NASB, NKJV, KJV) or "so" (NIV). The NET and NRSV omit the conjunction.

ἔδωκεν: The Greek word ἔδωκεν is a third-person singular aorist active indicative from the verb δίδωμι that means "to give" or "appoint" (BDAG, s.v. "δίδωμι" 7, p. 242). **Syntactically**, ἔδωκεν functions as the main verb of the independent conjunctive clause introduced by καί. The subject is the third-person personal pronoun: "he" (αὐτός). By including the pronoun, Paul places emphasis on Christ as the giver of gifts. The English versions bring out this emphasis in a number of different ways: "It was he who gave" (NET; cf. GNT); "So Christ himself gave" (NIV); "And he personally gave" (HCSB); "And he himself gave" (NKJV, CSB). The NLT conveys the idea of gifts: "Now these are the gifts Christ gave to the church." The phrase "apostles, prophets, evangelists, shepherds and teachers" (τοὺς μὲν ἀποστόλους, τοὺς δὲ προφήτας, τοὺς δὲ εὐαγγελιστάς, τοὺς δὲ ποιμένας καὶ διδασκάλους) functions as the direct object of the verb. The use of μὲν … δέ coordinates a series of items (BDAG, s.v. "μέν" 1c, p. 630). The article could make the noun definite ("he

gave the apostles, the prophets, the evangelists, the shepherds and teachers,"
ESV, NIV, NLT; Larkin, 78; Lincoln, 249). However, it is best to understand the
article as a pronoun ("he gave *some* to be apostles, *some* prophets, *some* evangelists, *some* pastors and teachers," HCSB, cf. NET, RSV, NRSV, NASB, NKJV, KJV;
W, 212–13; Porter, 113; Barth, 435). This option gives the list a distributive
sense alluding to verse 7 and the concept of Christ giving grace to the believer
according to the measure of the gift. **Semantically**, ἔδωκεν is a constative
aorist: "gave" (ESV, NRSV, NIV, NET, CSB, HCSB, NASB, NKJV, KJV). It describes
the action of the verb as a whole (W, 557–58). After his ascension, Christ gave
these offices as gifts for the church. Verse 11 begins a long sentence describing the purpose of these gifts—so that the church, the body of Christ, might
reach maturity. There is no structural marker in verse 12—it contains three
prepositional phrases that convey the purpose for Christ giving these gifts.
The structure of the prepositions is debated (see Syntactical Nugget below).

Syntactical Nugget: What is the best way to understand the relationship
between shepherds and teachers in verse 11? The last two items of the
accusative phrase: "shepherds and teachers." (τοὺς δὲ ποιμένας καὶ
διδασκάλους) fit the Granville-Sharp construction (article-noun-καί-
noun). The construction raises the question about the identity of the
group. Paul could refer to a single group who are both shepherds and
teachers. Or else he could refer to two distinct groups. Since the nouns
are plural, the phrase does not strictly fit the Granville Sharp construction, but it can denote some relationship between the two groups. In the
New Testament, pastors had a teaching function, but not all teachers were
pastors (Hoehner, 545; Lincoln, 250). The first three groups (apostles,
prophets, and evangelists) have a clear communicative role within the
church. The construction suggests that shepherds (or pastors) have a similar teaching role within their community (Thielman, 276–77). Because of
this, we might identify the first group is a subset of the second: "pastors
and *other teachers*" (W, 284).

Lexical Nugget: What were the roles of these leaders in the church? The
list of Christian leaders highlights the diversity within the Christian community. The community is unified (vv. 4–6), but the gift of the Spirit is expressed a number of different ways. First, Paul states that Christ appointed
"apostles" (ἀπόστολος). Within the context of Ephesians, Paul describes
the apostles as the foundation of the church, Jesus Christ himself being
the cornerstone (Eph. 2:20; cf. Heb. 3:1). In Ephesians 3, he describes his
apostolic role as proclaiming the gospel that he received from God (Eph.
3:5, 7–8). Second, Christ gave "prophets" (προφήτης). Paul most likely has
New Testament prophets in mind here since they edify the church (cf. Eph.
3:5). Just like Old Testament prophets, these probably served a predictive

role (cf. Acts 21:10–11). However, their main role was to build up the Christian body (1 Cor. 14:3). Within the context of Ephesians, Paul describes prophets as founding the church along with the apostles. Third, Christ gave "evangelists" (εὐαγγελιστής), those who proclaim the good news revealed to the apostles and prophets. Outside of the biblical literature, an evangelist had a religious connotation: one who proclaimed ocular visions (LSJ, s.v. "εὐαγγελιστής," p. 705). The word is used three times in the New Testament. Luke refers to Philip as an evangelist (Acts 21:6). And Paul calls Timothy to "do the work of an evangelist" (1 Tim. 4:5). The basic function of an evangelist is the proclamation of the gospel (cf. Eph. 1:13; 2:17; 3:6, 8; 6:15, 19). Within the scope of Ephesians, the role of the evangelist overlaps with the apostle and the prophet (Eph. 3:8–12). Fourth, Christ gave "shepherds" (ποιμήν). Ephesians 4:11 is the only text that describes Christian leaders as "shepherds." Hebrews refers to Christ as the great shepherd (Heb. 13:20; cf. John 10:11). In Acts 20, while addressing the Ephesian elders Paul refers to the Christian community as a flock (Acts 20:28–29). Peter gives a similar exhortation to the elders, urging them to take care of the flock that God entrusted to them (1 Pet. 5:2–3). Even though the term is not present in the New Testament, the concept of a pastor as a shepherd runs throughout the literature. Fifth, Christ gave "teachers" (διδάσκαλος). Teachers convey instruction. It appears that they played a formal role in the leadership structure of the New Testament church (Acts 13:1; 1 Cor. 12:28; James 3:1). Later in Ephesians, Paul will refer to "learning Christ" (Eph. 4:20–21). For Paul, this instruction about Christ includes an ethical dimension (Eph. 4:25–32).

Syntactical Nugget: What is the structure of the three prepositional phrases in verse 12? Paul continues his exposition in verse 12 with three additional prepositional phrases. The structure of the prepositional phrases is debated. The phrases could be parallel, each phrase modifying the main verb of the sentence: "he gave" (ἔδωκεν, v. 11):

v. 11: καὶ αὐτὸς <u>ἔδωκεν</u> …

    <u>πρὸς</u> τὸν καταρτισμὸν τῶν ἁγίων
    <u>εἰς</u> ἔργον διακονίας,
    <u>εἰς</u> οἰκοδομὴν τοῦ σώματος τοῦ Χριστοῦ

v. 11: "and he <u>gave</u> …

    <u>for</u> the equipping of the saints
    <u>for</u> the work of ministry,
    <u>in</u> the building up of the body of Christ"

By understanding the structure this way, the prepositions state that Christ gave apostles, prophets, evangelists, shepherds, and teachers for the purpose of equipping the saints, the work of ministry, and the building up of the body of Christ. This implies that those Christian leaders equip the saints *and* do the work of service. By inserting a comma between the first and second prepositional phrase, the KJV could be construed this way. Lincoln argues for this view by noting that Paul regularly uses prepositions in coordinating manner (Eph. 1:3, 20–21; 2:7; 4:13, 14) (Lincoln, 253–54). This reading keeps the emphasis on Christ's gift of the Christian leaders listed in verse 11.

Another option is that the prepositional phrases could be subordinating. The first phrase expresses the purpose of Christ giving these apostles, prophets, evangelists, shepherds, and teachers. The second phrase expresses the purpose for the equipping of the saints:

v. 11: καὶ αὐτὸς <u>ἔδωκεν</u> ...
    <u>πρὸς</u> τὸν καταρτισμὸν τῶν ἁγίων
     <u>εἰς</u> ἔργον διακονίας
      <u>εἰς</u> οἰκοδομὴν τοῦ σώματος τοῦ Χριστοῦ

v. 11: "and he <u>gave</u> ...
    <u>for</u> the equipping of the saints
     <u>for</u> the work of ministry
      <u>in</u> the building up of the body of Christ"

If the prepositional phrases are subordinating, then the purpose of equipping the saints (v. 12a) is for the saints to do the work of ministry (v. 12b). The strength of this understanding is that Paul changes the preposition from πρός to εἰς. Also, by inserting the genitive τῶν ἁγίων at the end of verse 12a, he may underscore the shift. Best notes that if the prepositions were parallel, then Paul would invert the phrases, putting the more general statement first (Best, 397–98). Finally, this understanding takes seriously the fact that grace has been given to all believers (v. 7) rather than those leaders listed in verse 11 (Barth, 178–81; Hoehner, 548–49; Thielman, 278–80; Arnold, 262–63). Most English translations present the prepositions this way, by omitting the comma between the two clauses (ESV, NET, NIV, RSV, NRSV, HCSB, NASB, NKJV). Even though the syntax may not be clear, understanding the structure of the prepositions like this coheres best with Paul's larger context.

The first phrase, "for the building up of the saints," (πρὸς τὸν καταρτισμὸν τῶν ἁγίων) expresses the purpose of Christ giving these gifts (BDAG, s.v. "πρός" 3cα, p. 874)—so that the saints can be equipped. Most English versions render the preposition as "to" (ESV, NET, NIV, RSV, NRSV) or "for" (HCSB, NASB, NKJV, KJV). The Greek word καταρτισμός expresses the idea of training or discipline (LSJ, s.v. "καταρτισμός," p. 910). The genitive τῶν ἁγίων is objective—the saints are equipped. To bring out the objective sense of the genitive, some English versions convert the head noun to an infinitive: "to equip" (ESV, NET, CSB, NIV, NLT). The NIV clarifies the referent to "the saints" (τῶν ἁγίων) by rendering it "his people."

The second prepositional phrase, "for the work of service," (εἰς ἔργον διακονίας) expresses the purpose or goal of the equipping of the saints (BDAG, s.v. "εἰς" 4f, p. 290). The genitive διακονίας is a genitive of apposition: "for the work, *namely service*" (W, 94–100).

The third prepositional phrase, "for the building up of the body of Christ," (εἰς οἰκοδομὴν τοῦ σώματος τοῦ Χριστοῦ) expresses either purpose or goal (BDAG, s.v. "εἰς" 4f, p. 290). The phrase can be parallel to the second prepositional phrase providing a second goal for the ministry of the saints (Arnold, 263–64). The NET translates the phrase as "the work of ministry, *that is*, to build up the body of Christ." However, it is best to understand it as expressing a final goal or purpose modifying the second prepositional phrase. The goal of the work is to build up the body of Christ (Hoehner, 548–49). The genitive τοῦ σώματος is an objective genitive referring to the church (cf. Eph. 1:23; 2:16; 5:23, 30).

4:13a μέχρι: The Greek word μέχρι is a conjunction that means "until" (BDAG, s.v. "μέχρι" 2b, p. 644). **Syntactically**, μέχρι introduces a dependent conjunctive clause "*until* we all attain the unity of the faith" (μέχρι καταντήσωμεν οἱ πάντες εἰς τὴν ἑνότητα τῆς πίστεως). The entire clause functions adverbially modifying the main verb in verse 11: "he gave" (ἔδωκεν). **Semantically**, μέχρι functions as a temporal marker indicating the continuation of an activity up to a specific point; the conjunction implicitly expresses goal as well. The work of the church will continue until some point in the future when the church will attain unity of faith (Arnold, 264).

καταντήσωμεν: The Greek word καταντήσωμεν is a first-person plural aorist active subjunctive from the verb καταντάω that means "to arrive at" or "attain to something"; the verb carries the notion of possession (BDAG, s.v. "καταντάω" 2a, p. 523). In Acts, Luke uses the term in travel narratives to describe the arrival to a new location (Acts 16:1; 18:19, 24; 20:15; 21:7; 25:13; 28:13). Paul can use the term eschatologically looking forward to the resurrection (Phil. 3:11; cf. Acts 26:7; 1 Cor. 10:11). Most English versions translate the verb as "attain" (ESV, NET, RSV, NASB) or "reach" (NIV, HCSB, CSB). **Syntactically**, καταντήσωμεν functions as the main verb of the dependent conjunctive clause introduced by μέχρι. The subject of the verb is implied by the verb: "we." The nominative οἱ πάντες modifies the implied subject: "we all," referring to all of God's people, including Paul (BDAG, s.v. "πᾶς" 4dα, p. 784; ESV, NIV, NET, RSV, HCSB, CSB, NASB, NKJV, KJV). **Semantically**, καταντήσωμεν is a constative aorist: "attain" (ESV). It describes the action of the verb as a whole (W, 557–58). The aorist tense along with μέχρι describes an undetermined, but certain event in the future (BDF §383.2)—there is no indication when the church will arrive at this unity, but it will certainly occur.

Semantical Nugget: What do the following three prepositional phrases related to verse 13 mean? Three prepositional phrases, each beginning with the preposition εἰς, state the goal, marking what the church will attain. The phrases are parallel, modifying the verb: "we will attain" (καταντήσωμεν). The phrases describe complementary, but distinct, goals (Larkin, 80; Best, 399; Lincoln, 255; Arnold, 264).

καταντήσωμεν …
<u>εἰς</u> τὴν ἑνότητα τῆς πίστεως καὶ τῆς ἐπιγνώσεως τοῦ υἱοῦ τοῦ θεοῦ
<u>εἰς</u> ἄνδρα τέλειον
<u>εἰς</u> μέτρον ἡλικίας τοῦ πληρώματος τοῦ Χριστοῦ

we attain …
<u>to</u> the unity of the faith and the knowledge of the Son of God
<u>to</u> the complete person
<u>to</u> the measure of maturity of the fullness of Christ

The first goal is "unity of faith and knowledge of the Son of God." Paul has already described that unity within the church comes from the Spirit (Eph. 4:3). The genitive τῆς πίστεως is most likely a genitive of reference, referring to the Christian message (cf. v. 5). The following genitive τῆς ἐπιγνώσεως is also a genitive of reference. The Greek word ἐπίγνωσις means "knowledge" or "recognition"; it infers experiential knowledge (BDAG, s.v. "ἐπίγνωσις," p. 369). The genitive τοῦ υἱοῦ is an objective genitive: "knowledge *about* the Son of God," referring to Jesus Christ. Within a Jewish context, the title has messianic implications. The Davidic heir was known as God's son (2 Sam. 7:14; Ps. 2:7). Within a Gentile context, the emperor was known as a "son of God." Even though Paul regularly refers to Christ as "Son," he rarely uses the phrase "the Son of God" (Rom. 1:3–4; 2 Cor. 1:19; Gal. 2:20). Paul most likely has the Old Testament context in mind, but both he and his audience would have known that the phrase also refers to the emperor (see Lexical Nugget at 1:5a).

The second goal, introduced by εἰς, is that the church attains the status of "a mature person" (ἄνδρα τέλειον). The concept of a mature person contrasts the image of an infant, which Paul describes in verse 14. Throughout Ephesians, he develops the theme of the church as a "new person" (καινὸν ἄνθρωπον; 2:15; 4:24), which is probably the referent here (Hoehner, 555–56; Arnold, 265; Lincoln, 256; Best, 401–2). However, by changing the language, he shifts the image. Rather than referring to this person as "new," he calls it "complete" or "mature" (BDAG, s.v. "τέλειος" 2a, p. 995). He also uses a different noun: ἀνήρ, which refers to a fully grown man, in contrast to a boy (BDAG, s.v. "ἀνήρ" 1b, p. 79). The shift in language seems to focus on the growth of the church (Thielman, 281–82).

The third goal, again introduced by εἰς, is that the church reach the "measure of the stature of the fullness of Christ." The genitive ἡλικίας is in apposition: "to a measure, *namely* the stature of the fullness of Christ" (Larkin, 80–81; Merkle, 130). The Greek word ἡλικία is best understood as "stature" (BDAG, s.v. "ἡλικία" 3, p. 436; cf. Luke 2:52; Thielman, 282; ESV, NET, RSV, NRSV, HCSB, NASB, NKJV, KJV) rather than "maturity" (BDAG, s.v. "ἡλικία" 2, p. 436; Hoehner, 557) since Paul's point hinges on spatial dimensions. However, these images do not need to be mutually exclusive: a mature person will have a larger body size (Arnold, 403). The genitive τοῦ πληρώματος could be a genitive of reference, but is most likely a genitive in apposition: "the measure of stature, *namely* the fullness of Christ." (Hoehner, 557); τοῦ Χριστοῦ is possessive: "Christ's fullness." Arnold states: "Paul wants all believers not only to grow, but to attain the 'size' of Christ, that is, to reflect his virtues and likeness in their lives" (Arnold, 266). The entire genitive chain could be rendered: "to the measure which is Christ's full stature" (NET; cf. HCSB, CSB; Hoehner, 557).

4:14 ἵνα: The Greek word ἵνα is a conjunction that means "that" in this context to denote purpose (BDAG, s.v. "ἵνα" 1aε, p. 475). **Syntactically**, ἵνα introduces a dependent conjunctive clause: "*so that* we are no longer infants" (ἵνα μηκέτι ὦμεν νήπιοι). The clause could modify the verb "we all attain" (καταντήσωμεν, v. 13) (Muddimann, 2001, 205). However, it is best viewed as a parallel clause modifying the main verb in verse 11: "he gave" (ἔδωκεν) (Hoehner, 559–60). **Semantically**, ἵνα expresses the purpose of the verb ἔδωκεν (W, 472). Christ gave the spiritual gifts so that we are no longer infants.

ὦμεν: The Greek word ὦμεν is a first-person plural present active subjunctive from the verb εἰμί that means "to be" (BDAG, s.v. "εἰμί" 2a, p. 283). **Syntactically**, ὦμεν functions as the main verb of the dependent conjunctive clause introduced by ἵνα. The subject is implied by the verb: "we," referring to the church. The adverb μηκέτι negates the clause. The predicate nominative is νήπιοι, which literally means "infant," but figuratively it means "immature," (BDAG, s.v. "νήπιος" 1bα, p. 671; cf. NLT). **Semantically**, ὦμεν functions as a customary present, describing an ongoing state (W, 521–22). According to Paul, Christ gave these gifts so that the church might no longer be immature.

κλυδωνιζόμενοι: The Greek word κλυδωνιζόμενοι is a masculine nominative plural present middle (deponent) participle from the verb κλυδωνίζομαι that means "to be tossed here and there by waves" (BDAG, s.v. "κλυδωνίζομαι," p. 550). The word is a *hapax legomenon*, appearing only once in the New Testament. The word is usually associated with a boat being carried by the motion of the waves (L&N, 16.12). Most English versions bring out the imagery of the word by including the phrase "by the waves" (ESV, NIV, HCSB, CSB, NASB; cf. NET), while other versions omit the phrase (RSV, NRSV, NKJV, KJV). **Syntactically**, κλυδωνιζόμενοι is an attributive participle modifying "infants" (νήπιοι) (Larkin, 81). **Semantically**, κλυδωνιζόμενοι is gnomic, expressing a timeless truth (W, 523–25). The participle offers an image of instability that is characteristic of immaturity.

περιφερόμενοι: The Greek word περιφερόμενοι is a masculine nominative plural present passive participle from the verb περιφέρω that means "to carry about" or "to carry here and there" (BDAG, s.v. "περιφέρω" b, p. 808). **Syntactically**, περιφερόμενοι is an attributive participle modifying νήπιοι, along with κλυδωνιζόμενοι. **Semantically**, περιφερόμενοι is gnomic, describing a timeless truth (W, 523–25). Hoehner states that both participles indicate the manner that exhibits their "childish lack of perception" (Hoehner, 561). The dative παντὶ ἀνέμῳ ("all wind") functions as means, describing how immature believers might be easily moved. The Greek word ἄνεμος literally means "wind," but figuratively, it can refer to an idea or trend that causes one to change their mind (BDAG, s.v. "ἄνεμος" 3, p. 77). The genitive τῆς διδασκαλίας is a genitive of apposition: "every wind, *namely teaching*." Paul uses διδασκαλία to refer to Christian teaching (Rom. 12:7; 15:4), but in this context the word suggests false teaching that comes from every direction. Paul mixes his metaphors by using κλυδωνιζόμενοι and περιφερόμενοι to describe a single image of instability. Lincoln describes the image conjured by the participles as "a little storm-tossed boat or of swirling flotsam and jetsam entirely at the mercy of the waves and the wind" (Lincoln, 257–58). The image contrasts the instability of a community without the work of the Christian leaders (v. 11) with the maturity that he hopes every Christian community will attain.

Semantical Nugget: What do the three prepositional phrases in verse 14 mean? Just as he did in verses 11–12 and 13, Paul ends the clause in verse 14 with three prepositional phrases. They could be structured this way:

περιφερόμενοι παντὶ ἀνέμῳ τῆς διδασκαλίας
<u>ἐν</u> τῇ κυβείᾳ τῶν ἀνθρώπων
<u>ἐν</u> πανουργίᾳ
<u>πρὸς</u> τὴν μεθοδείαν τῆς πλάνης

and being carried about by every wind of doctrine
<u>by</u> the craftiness of people
<u>by</u> trickery
<u>in</u> deceitful schemes

The first prepositional phrase, "by the craftiness of people" (ἐν τῇ κυβείᾳ τῶν ἀνθρώπων), expresses the means of creating this instability. Not only do the winds of changing doctrine create instability, but also the "craftiness of people." The Greek word κυβεία is a *hapax legomenon* that means "craftiness." The word refers to dice-playing, or figuratively, playing with loaded dice (BDAG, s.v. "κυβεία," p. 573; LSJ, s.v. "κυβεία," p. 1004). The genitive τῶν ἀνθρώπων is an attributive genitive: "*human* craftiness" (cf. ESV, NRSV, CSB; Larkin, 82). The second prepositional phrase, "by trickery" (ἐν πανουργίᾳ), is parallel to the first, also communicating means. The Greek word πανουργία meaning "cunningness" or "trickery" (BDAG, s.v. "πανουργία," p. 754) is also the means of instability. The third prepositional phrase, "in deceitful scheming" (πρὸς τὴν μεθοδείαν τῆς πλάνης), expresses standard. Craftiness and trickery are in line with deceitful scheming (Larkin, 82). The Greek word μεθοδεία only appears twice in the New Testament, both times in Ephesians (cf. Eph. 6:11). The term may have a negative connotation (BDAG, s.v. "μεθοδεία," 625), but it can just refer to a system of rules: "method" (GE, s.v. "μεθοδεία," 1296; Thielman, 284). The genitive τῆς πλάνης is attributive: "*deceitful* schemes," which gives the Greek term μεθοδεία a negative value. These prepositional phrases communicate an important message—maturity is essential for the Christian community, not just to overcome immaturity, but also to withstand deceit from the world. Earlier in the letter, Paul described believers as once "walking according to the ruler of authority" who is "now working in the sons of disobedience" (Eph. 2:2). Later, he will describe a spiritual struggle with the devil (Eph. 6:10–12). These forces in the world act with the intent to harm the church.

4:15a ἀληθεύοντες: The Greek word ἀληθεύοντες is a masculine nominative plural present active participle from the verb ἀληθεύω that means "to be truthful" or "to tell the truth" (BDAG, s.v. "ἀληθεύω," p. 43). The NET renders the participle as "practicing the truth," suggesting that the verb is more than a verbal confession (cf. Hoehner, 565) but most translations render the verb as "speaking the truth" (ESV, NIV, RSV, NRSV, CSB, NASB, NKJV, KJV; Arnold, 268–69). **Syn-

tactically, ἀληθεύοντες introduces a dependent participle clause. It functions adverbially modifying the following verb, the second verb in the ἵνα clause that Paul began in verse 14: "we might grow" (αὐξήσωμεν). **Semantically**, ἀληθεύοντες could function as manner, but most likely describes the means by which the action of the verb is accomplished: *by the means* of being truthful" (Hoehner, 566; Thielman, 285; W, 628–30). Paul will come back around to the idea of speaking the truth in the next section (Eph. 4:25). The prepositional phrase "in love" (ἐν ἀγάπη) modifies ἀληθεύοντες, expressing manner (Larkin, 82; Thielman, 285). The phrase describes how believers should speak the truth. Paul uses the phrase in verse 2 ("bearing one another in love"); his use here creates an *inclusio* (Larkin, 132). In Ephesians 5, Paul encourages the Ephesians to love one another just as Christ loved us—by handing himself over on our behalf (Eph. 5:1–2). Speaking truth with this kind of sacrificial love creates an environment in which the church can grow. More times than not, these two values conflict. Believers might defend the truth at the expense of love, or rather sacrifice truth in order to express love. Both are essential.

δέ: The Greek word δέ is a conjunction that means "but" or after a negative statement "rather" (BDAG, s.v. "δέ" 4c, p. 213). **Syntactically**, δέ is in the postpositive position that introduces an independent conjunctive clause. **Semantically**, δέ is a contrastive coordinating connector: "but" (NRSV, HCSB, CSB, NASB) or "rather" (ESV RSV). The NIV and NLT render the conjunction as "instead." Besides the conjunction, Paul underscores the contrast a number of ways. First, the participle "speaking the truth" (ἀληθεύοντες) stands in contrast with Paul's description of being tossed about with craftiness and deceit (v. 14). Second, Paul uses the preposition ἐν to express manner in both verses 14 and 15. In verse 14, the system of deceit takes advantage of the immature *in craftiness and trickery*; in verse 15, the church grows *in love* (Thielman, 285). Finally, Paul uses two verbs in the ἵνα clause he began in verse 14a. The first verb is a static verb "that we might no longer be infants" (ἵνα μηκέτι ὦμεν νήπιοι); the second verb is a dynamic verb "that we might grow in him" (αὐξήσωμεν εἰς αὐτόν) (Hoehner, 564).

4:15b αὐξήσωμεν: The Greek word αὐξήσωμεν is a first-person plural aorist active subjunctive from the verb αὐξάνω that means "to grow" or "to increase" (BDAG, s.v. "αὐξάνω" 2b, p. 151). **Syntactically**, αὐξήσωμεν functions as the main verb of the dependent conjunctive clause introduced by δέ. It is governed by the ἵνα in verse 14. The clause makes a positive statement in contrast to the negative statement in verse 14. The subject is implied by the verb: "we," referring to the church. **Semantically**, αὐξήσωμεν could be considered as a hortatory subjunctive ("let us grow") (W, 464–65; Larkin, 82; cf. HCSB, CSB), but it is best understood as a purpose subjunctive ("so that we might grow") since the parallel subjunctive expresses purpose (Arnold, 269;

Hoehner, 566; Merkle, 132). Some English versions translate the verb with a future tense: "we will in all things grow up" (NET; cf. NIV). The aorist tense functions as an ingressive aorist. The verb expresses entrance into a new state or condition (Hoehner, 566). Paul uses a similar image in Ephesians 2. He describes the church as a building growing into a holy temple (Eph. 2:20–22). The growth of a building may seem odd, but it allows him to underscore the believer's new relationship with God in Christ. In this context (vv. 15–16), his description of the church as a growing body better emphasizes the maturation process. The prepositional phrase "into him" (εἰς αὐτόν) expresses the goal of our growth (BDAG, s.v. "εἰς" 1aα, pp. 288–89). The accusative τὰ πάντα is an accusative of reference (W, 203–4; Porter, 90). We are to grow toward Christ in every possible way (Hoehner, 566).

4:15c ὅς: The Greek word ὅς is a masculine singular nominative from the relative pronoun ὅς that means "who" in this context (BDAG, s.v. "ὅς" 1a, p. 725). **Syntactically**, ὅς introduces a dependent adjectival relative clause "*who is the head*" (ὅς ἐστιν ἡ κεφαλή). The antecedent of the pronoun is αὐτόν (v. 15b), referring to Christ. The pronoun functions as the subject of the verb ἐστίν.

ἐστίν: The Greek word ἐστίν is a third-person singular present active indicative from the verb εἰμί that means "to be" (BDAG, s.v. "εἰμί" 2b, p. 283). **Syntactically**, ἐστίν functions as the main verb of the relative clause. The subject is the relative pronoun (ὅς). The predicate nominative is "the head" (ἡ κεφαλή); χριστός is in apposition to ἡ κεφαλή. **Semantically**, ἐστίν is an equative present: "is" (ESV, RSV, NRSV, NIV, CSB, HCSB, NASB, NKJV, KJV). Throughout the letter, Paul refers to Christ as the head to describe his supremacy (1:22; 5:23). Thielman notes that this careful logic might appear to be an odd image: believers do not grow into the head, but "up to Christ" as Paul describes in Ephesians 4:13, "but Christ, they must not forget, is still the head of his body, the church" (Thielman, 286).

4:16 οὗ: The Greek word οὗ is a masculine singular genitive from the relative pronoun ὅς that means "whom" in this context (BDAG, s.v. "ὅς" 1a, p. 725). **Syntactically**, οὗ introduces a dependent substantival relative clause "from *whom* the whole body … makes the body grow" (ἐξ οὗ πᾶν τὸ σῶμα … τὴν αὔξησιν τοῦ σώματος ποιεῖται). The antecedent of the pronoun is Christ (v. 15b, 15c). The pronoun functions as the object of the preposition ἐξ. The preposition expresses the source of growth (BDAG, s.v. "ἐκ" 3c, p. 296; Lenski, 1937, 545). The body plays an active role in its growth, but the relative clause emphasizes that this growth is ultimately from Christ (Arnold, 270).

συναρμολογούμενον: The Greek word συναρμολογούμενον is a neuter nominative singular present passive participle from the verb συναρμολογέω that means "to fit together" or "join together" (BDAG, s.v. "συναρμολογέω," p. 966). In the New Testament, the term only appears in Ephesians (cf. Eph. 2:21). **Syntactically**, συναρμολογούμενον is an attributive participle modifying "the body" (τὸ σῶμα) (Arnold, 270; Best, 410; Merkle, 133; Larkin, 83). **Semantically**, συναρμολογούμενον is a customary present, describing an ongoing process (W, 521–22). The verb is a divine passive, indicating that God is the agent that fits the body together. The participle describes how this body grows—by God fitting it together.

συμβιβαζόμενον: The Greek word συμβιβαζόμενον is a neuter nominative singular present passive participle from the verb συμβιβάζω that means "to bring together into a unit" or "unite" (BDAG, s.v. "συμβιβάζω" 1a, p. 596). Several English versions translate the verb as "knit together" (rsv, nrsv, hcsb, csb, nkjv); other versions render the verb as "held together" (esv, net, niv, nasb). The participle is an important part of Paul's metaphor, but it can also be used within the context of instruction (BDAG, s.v. "συμβιβάζω" 4, p. 597; 1 Cor. 2:16). This secondary meaning points us back to the importance of Christian teaching for the growth of the church, a theme that runs through this section (4:5, 11, 20–21) (Arnold, 270). **Syntactically**, συμβιβαζόμενον is an attributive participle modifying τὸ σῶμα, along with συναρμολογούμενον (Best, 410; Merkle, 133; Larkin, 83). **Semantically**, συμβιβαζόμενον is a customary present, describing an ongoing process (W, 521–22). The verb is a divine passive indicating that God is the agent who holds the body together. Just like the previous participle συναρμολογούμενον, συμβιβαζόμενον describes how the body grows—by being united. Paul uses the verb in a similar way in Colossians 2:19. There he describes the church as "nourished and held together" growing with a growth that comes from God.

> **Semantical Nugget**: What is the structure of the prepositional phrases in verse 16 and what do they mean? Paul inserts three prepositional phrases. The first two phrases modify the preceding participles. The last phrase most likely modifies the object of the second phrase. We could lay them out this way:
>
> πᾶν τὸ σῶμα <u>συναρμολογούμενον</u> καὶ <u>συμβιβαζόμενον</u>
>   <u>διὰ</u> πάσης ἀφῆς τῆς ἐπιχορηγίας
>   <u>κατ’</u> ἐνέργειαν
>   <u>ἐν</u> μέτρῳ ἑνὸς ἑκάστου μέρους
>
> The whole body, <u>joined</u> and <u>held together</u>,
>   <u>by</u> every supporting joint
>   <u>according</u> to the working
>   <u>in</u> the capacity of each part

The first prepositional phrase, "by every supporting joint" (διὰ πάσης ἁφῆς τῆς ἐπιχορηγίας), expresses the means by which the body is held together. The object of the preposition, ἁφή, might be best translated as "contact," referring to the connection between all believers (Hoehner, 572–73; LSJ, s.v. "ἁφή," p. 288). This view is underscored by the genitive at the end of the clause: "each part" (ἑνὸς ἑκάστου μέρους). The genitive τῆς ἐπιχορηγίας is an attributive genitive: "supporting ligament." Lincoln argues that Paul has in mind the church leaders listed in verse 11 (Lincoln, 263), but since Paul has shifted to discuss the body, he has all believers in view (Best, 411–12). The image implies that the members are connected to one another. The significance is important to understand the image. The members are distinct from one another, but make up a unified body.

The second prepositional phrase, "according to the working" (κατ' ἐνέργειαν), modifies the participles, not the previous prepositional phrase (*contra* Hoehner, 575). The preposition expresses the standard (Larkin, 84). The body is fitted together and joined "*according to* the working." The Greek word ἐνέργεια means "power" or "operation" (BDAG, s.v. "ἐνέργεια," p. 335). Earlier in Ephesians, Paul used the term to refer to divine power—the same power at work within the resurrection (Eph. 1:19; cf. 3:7).

The third prepositional phrase, "in the measure" (ἐν μέτρῳ), modifies the previous prepositional phrase. The phrase expresses manner describing the "working." The object of the preposition (μέτρον) alludes to verse 7: Christ gives to each of us "according to the measure" of his gift. Even though each member has different gifts, they should work to their capacity (Arnold, 271). BDAG renders the phrase as: "according to the functioning capacity of each individual part" (BDAG, s.v. "μέτρον" 2b, p. 644). English versions render the last two phrases a number of different ways. The ESV translates it: "when each part is working properly" (RSV; cf. NRSV). The CSB translates it: "by the proper working of each individual part" (HCSB; cf. NASB). The NIV translates it "as each part does its work." And the NLT translates it as "each part does its own special work."

Finally, the genitive construction ἑνὸς ἑκάστου μέρους ("each one of the parts") most likely modifies the second prepositional phrase (κατ' ἐνέργειαν), not the third (ἐν μέτρῳ). The genitive is subjective—each member is doing the work (Larkin, 84; Merkle, 133). Paul's language in this section is compact. Thielman summarizes the phrase well: "Christ measures out grace to each Christian in a way that is appropriate for that Christian's role in building up the body" (Thielman, 288). Paul uses a similar phrase in verse 7: "Grace was given to each one of us [ἑνὶ δὲ ἑκάστῳ ἡμῶν] according to the measure of Christ's gift [κατὰ τὸ μέτρον τῆς δωρεᾶς τοῦ Χριστοῦ].” Paul comes full circle with his argument. Even though Christ gives distinct and different gifts to the church, these gifts are given for a singular reason: for the church to be transformed in Christlikeness.

ποιεῖται: The Greek word ποιεῖται is a third-person singular present middle indicative from the verb ποιέω that means "to make" or "do for oneself" (BDAG, s.v. "ποιέω" 7a, pp. 841–42). **Syntactically**, ποιεῖται functions as the main verb of the relative clause. The subject is "the whole body" (πᾶν τὸ σῶμα). The direct object is "the growth of the body" (τὴν αὔξησιν τοῦ σώματος). The genitive τοῦ σώματος is a subjective genitive: "bodily growth" (W, 113–16; Merkle, 133; Larkin, 84). The ESV translates the phrase "the body grows" (cf. RSV, NRSV). **Semantically**, the present tense functions as a customary present; the action of the verb occurs regularly (W, 521–22). The middle voice is causative. The body causes its own growth—the reflexive pronoun (ἑαυτοῦ) highlights this; however, the preposition and relative pronoun (ἐξ οὗ) make it clear that this ability comes from Christ (W, 411–12; Arnold, 272). The KJV translates the phrase as: "causes growth of the body."

Ephesians 4:17–32

Big Greek Idea: Believers should walk in holiness, recalling the change in their lives in light of their new identity as Christians; and as a result, they should build up the community through their behavior and cease any conduct that breaks down the community.

Structural Overview: Just like the first section, Paul begins the second section with a verb of exhortation along with a complementary infinitive (cf. Eph. 4:1, 17). Without using an imperative, he effectively gives a command. In verse 1, he gives an exhortation to walk in light of the believer's call, but in verse 17 he gives an admonition to stop walking as they had done in the past—as the Gentiles walk. The first part of this section (vv. 17–19) gives an extensive description of this lifestyle. Paul describes them as callous, hard-hearted, darkened in their thinking. Ultimately they are estranged from God, leading them into a life of sensuality and greed.

In the second part of this section (vv. 20–24), Paul reminds the readers of the transformation that they underwent as they became believers. He contrasts their previous lifestyle (vv. 17–19) with their new position in Christ. Paul makes a similar contrast in Ephesians 2 (vv. 1–3 and 4–5; vv. 11–12 and 13). Here he reminds them of what they had been taught (vv. 20–21) with three infinitives in indirect discourse. These believers have: taken off the old self (v. 22), an allusion to their former behavior (vv. 17–19); renewed their minds (v. 23); and put on the new self (v. 24), a reference to the believers' new identity as members of the Christian community.

In the final part, Paul gives specific commands for believers, giving them concrete examples of taking off the old self and putting on the new self. The first command explicitly links the final section (vv. 25–32) to the second section (vv. 20–24). Paul tells the believers to "take off falsehood" (v. 25) The second command focuses on anger. After giving allowance for anger (v. 26a), he gives strict warnings about allowing anger to go unchecked. He gives the believers a time limit for their anger and warns them that extensive anger gives the devil an opportunity (vv. 26b–27). The third command is for those who steal to stop. Instead of theft, they should commit to work so that they can provide for those who are in need (v. 28). The fourth command is that believers should refrain from negative language, saying only what will edify others (v. 29). After four specific commands, Paul gives a more general command to "not grieve the Holy Spirit" (v. 30). Within the context, this command most likely refers to anything that breaks down the community, specifically harmful words. This section ends with a list of vices that believers should put away and a list of virtues they should adopt (vv. 31–32). These lists serve as an inclusive catch-all at the end of the list of commands. In short, believers should put away all bitterness, slander, and all wickedness. Rather they should be kind and compassionate, forgiving one another.

Outline:

The believers' former life, characterized by a hard heart alienates them from God and leads them to a life of sensuality and greed (vv. 17–19)

Believers have transformed their lives by renewing their minds and identifying with the community of believers, the new person (vv. 20–24)

In light of their new identity, believers should adopt conduct that builds up the community instead of tearing it down (vv. 25–32)

Believers should speak the truth (v. 25)

Believers should control their anger (vv. 26–27)

Believers should no longer steal, but provide for those in need (v. 28)

Believers should refrain from any speech that destroys the community (vv. 29–30)

Believers should put away evil and adopt an attitude of forgiveness (vv. 31–32)

CLAUSAL OUTLINE FOR EPHESIANS 4:17–32

4:17a Τοῦτο οὖν **λέγω**
4:17a Therefore, **I say** this

    4:17b καὶ **μαρτύρομαι** ἐν κυρίῳ,
    4:17b and **I testify** in the Lord,

        4:17c μηκέτι ὑμᾶς **περιπατεῖν**
        4:17c that you no longer **walk**

            4:17d **καθὼς** καὶ τὰ ἔθνη **περιπατεῖ** ἐν ματαιότητι τοῦ νοὸς αὐτῶν,
            4:17d **just as** the Gentiles also **walk** in the futility of their minds,

                4:18a **ἐσκοτωμένοι** τῇ διανοίᾳ **ὄντες**,
                4:18a **with the result of being darkened** in their understanding

                4:18b **ἀπηλλοτριωμένοι** τῆς ζωῆς τοῦ θεοῦ, διὰ (τὴν ἄγνοιαν τὴν οὖσαν ἐν αὐτοῖς), διὰ τὴν πώρωσιν τῆς καρδίας αὐτῶν,
                4:18b **with the result of being alienated** from the life that God gives, because of (the ignorance that is in them) due to the hardness of their heart,

[τὰ ἔθνη] (v. 17d)
[Gentiles (v. 17d)]
      |
4:19a οἵτινες **ἀπηλγηκότες**
4:19a who, **because they have become callous**,

4:19b ἑαυτοὺς **παρέδωκαν** τῇ ἀσελγείᾳ εἰς ἐργασίαν ἀκαθαρσίας πάσης ἐν πλεονεξίᾳ.
4:19b **gave themselves over** to sensuality for the practice of all uncleanliness with greed.

4:20 ὑμεῖς δὲ οὐχ οὕτως **ἐμάθετε** τὸν Χριστόν,
4:20 But you **have** not **learned** Christ in such a manner,

4:21a εἴ γε αὐτὸν **ἠκούσατε**
4:21a if indeed **you heard** about him

4:21b καὶ ἐν αὐτῷ **ἐδιδάχθητε**,
4:21b and **were taught** in him,

4:21c **καθώς ἐστιν** ἀλήθεια ἐν τῷ ’Ιησοῦ,
4:21c **just as** the truth **is** in Jesus,

[ἐδιδάχθητε (v. 21b)]
[you were taught (v. 21b)]
    |
4:22 **ἀποθέσθαι** ὑμᾶς κατὰ τὴν προτέραν ἀναστροφὴν (τὸν παλαιὸν ἄνθρωπον τὸν φθειρόμενον) κατὰ τὰς ἐπιθυμίας τῆς ἀπάτης,
4:22 **that you put off** (the old self who is corrupted) according to the former behavior according to the desires from deceit,

4:23 **ἀνανεοῦσθαι** δὲ τῷ πνεύματι τοῦ νοὸς ὑμῶν,
4:23 but **you are being renewed** in your spirit, your mind

4:24 καὶ **ἐνδύσασθαι** (τὸν καινὸν ἄνθρωπον τὸν κατὰ θεὸν κτισθέντα) ἐν δικαιοσύνῃ καὶ ὁσιότητι τῆς ἀληθείας.
4:24 and **you put on** (the new self who is created according to God's likeness) in righteousness and holiness from truth.

4:25a <u>Διὸ</u> **ἀποθέμενοι** τὸ ψεῦδος
4:25a <u>Therefore</u>, **since you have put away** falsehood

4:25b **λαλεῖτε** ἀλήθειαν ἕκαστος μετὰ τοῦ πλησίον αὐτοῦ,
4:25b **let** each of you **speak** the truth with their neighbor

4:25c **ὅτι ἐσμὲν** ἀλλήλων μέλη.
4:25c **because we are** members of one another.

4:26a **ὀργίζεσθε**
4:26a **Be angry**

4:26b <u>καὶ</u> μὴ **ἁμαρτάνετε·**
4:26b <u>and</u> **do** not **sin**

4:26c ὁ ἥλιος μὴ **ἐπιδυέτω** ἐπὶ τῷ παροργισμῷ ὑμῶν,
4:26c **Do** not **allow** the sun to set while you are angry

4:27 μηδὲ **δίδοτε** τόπον τῷ διαβόλῳ.
4:27 nor **give** the devil an opportunity.

4:28a (ὁ κλέπτων) μηκέτι **κλεπτέτω**,
4:28a (The one who steals) must no longer **steal**,

4:28b μᾶλλον δὲ **κοπιάτω**
4:28b <u>but</u> rather **must do work**

4:28c **ἐργαζόμενος** ταῖς ἰδίαις χερσὶν τὸ ἀγαθόν,
4:28c **by producing** what is good with his own hands,

4:28d **ἵνα ἔχῃ** <u>μεταδιδόναι</u> (τῷ χρείαν ἔχοντι).
4:28d **so that they may have** something <u>to share</u> with (the one who has need).

4:29a πᾶς λόγος σαπρὸς ἐκ τοῦ στόματος ὑμῶν μὴ **ἐκπορευέσθω**,
4:29a **Do** not **let** any unwholesome word **come out** of your mouth,

[ἐκπορευέσθω (v. 29b)]

4:29b <u>ἀλλὰ</u> εἴ τις [ἐστίν] ἀγαθὸς πρὸς οἰκοδομὴν τῆς χρείας,
4:29b <u>but</u> whatever [<u>is</u>] good for the edification of the need [let it come out],

[ἐκπορευέσθω (v. 29b)]
[let these words come out (v. 29b)]

4:29c **ἵνα δῷ** χάριν (τοῖς ἀκούουσιν).
4:29c **so that it may give** grace (to those who hear).

4:30a καὶ μὴ **λυπεῖτε** τὸ πνεῦμα τὸ ἅγιον τοῦ θεοῦ,
4:30a And **do** not **grieve** the Holy Spirit of God,

4:30b ἐν ᾧ **ἐσφραγίσθητε** εἰς ἡμέραν ἀπολυτρώσεως.
4:30b by **whom** **you were sealed** for the day of redemption.

4:31 πᾶσα πικρία καὶ θυμὸς καὶ ὀργὴ καὶ κραυγὴ καὶ βλασφημία **ἀρθήτω** ἀφ᾽ ὑμῶν σὺν πάσῃ κακίᾳ.
4:31 Let all bitterness, anger, wrath, shouting and slander **be put away** from you with all wickedness.

4:32a **γίνεσθε** δὲ εἰς ἀλλήλους χρηστοί, εὔσπλαγχνοι,
4:32a But **be** kind to one another, compassionate,

4:32b **χαριζόμενοι** ἑαυτοῖς
4:32b **by forgiving** one another

4:32c **καθὼς** καὶ ὁ θεὸς ἐν Χριστῷ **ἐχαρίσατο** ὑμῖν.
4:32c **just as** also God **forgave** us in Christ.

Syntax Explained for Ephesians 4:17–32

4:17a οὖν: The Greek word οὖν is a conjunction that means "therefore" or "consequently" (BDAG, s.v. "οὖν" 1a, p. 736). English versions render the conjunction as either "therefore" (CSB, HCSB, KJV, NKJV) or "Now" (RSV, NRSV, ESV) or "So" (NET, NIV). **Syntactically**, οὖν introduces an independent conjunctive clause "*Therefore* I say this" (Τοῦτο οὖν λέγω). **Semantically**, οὖν could be an inferential conjunction introducing an inference from the preceding context (BDAG, s.v. "οὖν" 1a, p. 736); however, it might be best considered resumptive, picking on Paul's use in verses 1–3, continuing Paul's exhortation to walk in a manner worthy of their calling (Hoehner, 582; Larkin, 68).

λέγω: The Greek word λέγω is a first-person singular present active indicative from the verb λέγω that means "to declare" or "maintain" (BDAG, s.v. "λέγω" 2e, p. 590). Most English versions render the verb as simply "I say" (ESV, NET, CSB, HCSB, NASB, NKJV, KJV). To bring out the strength of the affirmation the NRSV translates it as "I affirm" (cf. RSV). The NIV translates it as "I tell you."

Syntactically, λέγω functions as the main verb of the conjunctive clause introduced by οὖν. The subject of the verb is implied: "I," referring to Paul (cf. Eph. 4:1). **Semantically**, the present tense is progressive. The verb describes Paul's statement as the action unfolds (W, 518–19). If this represents content that Paul regularly teaches, then this could be construed as a customary present.

4:17b καί: The Greek word καί is a conjunction that means "and" (BDAG, s.v. "καί" 1ba, p. 494). **Syntactically**, καί introduces an independent conjunctive clause: "*and* testify in the Lord" (καὶ μαρτύρομαι ἐν κυρίῳ). **Semantically**, καί is a coordinating connective: "and" (ESV, NRSV, RSV, CSB, HCSB, NASB, NIV), connecting this clause to the previous one. The NLT renders both Greek verbs as one: "With the Lord's authority I say this." The conjunctive clause adds redundancy. The repetition, along with the prepositional phrase "in the Lord" (ἐν κυρίῳ), adds seriousness to what Paul is about to say.

μαρτύρομαι: The Greek word μαρτύρομαι is a first-person singular present middle (deponent) indicative from the verb μαρτύρομαι that means "to affirm," "to insist," or "to implore" (BDAG, s.v. "μαρτύρομαι" 2, p. 619). The CSB renders the verb literally as "I testify," which gives solemnity to what Paul expresses (cf. RSV, ESV, KJV, NKJV). The NIV renders it as "I insist" (cf. NET; Arnold, 280). **Syntactically**, μαρτύρομαι functions as the main verb of the conjunctive clause introduced by καί, parallel to λέγω. **Semantically**, the present tense functions as a progressive present. The verb describes Paul's assertion as he is making it (W, 518–19).

4:17c περιπατεῖν: The Greek word περιπατεῖν is a present active infinitive from the verb περιπατέω that means "to behave" or "live"; the word connotes a habit of conduct (BDAG, s.v. "περιπατέω" 2aγ, p. 803). Some English versions translate the verb literally as "to walk" (ESV, NKJV, KJV, HCSB, NASB); others present the metaphorical idea: "to live" (RSV, NRSV, NIV, CSB, NLT, NET). **Syntactically**, περιπατεῖν functions as the direct object of the verbs "I say and I testify" (λέγω καὶ μαρτύρομαι). The subject of the infinitive is "you" (ὑμᾶς), referring to the Ephesian believers. **Semantically**, περιπατεῖν is in indirect discourse; it can either carry the force of an indicative or imperative. Because of the main verb, the infinitive represents an imperative (W, 603–5). With the negative adverb, the present infinitive gives a prohibition. The present tense is a customary present: "walk." The present tense describes an ongoing state (W, 521–22; Fanning, 1990, 382–83). Paul anticipates that the Ephesians make this a way of life. Paul uses the verb περιπατέω as a significant structural marker for the second part of Ephesians (see Theological Nugget at 4:1b).

4:17d καθὼς καί: The Greek word καθώς is a conjunction that means "just as" or "even as" (BDAG, s.v. "καθώς" 1, p. 493). The Greek word καί is a conjunction that means "also" or "even" (BDAG, s.v. "καί" 2c, p. 495). Most English versions translate the phrase as "as" omitting καί (ESV, RSV, NRSV, NIV, NET, CSB, HCSB). **Syntactically**, καθώς introduces a dependent conjunctive clause "*just as* the Gentiles also walk" (καθὼς καὶ τὰ ἔθνη περιπατεῖ). The entire clause functions adverbially modifying the infinitive "to walk" (περιπατεῖν). **Semantically**, καί is ascensive (W, 670–71). The καθώς marks the clause as a comparison, in this case, it is a negative comparison. The Ephesian believers should avoid conducting their lives in the same way as the Gentiles.

περιπατεῖ: The Greek word περιπατεῖ is a third-person singular present active indicative from the verb περιπατέω that means "to behave" or "to live" (BDAG, s.v. "περιπατέω" 2aγ, p. 803). Several translations simply repeat the verb from verse 17c: "no longer live as the Gentiles live" (CSB, NRSV) or "no longer walk as the Gentiles walk" (HCSB, NKJV; cf. NASB). Some translations render the verb as "do" avoiding the redundancy of the verb: "no longer walk as the Gentiles *do*" (RSV, ESV; cf. NLT, NET, NIV). **Syntactically**, περιπατεῖ functions as the main verb of the dependent conjunctive clause introduced by καθώς. The subject of the verb is "Gentiles" (τὰ ἔθνη). The neuter plural normally takes a singular verb when it represents a collective whole (W, 399–400). **Semantically**, περιπατεῖ is a customary present: "walk." The present tense describes an ongoing state (W, 521–22). Paul has already used the verb as a prohibition: "no longer walk." The usage here describes exactly what he is prohibiting, namely that the Ephesian believers no longer walk as the Gentiles.

Lexical Nugget: Why does Paul refer to "Gentiles" in verse 17? Even though Paul uses the term "Gentiles," or literally, "nations," (BDAG, s.v. "ἔθνος" 2b, p. 277), he uses the term to refer to a group who does not profess faith in the God, unbelievers (BDAG, s.v. "ἔθνος" 2a, pp. 276–77). Undoubtedly, a large number of Gentiles, who responded to Paul's gospel message, made up a significant portion of the Ephesian church. A dominant theme in the first half of the book is that Gentiles have become heirs to God's promises given through Christ (Eph. 3:6)—Paul's apostolic message (Eph. 3:1, 8). In Ephesians 2, he specifies how the Gentiles once lived apart from Christ. Their estrangement from God left them godless and hopeless (Eph. 2:11–12). They lived their lives under satanic control, pursuing their own passions. Paul describes their situation as "children of wrath by nature" (Eph. 2:1–3). The current context (vv. 17–19) gives this previous behavior more description: these Gentiles walk in futility as in darkness, given over to their own greed. The Ephesian believers have stepped out of this lifestyle. Paul calls them to avoid going back to it.

Text-Critical Nugget: Does Paul use the adjective λοιπά to modify τὰ ἔθνη? Several Byzantine manuscripts insert λοιπά before τὰ ἔθνη (𝔐, K, L), which should be rendered: "the rest of the Gentiles" (NKJV) or "other Gentiles" (cf. MT; RP^{2005}). The insertion makes a clear delineation between non-Christian Gentiles and the Ephesian Gentiles. Several Alexandrian ($\mathfrak{P}^{46}$, ℵ, A, B) and Western manuscripts omit the adjective (D, F, G). He uses the adjective in a similar manner in Ephesians 2:3. In this case, the omission is found in better manuscripts. Since the insertion clarifies Paul's meaning, the omission is the shortest, harder reading, making it the best reading.

4:18a ἐσκοτωμένοι ... ὄντες: The Greek word ἐσκοτωμένοι is a masculine nominative plural perfect passive participle from the verb σκοτόω that means "to be inwardly darkened" (BDAG, s.v. "σκοτόω" 2, p. 932). The Greek word ὄντες is a masculine nominative plural present active participle from the verb εἰμί that means "to be" which is used as an auxiliary verb to the verbal idea (BDAG, s.v. "εἰμί" 11a, pp. 285–86). **Syntactically**, The perfect participle ἐσκοτωμένοι with a form of εἰμί is a periphrastic construction (BDF §352; Robertson, 910; Fanning, 1990, 417; W, 647–49; Merkle, 139). The periphrastic introduces the clause as a dependent participle clause: "being darkened in their understanding" (ἐσκοτωμένοι τῇ διανοίᾳ ὄντες). The entire clause is adverbial modifying the verb "walk" (περιπατεῖ). A number of English translations begin a new sentence at verse 18 by rendering the participle as an indicative: "They are darkened" (CSB, HCSB, NRSV, ESV, NIV, NET). The gender of the subject has shifted from neuter (τὰ ἔθνη) to masculine (ἐσκοτωμένοι ... ὄντες), which may suggest a shift from class to person (Hoehner, 585). **Semantically**, the perfect tense participle (ἐσκοτωμένοι) expresses a completed idea with ongoing results. The present tense participle (ὄντες) emphasizes the Gentiles present situation (BDF §352; Arnold, 282). In Romans 1:21, Paul makes a similar statement—because these Gentiles failed to give God his due honor, "their foolish hearts are darkened."

Text-Critical Nugget: Why does the MT use the verb σκοτίζω instead of the verb σκοτόω, which is found in the NA^{28}? Several Western (D, F, G) and Byzantine manuscripts (𝔐, K, L) read ἐσκοτισμένοι, while several Alexandrian manuscripts ($\mathfrak{P}^{46}$, $\mathfrak{P}^{49}$, ℵ, A, B) ἐσκοτωμένοι. The difference is subtle. The Greek word σκοτίζω means "to become inwardly darkened" (BDAG, s.v. "σκοτίζω" 2, p. 932); the Greek word σκοτόω means to "become darkened in the mind" (BDAG, s.v. "σκοτόω" 2, p. 932). Hoehner notes that scribes would be more likely to insert σκοτόω, the more classical form of the word, than σκοτίζω, making σκοτίζω the harder reading (Hoehner, 584 n. 3). This along with the external evidence suggests that ἐσκοτισμένοι is the more original reading, though there is no change in translation. However, we have followed the text of the NA^{28} in the clausal outline.

4:18b ἀπηλλοτριωμένοι: The Greek word ἀπηλλοτριωμένοι is a masculine nominative plural perfect passive participle from the verb ἀπαλλοτριόω that means "to estrange" or "alienate" (BDAG, s.v. "ἀπαλλοτριόω," p. 96). **Syntactically**, ἀπηλλοτριωμένοι is parallel with the participle ἐσκοτωμένοι (v. 18a), functioning as the second verb in a periphrastic construction (Arnold, 282; Best, 418; BDF §352). Just like the previous participle clause (v. 18a), the entire clause is adverbial, modifying the verb "the Gentiles walk" (τὰ ἔθνη περιπατεῖ). **Semantically**, the perfect tense expresses a completed idea with ongoing results. The presence of the present participle (ὄντες) emphasizes the present situation of the Gentiles (BDF §352; Arnold, 282). Most English versions translate the verb as "alienated" (NRSV, RSV, ESV, NET, NKJV, KJV), "separated" (NIV), or "excluded" (CSB, HCSB, NASB). The NLT translates the verb more actively: "They wandered far." Earlier, Paul described the spiritual state of these Gentiles as "estranged from the commonwealth of Israel" (Eph. 2:12). The present context describes a more comprehensive result: "estranged from a life from God," a summary of the Gentile state that Paul describes in Ephesians 2:12.

> **Semantical Nugget**: How should we classify the genitive chain τῆς ζωῆς τοῦ θεοῦ following the participle ἀπηλλοτριωμένοι? The first genitive (τῆς ζωῆς) is a genitive of separation (W, 107–9; Arnold, 282; Larkin, 87). These unbelievers are separated *from* life. The second genitive (τοῦ θεοῦ) is best understood as a genitive of source (W, 109–10; Best, 420; Larkin, 87): life that comes *from* God. Most English versions translate the phrase as "from the life of God" (NASB, HCSB, CSB, NKJV, KJV, ESV, NRSV, ESV, NIV). The NLT captures the meaning of both genitives: "from the life God gives."

οὖσαν: The Greek word οὖσαν is a present active participle feminine singular accusative from εἰμί that means "to be" (BDAG, s.v. "εἰμί" 3c, p. 284). **Syntactically**, οὖσαν is an attributive participle modifying the noun "ignorance" (τὴν ἄγνοιαν). The phrase serves as the object of the preposition "because of" (διά). The prepositional phrase modifies the previous participle phrases (vv. 18a, 18b). **Semantically**, οὖσαν is a customary present: "is" (NASB). The present tense describes an ongoing state (W, 521–22). The preposition διά expresses cause: "*because* of" (CSB, HCSB, NASB, NKJV, RSV, NRSV, ESV, NET, NIV). It provides the reason for their darkened understanding and alienation from God.

> **Lexical Nugget**: What does it mean to be "ignorant" (ἄγνοια)? The Greek word ἄγνοια literally means "ignorance" or "a lack of knowledge" (BDAG, s.v. "ἄγνοια" 1, p. 13), but the word characterizes sinners (Acts 17:30; 1 Pet. 1:14; 2:15). Because of their ignorance, they act contrary to God's will. The participle along with the prepositional phrase gives a deeper description of this ignorance—it is *in them* (ἐν αὐτοῖς). Hoehner calls this ignorance internal; he states it "is not innocent but also a flagrant refusal of the knowledge of God and his will" (Hoehner, 587).

Syntactical Nugget: What is the relationship between the prepositional phrase "because of the hardness of their heart" (διὰ τὴν πώρωσιν τῆς καρδίας αὐτῶν) and the context? The prepositional phrase could either be parallel to the previous prepositional phrase, modifying the participles in verse 18 (Larkin, 87; Best, 419–20; Thielman, 298) giving a second reason for why the Gentiles are alienated. Some English translations bring this out by inserting "and" between the two prepositional phrases (CSB, HCSB, NRSV, NLT). However, it most likely modifies the preceding prepositional phrase (v. 18c) (Arnold, 282–83; Hoehner, 587; Lincoln, 278; Merkle, 139). The preposition διά means "because" in this context (BDAG, s.v. "διά" B2a, p. 225). The first prepositional phrase provides the reason for the Gentiles' estrangement; the second prepositional phrase provides the reason for their ignorance: "*because of* the hardness of their heart." The Greek word πώρωσις means "obstinacy" or "dullness" (BDAG, s.v. "πώρωσις," p. 900). God is the one who blinds the hearts (cf. John 12:40; Rom. 11:25). This hardness keeps them from responding to God's message—they are not even able to understand it.

4:19a οἵτινες: The Greek word οἵτινες is a masculine plural nominative from the indefinite relative pronoun ὅστις that means "whoever" or "such a one." The pronoun can be used to define a characteristic of a person who belongs to a class (BDAG, s.v. "ὅστις" 2b, p. 729–30). **Syntactically**, οἵτινες introduces a dependent adjectival relative clause "*who* handed themselves over" (οἵτινες … ἑαυτοὺς παρέδωκαν). The antecedent of the pronoun is "the Gentiles" (τὰ ἔθνη; v. 17d). The pronoun functions as the subject of the relative clause. Due to the length of the sentence several English versions begin a new sentence and translate the relative pronoun as a personal pronoun: "They have given themselves over" (NIV; cf. ESV, NRSV, NET, HCSB, CSB).

ἀπηλγηκότες: The Greek word ἀπηλγηκότες is a masculine nominative plural perfect active participle from the verb ἀπαλγέω that could mean "to be despondent" or "becoming callous" (BDAG, s.v. "ἀπαλγέω" 1, p. 96). The word is a *hapax legomenon*, occurring only once in the New Testament. Within the context, Paul is not describing the Gentiles as despondent, but hard-hearted and alienated. The idea of being "callous" best fits the context. Hoehner states that the word "reflects their moral apathy" (Hoehner, 589). This callousness leads to self-abandonment (v. 19a). Most English versions bring this sense out in their translation: "having become callous" (NASB; cf. CSB, HCSB, RSV, NRSV, ESV, NET), "having lost all sensitivity" (NIV), or "being past feeling" (NKJV, KJV). **Syntactically**, ἀπηλγηκότες functions adverbially modifying the verb in the relative clause "have been handed over" (παρέδωκαν). **Semantically**, ἀπηλγηκότες conveys the idea of cause: "*because* they are callous" (NET). The perfect tense implies that the effects of this callousness are ongoing. Most English versions render the participle as attendant circumstance: "They became callous and gave themselves over" (CSB, HCSB; cf. ESV, RSV, NRSV).

4:19b παρέδωκαν: The Greek word παρέδωκαν is a third-person plural aorist active indicative from the verb παραδίδωμι that means "to hand over," "turn over," or "give up" (BDAG, s.v. "παραδίδωμι" 1b, p. 762). Most English versions translate the verb as "have given themselves over" (NIV, RSV; cf. ESV, NASB, CSB, HCSB, KJV, NKJV); the NRSV translates it as "have abandoned themselves." **Syntactically**, παρέδωκαν functions as the main verb of the relative clause. The relative pronoun (οἵτινες) is the subject. The direct object is "themselves" (ἑαυτούς). Paul emphasizes the reflexive pronoun by placing it before the verb. The indirect object is "sensuality" (τῇ ἀσελγείᾳ). **Semantically**, παρέδωκαν is a constative aorist: "gave" (CSB, HCSB) or "have given" (ESV, RSV, NIV, NET, NASB, NKJV, KJV). It describes the action of the verb as a whole (W, 557–58). In Romans, Paul writes that God handed these over as a result of their sin (Rom. 1:24, 26, 28); in our current context, Paul states that these Gentiles have handed themselves over, emphasizing their culpability (Best, 421–22).

Lexical Nugget: What does the term "sensuality" (ἀσέλγεια) mean? The Greek word ἀσέλγεια is translated a number of different ways in English versions. Some versions translate the noun as "licentiousness" (RSV, NRSV) or "indecency" (NET). The KJV translates it "lasciviousness," while the NKJV translates it as "lewdness." Other versions translate the word with a sexual connotation: "sensuality" (NASB, ESV, NIV) or "promiscuity" (CSB, HCSB). In Greek, the word can mean "self-abandonment," moving beyond the bounds of what is socially acceptable (BDAG, s.v. "ἀσέλγεια," p. 141). Elsewhere, Paul definitely uses the term to specify sexual promiscuity (Rom. 13:13; 2 Cor. 12:21; Gal. 5:19; cf. 2 Pet. 2:2, 18; Bauernfeind, 1964, 490). The concept of self-abandonment fits well with the following prepositional phrase: in the pursuit of all uncleanliness in greed (εἰς ἐργασίαν ἀκαθαρσίας πάσης). The phrase expresses purpose (Larkin, 89; Merkle, 140). The genitive ἀκαθαρσίας is objective: "the pursuit of uncleanliness." The Greek word ἀκαθαρσία refers to a moral corruption (BDAG, s.v. "ἀκαθαρσία" 2, p. 34). Paul also uses the term to describe sexual impurity (Rom. 1:24; Gal. 5:19; Col. 3:5). The final prepositional phrase, "with greed" (ἐν πλεονεξίᾳ), describes the manner with which they pursue this sexual uncleanliness (Larkin, 89; Hoehner, 592). English translations render the phrase a number of different ways. The ESV captures the essence well: "greedy to practice every kind of impurity" (cf. RSV, NRSV), as does the NLT: "eagerly practice every kind of impurity." The entire phrase describes an insatiable sexual desire.

4:20 δέ: The Greek word δέ is a conjunction that means "but" (BDAG, s.v. "δέ" 4c, p. 213). **Syntactically**, δέ is in the postpositive position introducing the independent conjunctive clause "*But* you did not learn Christ in such a manner" (ὑμεῖς δὲ οὐχ οὕτως ἐμάθετε τὸν Χριστόν). **Semantically**, δέ is a contrastive conjunction: "but" (ESV, NASB, CSB, HCSB, NKJV, KJV, NET, NLT). The NIV marks the contrast by translating the conjunction as "However." The NRSV and RSV omit the conjunction. The conjunction marks a shift in Paul's argument from discussing the state of the non-Christian to the current state of the believer. Paul underscores the contrast by inserting ὑμεῖς ("you"), shifting the subject from "the Gentiles" (τὰ ἔθνη) in verses 17–19.

ἐμάθετε: The Greek word ἐμάθετε is a second-person plural aorist active indicative from the verb μανθάνω that means "to learn" (BDAG, s.v. "μανθάνω" 1, p. 615). **Syntactically**, ἐμάθετε functions as the main verb of the independent conjunctive clause introduced by δέ. The clause functions as the apodosis of a first class conditional statement. Paul adds οὐχ οὕτως, creating a litotes—an affirmative expression made by negating the contrary (Hoehner, 593). The subject of the sentence is "you" (ὑμεῖς), referring to the Gentiles. By adding the pronoun and placing it before the verb, Paul emphasizes the subject. The direct object is "Christ" (τὸν Χριστόν). **Semantically**, ἐμάθετε is a constative aorist: "learned" (ESV, NIV, NRSV, HCSB, NKJV, KJV, NLT) or "came to know" (CSB). It describes the action of the verb as a whole (W, 557–58). Hoehner labels this as an ingressive aorist, describing the point of the believer's conversion (Hoehner, 594; Best, 427). However, the following verbs seem to describe the process by which they learned Christ, suggesting that the action is broader than just a point in time (Barth, 504; Larkin, 89–90; Merkle, 140).

Theological Nugget: What does it mean to "learn Christ" (ἐμάθετε τὸν Χριστόν)? Abbott states that the use of this verb with a person "seems to be without parallel" (Abbott, 1909, 134); we would anticipate that the object is content, such as doctrine (cf. Rom. 16:17). Nonetheless, most commentators note that this phrase is parallel to statements such as "preaching Christ" (Gal. 1:16; 1 Cor. 1:23; 2 Cor. 1:19; Phil. 1:15). The phrase describes the content of the preaching: the gospel message centered on the person of Christ. In Colossians, Paul makes a similar statement, but with a different verb: "Just as you received [παρελάβετε] Jesus Christ as Lord, continue to walk in him." The verb ἐμάθετε carries a similar connotation (Abbott, 1909, 135; Arnold, 284).

4:21a εἴ γε: The Greek word εἰ is an adverbial conjunction that means "if" in this context (BDAG, s.v. "εἰ" 6b, p. 278). The Greek word γέ is a particle that adds emphasis: "if indeed" (BDAG, s.v. "γέ" bα, p. 190; cf. NET, NASB, NKJV).

Syntactically, εἰ introduces a dependent conjunctive clause: "*if indeed* you have learned about him" (εἴ γε αὐτὸν ἠκούσατε). The entire clause functions adverbially. It modifies the verb "have learned" (ἐμάθετε). **Semantically**, εἰ introduces the protasis of a first class conditional clause: "if" (NET, NASB, NKJV, KJV). The conditional clause puts forward a statement of truth for the sake of an argument (W, 690–94). Paul assumes that the Ephesian believers "have heard" and "have been taught" the content that Paul presents in verses 22–24. Several English versions render the conjunction with the concessive idea: "assuming" (CSB, HCSB, RSV, ESV), "for surely" (NRSV), or simply as "since" (NLT).

ἠκούσατε: The Greek word ἠκούσατε is a second-person plural aorist active indicative from the verb ἀκούω that means "to learn about" (BDAG, s.v. "ἀκούω" 3b, p. 38). **Syntactically**, ἠκούσατε functions as the main verb of the dependent conjunctive clause introduced by εἰ. The subject is implied by the verb: "you," referring to the Ephesian believers. The direct object is "him" (αὐτόν). The antecedent of the pronoun is "Christ" (v. 20). Normally, ἀκούω takes the genitive case to refer to the words spoken by a person; however, the accusative communicates "the thing about which one hears" (BDF §173.1). The accusative implies that they did not hear Christ directly, but rather heard *about* him (cf. ESV, RSV, NRSV, NIV, NET, CSB, HCSB, NLT). **Semantically**, ἠκούσατε is a constative aorist: "heard" (CSB, HCSB, NASB, NET, NLT). It describes the action of the verb as a whole (W, 557–58). Presumably, this refers to Paul preaching the gospel. In Romans, Paul makes the point that faith comes from hearing and hearing from preaching (Rom. 10:14).

4:21b καί: The Greek word καί is a conjunction that means "and" (BDAG, s.v. "καί" 1bα, p. 494). **Syntactically**, καί introduces a dependent conjunctive clause: "*and* you were taught in him" (καὶ ἐν αὐτῷ ἐδιδάχθητε). The clause is parallel to the conjunctive clause introduced by εἰ. **Semantically**, καί is a coordinating connective: "and" (NRSV, RSV, ESV, NET, NIV, CSB, HCSB, NASB, NKJV, KJV). The conjunction notes that the believers have not just heard about Jesus, but that they also learned about him.

ἐδιδάχθητε: The Greek word ἐδιδάχθητε is a second-person plural aorist passive indicative from the verb διδάσκω that means "to teach" (BDAG, s.v. "διδάσκω" 2d, p. 241). **Syntactically**, ἐδιδάχθητε functions as the main verb of the dependent clause introduced by εἰ along with ἠκούσατε. The subject is implied by the verb: "you," referring to the Ephesian believers. **Semantically**, ἐδιδάχθητε is a constative aorist: "were taught" (RSV, NRSV, ESV, NIV, NET, CSB, HCSB). It describes the action of the verb as a whole (W, 557–58). The NLT translates the aorist actively: "you learned."

Semantical Nugget: What does the prepositional phrase "in him" (ἐν αὐτῷ) mean? The phrase could express means: "you were taught *by him*" (KJV, NKJV, CSB, HCSB). The problem is that Jesus most likely did not teach these believers directly. The preposition most likely expresses the sphere of the believer's learning, highlighting their relationship with Christ (Hoehner, 595). Most English versions render the prepositional phrase as "in him" (RSV, NRSV, ESV, NIV, NET, NASB).

4:21c καθώς: The Greek word καθώς is a conjunction that means "as" or "just as" (BDAG, s.v. "καθώς" 1, p. 493). **Syntactically**, καθώς introduces a dependent conjunctive clause "*just as* it is true in Jesus" (καθώς ἐστιν ἀλήθεια ἐν τῷ Ἰησοῦ). The entire clause functions adverbially modifying the verbs "have heard" (ἠκούσατε) and "have been taught" (ἐδιδάχθητε). **Semantically**, καθώς could provide the reason for why the Ephesians were taught, expressing cause: "because" (HCSB; cf. NLT; Best, 428–29; Arnold, 285). However, it is best understood as a comparison: "just as" (NASB) or "as" (CSB, NKJV, KJV, RSV, NRSV, ESV). The clause expresses the standard by which they were taught (Hoehner, 598; Larkin, 90; Lincoln, 283). The NIV renders the phrase: "in accordance with the truth that is in Jesus."

ἐστίν: The Greek word ἐστίν is a third-person singular present active indicative from the verb εἰμί that means "to be" (BDAG, s.v. "εἰμί" 3b, p. 284). **Syntactically**, ἐστίν functions as the main verb of the dependent conjunctive clause introduced by καθώς. "Truth" (ἀλήθεια) is the subject of the sentence, not the predicate nominative (BDF §258; Best, 429; Merkle, 141; Larkin, 91). Hoehner notes that this truth is best understood in light of the lies that dominate the life of the unbeliever (cf. vv. 18–19) (Hoehner, 597). In this context, truth most likely refers to the gospel message (cf. Eph. 1:13; Col. 1:15; Best, 429; Lincoln, 282–83). Paul will reiterate this contrast in verses 22 and 24. The predicate nominative is the prepositional phrase "in Jesus" (ἐν τῷ Ἰησοῦ). The preposition expresses sphere—the truth is in Jesus. **Semantically**, ἐστίν is a gnomic present: "is" (ESV, RSV, NRSV, NIV, NET, CSB, HCSB, NASB, NKJV, KJV). The present tense describes a timeless, or general statement (W, 523–24).

Theological Nugget: What's the significance that Paul only refers to Jesus without any other designation? This is the only occurrence in Ephesians where "Jesus" (Ἰησοῦς) appears without "Christ" or "Lord." Lincoln argues that this is due to stylistic variation (Lincoln, 381–82). On the other hand, several commentators indicate that Paul's use here may point to the historical Jesus. While it might be tenuous to draw this conclusion based on Paul's use of the name here, he does refer to Christ's death as an example for the believer (Eph. 5:2). Not only did Paul teach the truth as it is found in Jesus, but he also uses the life of Christ as an example to follow (Thielman, 302; Hoehner, 597; Arnold, 285; Best, 429–30).

4:22 ἀποθέσθαι: The Greek word ἀποθέσθαι is an aorist middle infinitive from the verb ἀποτίθημι that means "to take off" or "lay aside." The term literally means to take off clothes, but it takes a metaphorical meaning to describe the cessation of a behavior. Most English versions translate the verb literally: "to take off" (CSB; cf. HCSB); or metaphorically: "to put off" (ESV; cf. RSV, NRSV, NIV) (BDAG, s.v. "ἀποτίθημι" 1b, pp. 123–24). **Syntactically**, ἀποθέσθαι functions as the direct object of the verbs "have heard" (ἠκούσατε) and "have been taught" (ἐδιδάχθητε). The subject of the infinitive is "you" (ὑμᾶς), referring to the Ephesians. The direct object of the infinitive is "the old self that is corrupt" (τὸν παλαιὸν ἄνθρωπον). **Semantically**, the infinitive expresses indirect discourse, providing the content of Paul's teaching. In the original discourse, the infinitive represents the indicative: "you have taken off the old self" (see Semantical Nugget below). The infinitive is a constative aorist: "take off." It describes the action of the verb as a whole (W, 557–58).

Semantical Nugget: How should the infinitives in Ephesians 4:22–24 be treated? In Ephesians 4:22–24, Paul summarizes what he had taught in Ephesus with three infinitives: ἀποθέσθαι (v. 22), ἀνανεοῦσθαι (v. 23), and ἐνδύσασθαι (v. 24). A number of commentators identify these infinitives as epexegetical (Lincoln, 283; Arnold, 286; Moule, 127, 139). However, since the controlling verbs describe instruction, they are best understood as indirect discourse, giving the content of what Paul taught the Ephesian church (W, 603–5; Robertson, 1036–38; Merkle, 142; Larkin, 92). As infinitives in indirect discourse, these infinitives can represent either the *indicative*: "You took off ... you are being renewed ... you put on" (HCSB); or the *imperative*: "Take off ... be renewed ... and put on" (RSV; cf. NLT, GNT). Most English versions retain the infinitive, which gives an imperatival force: "you were taught ... to put off ... to be made new ... and to put on" (NIV, ESV, NRSV). Most commentators interpret these infinitives as imperatives, relying on Burton's comments: "There is apparently no instance in the New Testament of the Aorist Infinitive in indirect discourse representing the Aorist Indicative of the direct form" (Burton, 1898, 53). Nonetheless, the context of conveying instruction suggests that these should be taken as imperative (Lincoln, 283–84; Best, 430–31; Arnold, 286; Thielman, 302–3; Bock, 1994a, 162–63). On the other hand, Hoehner argues that the content of Paul's instruction is "the impartation of tradition." Even though the context suggests that this is instruction, he is communicating the positional status of the Ephesian believers, not giving them a command. This is consistent with Pauline theology (cf. Gal. 3:27; Rom. 6: 2, 4, 6; 2 Cor. 5:17). In Colossians 3:9–10,

Paul uses the same image with an aorist participle. In Colossians, the "taking off of the old self" and the "putting on of the new self" serves as the basis for the command (you should no longer lie). This suggests that the command is based on the position or status of the believer (Hoehner, 600–2). Finally, John Stott represents a mediating position. He argues that the infinitives could represent an initial command for believers when the gospel was originally proclaimed. After responding, the phrase could be viewed as a statement of their position (Stott, 1979, 180). Stott's observation gets to the heart of the issue. Underlying the difficulty is the eschatological tension in Paul's theology, what scholars call "already/not yet." On the one hand, the believer receives the benefit of their relationship with Christ. On the other hand, he looks forward to a time when the believer will receive their full inheritance. In the meantime, he exhorts believers to live a life worthy of their calling (Arnold, 286–87; Dunn, 1998, 461–98; Schreiner, 2001, 251–61).

φθειρόμενον: The Greek word φθειρόμενον is a masculine accusative singular present passive participle from the verb φθείρω that means "to ruin" or "corrupt" as it pertains to the inner life through erroneous teaching or immorality (BDAG, s.v. "φθείρω" 2a, p. 1054). **Syntactically**, φθειρόμενον is an attributive participle modifying "the old self" (τὸν παλαιὸν ἄνθρωπον). Most English versions render the participle with a relative pronoun: "your old self, which is being corrupt" (NIV, KJV, NKJV) or "the old self that is corrupted" (CSB, HCSB). **Semantically**, φθειρόμενον is a customary present: "being corrupted" (NIV, NASB, NET) or "is corrupted" (CSB, HCSB, NASB, NLT). The present tense describes an ongoing state (W, 521–22). The tense does not communicate the fact that the old self becomes more corrupt; it suggests that it exists in a continual state of corruption (Arnold, 288).

Syntactical Nugget: How do the prepositional phrases "according to the former behavior" (κατὰ τὴν προτέραν ἀναστροφήν) and "according to the deceitful desires" (κατὰ τὰς ἐπιθυμίας τῆς ἀπάτης) relate to the context? The first prepositional phrase is best understood as modifying "the old self," describing the conduct of the previous lifestyle of the believers (cf. Eph. 4:17–19) (cf. ESV, RSV, NRSV; Hoehner, 604–5; Best, 434; Merkle, 142). The second prepositional phrase modifies the attributive participle. It can convey the reason for the corruption: "the old self that is corrupted by deceitful desires" (CSB; BDAG, s.v. "κατά" 5aδ, p. 512–13; Thielman, 304). Or else it can be taken to express the standard: "the old man who is being corrupted in accordance with deceitful desires" (NET; cf. NASB, KJV, NKJV; Hoehner, 606). In essence, this old self is corrupt according to these deceitful desires. Most English versions render the genitive construction τὰς ἐπιθυμίας τῆς ἀπάτης as an attributive genitive: "deceitful desires" (CSB, HCSB, KJV, NKJV, RSV, ESV,

NIV, NET); however it could be rendered as a genitive of source: "desires *that come from* deceit" (Thielman, 304; Hoehner, 606).

Theological Nugget: What does Paul mean by the "old man"? Most English versions translate the phrase τὸν παλαιὸν ἄνθρωπον ("the old man"), metaphorically either rending it as "your old nature" (RSV) or "your old self" (NRSV, ESV, NIV; cf. CSB, HCSB, NASB). The NET renders the phrase literally: "the old man" (cf. NKJV, KJV). In Romans, Paul describes the old person as our sinful nature. In Romans 6, he states that "our old person has been crucified with Christ," rendering sin ineffective (Rom. 6:6). As a result, sin no longer rules the believer; we are free to present ourselves as instruments of righteousness (Rom. 6:12–13). In Ephesians—as well as Colossians—Paul changes the metaphor. The old person stands in contrast to the new person, which the believer has put on (see Theological Nugget at 4:24). Rather than describing the old person as crucified, he uses a clothing metaphor: taking off and putting on. While the image is less stark, the idea is the same. They have received a new identity in Christ, and with this new identity, they will act differently (Dockery, 1993, 628–29).

4:23   ἀνανεοῦσθαι: The Greek word ἀνανεοῦσθαι is a present passive infinitive from the verb ἀνανεόω that means "to renew" (BDAG, s.v. "ἀνανεόω" 1, p. 68). The term is a *hapax legomenon*, only occurring once in the New Testament. **Syntactically**, ἀνανεοῦσθαι functions as the direct object of the verbs "have heard" (ἠκούσατε) and "have been taught" (ἐδιδάχθητε). The subject of the infinitive is "you" (ὑμᾶς; v. 22). **Semantically**, ἀνανεοῦσθαι expresses indirect discourse, providing the content of Paul's teaching. In the original discourse, the infinitive represents the indicative: "your mind is being renewed." (see Semantical Nugget at 4:22). The infinitive is a customary present: "be renewed" (ESV, RSV, NRSV, NET, CSB, NASB, NKJV, KJV). The present tense describes an ongoing state (W, 521–22). The present tense infinitive stands out with the aorist infinitives before and after it. The clause temporally interrupts Paul's clothing metaphor to describe the believer's ongoing experience. This renewal is ongoing, while "taking off" and "putting on" are undefined actions (Hoehner, 607). The passive voice is a divine passive. Even though the agent is absent, God is the one who renews the believer (Thielman, 306).

Grammatical Nugget: What is the structure of verses 22 and 24 compared to verse 23? Compared to verses 22 and 24, verse 23 makes a simple statement. Both verses 22 and 24 contain an attributive participle modifying "old self" and "new self," as well as two prepositional phrases. The old self is corrupt according to their former behavior; the new self is created according to God. The old self lives according to deceitful desires; the new self lives in true righteousness and holiness.

v. 22: **ἀποθέσθαι** ὑμᾶς

<u>κατὰ</u> τὴν προτέραν ἀναστροφὴν τὸν παλαιὸν ἄνθρωπον τὸν **φθειρόμενον**

<u>κατὰ</u> τὰς ἐπιθυμίας τῆς ἀπάτης

v. 24: καὶ **ἐνδύσασθαι**

τὸν καινὸν ἄνθρωπον τὸν <u>κατὰ</u> θεὸν **κτισθέντα**

<u>ἐν</u> δικαιοσύνῃ καὶ ὁσιότητι τῆς ἀληθείας

v. 22: that you **have put off**

the old self who **is corrupted** <u>according</u> to the former behavior

<u>according</u> to the desires from deceit

v. 24: and that you **have put on**

the new self who **is created** <u>according</u> to God

<u>in</u> righteousness and holiness from truth

The repetition creates balance between the two statements, emphasizing the contrast. In contrast, Paul puts forward a simple statement in verse 23. The simple statement creates a rhetorical effect drawing the reader's attention to the renewal of the mind.

δέ: The Greek word δέ is a conjunction that means "but" or "rather" (BDAG, s.v. "δέ" 4a, p. 213). **Syntactically**, δέ is in the postpositive position and introduces the second infinitive clause: "*but* be renewed by the spirit of your mind" (ἀνανεοῦσθαι δὲ τῷ πνεύματι τοῦ νοὸς ὑμῶν). **Semantically**, δέ is adversative: "but" (W, 671–72; Merkle, 143). It introduces a positive statement after the negative statement. Most English versions render the conjunction as "and" (NASB, KJV, NKJV, RSV, NRSV, ESV) or simply omit it (NET, NIV, CSB, HCSB). The NLT brings out the shift in Paul's discussion by rendering the conjunction as "instead."

Semantical Nugget: What does Paul mean by being renewed "in the spirit of your mind" (τῷ πνεύματι τοῦ νοὸς ὑμῶν)? On the one hand, "spirit" could refer to God's Spirit. If this is the case, then the dative most likely expresses means: "be renewed *by the Spirit*." The NLT renders the phrase as "let the Spirit renew your thoughts and attitudes" (cf. Arnold, 288–89). On the other hand, this probably refers to the human spirit. The genitive τοῦ νοός is in apposition, describing τῷ πνεύματι: "the spirit, *namely* your mind." Most English versions render τῷ πνεύματι with a lower case: "spirit" (CSB, HCSB, NASB, KJV, NKJV, ESV, NRSV, RSV, NET) (Abbott, 1909, 137; Hoehner, 608; Lincoln, 287). The NIV translates it as "attitude." If this is the case, the dative most likely communicates sphere to describe an internal renewal.

4:24 καί: The Greek word καί is a conjunction that means "and" (BDAG, s.v. "καί" 1b, p. 494). **Syntactically**, καί introduces an independent conjunctive clause:

"*and* you have put on the new self" (καὶ ἐνδύσασθαι τὸν καινὸν ἄνθρωπον). **Semantically**, καί is a coordinating connective: "and" (RSV, NRSV, ESV, NIV, NET, CSB, NASB, KJV, NKJV). The conjunction brings the reader back to Paul's clothing metaphor, which he began in verse 22.

ἐνδύσασθαι: The Greek word ἐνδύσασθαι is an aorist middle infinitive from the verb ἐνδύω that means "to put on" or "to wear" (BDAG, s.v. "ἐνδύω" 2b, pp. 333–34). Most English versions render the verb as "put on"; the NRSV translates it as "clothe yourself." The verb expresses the opposite of "taking off" (ἀποθέσθαι, v. 22). Metaphorically, the verb communicates the idea of taking on some characteristic or virtue. **Syntactically**, ἐνδύσασθαι functions as the direct object of the verbs "have heard" (ἠκούσατε) and "have been taught" (ἐδιδάχθητε). The subject of the infinitive is "you" (ὑμᾶς; v. 22). The direct object of the infinitive is "the new self, created according to God" (τὸν καινὸν ἄνθρωπον τὸν κατὰ θεὸν κτισθέντα). **Semantically**, ἐνδύσασθαι expresses indirect discourse, providing the content of Paul's teaching. In the original discourse, the infinitive represents the indicative: "you have put on the new self." (see Semantical Nugget at 4:22). The infinitive is a constative aorist, describing the action of the verb as a whole (W, 557–58).

κτισθέντα: The Greek word κτισθέντα is a masculine accusative singular aorist passive participle from the verb κτίζω that means "to bring into existence" or "create" (BDAG, s.v. "κτίζω," p. 572). **Syntactically**, κτισθέντα is an attributive participle modifying "the new self" (τὸν καινὸν ἄνθρωπον). Most English versions render the participle with the relative pronoun: "the new self *which* was created" (NKJV, KJV; cf. NASB, NET). Several English versions translate the participle after the noun: "the new self, created" (ESV, NRSV, RSV, NLT). **Semantically**, κτισθέντα is an ingressive aorist, which focuses on the beginning of an action (W, 558–59). The passive participle is a divine passive; even though the agent is unexpressed; God is the one who creates this new self. This passive participle is in contrast to the passive participle in verse 22 ("being corrupted," φθειρόμενον). The old self is being corrupted by deceit, but God creates this new self according to his image.

Theological Nugget: How does the participle κτισθέντα ("created") connect the passage to the rest of Ephesians? In Ephesians, Paul describes God as the one who creates (Eph. 3:9). In Ephesians 2:10, he calls believers God's handiwork, "having been created in Christ Jesus." Later in the chapter, he sharpens this theme. Through the death of Christ, God "creates one new person" (ἕνα καινὸν ἄνθρωπον) from two groups—Jews and Gentiles (Eph. 2:15). In Ephesians 4, Paul begins to draw out the implications. This "new person, created according to God's likeness" is an allusion to

Ephesians 2:15, implying that the following ethical statements are born out of the believers' identity as members of the Christian community.

The participle phrase is modified by two prepositional phrases. The first prepositional phrase, "according to God" (κατὰ θεόν), expresses the standard of the creation. The preposition most likely refers to God creating the believer in his own image (cf. Col. 3:10) (Arnold, 290). Most English versions draw this idea out: "according to the *likeness of God*" (cf. ESV, RSV, NRSV, HCSB, CSB, NASB). The NET translates the phrase as "in God's image." The second, prepositional phrase "in true righteousness and holiness" (ἐν δικαιοσύνῃ καὶ ὁσιότητι τῆς ἀληθείας), expresses sphere. Righteousness and holiness are characteristic of God, which now characterize the believer. Paul modifies these terms with the genitive τῆς ἀληθείας ("the truth"). Several English versions translate the genitive as an attributive genitive: "true righteousness and holiness" (RSV, NRSV, ESV, NIV, NKJV), but it is most likely a genitive of source: "righteousness and holiness *that comes from* truth" (NET; Thielman, 307; Hoehner, 613; Arnold, 290). The genitive completes the contrast that Paul began in verse 22. The desires that corrupted the old self came from deceit, but righteousness and holiness that characterize the new self come from truth (Thielman, 307).

4:25a διό: The Greek word διό is a conjunction that means "therefore" (BDAG, s.v. "διό," p. 250). Most English versions translate the conjunction as "Therefore" (CSB, NASB, NKJV, RSV, ESV, NIV, NET) or "So" (NRSV, NLT). **Syntactically**, διό introduces an independent conjunctive clause: "*Therefore* … let each one of you speak the truth." **Semantically**, διό is inferential (W, 673). The following section rests on the previous one (vv. 17–24). Paul shifts the discussion from a general discussion to specific commands, which rest on what he has said before.

ἀποθέμενοι: The Greek word ἀποθέμενοι is a masculine nominative plural aorist middle participle from the verb ἀποτίθημι that means "take off" (BDAG, s.v. "ἀποτίθημι" 1b, pp. 123–24). **Syntactically**, ἀποθέμενοι introduces a dependent participle clause. It functions adverbially modifying the verb "let us speak" (λαλεῖτε). The direct object is "falsehood" (τὸ ψεῦδος). **Semantically**, a number of commentators argue that the participle is attendant circumstance. The NIV renders it this way; since the verb it modifies is an imperative, the participle communicates an imperative idea: "each of you must put off falsehood and speak truthfully" (NIV; cf. NLT). Paul's series of exhortations suggest the imperative as well (Arnold, 299; Merkle, 147). However, the word choice links this section to the previous section, suggesting that it has the same force as the inferential conjunction (Hoehner, 615; W, 605 n. 55; Larkin, 97). In this regard, the participle best expresses cause: "*Since* you put away lying, speak the truth" (HCSB).

Lexical Nugget: What does it mean to "take off falsehood" (ἀποθέμενοι τὸ ψεῦδος)? Paul repeats the verb "take off" from verse 22, where he describes the believer having "taken off the old self." The repetition draws a link between the believer's new position and the list of imperatives. Besides the repetition of the verb, Paul creates a thematic link to the previous section. In the previous section, he characterizes the life of the unbeliever as one full of falsehood, and as a result uncertainty (4:14, 17–19, 22). On the other hand, the believer grows in truth (4:15, 21, 24). Verse 25 brings the argument to the climax: the believer must put away lies and speak the truth.

4:25b λαλεῖτε: The Greek word λαλεῖτε is a second-person plural present active imperative from the verb λαλέω that means "to talk" or "speak" (BDAG, s.v. "λαλέω" 2b, pp. 582–83). **Syntactically**, λαλεῖτε functions as the main verb of the independent conjunctive clause introduced by διό. The subject is "each" (ἕκαστος). The demonstrative functions as a distributive pronoun: "each of you" (NIV; cf. RSV, ESV) or "each one" (CSB, HCSB, NASB, NKJV). The direct object is "truth" (ἀλήθειαν). **Semantically**, λαλεῖτε is a customary present: "speak" (NIV, NET, CSB, HCSB, NASB). The present imperative communicates a general precept. Paul wants the Ephesians to make speaking the truth habitual (Merkle, 147; W, 722).

Theological Nugget: What is the background to Zechariah 8:16, which is quoted in Ephesians 5:25? Even though he does not give an introduction, Paul's command to "speak the truth" is a close parallel to Zechariah 8:16.

Zechariah 8:16: λαλεῖτε ἀλήθειαν ἕκαστος <u>πρὸς</u> τὸν πλησίον αὐτοῦ
Ephesians 4:25: λαλεῖτε ἀλήθειαν ἕκαστος <u>μετὰ</u> τοῦ πλησίον αὐτοῦ

Zechariah 8:16: Let each of you speak truth <u>to</u> their neighbor
Ephesians 4:25: Let each of you speak truth <u>with</u> their neighbor

Paul makes one change: he uses the preposition μετά instead of πρός. The different preposition slightly alters the meaning, suggesting more of a mutual interaction between believers (BDAG, s.v. "μετά" A1aβ, pp. 636–37; Hoehner, 616). Even though Paul does not seem to take advantage of the wider context of Zechariah for his argument here, the original context might provide some insight. Zechariah 8 describes a point in the future when God returns to Jerusalem, bringing his people out of exile (Zech. 8:3–8). The time will be marked with peace (Zech. 8:12). The first command that God gives in this new age is verse 16: "speak the truth to your neighbor." And just like Zechariah, this is the first command that Paul gives for the believer who has put on the new self (Hoehner, 616; Thielman, 311–12).

⁴:²⁵ᶜ ὅτι: The Greek word ὅτι is a conjunction that means "because" in this context (BDAG, s.v. "ὅτι" 4a, p. 732). **Syntactically**, ὅτι introduces a dependent conjunctive clause "*because* we are members of one another" (ὅτι ἐσμὲν ἀλλήλων μέλη). The entire clause functions adverbially modifying the main verb "speak" (λαλεῖτε). **Semantically**, ὅτι marks the clause as the reason or basis for the action of the verb: "*because* we are members of one another" (CSB, HCSB). The clause gives the basis of why believers should speak the truth: namely, we are members with one another (W, 460–61).

ἐσμέν: The Greek word ἐσμέν is a first-person plural present active indicative from the verb εἰμί that means "to be" (BDAG, s.v. "εἰμί" 2b, p. 283). **Syntactically**, ἐσμέν functions as the main verb of the dependent conjunctive clause introduced by ὅτι. The subject is implied in the verb "we," referring to the believers. **Semantically**, the present tense functions as a gnomic present, expressing a general fact or statement: "we are members of one another" (ESV, NRSV, CSB, HCSB, NASB, NKJV, KJV) (W, 523–25).

> **Lexical Nugget**: What does being a "member" (μέλος) mean? The Greek word μέλος literally refers to a body part: a member of the body. Figuratively, it refers to the extension of a community, i.e., "the many-sided organism of the Christian community" (BDAG, s.v. "μέλος" 2, p. 628). Paul develops this image in Romans 12:5: "Even though we are many, we are one body in Christ, but individually members of one another" (cf. 1 Cor. 12:27). In Ephesians 5:30, he makes a similar argument: Christ will care for the church "because we are members of his body." Earlier in the chapter, he describes the church as an organism growing into Christ—each part (μέρος) working together to accomplish a unified goal (Eph. 4:15–16). Paul's word choice points to the close-knit relationship of the various members of the body. The consequences for one's action will impact the entire community. As Hoehner states: "Deception by one member not only harms that member, but the whole body suffers as well" (Hoehner, 618).

⁴:²⁶ᵃ ὀργίζεσθε: The Greek word ὀργίζεσθε is a second-person plural present passive imperative from the verb ὀργίζω that means "to be angry" (BDAG, s.v. "ὀργίζω," p. 721). **Syntactically**, ὀργίζεσθε is the main verb of an independent asyndeton clause: "be angry" (ὀργίζεσθε). The subject is implied by the verb: "you all," referring to the believers. **Semantically**, ὀργίζεσθε could be classified as a conditional imperative, in which the imperative states the condition, or the protasis, upon which the fulfillment of another verb depends (Best, 449; Lincoln, 301). The problem with this position is that if this is conditional, then the second imperative, ἁμαρτάνετε ("sin"), should be considered as a future indicative. Absurdly, it would be translated as "if you get angry, then you will not sin" (W, 489–92). It is best to understand both

imperatives as commands, the first as positive and the second as negative. The present tense functions as an iterative present, which expresses repeated action as opposed to a customary present, which would describe an attitude of anger (W, 722). In contrast to the other prohibitions in this section, which he absolutely condemns, Paul seems to give some room for anger (cf. Mark 3:5). However, he gives some warning about dangers of excessive anger in verses 26b and 27 (cf. James 1:19), which may lead to giving place for Satan in the life of the believer. Later in the passage, he will condemn rage (v. 31) (Hoehner, 620; Arnold, 300–301).

4:26b καί: The Greek word καί is a conjunction that means "and" (BDAG, s.v. "καί" 1b p. 494). **Syntactically**, καί introduces an independent conjunctive clause: "*and* do not sin" (καὶ μὴ ἁμαρτάνετε). **Semantically**, καί is a coordinating connective: "and" (csb, hcsb, nasb, nkjv, kjv, esv, net). The prohibition helps to balance the positive imperative: "Be angry" (v. 26a). While Paul gives some allowance for anger in the passage, the prohibition shows that there is some limit. It provides balance for the positive command in verse 26a: "be angry." Larkin labels the conjunction as "continuative, with an epexegetical quality:" "and yet." (Larkin, 98). The rsv renders the conjunction as "but do not sin" (nrsv). The niv shows the relationship between the two imperatives by rendering the first imperative as a noun: "In your anger, do not sin." The nlt follows a similar translation: "Don't sin by letting anger control you."

ἁμαρτάνετε: The Greek word ἁμαρτάνετε is a second-person plural present active imperative from the verb ἁμαρτάνω that means "to sin" (BDAG, s.v. "ἁμαρτάνω" a, p. 49). Most English versions translate the prohibition as "do not sin" (rsv, nrsv, esv, niv, net, nlt, csb, hcsb, nasb, nkjv). **Syntactically**, ἁμαρτάνετε functions as the main verb of the independent conjunctive clause introduced by καί, parallel with the verb ὀργίζεσθε. The subject is implied: "you all," referring to the Ephesians. **Semantically**, ἁμαρτάνετε functions as a customary present, which expresses the prohibition as a general precept to follow when the believer is angry (W, 724–25). Within the immediate context, the prohibition sets the limit of the believer's anger.

4:26c ἐπιδυέτω: The Greek word ἐπιδυέτω is a third-person singular present active imperative from the verb ἐπιδύω that means "to set (upon)," in reference to the movement of the sun (BDAG, s.v. "ἐπιδύω," p. 371). **Syntactically**, ἐπιδυέτω is the main verb in an asyndeton clause: "do not let." The clause is parallel with ὀργίζεσθε and ἁμαρτάνετε. The subject is "the sun" (ὁ ἥλιος). **Semantically**, ἐπιδυέτω functions as a customary present, which expresses the prohibition as a general precept to follow when the believer is angry (W, 724–25). Most English versions render the phrase as "do not let the sun go down" (rsv, nrsv, esv, niv, net, csb, hcsb, nasb, nkjv). Just like the previous phrase ("and do not sin"), the prohibition sets a limit on the believer's anger. In this case, it gives a temporal limit. The phrase should be taken somewhat figuratively. Best points out that if we take the phrase literally then "those who lived in the Arctic or Antarctic would at certain times of the year have no temporal limitation on their anger!" (Best, 450). Believers should avoid harboring anger over a long period of time—Paul sets the limit to a single day (Hoehner, 621–22). The verb is modified by the prepositional phrase "on your anger" (ἐπὶ τῷ παροργισμῷ ὑμῶν). The preposition ἐπί is a temporal marker expressing the idea of "at the time of" or "during" (BDAG, s.v. "ἐπί" 18b, p. 367). Most English versions render the preposition literally: "on your anger" (CSB, HCSB, NASB, NKJV, RSV, NRSV, ESV; cf. NET); however, it might be best rendered "while you are angry" (cf. NIV, NLT). The Greek word παροργισμός ("anger") has the connotation of provocation (BDAG, s.v. "παροργισμός," p. 780), or the source of one's anger. The NET renders the noun as "the cause of your anger."

4:27   δίδοτε: The Greek word δίδοτε is a second-person plural present active imperative from the verb δίδωμι that means "to give," or here "to allow" (BDAG, s.v. "δίδωμι" 17a, p. 242). Most English versions render the verb as "give" (RSV, ESV, NIV, NET, NLT, CSB, HCSB, NASB, NKJV, KJV). The NRSV translates it: "make room." **Syntactically**, δίδοτε functions as the main verb of the independent clause. The verb is parallel with ὀργίζεσθε, ἁμαρτάνετε, and ἐπιδυέτω, but it logically relates the to the first imperative, ὀργίζεσθε ("be angry"). It provides the rationale for the limits that Paul sets on anger: to avoid giving the devil a place through prolonged and unchecked anger (Arnold, 302–3; Thielman, 314). The subject is implied by the verb "you all," referring to the Ephesians. The direct object is "place" (τόπον), or figuratively "opportunity" (BDAG, s.v. "τόπος" 4, p. 1012). The indirect object is "the devil" (τῷ διαβόλῳ). **Semantically**, δίδοτε functions as a customary present, which expresses the prohibition as a general precept. Paul anticipates that the believer will not give the devil an opportunity (W, 724–25). Anger leaves the believer open to being exploited by the devil. By avoiding sin and setting a reasonable amount of time on one's anger, the believer takes away the chance that the devil may have in the life of the believer.

Theological Nugget: What does it mean to "give the devil an opportunity?" Throughout the letter, Paul describes evil spirits at work within the world scheming against believers. In Chapter 2, he describes unbelievers as "sons of disobedience" living a life under control of the "ruler of authority." These unbelievers are "by nature children of wrath" (Eph. 2:1–3). Later in Ephesians, he describes the relationship between believers and the devil as a struggle or a battle (Eph. 6:12). Not only has God redeemed the believer (Eph. 2:4–6); he has given the believer victory in this battle through their relationship with Christ (Eph. 1:19–23; 2:4–6). Regardless, the devil still looks for opportunities. At the end of the letter, Paul tells the believer to put on the full armor of God to withstand "the craftiness of the devil" (Eph. 6:11). Here in Ephesians 4:27, Paul gives a specific way to stifle the aims of the devil: to limit anger. On the surface, anger may seem to us as an emotional reaction to things that annoy us. But anger can have spiritual implications—particularly from the perspective of the devil. And even though Paul gives some license for anger in the current passage, later he warns the believer against the kind of anger that leads to bitterness, rage, and blasphemy (Eph. 4:31).

4:28a κλέπτων: The Greek word κλέπτων is a masculine nominative singular present active participle from the verb κλέπτω that means "to steal" (BDAG, s.v. "κλέπτω," p. 547). **Syntactically**, κλέπτων is a substantival participle: "the one who steals" (NET; cf. NASB, KJV, NKJV). Several English versions render the participle as a noun: "thief" (CSB, HCSB, RSV, ESV, NLT). The substantival participle functions as the subject of the verb "no longer steal" (μηκέτι κλεπτέτω). **Semantically**, κλέπτων is a customary present, describing an ongoing or habitual action (W, 521–22). Paul is addressing those who steal habitually. Of course, this does not limit Paul's admonition to only those who habitually steal. He gives the same command to his general readers in Romans (13:9) and 1 Corinthians (6:10) (Arnold, 303–4).

κλεπτέτω: The Greek word κλεπτέτω is a third-person singular present active imperative from the verb κλέπτω that means "to steal" (BDAG, s.v. "κλέπτω," p. 547). **Syntactically**, κλεπτέτω functions as the main verb of the asyndeton clause: "The one who steals must no longer steal" (ὁ κλέπτων μηκέτι κλεπτέτω). The subject of the verb is the substantival participle "the one who steals" (ὁ κλέπτων). **Semantically**, the present tense functions as a progressive present. In this case, the prohibition is directed to the one who steals. The force of the prohibition is that this type of action is already in progress, but needs to stop (W, 724).

4:28b δέ: The Greek word δέ is a conjunction that means "but" (BDAG, s.v. "δέ" 4c, p. 213). **Syntactically**, δέ introduces an independent conjunctive clause: "*but* rather let him labor" (μᾶλλον δὲ κοπιάτω). **Semantically**, δέ is a contrastive conjunction: "but" (RSV, ESV, NIV, KJV, NKJV) or "rather" (NRSV, NET; cf. NASB). The CSB begins a new sentence and translates the conjunction as "Instead, he is to do honest work" (cf. HCSB, NLT). The clause introduces an alternative to theft—to do honest labor.

κοπιάτω: The Greek word κοπιάτω is a third-person singular present active imperative from the verb κοπιάω that means "to work," "toil," or "strive"

(BDAG, s.v. "κοπιάω" 2, p. 558). Most English versions render the verb as "labor" or "work." **Syntactically**, κοπιάτω functions as the main verb of the conjunctive clause: "but rather let him labor" (μᾶλλον δὲ κοπιάτω). The subject of the verb is the substantival participle "the one who steals" (ὁ κλέπτων). **Semantically**, The present tense functions as an ingressive-progressive present. The force of the tense is that the one who steals should begin and continue to work (W, 721–22).

> **Grammatical Nugget**: Is there any significance for Paul's word choice in verse 28b? Paul creates an alliteration that is lost in English by repeating words that contain *kappa*, *pi*, *tau*, and *omega*: κλέπτων … κλεπτέτω … κοπιάτω. Paul could have used the noun (κλέπτης), but the substantival participle creates a link with the prohibition. And he certainly could have chosen other words for labor, which suggests that the alliteration was intentional. The alliteration underscores the connection between the prohibition and the positive command, making the contrast more pronounced.

4:28c ἐργαζόμενος: The Greek word ἐργαζόμενος is a masculine nominative singular present middle (deponent) participle from the verb ἐργάζομαι that means "to do" or "accomplish through work" (BDAG, s.v. "ἐργάζομαι" 2a, p. 389). **Syntactically**, ἐργαζόμενος introduces a dependent participle clause. It functions adverbially modifying the verb "labor" (κοπιάτω; v. 28b). The direct object is "the good" (τὸ ἀγαθόν). **Semantically**, ἐργαζόμενος could function as manner, describing how the labor should be accomplished, but it is most likely expresses means "*by the means* of working with his own hands." Some English versions treat the participle as attendant circumstance, translating it as an imperative: "let them labor and work honestly with their hands" or "he must do honest *work*" (HCSB, RSV).

> **Text-Critical Nugget**: Why does the NA[28] place brackets around ἰδίαις? There are a number of variations in the text of verse 28 at this point. First, a number of manuscripts rearrange the order of the words and omit the adjective ἰδίαις: τὸ ἀγαθόν ταῖς χερσὶν (L, Ψ, 323, 326, 614, 630, 945; K and 1505 support this word order, but insert ἰδίαις). This reading, found in MT and RP[2005], places emphasis on the good work of the thief, not his hands. However, it is more probable that a scribe moves the object (τὸ ἀγαθόν) closer to the participle rather than separating them (Metzger, 537). Second, a number of significant Alexandrian manuscripts (𝔓[46] and B) seem to support the word order found in the NA[28] but omit the adjective ἰδίαις. This reading might be found in 𝔓[49], but the manuscript is damaged at this point in the text (see Comfort and Barrett, 2001, 359). The longer reading is supported by good Alexandrian (ℵ, A ,81, 104, 1175) and Western (D, F, G) manuscripts. It is possible that ἰδίαις is an interpolation from 1 Corinthians 4:12; it is

equally possible that the word was omitted as superfluous (Lincoln, 292–93). The external evidence seems to suggest that the longer reading is original. The adjective emphasizes the contrast—these thieves should produce with their own hands, rather than steal the work from others.

Lexical Nugget: What does Paul mean by "honest work" (τὸ ἀγαθόν)? This literally means "a good thing," referring to something helpful or useful: "what is good" (BDAG, s.v. "ἀγαθός" 2bα, p. 4). Most English versions render the accusative τὸ ἀγαθόν as "honest work" (RSV, ESV, CSB, HCSB) or "something useful" (NIV). The NET renders the word as "good" (cf. NKJV, KJV, NASB). Paul probably has a more general idea in mind referring to anything good that might lead to the benefit of the community: a good work (cf. Gal. 6:10; 1 Thess. 5:15; 2 Thess. 2:17) (Lincoln, 304). He uses this word to link this command with the following context. He will tell the Ephesians to have something *good* to say (BDAG, s.v. "ἀγαθός" 1a, p. 4). While translating this word in verse 28c as "honest work" makes sense of the context, it removes the link. These commands allude to the first part of the book: Paul states that God creates good works for believers to walk in them (Eph. 2:10; cf. 6:8).

4:28d ἵνα: The Greek word ἵνα is a conjunction that means "so that" in this context (BDAG, s.v. "ἵνα" 1aγ, p. 475). **Syntactically**, the conjunction ἵνα introduces a dependent conjunctive clause: "*that* you might have something to share with the one who has need" (ἵνα ἔχη μεταδιδόναι τῷ χρείαν ἔχοντι). The entire clause functions adverbially modifying the main verb "labor" (κοπιάτω). **Semantically**, ἵνα expresses purpose: "so that" (ESV, RSV, NET, CSB, HCSB, NASB) or "that" (NIV, NKJV, KJV).

ἔχη: The Greek word ἔχη is a third-person singular present active subjunctive from the verb ἔχω. BDAG notes that verb could mean to be in a position to do something: "to be able" (BDAG, s.v. "ἔχω" 5, p. 421; cf. RSV). However, it is best to render the verb with the normative meaning: "to have" (BDAG, s.v. "ἔχω" 1aα, p. 420). Most English versions render the verb this way, creating a link with the following participle (ESV, NRSV, NIV, NET, NASB, NKJV, KJV; cf. CSB, HCSB). The RSV renders it: "he may be able" (cf. GNT); the NLT drops the verb altogether and translates the infinitive as the main verb. **Syntactically**, ἔχη functions as the main verb of the dependent conjunctive clause introduced by ἵνα. The subject of the verb is the substantival participle "the one who steals" (ὁ κλέπτων; v. 28a). Even though there is no accusative, English versions have to supply a direct object: "they may have *something*" (see NRSV, ESV, NIV, NET, NKJV, CSB, HCSB, NASB). **Semantically**, ἔχη is a customary present: "they may have" (ESV, NET, NKJV, KJV). The present tense describes an ongoing state (W, 521–22). Paul's command for them to continue working should leave them in a position to help anyone with a need.

μεταδιδόναι: The Greek word μεταδιδόναι is a present active infinitive from the verb μεταδίδωμι that means "to give" or "share" (BDAG, s.v. "μεταδίδωμι," p. 638). **Syntactically**, μεταδιδόναι introduces a dependent adverbial infinitive clause modifying the verb: "they may have something" (ἔχῃ). **Semantically**, this could be a complementary infinitive following ἔχῃ (cf. BDAG, s.v. "ἔχω" 5, p. 421): "he may be able to give" (rsv). However, we have interpreted ἔχῃ as referring to holding an implicit direct object; this indicates that the infinitive expresses purpose: "that they might have something *to give* to those who are in need" (Larkin, 101).

ἔχοντι: The Greek word ἔχοντι is a masculine dative singular present active participle from the verb ἔχω that means "to have" (BDAG, s.v. "ἔχω" 7aδ, p. 421). **Syntactically**, ἔχοντι is a substantival participle: "the one who has a need." The substantival participle functions as the indirect object of the infinitive "to share" (μεταδιδόναι; v. 28d). The direct object of the participle is "need" (χρείαν). In the sentence, the phrase τῷ χρείαν ἔχοντι ("the one who has need") functions as the direct object of the infinitive. **Semantically**, ἔχοντι is a customary present: "has" (nasb, net, nkjv). The present tense describes an ongoing state (W, 521–22). English versions translate the participle a number of different ways: "anyone in need" (esv, csb, hcsb); "those in need" (rsv, niv); or simply "the needy" (nrsv). The participle creates a contrast with the main verb in the clause. Paul wants believers to work in order to *have* something to give to those who *have* a need. The early Christian community regularly collected their goods and shared with those who were in need (Acts 2:45; 4:35; cf. 1 John 3:17).

4:29a ἐκπορευέσθω: The Greek word ἐκπορευέσθω is a third-person singular present middle (deponent) imperative from the verb ἐκπορεύομαι that means "to come out" or "go out" (BDAG, s.v. "ἐκπορεύομαι" 2, pp. 308–9). Most English versions render the verb as "come out of" (nrsv, rsv, esv, niv, net) or "come from" (csb, hcsb). **Syntactically**, ἐκπορευέσθω functions as the main verb of the asyndeton clause. The subject is "all unwholesome words" (πᾶς λόγος σαπρός). The use of πᾶς with the negative μή is a Hebrew idiom (BDF §302.1; Turner², 158). We might translate it as "do not let any unwholesome words." The prepositional phrase "from your mouth" (ἐκ τοῦ στόματος ὑμῶν) with the verb ἐκπορευέσθω is circumlocution that means to talk (cf. Matt. 4:4; Luke 4:22; 11:54; cf. Eph. 6:19; BDF §217.2; Turner², 84). **Semantically**, ἐκπορευέσθω is a progressive present indicating that this action is ongoing and should stop (W, 724–25; Hoehner, 629). Believers should keep from unwholesome speech.

Lexical Nugget: What does "unwholesome talk" (λόγος σαπρός) mean? In Greek, the word σαπρός modifies λόγος attributively: "unwholesome talk" (BDAG, s.v. "λόγος" 1aγ, p. 600). The adjective is primarily used to refer to food, meaning "rotten," indicating poor quality (Matt. 13:48; BDAG, s.v. "σαπρός" 1a, p. 913). The Gospel writers use the term to refer to rotten fruit, which comes from rotten trees (Matt. 12:33; Luke 6:43). In the Gospels, the image draws a link between one's internal reality and what they might produce. Elsewhere, Jesus teaches that what enters a person does not defile him, but what comes out (Mark 7:17–23). Just as in the Gospels, the word in this context takes on a moral connotation. In the following clause, Paul gives a positive command, stating that believers should use their words to build up in the time of need. He makes a similar contrast in verse 28: instead of stealing, believers should work so that they can give to those who have a need.

4:29b ἀλλ᾽: The Greek word ἀλλά is a conjunction that means "but" (BDAG, s.v. "ἀλλά" 1a, p. 45). **Syntactically**, ἀλλά introduces an independent conjunctive clause: "*but* what is good for the edification of the need" (ἀλλ᾽ εἴ τις ἀγαθὸς πρὸς οἰκοδομὴν τῆς χρείας). **Semantically**, ἀλλά is a contrastive conjunction: "but" (RSV, NRSV, ESV, NIV, NET, CSB, HCSB, NKJV, KJV). After giving a prohibition, the conjunction introduces a positive command—to speak in a way to build up others.

[ἐκπορευέσθω]: The Greek word ἐκπορευέσθω is a third-person singular present middle (deponent) imperative from the verb ἐκπορεύομαι that means "to come out" or "go out" (BDAG, s.v. "ἐκπορεύομαι" 2, pp. 308–9). **Syntactically**, [ἐκπορευέσθω] is an ellipsis; even though there is no verb in the clause, it is assumed from verse 29a. It serves as the main verb of the conjunctive clause introduced by ἀλλ᾽. The NLT begins a new sentence with verse 29b by omitting the conjunction and repeating the verb: "Let everything *you say* be good." **Semantically**, the elliptical verb describes an ongoing state (W, 521–22). The Ephesian believers should make this type of talk habitual.

εἰ: The Greek word εἰ is a conjunction that means "if." With the indefinite pronoun τις, the conjunction functions like an indefinite relative clause: "whatever" (BDAG, s.v. "εἰ" 7, p. 279). **Syntactically**, the conjunction εἰ introduces the protasis of a first class conditional statement. The clause modifies the elliptical verb ἐκπορευέσθω (v. 29b). Most English versions render the phrase as "only what is" (CSB, HCSB, NRSV, NIV, NET) or "only such as is" (RSV, ESV).

[ἐστίν]: The Greek word ἐστίν is a third-person singular present indicative from the verb εἰμί that means, "to be" (BDAG, s.v. "εἰμί" 2a, p. 283). **Syntactically**, ἐστίν is an ellipsis; it is the main verb of the dependent conjunctive clause introduced by εἰ. The indefinite pronoun τις functions as the subject of the clause. The predicate nominative is "good" (ἀγαθός): "what is good" (CSB, HCSB, NKJV). **Semantically**, [ἐστίν] is an equative present tense: "is" (ESV, NIV, RSV, NRSV, NET, CSB, HCSB, NASB, NKJV, KJV). In verse 28, Paul states that believers should work in order to have something good for those who are in need; in the current context, the believer should use their speech for the good of the community.

> **Semantical Nugget**: What does the prepositional phrase "for the building up of the need" (πρὸς οἰκοδομὴν τῆς χρείας) mean? The preposition πρός expresses the goal or purpose for this beneficial speech (BDAG, s.v. "πρός" 3cβ, p. 874). The object of the preposition is οἰκοδομήν, which refers to the process of building: "building" or "construction" (BDAG, s.v. "οἰκοδομή" 1bα, p. 696). In this context, the word takes a figurative meaning to refer to the spiritual edification. Paul threads the spiritual edification of the church throughout the letter (Eph. 2:20–21; 4:12, 15–16; Merkle, 150). Finally, the genitive τῆς χρείας ("need" or "difficulty"; BDAG, s.v. "χρεία" 2a, p. 1088) could possibly be an attributive genitive: "*necessary* edification" (KJV) (Lincoln, 306). But it is probably best understood as an objective genitive: use words that edify *the need* (Hoehner, 630; Larkin, 102). Some English versions translate the genitive as a person: "someone in need" (HCSB, CSB, NET). The genitive creates a link with verse 28. In verse 28 the believer does honest work to share with those who have a need (τῷ χρείαν ἔχοντι); in verse 29, the believer should use their words to build up the needs.

4:29c ἵνα: The Greek word ἵνα is a conjunction that means "so that" in this context (BDAG, s.v. "ἵνα" 1aγ, p. 475). **Syntactically**, the conjunction ἵνα introduces a dependent conjunctive clause "*so that* you might give grace to those who hear" (ἵνα δῷ χάριν τοῖς ἀκούουσιν). The entire clause functions adverbially modifying the implied verb from verse 29b: "let what is good come out" (ἐκπορευέσθω). **Semantically**, ἵνα expresses the purpose of this edifying speech: "so that" (NRSV, CSB, HCSB, NASB, NLT) or "that" (ESV, NIV, NET, NKJV). The intent of edifying speech is to give grace to those who hear.

δῷ: The Greek word δῷ is a third-person singular aorist active subjunctive from the verb δίδωμι that means "to give" or "donate" (BDAG, s.v. "δίδωμι" 4, p. 242). Most English versions translate the verb as "may give" (NRSV, ESV, NET; cf. CSB, HCSB). **Syntactically**, δῷ functions as the main verb of the dependent conjunctive clause introduced by ἵνα. The subject is implied by the verb: "it," referring to those good words spoken by the believers. The direct object is "grace" (χάριν). The word could refer to either "grace" on the part of believers (BDAG, s.v. "χάρις" 3a, pp. 1079–80), but throughout the book, Paul only refers to grace as it comes from God to the believer (cf. Eph. 1:2,

6–7; 2:5–8; 3:2, 7, 8; 4:7; 6:24; Best, 457; Merkle, 151). If the believer is in view here, then this most likely refers to God's grace conveyed through the believer. **Semantically**, δῷ is a constative aorist: "give" (ESV, NRSV, NET, CSB, HCSB). It describes the action of the verb as a whole (W, 557–58).

ἀκούουσιν: The Greek word ἀκούουσιν is a masculine dative plural present active participle from the verb ἀκούω that means "to hear" (BDAG, s.v. "ἀκούω" 1a, p. 37). **Syntactically**, ἀκούουσιν is a substantival participle, functioning as the indirect object of the verb "it may give" (δῷ). It refers to those who hear the words of the believer: "to those who hear" (RSV, NRSV, ESV, NET, CSB, HCSB, NASB; cf. NKJV, KJV). **Semantically**, ἀκούουσιν is a progressive present describing the action of the verb as it unfolds (W, 518–19).

4:30a κα í: The Greek word καί is a conjunction that means "and" (BDAG, s.v. "καί" 1b p. 494). **Syntactically**, καί introduces an independent conjunctive clause: "*and* do not grieve the Holy Spirit of God" (καὶ μὴ λυπεῖτε τὸ πνεῦμα τὸ ἅγιον τοῦ θεοῦ). **Semantically**, καί is a coordinating connective: "and" (ESV, NRSV, RSV, NIV, NET, CSB, HCSB, KJV, NKJV; the NASB omits the conjunction). Because the prohibition is broad enough to touch on each command that Paul lists in verses 25–29, Best and Larkin argue that the clause serves as a summary statement (Best, 459–60; Larkin, 103). The NLT gives the phrase this broad range by rendering it as "And do not bring sorrow to God's Holy Spirit by the way you live." However, the coordinating conjunction naturally links the prohibition to the preceding instruction about speech (v. 29), giving another reason for the believer to keep from harmful speech. Verse 27 serves a similar function in conjunction with the instruction on anger (cf. v. 26). In verse 27, Paul's reason for placing limits on anger is to avoid giving an opportunity to the devil; in verse 30, his reason to avoid harmful speech is to avoid offending the Spirit (Arnold, 305–6; Hoehner, 631; Lincoln, 307; Thielman, 317).

λυπεῖτε: The Greek word λυπεῖτε is a second-person plural present active imperative from the verb λυπέω that means "to offend" or "insult" (BDAG, s.v. "λυπέω" 1, p. 604). **Syntactically**, λυπεῖτε functions as the main verb of the independent conjunctive clause introduced by καί. The subject is an implied "you all," referring to the believers. The direct object is "the Holy Spirit" (τὸ πνεῦμα τὸ ἅγιον). **Semantically**, λυπεῖτε is a customary present: "grieve." The present tense describes an ongoing state (W, 521–22, 724–25; Hoehner, 631). Paul does not want the believer to habitually live a life that grieves the Spirit.

Theological Nugget: What does it mean to "grieve the Holy Spirit"? The Greek word λυπέω means to "vex," "irritate," "offend," or "insult" (BDAG, s.v. "λυπέω" 1, p. 604). Most English versions render the verb as "grieve"; the NLT translates the verb: "do not bring sorrow to God's Holy Spirit." The actions of the believer can sadden the Spirit, implying that the Spirit is personal (Hoehner, 632; Arnold, 306). The prohibition may allude to Isaiah 63:10, where the prophet describes the rebellion of the Jewish people after the exodus, which "grieved his Holy Spirit" (παρώξυναν τὸ πνεῦμα τὸ ἅγιον αὐτοῦ). The believer faces a similar danger: even though they have been sealed for the day of redemption (cf. Eph. 1:13–14), their actions may still inflict pain on the Spirit. The prohibition points to the spiritual implications for harmful speech. This kind of talk not only hurts others, but it also breaks down the community that the Spirit works to build (Eph. 2:21–22; 4:11–12).

4:30b ᾧ: The Greek word ᾧ is a neuter singular dative from the relative pronoun ὅς that means "whom" (BDAG, s.v. "ὅς" 1a, p. 725). **Syntactically**, ᾧ functions as the object of the preposition ἐν. The relative pronoun introduces a dependent adjectival relative clause, "in *whom* you have been sealed for the day of redemption" (ἐν ᾧ ἐσφραγίσθητε εἰς ἡμέραν ἀπολυτρώσεως). The antecedent of the pronoun is "the Holy Spirit" (τὸ πνεῦμα τὸ ἅγιον). **Semantically**, ἐν is instrumental, not locative (*contra* RSV). God seals the believer with the Holy Spirit: "*by* whom" (NASB, NKJV, ESV, NET; cf. CSB, HCSB) or "*with* whom" (NRSV, NIV) (Arnold, 306; Best, 458; Larkin, 103; Merkle, 152). Earlier in the letter, Paul states that the Spirit serves as the seal (Eph. 1:13). In Ephesians 1, the seal serves as a guarantee for God's future blessing.

ἐσφραγίσθητε: The Greek word ἐσφραγίσθητε is a second-person plural aorist passive indicative from the verb σφραγίζω that means "to mark" or "seal." The word suggests that the mark denotes ownership and carries the protection of the owner (BDAG, s.v. "σφραγίζω" 3, p. 980). The NRSV renders the verb as "you were marked with a seal." **Syntactically**, ἐσφραγίσθητε functions as the main verb of the relative clause, "in whom you were sealed for the day of redemption" (ἐν ᾧ ἐσφραγίσθητε εἰς ἡμέραν ἀπολυτρώσεως). The subject is implied: "you all," referring to the believers. **Semantically**, ἐσφραγίσθητε is an ingressive aorist, emphasizing the entrance into a new state: "were sealed" (ESV, RSV, NRSV, NIV, NET, NASB, NKJB, CSB; W, 558–59). The verb describes the point at which the believer was sealed. The voice is a divine passive. Even though the voice obscures the actor, God is the one who seals the believer (cf. Eph. 1:13).

Semantical Nugget: What does the prepositional phrase "for the day of redemption" mean? The prepositional phrase, "for the day of redemption" (εἰς ἡμέραν ἀπολυτρώσεως) modifies the verb ἐσφραγίσθητε. The preposition εἰς most likely expresses a temporal element: "*for* the day of redemption" (Merkle, 152; Larkin, 103; BDAG, s.v. "εἰς" 2aβ, p. 289). The NLT renders the preposition as: "*on* the day of redemption." The term "redemption" (ἀπολύτρωσις) has a military background. Prisoners of war could be redeemed with a price, or a ransom (BDAG, s.v. "ἀπολύτρωσις" 2a, p. 117; Morris, 1993, 785–86). This is best understood as a reference to a future point in time when Christ will return to deliver his people. Believers are sealed for redemption on this final day (Eph. 1:14). On the other hand, God will give those who have rebelled against him to his wrath (Eph. 5:6) (Thielman, 318). This is the only instance where Paul refers to the "day of redemption." Elsewhere he can refer to the "day of the Lord" (1 Cor. 5:5; 1 Thess. 5:2; 2 Thess. 2:2) or the "day of Christ" (Phil. 1:6, 10; 2:16; cf. 1 Cor. 1:8; 2 Cor. 1:14). In Romans, he refers to the "day of wrath" (2:2). This day marks a specific point in the future when Christ will come to judge.

4:31   ἀρθήτω: The Greek word ἀρθήτω is a third-person singular aorist passive imperative from the verb αἴρω that means "to take away" or "remove" (BDAG, s.v. "αἴρω" 3, pp. 28–29). The verb is synonymous with the concept of "taking off" (ἀποτίθημι) drawing the reader's attention back to Paul's understanding that the believer has "taken off the old self" (Eph. 4:22) (Arnold, 307; Lincoln, 308). **Syntactically**, ἀρθήτω is the main verb of the independent asyndeton clause: "*Let* all bitterness, anger, wrath, shouting, and slander *be put away*" (πᾶσα πικρία καὶ θυμὸς καὶ ὀργὴ καὶ κραυγὴ καὶ βλασφημία ἀρθήτω). The list of negative character qualities (bitterness, anger, wrath, shouting, and blasphemy) serves as the subject of the verb. Without a conjunction, the connection of the list is not clear, but it most likely serves as a summary statement of the passage. The vice list brings together both the theme of anger (Eph. 4:26–28) and unwholesome talk (Eph. 4:29) (Larkin, 103–4; Best, 460). **Semantically**, the aorist tense imperative stands in contrast with the present tense imperatives that Paul uses throughout this unit. It is doubtful that this is a specific, one-time command (Merkle, 153). The aorist tense imperative expresses an ingressive idea, marking a change in the believer's behavior. However, this change is appropriate throughout the believer's life (W, 719–20; Hoehner, 636; Fanning, 1990, 359–61).

Theological Nugget: What is a "vice list"? Throughout his letters, Paul offers several lists of virtues and vices. In verse 31, he lists a number of vices that believers should "put away"; in verse 32, he gives a positive list. Generally, New Testament writers either give a list of virtues or vices; however, in four instances Paul gives two distinct lists simultaneously (Gal. 5:19–21 and 22–23; Eph. 4:31 and 32; Col. 3:5–8 and 12; Titus 1:7 and 8). In these instances, Paul lists a number of vices before the virtues (Kruse, 1993, 962–63). In this situation, the list is designed to encourage the reader to leave behind one set of behaviors and pick up another set. Paul's list of vices seems to have a progression moving from bitterness (πικρία)—an internal resentment—to an outward expression of anger: shouting and blasphemy (κραυγή and βλασφημία) (Arnold, 307; Best, 461; Hoehner, 636). The final prepositional phrase summarizes the vice list: "with all wickedness" (σὺν πάσῃ κακίᾳ). Even though some of these characteristics may not have a negative connotation (i.e., "shouting"), Hoehner notes that the final prepositional phrase "colors all the other words mentioned" to "denote a malicious anger and wrath" (Hoehner, 637). Earlier in the passage, Paul seemed to give some license for anger (Eph. 4:26–27), while here he states that anger and wrath (θυμός and ὀργή) should be put away. The context signals the significant shift between the two commands. In verse 26, he gives some room for anger, but with strict limitations: to not sin; to limit the time of anger, and ultimately to avoid giving the devil opportunity. In verse 31, he describes anger in the context of bitterness, which gives way to shouting and blasphemy.

4:32a γίνεσθε: The Greek word γίνεσθε is a second-person plural present middle (deponent) imperative from the verb γίνομαι that means "to become something" (BDAG, s.v. "γίνομαι" 5b, p. 198). Most English versions render the verb as "be" (NRSV, RSV, ESV, NET, CSB, HCSB, NASB, KJV, NKJV). **Syntactically,** γίνεσθε functions as the main verb of the conjunctive clause introduced by the postpositive conjunction δέ. The predicate nominatives are "kind" (χρηστοί) and "compassionate" (εὔσπλαγχνοι). χρηστός conveys the notion of morally good or benevolent (BDAG, s.v. "χρηστός" 3bα, p. 1090). εὔσπλαγχνος appears only twice in the New Testament (1 Pet. 3:8). It refers to having tender feelings for someone, to be "tenderhearted" or "compassionate" (BDAG, s.v. "εὔσπλαγχνος," p. 413). The prepositional phrase "to one another" (εἰς ἀλλήλους) expresses to whom this kindness is directed. Paul places it before the predicate nominatives for emphasis (Merkle, 153). **Semantically,** γίνεσθε is a customary present: "be" (ESV, RSV, NRSV, NIV, NET, CSB, HCSB NASB NKJV KJV). The present tense describes an ongoing state (W, 521–22; 722). Believers are to habitually show kindness and compassion to others. Earlier in the letter, Paul describes God's salvation for the believer as "kindness" (Eph. 2:7); here he calls believers to be kind to one another. Even though the command is wide-sweeping—be compassionate with everyone—the parallel command (v. 31) specifically draws our attention to those who make us angry.

δέ: The Greek word δέ is a conjunction in the postpositive position that means "but" (BDAG, s.v. "δέ" 4c, p. 213). **Syntactically,** δέ introduces an independent conjunctive clause: "*but* become kind to one another" (γίνεσθε δὲ εἰς ἀλλήλους χρηστοί). **Semantically,** δέ is a contrastive conjunction: "instead" (NET, NLT). Most English versions render the conjunction as a connective conjunction: "and" (RSV, NRSV, CSB, HCSB, NKJV, KJV). Just as Paul alternates from a prohibition to an imperative throughout this section, δέ introduces a positive imperative following the prohibition.

> **Text-Critical Nugget**: Why does the NA[28] place brackets around the conjunction δέ? A few key Alexandrian manuscripts omit the conjunction (𝔓[46], B, 1739, 1881) (cf. NASB, NIV, ESV). A handful of Western manuscripts insert οὖν (D, F, G). However, the majority of Alexandrian and Byzantine manuscripts (𝔓[49], ℵ, A, K, 33, 81, 365, 630, 1241, 1505, 2464, lat, 𝔐) insert the conjunction δέ. The asyndetic reading is only found in the Alexandrian text type and the reading with οὖν is only found in the Western text type. Despite the quality of these manuscripts, the fact that the reading with δέ is found in both the Alexandrian and Byzantine text types suggests that it is original.

χαριζόμενοι: The Greek word χαριζόμενοι is a masculine nominative plural present middle (deponent) participle from the verb χαρίζομαι that means "to forgive" or "pardon" (BDAG, s.v. "χαρίζομαι" 3, p. 1078). The normal meaning of the word is to "give graciously" (cf. Phil. 1:29; 2:9; cf. Hoehner, 640). Most English versions render the participle as "forgiving" (ESV, NRSV, RSV, NIV, NET, CSB, HCSB, NASB, NKJV, KJV), which is best suited within the context of Paul's command to put away anger (v. 31). **Syntactically**, χαριζόμενοι introduces a dependent participle clause. It functions adverbially modifying "Be kind and compassionate to one another" (γίνεσθε δὲ εἰς ἀλλήλους χρηστοί, εὔσπλαγχνοι). The direct object is "one another" (ἑαυτοῖς). Paul uses the reflexive pronoun in the place of the reciprocal pronoun (ἀλλήλων) (BDAG, s.v. "ἑαυτοῦ" 2, p. 269; Merkle, 153; Hoehner, 640). **Semantically**, χαριζόμενοι functions as means describing how these believers should be kind: "*by* forgiving one another." Since both the participle and indicative verbs are present tense, they describe a simultaneous action. Believes show compassion to others when they forgive one another.

4:32c καθὼς καί: The Greek word καθώς is a conjunction that means "just as" (BDAG, s.v. "καθώς" 1, p. 493). The Greek word καί is a conjunction that means "also" (BDAG, s.v. "καί" 2b, p. 494). The two conjunctions are best rendered: "just as also" (cf. CSB, HCSB, NASB). Most English versions simply translate καθώς: "as" (RSV, NRSV, ESV; cf. NET, NIV). **Syntactically**, καθώς introduces a dependent conjunctive clause "*just as* also God forgave you in Christ" (καθὼς καὶ ὁ θεὸς ἐν Χριστῷ ἐχαρίσατο ὑμῖν). The entire clause functions adverbially modifying the participle "forgiving" (χαριζόμενοι). **Semantically**, καθώς can express cause: "forgive one another *because* God forgave you" (BDAG, s.v. "καθώς" 3, p. 494; Arnold, 309; Best, 464; Lincoln, 310); however it is best to understand the conjunction as marking a comparison (W, 675; Hoehner, 640; Larkin, 105). καί is a connective emphasizing the comparison: "also" (CSB, HCSB, NASB). God's forgiveness for the believer has become axiomatic for the believer.

ἐχαρίσατο: The Greek word ἐχαρίσατο is a third-person singular aorist middle (deponent) indicative from the verb χαρίζομαι that means "to forgive" or "pardon" (BDAG, s.v. "χαρίζομαι" 3, p. 1078). Paul used the same verb in the previous clause. **Syntactically**, ἐχαρίσατο functions as the main verb of the dependent conjunctive clause introduced by καθώς. The subject is "God" (ὁ θεός). The direct object is "you" (ὑμῖν), referring to the believers. **Semantically**, ἐχαρίσατο is a constative aorist: "forgave" (ESV, RSV, NIV, NET, CSB, HCSB, NKJV). It describes the action of the verb as a whole (W, 557–58). The prepositional phrase "in Christ" (ἐν Χριστῷ) is sphere marking the location in which this forgiveness takes place. The phrase refers to Christ's death, to which Paul alludes in the following section (Eph. 5:1–2).

Text-Critical Nugget: Was this forgiveness for "us" (ἡμῖν) or "you" (ὑμῖν)? A number of manuscripts replace the phrase "just as God forgave *you*" (cf. NA[28] SBL) with "just as God forgave *us*" (ἡμῖν) (cf. MT; RP[2005]; THGNT). The reading with the first-person pronoun appears in every major text type: Alexandrian (𝔓[49], B, 33, 104, 1175, 1739, 1881), Western (D), and Byzantine (K, L, 𝔐). On the other hand, the textual reading is found in both early Alexandrian (𝔓46 and ℵ) and Western (F and G) manuscripts. While the external evidence is split, the internal evidence is split as well. Paul uses the second person throughout this section, but he normally uses the first person in reference to what Christ has done for the believer. A scribe could have changed the second-person pronoun to align with Paul's style outside of the context, just as easy as changing the first-person pronoun to align with his style throughout the passage (Thielman, 323). Because the external evidence is slightly in favor of the first-person pronoun, it is preferred (Hoehner, 640 n. 2). We have retained the NA[28] reading in the structural layout.

Ephesians 5:1–6

Big Greek Idea: Believers should imitate God by loving one another like Christ, who loved us by sacrificing himself for us. They should abstain from any sign of sexual deviancy or harsh words, since these types of people will not inherit the kingdom; rather, believers should be known for thanksgiving.

Structural Overview: In the previous section, Paul admonishes believers not to act like unbelievers. He ends the previous section by encouraging believers to forgive one another—"just as God forgave you." He begins this section by explicitly calling the believers to imitate God by loving one another. Believers should love one another the way Christ loved us, by sacrificing himself on the cross.

In light of this command to love one another, Paul gives two extensive lists of character qualities that do not cohere with a life of love (vv. 3–4). They should not even be hinted at within the community. Both lists give three elements each. The first list describes sexual deviancy: sexual immorality, uncleanliness, and greediness (v. 3). The second list describes speech: obscenity, foolish talk, sarcastic ridicule (v. 4). In contrast to these lists of qualities, Paul simply designates thanksgiving as what should characterize the community.

He ends this section with a warning: those who conduct themselves in this manner will not inherit the kingdom (v. 5). He repeats the adjectives from the first list (v. 4) but uses the personal forms to specifically refer to those who practice sexual immorality, uncleanliness, and greed. Not only will they fail to inherit the kingdom, but the wrath of God will come upon them (cf. Eph. 2:3).

Outline:

> Believers should imitate God by loving one another with a self-sacrificing love, like Christ's love for the believer (vv. 1–2)
> Believers should avoid any characterization of sexual deviancy or harmful language, but rather be known for thanksgiving (vv. 3–4)
> Those who are sexually immoral, unclean, or greedy will not inherit the kingdom (vv. 5–6)

Clausal Outline for Ephesians 5:1–6

5:1 **γίνεσθε** οὖν μιμηταὶ τοῦ θεοῦ, ὡς τέκνα ἀγαπητά,
5:1 Therefore **be** imitators of God, as beloved children,

|

5:2a καὶ **περιπατεῖτε** ἐν ἀγάπῃ,
5:2a and **walk** in love,

|

    5:2b **καθὼς** καὶ ὁ Χριστὸς **ἠγάπησεν** ἡμᾶς
    5:2b **just as** also Christ **loved** us

    5:2c καὶ **παρέδωκεν** ἑαυτὸν ὑπὲρ ἡμῶν προσφορὰν καὶ θυσίαν τῷ θεῷ εἰς ὀσμὴν εὐωδίας.
    5:2c and **gave** himself **up** for us as a offering and sacrifice to God for a fragrant offering.

5:3a πορνεία **δὲ** καὶ ἀκαθαρσία πᾶσα ἢ πλεονεξία μηδὲ **ὀνομαζέσθω** ἐν ὑμῖν,
5:3a But also **do** not **let** sexual immorality, any uncleanliness, or greediness **be named** among you,

|

    5:3b **καθὼς πρέπει** ἁγίοις,
    5:3b **because it is not proper** among the saints

5:4a καὶ αἰσχρότης καὶ μωρολογία ἢ εὐτραπελία [μηδὲ **ὀνομαζέσθω**],
5:4a nor let obscenity, foolish talk, or sarcastic ridicule [**be named**]

|

    5:4b ἃ οὐκ **ἀνῆκεν**,
    5:4b which **is** not **fitting**,

5:4c ἀλλὰ μᾶλλον εὐχαριστία [**ὀνομαζέσθω**].
5:4c but rather let thanksgiving [**be named**].

5:5a τοῦτο γὰρ **ἴστε γινώσκοντες**
5:5a For you **certainly know** this

    5:5b **ὅτι** πᾶς πόρνος ἢ ἀκάθαρτος ἢ πλεονέκτης, (ὅ ἐστιν εἰδωλολάτρης,) οὐκ **ἔχει** κληρονομίαν ἐν τῇ βασιλείᾳ τοῦ Χριστοῦ καὶ θεοῦ
    5:5b **that** every immoral, unclean, or greedy person (that is an idolater) **does** not **have** an inheritance in the kingdom of Christ and God.

5:6a Μηδεὶς ὑμᾶς **ἀπατάτω** κενοῖς λόγοις,
5:6a **Let** no one **deceive** you with empty words,

    |

5:6b διὰ ταῦτα γὰρ **ἔρχεται** ἡ ὀργὴ τοῦ θεοῦ ἐπὶ τοὺς υἱοὺς τῆς ἀπειθείας.
5:6b for because of these things the wrath of God **comes** upon the sons of disobedience.

Syntax Explained for Ephesians 5:1–6

5:1 γίνεσθε: The Greek word γίνεσθε is a second-person plural present middle (deponent) imperative from the verb γίνομαι that means "to become something" (BDAG, s.v. "γίνομαι" 5a, p. 198). Paul uses the same form of the verb in Ephesians 4:32, creating a link to the previous section. Most English versions render the verb as a stative verb: "Be imitators" (CSB, HCSB, NASB, NKJV, RSV, NRSV, ESV, NET). The NIV renders the verb conceptually: "Follow God's example." The NLT shifts the predicate nominative into an imperative: "Imitate God." **Syntactically**, γίνεσθε functions as the main verb of the dependent conjunctive clause introduced by οὖν. The subject is implied in the verb: "you all," referring to the Ephesian believers. The phrase "imitators of God" (μιμηταὶ τοῦ θεοῦ) is the predicate nominative. **Semantically**, γίνεσθε is a customary present: "be" (ESV, RSV, NRSV, NET, CSB, HCSB, NASB, NKJV, KJV). The present tense describes an ongoing state (W, 521–22). Believers are to make imitating God habitual (Hoehner, 644; Arnold, 309).

οὖν: The Greek word οὖν is a conjunction that means "therefore" or "consequently" (BDAG, s.v. "οὖν" 1b, p. 736). Most English versions translate the conjunction as "therefore" (NASB, CSB, HCSB, NKJV, KJV, RSV, NRSV, ESV, NET, NIV). **Syntactically**, οὖν introduces an independent conjunctive clause: "*Therefore* become imitators of God" (γίνεσθε οὖν μιμηταὶ τοῦ θεοῦ). **Semantically**, Hoehner considers the conjunction resumptive, referring back to Ephesians 4:1, inserting a new application of Ephesians 1–3 (Hoehner, 643; Larkin, 106). On the other hand, Paul may link this new command to the previous section, which he concludes with a command for believers to forgive "just as God forgave you" (Eph. 4:32). In this case, the conjunction is probably inferential—drawing conclusions from the previous section (Arnold, 309; Abbott, 1909, 146; Thielman, 320). This makes the most sense in light of the comparison that Paul makes at the end of the previous section (Eph. 4:32).

Theological Nugget: What does it mean to "imitate God"? The genitive τοῦ θεοῦ is best rendered as an objective genitive: believers should imitate

God (Hoehner, 644). Elsewhere, Paul calls believers to imitate himself as he imitates Christ (1 Cor. 4:16; 11:1; 1 Thess. 1:6; 2 Thess. 3:7, 9) or to imitate other churches (2 Thess. 2:14). This is the only instance where he calls believers to imitate God. Paul concludes the previous section with a comparative statement: believers should forgive one another just as God forgave them (Eph. 4:32). The comparative statement looks forward to his command to become imitators of God. The verse ends with another comparative statement expressing the manner in which believers should imitate God: "*as* beloved children" (ὡς τέκνα ἀγαπητά). Paul describes believers as recipients of God's love—the motivation for his salvation (Eph. 1:4–6; 2:4–6). Believers should respond as beloved children. In the following verse, Paul puts forward Christ's death as an example of this type of love (cf. Eph. 5:25). The comparison gives the depth of love: just as Christ loved us to the point of death, we should love others.

5:2a καί: The Greek word καί is a conjunction that means "and" (BDAG, s.v. "καί" 1bγ, pp. 495–96). **Syntactically**, καί introduces an independent conjunctive clause: "*and* walk in love" (καὶ περιπατεῖτε ἐν ἀγάπῃ). The conjunction connects the following clause to the previous clause in verse 1: "become imitators of God." Most English versions render the conjunction as "and" (RSV, NRSV, ESV, NIV, NET, HCSB, CSB, NASB, NKJV, KJV). **Semantically**, καί is epexegetical, giving more detail about how the believer can imitate God (Hoehner, 646; Merkle, 154; Larkin, 106). As beloved children, believers should walk in love.

περιπατεῖτε: The Greek word περιπατεῖτε is a second-person plural present active imperative from the verb περιπατέω that means "to live" or "behave" (BDAG, s.v. "περιπατέω" 2aδ, p. 803). Most English versions render the verb literally: "walk," which carries a figurative meaning in English (CSB, HCSB, NIV, NASB, NKJV, KJV, RSV, ESV). Some versions render the verb with the figurative meaning: "live" (NRSV, NET, NLT). **Syntactically**, περιπατεῖτε functions as the main verb of the independent conjunctive clause introduced by καί. The subject is implied by the verb: "you all," referring to the Ephesian believers. **Semantically**, περιπατεῖτε is a customary present: "walk" (ESV, RSV, NIV, CSB, HCSB, NASB, NKJV, KJV). The present tense describes an ongoing state (W, 521–22, 722). Paul's command here is more of a general precept. Earlier in the book, he commends them for their love for one another (Eph. 1:15). Here he expresses the idea that they should continue this way of life—he expects them to make it habitual. Paul uses the verb in Ephesians 2:10—God created the believer to walk in good works. The second part of the letter gives this command definition (see Theological Nugget at 4:1b). The following prepositional phrase "in love" (ἐν ἀγάπῃ) modifies the verb. It expresses the sphere in which believers should lead their lives (BDAG, s.v. "περιπατέω" 2aδ, p. 803; Hoehner, 646). Paul is most likely referring to the believer's love for one another (cf. Eph. 1:15). Just as they have received love from God, they should live a life of love for others.

5:2b καθὼς καί: The Greek word καθώς is a conjunction that means "just as" (BDAG, s.v. "καθώς" 1, p. 493). The Greek word καί is a conjunction that means "also" (BDAG, s.v. "καί" 2b, pp. 495–96). The two conjunctions are best rendered: "just as also" (cf. CSB, HCSB, NASB, NJKV, KJV, NET). Some English versions simply translate καθώς: "as" (RSV, NRSV, ESV), or "just as" (NIV). Paul introduced a comparative in Ephesians 4:32 with the same combination of conjunctions. **Syntactically**, καθώς introduces a dependent conjunctive clause *"just as also* Christ loved us" (καθὼς καὶ ὁ Χριστὸς ἠγάπησεν ἡμᾶς). The entire clause functions adverbially modifying the previous imperatives: "walk in love" (περιπατεῖτε ἐν ἀγάπῃ) (v. 2). **Semantically**, καθώς could express cause: "walk in love *because* Christ loved us" (cf. Arnold, 310; Best, 468; Lincoln, 310), but it is best understood as expressing a comparison. The clause shows the manner in which the believer should love—*as Christ loved us*. καί is an adjunctive conjunction (Hoehner, 647; Merkle, 154–55).

ἠγάπησεν: The Greek word ἠγάπησεν is a third-person singular aorist active indicative from the verb ἀγαπάω that means "to cherish" or "love" (BDAG, s.v. "ἀγαπάω" 1bα, p. 5). **Syntactically**, ἠγάπησεν functions as the main verb of the dependent conjunctive clause introduced by καθώς. The subject of the verb is "Christ" (ὁ Χριστός). The direct object is "us" (ἡμᾶς), referring to believers. **Semantically**, ἠγάπησεν is a constative aorist: "loved" (ESV, RSV, NRSV, NIV, NET, CSB, HCSB, NASB, NKJV, KJV, NLT). It describes the action of the verb as a whole (W, 557–58). Earlier in the letter, Paul states that it is God who loves the believer (Eph. 2:4); God shows his love by saving us through Christ's sacrificial death (cf. Eph. 2:13), which he describes in the following phrase.

5:2c καί: The Greek word καί is a conjunction that means "and" (BDAG, s.v. "καί" 1bγ, p. 494). **Syntactically**, καί introduces a dependent conjunctive clause: *"and* handed himself over for us as an offering and sacrifice to God for a fragrant offering" (καὶ παρέδωκεν ἑαυτὸν ὑπὲρ ἡμῶν προσφορὰν καὶ θυσίαν τῷ θεῷ εἰς ὀσμὴν εὐωδίας). The clause is parallel to the previous clause ("just as Christ loved us"), a dependent conjunctive clause introduced by καθώς. **Semantically**, καί is epexegetical: "and" (RSV, NRSV, ESV, NET, NIV, HCSB, CSB, NASB, NKJV, KJV). The clause gives further explanation about Christ's love. He demonstrates his love for the believer by handing himself over—an allusion to his sacrificial death.

παρέδωκεν: The Greek word παρέδωκεν is a third-person singular aorist active indicative from the verb παραδίδωμι that means "to hand over" or "give up." This is a technical term used by officials of the court: "*to hand one into the custody of*" (BDAG, s.v. "παραδίδωμι" 1b, p. 762). **Syntactically**, παρέδωκεν functions as the main verb of the dependent conjunctive clause introduced by καί. The subject is implied by the verb: "he," referring to Christ. The direct object is "himself" (ἑαυτόν). The reflexive pronoun suggests that Christ took the initiative to give himself up (Hoehner, 648). The two accusatives "offering" (προσφοράν) and "sacrifice" (θυσίαν) are object complements in a double accusative construction: "he gave himself up *as* an offering and sacrifice" (W, 187). The indirect object is "God" (τῷ θεῷ) **Semantically**, παρέδωκεν is a constative aorist: "gave himself up" (ESV, RSV, NRSV, NIV, NASB) or "gave himself" (NET, CSB, HCSB). It describes the action of the verb as a whole (W, 557–58). The Gospel writers use the Greek verb παραδίδωμι to refer to Judas's betrayal of Jesus (Mark 14:10–11, 18, 21, 41–44; John 6:64, 71; 12:4; 13:2, 11; 18:2, 5). Paul uses the verb to refer to Christ's death on our behalf (Rom. 8:32; Gal. 2:20). Here Paul states that Christ handed himself over on our behalf (ὑπὲρ ἡμῶν).

Theological Nugget: What does it mean that Christ "gave himself up for us"? Later in the chapter, Paul makes a similar statement: "just as Christ loved the church and gave himself up for her" (v. 25). Besides changing the direct object from the pronoun ("Christ loved us") to the noun ("Christ loved the church"), Paul adds the phrase: προσφορὰν καὶ θυσίαν τῷ θεῷ εἰς ὀσμὴν εὐωδίας ("offering and sacrifice to God for a fragrant scent"). Both προσφοράν ("offering") and θυσίαν ("sacrifice") refer to Old Testament sacrifices (cf. Num. 7:13–88). προσφορά refers to a gift but is generally used in reference to sacrifices (BDAG, s.v. "προσφορά" 2, p. 887; cf. Acts 21:26; 24:17). θυσία refers to the burnt offering (BDAG, s.v. "θυσία" 2aγ, p. 462). Paul may have used both nouns to refer to the range of sacrifices throughout the Jewish calendar (Hoehner, 649), but it is best to consider this as a hendiadys—two words referring to a single idea (Arnold, 311; Best, 470; Lincoln, 312). Finally, the prepositional phrase εἰς ὀσμὴν εὐωδίας ("for a fragrant scent") generally refers to the aroma from burnt sacrifices in the temple. It emphasizes God's acceptance of the sacrifice (cf. Exod. 29:18, 25; Lev. 1:9; 2:12). These additional elements clarify the allusion. When Paul states that Christ "gave himself up," he refers to his sacrificial death (cf. Eph. 2:13). Christ does all of this on our behalf (ὑπὲρ ἡμῶν)

5:3a δέ: The Greek word δέ is a conjunction that means "but" (BDAG, s.v. "δέ" 4a, p. 213). **Syntactically**, δέ introduces an independent conjunctive clause: "*but* do not allow immorality, all uncleanliness, and all greed to be named among you" (πορνεία δὲ καὶ ἀκαθαρσία πᾶσα ἢ πλεονεξία μηδὲ ὀνομαζέσθω ἐν ὑμῖν). **Semantically**, δέ is a marker of contrast: "but" (HCSB, CSB, NASB, NKJV, KJV, RSV, NRSV, ESV, NIV, NET). After giving a positive command (v. 2), the conjunction introduces a negative prohibition.

ὀνομαζέσθω: The Greek word ὀνομαζέσθω is a third-person singular present passive imperative from the verb ὀνομάζω that means "to name a name" or "use a word" (BDAG, s.v. "ὀνομάζω" 2, p. 714). Most English versions render the verb literally: "must not even be named" (RSV, ESV, NASB; cf. KJV, NKJV). The verb certainly indicates that believers should not practice these behaviors, but it implies much more—there should not even be a rumor of these activities. The CSB renders the verb actively: "should not even be heard" (cf. HCSB). The NIV captures the metaphor well: "there must not even be a hint." **Syntactically**, ὀνομαζέσθω functions as the main verb of the dependent conjunctive clause introduced by δέ. The subject is complex, made up of a series of nouns: "sexual immorality" (πορνεία), "immorality" (ἀκαθαρσία), "greediness" (πλεονεξία). **Semantically**, ὀνομαζέσθω is a customary present: "be named" (ESV, RSV, NASB). The present tense describes an ongoing state (W, 521–22, 722; Fanning, 1990, 337; Hoehner, 653). Paul wants this attitude toward sin to be habitual.

> **Lexical Nugget**: What do the terms "immorality" (πορνεία), "uncleanliness" (ἀκαθαρσία), and "greediness" (πλεονεξία) mean? The Greek term πορνεία generally refers to unlawful sexual intercourse—generally, sex outside of marriage (BDAG, s.v. "πορνεία" 1, p. 854). The second Greek term ἀκαθαρσία can generally refer to any type of uncleanliness, but Paul regularly pairs it with πορνεία (2 Cor. 12:21; Gal. 5:19; Col. 3:5; BDAG, s.v. "ἀκαθαρσία" 2, p. 34). In these situations, the word usually connotes sexual immorality. Paul uses the term in Ephesians 4:19 where it could refer to more general uncleanliness, but in the current context, a sexual connotation is clear (Arnold, 320). The adjective πᾶς modifies the noun suggesting that Paul has all sorts of sexual uncleanliness in mind (BDAG, s.v. "πᾶς" 5, p. 784). Finally, Paul indicates that "greed" (πλεονεξία) should not be named within the Christian community. Within the context of the first two nouns, it is possible that Paul describes "sexual greediness," a concept that he described in Ephesians 5:19 (cf. Lincoln, 322). Most commentators note that Paul separates the last item with the conjunction ἤ, setting it off as a different type of sin. The term includes sexual greed, but it is not limited by it—Paul could have in mind all types of greed (Hoehner, 653; Arnold, 320–21; Best, 476; Thielman, 328).

5:3b καθώς: The Greek word καθώς is a conjunction that means "as" or "just as" (BDAG, s.v. "καθώς" 1, p. 493). **Syntactically**, καθώς introduces a dependent conjunctive clause "*just as* is fitting among the saints" (καθὼς πρέπει ἁγίοις).

The entire clause functions adverbially modifying the prohibition "do not allow it to be named" (μηδὲ ὀνομαζέσθω). **Semantically**, most English versions render the conjunction as a comparative: "as is proper among the saints" (ESV; cf. RSV, NRSV, NET, CSB, HCSB, NASB, NKJV, KJV; Merkle, 160; Larkin, 108). However, it might be best understood as expressing cause: "*because* these things are improper for God's holy people" (NIV; Hoehner, 653; Arnold, 321; Best, 477). In this case, the clause provides the rationale for Paul's prohibition that these acts of immorality be named within the Christian community.

πρέπει: The Greek word πρέπει is a third-person singular present active indicative from the verb πρέπω that means "to be fitting" or "suitable" (BDAG, s.v. "πρέπω," p. 861). **Syntactically**, πρέπει functions as the main verb of the dependent conjunctive clause introduced by καθώς. **Semantically**, πρέπει is a gnomic present: "is proper" (ESV, NRSV, CSB, HCSB, NASB). This conduct should not be a part of the community (W, 523–24).

5:4a καί: The Greek word καί is a conjunction that means "and" (BDAG, s.v. "καί" 1bα, p. 494). **Syntactically**, καί introduces an independent conjunctive clause: "*and* filthiness and foolish talk or crude joking" (καὶ αἰσχρότης καὶ μωρολογία ἢ εὐτραπελία). **Semantically**, καί is a coordinating connective: "and" (NASB), introducing a second set of three vices. Since Paul continues his list of vices that believers should avoid, many versions render the conjunction as "neither" (NET, NKJV, KJV) or "nor" (NIV). Several translations begin a new sentence at this point and omit the conjunction (RSV, NRSV, ESV, NLT, CSB, HCSB).

[ὀνομαζέσθω]: The Greek word ὀνομαζέσθω is a third-person singular present passive imperative from the verb ὀνομάζω that means "to name a name" or "to use a word" (BDAG, s.v. "ὀνομάζω" 2, p. 714). Without a verb, the clause picks up the force from the verb in the previous context—an ellipsis (Arnold, 321; Larkin, 109). Several English versions begin a new sentence at this point rendering the relative clause as the main verb: "are not suitable" (CSB, HCSB; cf. NRSV, NLT). **Syntactically**, [ὀνομαζέσθω], the ellipsis, functions as a dependent clause introduced by καί. The subject is complex, made up of a series of nouns: "obscenity" (αἰσχρότης), "foolish talk" (μωρολογία), and "coarse joking" (εὐτραπελία). **Semantically**, the present tense is a customary present. There is no indication that the Ephesians practice these activities; the present tense communicates a general precept. Just like the previous list of negative qualities (v. 3), Paul wants the believer to avoid making these types of behaviors habitual.

Lexical Nugget: What do the terms "obscenity" (αἰσχρότης), "foolish talk" (μωρολογία), and "coarse joking" (εὐτραπελία) mean? All of these words are *hapax legomena*—words that only occur once in the New Testament. The first Greek term αἰσχρότης is rare even outside of biblical literature. Some translations render the word in conjunction with the following word: "obscene and foolish talking" (CSB; cf. HCSB, NET), giving the sense that Paul is referring to speech. However, the term seems to have a broader meaning, referring to obscene behavior (BDAG, s.v. "αἰσχρότης," p. 29; LSJ, s.v. "αἰσχρότης," p. 43; Hoehner, 655; Arnold, 322; cf. NIV). The second term, μωρολογία, is even rarer. The word is derived from the words μωρός and λογία, which means "foolish talk" (NLT, NET, NIV, CSB, HCSB, NKJV, KJV, NLT) or "silly talk" (RSV, NRSV, NASB) (BDAG, s.v. "μωρολογία," p. 663). The word connotes empty or futile speculation—ultimately harmful to the Christian community. Jesus calls those who reject his teaching foolish (Matt. 7:26; cf. 1 Cor. 1:23). The third term, εὐτραπελία, refers to joking but taken too far. BDAG suggests the translation: "risqué wit" (BDAG, s.v. "εὐτραπελία," p. 414). Joking is fine, but this refers to joking too much, and beyond the point of ridicule and sarcasm. This kind of joking breaks down the community, standing at odds with the work of the Spirit to build up the community.

5:4b ἅ: The Greek word ἅ is a neuter plural nominative from the relative pronoun ὅς that means "which" in this context (BDAG, s.v. "ὅς" 1gβ, p. 725). **Syntactically**, ἅ introduces a dependent adjectival relative clause "*which is not fitting*" (ἃ οὐκ ἀνῆκεν). Due to the shift of the gender from the feminine nouns to the neuter relative pronoun, the pronoun most likely refers to the complete list of nouns: "obscenity," "foolish talk," and "sarcastic ridicule" (αἰσχρότης, μωρολογία, εὐτραπελία). The relative pronoun functions as the subject of the verb ἀνῆκεν ("it is proper").

ἀνῆκεν: The Greek word ἀνῆκεν is a third-person singular imperfect active indicative from the verb ἀνήκω that means "it is fitting" or "it is proper" (BDAG, s.v. "ἀνήκω" 2, p. 79). **Syntactically**, ἀνῆκεν functions as the main verb of the relative clause. **Semantically**, the imperfect tense functions as a customary imperfect, which emphasizes the regularity of the action of the verb. In this case, the described behavior should not be tolerated within the Christian community. Even though the verb is in the imperfect tense, it should be translated in the present tense (Turner[1], 90; Robertson, 886): "which are out of place" (ESV, NIV; cf. NASB, NET).

Grammatical Nugget: What is the structure of Paul's vice list in verses 3 and 4? Within this short section, Paul gives three different vice lists (vv. 3, 4, 5), each containing three different behaviors. Paul presents the first two lists with similar features. He uses similar conjunctions and comments on the suitability in both lists:

> v. 3:   πορνεία δὲ
>   <u>καὶ</u> ἀκαθαρσία πᾶσα
>   <u>ἢ</u> πλεονεξία μηδὲ ὀνομαζέσθω ἐν ὑμῖν
>   <u>καθὼς</u> πρέπει ἁγίοις
> v. 4:   <u>καὶ</u> αἰσχρότης
>   <u>καὶ</u> μωρολογία
>   <u>ἢ</u> εὐτραπελία
>   <u>ἃ</u> οὐκ ἀνῆκεν
>
> v. 3:   But <u>also</u> sexual immorality
>   and all uncleanliness
>   or greed neither be named among you,
>   just as it is proper among the saints
> v. 4:   and obscenity,
>   and foolish talk,
>   or sarcastic ridicule,
>   <u>which</u> are out of place.

Paul's comment about how inappropriate this conduct is for the community reflects the command that he gave at the beginning of the section: "walk in love." These behaviors have no place within a community that imitates God's love for them. Paul gives a very different rational following the final vice list: the people who make these behaviors habitual "have no inheritance in the kingdom of Christ and God" (v. 5).

5:4c ἀλλά: The Greek word ἀλλά is a conjunction that means "but" (BDAG, s.v. "ἀλλά" 2, p. 45). **Syntactically**, ἀλλά introduces an independent conjunctive clause: "*but* rather thanksgiving" (ἀλλὰ μᾶλλον εὐχαριστία). **Semantically**, ἀλλά is a contrastive conjunction: "but." Along with μᾶλλον, the conjunction can be rendered as "but rather" (CSB, HCSB, NASB, NKJV, KJV, NIV, NET) or "but instead" (RSV, NRSV, ESV). Rather than the kind of talk that tears down others in the community, believers should give thanks.

[ὀνομαζέσθω]: The Greek word ὀνομαζέσθω is a third-person singular present passive imperative from the verb ὀνομάζω that means "to name a name" or "use a word" (BDAG, s.v. "ὀνομάζω" 2, p. 714). Just as in the previous clause (v. 4b), the clause picks up the force of the verb ὀνομαζέσθω (Arnold, 323; Larkin, 109). Most English versions insert "let there be" (RSV, NRSV, ESV, NLT) or translate the noun as a verb: "giving thanks" (CSB, HCSB, NASB, KJV, NKJV). **Syntactically**, ὀνομαζέσθω, the ellipsis, functions as a dependent clause introduced by ἀλλά. The subject is "thanksgiving" (εὐχαριστία). **Semantically**, the present tense is a customary present. There is no indication that the Ephesians practice these activities; the present tense communicates a general precept. Paul wants

the believers to regularly give thanks. Rather than give a list of positive qualities, Paul gives a simple contrast: thanksgiving. The Greek word εὐχαριστία refers to an "expression of gratitude" (BDAG, s.v. "εὐχαριστία" 2, p. 416), which
stands in contrast to the offenses of speech that make up Ephesians 5:4a. By
giving thanks, the believers reorientate their lives from self-centeredness to an
admission that what we have comes from God (Osborne, 163).

5:5a γάρ: The Greek word γάρ is a conjunction that means "for" or "therefore"
(BDAG, s.v. "γάρ" 1a, p. 189). Most English versions translate the conjunction
as "for" (ESV, NIV, NET, CSB, HCSB, NASB, NKJV, KJV). **Syntactically**, γάρ is in
a postpositive position introducing an independent conjunctive clause: "*For
you know this*" (τοῦτο γὰρ ἴστε γινώσκοντες). **Semantically**, γάρ expresses the reason for Paul's prohibition (Arnold, 323; Hoehner, 659; Thielman,
332; Merkle, 161). He introduces a third vice list, but with verse 5 he gives the
ultimate reason to put away these sins. Those who conduct their lives in this
manner will not inherit the kingdom.

ἴστε γινώσκοντες: The Greek word ἴστε is a second-person plural perfect
active imperative from the verb οἶδα that means "to respect" or "honor"; the
connotation is to "recognize merit" (BDAG, s.v. "οἶδα" 6, p. 694). The Greek
word γινώσκοντες is a masculine nominative plural present active participle
from the verb γινώσκω that means "to have come to know" or "know" (BDAG,
s.v. "γιγνώσκω" 6c, p. 200). The phrase is periphrastic, which is usually formed
with εἰμί, but here used with οἶδα. Due to the frequency of the imperative
throughout this section some English versions have rendered the phrase as an
imperative: "Be sure of this" (RSV, NRSV, HCSB, CSB; Best, 480; Thielman, 332).
However, the indicative might be better: "you know this" (NASB, NKJV, KJV, NIV,
ESV, NET). Paul uses the indicative following the conjunction γάρ to express the
reason (Hoehner, 659; Arnold, 324). The periphrastic construction adds certainty. The NLT renders it: "You can be sure." **Syntactically**, the periphrastic ἴστε
γινώσκοντες functions as the main verb of the independent conjunctive clause
introduced by the conjunction γάρ. The subject is implied by the verb "you
all," referring to the Ephesian believers. The direct object is the demonstrative:
"this" (τοῦτο). **Semantically**, the combination of the perfect with the present
participle results in a present tense (Robertson, 330), expressing a continuous
action. Paul draws believers to the truth that they already know, that these types
of people will not inherit the kingdom.

5:5b ὅτι: The Greek word ὅτι is a conjunction that means "that" in this context
(BDAG, s.v. "ὅτι" 2c, p. 732). **Syntactically**, ὅτι introduces a dependent conjunctive clause "*that all who are immoral … do not have an inheritance in the
kingdom of Christ and God*" (ὅτι πᾶς πόρνος … οὐκ ἔχει κληρονομίαν ἐν
τῇ βασιλείᾳ τοῦ Χριστοῦ καὶ θεοῦ). The entire clause functions substantively

in apposition to the demonstrative pronoun τοῦτο: "you know this, *namely that*" (W, 458–59). **Semantically**, ὅτι is in apposition to the demonstrative pronoun "that" (NASB, NKJV, KJV, ESV, NRSV, RSV, NET). The clause introduces the content of Paul's reminder.

> **Lexical Nugget**: Why does Paul repeat the vice list from verse 3, but change the form? Paul gives his third list of three vices (cf. vv. 3, 4). This final list repeats the vices from verse 3, but here he gives the personal forms instead of the abstract terms. For example, in verse 3 he condemns "sexual immorality," but in verse 5 he condemns those who are sexually immoral. The context is a significant difference. In verse 3, Paul uses the terms to describe those behaviors not proper for the Christian community. In verse 5, he refers to specific types of people who have no inheritance in the kingdom (Arnold, 324). See the Lexical Nugget 5:3a for a description of each term.

ὅ: The Greek word ὅ is a neuter singular nominative from the relative pronoun ὅς that means "who" or introduces an explanation "that is" (BDAG, s.v. "ὅς" 1gα, p. 727). Several English translations offset the phrase with dashes or parentheses (cf. ESV, RSV, NRSV, NIV, NET). **Syntactically**, ὅ introduces a dependent adjectival relative clause "*who* is an idolater" (ὅ ἐστιν εἰδωλολάτρης). Since the pronoun is singular, the antecedent is most likely limited to the last item of the list: "a greedy person" (πλεονέκτης) (cf. Col. 3:5) (Hoehner, 660; Best, 481; Arnold, 324). The neuter pronoun lacks concord—the antecedent is masculine. Paul may use the neuter pronoun as a part of an explanation (BDF §132): "*that is* an idolater" (cf. ESV, RSV, NRSV). The relative pronoun functions as the subject of the relative clause.

> **Text-Critical Nugget**: Should the relative pronoun in verse 5 be masculine or neuter? The majority of Byzantine manuscripts (𝔐) along with a few key Alexandrian and Western manuscripts (A and D) replace the neuter relative pronoun (ὅ) with the masculine relative pronoun (ὅς). On the other hand, the reading with the neuter relative pronoun (ὅ) is found in a number of good Alexandrian (𝔓⁴⁶, ℵ, B, 1739) and Western (F, G, latt) manuscripts. Besides having strong external support in two text types, the reading with the neuter relative pronoun is harder. A scribe more likely changed the relative pronoun to agree with the personal nature of the nouns (Metzger, 539).

ἐστίν: The Greek word ἐστίν is a third-person singular present active indicative from the verb εἰμί that means "to be" (BDAG, s.v. "εἰμί" 2cα, p. 284). **Syntactically**, ἐστίν functions as the main verb of the relative clause. The subject of the verb is the relative pronoun "who" (ὅ). The predicate nominative is "idolater" (εἰδωλολάτρης). **Semantically**, ἐστίν is an equative present: "is" (cf. RSV, NRSV, ESV, HCSB, CSB, NASB, NKJV, KJV, NIV, NET). Paul equates greed with idolatry. In Romans 1, Paul explains how greed for something can easily take over God's rightful place in a person's life. Out of greed, we exchange the glory of the creator for the glory of what he created (Rom. 1:23–25; Hoehner, 660).

ἔχει: The Greek word ἔχει is a third-person singular present active indicative from the verb ἔχω that means "to own" or "possess" (BDAG, s.v. "ἔχω" 1aα, p. 420). **Syntactically**, ἔχει functions as the main verb of the dependent conjunctive clause introduced by ὅτι (v. 5b). The subject is complex, made up with a series of nouns: "sexually immoral" (πόρνος), "morally unclean" (ἀκάθαρτος), and "greedy" (πλεονέκτης). The direct object is "inheritance" (κληρονομίαν). The adjective πᾶς along with the negative adverb οὐκ is a Semitic construction. The verb should be negated and πᾶς refers to each individual class: "everyone who is sexually immoral, impure, or greedy … has no inheritance (cf. ESV, CSB, HCSB). **Semantically**, ἔχει could function as a futuristic present, which describes an event that has begun in the present but will culminate in the future (Hoehner, 661). On the other hand, Arnold argues that elsewhere Paul describes the inheritance for the believer as a present reality (Eph. 1:13–14, 18, cf. 2:6) (Arnold, 325). In this case, ἔχει could be classified as a customary present, which describes an ongoing action. Thielman notes that this is the only occurrence of the phrase "the kingdom of Christ and God." Paul normally refers to the "kingdom of God." Even though he can talk about the future of the kingdom of God (1 Cor. 6:10; 15:50; Gal. 5:21), this reference to the kingdom of Christ and God may point to Christ's present reign (Thielman, 333–34). The problem with these arguments is that the object of the verb is "inheritance." Earlier in Ephesians, Paul described this inheritance as a future reality for the believer—of which they have received a down payment (Eph. 1:14) (Best, 481–82). Nonetheless, both options—the futuristic present or the customary present—touch on the tension within Paul's eschatology. The believer currently has a foretaste of a future reality, but the unbeliever does not (cf. Eph. 2:1–3; 4:17b–19, 22).

Syntactical Nugget: What is the relationship between "Christ" and "God" in verse 5? The phrase τοῦ Χριστοῦ καὶ θεοῦ ("of Christ and God") fits the TSKS (or the Granville Sharp) construction and may have significant christological implications. Generally, when two nouns are brought together with καί and governed by a single article, both substantives refer to the same person. In this case, the phrase might be translated: "the kingdom of Christ, who is God" (Larkin, 111; Turner, 1965, 16). However, since both nouns should probably be either considered as a proper name or title it does not fit the strict rules of the Granville Sharp construction (W, 276; Merkle, 162; Hoehner, 661; Arnold, 325). Even though the construction may not point to identity, the construction with two distinct people describes the two as a coherent group with a singular purpose (W, 277–78). In this case, the kingdom belongs to both Christ and God. Elsewhere Paul describes the relationship with more depth. God subjects all things to Christ, and Christ rules at the right hand of God (Eph. 1:20–22).

5:6a ἀπατάτω: The Greek word ἀπατάτω is a third-person singular present active imperative from the verb ἀπατάω that means "to deceive" or "mislead" (BDAG, s.v. "ἀπατάω" 1, p. 98). **Syntactically**, ἀπατάτω is the main verb of the independent asyndeton clause. The subject is "no one" (μηδείς). The direct object is "you" (ὑμᾶς), referring to the believers: "let no one deceive you" (RSV, NRSV, ESV, NIV, CSB, HCSB, NASB, KJV, NKJV). The NLT renders the phrase as "don't be fooled." **Semantically**, ἀπατάτω is a customary present: "deceive" (ESV, RSV, NRSV, NIV, NET, CSB, HCSB, NASB, NKJV, KJV). The present tense describes an ongoing state (W, 521–22). The prohibition in this context refers to a general precept—believers should avoid deception. The dative phrase κενοῖς λόγοις, literally, "empty words," or figuratively, "words devoid of any moral or spiritual value" (BDAG, s.v. "κενός" 2a, p. 539) expresses means by which this deception might take place: "*with* empty words" (RSV, NRSV, ESV, NIV, NET, NASB, NKJV; cf. CSB, HCSB, KJV). In Ephesians 4, Paul expresses his desire for the believers to grow to keep from being "tossed about and carried along" by deceit (Eph. 4:14). Here he gives a similar command with explicit language.

5:6b διὰ ταῦτα: The Greek word ταῦτα is a neuter plural accusative from the demonstrative pronoun οὗτος. The pronoun with the preposition διά expresses a causal relation to the preceding context (Runge, 2010, 48). Most English translations render the phrase: "because of these things" (ESV, RSV, NRSV, CSB, HCSB, NASB, NKJV, KJV) or "for this reason" (BDAG, s.v. "διά" B2b, pp. 225–26). **Syntactically**, the pronoun does not refer to "empty words" (κενοῖς λόγοις), which is masculine, but to sexually perverse and greedy conduct described in verses 3–5 (Hoehner, 664; Thielman, 335). Most English versions translate the phrase as "because of these things" (CSB, HCSB, NASB, KJV, NKJV, RSV, NRSV, ESV, NET).

γάρ: The Greek word γάρ is a conjunction that means "for" or "therefore" (BDAG, s.v. "γάρ" 1a, p. 189). **Syntactically**, γάρ is in a postpositive position introducing an independent conjunctive clause: "*For* because of these things the wrath of God comes on the sons of disobedience" (διὰ ταῦτα γὰρ ἔρχεται ἡ ὀργὴ τοῦ θεοῦ ἐπὶ τοὺς υἱοὺς τῆς ἀπειθείας). **Semantically**, γάρ expresses the reason for Paul's prohibition: "for" (ESV, NRSV, RSV, NIV, NET, CSB, HCSB, NASB, NKJV, KJV; Hoehner, 664; Merkle, 163; Larkin, 113).

ἔρχεται: The Greek word ἔρχεται is a third-person singular present middle (deponent) indicative from the verb ἔρχομαι that means "to come" (BDAG, s.v. "ἔρχομαι" 5, p. 395). **Syntactically**, ἔρχεται functions as the main verb of the independent conjunctive clause introduced with γάρ. The phrase "the wrath of God" (ἡ ὀργὴ τοῦ θεοῦ) functions as the subject. **Semantically**, ἔρχεται functions as a futuristic present: "comes" (ESV, RSV, NRSV, NIV, NET, NASB, NKJV). The NLT translates the verb "will fall." The present tense expresses confidence that the action of the verb will come to pass in the future. Elsewhere, Paul uses the present tense to describe God's future wrath (1 Thess. 1:10; 5:9; Col. 3:6; BDF §323; Arnold, 327; Larkin, 113; Lincoln, 326–26; Thielman, 335). Some argue that Paul means to convey both a future and present idea behind the present tense. In some ways, these sons of disobedience already experience God's wrath through their hard hearts (Eph. 4:17–19; cf. Rom. 1:18), but Paul envisions a day when this wrath will be fully realized (cf. Rom. 2:5) (Best, 485–86; Hoehner, 664). The verb is modified by the prepositional phrase "on the sons of disobedience" (ἐπὶ τοὺς υἱοὺς τῆς ἀπειθείας). The preposition ἐπί marks the direction to which God's wrath is directed (BDAG, s.v. "ἐπί" 14bβ, p. 366). The object of the preposition is "the sons of disobedience" (τοὺς υἱοὺς τῆς ἀπειθείας). The phrase is a Hebrew idiom. The idea is that these people are characterized by disobedience (Moule, 174–75; Robertson, 651–52). Paul uses a similar phrase in Ephesians 2:3 where he describes these people under the sway of the ruler of this world—they are destined for wrath. In Ephesians 5:6, he clarifies that they are destined for God's wrath.

Ephesians 5:7–14

Big Greek Idea: Believers should walk as children of light, characterized by goodness, justice, and truth, not associating with those who do shameful deeds of evil, but rather exposing them.

Structural Overview: The fourth section is closely related to the previous section. Paul ends the previous section warning that the unbelievers will not inherit the kingdom, rather the wrath of God will come upon them. He begins this section by commanding the believers not to associate with these people (v. 7) and reminds them that they once lived a similar life. In verse 8 he changes the metaphor, signaling a new section. Instead of walking in love as beloved children (v. 2), believers should "walk as children of light" (v. 8). As children of light the Christian community should be marked with goodness, righteousness, and truth (v. 9).

Not only should believers abstain from interacting with these unbelievers, Paul suggests that as children of light, they should also expose these shameful deeds (vv. 11–13). Ultimately, the light will shine on all things, revealing all of their actions. The idea is that through exposing these deeds, the unbeliever will convert. He supports this by quoting an early Christian hymn. When Christ shines his light on those who are spiritually dead, they will rise (v. 14).

Outline:

Believers should walk as children of the light, marked by goodness, justice, and truth, exposing the evil deeds in the world (vv. 7–11)

Believers, who were once in the darkness, should walk as children of the light (vv. 7–8)

As children of the light, the Christian community should be marked by goodness, justice, and truth, seeking what pleases God (vv. 9–10)

Believers should no longer associate with these unbelievers, but rather expose their deeds (v. 11)

Believers should seek to expose evil deeds with the intent of bringing these to Christ (vv. 12–14)

Despite how shameful these deeds are, believers should expose them with the intent that they turn to the light as well (vv. 12–13)

Conclusion: the light Christ shines leads to resurrection (v. 14)

Clausal Outline for Ephesians 5:7–14

5:7 μὴ <u>οὖν</u> **γίνεσθε** συμμέτοχοι αὐτῶν·
5:7 <u>Therefore</u> **do** not **become** partners with them;

5:8a **ἦτε** γάρ ποτε σκότος,
5:8a <u>for</u> you **were** once darkness,

5:8b νῦν <u>δέ</u> [**ἐστε**] φῶς ἐν κυρίῳ·
5:8b <u>but</u> now you [**are**] light in the Lord;

5:8c <u>ὡς</u> τέκνα φωτὸς
5:8c <u>as</u> children of the light

5:8d **περιπατεῖτε**
5:8d **walk**

5:9 —ὁ <u>γὰρ</u> καρπὸς τοῦ φωτός [**ἐστίν**] ἐν πάσῃ ἀγαθωσύνῃ καὶ δικαιοσύνῃ καὶ ἀληθείᾳ—
5:9 —<u>for</u> the fruit of the light [**is**] in all goodness, righteousness, and truth—

[περιπατεῖτε (v. 8d)]
[walk (v. 8d)]

5:10 **δοκιμάζοντες** (<u>τί</u> <u>ἐστιν</u> εὐάρεστον τῷ κυρίῳ)·
5:10 **by testing** (<u>what</u> <u>is</u> pleasing to the Lord);

5:11a <u>καὶ</u> μὴ **συγκοινωνεῖτε** τοῖς ἔργοις τοῖς ἀκάρποις τοῦ σκότους,
5:11a <u>And</u> **do** not **participate** in the unfruitful works of darkness,

5:11b μᾶλλον <u>δὲ καὶ</u> **ἐλέγχετε**,
5:11b <u>but</u> rather **expose** them.

5:12 (τὰ γὰρ κρυφῇ γινόμενα ὑπ' αὐτῶν) αἰσχρόν **ἐστιν** καὶ **λέγειν**
5:12 <u>For</u> even **to say** (the things done by them in secret) **is** shameful

5:13 (τὰ δὲ πάντα ἐλεγχόμενα) ὑπὸ τοῦ φωτὸς **φανεροῦται**,
5:13 <u>but</u> (all things that are exposed) by the light **become clear**,

5:14a (πᾶν <u>γὰρ</u> τὸ φανερούμενον) φῶς **ἐστιν**.
5:14a <u>for</u> (all things that are made clear) **are** light.

5:14b διὸ **λέγει**,
5:14b Therefore **it says**:

|
5:14c **Ἔγειρε**, (ὁ καθεύδων),
5:14c **Get up**, (sleeper),

|
5:14d καὶ **ἀνάστα** ἐκ τῶν νεκρῶν,
5:14d and **rise up** from the dead,

|
5:14e καὶ **ἐπιφαύσει** σοι ὁ Χριστός.
5:14e and Christ **will shine** on you.

SYNTAX EXPLAINED FOR EPHESIANS 5:7–14

5:7 οὖν: The Greek word οὖν is a conjunction that means "therefore" or "consequently" (BDAG, s.v. "οὖν" 1b, p. 736). **Syntactically**, οὖν introduces an independent conjunctive clause: "*Therefore* do not become partakers with them" (μὴ οὖν γίνεσθε συμμέτοχοι αὐτῶν). **Semantically**, οὖν is an inferential conjunction, drawing an inference from the previous verse: "therefore" (CSB, HCSB, NASB, KJV, NKJV, RSV, NRSV, ESV, NET, NIV). Believers should have no part with these sons of disobedience since God's wrath is coming down on them (Hoehner, 668).

γίνεσθε: The Greek word γίνεσθε is a second-person plural present middle (deponent) imperative from the verb γίνομαι that means "to become something" (BDAG, s.v. "γίνομαι" 5a, p. 198). **Syntactically**, γίνεσθε functions as the main verb of the independent conjunctive clause introduced by οὖν. The subject is implied by the verb: "you all," referring to believers. The predicate nominative is the phrase: "having a share with them" (συμμέτοχοι αὐτῶν). The genitive αὐτῶν is a genitive of association: "having a share *with them*" (RSV, NRSV, ESV, NIV, NET, NASB, NKJV, KJV). **Semantically**, γίνεσθε is a customary present: "be" (NRSV, NIV, NASB) or "become" (ESV, CSB, HCSB). Some versions translate the predicate nominative as the verb: "do not associate" (RSV) or "Don't participate" (NLT). The present tense describes an ongoing state. Paul wants the Ephesian believers to habitually avoid these sons of disobedience (W, 521–22).

> **Lexical Nugget:** What does it mean to be "partakers" (συμμέτοχος)? The Greek word συμμέτοχος only appears in Ephesians (3:6; 5:7). It means to have a share in something (BDAG, s.v. "συμμέτοχος," p. 958). Paul is not prohibiting all association with unbelievers, but rather believers partaking in their lifestyle (Hoehner, 668–69; Thielman, 335–36). In Ephesians 3:6, Paul describes Gentiles as partners with Christ and his

people—the church. Through their relationship with Christ, they have changed their association. They are no longer "sons of disobedience" (cf. Eph. 2:1–3; cf. 2:11–12). Their new allegiance with Christ has called for a new worldview completely distinct from their former way of life—the two are incompatible (cf. Eph. 4:17–24).

Grammatical Nugget: What is the antecedent of the pronoun αὐτῶν in verse 7? The pronoun could be understood as neuter, in which case the antecedent would be the demonstrative pronoun ταῦτα—itself a referent to the evil deeds. Paul commands the believers to not partake in these evil deeds (Best, 486). However, the pronoun is best understood as masculine, referring to the "sons of disobedience" themselves (cf. Hoehner, 668; Lincoln, 326; Abbott, 1909, 152).

5:8a ἦτε: The Greek word ἦτε is a second-person plural imperfect active indicative from the verb εἰμί that means "to be" (BDAG, s.v. "εἰμί" 2a, p. 283). **Syntactically**, ἦτε functions as the main verb of the independent conjunctive clause introduced by the postpositive γάρ. The subject is implied by the verb: "you all," referring to the Ephesians. The predicate nominative is "darkness" (σκότος). **Semantically**, the imperfect tense functions as a customary imperfect, which expresses the action of the verb as a continual state. Paul uses the verb to describe the believer's former state. Later he will refer to the unbeliever's behavior as "fruit of darkness" (Eph. 5:11), but here he refers to them as "darkness."

γάρ: The Greek word γάρ is a conjunction that means "for" or "therefore" (BDAG, s.v. "γάρ" 1a, p. 189). Most English versions translate the conjunction "for" (RSV, NRSV, ESV, NIV, NET, CSB, HCSB, NASB, NKJV, KJV). **Syntactically**, γάρ is in a postpositive position introducing an independent conjunctive clause: "*For* you were once in the dark" (ἦτε γάρ ποτε σκότος). **Semantically**, γάρ expresses the reason for Paul's prohibition: "for" (Larkin, 114; Merkle, 163; Arnold, 327; Lincoln, 326). Paul prohibits believers from partnering with these sons of disobedience because their identity has changed. They are no longer in the darkness with these sons of disobedience, but they are "sons of light."

5:8b δέ: The Greek word δέ is a conjunction that means "but" (BDAG, s.v. "δέ" 4a, p. 213). **Syntactically**, δέ is in the postpositive position introducing an independent conjunctive clause "*but* now you are in the in the light, in the Lord" (νῦν δὲ φῶς ἐν κυρίῳ). **Semantically**, δέ along with νῦν as a temporal maker, creating a contrast with the adverb ποτέ in verse 8a: "*once* you were … *but now*" (RSV, NRSV, ESV, NIV, NET, NLT, CSB, HCSB, NASB, NKJV, KJV). The contrast marks a change in the believer's eschatological reality. Paul makes a similar contrast in Ephesians 2. In Ephesians 2:2–3, he describes the believer's *former* behavior before God saved them before describing how God saved them (See Theological Nugget at 2:2a). In Ephesians 5, he uses the temporal markers to describe this eschatological shift in conceptual terms: they *once* were in darkness, but *now* they walk in light.

[ἐστέ]: The Greek word [ἐστέ] is a second-person plural present active indicative from the verb εἰμί that means "to be" (BDAG, s.v. "εἰμί" 2a, p. 283). **Syntactically**, [ἐστέ] is an ellipsis. It is the main verb of the independent conjunctive clause introduced by δέ. The subject is implied in the verb: "you all," referring to the Ephesians. The predicate nominative is "light" (φῶς). **Semantically**, the present tense is a customary present, expressing the action of the verb as a continual state. The present tense describes the believer's current situation: "you are light" (RSV, NRSV, ESV, NIV, NET, CSB, HCSB, NASB, NKJV). The elliptical verb is modified by the prepositional phrase "in the Lord" (ἐν κυρίῳ). The preposition expresses sphere. Due to the believers' new relationship with the Lord, they are no longer in darkness—they are in light.

5:8c ὡς: The Greek word ὡς is a conjunction that means "as" in this context (BDAG, s.v. "ὡς" 1bα, pp. 1103–4). **Syntactically**, ὡς introduces a dependent conjunctive clause "*as* children of light" (ὡς τέκνα φωτός). The entire clause functions adverbially modifying the verb "walk" (περιπατεῖτε). **Semantically**, ὡς expresses a comparison: "as" (RSV, NRSV, ESV, NIV, NET, CSB, HCSB, NASB, NKJV, KJV). The clause describes the manner in which believers should walk. As children of light, believers should walk in the light.

5:8d περιπατεῖτε: The Greek word περιπατεῖτε is a second-person plural present active imperative from the verb περιπατέω that means "to live" or "behave"; the word figuratively describes a habit of conduct (BDAG, s.v. "περιπατέω" 2aγ, p. 803). Some English versions translate the verb literally as "walk" (HCSB, NASB, KJV, NKJV, RSV, ESV, NET); others present the word metaphorically as "live" (CSB, NIV, NRSV, NLT). **Syntactically**, περιπατεῖτε functions as the main verb of an asyndetic clause. The subject is implied in the verb: "you all," referring to the believers. The direct object is "children of the light." **Semantically**, περιπατεῖτε is a customary present: "walk" (ESV, RSV, NET, HCSB, NASB, NKJV, KJV) or "live" (NIV, NRSV, CSB, NLT). The present tense describes an ongoing state. The imperative conveys the idea of a general precept: Paul wants believers to habitually live in the light (W, 521–22, 722). Paul uses the Greek verb περιπατέω as a keyword that provides the structure for the second part of the letter (see the Theological Nugget in 4:1b).

^{5:9} γάρ: The Greek word γάρ is a conjunction that means "for" or "therefore" (BDAG, s.v. "γάρ" 1a, p. 189). **Syntactically**, γάρ is in a postpositive position, introducing an independent conjunctive clause: "*For* the fruit of the light is in all goodness, righteousness, and truth" (ὁ γὰρ καρπὸς τοῦ φωτὸς ἐν πάσῃ ἀγαθωσύνῃ καὶ δικαιοσύνῃ καὶ ἀληθείᾳ). **Semantically**, γάρ explains the previous clause: "for" (RSV, NRSV, ESV, NIV, NET, CSB, HCSB, NASB, NKJV, KJV). The shift from the second person to the third indicates that the phrase is parenthetical, providing more information about what it means to walk in the light (Hoehner, 672; Best, 489).

[ἐστίν]: The Greek word ἐστίν is a third-person singular present active indicative from the verb εἰμί that means "to be" (BDAG, s.v. "εἰμί" 2c, p. 283). **Syntactically**, [ἐστίν] is an ellipsis. It serves as the main verb in the independent conjunctive clause introduced by γάρ: "For the fruit of the light is in all goodness, righteousness, and truth" (ὁ γὰρ καρπὸς τοῦ φωτὸς ἐν πάσῃ ἀγαθωσύνῃ καὶ δικαιοσύνῃ καὶ ἀληθείᾳ). The subject of the verb is "fruit" (καρπός). The predicate nominative is the prepositional phrase "in all goodness, righteousness, and truth" (ἐν πάσῃ ἀγαθωσύνῃ καὶ δικαιοσύνῃ καὶ ἀληθείᾳ). **Semantically**, [ἐστίν] is an equative present tense: "is." English requires a noun for the ellipsis. English translations render the verb a number of different ways: "is found in" (RSV, NRSV, ESV); "consists in" (NIV, NET, NASB); "consists of" (CSB); "results in" (HCSB); or "is in" (KJV, NKJV). The genitive τοῦ φωτός is best understood as a genitive of production: "fruit produced by light" (W, 105). The character of these children of light (v. 8) should be characterized by goodness, righteousness, and truth.

> **Text-Critical Nugget**: Does Paul write "fruit of the light" or "fruit of the Spirit" in verse 9? In addition to a number of Byzantine manuscripts (𝔐), a handful of key manuscripts (𝔓⁴⁶, D², Ψ, 1505) read πνεύματος (i.e., "the fruit of the Spirit") instead of φωτός (i.e., "the fruit of the light"). The reading most likely came about due to the influence of Galatians 5:22 (Metzger, 539–40). The reading with φωτός is found in the majority of Alexandrian (𝔓⁴⁹, ℵ, A, B, 1739, 1881) and Western (D, F, G, latt) manuscripts. The internal evidence along with the diverse set of manuscripts suggests that the original reading is καρπός τοῦ φωτός.

> **Lexical Nugget**: What do the terms "goodness" (ἀγαθωσύνη), "righteousness" (δικαιοσύνη), and "truth" (ἀλήθεια) mean? Each term is the object of the preposition ἐν, which marks specification or substance (BDAG, s.v. "ἐν" 12, p. 330): "fruit of light *consists in* goodness, righteousness, and truth." Each term relates to a theme that Paul develops throughout the letter. The first Greek term (ἀγαθωσύνη) only occurs four times in the New Testament (Rom. 15:14; Gal. 5:22; Eph. 5:9; 2 Thess. 1:11). The term refers

to the quality of a person who is good (ἀγαθός) (Grundmann, 1964, 18). Throughout the letter, Paul describes the believer as "doing good works," which come from God (Eph. 2:10) and build up the community (4:28, 29; 6:8). The second Greek term (δικαιοσύνη) refers to an attitude of uprightness or justice (BDAG, s.v. "δικαιοσύνη" 3a, p. 248). Earlier in the letter, Paul associates righteousness with God (Eph. 4:24; cf. 6:14). Because God is righteous, believers should also be righteous. The final Greek term (ἀλήθεια) means "trustfulness" or "dependability" (BDAG, s.v. "ἀλήθεια" 1, p. 42). Truth was the dominant theme in Ephesians 4 (4:21, 24, 25). He calls the believers to treat one another with truth. He refers to the gospel as the "word of truth" (Eph. 1:3; cf. 4:21).

5:10 δοκιμάζοντες: The Greek word δοκιμάζοντες is a masculine nominative plural present active participle from the verb δοκιμάζω that means "to put to the test" or "examine" with the connotation of determining the genuineness of something (BDAG, s.v. "δοκιμάζω" 1, p. 255). **Syntactically**, δοκιμάζοντες introduces a dependent participle clause. It functions adverbially modifying the verb "walk" (περιπατεῖτε) (v. 8). **Semantically**, δοκιμάζοντες expresses either manner (Hoehner, 675; Larkin, 115) or means (Arnold, 330; Merkle, 165): "*by testing*." Believers walk in light by examining what is pleasing to the Lord. Several English versions render the participle as an imperative: "find out what pleases the Lord" (NIV; cf. RSV, NRSV, ESV, NLT; cf. Barth, 569). This is unlikely since the verb it modifies (περιπατεῖτε, v. 8), as well as the following verbs (συγκοινωνεῖτε and ἐλέγχετε, v. 11), are imperatives (Abbott, 1909, 153).

τί: The Greek word τί is an indefinite pronoun from the word τίς that means "what" or "what sort of" (BDAG, s.v. "τίς" 1aβ⸃, p. 1007; W, 345–46). **Syntactically**, τί introduces the clause as the direct object of the participle "testing" (δοκιμάζοντες): "testing *what* is pleasing to the Lord."

ἐστίν: The Greek word ἐστίν is a third-person singular present active indicative from the verb εἰμί that means "to be" (BDAG, s.v. "εἰμί" 2ca, p. 284). **Syntactically**, ἐστίν functions as the main verb of the dependent conjunctive clause introduced by τί related to the participle δοκιμάζοντες. The interrogative pronoun functions as the subject. The predicate nominative is "pleasing" (εὐάρεστον). The term refers to "God's attitude towards human conduct" (Foerster, 1964, 457). Elsewhere, Paul uses the term to refer to understanding and doing the will of God (Rom. 12:1–2). The indirect object is "the Lord" (τῷ κυρίῳ), referring to Jesus Christ. **Semantically**, ἐστίν is an equative present: "is" (CSB, HCSB, NASB, NKJV, KJV, RSV, NRSV, ESV, NET). The NIV renders the adjective as a verb: "what pleases the Lord" (cf. NLT). The clause expresses the standard by which believers should behave—they should seek to please the Lord.

5:11a καί: The Greek word καί is a conjunction that means "and" (BDAG, s.v. "καί" 1ba, p. 494). **Syntactically**, καί introduces an independent conjunctive clause: "*and* do not participate in their unfruitful works of darkness" (καὶ μὴ συγκοινωνεῖτε τοῖς ἔργοις τοῖς ἀκάρποις τοῦ σκότους). **Semantically**, καί is a coordinating connective: "and" (KJV, NKJV). Most English versions simply omit the conjunction, beginning a new sentence with the imperative: "Do not participate" (NASB, NET; cf. CSB, HCSB) or "Take no part" (RSV, NRSV, ESV, NLT). After describing the believer's life in light (vv. 9–10), the conjunction brings Paul back to a new prohibition, similar to his command in verse 7.

συγκοινωνεῖτε: The Greek word συγκοινωνεῖτε is a second-person plural present active imperative from the verb συγκοινωνέω that means "to be connected" (BDAG, s.v. "συγκοινωνέω" 1a, p. 952). **Syntactically**, συγκοινωνεῖτε is the main verb of the independent conjunctive clause introduced by καί. The verb is parallel to the imperative γίνεσθε (v. 7). The subject is implied in the verb: "you all," referring to believers. The indirect object is "unfruitful works of darkness" (τοῖς ἔργοις τοῖς ἀκάρποις τοῦ σκότους). **Semantically**, συγκοινωνεῖτε is a customary present: "participate" (NET, CSB, HCSB, NASB) or "take part" (ESV, RSV, NRSV, NLT). The NIV renders the imperative as "do not participate." The present tense describes an ongoing state. Paul commands believers to make this attitude habitual (W, 521–22, 722). Just as believers are not to partner with unbelievers (v. 7), they are not to participate in their deeds, which Paul calls unfruitful. Darkness refers to the darkness in which Gentiles once lived (v. 8).

Semantical Nugget: What does the phrase "unfruitful works of darkness" mean? The genitive τοῦ σκότους is a genitive of production: "unfruitful work *produced by* the darkness" (W, 106–7). This is similar to the genitive construction that Paul uses in verse 9: ὁ καρπὸς τοῦ φωτός ("fruit *produced by* light"), creating a contrast between the "sons of darkness" and "children of light." In verse 11, he adds the dative τοῖς ἔργοις (deeds) to refer specifically to their actions (BDAG, s.v. "ἔργον" 1cβ, pp. 390–91). Even though he does not specifically outline these deeds, he probably envisions a contrast with the fruit of light that he lists in verse 9: goodness, righteousness, and truth. Earlier in the letter he gives a detailed description of this type of behavior (Eph. 2:1–3; 4:17–19; particularly 4:18). They follow their own desires living apart from God. Finally, since he is comparing the Christian community to those "sons of disobedience," he most likely has in mind the vices that he lists in the previous section (Eph. 5:3–5), consisting of sexual perversion and greed.

5:11b δὲ καί: The Greek word δέ is a conjunction that means "but" in this context (BDAG, s.v. "δέ" 5a, p. 213). The Greek word καί is a conjunction that means "and" or "even" (BDAG, s.v. "καί" 1bε, p. 495). **Syntactically**, δὲ καί introduces the independent conjunctive clause: "but rather expose them" (μᾶλλον δὲ καὶ ἐλέγχετε). **Semantically**, δέ is a contrastive conjunction. Together with καί, the two conjunctions create a heightened emphasis: "but even" (cf. NASB). The adverb μᾶλλον heightens the contrast even more: "but rather" (ESV, RSV, NRSV, NIV, NET, CSB, HCSB). After giving a prohibition—do not associate with these deeds—he gives a positive command: expose them.

ἐλέγχετε: The Greek word ἐλέγχετε is a second-person plural present active imperative from the verb ἐλέγχω that means "to bring to light," "expose," or "set forth" (BDAG, s.v. "ἐλέγχω" 1, p. 315). **Syntactically**, ἐλέγχετε functions as the main verb of the independent conjunctive clause introduced by δὲ καί: "but rather expose them" (μᾶλλον δὲ καὶ ἐλέγχετε). The subject is implied in the verb: "you all," referring to believers. Since there is no object for the verb, Paul could be calling believers to rebuke these people or their deeds. In verse 12, he refers specifically to those who do such things (Larkin, 117), but it is best to understand that he has the deeds themselves in mind since he refers to them specifically in verses 11a and 13 (Best, 492; Lincoln, 329; Thielman, 343–44; Merkle, 165–66). **Semantically**, ἐλέγχετε is an iterative present expressing a repeated action (W, 520–21, 722). Believers should expose these deeds whenever they are confronted with them. The command stands in contrast with the previous prohibition (v. 11a). Paul began this section in a similar manner, contrasting a prohibition (v. 7) with a command (v. 8). While the prohibitions are similar (not to join yourself with these sons of disobedience), the imperatives are somewhat distinct: "walk as children of the light" (v. 8c) and "expose these evil deeds" (v. 11b).

Theological Nugget: Does Paul refer to exposing the sin of those inside the church or outside? When Paul commands believers to expose these unfruitful deeds, does he mean those deeds done by believers or unbelievers? By excluding the object of the verb, his intent is not clear. Some commentators argue that Paul limits his command to those within the church since the larger context of the passage is directed to how believers should live within their community of faith. Furthermore, Paul always uses the verb ἐλέγχω to refer to believers (1 Tim. 5:20; Titus 1:9, 13; 2:15) (Arnold, 331–32; Hoehner, 679–80). On the other hand, Paul does discuss how believers should relate to those outside of the community (v. 7). In verse 11, he specifically commands believers to have no part in these evil deeds. By giving the command, he suggests that believers are still susceptible to this behavior; however, this darkness characterizes the unbeliever (Eph. 4:18; 5:8). In the narrow context, his focus is on deeds of darkness—not those who commit them. As children of light, believers should expose these types of deeds, whether they are committed inside the church or outside (Thielman, 343–44; cf. Schreiner, 2001, 69; Lincoln, 330; Bock, 1994b, 317).

^{5:12} γάρ: The Greek word γάρ is a conjunction that means "for" or "therefore" (BDAG, s.v. "γάρ" 2, pp. 189–90). **Syntactically**, γάρ is in a postpositive position, introducing an independent conjunctive clause: "*for* the things done in secret by them are shameful" (τὰ γὰρ κρυφῇ γινόμενα ὑπ' αὐτῶν αἰσχρόν ἐστιν). **Semantically**, γάρ introduces a parenthetical explanation of the previous section: "for" (CSB, HCSB, NASB, NKJV, KJV, RSV, NRSV, ESV, NET). Some argue that the conjunction introduces the reason for Paul's command for the believer to have nothing to do with these evil deeds—they are shameful even to discuss (Lincoln, 330; Hoehner, 680; Thielman, 344). On the other hand, it can explain the effectiveness of such a rebuke that Paul describes in verse 12. By calling attention to these actions in public those who do them are shamed (Lenski, 1937, 609; Best, 494–95).

γινόμενα: The Greek word γινόμενα is a neuter accusative plural present passive (deponent) participle from the verb γίνομαι that means "to be made" or "be created" (BDAG, s.v. "γίνομαι" 2a, p. 197). **Syntactically**, γινόμενα is a substantival participle. The phrase "the things done in secret by them" (τὰ κρυφῇ γινόμενα ὑπ' αὐτῶν) functions as the direct object of the infinitive λέγειν. **Semantically**, γινόμενα is a customary present—these actions are done habitually in secret. The dative κρυφῇ expresses manner: "what such people do *secretly*" (NRSV; BDAG, s.v. "κρυφῇ," p. 572). The preposition ὑπό expresses agency: "what is done by them in secret" (CSB, HCSB; cf. NASB); however some translations render the participle in the active voice: "the things they do in secret" (ESV, RSV, NET; cf. NRSV, NIV, NLT). The participle clause refers to "unfruitful deeds" (cf. v. 11).

ἐστίν: The Greek word ἐστίν is a third-person singular present active indicative from the verb εἰμί that means "to be" (BDAG, s.v. "εἰμί" 2b, p. 283). **Syntactically**, ἐστίν functions as the main verb of the independent conjunctive clause introduced by γάρ. The subject of the verb is the substantival infinitive clause: "even to say the things secretly done by them" (τὰ γὰρ κρυφῇ γινόμενα ὑπ' αὐτῶν ... καὶ λέγειν). The predicate nominative is "shameful" (αἰσχρόν). **Semantically**, ἐστίν is an equative present: "is." Most English versions render the verb as "it is" (RSV, NRSV, ESV, NIV, CSB, HCSB, NASB, NKJV, KJV).

λέγειν: The Greek word λέγειν is a present active infinitive from the verb λέγω that means "to speak" or "to report" (BDAG, s.v. "λέγω" 3, p. 590). **Syntactically**, λέγειν is a substantival infinitive functioning as the subject of the verb ἐστιν. The conjunction καί is ascensive emphasizing the infinitive: "*even* to speak of the things secretly done by them" (BDAG, s.v. "καί" 2b, pp. 495–96). **Semantically**, λέγειν is an iterative present describing a repetitive event (W, 520–21). Not only is it shameful to do these things, but it is also shameful to speak of them.

5:13 δέ: The Greek word δέ is a conjunction that means "but" (BDAG, s.v. "δέ" 4a, p. 213). **Syntactically**, δέ introduces an independent conjunctive clause: "*but* all things that are exposed by the light are made clear" (Τὰ δὲ πάντα ἐλεγχόμενα ὑπὸ τοῦ φωτὸς φανεροῦται). **Semantically**, δέ marks a contrast: "but" (RSV, NRSV, ESV, NIV, NET, NASB, NKJV, KJV). The clause contrasts with those things done in secret (v. 12), giving further explanation for his command for believers to expose these behaviors (v. 11) (Hoehner, 682; Thielman, 346; Merkle, 167; contra Larkin, 118, who takes the conjunction as resumptive).

ἐλεγχόμενα: The Greek word ἐλεγχόμενα is a neuter nominative plural present passive participle from the verb ἐλέγχω that means "to bring to light," "expose," or "set forth" (BDAG, s.v. "ἐλέγχω" 1, p. 315). Paul uses the same verb in verse 11. **Syntactically**, ἐλεγχόμενα is an attributive participle modifying "all the things" (τὰ πάντα). The participle phrase τὰ πάντα ἐλεγχόμενα ("all the things that are exposed") functions as the subject of the verb "are made clear" (φανεροῦται). The participle refers to those deeds that were done in secret (v. 11), not all things in general (Hoehner, 682; Merkle, 167). **Semantically**, ἐλεγχόμενα is a gnomic present: "everything exposed" (NRSV, NIV, CSB, HCSB; cf. NET, NKJV, KJV). Some versions render the participle with a temporal marker: "*when* anything is exposed" (ESV, RSV, NASB).

> **Syntactical Nugget**: What is the relationship of the prepositional phrase "by the light" (ὑπὸ τοῦ φωτός) to the context? The preposition ὑπό following a passive verb expresses agency. The prepositional phrase could either modify the indicative φανεροῦται: "but all things that are exposed are made clear *by the light*" (cf. KJV, NKJV; cf. NLT) or the participle ἐλεγχόμενα: "but all things that are exposed *by the light* are made clear" (RSV, NRSV, ESV, NIV, NET, CSB, HCSB, NASB). Some commentators argue that the phrase best modifies the indicative since light is not associated with reproof in verse 11 and the phrase makes a good transition to verse 14 (Arnold, 333; Lincoln, 330–31; Larkin, 118). On the other hand, it is best to understand that it modifies the participle. Paul uses ὑπό with a genitive object three times throughout the letter. In each occurrence, the prepositional phrase modifies the preceding verb (Eph. 2:11; 5:12). In verse 8, Paul calls believers to live as "children of light," which entails reproof. In verse 13, he describes believers as this light that exposes these evil deeds. He will expand the referent in verse 14 to include Christ (Best, 496; Hoehner, 684; Thielman, 346–47; Merkle, 167).

φανεροῦται: The Greek word φανεροῦται is a third-person singular present passive indicative from the verb φανερόω that means "to reveal" or "expose publicly" (BDAG, s.v. "φανερόω" 1b, p. 1048). The verb could be understood as a middle voice verb and rendered with an active meaning: "the light shines on them" (NLT) or "everything made manifest" (ASV); however it is best understood as a passive voice verb: "become visible" (NASB, RSV, NRSV, NIV; Hoehner, 684; Larkin, 118). **Syntactically**, φανεροῦται functions as the verb of the independent conjunctive clause introduced by δέ. The subject of the verb is the participle phrase "all things that are exposed" (τὰ πάντα ἐλεγχόμενα). The lack of concord between the subject and the verb suggests that Paul sees these things as a collective (W, 399). **Semantically**, the present tense functions as a gnomic present, which describes a timeless fact (W, 523–24). In this context, all things that are exposed are revealed.

5:14a γάρ: The Greek word γάρ is a conjunction that means "for" or "therefore" (BDAG, s.v. "γάρ" 2, pp. 189–90). **Syntactically**, γάρ is in a postpositive position, introducing an independent conjunctive clause: "*for* all things that are made clear are light" (πᾶν γὰρ τὸ φανερούμενον φῶς ἐστιν). **Semantically**, γάρ provides an explanation of the previous section: "for" (CSB, HCSB, NRSV, ESV, NET, NLT, NASB, RSV). Because of the connection of the clause with the previous verse, some English versions include this clause with verse 13 (NIV, RSV, NASB, KJV, NKJV). This allows the quotation in verse 14 to conclude Paul's argument throughout this section.

φανερούμενον: The Greek word φανερούμενον is a neuter nominative singular present passive participle from the verb φανερόω that means "to reveal" or "expose publicly" (BDAG, s.v. "φανερόω" 1b, p. 1048). Paul uses the same verb in verse 13. The verb could be considered as a middle voice verb and rendered with an active verb: "the light makes everything visible" (NLT; Arnold, 333–34; Abbott, 1909, 156). However, it is best to understand the voice of the participle to be consistent with the same verb in the previous verse: "for anything that becomes visible is light" (ESV, RSV, NRSV, CSB, NASB). **Syntactically**, φανερούμενον is an attributive participle modifying "all things" (πᾶν). The participle phrase πᾶν τὸ φανερούμενον ("all things that are made clear") functions as the subject of the verb "is" (ἐστίν). **Semantically**, φανερούμενον is an iterative present, expressing a repeated idea: "everything that becomes visible." Paul seems to be discussing the deeds that are done at this point, not those who do them. The following quotation makes the move back to those who do these deeds clear (Thielman, 347–48).

ἐστίν: The Greek word ἐστίν is a third-person singular present active indicative from the verb εἰμί that means "to be" (BDAG, s.v. "εἰμί" 2b, p. 283). **Syntactically**, ἐστίν functions as the verb of the independent conjunctive clause introduced by γάρ. The subject is the participle phrase: "all things that are made clear" (πᾶν τὸ φανερούμενον). The predicate nominative is "light" (φῶς). **Semantically**, ἐστίν is an equative present: "is" (RSV, NRSV, ESV, CSB,

HCSB, NASB, NET). The deeds that are made known are light. The phrase seems
to refer to those who respond positively to the reproof that Paul describes in
verse 11b. We do not need to limit the scope to just either believers or unbelievers. The clause can refer to either group of people. Osborne states: "The
light shines in the lives of the unsaved as well as of the saved, transforming
the first into a Christian and the second into a victorious Christian. In both
cases the light of God exposes sin and transforms the person into a true child
of God—that is, into light" (Osborne, 173).

5:14b διό: The Greek word διό is a conjunction that means "therefore" or "for this
reason" (BDAG, s.v. "διό," p. 250). **Syntactically**, διό introduces an independent conjunctive clause: "*therefore* it says" (διὸ λέγει). **Semantically**, διό
draws an inference from verse 13: "therefore" (RSV, NRSV, ESV, CSB, HCSB,
NKJV). The NIV renders the conjunction as "this is why"; the NASB renders
it as "for this reason" (cf. NET). The clause: "therefore it says" introduces a
quotation that concludes this section.

λέγει: The Greek word λέγει is a third-person singular present active indicative from the verb λέγω that means "to say," "tell," or "give expression to"
(BDAG, s.v. "λέγω" 1bη, p. 589). **Syntactically**, λέγει functions as the main
verb of the independent conjunctive clause introduced by διό. The subject is
implied in the verb: "it says," referring to the following quotation. **Semantically**, the present tense functions as a perfective present, which emphasizes
the present results of a past action (W, 532–33). Paul uses the same formula
to introduce an Old Testament quotation in Ephesians 4:8 (cf. James 4:6),
which suggests that he views verse 14 as an authority; however, the source of
the quotation is not clear. Most commentators note that the quotation seems
to rely on texts from Isaiah (Isa. 9:2; 26:19; 60:1–2); however, the variety of
possible parallels suggest that Paul is not drawing from the Old Testament.
The parallelism of the lines reflects Hebrew poetry, suggesting that the citation is a hymn (cf. Eph. 5:19). It is possible that Paul is drawing from an
early Christian hymn influenced by these Old Testament themes (Thielman,
348–51; Hoehner, 686–87; Arnold, 334).

5:14c ἔγειρε: The Greek word ἔγειρε is a second-person singular present active
imperative from the verb ἐγείρω that means as a command "to get up" or
"come" (BDAG, s.v. "ἐγείρω" 13a, p. 272). **Syntactically**, ἔγειρε functions as the main verb of the asyndeton clause: "get up, sleeper" (ἔγειρε, ὁ
καθεύδων). The subject is implied in the verb: "you," referring to the "sleeper"
(ὁ καθεύδων). **Semantically**, ἔγειρε could be considered as an iterative present, describing someone waking up every morning; however, Paul has a single
event in mind—the resurrection. This raises the question: Why did he use the
present? He may use the present tense to convey a general precept. Or else he

simply follows his source but changes the referent. Merkle cautions us against pushing the meaning of the tense too far: the imperative form of ἐγείρω regularly appears in the present form (it occurs eighteen times in the present, only twice in the aorist), suggesting that this represents the "default or expected form" (Merkle, 168). Wallace classifies ἔγειρε and ἀνάστα as conditional imperatives contingent on the future verb ἐπιφαύσει. The imperatives function as the protasis; the future indicative functions as the apodosis: "*if* you wake up and arise from the dead, *then* Christ will shine on you" (W, 489–90).

> **Theological Nugget**: Is Paul calling unbelievers to faith? Or is he calling believers to wake up from a spiritual lethargy? On the one hand, Paul is addressing believers throughout the passage. If he has believers in mind, then this spiritual awakening does not represent an ontological change but the recognition of sin in their own lives and a realignment with their call (Eph. 4:1). Elsewhere New Testament writers use sleeping metaphors to refer to listless spirituality (Mark 14:37–38; Rom. 13:11; 1 Thess. 5:6). If this is the case, he uses the language of their conversion as a call for them to put away sin. He makes a similar argument in Romans 6: if the believer has died to sin (Rom. 6:2) we can walk in the newness of life (Rom. 6:4) (Arnold, 335; Best, 498–99; Hoehner, 687; Osborne, 174). On the other hand, the resurrection language (ἐγείρω, ἀνίστημι, νεκρός) suggests that he is referring to unbelievers and the point in which they come to faith. Earlier in the letter, he refers to unbelievers as dead (Eph. 2:1, 5). He says that believers have been raised together with Christ (Eph. 2:5–6). He describes believers as having lived in the dark at one point (Eph. 4:18; 5:8), but now are "children of light" (Eph. 5:8). Even though he addresses believers throughout the section, he shifts his attention to deeds done by the sons of disobedience. For this reason, Paul most likely has unbelievers in mind here (Lincoln, 318–19; Thielman, 350–51).

καθεύδων: The Greek word καθεύδων is a masculine nominative singular present active participle from the verb καθεύδω that means "to sleep" or metaphorically "to be spiritually indifferent" (BDAG, s.v. "καθεύδω" 2, p. 490). **Syntactically**, καθεύδων is a substantival participle. **Semantically**, καθεύδων is a customary present: "sleeper." The present tense describes an ongoing state, portraying an ongoing state of lethargic spirituality (W, 521–22). The participle is a nominative functioning as a vocative (W, 56–59; Turner[1], 34). Most English versions render the participle as "sleeper" (CSB, HCSB, NASB, NRSV, NIV) or "O sleeper" (RSV, ESV, NLT, NET). The NKJV renders the participle as an attributive participle: "you who sleep" (cf. KJV). The vocative is in apposition to the subject implied in the second-person singular imperatives (ἔγειρε and ἀνάστα): "you." Paul directs these commands to those who are spiritually asleep.

5:14d καί: The Greek word καί is a conjunction that means "and" (BDAG, s.v. "καί" 1bγ, p. 494). **Syntactically**, καί introduces an independent conjunctive clause: "*and* rise from the dead" (καὶ ἀνάστα ἐκ τῶν νεκρῶν). **Semantically**, καί is a coordinating connective: "and" (RSV, ESV, CSB, HCSB, NASB, KJV). Several versions omit the conjunction (NRSV, ESV, NET, NLT, NKJV). The conjunction gives an additional command to the one who is asleep: get up and rise.

ἀνάστα: The Greek word ἀνάστα is a second-person singular aorist active imperative from the verb ἀνίστημι that means "to rise up" or "come back from the dead" (BDAG, s.v. "ἀνίστημι" 7, p. 83). **Syntactically**, ἀνάστα functions as the main verb of the independent conjunctive clause introduced by καί. The verb is parallel to the previous imperative ἔγειρε. The subject is implied by the verb: "you," referring to the "sleeper" (ὁ καθεύδων). **Semantically**, ἀνάστα functions as an ingressive aorist (W, 558–59; 719–20). The aorist tense expresses some level of urgency. Just like ἔγειρε, ἀνάστα functions as a conditional imperative. The imperative functions as the condition (or the protasis), the future indicative (ἐπιφαύσει) in the following clause functions as the apodosis (W, 489–90). The phrase describes a physical resurrection, but the context suggests that Paul has a spiritual awakening in mind.

5:14e καί: The Greek word καί is a conjunction that means "and" (BDAG, s.v. "καί" 1bζ, p. 494). **Syntactically**, καί introduces an independent conjunctive clause: "*and* Christ will shine on you" (καὶ ἐπιφαύσει σοι ὁ Χριστός). **Semantically**, καί is a coordinating connective: "and" (ESV, NRSV, RSV, NIV, NET, CSB, HCSB, NASB, NKJV, KJV, NLT). Grammatically, the clause is parallel to the previous clauses introduced with the coordinating conjunction. However, since the first two imperatives are conditional imperatives, the conjunction introduces the future indicative, which functions as the apodosis. The NIRV translates the clause as "*Then* Christ will shine on you."

ἐπιφαύσει: The Greek word ἐπιφαύσει is a third-person singular future active indicative from the verb ἐπιφαύσκω that means "to shine"; or referring to the sun or moon "to arise" or "appear" (BDAG, s.v. "ἐπιφαύσκω," p. 386). **Syntactically**, ἐπιφαύσει functions as the verb of the independent conjunctive clause introduced by καί. The subject of the verb is "Christ" (ὁ Χριστός). The direct object is "you" (σοι), referring to "sleeper" (v. 14b). **Semantically**, the future tense functions as a predictive future (W, 568). The action expressed by the verb, namely Christ shining, depends on conditions expressed by the imperatives.

Text-Critical Nugget: What is the original reading in verse 14e? Some Western manuscripts (D and a few Latin manuscripts) replace the phrase ἐπιφαύσει σοι ὁ Χριστός with ἐπιψαύσεις τοῦ Χριστοῦ ("you will touch Christ"). On the other hand, the majority of Alexandrian manuscripts ($\mathfrak{P}^{46}$, ℵ, A, B, 1739), Byzantine manuscripts ($\mathfrak{M}$), and several Western manuscripts (F and G) read ἐπιφαύσει σοι ὁ Χριστός. Besides having superior external evidence, the reading "Christ will shine on you" (ἐπιφαύσει σοι ὁ Χριστός) makes good sense within the wider context. The idea of shining connects the quotation to the light/darkness theme that runs throughout the passage.

EPHESIANS 5:15–21

Big Greek Idea: Believers should walk in wisdom to understand the will of God, because the age is evil, and submit to the Holy Spirit with the result that they speak to one another with psalms, sing praise to God, give thanks always, and submit to one another.

Structural Overview: In the fifth section, Paul directs believers to walk in wisdom. He gives two reasons for this attitude. The first reason is that believers should live a life of wisdom because the days are evil (v. 16). The second reason is that they need to understand the will of God (v. 17).

As an example, Paul states that believers should avoid drinking wine in a way that leads to a reckless lifestyle. The command creates a foil for his positive statement: believers should be filled with the Spirit (v. 18). Paul lists five participles that describe the result of the Spirit impacting their lives: they speak to one another with psalms and hymns, they sing, they praise God, they give thanks always, and they submit to one another (vv. 19–21).

The next three sections (5:22–33; 6:1–4; and 6:5–9), known as the household code or rules for the household, are actually subsections that begin with this section. Paul omits the verb in verse 22, requiring the final participle "submitting" (ὑποτασσόμενοι) to be supplied, creating a link between the two sections. Each subsection addresses a specific relationship (husbands and wives, children and parents, slaves and masters) showing what mutual submission looks like.

Outline:

> Believers should walk in wisdom to understand God's will in the midst of this evil age (vv. 15–17)
>> Believers should walk in wisdom to redeem the time since the age is evil (vv. 15–16)
>> Believers should walk in wisdom to understand the will of God (v. 17)
> Believers should walk in wisdom by submitting to the will of the Holy Spirit (vv. 18–21)
>> Believers should avoid wine, but submit to the Holy Spirit (v. 18)
>> As a result of the Spirit's work, believers speak to one another with psalms, sing praises, give thanks, and submit to one another (vv. 19–21)

Clausal Outline for Ephesians 5:15–21

5:15a **Βλέπετε** <u>οὖν</u> ἀκριβῶς
5:15a <u>Therefore</u> **watch** carefully

    5:15b <u>πῶς</u> **περιπατεῖτε**,
    5:15b <u>how</u> **you walk**,

        5:15c μὴ <u>ὡς</u> ἄσοφοι
        5:15c not <u>as</u> the foolish,

        5:15d ἀλλ' <u>ὡς</u> σοφοί,
        5:15d but <u>as</u> the wise

        5:16a **ἐξαγοραζόμενοι** τὸν καιρόν,
        5:16a **by making the most of** the opportunity,

            5:16b **ὅτι** αἱ ἡμέραι πονηραί **εἰσιν**.
            5:16b **because** the days **are** evil.

5:17a <u>διὰ τοῦτο</u> μὴ **γίνεσθε** ἄφρονες,
5:17a <u>For this reason,</u> **do** not **become** foolish,

5:17b <u>ἀλλὰ</u> **συνίετε** (<u>τί</u> [<u>ἐστιν</u>] τὸ θέλημα τοῦ κυρίου).
5:17b <u>but</u> **understand** (<u>what</u> [<u>is</u>] the will of the Lord).

5:18a <u>καὶ</u> μὴ **μεθύσκεσθε** οἴνῳ,
5:18a <u>and</u> **do** not **get drunk** with wine,

        5:18b ἐν <u>ᾧ</u> **ἐστιν** ἀσωτία,
        5:18b in <u>which</u> **is** debauchery

5:18c <u>ἀλλὰ</u> **πληροῦσθε** ἐν πνεύματι,
5:18c <u>but</u> **be filled** by the Spirit,

      5:19a **λαλοῦντες** ἑαυτοῖς ἐν ψαλμοῖς καὶ ὕμνοις καὶ ᾠδαῖς
        πνευματικαῖς,
      5:19a **with the result of speaking** to one another with psalms, hymns,
        and spiritual songs,

      5:19b **ᾄδοντες**
      5:19b **with the result of singing**

5:19c καὶ **ψάλλοντες** τῇ καρδίᾳ ὑμῶν τῷ κυρίῳ,
5:19c and **with the result of making music** with your heart to the Lord,

5:20 **εὐχαριστοῦντες** πάντοτε ὑπὲρ πάντων ἐν ὀνόματι τοῦ κυρίου ἡμῶν Ἰησοῦ Χριστοῦ τῷ θεῷ καὶ πατρί,
5:20 **with the result of giving thanks** always for all things in the name of our Lord Jesus Christ to God and Father,

5:21 **ὑποτασσόμενοι** ἀλλήλοις ἐν φόβῳ Χριστοῦ.
5:21 **with the result of submitting** to one another in the fear of Christ.

SYNTAX EXPLAINED FOR EPHESIANS 5:15–21

5:15a βλέπετε: The Greek word βλέπετε is a second-person plural present active imperative from the verb βλέπω that means "to consider" or "notice" (BDAG, s.v. "βλέπω" 6c, p. 179). **Syntactically**, βλέπετε functions as the verb of the independent conjunctive clause introduced by οὖν. The subject is implied by the verb: "you all," referring to the Ephesian believers. The quotation in verse 14 used singular verbs; in verse 15 Paul reverts back to the plural. **Semantically**, βλέπετε is a customary present: "watch." The present tense describes an ongoing state (W, 521–22, 722). Paul expects that the believer should habitually watch their behavior: "be careful" (NRSV, NLT, NASB; cf. NIV, NET) or "look carefully" (RSV, ESV). The CSB renders it as "pay careful attention." Paul easily could have used the imperatival form of περιπατέω (cf. Eph. 5:2), but by inserting βλέπετε he emphasizes the importance of the believer's behavior.

οὖν: The Greek word οὖν is a conjunction that means "therefore" or "consequently" (BDAG, s.v. "οὖν" 1b, p. 736). **Syntactically**, οὖν introduces a conjunctive independent clause: "*Therefore* watch carefully" (Βλέπετε οὖν ἀκριβῶς). **Semantically**, οὖν should be considered resumptive. Hoehner argues that the conjunction marks a new hortatory section and refers to Ephesians 4:1. Paul concludes the previous section with a quotation introduced with the conjunction διό. The fact that he drops the light/darkness theme gives another signal that the argument has shifted (Hoehner, 690–91). Other commentators agree, but note that Paul's preceding discussion about the believer's response to evil within the community of faith leads to his solemn warning to watch one's behavior (Arnold, 345; Best, 502; Lincoln, 341; Merkle, 171). Most English versions translate the conjunction as "then" (CSB, HCSB, RSV, NRSV, ESV, NIV, NKJV, KJV), creating a closer link with the previous section. The NASB and NET render the conjunction as "therefore."

Text-Critical Nugget: What does the adverb ἀκριβῶς modify? A number of Western (D, F, G) and Byzantine (𝔐, K, L) manuscripts read οὖν πῶς ἀκριβῶς. This reading suggests that the adverb ἀκριβῶς modifies the indicative περιπατεῖτε: "See that you walk carefully" (cf. KJV, NKJV). On the other hand, the textual reading (οὖν ἀκριβῶς πῶς) is found in a number of good Alexandrian manuscripts (𝔓46, ℵ, B, 33, 81, 104, 1175, 1739). In this case, the adverb ἀκριβῶς modifies the imperative Βλέπετε: "Look carefully" (ESV; cf. RSV, NRSV, NIV, CSB, HCSB, NASB). Hoehner opts for the Western/Byzantine reading due to the geographical distribution of the manuscripts (Hoehner, 690 n. 1). However, the Alexandrian reading is found in a better set of manuscripts (Lincoln, 337). Metzger notes that the adverb πῶς may have been accidentally omitted and subsequently added in the wrong location (Metzger, 540).

5:15b πῶς: The Greek word πῶς is a conjunction that means "how" (BDAG, s.v. "πῶς" 1bα, p. 901). **Syntactically**, πῶς introduces a dependent conjunctive clause: "how you walk" (πῶς περιπατεῖτε). The conjunction introduces an indirect question (Larkin, 122). **Semantically**, πῶς can have the same semantic thrust as ὅτι: "that" (KJV), but here it is best rendered as "how" (ESV, RSV, NRSV, NIV, NET, CSB, HCSB, NASB) describing how one should walk: "how you walk" (cf. Hoehner, 691).

περιπατεῖτε: The Greek word περιπατεῖτε is a second-person plural present active indicative from the verb περιπατέω that means "to live" or "behave" (BDAG, s.v. "περιπατέω" 2aγ, p. 803). Many English versions render the verb metaphorically: "you live" (NRSV, NIV, NET, CSB, NLT), while others render it literally: "you walk" (RSV, ESV, HCSB, NASB, KJV, NKJV). **Syntactically**, περιπατεῖτε functions as the main verb of the dependent conjunctive clause introduced by πῶς ("how"). The subject is implied by the verb: "you all," referring to the Ephesian believers. **Semantically**, περιπατεῖτε is a customary present: "walk." The present tense describes an ongoing state (W, 521–22). The believer should make it a habit to conduct their lives in wisdom.

5:15c ὡς: The Greek word ὡς is a conjunction that means "as" in this context (BDAG, s.v. "ὡς" 1bα, pp. 1103–4). **Syntactically**, ὡς introduces a dependent conjunctive clause. The entire clause "not as the foolish" (μὴ ὡς ἄσοφοι), functions adverbially modifying the verb "walk" (περιπατεῖτε). **Semantically**, ὡς expresses a comparison: "as" (ESV, RSV, NRSV, NIV, NET, CSB, HCSB, NASB, NKJV, KJV). The negative statement describes what the believer should avoid. The following positive statement creates a contrast.

5:15d ἀλλ᾽ ὡς: The Greek word ἀλλά is a conjunction that means "but" in this context (BDAG, s.v. "ἀλλά" 1a, pp. 44–45). The Greek word ὡς is a conjunction that means "as" in this context (BDAG, s.v. "ὡς" 1bα, pp. 1103–4). **Syntactically**, ὡς introduces a dependent conjunctive clause. The entire clause, "but as the wise" (ἀλλ᾽ ὡς σοφοί), functions adverbially modifying the verb "walk" (περιπατεῖτε). **Semantically**, ἀλλά expresses a contrast with the negative comparative statement in verse 15c. Believers are not to walk as the foolish, "*but as* the wise" (ESV, RSV, NRSV, NIV, NET, CSB, HCSB, NASB, NKJV, KJV).

5:16a   ἐξαγοραζόμενοι: The Greek word ἐξαγοραζόμενοι is a masculine nominative plural present middle participle from the verb ἐξαγοράζω that means "to make the most of" (BDAG, s.v. "ἐξαγοράζω" 2, p. 343). The term literally refers to buying something: "to pay a price" (L&N, 37.131). Idiomatically, it means to "work urgently, to redeem the time" (L&N, 68.73). The KJV renders the verb more literally: "redeeming" (cf. NKJV), while most English versions offer a more equivalent translation: "making the most" (RSV, NRSV, NIV, CSB, HCSB, NASB, NLT). The NET translates the participle as "taking advantage of." **Syntactically**, ἐξαγοραζόμενοι introduces a participle dependent clause. It functions adverbially modifying "walk" (περιπατεῖτε, v. 15b). The direct object of the participle is "the time" (τὸν καιρόν). The term can have a broader meaning: "the right time" or "opportunity" (BDAG, s.v. "καιρός" 1b, pp. 497–98; cf. NIV, NET). **Semantically**, ἐξαγοραζόμενοι functions as a participle of manner (Hoehner, 692; Arnold, 346) or means (Merkle, 172; Larkin, 122–23): "*by* redeeming the time." The participle describes how the wise walk—by taking advantage of every opportunity. The voice of the verb is middle and should be treated reflexively: "for yourself" (W, 421), which most English versions omit. Taking advantage of opportunities characterize the behavior of the wise.

5:16b   ὅτι: The Greek word ὅτι is a conjunction that means "because" in this context (BDAG, s.v. "ὅτι" 4a, p. 732). **Syntactically**, ὅτι introduces a dependent conjunctive clause: "*because* the days are evil" (ὅτι αἱ ἡμέραι πονηραί εἰσιν). The clause functions adverbially modifying the participle "redeeming the time" (ἐξαγοραζόμενοι). **Semantically**, ὅτι marks the reason for the action of the participle: "because" (ESV, RSV, NRSV, NIV, NET, CSB, HCSB, NASB, NKJV, KJV). Believers should redeem the time because the days are evil.

εἰσίν: The Greek word εἰσίν is a third-person plural present active indicative from the verb εἰμί that means "to be" (BDAG, s.v. "εἰμί" 2b, p. 283). **Syntactically**, εἰσίν functions as the main verb of the dependent conjunctive clause introduced by ὅτι. The subject is "days" (αἱ ἡμέραι). The predicate nominative is "evil" (πονηραί). **Semantically**, εἰσίν is an equative present: "are" (ESV, RSV, NRSV, NIV, NET, CSB, HCSB, NASB, KJV, NKJV). Later, Paul tells believers to prepare themselves for the "evil day," when they will come under attack from Satan (Eph. 6:13; cf. Gal. 1:4). Throughout the letter, Paul describes believers as victorious through their relationship with Christ (Eph. 2:4–6); nonetheless, we live in a world under Satan's control (Eph. 2:2). Even though there is victory, believers must remain vigilant.

5:17a διὰ τοῦτο: The Greek word τοῦτο is a neuter singular accusative from the demonstrative pronoun οὗτος. The pronoun with the preposition διά functions as a conjunction (Runge 2010, 48; BDAG, s.v. "διά" B2a, p. 225). **Syntactically**, the phrase introduces the independent conjunctive clause: "*Therefore*, do not be foolish" (διὰ τοῦτο μὴ γίνεσθε ἄφρονες). **Semantically**, the phrase possibly creates a causal link with the preceding phrase: "*For this reason* do not become foolish" (NET; Runge 2010, 50; Larkin, 123; Thielman, 357).

γίνεσθε: The Greek word γίνεσθε is a second-person plural present middle (deponent) imperative from the verb γίνομαι that means "to be made" or "created" (BDAG, s.v. "γίνομαι" 2a, p. 197). **Syntactically**, γίνεσθε is the main verb of the independent conjunctive clause introduced by διὰ τοῦτο. The subject is implied by the verb "you all," referring to the Ephesian believers. The predicate nominative is "foolish" (ἄφρονες). **Semantically**, γίνεσθε is best understood as an ingressive present. Paul encourages believers to walk as the wise (v. 15) and likewise do not *begin* to become foolish. Most English versions render the phrase as "do not *be* foolish" (ESV, RSV, NRSV, NIV, NET, CSB, HCSB, NASB), but the verb carries the notion of entering into a state: "become" (Hoehner, 696; W, 717, 721–22). In Proverbs, the fool is often contrasted with the one who walks in the ways of the Lord (Prov. 10:23; 23:9; 24:7; Arnold, 347). Paul seems to make a similar contrast with the fool by encouraging the believer to come to understand the will of God—and presumably to do it.

5:17b ἀλλά: The Greek word ἀλλά is a conjunction that means "but" in this context (BDAG, s.v. "ἀλλά" 1a, pp. 44–45). **Syntactically**, ἀλλά introduces an independent conjunctive clause: "*but* understand what is the will of God" (ἀλλὰ συνίετε τί τὸ θέλημα τοῦ κυρίου). **Semantically**, ἀλλά is a contrastive conjunction: "but" (ESV, RSV, NRSV, NIV, NET, CSB, HCSB, NASB, NKJV, KJV). The conjunction establishes a similar contrast that Paul makes in verse 15 between the foolish and the wise. He uses synonyms for "foolishness" (ἄσοφος in v. 15; ἄφρων in v. 17). Because of the parallelism, we might anticipate a command for believers to become wise (cf. v. 15d), but he tells the believers to "understand the will of the Lord." The shift in parallelism implies that a key facet of wisdom is understanding God's will and responding appropriately.

συνίετε: The Greek word συνίετε is a second-person plural present active imperative from the verb συνίημι that means "to understand" or "comprehend" (BDAG, s.v. "συνίημι," p. 972). Earlier in the letter, Paul uses the nominal form of the word (σύνεσις), referring to the divine revelation concerning the mystery of Christ as an insight (Eph. 3:4; cf. Col. 2:2; Conzelmann, 1971, 896). **Syntactically**, συνίετε functions as the verb of the independent conjunctive clause introduced by the conjunction ἀλλά. The subject is implied by the verb: "you all," referring to the Ephesian believers. **Semantically**, συνίετε is a customary present: "understand" (ESV, RSV, NRSV, NIV, CSB, HCSB, NASB, NKJV, NLT). The present tense describes the action of the verb to be ongoing. Paul wants believers to continually seek out God's will for their lives (W, 521–22, 722). His word choice points beyond a factual knowledge and toward a deeper understanding with consequences (Hoehner, 698; Arnold, 347–48).

τί: The Greek word τί is an indefinite pronoun from the word τί that means "what" or "what sort of" (BDAG, s.v. "τίς" 1aβ‫ב‬, p. 1007; W, 345–46). **Syntactically**, τί is a dependent conjunctive clause functioning as the direct object of the verb "understand" (συνίετε). The clause provides the content that Paul wants the believers to understand.

[ἐστίν]: The Greek word ἐστίν is third-person singular present active indicative from the verb εἰμί that means "is" (BDAG, s.v. "εἰμί" 1, pp. 282–83). **Syntactically**, the ellipsis [ἐστίν] is the main verb of the substantival clause introduced by τί. The subject of the verb is the indefinite pronoun τί. The predicate nominative is "will" (τὸ θέλημα). The genitive τοῦ κυρίου is subjective: "what the Lord wills" (BDAG, s.v. "θέλημα" 1cγ, p. 447). **Semantically**, [ἐστίν] is an equative present tense: "what the will of the Lord *is*" (ESV, RSV, NRSV, NIV, NET, CSB, HCSB, NASB, KJV, NKJV). The NLT omits the equative verb rendering the phrase as: "what the Lord wants you to do." In verse 10, Paul gives a similar exhortation for believers: as children of light, they should test "what is pleasing to the Lord."

5:18a καί: The Greek word καί is a conjunction that means "and" (BDAG, s.v. "καί" 1b, p. 494). **Syntactically**, καί introduces an independent conjunctive clause: "*and* do not get drunk with wine" (καὶ μὴ μεθύσκεσθε οἴνῳ). **Semantically**, καί is a connective conjunction: "and" (ESV, RSV, NET, CSB, HCSB, NASB, KJV, NKJV). Several translations omit the conjunction (NIV, NRSV, NLT). It introduces a third contrast between the wise and foolish (cf. vv. 15, 17). Unlike the first two statements, the third contrast gives a concrete example of the fool and wise: a contrast between a life led by reckless abandonment and one characterized by control by the Spirit (Hoehner, 699).

μεθύσκεσθε: The Greek word μεθύσκεσθε is a second-person plural present passive imperative from the verb μεθύσκω that means "cause to become intoxicated" or "get drunk" (BDAG, s.v. "μεθύσκω," p. 625). **Syntactically**, μεθύσκεσθε functions as the main verb of the independent conjunctive clause introduced by καί. The subject is implied by the verb: "you all," referring to the Ephesian believers. The dative οἴνῳ functions as a dative of means: "*with wine*." **Semantically**, μεθύσκεσθε is a customary present: "get drunk" (ESV, RSV, NRSV, NIV, NET, CSB, HCSB, NASB). The present tense describes an ongoing state. The imperative is a general precept. There is no indication in the letter that alcoholism is a problem in the church. But Paul encourages them not to make this lifestyle habitual (W, 521–22, 722). A similar command is found in the Proverbs (Prov. 23:31), but the command seems out of step with the thrust of Paul's argument. He might have added the command to establish a contrast with the following command: to be filled with the Spirit (for examples of the impact of drunkenness within first-century religious circles, see Arnold, 348–49).

5:18b ᾧ: The Greek word ᾧ is a masculine singular dative from the relative pronoun ὅς that means "whom" (BDAG, s.v. "ὅς" 1, pp. 725–26). **Syntactically**, ᾧ functions as the object of the preposition ἐν. The relative pronoun introduces a dependent adjectival relative clause: "in *which* is debauchery" (ἐν ᾧ ἐστιν ἀσωτία) (cf. KJV). The antecedent of the pronoun is not just "wine" (οἴνῳ), but the entire command (Larkin, 124; Hoehner, 700).

ἐστίν: The Greek word ἐστίν is a third-person singular present active indicative from the verb εἰμί that means "to be" (BDAG, s.v. "εἰμί" 3b, p. 284). **Syntactically**, ἐστίν functions as the main verb of the relative clause. The subject is "debauchery" (ἀσωτία). **Semantically**, ἐστίν is an equative present tense: "is" (ESV, RSV, NRSV, NET, NASB, NKJV, KJV). Several translations exchange the equative verb with a verb of motion: "which *leads* to debauchery" (NIV; cf. CSB, HCSB). The NLT renders the phrase: "will ruin your life." The Greek word ἀσωτία refers to wastefulness. It carries the notion of wild living or "reckless abandonment" (BDAG, s.v. "ἀσωτία," p. 148). Louw and Nida define the word as "behavior which shows lack of concern or thought for the consequences of an action" (L&N, 88.96). Luke uses a similar term to describe the life of the prodigal son: ζῶν ἀσώτως ("wasteful living") (Luke 15:13). Eventually, habitual intoxication will bring one to ruin.

5:18c ἀλλά: The Greek word ἀλλά is a conjunction that means "but" (BDAG, s.v. "ἀλλά" 1a, pp. 45–44). **Syntactically**, ἀλλά introduces an independent conjunctive clause: "*but* be filled with the Spirit" (ἀλλὰ πληροῦσθε ἐν πνεύματι). **Semantically**, ἀλλά is a contrastive conjunction: "but" (ESV, RSV, NRSV, NET, CSB, HCSB, NASB, NKJV, KJV). The NIV and NLT begin a new sentence with the clause and mark the contrast with "instead."

πληροῦσθε: The Greek word πληροῦσθε is a second-person plural present passive imperative from the verb πληρόω that means "to fill" (BDAG, s.v. "πληρόω" 1b, p. 828). Paul's word choice suggests that the believer is marked by what fills them, in this case, the Spirit (Delling, 1968, 291) **Syntactically**, πληροῦσθε functions as the main verb of the independent conjunctive clause introduced by ἀλλά. The subject is implied by the verb: "you all," referring to the Ephesian believers. **Semantically**, πληροῦσθε is a customary present: "be filled" (ESV, RSV, NRSV, NIV, NET, CSB, HCSB, NASB, NKJV, KJV, NLT). The present tense describes an ongoing state (W, 521–22; Hoehner, 704). The passive voice indicates that believers cannot fill themselves, but the imperative suggests that the believer is responsible to be filled. At the point of their salvation, the believer is sealed by the Holy Spirit (Eph. 1:13). In Romans, Paul states that unless you are indwelt by the Holy Spirit, you are not a believer (Rom. 8:9). However, the present imperative suggests that this is distinct from the reception of the Spirit at the point of salvation. Hoehner states: "this is not an automatic bestowment at the time of salvation but an injunction for every believer to follow continually. The filling by the Spirit is more than the Spirit's indwelling—it is his activities realized in and through us" (Hoehner, 705).

> **Semantical Nugget**: What does it mean to be filled "with the Spirit" (ἐν πνεύματι)? The prepositional phrase has been hotly debated. First, the preposition could express content: "*with* the Spirit" (ESV, RSV, NRSV, NIV, NASB, KJV, NKJV, NLT). This interpretation makes good sense of the temple imagery that Paul developed in Ephesians 2:22. Just as the presence of God filled the temple, Paul describes the church as a temple filled with God's Spirit. The contrasting prohibition against getting drunk with wine suggests that Paul has content in mind as well (Arnold, 349–51). Lincoln notes that if the believer is filled *by* the Spirit, they are filled *with* the Spirit (Lincoln, 344). On the other hand, it is probably best to understand the preposition as means: "*by* the Spirit" (NET, CSB, HCSB). Generally, the genitive follows πληρόω to express content (cf. Acts 2:28; 13:52; Rom. 15:13), not ἐν with the dative. In the parallel statement, Paul's injunction to not get drunk is modified with a dative of means: "*with* wine" (οἴνῳ). It would make sense that he is making a similar statement here. Understanding the preposition as means makes sense of the scope of Paul's letter. In Ephesians 3:19 he specifies that the believer will be filled with "the fullness of God;" in Ephesians 4:10 he specifies who will fill them: Christ. Finally, in Ephesians 5:18, we receive the means. Wallace states: "Believers are to be filled *by* Christ *by means of* the Spirit *with* the content of the fullness of God" (W, 375; cf. Hoehner, 703–4).

5:19a λαλοῦντες: The Greek word λαλοῦντες is a masculine nominative plural present active participle from the verb λαλέω that means "to talk" or "speak" (BDAG, s.v. "λαλέω" 2aδ, p. 582). Because the context describes music, the NRSV renders the verb: "as you sing" (cf. NLT). Most English versions render the verb as either "speaking" (NIV, NET, CSB, HCSB, NASB, KJV, NKJV) or "addressing" (ESV, RSV). **Syntactically**, λαλοῦντες introduces a participle dependent clause. It functions adverbially modifying the main verb: "be filled" (πληροῦσθε). The indirect object is the reciprocal pronoun "to one another" (ἑαυτοῖς) (W, 351). **Semantically**, λαλοῦντες could function as means describing how the believer is filled: "*by* speaking to one another (Arnold, 351–52). However, it is best understood as the result of the believer being filled: "*with the result of* speaking to one another" (W, 639; Hoehner, 706; Lincoln, 345; Arnold, 361). The preposition ἐν expresses means: "*with* psalms, hymns, and spiritual songs" (NIV). The LXX uses all three terms (ψαλμός, ὕμνος, and ᾠδή) to refer to religious songs. Paul most likely uses the terms synonymously rather than distinguishing between different types of songs (Thielman, 361). He uses the verbal forms of ψαλμός (ψάλλω) and ᾠδή (ᾄδω) in the following clauses. Earlier in the letter, Paul instructs believers to engage one another with truth; here having been filled with the Spirit, they are to engage one another with an attitude of praise and thanksgiving.

> **Text-Critical Nugget**: Is the preposition ἐν found in verse 19a? A number of significant Alexandrian (ℵ, A, 81, 104, 1175, 1881), Western (D, F, G), and Byzantine (𝔐, K, L) manuscripts omit the preposition ἐν. Besides the NA[28], none of the modern Greek texts include the preposition (THGNT; SBL; RP[2005]; MT). However, a handful of key Alexandrian manuscripts (𝔓[46], B, 33, 1739) include it. The prepositional phrase in the previous clause may have influenced a scribe to insert the preposition here. Regardless, the external evidence strongly suggests that the reading with the preposition is secondary. The dative alone can still express means, so the meaning does not change.

> **Text-Critical Nugget**: Does Paul call believers to sing "spiritual songs"? Some manuscripts omit the adjective πνευματικαῖς, so Paul only refers to "songs" (𝔓[46] and B). These are significant manuscripts, but the majority of Alexandrian (ℵ, 33, 81, 104, 1175, 1739, 1881), Western (D, F, G), and Byzantine (𝔐, K, L) manuscripts include the adjective: "spiritual songs." It is possible that a scribe added the adjective based on Colossians 3:16, but the weight of the external evidence suggests that the adjective is more original. Metzger suggests that it was accidentally omitted based on homoeoteleuton (Metzger, 540–41).

5:19b ᾄδοντες: The Greek word ᾄδοντες is a masculine nominative plural present active participle from the verb ᾄδω that means "to sing" (BDAG, s.v. "ᾄδω," p. 22). **Syntactically**, ᾄδοντες introduces a participle dependent clause. It functions adverbially modifying the main verb: "be filled" (πληροῦσθε). **Semantically**, just like λαλοῦντες, ᾄδοντες expresses the result of being filled by the Spirit (W, 639).

καί: The Greek word καί is a conjunction that means "and" (BDAG, s.v. "καί" 1bδ, p. 494). **Syntactically**, καί introduces a dependent conjunctive clause: "*and* singing praises in your heart to the Lord" (καὶ ψάλλοντες τῇ καρδίᾳ ὑμῶν τῷ κυρίῳ). **Semantically**, καί is a coordinating connective: "and" (ESV, RSV, NRSV, NIV, NET, CSB, HCSB, NASB, NKJV, KJV). The conjunction joins the previous participle (ᾄδοντες) with the following participle (ψάλλοντες). The two participles—"singing and psalming"—create a single thought and the second result of being filled (Hoehner, 711; Merkle, 175).

5:19c ψάλλοντες: The Greek word ψάλλοντες is a masculine nominative plural present active participle from the verb ψάλλω that means "to sing" or "to sing praise" (BDAG, s.v. "ψάλλω," p. 1096). Several English versions render the participle as "making melody" (ESV, RSV, NRSV, NASB, NKJV, KJV) or "making music" (CSB, HCSB, NIV, NET, NLT). **Syntactically**, ψάλλοντες is a participle dependent clause introduced by καί. It functions adverbially modifying the main verb: "be filled" (πληροῦσθε). The indirect object is "the Lord" (τῷ κυρίῳ), referring to Jesus Christ. The dative τῇ καρδίᾳ ("heart," referring to one's inner life; BDAG, s.v. "καρδία" 1bα, p. 508) expresses means. Since καί joins the two participles (ᾄδοντες and ψάλλοντες), the datives modify both participles. **Semantically**, just like λαλοῦντες and ᾄδοντες, ψάλλοντες expresses the result of being filled by the Spirit (W, 639). This attitude of praise is directed to others within the community (v. 19a), but also to the Lord himself (v. 19b).

> **Semantical Nugget**: What does it mean to sing psalms "in your heart" (τῇ καρδίᾳ)? The dative τῇ καρδίᾳ could be interpreted a number of ways. First, it could express sphere: "*in* your heart" (NRSV, NET, NLT, KJV, NKJV). This interpretation conveys the idea that believers sing privately; however, this is an outward expression of praise (Best, 513). Second, Delling argues that the preposition ἐν was original and corresponds to the Hebrew בְּ, meaning "engagement of the heart," or "*from* the heart" (Delling, 1972, 498 n. 66; HCSB, NIV). However, the preposition ἀπό would have best expressed this idea (Hoehner, 713). Third, it is best to understand the dative as means: "*with* your heart" (ESV, RSV, CSB, NASB). The idea is that believers sing with sincerity (Stott, 1979, 206). The dative τῷ κυρίῳ expresses direction: "*to* the Lord." The first clause ("speaking to one another") has a horizontal dimension describing how believers should address one another; the second clause ("singing and making music") has a vertical focus between the believer and the Lord (Lincoln, 346).

5:20 εὐχαριστοῦντες: The Greek word εὐχαριστοῦντες is a masculine nominative plural present active participle from the verb εὐχαριστέω that means "to give thanks" or "express thanks" (BDAG, s.v. "εὐχαριστέω" 2, p. 415).

Syntactically, εὐχαριστοῦντες introduces a participle dependent clause. It functions adverbially, modifying the main verb: "be filled" (πληροῦσθε). The indirect objects are "God and Father" (τῷ θεῷ καὶ πατρί). The phrase is an example of the Granville Sharp rule—when two nouns are governed by a single article and joined by καί, both nouns can refer to the identical person or show some type of unified purpose. Here Paul is referring to the same person—God the Father (W, 270–74). **Semantically**, just like the previous participles that modify πληροῦσθε (λαλοῦντες, ᾄδοντες, and ψάλλοντες), εὐχαριστοῦντες expresses the result of being filled by the Spirit (W, 639): "*with the result of* giving thanks." Most English versions simply render the participle as "giving thanks" (ESV, RSV, NRSV, NIV, NET, CSB, HCSB, NASB, KJV, NKJV). The participle picks up a theme that Paul begins in Ephesians 5:4. Thanksgiving should characterize the Christian community. Paul himself gives thanks to God on behalf of the Ephesian believers (Eph. 1:15–16; cf. Eph. 1:16; Phil. 1:4; Col. 1:3; 1 Thess. 1:2; 2 Thess. 1:3, 11; 2:13; Philem. 4).

Theological Nugget: What does Paul mean when he says "giving thanks" (εὐχαριστοῦντες)? Some have suggested that Paul describes prayer within a corporate setting. The previous verse describing Christian worship might refer to a corporate setting. Thanksgiving was an important part of the Christian worship service (cf. 1 Cor. 11:24; 14:16–17) (Thielman, 362; Best, 513). On the other hand, the corporate notion is not clear within the context. He states that this thanksgiving should be "always" (πάντοτε). This suggests that Paul has a wider context in mind than just a corporate setting (Arnold, 355; Hoehner, 714). Rather than a corporate prayer, Paul most likely has a prayer of thanksgiving in mind.

Paul adds a number of elements to this thanksgiving. First, he states that believers should give thanks "always for all things" (πάντοτε ὑπὲρ πάντων). The adjective πάντων could be masculine, referring to all people (NET: "each other"), but the context does not clearly point to a specific group. It is best to understand the adjective as neuter: "for everything" (ESV, RSV, NRSV, NIV, CSB, HCSB, NASB, KJV, NKJV; Best, 513), referring to all of life's circumstances. Hoehner states: "Thus, thanksgiving to God should encompass all things that come into life's path, and when believers are filled by the Spirit this will be their response in lieu of dissatisfaction and complaints. In difficult circumstances, an attitude of thanksgiving is easier to achieve with the knowledge that God is always in control" (Hoehner, 714). Second, believers should give thanks to God "in the name of our Lord Jesus Christ" (ἐν ὀνόματι τοῦ κυρίου ἡμῶν Ἰησοῦ Χριστοῦ). The name of Christ is the authority by which believers can approach the Father through prayer. In the New Testament, the formula is normally associated with exorcism (Luke 10:17; Acts 3:6; 4:10; 16:18) or preaching

(Acts 9:27–28) (Larkin, 127). In John's Gospel, Jesus instructs the disciples to pray to the Father in his name (John 14:13, 14; 15:16; 16:23, 26) (Hoehner, 715). Within the context of Ephesians, Paul describes Jesus as one who has ascended above all other names (Eph. 1:20–22; cf. Phil. 2:9–10). It is by this authority that believers give thanks. Finally, this thanksgiving is directed toward God.

5:21 ὑποτασσόμενοι: The Greek word ὑποτασσόμενοι is a masculine nominative plural present middle participle from the verb ὑποτάσσω that means "to subject oneself" or "be subordinated" (BDAG, s.v. "ὑποτάσσω" 1bβ, p. 1042). The word could be construed as a passive voice: "be subject" (RSV, NASB, NRSV), but the middle voice is better: "submit" (NIV, ESV) or "submit yourself" (KJV). The difference is slight, but the passive voice suggests that the subject has no control, while the middle voice connotes some type of cooperation (Hoehner, 717). **Syntactically**, ὑποτασσόμενοι introduces a participle dependent clause. It functions adverbially modifying the main verb: "be filled" (πληροῦσθε). The indirect object is "one another" (ἀλλήλοις). **Semantically**, just like the previous participles that modify πληροῦσθε (λαλοῦντες, ἄδοντες, ψάλλοντες, and εὐχαριστοῦντες) ὑποτασσόμενοι expresses the result of being filled by the Spirit (W, 639): "*with the result of* submitting." The prepositional phrase conveys the reason believers should submit to one another: because they fear the Lord (Larkin, 130; Merkle, 178; Hoehner, 719). The term φόβος ("fear"; BDAG, s.v. "φόβος" 2bα, p. 1062) can describe a terror; however, since Paul is describing a believer, who is "in Christ," it is best to understand the term as referring to reverential awe: "out of reverence for Christ" (ESV, RSV, NRSV, NIV, NET, NLT).

Syntactical Nugget: How does verse 21 connect to the context? Even though the participle modifies πληροῦσθε ("be filled," v. 18), the NA[28] begins a new paragraph with verse 21. Verse 22 begins a new subject—the relationship between husbands and wives, but since the clause in verse 22 is missing a verb we have to supply some form of ὑποτάσσω. Because of this, it is best to understand the verse as a hinge. It concludes the current section (Eph. 5:15–21): the believer should walk in wisdom by pursuing God's will, leading to submission to one another. But it also establishes the baseline for what follows. As Paul discusses the relationship between husbands and wives, children and parents, and slaves and masters, he presents mutual submission as a guiding principle.

Lexical Nugget: What does it mean to "submit"? Today in English the term "submission" can be controversial, particularly as it applies to women—an issue that Paul touches on in the next section (Eph. 5:22–24). Some have argued that the verb does not refer to mutual submission, but to submission to an authority. The verb normally describes the relationship between an inferior and superior (cf. 1 Cor. 15:27; Eph. 1:22). Furthermore, the following sections seem to describe these types of relationships: wives submitting to husbands, children to parents, and slaves to masters (Hoehner, 732–34). The significant problem with this position is the presence of the reciprocal pronoun: ἀλλήλοις ("to one another" or "mutually"; BDAG, s.v. "ἀλλήλων," p. 46). If we interpret the participle to refer to specific relationships, then this limits the scope of the pronoun. The relationship of the participle to the main verb presents another problem. The command to be filled with the Spirit applies to all believers, suggesting that Paul has the submission of all believers in mind. Finally, it is important to note that when Paul shifts the discussion from husbands and wives to parents and children, he uses a different verb. He directs wives to submit (ὑποτάσσω) to their husbands, but children and slaves to obey (ὑπακούω) the head of the household (cf. Eph. 6:1, 5) (Arnold, 356–57; Lincoln, 365–66; Thielman, 372–74). Elsewhere Paul encourages believers to become mutually submissive (Rom. 12:10; Gal. 5:13; 6:2; Eph. 4:2; Phil. 2:2; 1 Thess. 5:13). Paul gives the same instructions here. Even though all people relate to one another through certain social structures, believers should engage these relationships by continually putting the needs of others ahead of their own.

Ephesians 5:22–33

Big Greek Idea: Wives should voluntarily submit to their husbands as they would to the Lord because he is the head; husbands should love their wives self-sacrificially as they would care for their own bodies, just as Christ loved the church.

Structural Overview: Ephesians 5:22–33 is a part of a larger section that Paul began in Ephesians 5:15. Verse 21 serves as a hinge between the two passages. Grammatically, the participle "submit" (Ὑποτασσόμενοι) modifies the main verb in verse 18 describing the final result of being filled by the Spirit. But since there is no verb in verse 22, the participle should be supplied. The marriage relationship that Paul describes in verses 22–33 provides a glimpse of what mutual submission looks like. Throughout the passage, Paul uses the comparative conjunction ὡς or καθώς to compare the marriage relationship to Christ's relationship with the church. On the surface, Paul is addressing husbands and wives, but he has just as much to say about Christ and the church.

First, Paul addresses wives. He does not explicitly command wives to submit to their husbands. The verb is omitted in both verses 22a and 24b. The imperative is undoubtedly implied since he uses it in verse 24a in a comparative statement describing how the church submits to Christ. He gives the reason for this submission in verse 23: wives should submit because their husbands are in authority, just as Christ has been given authority over the church.

Second, Paul addresses husbands. He commands them to love their wives (v. 25). In the same way he related a wife's submission to the church, he relates the husband's love to Christ's love for the church. Christ went to the cross on behalf of the church in order to present the church to God as holy and blameless (vv. 26–27). Husbands should love their wives with the same selfless kind of love. He gives the reason for the command in verses 28–32: husbands and wives are one flesh. Men should take care of their wives as they take care of themselves (vv. 28–29c). This serves as another point of departure to discuss Christ and the church: believers are members of the body of Christ (vv. 29d–30). He ends the lengthy discussion by repeating the commands (v. 33). The summary first addresses husbands and then wives, creating a chiastic pattern with the text.

Outline:

> Wives should submit to their husbands as to the Lord, because they are in authority (vv. 22–24)
> Husbands should love their wives as Christ loved the church, because they are one body (vv. 25–32)

Husbands should love their wives sacrificially, illustrated by Christ's
death on the cross (vv. 25–27)
Husbands should love their wives because they are one body (vv. 28–32)
Summary statement: husbands, love your wives; wives, respect your
husbands (v. 33)

CLAUSAL OUTLINE FOR EPHESIANS 5:22–33

5:22a Αἱ γυναῖκες [**ὑποτάσσεσθε**] τοῖς ἰδίοις ἀνδράσιν
5:22a Wives, [**submit**] to your own husbands

      |

    5:22b ὡς τῷ κυρίῳ [**ὑποτάσσεσθε**],
    5:22b as [**you submit**] to the Lord,

      |

    5:23a **ὅτι** ἀνήρ **ἐστιν** κεφαλὴ τῆς γυναικὸς
    5:23a **because** the husband **is** the head of his wife

        5:23b ὡς καὶ ὁ Χριστός [**ἐστιν**] κεφαλὴ τῆς ἐκκλησίας,
        5:23b as Christ also [**is**] the head of the church,

            5:23c αὐτός [**ἐστιν**] σωτὴρ τοῦ σώματος.
            5:23c he [**is**] the savior of the body.

        5:24a ἀλλὰ ὡς ἡ ἐκκλησία **ὑποτάσσεται** τῷ Χριστῷ,
        5:24a But as the church **submits** to Christ,
            5:24b οὕτως καὶ αἱ γυναῖκες [**ὑποτασσέσθωσαν**] τοῖς
                ἀνδράσιν ἐν παντί.
            5:24b thus also wives [**submit**] to their husbands in all
            things.

5:25a Οἱ ἄνδρες, **ἀγαπᾶτε** τὰς γυναῖκας,
5:25a Husbands, **love** your wives,

        5:25b **καθὼς** καὶ ὁ Χριστὸς **ἠγάπησεν** τὴν ἐκκλησίαν
        5:25b **just as** Christ also **loved** the church

        5:25c καὶ ἑαυτὸν **παρέδωκεν** ὑπὲρ αὐτῆς,
        5:25c and **gave** himself for her,

           |

          5:26a **ἵνα** αὐτὴν **ἁγιάσῃ**
          5:26a **so that he might sanctify** her

|
5:26b **καθαρίσας** τῷ λουτρῷ τοῦ ὕδατος
ἐν ῥήματι,
5:26b **by cleansing** her with the washing of
the water by the word,

[ἀγιάσῃ (v. 26a)]
[he might sanctify her (v. 26a)]
|
5:27a **ἵνα παραστήσῃ** αὐτὸς ἑαυτῷ ἔνδοξον (τὴν ἐκκλησίαν, μὴ
ἔχουσαν σπίλον ἢ ῥυτίδα ἤ τι τῶν τοιούτων),
5:27a **so that** he **might present** the church to himself as glorious, (not
having a spot, wrinkle, or any such thing),

[παραστήσῃ (v. 27a)]
[he might present (v. 27a)]
|
5:27c **ἀλλ᾽ ἵνα ᾖ** ἁγία καὶ ἄμωμος.
5:27c **but that she might be** holy and blameless,

[ἠγάπησεν (v. 25b)]
[loved (v. 25b)]
|
5:28a **οὕτως ὀφείλουσιν** καὶ οἱ ἄνδρες **ἀγαπᾶν** τὰς ἑαυτῶν γυναῖκας
5:28a **thus** husbands also **ought to love** their wives
|
5:28b **ὡς** [**ἀγαπῶσιν**] τὰ ἑαυτῶν σώματα
5:28b **as** [**they love**] their own bodies.

5:28c (ὁ ἀγαπῶν τὴν ἑαυτοῦ γυναῖκα) ἑαυτὸν **ἀγαπᾷ**.
5:28c (He who loves his wife) **loves** himself.

5:29a **οὐδεὶς γάρ** ποτε τὴν ἑαυτοῦ σάρκα **ἐμίσησεν**,
5:29a **For** no one ever **hates** his own flesh,
|
5:29b **ἀλλὰ ἐκτρέφει**
5:29b **but nourishes**
|
5:29c **καὶ θάλπει** αὐτήν,
5:29c **and cherishes** it,
|

5:29d **καθὼς** καὶ ὁ Χριστὸς [**ἐκτρέφει** καὶ **θάλπει**] τὴν
ἐκκλησίαν,
5:29d **just as** Christ <u>also</u> [**nourishes** and **cherishes**] the church,

5:30 **ὅτι** μέλη **ἐσμὲν** τοῦ
σώματος αὐτοῦ.
5:30 **because** <u>we are</u> members of
his body.

5:31a <u>ἀντὶ τούτου</u> **καταλείψει** ἄνθρωπος τὸν πατέρα καὶ τὴν μητέρα
5:31a <u>For this reason</u>, a man **shall leave** his father and mother

5:31b <u>καὶ</u> **προσκολληθήσεται** πρὸς τὴν γυναῖκα αὐτοῦ,
5:31b <u>and</u> **be joined** to his wife,

5:31c <u>καὶ</u> **ἔσονται** οἱ δύο εἰς σάρκα μίαν.
5:31c <u>and</u> the two **will become** one flesh.

5:32a Τὸ μυστήριον τοῦτο μέγα **ἐστίν**,
5:32a This mystery **is** great,

5:32b ἐγὼ <u>δὲ</u> **λέγω** εἰς Χριστὸν καὶ εἰς τὴν ἐκκλησίαν.
5:32b <u>but</u> I **am speaking** about Christ and about the church.

5:33a <u>πλὴν καὶ</u> ὑμεῖς οἱ καθ' ἕνα ἕκαστος τὴν ἑαυτοῦ γυναῖκα οὕτως **ἀγαπάτω**
5:33a <u>Nevertheless</u> each of you, **love** his own wife

33b <u>ὡς</u> [**ἀγαπᾷ**] ἑαυτόν,
33b <u>as</u> [**he loves**] himself,

5:33c ἡ <u>δὲ</u> γυνὴ ἵνα **φοβῆται** τὸν ἄνδρα.
5:33c <u>and</u> the wife **should respect** her husband.

Syntax Explained for Ephesians 5:22–33

5:22a [ὑποτάσσεσθε]: The Greek word [ὑποτάσσεσθε] is a second-person plural present middle imperative from the verb ὑποτάσσω that means "to be
subject" or "be subordinated" (BDAG, s.v. "ὑποτάσσω" 1bβ, p. 1042). Even
though the verb could be passive, the context suggests that it is middle. The
participle in verse 21 (ὑποτασσόμενοι) and the repeated verb in verse 24
should be understood as middle-voice verbs. The middle voice expresses
cooperation—Paul exhorts women to make the choice to submit to their

husband. **Syntactically**, [ὑποτάσσεσθε] is an ellipsis. The clause does not contain a verb, so the force of the participle in verse 21 governs this clause (cf. Eph. 5:24) (W, 658 n. 6; Robertson, 946). The subject is implied by the verb: "you all." The nominative αἱ γυναῖκες functions as a vocative (W, 58). The vocative signals a specific address. Paul uses a similar technique throughout this section (cf. Eph. 5:25; 6:1, 4, 9). The direct object is "to your own husbands" (τοῖς ἰδίοις ἀνδράσιν). Since Paul adds ἰδίοις, he most likely refers to wives specifically, not women (Hoehner, 732). **Semantically**, the present tense is a customary present: "be subject" (RSV, NRSV, NASB) or "submit" (ESV, NIV, NET, CSB, HCSB, NKJV, NLT). The present tense describes an ongoing state. The imperative conveys a general precept. Paul expects that this is an ongoing characteristic of these Christian wives (W, 521–22, 722).

> **Text-Critical Nugget**: Is the command to "submit" (ὑποτάσσεσθε) in the earliest manuscripts? Every manuscript except for two inserts some form of ὑποτάσσω. Two significant Alexandrian manuscripts omit the verb (B and 𝔓⁴⁶). Most manuscripts either insert the third-person plural present passive imperative (ὑποτασσέσθωσαν) (ℵ, A, I, P, Ψ, 0278, 6, 33, 81, 104, 365, 1175, 1505, 1739, 1881, 2464) or the second-person plural present passive imperative (ὑποτάσσεσθε) (D, F, G, K, L, 630, 𝔐). These manuscripts will insert the verb after either γυναῖκες or ἀνδράσιν. Even though the reading with the omission is found in only two manuscripts, it is the shorter, more difficult reading. And it accounts for the rise of the other readings. Given the omission, it makes sense for later scribes to add a verb. This also explains the inconsistency of the person and the location of the verb. Metzger notes that most lectionaries begin a new reading with verse 22, which would require some verb (Metzger, 541).

5:22b ὡς: The Greek word ὡς is a conjunction that means "as" in this context (BDAG, s.v. "ὡς" 3aα, pp. 1104–5). **Syntactically**, ὡς introduces a dependent conjunctive clause: "as to the Lord" (ὡς τῷ κυρίῳ). The clause functions adverbially modifying the preceding verb "submit yourself" (ὑποτάσσεσθε). **Semantically**, ὡς could express cause: "because you submit yourself to the Lord" (Lincoln, 368); however the following conjunction (ὅτι) states the cause. This conjunction most likely expresses a comparison: "as" (ESV, RSV, NRSV, NIV, NET, CSB, HCSB, NASB, NKJV, KJV). The conjunction most likely communicates a comparison in kind, not degree. As the wife submits to her husband, she also submits to the Lord (Hoehner, 738).

[ὑποτάσσεσθε]: The Greek word [ὑποτάσσεσθε] is a second-person plural present middle imperative from the verb ὑποτάσσω that means "to be subject" or "be subordinated" (BDAG, s.v. "ὑποτάσσω" 1bβ, p. 1042). **Syntactically**, [ὑποτάσσεσθε] is an ellipsis. The implied verb in verse 22a must be inserted here as well. The subject is implied by the verb: "you all," referring to the Ephesian wives. The dative τῷ κυρίῳ functions as the dative direct object. It refers to Christ as Lord, not their husbands, as "lords" (cf. BDAG, s.v. "κύριος" 2a, p. 577). If Paul had husbands in mind, he would have used the plural. **Semantically**, the present tense is a customary present: "submit." The present tense describes an ongoing state. Submission should characterize the woman's relationship to the Lord (W, 521–22). Most English versions omit the elliptical verb and render the phrase "as to the Lord" (ESV, RSV, NET, CSB, HCSB, NASB, NKJV, NLT). The NIV renders the ellipsis as "as you *do* to the Lord"; the RSV translates it "as you *are* to the Lord."

5:23a ὅτι: The Greek word ὅτι is a conjunction that means "because" in this context (BDAG, s.v. "ὅτι" 4a, p. 732). **Syntactically**, the conjunction ὅτι introduces a dependent clause: "*because* the man is the head of the woman" (ὅτι ἀνήρ ἐστιν κεφαλὴ τῆς γυναικός). The clause functions adverbially modifying the implied verb from verse 22a: "submit yourself" (ὑποτάσσεσθε). **Semantically**, the ὅτι conveys the cause or reason for the previous section: "because" (NET, CSB). Several English versions begin a new sentence with verse 23, rendering the conjunction as "for" (ESV, RSV, NRSV, NIV, HCSB, NASB, KJV, NKJV). The clause provides the rationale for Paul's instruction for wives to submit to their own husbands.

ἐστίν: The Greek word ἐστίν is a third-person singular present active indicative from the verb εἰμί that means "to be" (BDAG, s.v. "εἰμί" 2b, p. 283). **Syntactically**, ἐστίν functions as the main verb of the dependent conjunctive clause introduced by ὅτι. The subject of the verb is "man" or "husband" (ἀνήρ); the predicate nominative is "head" (κεφαλή). **Semantically**, ἐστίν is an equative present: "is" (ESV, RSV, NRSV, NIV, NET, CSB, HCSB, NASB, KJV, NKJV). The genitive τῆς γυναικός conveys the notion of subordination: "the head *over* the wife."

> **Lexical Nugget**: What does Paul mean by calling husbands the "head over his wife" (κεφαλὴ τῆς γυναικός)? The Greek word κεφαλή ("head") can either express a superior status, such as a superior rank (BDAG, s.v. "κεφαλή" 2a, p. 542), or "source," such as a "river head" (Bedale, 1954, 211–15). Paul evokes both metaphors throughout the letter: in Ephesians 1:22, he describes Jesus as with authority—as all things are subjected to him. But in Ephesians 4:15–16, Christ is the head—the source of the church's growth. The context of the passage presents problems for understanding κεφαλή as source. Both verses 22 and 24 reiterate Paul's instruction for both wives to submit to their husbands as well as the church to submit to Christ. Furthermore, the entire section (Eph. 5:22–6:9) comments on authority within various relationships (Best, 535; Lincoln, 369–70). Paul's usage does not indicate an ontological superiority, but one that

is functional. Hoehner states that "In God's administration the role of the husband's headship is positional power. His headship and the wife's submission are for the sake of harmony" (Hoehner, 740).

5:23b ὡς καί: The Greek word ὡς is a conjunction that means "as" in this context (BDAG, s.v. "ὡς" 3aα, pp. 1104–5). The Greek word καί is a conjunction that means "also" in this context (BDAG, s.v. "καί" 2c, pp. 495–96). **Syntactically**, ὡς introduces a dependent conjunctive clause: "as also Christ is the head of the church" (ὡς καὶ ὁ Χριστὸς κεφαλὴ τῆς ἐκκλησίας). The clause functions adverbially modifying the verb in the previous clause: "is" (ἐστίν). **Syntactically**, ὡς expresses a comparison: "as" (RSV, NIV, NLT, CSB, HCSB). καί functions adjunctively, emphasizing the comparison: "even as" (ESV, KJV), "just as" (NRSV), or "as also" (NET, NASB, NKJV).

[ἐστίν]: The Greek word ἐστίν is a third-person singular present active indicative from the verb εἰμί that means "to be" (BDAG, s.v. "εἰμί" 2b, p. 283). **Syntactically**, [ἐστίν] is an ellipsis. The implied verb functions as the main verb of this dependent conjunctive clause introduced by ὡς καί. The subject of the verb is "Christ" (ὁ Χριστός); the predicate nominative is "head" (κεφαλή). **Semantically**, [ἐστίν] is an equative present: "is" (ESV, RSV, NRSV, NIV, NET, CSB, HCSB, NASB, KJV, NKJV). The genitive τῆς ἐκκλησίας should be rendered as a genitive of subordination: "head *over* the church."

5:23c [ἐστίν]: The Greek word [ἐστίν] is a third-person singular present active indicative from the verb εἰμί that means "to be" (BDAG, s.v. "εἰμί" 2b, p. 283). **Syntactically**, [ἐστίν] is an ellipsis. The implied verb functions as the main verb of the asyndeton clause. The subject is "he" (αὐτός), referring to Christ. The predicate nominative is "savior" (σωτήρ). **Semantically**, [ἐστίν] is an equative present: "is" (CSB, HCSB, KJV, NKJV). Some versions render the pronoun emphatically: "he *himself*" (cf. NASB, RSV, ESV, NET; Robertson, 399). The phrase is in apposition to ὁ Χριστός, not ἀνήρ. The position of αὐτός suggests that it modifies the preceding clause. New Testament writers exclusively refer to either God or Jesus as "savior," never human beings. If Paul intends for the husband to act as a savior for his wife, then it is probably as provider and protector, which he describes in the following section (Eph. 5:25–33; Thielman, 379). However, it is best to restrict the phrase to Christ and the church without any analogous role for husbands and wives (Best, 535–36; Hoehner, 742–43; Arnold, 382; Larkin, 132).

5:24a ἀλλὰ ὡς: The Greek word ἀλλά is a conjunction that means "but" (BDAG, s.v. "ἀλλά" 4b, p. 45). The Greek word ὡς is a conjunction that means "as" in this context (BDAG, s.v. "ὡς" 1a, p. 1103). **Syntactically**, ἀλλὰ ὡς introduces a dependent conjunctive clause: "*but as* the church submits to Christ" (ἀλλὰ ὡς ἡ ἐκκλησία ὑποτάσσεται τῷ Χριστῷ). **Semantically**, the significant issue is how to understand ἀλλά. On the one hand, it could be interpreted as resumptive: "therefore" (KJV, NKJV) or "now" (ESV, NIV, CSB, HCSB). Some versions omit the conjunction (NRSV, RSV). In this case, the clause relates to verse 23b ("as also Christ is the head of the church") and verse 23c ("he is the savior of the body") an aside (Larkin, 133; Thielman, 379). On the other hand, ἀλλά could be understood as an adversative conjunction: "but" (NASB, NET). After making a statement limited to Christ and the church (Eph. 5:23c), he brings the reader back to the comparison (Arnold, 382; Lincoln, 372; Merkle, 183). Hoehner suggests rendering the conjunction: "notwithstanding this difference" (Hoehner, 744). The conjunction ὡς expresses a comparison. Just as the church submits herself to Christ, wives should do the same.

ὑποτάσσεται: The Greek word ὑποτάσσεται is a third-person singular present middle indicative from the verb ὑποτάσσω that means "to be subject" or "be subordinated" (BDAG, s.v. "ὑποτάσσω" 1bβ, p. 1042). **Syntactically**, ὑποτάσσεται functions as the main verb of the dependent conjunctive clause introduced by ἀλλὰ ὡς. The subject of the verb is "the church" (ἡ ἐκκλησία). The direct object is "Christ" (τῷ Χριστῷ). **Semantically**, ὑποτάσσεται is a customary present: "submits" (ESV, NIV, NET, CSB, HCSB, NLT) or "is subject" (RSV, NRSV, NASB, NKJV, KJV). The present tense describes the action of the verb as ongoing. The church should habitually submit to Christ (W, 521–22). Even though the verb could be passive, the middle is preferred. The middle voice suggests a volitional subordination (see Lexical Nugget at 5:21).

5:24b oὕτως καί: The Greek word oὕτως is a conjunction that means "so" (BDAG, s.v. "oὕτως" 1a, p. 741). The Greek word καί is a conjunction that means "also" in this context (BDAG, s.v. "καί" 2c, p. 496). **Syntactically**, oὕτως καί introduces the dependent conjunctive clause "*so also* wives should submit to their husbands in all things" (oὕτως καὶ αἱ γυναῖκες τοῖς ἀνδράσιν ἐν παντί). **Semantically**, oὕτως καί correlates with the previous clause, introducing the second half of the comparison: "so also" (ESV, RSV, NRSV, NIV, NET, CSB, HCSB, NASB; Merkle, 183; Larkin, 133).

[ὑποτασσέσθωσαν]: The Greek word [ὑποτασσέσθωσαν] is a third-person plural present middle imperative from the verb ὑποτάσσω that means "to be subject" or "be subordinated" (BDAG, s.v. "ὑποτάσσω" 1bβ, p. 1042). **Syntactically**, [ὑποτασσέσθωσαν] is an ellipsis (Robertson, 394). The subject of the verb is "wives" (αἱ γυναῖκες). The direct object is "husbands" (τοῖς ἀνδράσιν). **Semantically**, the present tense is a customary present: "should submit" (ESV, NIV, NET, NLT) or "are to submit" (CSB, HCSB). The present tense describes an ongoing state. The imperative describes a general precept (W, 521–22, 722).

Semantical Nugget: What does Paul mean when he states that wives should submit "in all things" (ἐν παντί)? The prepositional phrase modifies the elliptical imperative. Wives should submit in all things. The phrase is comprehensive. Wives should submit to their husbands in every aspect of their marriage. Most interpreters agree that Paul would understand that the phrase needs to be qualified. He does not envision women following their husbands into sinful behavior or tolerating abuse (Thielman, 380–81; Hoehner, 745–46). The following section addresses husbands—to love their wives. However, the command for wives to submit to their husbands is not contingent on how their husbands might treat them. Wives submit as a response to Christ. On the other hand, husbands are commanded to love their wives, regardless if they choose to submit.

5:25a ἀγαπᾶτε: The Greek word ἀγαπᾶτε is a second-person plural present active imperative from the verb ἀγαπάω that means "to cherish" or "love" (BDAG, s.v. "ἀγαπάω" 1aα, p. 5). **Syntactically**, ἀγαπᾶτε functions as the main verb of an asyndeton clause. The nominative οἱ ἄνδρες functions as a vocative (W, 56–59). The use of the vocative here signals a change in address. Paul uses a similar technique throughout this section (Eph. 5:22; 6:1, 4, 5, 9). Even though this could refer to men in general, Paul most likely has husbands in mind since he has referred to wives in verses 22–24 (see specifically his use of ἰδίοις at verse 22a). The subject is implied by the verb "you all," referring to the husbands. The direct object is "women," or better "wives" (τὰς γυναῖκας; BDAG, s.v. "γυνή" 2, p. 209). **Semantically**, ἀγαπᾶτε is a customary present: "love" (ESV, RSV, NRSV, NIV, NET, CSB, HCSB, NASB, NKJV, KJV, NLT). The present tense describes the action of the verb as ongoing. The imperative suggests that husbands should continually love their wives, making this habitual (W, 521–22).

Text-Critical Nugget: Does Paul add a pronoun after "wives" (τὰς γυναῖκας)? The majority of manuscripts add either the second-person personal pronoun ὑμῶν (F and G) or the reflexive pronoun ἑαυτῶν (D, K, L, 𝔐). On the other hand, our earliest manuscripts (ℵ, A, B) do not contain a pronoun. Hoehner argues that the reading with the reflexive pronoun is original based on the external evidence—it is found in both the Western and Byzantine text types (Hoehner, 747 n. 1). On the other hand, the omission is shorter and harder. Even without the pronoun, the article can convey the notion of possession (W, 215–16). A scribe more likely added the pronoun to clarify the text rather than omit it.

Theological Nugget: Why does Paul focus so much attention on his command for husbands to love their wives? A significant amount of space focuses on the husband's role in marriage (nine verses; vv. 25–33), compared to the wife's role (three verses; vv. 22–24). In the remainder of the household code, he spends more space encouraging those in the subordinated position (children: three verses [Eph. 6:1–3], and parents: one verse [Eph. 6:4]; slaves: four verses [Eph. 6:5–8], and masters: one verse [Eph. 6:9]). In the previous section (vv. 22–24), Paul implicitly uses an imperative to command wives to submit to their husbands. The command is implied from Paul's description of all believers submitting to one another (v. 21). He never explicitly uses the verb in reference to wives, though he does use the verb once to describe the church's submission to Christ (v. 24a). In contrast, Paul commands husbands to love their wives three times throughout the passage (Eph. 5:25, 28, 33). The length of the section may have to do with the analogy that Paul draws between Christ's love for the church and the husband's love for his wife (Hoehner, 746). On the other hand, it might have to do with the fact that his command was countercultural for the Ephesian believers. In a Greco-Roman context, wives would have to manage home affairs in a way to free their husbands to develop their social standing. Paul here calls husbands to love their wives just as Christ loved the church—with a sacrificial love (Thielman, 381–82; Arnold, 383).

5:25b καθὼς καί: The Greek word καθώς is a conjunction that means "as" or "just as" (BDAG, s.v. "καθώς" 1, p. 493). The Greek word καί is a conjunction that means "also" in this context (BDAG, s.v. "καί" 2c, p. 496). **Syntactically**, καθὼς καί introduces a dependent conjunctive clause: "*just as also* Christ loved the church" (καθὼς καὶ ὁ Χριστὸς ἠγάπησεν τὴν ἐκκλησίαν). The clause functions adverbially modifying the verb in the previous clause: "love" (ἀγαπᾶτε). **Semantically**, καθώς could express cause, giving the reason why husbands should love their wives: "*because* Christ loved the church" (Lincoln, 374; Best, 539); however, it is best understood as marking a comparison, indicating the manner or extent to which men should love their wives (Hoehner, 748). The conjunction καί is adjunctive, emphasizing the comparison: "*just as also* Christ loved the church" (cf. NASB, NKJV, KJV). Most English versions simply omit καί (cf. CSB, HCSB, RSV, NRSV, ESV, NIV, NET).

ἠγάπησεν: The Greek word ἠγάπησεν is a third-person singular aorist active, indicative from the verb ἀγαπάω that means "to cherish" or "to love" (BDAG, s.v. "ἀγαπάω" 1bα, p. 5). **Syntactically**, ἠγάπησεν functions as the main verb of the dependent conjunctive clause introduced by καθὼς καί. The subject is "Christ" (ὁ Χριστός). The direct object is "the church" (τὴν ἐκκλησίαν). **Semantically**, ἠγάπησεν is a constative aorist: "loved" (ESV, RSV, NRSV, NIV, NET, CSB, HCSB, NASB, KJV, NKJV). It describes the action of the verb as a whole (W, 557–58). In the following clause, Paul indicates that Christ demonstrated this love by giving himself up for her. Paul uses the present tense to address husbands (v. 25a), but shifts to the aorist here. Husbands should continually love their wives, but Christ expressed this love through his life and death.

5:25c καί: The Greek word καί is a conjunction that means "and" (BDAG, s.v. "καί" 1bγ, p. 494). **Syntactically**, καί introduces a dependent conjunctive clause: "*and* gave himself for her" (καὶ ἑαυτὸν παρέδωκεν ὑπὲρ αὐτῆς). The clause is parallel to the previous clause ("Christ loved the church"), a dependent conjunctive clause introduced by καθὼς καί. **Semantically**, καί is epexegetical, providing additional information about Christ's love for us: "and" (ESV, RSV, NRSV, NIV, NET, CSB, HCSB, NASB, KJV, NKJV; Merkle, 184).

παρέδωκεν: The Greek word παρέδωκεν is a third-person singular aorist active indicative from the verb παραδίδωμι that means "to hand over," "to turn over," or "to give up a person" (BDAG, s.v. "παραδίδωμι" 1b, p. 762). **Syntactically**, παρέδωκεν functions as the main verb of the dependent conjunctive clause introduced by καί. The clause is parallel to the previous clause ("Christ loved the church"). The subject is implied by the verb: "he," referring to Christ (v. 25b). The direct object is the reflexive pronoun "himself" (ἑαυτόν). **Semantically**, παρέδωκεν is a constative aorist: "gave himself up" (ESV, RSV, NRSV, NIV, NASB) or "he gave himself" (NET, CSB, HCSB, KJV, NKJV). It describes the action of the verb as a whole (W, 557–58). The verb refers to Christ's death on the cross. The NLT makes this explicit by rendering the clause as: "He gave up his life for her."

> **Semantical Nugget**: What does the prepositional phrase "for her" (ὑπὲρ αὐτῆς) mean? The phrase "for her" modifies the verb "he gave himself up." The preposition expresses representation: "for," "in behalf of," or "for the sake of someone" (BDAG, s.v. "ὑπέρ" A1aε, p. 1030). The antecedent of the pronoun αὐτῆς is "the church" (ἐκκλησία). Paul uses a similar phrase in Ephesians 5:2. In that context, he commands believers to love one another "just as Christ loved us and gave himself for us." In Ephesians 5:2, he describes Christ's love in sacrificial terms (see Theological Nugget at 5:2c). Interestingly, Paul commands wives to submit within the context of the mutual submission of all believers (cf. Eph. 5:21); he also commands husbands to love their wives after exhorting all believers to love one another.

5:26a ἵνα: The Greek word ἵνα is a conjunction that means "that" in this context to denote purpose (BDAG, s.v. "ἵνα" 1aε, p. 475). This is the first of three ἵνα clauses in this context that express purpose (cf. Eph. 5:26a, 27a, and 27c). **Syntactically**, ἵνα introduces a dependent conjunctive clause: "*so that* he might sanctify her" (ἵνα αὐτὴν ἁγιάσῃ). The clause functions adverbially modifying both ἠγάπησεν and παρέδωκεν (v. 26a), the two main verbs of the sentence.

Semantically, ἵνα marks the clause as purpose clause: "that" (ESV, RSV, KJV, NKJV) or "to" (CSB, HCSB, NIV, NET, NLT). The clause expresses the first purpose for Christ's love expressed through the cross, that he might sanctify her.

ἁγιάσῃ: The Greek word ἁγιάσῃ is a third-person singular aorist active subjunctive from the verb ἁγιάζω that means "to consecrate," "dedicate," or "sanctify" (BDAG, s.v. "ἁγιάζω" 2, p. 10). **Syntactically**, ἁγιάσῃ functions as the main verb of the dependent conjunctive clause introduced by ἵνα. The subject is implied by the verb: "he," referring to Christ. The direct object is "her" (αὐτήν); the antecedent of the pronoun is the church (ἐκκλησία, v. 25c). **Semantically**, ἁγιάσῃ is a constative aorist: "sanctify" (ESV, RSV, NASB, NKJV, KJV) or "make her holy" (NRSV, NIV, CSB, HCSB). It describes the action of the verb as a whole (W, 557–58). This could refer to Christ's death, the basis of God setting apart the church. But it can also refer to the ultimate consummation. Finally, it can refer to the ongoing process of believers becoming like Christ (Eph. 4:11–16) (Arnold, 386).

5:26b καθαρίσας: The Greek word καθαρίσας is a masculine nominative singular aorist active participle from the verb καθαρίζω that means "to cleanse" or "purify" (BDAG, s.v. "καθαρίζω" 3bα, pp. 488–89). **Syntactically**, καθαρίσας introduces a participle dependent clause. It functions adverbially modifying the verb "he might sanctify" (ἁγιάσῃ). **Semantically**, καθαρίσας could express cause: "*because* he cleansed;" or means: "*by* cleansing" (NRSV, NET; Thielman, 383; Arnold, 387). Hoehner notes that since there is no temporal aspect with the subjunctive (ἁγιάσῃ) grammatically, these actions occurred simultaneously. But logically the action of the participle precedes the action of the subjunctive verb (Hoehner, 752; cf. Abbott, 168). The dative τῷ λουτρῷ ("washing" or "bath"; see BDAG, s.v. "λουτρόν," p. 603) functions as a dative of means: "*by* the washing" (ESV, RSV, NRSV, NIV, NASB, cf. NLT) or "*with* the washing" (CSB, HCSB, NET, NKJV, KJV). This washing might refer specifically to the believer's baptism (Best, 542). The problem is that λουτρόν does not normally refer to baptism. Rather, Paul uses the term βαπτισμά (cf. Eph. 4:5). This could refer to a metaphorical washing, referring to a bridal bath. Ezekiel uses a similar image to describe God's redemption of Israel (Ezek. 16:8–14). This makes the best sense of the background of the passage (Hoehner, 753–54; Thielman, 383–84; Arnold, 387–88).

> **Syntactical Nugget**: What does the prepositional phrase "by the word" (ἐν ῥήματι) modify? The preposition ἐν conveys the idea of means: "*by* the word" (CSB, HCSB, KJV, NKJV, NRSV, NET) or "*with* the word" (ESV, RSV, NASB). The "word" most likely refers to the gospel message that Christ "loved the church and gave himself up for her" (Hoehner, 756). The phrase could modify either "the washing" (τῷ λουτρῷ τοῦ ὕδατος) or

the particle "by cleansing" (καθαρίσας). If it modifies the noun, then the word bathes the believer (Thielman, 384–85; Best, 544). However, we might anticipate that an article precedes the prepositional phrase. It most likely modifies the participle καθαρίσας ("by cleansing"). With this interpretation, the prepositional phrase adds more description to the metaphorical bath. Arnold states: "What formerly took place through ritual cleansing with water now happens through the proclamation of the Word of God" (Arnold, 388; cf. Hoehner, 756–57).

5:27a ἵνα: The Greek word ἵνα is a conjunction that means "that" in this context to denote purpose (BDAG, s.v. "ἵνα" 1aε, p. 475). This is the second of three ἵνα clauses that express purpose (cf. Eph. 5:26a, 27a, and 27c). **Syntactically**, ἵνα introduces a dependent conjunctive clause: "*so that* he might present to himself the glorious church" (ἵνα παραστήσῃ αὐτὸς ἑαυτῷ ἔνδοξον τὴν ἐκκλησίαν). The clause could be parallel to the previous ἵνα clause (v. 26a) modifying ἠγάπησεν and παρέδωκεν (v. 25). But since there is no coordinating conjunction introducing the clause it most likely modifies the verb in the first ἵνα clause: "he might sanctify" (ἁγιάσῃ) (Hoehner, 757; Arnold, 389). **Semantically**, the ἵνα marks the clause as purpose clause: "that" (RSV, NASB, KJV, NKJV) or "so that" (ESV, NET). Due to the length of the sentence in Greek, the CSB begins a new sentence: "He did this to present" (cf. HCSB, NLT). The clause presents the second purpose for Christ's love and giving himself up—to present the church to himself.

παραστήσῃ: The Greek word παραστήσῃ is a third-person singular aorist active subjunctive from the verb παρίστημι that means "to make" or "to render" (BDAG, s.v. "παρίστημι" 1c, p. 778). **Syntactically**, παραστήσῃ functions as the main verb of the dependent conjunctive clause introduced by ἵνα. The subject is "he" (αὐτός). The antecedent of the pronoun is "Christ" (v. 25b). The indirect object is the reflexive pronoun "himself" (ἑαυτῷ). The direct object is "the church" (τὴν ἐκκλησίαν); the accusative ἔνδοξον ("glorious"; BDAG, s.v. "ἔνδοξον" 2, pp. 332–33) functions as the object complement (W, 182–89): "so that he might present the church to himself as glorious." **Semantically**, παραστήσῃ is a constative aorist: "present" (ESV, RSV, NRSV, NIV, NET, CSB, HCSB, NASB, NKJV, KJV, NLT). It describes the action of the verb as a whole (W, 557–58). Since this presentation is linked to Christ's death, some commentators argue that this refers to the present reality of the church (Thielman, 393; Best, 545–46; Lincoln, 377). However, Paul seems to describe a future state of the church. The church is still growing (cf. Eph. 4:15–16); at a future point, it will be completed (Hoehner, 761; Arnold, 389).

ἔχουσαν: The Greek word ἔχουσαν is a feminine accusative singular present active participle from the verb ἔχω that means "to have" related to a characteristic

(BDAG, s.v. "ἔχω" 7aβ, p. 421). **Syntactically**, ἔχουσαν is an attributive participle modifying the noun "the church" (ἐκκλησίαν). The participle phrase, "not having a spot, a wrinkle, or any such thing" (μὴ ἔχουσαν σπίλον ἢ ῥυτίδα ἢ τι τῶν τοιούτων), describes the church. **Semantically**, ἔχουσαν is a customary present: "having" (NASB, NET, NKJV, KJV). The present tense describes an ongoing state of the church as a result of Christ washing her (W, 521–22). Since the verb describes a characteristic of the church several versions render the verb as: "without spot or wrinkle" (ESV, RSV, NRSV, CSB, HCSB, NLT; cf. NIV).

5:27b ἀλλ' ἵνα: The Greek word ἀλλά is a conjunction that means "but" (BDAG, s.v. "ἀλλά" 1a, p. 45). The Greek word ἵνα is a conjunction that means "that" in this context to denote purpose (BDAG, s.v. "ἵνα" 1aε, p. 475). This is the third of three ἵνα clauses that express purpose (cf. Eph. 5:26a, 27a, and 27c). **Syntactically**, ἵνα introduces a conjunctive dependent clause: "*but that* it should be holy and blameless" (ἵνα ᾖ ἁγία καὶ ἄμωμος). The clause functions adverbially modifying the verb in the previous ἵνα clause: "he might present" (παραστήσῃ) (Hoehner, 760). **Semantically**, the adversative conjunction ἀλλά marks a contrast with the preceding clause, which gives a negative description. ἵνα specifies the third and ultimate purpose for Christ's death—that rather than having a spot or wrinkle, the church be holy and blameless.

ᾖ: The Greek word ᾖ is a third-person singular present active subjunctive from the verb εἰμί that means "to be" (BDAG, s.v. "εἰμί" 2a, p. 283). **Syntactically**, ᾖ functions as the main verb of the dependent conjunctive clause introduced by ἵνα. The subject is implied by the verb: "she" or "it" referring to the church. The predicate nominatives are "holy and blameless" (ἁγία καὶ ἄμωμος). **Semantically**, ᾖ is an equative present tense: "she *should be* holy and blameless" (cf. ESV, RSV, NRSV, NASB, NKJV, KJV). Several English versions simply omit the verb emphasizing the contrast: "but holy and blameless" (CSB, HCSB, NIV, NET). The clause alludes to the earlier part of the book. Paul describes believers as chosen to be "holy and blameless before him" (Eph. 1:4).

5:28a οὕτως: The Greek word οὕτως is a conjunction that means "so" (BDAG, s.v. "οὕτως" 1a, p. 741). **Syntactically**, οὕτως introduces a dependent conjunctive clause: "*so also* husbands ought to love their own wives" (οὕτως ὀφείλουσιν καὶ οἱ ἄνδρες ἀγαπᾶν τὰς ἑαυτῶν γυναῖκας). The conjunction could introduce a new section, looking forward to the following ὡς. However, it most likely relates to the preceding clause introduced by καθώς (v. 25b): "Just as Christ loved the church … *thus* also husbands ought to love their own wives." Paul makes a similar comparative in verse 24 (Arnold, 390–91; Hoehner, 762–63; Larkin, 137). **Semantically**, οὕτως introduces a comparison of a husband's love for his wife with Christ's love for the church: "so" (NASB, KJV, NKJV; cf. RSV) or "in the same way" (ESV, NRSV, NIV, NET, CSB, HCSB, NLT).

> **Text-Critical Nugget**: Why does the NA²⁸ place brackets around the conjunction καί? The MT and RP²⁰⁰⁵ both omit the conjunction, while THGNT and SBL along with the NA²⁸ insert it. Several Alexandrian (ℵ, 81, 104, 1739, 1881) and Byzantine (K, L, 𝔐) manuscripts omit καί following ὀφείλουσιν. Several Western (D, F, G, lat) and secondary Alexandrian manuscripts (A 0285) insert καί after οὕτως. While a handful of key Alexandrian manuscripts (𝔓⁴⁶, B, 33, 1175) insert καί after ὀφείλουσιν. The omission might suggest that the phrase correlates with the following ὡς clause, while the insertion emphasizes the link to the preceding clause. Based on the external evidence, the insertion of the conjunction is superior. Paul frequently places καί after οὕτως, rarely inserting a word between the two. Therefore the reading found in the NA²⁸ is more difficult. A scribe more likely placed the καί before ὀφείλουσιν than after it (Hoehner, 762 n. 2).

ὀφείλουσιν: The Greek word ὀφείλουσιν is a third-person plural present active indicative from the verb ὀφείλω that means "to owe" or "be obligated" particularly with the following infinitive (BDAG, s.v. "ὀφείλω" 2aβ, p. 743). **Syntactically**, ὀφείλουσιν functions as the main verb of the dependent conjunctive clause introduced by οὕτως. The subject is "husbands" (οἱ ἄνδρες). **Semantically**, the indicative functions as a potential indicative. The element of potentiality comes from the verb root itself rather than the mood (W, 451–52). The present tense functions as a customary present, expressing a continuous state for Christian husbands (W, 521–22). Paul anticipates that husbands make loving their wives a habitual act.

ἀγαπᾶν: The Greek word ἀγαπᾶν is a present active infinitive from the verb ἀγαπάω that means "to cherish" or "love" (BDAG, s.v. "ἀγαπάω" 1aα, p. 5). **Syntactically**, ἀγαπᾶν functions adverbially, modifying the main verb of the clause: "so also husbands ought" (ὀφείλουσιν). The direct object is "their own wives" (τὰς ἑαυτῶν γυναῖκας). **Semantically**, ἀγαπᾶν is a complementary infinitive, completing the verbal idea of the previous verb (ὀφείλουσιν) (W, 598–99). Along with the previous verb, the present tense is customary, expressing a continuous state: "husbands *ought to love* their wives" (NIV, NET, KJV, NKJV, NLT) or "husbands *should love* their wives" (ESV, RSV, NRSV). The CSB draws out the obligation: "Husbands *are to love* their wives" (CSB, HCSB). The clause brings the reader back to the point that he makes in verse 25—husbands are to love their wives.

5:28b ὡς: The Greek word ὡς is a conjunction that means "as" in this context (BDAG, s.v. "ὡς" 1bα, pp. 1103–4). **Syntactically**, ὡς introduces a dependent conjunctive clause: "*as* their own body" (ὡς τὰ ἑαυτῶν σώματα). The clause functions adverbially modifying the verbal idea in the previous clause: "ought to love" (ὀφείλουσιν … ἀγαπᾶν). **Semantically**, ὡς expresses a comparison: "as" (ESV, RSV, NRSV, NIV, NET, CSB, HCSB, NASB, NKJV, KJV). The comparative statement begins a new argument for Paul's command for husbands to love their wives. In verses 25–27, Paul argues that Christian husbands should love their wives sacrificially, just as Christ gave himself up for the church. In the remainder of the section (vv. 28–33) he gives a second reason for husbands to love their wives—they are one flesh. Just as Christ nourishes and cares for his body, the church, Christian husbands should care for their wives.

[ἀγαπῶσιν]: The Greek word [ἀγαπῶσιν] is a third-person plural present active indicative from the verb ἀγαπάω that means "to cherish" or "to love" (BDAG, s.v. "ἀγαπάω" 1aα, p. 5). **Syntactically**, [ἀγαπῶσιν] is an ellipsis, assumed from the previous clause. It is the main verb of the dependent conjunctive clause introduced by ὡς. The subject of the ellipsis is implied: "they," referring to Christian husbands (cf. v. 28a). The direct object is "their own bodies" (τὰ ἑαυτῶν σώματα). **Semantically**, [ἀγαπῶσιν] functions as a gnomic present describing a general, timeless fact (W, 523). Paul describes this type of self-care in verse 29. People regularly take care of themselves. The following clause (v. 29c) brings out the implication for this statement. The husband's care for his wife should be just as natural as one might care for his own body.

5:28c ἀγαπῶν: The Greek word ἀγαπῶν is a masculine nominative singular present active participle from the verb ἀγαπάω that means "to cherish" or "love" (BDAG, s.v. "ἀγαπάω" 1aα, p. 5). **Syntactically**, ἀγαπῶν is a substantival participle. The participle phrase "the one who loves his wife" (ὁ ἀγαπῶν τὴν ἑαυτοῦ γυναῖκα) functions as the subject of the asyndeton clause. **Semantically**, ἀγαπῶν functions as a customary present describing a continuous state: "he who loves his wife" (ESV, RSV, NRSV, NIV, NET, CSB, HCSB, NASB, NKJV).

ἀγαπᾷ: The Greek word ἀγαπᾷ is a third-person singular present active indicative from the verb ἀγαπάω that means "to cherish" or "love" (BDAG, s.v. "ἀγαπάω" 1aα, p. 5). **Syntactically**, ἀγαπᾷ is the main verb in an asyndeton clause: "he who loves his wife loves himself." The clause is a parenthetical, clarifying the preceding clause. **Semantically**, the present tense functions as a gnomic present, describing a general, timeless fact (W, 523). Since a husband and wife are one flesh (Eph. 5:31; cf. Gen. 2:24), a husband should treat his wife with the same depth of care. Paul draws the focus on the husband's love for his wife, not his own self-care. Hoehner states: "This love is not to be seen as a duty but as something that is consistent with his nature" (Hoehner, 765).

5:29a γάρ: The Greek word γάρ is a conjunction that means "for" or "therefore" (BDAG, s.v. "γάρ" 2, pp. 189–90). **Syntactically**, γάρ is in the postpositive position, introducing an independent conjunctive clause: "*For* no one ever hates his own flesh" (οὐδεὶς γάρ ποτε τὴν ἑαυτοῦ σάρκα ἐμίσησεν). **Semantically**, γάρ introduces a clause that explains the previous clause (v. 28b) (Hoehner, 766; Merkle, 187), or possibly the entire verse (Best, 549): "for" (ESV, RSV, NRSV, NET, CSB, HCSB, NASB, NKJV, KJV).

ἐμίσησεν: The Greek word ἐμίσησεν is a third-person singular aorist active indicative from the verb μισέω that means "to hate," or "to detest" (BDAG, s.v. "μισέω" 1b, pp. 652–53). **Syntactically**, ἐμίσησεν functions as the main verb of the independent conjunctive clause introduced by γάρ. The subject is "no one" (οὐδείς). The direct object is "his own flesh" (τὴν ἑαυτοῦ σάρκα). Paul shifts from σῶμα (v. 28) to σάρξ, which looks forward to the Genesis 2:24 citation in Ephesians 5:31. **Semantically**, ἐμίσησεν functions as a gnomic aorist (W, 562; Hoehner, 766; Porter, 38–39). Paul presents this timeless fact that people do not mistreat their bodies, and applies it to the marriage relationship. Due to the semantics of the verb, it is best to render the verb in the present tense: "hates" (RSV, NRSV, CSB, HCSB, NLT).

5:29b ἀλλά: The Greek word ἀλλά means "but" (BDAG, s.v. "ἀλλά" 1a, p. 45). **Syntactically**, ἀλλά introduces an independent conjunctive clause: "*but* nourishes" (ἀλλὰ ἐκτρέφει). **Semantically**, ἀλλά is a contrastive conjunction: "but" (ESV, RSV, NRSV, NIV, NET, CSB, HCSB, NASB, NKJV, KJV). The following two clauses (vv. 29b and 29c) provide a positive statement after the initial negative statement (v. 29a). In contrast to treating one's own body with disregard, the following verbs describe the kind of care that parents would give their children (Arnold, 391–92).

ἐκτρέφει: The Greek word ἐκτρέφει is a third-person singular present active indicative from the verb ἐκτρέφω that means "to provide food" or "nourish" (BDAG, s.v. "ἐκτρέφω" 1, p. 311). The word occurs twice in the New Testament, both in Ephesians. In Ephesians 6:4, Paul uses the word to describe how fathers should raise their children. **Syntactically**, ἐκτρέφει functions as the main verb of the independent conjunctive clause introduced by ἀλλά. The subject is implied by the verb: "he" or "she." The direct object is "it" (αὐτήν). The antecedent of the pronoun is "flesh" (σάρξ). **Semantically**, ἐκτρέφει is a gnomic present, stating a timeless truth (W, 523–24).

5:29c καί: The Greek word καί is a conjunction that means "and" (BDAG, s.v. "καί" 1bδ, p. 494). **Syntactically**, καί introduces an independent conjunctive clause: "*and* cherishes it" (θάλπει αὐτήν). **Semantically**, καί is a coordinating connective: "and" (ESV, RSV, NRSV, NIV, NET, HCSB, CSB, NASB, KJV, NKJV). The conjunction joins ἐκτρέφει with θάλπει ("nourish and cherish"). The two terms function together to describe the care that one gives his own body.

θάλπει: The Greek word θάλπει is a third-person singular present active indicative from the verb θάλπω that means "to cherish" or "comfort" (BDAG, s.v. "θάλπω," p. 442). **Syntactically,** θάλπει functions as the main verb of the independent conjunctive clause introduced by καί. The subject is implied by the verb: "he" or "she." The direct object is "it" (αὐτήν). The antecedent of the pronoun is "flesh" (σάρξ). **Semantically,** θάλπει functions as the gnomic present. Just like ἐκτρέφει, the verb expresses a timeless fact: people nourish and cherish their own bodies (W, 523–24).

5:29d καθὼς καί: The Greek word καθώς is a conjunction that means "as" or "just as" (BDAG, s.v. "καθώς" 1, p. 493). The Greek word καί is a conjunction that means "also" in this context (BDAG, s.v. "καί" 2c, p. 496). **Syntactically,** καθὼς καί introduces a dependent conjunctive clause: "*just as* Christ also nourishes and cherishes the church" (καθὼς καὶ ὁ Χριστὸς τὴν ἐκκλησίαν). The clause functions adverbially modifying the verbs in the previous clause: "nourish" and "cherish" (ἐκτρέφει and θάλπει). **Semantically,** καθώς marks a comparison. καί functions adjunctively: "just as also" (cf. NASB). Most English versions omit καί: "just as" (ESV, NIV, NET, CSB). Christ's care for the church becomes exemplary. Earlier in the letter, Paul developed this metaphor describing the church as a body growing into Christ, her head (Eph. 4:16; Arnold, 392).

[ἐκτρέφει καὶ θάλπει]: The Greek word ἐκτρέφει is a third-person singular present active indicative from the verb ἐκτρέφω that means "to provide food" or "to nourish" (BDAG, s.v. "ἐκτρέφω" 1, p. 311). The Greek word θάλπει is a third-person singular present active indicative from the verb θάλπω that means "to cherish" or "comfort" (BDAG, s.v. "θάλπω," p. 442). **Syntactically,** [ἐκτρέφει καὶ θάλπει] is an ellipsis, implied from the preceding clause. The verbs function as the main verbs of the dependent conjunctive clause introduced by καθώς. Most English versions render the ellipsis as "does" (ESV, RSV, NRSV, NIV, NET, CSB, HCSB, NASB, NKJV). The NLT supplies the second verb: "cares." The subject is "Christ" (ὁ Χριστός); the direct object is "the church" (τὴν ἐκκλησίαν). **Semantically,** both verbs are customary presents: "nourishes and cherishes." The present tense describes an ongoing state (W, 521–22). Just as anyone provides care for his or her own body, Christ actively cares for the church.

5:30 ὅτι: The Greek word ὅτι is a conjunction that means "because" in this context (BDAG, s.v. "ὅτι" 4a, p. 732). **Syntactically,** ὅτι introduces the clause as a dependent conjunctive clause: "*because* we are members of his body" (ὅτι μέλη ἐσμὲν τοῦ σώματος αὐτοῦ) functions adverbially modifying the implied verbs in verse 29d: "just as Christ *nourishes* and *cherishes* the church" (ἐκτρέφει καὶ θάλπει). **Semantically,** ὅτι explains why Christ nourishes and cherishes the church: "*because* we are members of his body" (ESV, RSV, NRSV, NASB) or "*since* we are members of his body" (CSB, HCSB).

ἐσμέν: The Greek word ἐσμέν is a first-person plural present active indicative from the verb εἰμί that means "to be" (BDAG, s.v. "εἰμί" 2b, p. 283). **Syntactically**, ἐσμέν functions as the main verb of the dependent conjunctive clause introduced by ὅτι. The subject is implied in the verb "we," referring to all believers. The predicate nominative is "members" (μέλη). The Greek term μέλος refers to an extension of a living organism (BDAG, s.v. "μέλος" 2, p. 628). **Semantically**, ἐσμέν is an equative present: "we *are*" (ESV, RSV, NRSV, NIV, NET, CSB, HCSB, NASB, KJV, NKJV). Paul has developed this body theme throughout the letter by referring to Christ as the head and the church as the body (Eph. 1:22–23; 5:23). In Ephesians 4:25 he uses the same image to describe the relationship between believers. Believers should speak to one another truthfully "because we are members of one another." In this context, Paul shifts the image to describe Christ's care for the church because we are members of his body.

> **Text-Critical Nugget**: Does Paul allude to Genesis 2:23 in verse 30? A number of Western (D, F, G, lat) and Byzantine manuscripts (K, L, 𝔐) insert a citation from Genesis 2:23, or some variation, after αὐτοῦ: ἐκ τῆς σαρκὸς αὐτοῦ καὶ ἐκ τῶν ὀστέων αὐτοῦ ("from his flesh and from his bone") (RP[2005]; MT; cf. KJV, NKJV). Most Alexandrian manuscripts (𝔓[46], ℵ, A, B, 048, 33, 81, 1739, 1881) contain the shorter reading (cf. NA[28], SBL, THGNT). Metzger speculates that the citation could have been accidentally omitted, but that it more likely was inserted due to Paul's citation of Genesis 2:24 in verse 31 (Metzger, 541). Hoehner argues that the insertion of the Genesis text is most likely original since the passage is inconsistent with Paul's argument and thus more difficult (Hoehner, 769 n. 3). However, the reading might be too difficult. Paul's image describes a spiritual connection between the Christ and the church; Genesis 2:23 emphasizes a physical connection (cf. Thielman, 393–94).

5:31a ἀντὶ τούτου: The Greek word ἀντί is a preposition that means "because" in this context (BDAG, s.v. "ἀντί" 4, p. 88). The Greek word τούτου is a neuter genitive singular demonstrative pronoun, which means "this" in this context (BDAG, s.v. "οὗτος" 1bα, p. 741). Together, the phrase means: "Because of this" or "For this reason." Paul quotes Genesis 2:24 in verse 31 following closely to the LXX. The introduction is the only alteration; instead of ἀντὶ τούτου, the LXX reads ἕνεκεν τούτου, which also expresses cause or reason (BDAG, s.v. "ἕνεκα" 1, p. 334). **Syntactically**, the phrase is debated (see Syntactical Nugget below). The phrase most likely provides a transition from Paul's argument to the citation. **Semantically**, ἀντὶ τούτου expresses cause, providing a rationale for his statement that "we are members of his body" (v. 30): "For this reason" (RSV, NRSV, NIV, NET, CSB, HCSB, NASB, NKJV).

> **Syntactical Nugget**: How does Paul's citation of Genesis 2:23 relate to the context? Paul does not introduce his citation of Genesis 2:23 as he would other passages. For example, in Ephesians 4:8 he introduces Psalm 68:18 with the phrase διὸ λέγει ("therefore, it says"). He closely follows the LXX but alters the conjunction. Instead of ἕνεκεν τούτου, Paul writes ἀντὶ τούτου, both phrases mean "for this reason." The phrase could simply be a part of the quotation linking the citation to Genesis 2:23—the formation of the woman (Larkin, 140). This interpretation would limit the scope of the application to the relationship between a husband and his wife. On the other hand, the clause could provide a transition from Paul's argument to the citation. In this case, Paul applies Genesis 2:24 to both to the marriage relationship as well as the relationship between Christ and the church. Hoehner argues that the clause modifies verses 28–30 and applies the citation to the relationship between husband and wife and secondarily to the relationship between Christ and the church (Hoehner, 772). Arnold argues that the clause modifies verses 29b–30 and limits the scope to Christ and the church and secondarily to the relationship between husband and wife. This makes the most sense since he applies the passage to Christ and the church in the next verse (v. 32) and the conjunction πλήν ("in any case") in verse 33 seems to shift his discussion of Christ and the church back to husband and wife (Arnold, 392–93; Thielman, 388–89; Best, 553; Lincoln, 380).

καταλείψει: The Greek word καταλείψει is a third-person singular future active indicative from the verb καταλείπω that means "to leave" (BDAG, s.v. "καταλείπω" 1aα, p. 520). **Syntactically**, καταλείψει functions as the main verb of the independent conjunctive clause introduced by ἀντὶ τούτου. The subject is "husband" (ἄνθρωπος); "his father and his mother" (τὸν πατέρα καὶ τὴν μητέρα) function as the direct object. **Semantically**, the future tense functions as gnomic future, which describes a generic event that will likely occur rather than a particular event (Hoehner, 774; Arnold, 393; Lincoln, 380).

5:31b καί: The Greek word καί is a conjunction that means "and" (BDAG, s.v. "καί" 1bγ, p. 494). **Syntactically**, καί introduces an independent conjunctive clause: "*and* be joined to his wife" (καὶ προσκολληθήσεται πρὸς τὴν γυναῖκα αὐτοῦ). **Semantically**, καί is a coordinating connective: "and" (ESV, RSV, NRSV, NIV, NET, CSB, HCSB, NASB, KJV, NKJV). The nature of the verbs along with the conjunction suggests that both verbs describe a single move— by joining his wife, a man leaves his parents.

προσκολληθήσεται: The Greek word προσκολληθήσεται is a third-person singular future passive indicative from the verb προσκολλάω that means "to be faithfully devoted to" or "to join" (BDAG, s.v. "προσκολλάω," pp. 881–82). Literally, the word means to "stick" (LSJ, s.v. "προσκολλάω," p. 1517). **Syntactically**, προσκολληθήσεται functions as the main verb of the independent conjunctive clause introduced by καί. The subject is implied by the context: "he," referring to husbands (ἄνθρωπος) **Semantically**, the future tense functions as a gnomic future, which describes a generic event that will likely occur rather than a particular event (Hoehner, 774).

5:31c καί: The Greek word καί is a conjunction that means "and" (BDAG, s.v. "καί" 1bζ, p. 494). **Syntactically**, καί introduces an independent conjunctive clause: "*and* the two will become one flesh" (καὶ ἔσονται οἱ δύο εἰς σάρκα μίαν). **Semantically**, καί is ascensive introducing the result of the previous action (Larkin, 140). Most English versions translate the conjunction as "and" (ESV, RSV, NRSV, NIV, NET, CSB, HCSB, NASB, KJV, NKJV). The following clause expresses the result of a man leaving his parents and joining his wife: the two become one flesh.

ἔσονται: The Greek word ἔσονται is a third-person plural future middle indicative from the verb εἰμί that means "to be" describing an event that will take place (BDAG, s.v. "εἰμί" 6, p. 285). **Syntactically**, ἔσονται functions as the main verb in the independent conjunctive clause introduced by καί. The subject of the verb is the substantive "the two" (οἱ δύο) referring to both husband and wife. The prepositional phrase εἰς σάρκα μίαν ("into one flesh") is a Hebraism. The construction functions as the predicate nominative (W, 47–48). **Semantically**, the future tense functions as gnomic future, which describes a generic event that will likely occur rather than a particular event (Hoehner, 774).

5:32a ἐστίν: The Greek word ἐστίν is a third-person singular present active indicative from the verb εἰμί that means "to be" (BDAG, s.v. "εἰμί" 2ca, p. 284). **Syntactically**, ἐστίν functions as the main verb of an independent asyndeton clause: "This mystery is great" (τὸ μυστήριον τοῦτο μέγα ἐστίν). The subject is "this mystery" (τὸ μυστήριον τοῦτο). The predicate nominative is the adjective "great" (μέγα). **Semantically**, the present tense functions as a gnomic present, which describes the action of the verb as a timeless fact. Throughout the letter, Paul develops the theme of a mystery (see Theological Nugget at 1:9a and 3:3a). In Ephesians 3, he reveals the mystery that God revealed to him—through the gospel Gentiles have become "fellow heirs, fellow members, fellow partakers of the promise in Christ Jesus" (Eph. 3:6). Paul's description of the marriage relationship provides a different facet of the mystery: the relationship between the church—made up of Jews and Gentiles—and Jesus.

Syntactical Nugget: What is the reference to "this mystery" (τὸ μυστήριον τοῦτο)? On the one hand, the mystery could refer to the marriage relationship, alluding to the Genesis 2:24 citation in verse 31. This interpretation makes the most sense of the flow of Paul's argument (Best, 553–54). On the other hand, it is best understood as referring to Christ and the church. First, Paul uses the citation as evidence for his statement in verse 30: "We are members of his body." Second, the following clause in verse 32b offsets a specific application of Genesis 2:24 to Christ and the church from the wider discussion of marriage. He brings the focus back to the marriage relationship in verse 33 with the conjunction πλήν ("nevertheless"). Finally, Paul uses comparative particles ὡς and καθώς to show the connection between the marriage relationship and the Christ/church relationship (Eph. 5:22, 23, 24, 25, 28, 33). However, he restricts his comments in verses 30–32 to discuss Christ and the church. Verse 33 concludes the section by picking up the specific commands for husbands and wives (Hoehner, 779–80; Arnold, 395–96; Lincoln, 382; Thielman, 389–90).

5:32b δέ: The Greek word δέ is a conjunction that means "but" (BDAG, s.v. "δέ" 2, p. 213). **Syntactically**, δέ is in the postpositive position introducing an independent conjunctive clause: "*But* I am speaking about Christ and about the church " (ἐγὼ δὲ λέγω εἰς Χριστὸν καὶ εἰς τὴν ἐκκλησίαν). **Semantically**, δέ is adversative, introducing a contrast with the previous context: "but" (NIV, NET, CSB, HCSB, NASB, NKJV, KJV). Jesus uses this phrase ("But I say") in the Sermon on the Mount to contrast his interpretation of the law with the Jewish interpretation (Matt. 5:22, 28, 32, 34, 39, 44). Paul uses the phrase to distinguish his interpretation of Christ and the church from the command for husbands and wives in verse 33.

λέγω: The Greek word λέγω is a first-person singular present active indicative from the verb λέγω that means "to say," "to tell," or "to give expression to" (BDAG, s.v. "λέγω" 1bα, p. 588). **Syntactically**, λέγω functions as the main verb of the independent conjunctive clause. The subject is "I" (ἐγώ) referring to Paul. **Semantically**, the present tense functions as an instantaneous present referring to the specific point of Paul's writing (W, 517–18). The preposition εἰς expresses a point of reference (BDAG, s.v. "εἰς" 5, p. 291). Paul limits his discussion to Christ and the church.

5:33a πλὴν καί: The Greek words πλήν is a conjunction that means "in any case" (BDAG, s.v. "πλήν" 1c, p. 826). The Greek word καί is a conjunction that means "also" in this context (BDAG, s.v. "καί" 2i, p. 496). **Syntactically**, the conjunctions πλὴν καί introduce an independent conjunctive clause: "*Nevertheless* each of you, love your own wife" (πλὴν καὶ ὑμεῖς οἱ καθ᾽ ἕνα ἕκαστος τὴν ἑαυτοῦ γυναῖκα οὕτως ἀγαπάτω). **Semantically**, πλήν is adversative. Robertson states that "Paul uses it at the end of an argument to single out the main point" (Robertson, 1187; BDF §449.2). The conjunction καί is adjunctive. The phrase marks a shift in Paul's discussion back to the relationship between husbands and wives. The shift to the second person underscores this change. The phrase "each one of you" (ὑμεῖς) brings the focus specifically to husbands and wives. The pronoun ὑμεῖς functions as a vocative. The prepositional phrase is modified with an article, making it substantival. The phrase functions distributively: "each one" (Robertson, 769; BDAG, s.v. "κατά" B3b, p. 512).

ἀγαπάτω: The Greek word ἀγαπάτω is a third-person singular present active imperative from the verb ἀγαπάω that means "to cherish," or "love" (BDAG, s.v. "ἀγαπάω" 1aα, p. 5). **Syntactically**, ἀγαπάτω functions as the main verb of the independent conjunctive clause. The subject is "each" (ἕκαστος). Even though Paul is not clear, he refers specifically to husbands. The direct object is "his own wife" (τὴν ἑαυτοῦ γυναῖκα). **Semantically**, ἀγαπάτω is a customary present: "let each one of you love" (ESV, RSV, cf. NKJV, KJV) or "each one of you also must love" (NIV, NET, NLT). The action of the verb should be ongoing. Paul expects husbands to habitually love their wives. (W, 521–22).

^{5:33b} ὡς: The Greek word ὡς is a conjunction that means "as" in this context (BDAG, s.v. "ὡς" 1a, p. 1103). **Syntactically**, ὡς introduces a dependent conjunctive clause: "as yourself" (ὡς ἑαυτόν). The clause functions adverbially modifying the preceding verb "love" (ἀγαπάτω). The conjunction corresponds with the adverb οὕτως (BDAG, s.v. "οὕτως" 2, p. 742). **Semantically**, ὡς expresses a comparison: "as" (ESV, RSV, NRSV, NIV, NET, CSB, HCSB, NASB, NKJV, NLT). The command, along with the comparison, is close to the command in verse 28: "husbands ought to love their own wives as they love their own bodies." Here Paul drops the reference to the body and simply inserts the reflexive pronoun: "as himself."

[ἀγαπᾷ]: The Greek word [ἀγαπᾷ] is a third-person singular present active indicative from the verb ἀγαπάω that means "to cherish," or "love" (BDAG, s.v. "ἀγαπάω" 1aα, p. 5). **Syntactically**, [ἀγαπᾷ] is an ellipsis, functioning as the verb of the dependent conjunctive clause introduced by ὡς. The subject is implied: "he," referring to Christian husbands. The direct object is "himself" (ἑαυτόν). **Semantically**, [ἀγαπᾷ] functions as a gnomic present describing a general, timeless fact (W, 523). Paul makes a similar ellipsis in verse 28b. The comparison provides a description of the husband's love for his wife. It should be as natural as one cares for his own body (cf. v. 29).

^{5:33c} δέ: The Greek word δέ is a conjunction that means "and" (BDAG, s.v. "δέ" 3, p. 213). **Syntactically**, δέ is in the postpositive position, introducing an

independent conjunctive clause: "but the wife should respect her husband" (ἡ δὲ γυνὴ ἵνα φοβῆται τὸν ἄνδρα). **Semantically**, δέ marks additional information: "and" (ESV, RSV, NRSV, NIV, NET, HCSB, CSB, NASB, NKJV, KJV). After repeating his command for men to love their wives (cf. vv. 25–28), he repeats his command for women to respect their husbands (cf. vv. 22–24).

ἵνα: The Greek word ἵνα is a conjunction that means "that" in this context (BDAG, s.v. "ἵνα" 2g, pp. 476–77). **Syntactically**, the conjunction ἵνα marks the clause as an imperatival ἵνα. Normally the conjunction introduces a dependent clause. If this is the case, the conjunction would modify an implied verb: "I wish" (θέλω) or "watch" (βλέπετε) (Larkin, 143; cf. ESV, NASB, NKJV, KJV). However, it might be best understood as introducing an imperative (W, 476–77; Robertson, 933; BDF §387.3; Moule, 144–45). In this case, the entire clause "a wife ought to respect her husband" (ἡ δὲ γυνὴ ἵνα φοβῆται τὸν ἄνδρα) functions as an independent clause in a parallel position to the previous command for men (Hoehner, 783; Arnold, 398). **Semantically**, the ἵνα clause marks the phrase as imperatival. The use of the subjunctive softens the tone of the command, which coheres with his subtle approach in the earlier portion of the passage (Eph. 5:22–24) (Thielman, 391; Barth, 648).

φοβῆται: The Greek word φοβῆται is a third-person singular present middle subjunctive from the verb φοβέω that means "to have reverence" or "respect," particularly for another person (BDAG, s.v. "φοβέω" 2b, p. 1062). **Syntactically**, φοβῆται functions as the main verb of the imperatival ἵνα clause introduced by δέ. The subject is "the wife" (ἡ γυνή). The direct object is "husband" (τὸν ἄνδρα). Even though there is no personal pronoun present in the Greek text, the article implies possession (W, 215–16). **Semantically**, the present tense functions as a customary present; Paul expects that wives habitually show their husbands respect. Some English versions render the verb as a command: "the wife *must respect* her husband" (NIV, NET), but the subjunctive should be softened: "the wife *is to respect* her husband" (CSB) or "a wife *should respect* her husband" (NRSV).

Lexical Nugget: What does Paul mean when he commands wives to "respect" their husbands? The section ends with a final command for wives to "respect" (φοβέω) their husbands. Earlier, Paul commanded wives to "submit" (ὑποτάσσω). By changing the verb from "submit" to "respect," he creates an *inclusio* with verse 21—all believers submitting to one another "in the fear of Christ" (ἐν φόβῳ Χριστοῦ). The Greek word φοβέω often carries the notion of fear as terror (Matt. 17:6; Acts 5:26). Both notions appear in the Old Testament. In Genesis, Jacob was afraid of Esau (Gen. 32:8, 12) because of the wrong he did against him. On the other hand, the righteous "fear the Lord" (Gen. 42:18; Prov. 3:7; 14:2; 24:21). For the righteous, this fear of the Lord provides an impetus to act—not out of fear, but from deep respect. In the same way, wives should show respect to their husbands. Finally, it is important to note that the commands are parallel to one another. Paul expects women to respect their husbands due to their position in the family, not as a response to their husbands' love. Likewise, men are to love their wives, even when they do not receive respect from their wives.

EPHESIANS 6:1–4

Big Greek Idea: Children should obey and honor their parents; fathers should raise their children without provoking them to anger, disciplining them and teaching them with Christian instruction.

Structural Overview: Ephesians 6:1–4 is a part of a larger section that Paul began in Ephesians 5:15. At the end of that section, Paul exhorts believers to be filled by the Spirit and as a result submit to one another. The participle "submit" in Ephesians 5:21 serves as the impetus behind the household code. The second part of the household code, or this third subsection, addresses children and their parents.

Paul addresses children first. He gives them two overlapping commands: to obey their parents (v. 1) and to honor them (v. 2). He gives the second command to link the exhortation to the Old Testament (Exod. 20:12; Deut. 5:16). He gives two reasons for the command. The first reason is that it is right (v. 1). The second reason is that the Old Testament links it to a promise: that you will live long in the land.

In verse 4, Paul addresses fathers. He shifts the address from parents to fathers since the father would have had ultimate responsibility for their children. He commands these fathers to avoid provoking their children to anger. Rather they should nurture their children, giving them Christian instruction. Paul does not give a reason for the command. This is the only command throughout the household code without some rationale. He may have assumed that parents understood their role in raising their children, but felt the need to frame their parenting within a Christian context.

Outline:

> Children should obey their parents because it is right (vv. 1–3)
>> Children should obey their parents because it is right (v. 1)
>> Children should honor their parents so they will have a long life (vv. 2–3)
>
> Fathers should not provoke their children to anger, but raise them within a Christian context (v. 4)

CLAUSAL OUTLINE FOR EPHESIANS 6:1–4

6:1a Τὰ τέκνα, **ὑπακούετε** τοῖς γονεῦσιν ὑμῶν ἐν κυρίῳ,
6:1a Children, **obey** your parents in the Lord,

6:1b τοῦτο γὰρ **ἐστιν** δίκαιον.
6:1b <u>for</u> this **is** right.

6:2a **τίμα** τὸν πατέρα σου καὶ τὴν μητέρα,
6:2a **Honor** your father and mother,

    |

    6:2b ἥτις **ἐστὶν** ἐντολὴ πρώτη ἐν ἐπαγγελίᾳ,
    6:2b as it **is** the first commandment with a promise,

[ὑπακούετε (v. 1a), τίμα (v. 2a]
[obey (v. 1a), honor (v. 2a)]

    |

    6:3a **ἵνα** εὖ σοι **γένηται**
    6:3a **that it may be** well for you

    6:3b <u>καὶ</u> **ἔσῃ** μακροχρόνιος ἐπὶ τῆς γῆς.
    6:3b <u>and</u> **you will** live long in the land.

6:4a <u>Καὶ</u> οἱ πατέρες, μὴ **παροργίζετε** τὰ τέκνα ὑμῶν,
6:4a <u>And</u> fathers, **do** not **anger** your children,

6:4b <u>ἀλλὰ</u> **ἐκτρέφετε** αὐτὰ ἐν παιδείᾳ καὶ νουθεσίᾳ κυρίου.
6:4b <u>but</u> **bring them up** with discipline and instruction from the Lord.

Syntax Explained for Ephesians 6:1–4

6:1a ὑπακούετε: The Greek word ὑπακούετε is a second-person plural present active imperative from the verb ὑπακούω that means, "to obey," "follow," or "be subject" (BDAG, s.v. "ὑπακούω" 1, pp. 1028–29). **Syntactically**, ὑπακούετε functions as the main verb of the asyndeton clause: "Children, obey your parents in the Lord" (Τὰ τέκνα, ὑπακούετε τοῖς γονεῦσιν ὑμῶν ἐν κυρίῳ). The subject is implied: "you." The nominative "children" (Τὰ τέκνα) functions as a nominative for vocative. The vocative signals a change in address to discuss the relationship between children and their parents. Paul uses a similar technique throughout this section (Eph. 5:22, 25; 6:4, 5, 9). The direct object is "your parents" (τοῖς γονεῦσιν ὑμῶν). **Semantically**, ὑπακούετε is a customary present: "obey" (ESV, RSV, NRSV, NIV, NET, CSB, HCSB, NASB, NKJV, KJV, NLT). The action of the verb is ongoing. Paul wants children to habitually obey their parents (W, 521–22, 722).

Syntactical Nugget: How does the prepositional phrase "in the Lord" (ἐν κυρίῳ) relate to the context? The phrase could either modify "your parents" (τοῖς γονεῦσιν ὑμῶν), suggesting that Paul limits this command to Christian parents, or the verb "obey" (ὑπακούετε), expressing the sphere in which children should obey their parents. While the first option is possible, it is unlikely that Paul would have limited the command to only Christian parents. Paul gives a similar command in Colossians: "Children obey your parents in all things, for this is pleasing in the Lord" (Col. 3:20). In Colossians, Paul suggests that a child's obedience is a response to Christ. This interpretation is consistent with his commands to wives and slaves, who are to submit as they would to the Lord (Eph. 5:22; 6:5) (Hoehner, 786–87).

Text-Critical Nugget: Is the prepositional phrase "in the Lord" (ἐν κυρίῳ) part of the text? Several Western manuscripts (D, F, G) along with a significant Alexandrian manuscript (B) omit the prepositional phrase "in the Lord" (ἐν κυρίῳ). However, the majority of Alexandrian (𝔓⁴⁶, א, A, 33, 81, 104, 1175, 1739, 1181) and Byzantine manuscripts (K, L, 𝔐) include the prepositional phrase. In Ephesians 5:22, Paul gives women a command to submit to their husbands "as to the Lord" (ὡς τῷ κυρίῳ); likewise, in 6:5 slaves are commanded to obey their masters "as to Christ" (ὡς τῷ Χριστῷ). It is possible that these commands influenced a scribe to insert the prepositional phrase; however, if this is the case, we would anticipate the comparative conjunction "as" (ὡς), not the prepositional phrase. Even though the omission is supported by impressive manuscripts, the external evidence points to the inclusion. Internally, it is more probable that a scribe omitted the phrase rather than inserting it.

^{6:1b} γάρ: The Greek word γάρ is a conjunction that means "for" or "therefore" (BDAG, s.v. "γάρ" 1b, p. 189). **Syntactically**, γάρ is in a postpositive position, introducing an independent conjunctive clause: "*For* this is right" (τοῦτο γάρ ἐστιν δίκαιον). **Semantically**, γάρ expresses the reason for Paul's command: "for" (ESV, RSV, NRSV, NIV, NET, NASB, NKJV, KJV, NLT) or "because" (CSB, HCSB). Children should obey their parents because it is right.

ἐστίν: The Greek word ἐστίν is a third-person singular present active indicative from the verb εἰμί that means "to be" (BDAG, s.v. "εἰμί" 2b, p. 283). **Syntactically**, ἐστίν functions as the main verb of the independent conjunctive clause introduced by γάρ. The subject is "this" (τοῦτο). The antecedent of the neuter demonstrative pronoun refers to the previous command. The adjective "right" (δίκαιον) functions as the predicate nominative. **Semantically**, the present tense functions as a gnomic present, which describes the action of the verb as a general, timeless fact (W, 523). In verse 2, Paul cites the Old Testament command for children to honor their parents, highlighting the abiding nature of the command.

^{6:2a} τίμα: The Greek word τίμα is a second-person singular present active imperative from the verb τιμάω that means "to honor" or "to revere" (BDAG, s.v. "τιμάω" 2, pp. 1004–5). **Syntactically**, τίμα functions as the main verb of the asyndeton clause: "Honor your father and mother" (τίμα τὸν πατέρα

σου καὶ τὴν μητέρα). The subject is implied by the verb: "you," referring to the Ephesian children. The direct objects are "your father and mother" (τὸν πατέρα σου and τὴν μητέρα). **Semantically**, τίμα is a customary present: "honor" (ESV, RSV, NRSV, NIV, NET, CSB, HCSB, NASB, NKJV, KJV, NLT). The action of the verb is ongoing. Paul wants children to habitually obey their parents (W, 521–22, 722).

> **Lexical Nugget**: What does Paul mean when he instructs children to "honor" their parents? By citing the Old Testament passage (Exod. 20:12; Deut. 5:16), Paul changes the command for children to "obey" (ὑπακούω) your parents to "honor" (τιμάω) them. There is a significant overlap between the two terms—obedience carries an outward action, while honor describes an internal motivation. Within the Old Testament context, the concept of honor would have been broader than obedience, but it would have encompassed it as well. A child showed honor to their parents by obeying them; likewise, they would have shown them dishonor through disobedience (Deut. 21:18–21; 27:16) (Hoehner, 788; Best, 565).

6:2b ἥτις: The Greek word ἥτις is a feminine singular nominative from the indefinite relative pronoun ὅστις that means "which" in this context. The relative pronoun emphasizes the quality of the command (BDAG, s.v. "ὅστις" 2b, pp. 729–30). Most English versions render the pronoun as "which" (NIV, NET, CSB, HCSB, NASB, KJV, NKJV), but it might be better translated as "as it is" (Hoehner, 789; W, 343–44). **Syntactically**, ἥτις introduces a dependent adjectival relative clause: "*which* is the first command with a promise" (ἥτις ἐστὶν ἐντολὴ πρώτη ἐν ἐπαγγελίᾳ). The phrase modifies the command in verse 2a, but the gender comes from the feminine noun ἐντολή ("command"). The relative clause breaks the Old Testament quote, which he picks up in verse 3. Since the relative clause is a digression several English versions render the relative pronoun as a demonstrative and offset the clause with parentheses or dashes: "(this is the first commandment with a promise)" (ESV, RSV; cf. NRSV, NLT).

ἐστίν: The Greek word ἐστίν is a third-person singular present active indicative from the verb εἰμί that means "to be" (BDAG, s.v. "εἰμί" 2ca, p. 284). **Syntactically**, ἐστίν functions as the main verb of the relative clause: "which is the first commandment with a promise" (ἥτις ἐστὶν ἐντολὴ πρώτη ἐν ἐπαγγελίᾳ). The subject is the relative pronoun (ἥτις). The predicate nominative is "the first commandment" (ἐντολὴ πρώτη). **Semantically**, the present tense functions as a gnomic present, which describes the action of the verb as a general, timeless fact (W, 523–24).

> **Lexical Nugget**: What does Paul mean by the "first command" (ἐντολὴ πρώτη)? The adjective "first" (πρῶτος) could either mean the first in a

series (BDAG, s.v. "πρῶτος" 1bα, p. 893) or the foremost, most prominent (BDAG, s.v. "πρῶτος" 2aα, p. 893; Best, 566–67). The most obvious problem with seeing this as the first in a series is that it is neither the first command (it is the fifth) nor the first command with a promise (the second command gives a negative promise—a warning against worshiping other gods). However, there are problems with understanding this as the foremost command. Jesus states that the "greatest and first" command is to "love the Lord your God with your whole heart and your whole soul, and your whole mind" (Matt. 22:37–38). The first option is perhaps the simplest. Most commentators note that the promise attached to the second command is actually a broad statement applicable to all of the commands (Lincoln, 404). The command to honor one's parents appears to be the first with a specific promise attached to it (Thielman, 398–99; Hoehner, 790–91).

6:3a ἵνα: The Greek word ἵνα is a conjunction that means "that" or "so that" in this context (BDAG, s.v. "ἵνα" 1aα, p. 475). **Syntactically**, ἵνα introduces a dependent conjunctive clause: "that it might go well with you" (ἵνα εὖ σοι γένηται). The clause functions adverbially, modifying the imperatives ὑπακούετε and τίμα. **Semantically**, the ἵνα expresses purpose: "so that" (NRSV, NIV, CSB, HCSB, NASB) or "that" (ESV, RSV, NET, NKJV, KJV). Children should honor their parents to reap the benefit of blessing in the land. The NLT renders the phrase as a conditional statement: "If you honor your father and mother, things will go well for you."

γένηται: The Greek word γένηται is a third-person singular aorist middle (deponent) subjunctive from the verb γίνομαι that means "to happen," "turn out," or "take place" (BDAG, s.v. "γίνομαι" 4bβ, pp. 197–98). **Syntactically**, γένηται functions as the main verb of the conjunctive dependent ἵνα clause. The subject is implied by the verb: "It may be well for you." The adverb εὖ is an adverb of manner describing something relationally or experientially "good" (BDAG, s.v. "εὖ" 1, pp. 401–2; BDF §102.3). **Semantically**, γένηται is a constative aorist: "may be" (RSV, NRSV, NASB, NKJV, KJV). It describes the action of the verb as a whole (W, 557–58). Some English versions capture this by rendering the verb: "it may go well" (ESV, NIV, NET, CSB, HCSB, NLT).

6:3b καί: The Greek word καί is a conjunction that means "and" (BDAG, s.v. "καί" 1bγ, p. 494). **Syntactically**, καί introduces an independent conjunctive clause: "*And* you will live long in the land" (καὶ ἔσῃ μακροχρόνιος ἐπὶ τῆς γῆς). **Semantically**, καί is a coordinating connective: "and" (ESV, RSV, NRSV, NIV, NET, CSB, HCSB, NASB, KJV, NKJV). The clause echoes the blessing in verse 3a, specifying that this will occur "in the land."

ἔσῃ: The Greek word ἔσῃ is a second-person singular future middle indicative from the verb εἰμί that means "to be" (BDAG, s.v. "εἰμί" 6, p. 285).

Syntactically, ἔση functions as the main verb of the dependent conjunctive clause introduced by ἵνα. The subject is implied by the verb: "you," referring to those children who obey their parents. The predicate adjective is "long-lived" (μακροχρόνιος). This is the only occurrence of the term in the New Testament. It refers to a "long duration of time" (L&N, 67.89; BDAG, s.v. "μακροχρόνιος," p. 613). **Semantically**, the future tense functions as a predictive future. Generally, a subjunctive verb follows a ἵνα. The original Old Testament quote (Exod. 20:12; Deut. 5:16) contains the aorist subjunctive form of γίνομαι (ἵνα μακροχρόνιος γένῃ). However, Paul uses the future indicative form elsewhere (Gal. 2:4; 1 Cor. 9:18). Paul's use of the future indicative form instead of the aorist subjunctive points to the expectation of the promised reward (Hoehner, 792; Robertson, 875).

> **Theological Nugget**: What does the prepositional phrase "in the land" mean? In the original context, the promise refers to a life of blessing in the land of Israel—the Promised Land. In the present context, Paul applies the promise to Gentile believers. It is possible that he generalizes the promise by omitting the following relative clause; "which the Lord your God gave to you" (Arnold, 417; Hoehner, 793). Some have suggested that the promise refers to eternal life; however, it is best to understand that the promise refers to physical life on the earth. The adjective μακροχρόνιος ("long-lived") does not seem to have an immortal duration and the prepositional phrase "on the earth" (ἐπὶ τῆς γῆς) indicates the sphere in which this life occurs. There is a danger in pressing the promise too far—obedient children, for inexplicable reasons have died untimely deaths. Like other proverbs, the statement follows a general pattern. Children who follow the advice of their parents will fare better in life than those who do not (Osborne, 211; Arnold, 417; Thielman, 400–401).

6:4a καί: The Greek word καί is a conjunction that means "and" (BDAG, s.v. "καί" 1e, p. 495). **Syntactically**, καί introduces an independent conjunctive clause: "*And* fathers, do not anger your children" (Καὶ οἱ πατέρες, μὴ παροργίζετε τὰ τέκνα ὑμῶν). **Semantically**, καί is transitional, moving from the command for children (Eph. 6:1–2) to the command given to fathers: "and" (NRSV, NKJV, KJV). Paul makes the same connection in verse 9. Several English versions omit the conjunction since there is no coordination (ESV, RSV, NIV, NET, CSB, HCSB, NASB).

παροργίζετε: The Greek word παροργίζετε is a second-person plural present active imperative from the verb παροργίζω that means "to make angry" (BDAG, s.v. "παροργίζω," p. 780) or "provoke to anger" (ESV, NRSV, RSV, NET, NASB). The NIV renders the verb as "exasperate." **Syntactically**, παροργίζετε functions as the main verb of the independent conjunctive clause introduced by καί. The subject is implied by the verb: "you." The nominative "fathers" (οἱ πατέρες) functions as a nominative for vocative. The vocative signals a change in address (cf. Eph. 5:22, 25; 6:1, 5, 9). The direct object is "your children" (τὰ τέκνα ὑμῶν). **Semantically**, παροργίζετε functions as a customary present, which expresses the prohibition as a general precept for fathers to follow (W, 724–25). Paul wants fathers to make it a habit to avoid angering their children.

Lexical Nugget: Why does Paul change his address from "parents" to "fathers"? In verse 1, Paul indicates that children should obey both parents. He uses the Greek term γονεύς, a reference to both parents (BDAG, s.v. "γονεύς," p. 205). He confirms this by citing Exodus 20:12. But in verse 4, he addresses only "fathers" (οἱ πατέρες) (cf. ESV, NRSV, RSV, NET, CSB, HCSB, NASB, NKJV, KJV, NLT). It is possible that Paul has both parents in mind, since he addressed both parents in the earlier section (BDAG, s.v. "πατήρ" 1b, p. 786; Larkin, 147). On the other hand, he most likely has men in mind. Within both a Jewish and Roman context, the father would have held ultimate responsibility for their children.

6:4b ἀλλά: The Greek word ἀλλά is a conjunction that means "but" (BDAG, s.v. "ἀλλά" 1a, p. 45). **Syntactically**, ἀλλά introduces an independent conjunctive clause: "*but* bring them up in discipline and instruction of the Lord" (ἀλλὰ ἐκτρέφετε αὐτὰ ἐν παιδείᾳ καὶ νουθεσίᾳ κυρίου). **Semantically**, ἀλλά is a contrastive conjunction: "but" (ESV, NRSV, RSV, NET, CSB, HCSB, NASB, NKJV, KJV) or "rather" (NIV, NLT). After giving a prohibition to these fathers, Paul gives a positive command for them to raise them with discipline and instruction.

ἐκτρέφετε: The Greek word ἐκτρέφετε is a second-person plural present active imperative from the verb ἐκτρέφω that means "to rear" or "bring up" (BDAG, s.v. "ἐκτρέφω" 2, p. 311). The word appears twice in the New Testament, both times in Ephesians. In Ephesians 5:29, Paul uses the same term to describe how one might treat his own body—by feeding it. **Syntactically**, ἐκτρέφετε functions as the main verb of the independent conjunctive clause introduced by ἀλλά. The subject is implied by the verb: "you," referring to "fathers" (cf. v. 4a). The direct object is "them" (αὐτά), referring to the children. The demonstrative is neuter, because of the gender of the antecedent (τὰ τέκνα; cf. v. 1). **Semantically**, ἐκτρέφετε functions as a customary present: "bring up" (ESV, RSV, NRSV, NIV, CSB, HCSB, NASB, NKJV, KJV, NLT). The NET translates it "raise them up." The present imperative expresses a general precept (W, 724–25). The following prepositional phrase "in discipline and instruction" expresses instrument—fathers should raise their children *"with* discipline and instruction" (NLT). Finally, the genitive κυρίου ("Lord") refers to Christ. The genitive most likely functions as a subjective genitive (or a genitive of source): "instruction that comes *from* the Lord" (NLT) (Arnold, 418; Thielman, 402).

EPHESIANS 6:5–9

Big Greek Idea: Slaves should obey their masters wholeheartedly as if they are serving the Lord himself; masters should treat their slaves with the same respect, knowing that they also serve the Lord, who judges without partiality.

Structural Overview: Ephesians 6:5–9 is the final part of a section that Paul began in Ephesians 5:15. At the end of the section, Paul encourages believers to be filled by the Spirit and as a result submit to one another. The participle "submit" in Ephesians 5:21 serves as the impetus behind the household code. The third part of the household code, or this fourth subsection, addresses slaves and masters.

Paul first addresses slaves. He commands them to serve their earthly masters with a wholehearted devotion as they are serving the Lord (vv. 6–7). This service should be sincere, not just when people are watching. He gives the reason for this obedience in verse 8: God will reward both those who are free and slaves for what they have done (v. 8).

Paul's rationale for the slave's service looks forward to his command for masters as well—God will give back to those according to their work. He commands these masters to "do the same" for their slaves (v. 9). The intention is not clear, but Paul probably has verse 8 in mind: "doing good." Specifically, he states that masters should stop threatening their slaves. The reason for this command is that their Lord will judge both slaves and masters without partiality. At this point, Paul inserts a wordplay with the Greek word κύριος, which is lost in English. On the one hand, slaves should do what is good, knowing that they will receive this back from the Lord (κύριος). On the other hand, masters (κύριος) should treat their slaves well, because their Lord (or "Master" [κύριος]) is in heaven.

Outline:

> Slaves should obey their masters as if they were serving the Lord (vv. 5–8)
> Masters should treat their slaves with the same respect given to them (v. 9)

CLAUSAL OUTLINE FOR EPHESIANS 6:5–9

6:5a Οἱ δοῦλοι, **ὑπακούετε** τοῖς κατὰ σάρκα κυρίοις μετὰ φόβου καὶ τρόμου ἐν ἁπλότητι τῆς καρδίας ὑμῶν

6:5a Slaves, **obey** your humanly masters with fear and trembling in sincerity of your heart

6:5b ὡς [**ὑπακούετε**] τῷ Χριστῷ,

6:5b as [**you obey**] Christ,

6:6a μὴ κατ᾽ ὀφθαλμοδουλίαν

6:6a not by being watched,

6:6b ὡς [**ὑπάκουσι**] ἀνθρωπάρεσκοι

6:6b as people pleasers,

6:6c ἀλλ᾽ ὡς [**ὑπάκουσι**] δοῦλοι Χριστοῦ

6:6c but as slaves of Christ

6:6d **ποιοῦντες** τὸ θέλημα τοῦ θεοῦ ἐκ ψυχῆς,

6:6d **by doing** the will of God from your heart,

6:7a μετ᾽ εὐνοίας **δουλεύοντες**,

6:7a **by serving** with goodwill

6:7b ὡς [**δουλεύετε**] τῷ κυρίῳ καὶ οὐκ ἀνθρώποις,

6:7b as [**you are serving**] the Lord and not men,

[ὑπακούετε (v. 5a)]

6:8a **εἰδότες**

6:8a **because you know**

6:8b **ὅτι** ἕκαστος … τοῦτο **κομίσεται** παρὰ κυρίου, εἴτε δοῦλος εἴτε ἐλεύθερος.

6:8b **that** each of you, whether slave or free,… **will receive** this **back** from the Lord.

6:8c ἐάν τι **ποιήσῃ** ἀγαθόν

6:8c **if you do** something good

[6:9a] Καὶ οἱ κύριοι, τὰ αὐτὰ **ποιεῖτε** πρὸς αὐτούς,

[6:9a] __And__ masters, __do__ the same to them,

      [6:9b] **ἀνιέντες** τὴν ἀπειλήν,

      [6:9b] __by stopping__ your threats,

      [6:9c] **εἰδότες**

      [6:9c] __because you know__

        [6:9d] **ὅτι** καὶ αὐτῶν καὶ ὑμῶν ὁ κύριός **ἐστιν** ἐν οὐρανοῖς,

        [6:9d] __that__ also their Lord and yours __is__ in heaven

        [6:9e] καὶ προσωπολημψία οὐκ **ἔστιν** παρ᾽ αὐτῷ.

        [6:9e] __and__ there __is__ no partiality with him.

SYNTAX EXPLAINED FOR EPHESIANS 6:5–9

[6:5a] ὑπακούετε: The Greek word ὑπακούετε is a second-person plural present active imperative from the verb ὑπακούω that means "to obey," "to follow," or "to be subject" (BDAG, s.v. "ὑπακούω" 1, pp. 1028–29). **Syntactically**, ὑπακούετε functions as the main verb of the asyndeton clause. The subject is implied by the verb: "you." The nominative "slaves" (οἱ δοῦλοι) functions as a nominative for vocative. The vocative signals a change in address to discuss the relationship between slaves and their masters. Paul uses a similar technique throughout this section (cf. Eph. 5:22, 25; 6:1, 4, 9). The dative "masters" (τοῖς κυρίοις) functions as the direct object. The prepositional phrase "according to flesh" (κατὰ σάρκα) modifies the dative, clarifying the kind of master: "*human* masters" (NET, CSB, HCSB) or "*earthly* masters" (ESV, RSV, NRSV, NIV) (BDAG, s.v. "σάρξ" 5, p. 916) **Semantically**, ὑπακούετε is a customary present: "obey" (ESV, NRSV, NIV, NET, CSB, HCSB) or "be obedient" (RSV, NASB, KJV, NKJV). Paul wants this kind of obedience to be habitual (W, 521–22). The verb is modified by two prepositional phrases. Both express manner. First, these slaves should obey their masters with "with fear and trembling" (μετὰ φόβου καὶ τρόμου). "Fear" can carry the notion of terror, but here most likely means "respect" (BDAG, s.v. "φόβος" 2ba, p. 1062; cf. Eph. 5:21, 33). The Greek word τρόμος means "trembling" (BDAG, s.v. "τρόμος" p. 1016). This is the outward appearance of fear. The word is often combined with φόβος (1 Cor. 2:3; 2 Cor. 7:15; Phil. 2:12; Hoehner, 806–7). Second, these slaves should obey "in sincerity of your heart" (ἐν ἁπλότητι τῆς καρδίας ὑμῶν). The Greek word ἁπλότης means "sincerity" or "uprightness" (BDAG, s.v. "ἁπλότης" 1, p. 104). The genitive τῆς καρδίας is an attributed genitive: "sincere *heart*" (ESV). Paul will present the opposite in the following verse—in outward appearance to please men. Here he indicates that this is without ulterior motives.

Theological Nugget: Did Paul condone slavery? Paul's comments about slavery seem to approve of the institution, at least implicitly, raising the question about his view of slavery. To begin with, slavery in a Greco-Roman context differs from slavery in a Western context. American slavery in the nineteenth century was race-based. In a Greco-Roman context, anyone could be a slave. Most were either sold into slavery to repay debt (Matt. 18:25) or else were prisoners of war. Roman law allowed for the emancipation of slaves—either after a debt was repaid (Matt. 18:34) or once a slave reached a certain age (Richards and O'Brien, 2016, 77–79). Despite these differences, slavery within a Greco-Roman context was just as horrific. In *Nicomachean Ethics*, Aristotle compares slaves to other tools: "there can be no friendship, nor justice, towards inanimate things; indeed not even towards a horse or an ox, nor yet towards a slave as a slave. For master and slave have nothing in common: a slave is a living tool, just as a tool is an inanimate slave" (*Eth. nic.* 8.11.6). Most considered slaves with diminished capacity—they were less than human. Owners could abuse slaves with no retribution. Paul certainly would have been aware of the treatment of slaves, and he instructs slaves to seek freedom if possible (1 Cor. 7:20–21), but he did not condemn the institution. Regardless, his comments about slavery are stark when read against the cultural background. Even though there might be a hierarchy between slaves and masters within the household structure, Paul evens the playing field. He instructs slaves to work as "slaves of Christ" (Eph. 6:6). In the following section, he reminds slave owners that they have a "master in heaven" (Eph. 6:9). Despite this structure, both slaves and slave owners are brothers and slaves to Christ (cf. Philem. 16; Richards and O'Brien, 2016, 89–91).

6:5b ὡς: The Greek word ὡς is a conjunction that means "as" in this context (BDAG, s.v. "ὡς" 1bα, p. 1103–4). **Syntactically**, ὡς introduces a dependent conjunctive clause "*as* to the Christ" (ὡς τῷ Χριστῷ). The entire clause functions adverbially, modifying the verb "obey" (ὑπακούετε; v. 5a). **Semantically**, ὡς expresses comparison: "as" (ESV, RSV, NRSV, NET, CSB, HCSB, NASB, NKJV, KJV). Slaves should obey their masters as they would obey Christ himself. Paul bears this out in his following comments (vv. 6–7).

[ὑπακούετε]: The Greek ellipsis ὑπακούετε is a second-person plural present active imperative from the verb ὑπακούω that means "to obey," "to follow," or "to be subject" (BDAG, s.v. "ὑπακούω" 1, p. 1028–29). **Syntactically**, the elliptical ὑπακούετε is the main verb of the dependent conjunctive clause introduced by ὡς. The subject is implied by the verb: "you," referring to slaves. The direct object is "Christ" (τῷ Χριστῷ). **Semantically**, ὑπακούετε is a customary present: "obey" (NRSV, NIV). The present tense describes an ongoing state (W, 521–22). Most English versions omit the elliptical verb: "as to Christ" (RSV, HCSB, NASB, NET, NKJV) or "as you would Christ" (ESV, CSB).

Syntactical Nugget: What does the prepositional phrase κατ' ὀφθαλμοδουλίαν modify? While the prepositional phrase could modify the elliptical verb ὑπακούετε, it most likely modifies the main verb of the sentence in verse 5a: "Slaves, obey your humanly masters" (Οἱ δοῦλοι, ὑπακούετε τοῖς κατὰ σάρκα κυρίοις). The preposition κατά expresses the standard by which a slave should obey his or her master (BDAG, s.v. "κατά" B5bβ, p. 513). The object of the preposition (ὀφθαλμοδουλίαν) literally means "eye-service." The idea is that slaves do not work only when the owner is present (BDAG, s.v. "ὀφθαλμοδουλία", pp. 743–44; cf. RSV, ESV, NASB, KJV, NKJV).

6:6b ὡς: The Greek word ὡς is a conjunction that means "as" in this context (BDAG, s.v. "ὡς" 1bα, p. 1103–4). **Syntactically**, ὡς introduces a dependent conjunctive clause "*as* people pleasers" (ὡς ἀνθρωπάρεσκοι). The entire clause functions adverbially, modifying the prepositional phrase "not by being watched" (μὴ κατ' ὀφθαλμοδουλίαν). The nominative ἀνθρωπάρεσκοι functions as the subject of an implied verb: ὑπάκουσι (as people pleasers *obey*) (Larkin, 151). **Semantically**, ὡς expresses comparison: "as" (ESV, RSV, NET, CSB, NASB, NKJV, KJV). The clause describes those who serve only while they are being watched. Believers are not to work like this.

6:6c ἀλλ': The Greek word ἀλλά is a conjunction that means "but" (BDAG, s.v. "ἀλλά" 1a, p. 45). **Syntactically**, ἀλλά introduces a dependent conjunctive clause: "*but* as slaves of Christ" (ἀλλ' ὡς δοῦλοι Χριστοῦ). **Semantically**, ἀλλά is a contrastive conjunction: "but" (ESV, RSV, NRSV, NIV, NET, CSB, HCSB, NASB, NKJV, KJV). After giving a negative description of how these slaves should serve their masters, Paul gives a positive description.

ὡς: The Greek word ὡς is a conjunction that means "as" in this context (BDAG, s.v. "ὡς" 1bα, p. 1103–4). **Syntactically**, ὡς introduces a dependent conjunctive clause "*as* slaves of Christ" (ὡς δοῦλοι Χριστοῦ). The clause functions adverbially, modifying the main verb of the sentence: "obey your humanly masters" (ὑπακούετε τοῖς κατὰ σάρκα κυρίοις). **Semantically**, ὡς expresses comparison: "as" (ESV, RSV, NET, CSB, NASB, NKJV, KJV). The clause describes a positive contrast to verse 6b.

[ὑπάκουσι]: The Greek ellipsis ὑπάκουσι is a third-person plural present active imperative from the verb ὑπακούω that means "to obey," "to follow," or "to be subject" (BDAG, s.v. "ὑπακούω" 1, p. 1028–29). **Syntactically**, the elliptical ὑπάκουσι is the main verb of the dependent conjunctive clause introduced by ὡς. The subject is implied by the verb: "slaves of Christ" (δοῦλοι Χριστοῦ). **Semantically**, ὑπάκουσι is a customary present. The present tense describes an ongoing state (W, 521–22). Most English versions omit the elliptical verb.

6:6d ποιοῦντες: The Greek word ποιοῦντες is a masculine nominative plural present active participle from the verb ποιέω that means "to do," "to keep," or "to practice" (BDAG, s.v. "ποιέω" 3a, pp. 840–41). **Syntactically**, ποιοῦντες introduces a dependent participle clause. Some argue that the participle is attributive modifying δοῦλοι: "slaves of Christ *who* do the will of God" (Larkin, 151; Merkle, 203). However, it might be best understood as an adverbial participle modifying the main verb: "obey" (ὑπακούετε; v. 5), describing how these slaves should obey their earthly masters (Hoehner, 809). The phrase "the will of God" (τὸ θέλημα τοῦ θεοῦ) functions as the direct object of the participle. **Semantically**, the present tense indicates that the action of the participle is simultaneous with the action of the main verb. The participle functions as manner, describing how the action of the main verb is completed: "*by* doing the will of God from the heart."

> **Lexical Nugget**: What does the prepositional phrase "from the heart" (ἐκ ψυχῆς) mean? The prepositional phrase modifies the participle phrase "doing the will of God." The preposition ἐκ best expresses the source from which one does the will of God (BDAG, s.v. "ἐκ" 3gγ, p. 297) The object of the preposition, ψυχῆς ("soul"), can refer to the center of one's inner life of their feelings and emotions—the soul (BDAG, s.v. "ψυχή" 2c, p. 1099). The phrase means that the slave should serve "wholeheartedly." The NLT renders the phrase as "with all your heart." Paul uses a synonymous phrase in verse 5—obey "with a sincere heart." This inner motivation contrasts those who only serve to please others (vv. 6a–6b).

6:7a δουλεύοντες: The Greek word δουλεύοντες is a masculine nominative plural present active participle from the verb δουλεύω that means, "to perform the duties of a slave," or "to serve" (BDAG, s.v. "δουλεύω" 2aα, p. 259). **Syntactically**, δουλεύοντες introduces a dependent participle clause. Larkin classifies this as an attributive participle parallel to ποιοῦντες modifying δοῦλοι: "slaves of Christ … *who* serve with good will" (Larkin, 151; Best, 578). However, it might be best to understand the participle as an adverbial participle modifying the main verb "obey" (ὑπακούετε; v. 5), describing how these slaves should obey their earthly masters (Hoehner, 810; Arnold, 424). **Semantically**, the present tense indicates that the action of the participle is simultaneous with the action of the main verb. The participle functions as manner: "*by* serving with a good attitude." The participle phrase describes the attitude of the slave as they serve their master. The prepositional phrase "with goodwill" (μετ᾽ εὐνοίας) describes the manner in which they should serve. The Greek word εὔνοια refers to a positive attitude within a relationship (BDAG, s.v. "εὔνοια" 2, p. 409). The opposite idea is to serve with ill will or harboring resentment. This attitude might be hard for slaves to maintain within a system filled with injustice (Thielman, 407; Hoehner, 810–11).

6:7b ὡς: The Greek word ὡς is a conjunction that means "as" in this context (BDAG, s.v. "ὡς" 1bα, p. 1103–4). **Syntactically**, ὡς introduces a dependent conjunctive clause: "*as* to the Lord and not to men" (ὡς τῷ κυρίῳ καὶ οὐκ ἀνθρώποις). The entire clause functions adverbially, modifying the participle δουλεύοντες (v. 7a). Most English versions omit the elliptical verb: "as to the Lord" (ESV, RSV, NRSV, CSB, HCSB, NASB, NKJV, KJV). The NIV supplies the verb, rendering the phrase: "as if *you were serving* the Lord" (cf. NET). **Semantically**, ὡς expresses a comparison. The following phrase presents a negative contrast: "and not to men." The clause describes how slaves should serve their masters—as they might serve Christ and not men.

[δουλεύετε]: The Greek word [δουλεύετε] is a second-person present active indicative from the verb δουλεύω that means, "to perform the duties of a slave," or "to serve" (BDAG, s.v. "δουλεύω" 2aα, p. 259). **Syntactically**, the elliptical δουλεύετε is the main verb of the dependent conjunctive clause introduced by ὡς. The subject is implied by the verb "you," referring to those slaves Paul is addressing. The datives τῷ κυρίῳ "the Lord" and ἀνθρώποις "men" function as the direct object of the implied verb δουλεύετε: "serve the Lord and not men," (Larkin, 152). **Semantically**, δουλεύετε is a customary present. The present tense describes an ongoing state (W, 521–22). Most English versions omit the elliptical verb: "as to the Lord" (ESV, RSV, NRSV, CSB, CSB, NASB, NKJV, KJV). The NLT renders the phrase: "as though you were working for the Lord" (cf. NIV, NET).

> **Semantical Nugget**: Who is the referent of "the Lord" in verse 7b? Paul can refer to God the Father as the Lord; however, the context suggests that he has Christ in mind. Paul has made a similar comparison in verses 5 and 6. Slaves should serve their masters "as they serve Christ" (v. 5) or "as slaves of Christ" (v. 6). This suggests that Paul has Christ in mind here as well. The word change looks forward to a play on words with the term κύριος in verse 8, reminding both slaves and free that they have a master. Paul carries the wordplay further in verse 9 when he reminds masters that they too are slaves—their master is in heaven.

6:8a εἰδότες: The Greek word εἰδότες is a masculine nominative plural perfect active participle from the verb οἶδα that means "to know" (BDAG, s.v. "οἶδα" 1e, pp. 693–94). **Syntactically**, εἰδότες introduces a dependent participle clause. It functions adverbially, modifying the main verb in verse 5: "obey" (ὑπακούετε). **Semantically**, the perfect tense indicates that the action of the participle is antecedent to the action of the main verb. The participle expresses cause, stating the grounds or motivation for the slaves' obedience: "*because* you know" (NIV, NET).

6:8b ὅτι: The Greek word ὅτι is a conjunction that means "that" in this context (BDAG, s.v. "ὅτι" 1c, p. 732). **Syntactically**, ὅτι introduces a dependent conjunctive clause "*that* each, whether you are a slave or free … then you will receive it back from the Lord" (ὅτι ἕκαστος … τοῦτο κομίσεται παρὰ κυρίου, εἴτε δοῦλος εἴτε ἐλεύθερος). The entire clause functions substantively as the direct object of the participle "knowing" (εἰδότες). **Semantically**, ὅτι marks the clause as indirect discourse (W, 456–58). It marks the content that Paul wants the slaves to call to mind.

6:8c ἐάν: The Greek word ἐάν is an adverbial conjunction that means "if" in this context (BDAG, s.v. "ἐάν" 1aα, p. 267). **Syntactically**, ἐάν introduces a dependent conjunctive clause "*if* you do something good" (ἐάν τι ποιήσῃ ἀγαθόν). The clause functions adverbially, modifying the main verb of the substantival clause: "will receive back" (κομίσεται). **Semantically**, ἐάν introduces the protasis of a third class conditional clause. It presents a hypothetical situation of probability (W, 696).

ποιήσῃ: The Greek word ποιήσῃ is a third-person singular aorist active subjunctive from the verb ποιέω that means "to do," "to keep," or "to practice" (BDAG, s.v. "ποιέω" 3b, p. 840). **Syntactically**, ποιήσῃ is the main verb of the dependent conjunctive clause introduced by ἐάν. The subject is implied by the verb: "he," an indefinite reference. The direct object is "whatever good" (τι … ἀγαθόν). **Semantically**, ποιήσῃ is a constative aorist: "does" (ESV, NET, CSB, HCSB, NASB, NKJV). It describes the action of the verb as a whole (W, 557–58).

κομίσεται: The Greek word κομίσεται is a third-person singular future middle indicative from the verb κομίζω that means "to receive" (BDAG, s.v. "κομίζω" 3, p. 557). **Syntactically**, κομίσεται is the main verb of the dependent conjunctive clause introduced by ὅτι. The clause functions as the apodosis of the third class conditional statement. The subject of the verb is "each one" (ἕκαστος). The demonstrative pronoun "this" (τοῦτο) is the direct object. The antecedent of the pronoun is "whatever good" (τι … ἀγαθόν). **Semantically**, the future tense functions as a predictive future. Anyone who does a good work now will receive it back from the Lord. The disjunctive conjunctions εἴτε … εἴτε makes this true for all people "whether slaves or free" (BDAG, s.v. "εἰ" 6oβ, p. 279). By pointing out that God will give to all people according to their work, Paul creates a transition from his exhortation for slaves to an exhortation to masters in verse 9.

6:9a καί: The Greek word καί is a conjunction that means "and" (BDAG, s.v. "καί" 2e, p. 495). **Syntactically**, καί introduces an independent conjunctive clause: "*And* masters, do the same to them" (Καὶ οἱ κύριοι, τὰ αὐτὰ ποιεῖτε πρὸς αὐτούς). **Semantically**, καί is a transitional conjunction, moving from the command to slaves (Eph. 6:5–8) to the command given to masters: "and" (NRSV, NIV, CSB, HCSB, NASB, NKJV, KJV). Paul makes the same connection in verse 4, linking the command to children to the command for parents. Some English versions omit the conjunction since there is no coordination (ESV, RSV, NET, NLT).

ποιεῖτε: The Greek word ποιεῖτε is a second-person plural present active indicative from the verb ποιέω that means "to do," "keep," or "practice" (BDAG, s.v. "ποιέω" 3b, p. 840). **Syntactically**, ποιεῖτε functions as the main verb of the independent conjunctive clause introduced by καί. The subject is implied by the verb "you." The nominative "masters" (οἱ κύριοι) functions as a nominative for vocative, signaling a change in address (cf. Eph. 5:22, 25; 6:1, 4, 5). The direct object is "the same thing" (τὰ αὐτά); by placing the object before the verb, Paul emphasizes the object (Larkin, 153). **Semantically**, ποιεῖτε is a customary present: "do" (ESV, RSV, NRSV, NASB, NKJV, KJV) or "treat" (NIV, NET, CSB, HCSB, NLT). The present tense describes an ongoing state (W, 521–22). Paul wants these masters to make treating their slaves well habitual.

> **Semantical Nugget:** What does Paul mean when he commands masters to do "the same" (τὰ αὐτά)? Chrysostom thought that this command meant that masters should obey their slaves, connecting this command to Paul's command in verse 5 (Chrysostom, *Hom. Eph.* 6:9). This is probably not the case since they were in an asymmetrical relationship (Merkle, 205). Slaves and masters had distinct roles (Best, 580). Nonetheless, it would have been a radical suggestion for slaveowners to treat their slaves with the same deference—just like Jesus's command for leaders to become servants, not lording their authority over them (Mark 10:42–45; cf. Luke 12:37) (Thielman, 409). And the overarching command is for believers to submit to one another (Eph. 5:21). In the next breath, Paul reminds these masters that they too are slaves. Another option is that the referent is to "doing what is good" (τι … ἀγαθόν) because Paul refers to both masters and slaves in the passage (Best, 580). However, since the pronoun is plural, the referent is probably wider than just verse 8 (Arnold, 425). Paul most likely has a more general attitude in how they treat their slaves. In Colossians 4:1, he offers a similar command to masters to "treat their slaves justly and fairly, knowing that you also have a master [or Lord; κύριον] in heaven" (Hoehner, 813; Arnold, 425–26; Lincoln, 423).

6:9b ἀνιέντες: The Greek word ἀνιέντες is a masculine nominative plural present active participle from the verb ἀνίημι that means "to give up" or "to cease from" (BDAG, s.v. "ἀνίημι" 3, p. 83). **Syntactically**, ἀνιέντες introduces a dependent participle clause. It functions adverbially, modifying the main verb "do" (ποιεῖτε; v. 9). The direct object is "threats" (τὴν ἀπειλήν). **Semantically**, the present tense indicates that the action of the participle is simultaneous with the action of the main verb. Most English versions translate the participle as an imperative: "Do not threaten them" (NIV; cf. ESV, NRSV, NASB, NLT; cf. Thielman, 408–9). The participle functions as manner, describing how the action of the verb is completed: "*by* stopping your threats." Violence, or the threat of violence, against slaves was commonplace in antiquity as a way of control. As believers, these threats should stop (Arnold, 426). Interestingly, the following clause describes these slaveowners as slaves who have a Lord in heaven—Jesus (v. 9d). Paul goes on to describe Jesus as one with no partiality—a reference to judgment (cf. Rom. 2:6–11).

⁶ˑ⁹ᶜ εἰδότες: The Greek word εἰδότες is a masculine nominative plural perfect active participle from the verb οἶδα that means, "to know" (BDAG, s.v. "οἶδα" 1e, pp. 693–94). **Syntactically**, εἰδότες introduces a dependent participle clause. It functions adverbially, modifying the imperative in verse 9: "do the same to them" (ποιεῖτε). **Semantically**, the perfect tense indicates that the action of the participle is antecedent to the action of the main verb. The participle expresses cause: "*because* you know that" (NET; cf. NIV). The participle phrase serves as the rationale for the master's treatment of the slave, namely that they recall that they too have a master in heaven.

⁶ˑ⁹ᵈ ὅτι: The Greek word ὅτι is a conjunction that means "that" in this context (BDAG, s.v. "ὅτι" 1c, p. 732). **Syntactically**, the conjunction ὅτι introduces a dependent conjunctive clause "*that* also their Lord and yours is in heaven and there is no partiality with him" (ὅτι καὶ αὐτῶν καὶ ὑμῶν ὁ κύριός ἐστιν ἐν οὐρανοῖς, καὶ προσωπολημψία οὐκ ἔστιν παρ᾽ αὐτῷ). The entire clause functions substantively as the direct object of the participle "knowing" (εἰδότες). **Semantically**, ὅτι marks the clause as indirect discourse (W, 456–58). It marks the content of what Paul wants these masters to remember.

ἐστίν: The Greek word ἐστίν is a third-person singular present active indicative from the verb εἰμί that means "to be" (BDAG, s.v. "εἰμί" 3a, p. 284). **Syntactically**, ἐστίν functions as the main verb of the dependent conjunctive clause introduced by ὅτι. The subject is "Lord" (ὁ κύριος). The genitive pronouns αὐτῶν and ὑμῶν are genitives of subordination: "Lord *over* them and *over* you" (Merkle, 205). English readers lose Paul's wordplay at this point by referring to Jesus as "Lord." Most English versions simply render this "Master" to keep the wordplay (ESV, RSV, NRSV, NIV, NET, CSB, HCSB, NASB, NKJV, KJV), but these versions lose the sense of "Lord" from the Greek word κύριος. **Semantically**, ἐστίν is as a gnomic present, which describes the action of the verb as a timeless fact (W, 523–24). The prepositional phrase "in heaven" (ἐν οὐρανοῖς) expresses sphere, describing where the Lord is. Paul makes a similar statement in Colossians 4:1; however in Ephesians, his description of Jesus as Lord in heaven is a theme that he begins in Ephesians 1:20–22.

[6:9e] καί: The Greek word καί is a conjunction that means "and" (BDAG, s.v. "καί" 1bα, p. 494). **Syntactically**, καί introduces a dependent conjunctive clause: "*and* there is no partiality with him" (καὶ προσωπολημψία οὐκ ἔστιν παρ' αὐτῷ). **Semantically**, καί is a coordinating connective: "and" (ESV, RSV, NRSV, NIV, NET, CSB, HCSB, NASB, NKJV). The conjunctive gives a further explanation, not only is their master in heaven, he is impartial.

ἐστίν: The Greek word ἐστίν is a third-person singular present active indicative from the verb εἰμί that means, "to be" (BDAG, s.v." εἰμί" 2a, p. 283). **Syntactically**, ἐστίν functions as the main verb of the dependent conjunctive clause introduced by ὅτι. It is parallel to the previous clause, giving a further explanation. The subject of the verb is "partiality" (προσωπολημψία) (Larkin, 154), but most English versions treat it as the predicate nominative: "*there is* no partiality" (ESV, RSV, NRSV, NASB, NKJV) or "*there is* no favoritism" (NIV, NET, CSB, HCSB). **Semantically**, ἐστίν is as a gnomic present, which describes the action of the verb as a timeless fact (W, 523–24).

Lexical Nugget: What does it mean to be "partial" (προσωπολημψία)? Paul makes a similar statement in Romans 2:11: "For there is no partiality with God" (cf. Col. 3:25; BDAG, s.v. "προσωπολημψία," p. 887). The word literally means "to receive the face" and is close to the Hebrew idiom, which refers to making a judgment based on some external aspect. The Old Testament regularly describes God as a judge who does not show partiality (Deut. 10:17) (Lohse, 1968, 779–80). Throughout this section, Paul encourages both slaves and masters to avoid acting on external motivation. Ultimately, when Christ judges, he will do so not on any external factors, but their internal motivation (Hoehner, 815–16).

EPHESIANS 6:10–20

Big Greek Idea: Believers must empower themselves through prayer by taking advantage of the spiritual provision that God has provided, in order to withstand the devil and his attacks on them.

Structural Overview: Paul begins the final section of the body of the letter with the phrase τοῦ λοιποῦ ("Finally"). Throughout the second half of the book (Eph. 4–6), Paul has used the keyword "walk" (περιπατέω) to describe how the believers should conduct their lives (Eph. 4:1, 17; 5:2, 8, 15). He breaks this pattern in this section. The keyword throughout this paragraph is ἵστημι (or ἀνθίστημι). He uses some form of the verb four times (Eph. 6:11, 13 [2x], 14). Rather than walk, he wants the believers to "stand" against the evil one. Even though Paul might refer to evil forces at work against the believer (Eph. 2:1–3; 4:14, 17–19; 5:16), the focus is on how the believer engages the world. This final section addresses how the believer might engage these satanic forces.

Paul begins the first section (vv. 10–13) with the present imperative "be strengthened" (ἐνδυναμοῦσθε), which becomes the dominant exhortation throughout the passage. The believer is empowered "in his mighty strength" (v. 10), an allusion to the power at work in Christ's resurrection (Eph. 1:19–20). This empowerment is critical to stand against our opponent. Paul uses the preposition πρός ("against") to outline our opponents: rulers, authorities, world powers, and spiritual forces of evil (v. 12). All of these are subsumed under the "schemes of the devil" (v. 11b).

In the second section (vv. 14–17), Paul shifts his attention to how the believer might oppose the devil (στῆτε), namely by putting on the armor of God (cf. vv. 11, 13). Each piece of the armor corresponds to some aspect of the Christian life designed to thwart the devil: the belt of truth (v. 14b), the breastplate of righteousness (v. 14c), the shoes of the gospel (v. 15), the shield of faith (v. 16a), the helmet of salvation (v. 17a), and the sword of the Spirit (v. 17a). The imagery comes from Isaiah's depiction of Yahweh as a divine warrior (Isa. 11:4–5; 52:7; 59:17).

The final section (vv. 18–20) is grammatically connected to the second section, but he breaks the extended metaphor of the armor of God. In this section, prayer becomes critical to withstanding the devil. He refers to prayer four times in verse 18. The believer must pray all the time and in every way. He concludes the paragraph with a personal request, that God will strengthen his resolve to boldly preach the gospel.

Outline:

> The power that Christ provides allows the believer to withstand the devil (vv. 10–17)
>> Christ's power strengthens the believer to withstand the devil (vv. 10–13)
>> The believer can withstand the devil by taking advantage of the spiritual provision from God (vv. 14–17)
> Paul asks that they pray for boldness for him as he preaches the gospel (vv. 18–20)

CLAUSAL OUTLINE FOR EPHESIANS 6:10–20

6:10 Τοῦ λοιποῦ **ἐνδυναμοῦσθε** ἐν κυρίῳ καὶ ἐν τῷ κράτει τῆς ἰσχύος αὐτοῦ.

6:10 <u>Finally</u>, **be strengthened** in the Lord and in his mighty strength.

6:11a **ἐνδύσασθε** τὴν πανοπλίαν τοῦ θεοῦ

6:11a **Put on** the whole armor of God

|

6:11b **πρὸς τὸ δύνασθαι** ὑμᾶς <u>στῆναι</u> πρὸς τὰς μεθοδείας τοῦ διαβόλου·

6:11b **so that** you **can** <u>stand</u> against the schemes of the devil

[ἐνδύσασθε (v. 11a)]
[Put on (v. 11a)]

|

6:12 **ὅτι** οὐκ **ἔστιν** ἡμῖν ἡ πάλη πρὸς αἷμα καὶ σάρκα, ἀλλὰ πρὸς τὰς ἀρχάς, πρὸς τὰς ἐξουσίας, πρὸς τοὺς κοσμοκράτορας τοῦ σκότους τούτου, πρὸς τὰ πνευματικὰ τῆς πονηρίας ἐν τοῖς ἐπουρανίοις.

6:12 **because** our struggle **is** not against blood and flesh, but against rulers, against authorities, against the world rulers of this darkness, against the spiritual forces of evil in the heavens.

6:13a διὰ τοῦτο **ἀναλάβετε** τὴν πανοπλίαν τοῦ θεοῦ,
6:13a For this reason, **take up** the whole armor of God

6:13b **ἵνα δυνηθῆτε** ἀντιστῆναι ἐν τῇ ἡμέρᾳ τῇ πονηρᾷ
6:13b **so that you may be able** to withstand in the evil day

6:13c καὶ ἅπαντα **κατεργασάμενοι**
6:13c and **after you have done** everything,

6:13d **στῆναι**.
6:13d **to stand**.

6:14a **στῆτε** οὖν
6:14a Therefore, **stand**

6:14b **περιζωσάμενοι** τὴν ὀσφὺν ὑμῶν ἐν ἀληθείᾳ,
6:14b **by girding** your waist with truth,

6:14c καὶ **ἐνδυσάμενοι** τὸν θώρακα τῆς δικαιοσύνης,
614c and **by putting on** the breastplate of righteousness,

6:15 καὶ **ὑποδησάμενοι** τοὺς πόδας ἐν ἑτοιμασίᾳ τοῦ εὐαγγελίου
τῆς εἰρήνης,
6:15 and **by binding** your feet with the preparation of the gospel of peace,

6:16a ἐν πᾶσιν **ἀναλαβόντες** τὸν θυρεὸν τῆς πίστεως,
6:16a in all things, by taking up the shield of faith,

6:16b ἐν ᾧ **δυνήσεσθε** πάντα (τὰ βέλη τοῦ πονηροῦ τὰ πεπυρωμένα) σβέσαι·
6:16b with which **you will be able** to extinguish all of (the fiery arrows of the evil
one)

6:17a καὶ τὴν περικεφαλαίαν τοῦ σωτηρίου **δέξασθε**, καὶ τὴν μάχαιραν τοῦ
πνεύματος,
6:17a and **take** the helmet of salvation and the sword of the Spirit

6:17b ὅ **ἐστιν** ῥῆμα θεοῦ,
6:17b which **is** the word of God,

[δέξασθε (v. 17a)]
[take (v. 17a)]

> 6:18a διὰ πάσης προσευχῆς καὶ δεήσεως **προσευχόμενοι** ἐν παντὶ καιρῷ ἐν πνεύματι,
> 6:18a **by praying** through all prayers and petitions, in every season by the Spirit,

> 6:18b καὶ εἰς αὐτὸ **ἀγρυπνοῦντες** ἐν πάσῃ προσκαρτερήσει καὶ δεήσει περὶ πάντων τῶν ἁγίων, 6:19a καὶ ὑπὲρ ἐμοῦ,
> 6:18b and to this end **by being alert** with all perseverance and all petition concerning the saints 6:19a and for me

[προσευχόμενοι (v. 18a)]
[by praying (v. 18a)]

> 6:19b **ἵνα** μοι **δοθῇ** λόγος ἐν ἀνοίξει τοῦ στόματός μου,
> 6:19b **that** a word **may be given** to me when I speak

> 6:19c ἐν παρρησίᾳ **γνωρίσαι** τὸ μυστήριον τοῦ εὐαγγελίου
> 6:19c **to make known** with boldness the mystery of the gospel

> 6:20a ὑπὲρ οὗ **πρεσβεύω** ἐν ἁλύσει,
> 6:20a for which **I work as an ambassador** in chains,

[προσευχόμενοι (v. 18a)]
[by praying (v. 18a)]

> 6:20b **ἵνα** ἐν αὐτῷ **παρρησιάσωμαι**
> 6:20b **that I may boldly proclaim** in it

> 6:20c ὡς **δεῖ** με λαλῆσαι.
> 6:20c as **it is necessary** for me to speak.

SYNTAX EXPLAINED FOR EPHESIANS 6:10–20

6:10 τοῦ λοιποῦ: The Greek word λοιπός is an adjective, but in this context functions as an adverbial conjunction that means "finally" (BDAG, s.v. "λοιπός" 3aβ, p. 602). **Syntactically**, τοῦ λοιποῦ introduces a dependent conjunctive clause: "*Finally*, be strengthened" (Τοῦ λοιποῦ ἐνδυναμοῦσθε). **Semantically**, τοῦ λοιποῦ functions inferentially. Paul uses the phrase to indicate that this is his final exhortation of the letter: "Finally" (ESV, RSV, NRSV, NIV, NET, CSB, HCSB, NASB, NKJV, KJV). The NLT translates it as "A final word."

ἐνδυναμοῦσθε: The Greek word ἐνδυναμοῦσθε is a second-person plural present middle imperative from the verb ἐνδυναμόω that means "to become strong," in this context an inner or moral strength (BDAG, s.v. "ἐνδυναμόω" 2b, p. 333). **Syntactically**, ἐνδυναμοῦσθε functions as the main verb of the independent conjunctive clause introduced by τοῦ λοιποῦ. The subject is implied by the verb: "you," referring to the Ephesian believers. **Semantically**, ἐνδυναμοῦσθε is a customary present: "be strong" (ESV, RSV, NRSV, NIV, NASB, NKJV, KJV, NLT) or "be strengthened" (NET, CSB, HCSB). The present tense describes an ongoing state (W, 521–22). The tense contrasts the following aorist verbs, which seem to describe this empowerment (Porter, 227). Paul wants the Ephesian believers to make strengthening habitual. Larkin argues that this should be understood as a direct middle with a causative force. It is a call to arms for believers to strengthen themselves (Larkin, 156). However, it is best to understand the middle verb with an active meaning (BDAG, s.v. "ἐνδυναμόω" 2b, p. 333; Thielman, 417; Hoehner, 820). The verb is modified by two prepositional phrases. The first prepositional phrase "in the Lord" (ἐν κυρίῳ) communicates sphere. The believer is strengthened through their relationship with Christ. The second prepositional phrase (ἐν τῷ κράτει τῆς ἰσχύος αὐτοῦ) could express means: "by his might," but probably means sphere: "in his might." The genitive τῆς ἰσχύος could either be an attributive genitive ("mighty strength"; cf. NIV, NLT) or an attributed genitive ("strong might"; cf. CSB, HCSB). The redundancy of synonymous terms emphasizes the strength. Paul uses a series of similar synonymous in Ephesians 1:19–20 to describe the power at work in Christ's resurrection (see Semantical Nugget at 1:19).

6:11a ἐνδύσασθε: The Greek word ἐνδύσασθε is a second-person plural aorist middle imperative from the verb ἐνδύω that means "to clothe oneself in," "put on," or "wear" (BDAG, s.v. "ἐνδύω" 2a, pp. 333–34). **Syntactically**, ἐνδύσασθε functions as the main verb of the asyndeton clause. Even though there is no conjunction that links this clause to the context, it is most likely parallel to the previous verb "be strengthened" (ἐνδυναμοῦσθε; v. 10), giving further explanation of the command to be strengthened, specifically from a divine strength (Thielman, 443). The direct object is "the full armor of God" (τὴν πανοπλίαν τοῦ θεοῦ). **Semantically**, ἐνδύσασθε is a constative aorist: "put on" (ESV, RSV, NRSV, NIV, CSB, HCSB, NASB, NKJV, KJV). It describes the action of the verb as a whole (W, 557–58). The aorist imperative contrasts with the present imperative that began this section: "be strengthened" (ἐνδυναμοῦσθε). The aorist verbs describe how the believer is strengthened. The command looks forward to verse 14 and Paul's description of the believer equipping themselves with each piece of armor. The command alludes back to Paul's instruction that the believer has put on "the new self" (cf. Eph. 4:24; see Theological Nugget at 4:24).

6:11b πρὸς τὸ δύνασθαι: The Greek word δύνασθαι is a present middle (deponent) infinitive from the verb δύναμαι that means "to be able to" or "to be capable" introducing an aorist infinitive (BDAG, s.v. "δύναμαι" aβ, p. 262). **Syntactically**, δύνασθαι introduces an infinitival dependent clause. The clause, "so that you stand against the schemes of the devil" (πρὸς τὸ δύνασθαι ὑμᾶς στῆναι πρὸς τὰς μεθοδείας τοῦ διαβόλου), functions adverbially, modifying the main verb "clothe yourself" (ἐνδύσασθε). The subject of the infinitive is "you" (ὑμᾶς), referring to the believer. **Semantically**, δύνασθαι is a purpose infinitive: "so that you can stand" (CSB, HCSB; cf. NIV, NRSV, NET, NASB, ESV, KJV, NKJV). Believers should put on the full armor of God so that they can stand. Paul makes a similar exhortation in Ephesians 4:14. The maturity of the believer is essential due to the spiritual struggle that the believer faces.

στῆναι: The Greek word στῆναι is an aorist active infinitive from the verb ἵστημι that means "to resist" (BDAG, s.v. "ἵστημι" B3, p. 482,). **Syntactically**, στῆναι introduces a dependent adverbial infinitive clause functioning as the direct object of the infinitive clause "you are able" (δύνασθαι). **Semantically**, the infinitive is a complementary infinitive, completing the idea that the infinitive begins: "so that you can *stand*" (CSB, HCSB; cf. NIV) or "that you may be able *to stand*" (ESV, RSV, NKJV; W, 598–99). The prepositional phrase "against the schemes of the devil" (πρὸς τὰς μεθοδείας τοῦ διαβόλου) modifies the infinitive clause. The preposition πρός expresses opposition (BDAG, s.v. "πρός" 3da, p. 874). Paul will repeat the preposition in verse 12 five times to explicitly describe the enemies that face the believer. The object of the preposition is "schemes" and may have a negative connotation, or it might simply refer to a plan or system of rules: "method" (GE, s.v. "μεθοδεία," p. 1296). The genitive τοῦ διαβόλου gives it a negative color. This is a subjective genitive: "the devil's schemes." Paul provides clear reasons for why the believer must continue to grow—the devil is actively scheming against them. The word μεθοδεία only occurs twice in the New Testament, both times in Ephesians. Paul uses it similarly in Ephesians 4:14.

6:12 ὅτι: The Greek word ὅτι is a conjunction that means "because" in this context (BDAG, s.v. "ὅτι" 4a, p. 732). **Syntactically**, ὅτι introduces a dependent conjunctive clause "*because* our struggle is not against blood and flesh" (ὅτι οὐκ ἔστιν ἡμῖν ἡ πάλη πρὸς αἷμα καὶ σάρκα). The entire clause functions adverbially, modifying the main verb in verse 11: "clothe" (ἐνδύσασθε). **Semantically**, ὅτι is causal: "because." The clause provides the reason why believers should clothe themselves with the armor of God (W, 460–61). Most English versions begin a new sentence with verse 12 and translate the conjunction as "for" (ESV, RSV, NRSV, NIV, NET, CSB, HCSB, NASB, NKJV, KJV).

ἐστίν: The Greek word ἐστίν is a third-person singular present active indicative from the verb εἰμί that means "to be" (BDAG, s.v. "εἰμί" 3a, p. 284). **Syntactically**, ἐστίν functions as the main verb of the conjunctive dependent ὅτι clause. The subject of the verb is "struggle" (ἡ πάλη). The Greek word πάλη is a *hapax legomenon*, occurring once in the New Testament. The word originally referred to wrestling matches, but can refer to a military struggle, which makes good sense of the armor language in verses 14–17. The following preposition πρός identifies the opponent (BDAG, s.v. "πάλη," p. 752). The dative ἡμῖν is a dative of possession, literally "the struggle is *to us*" or "*our* struggle" (W, 149–50). **Semantically**, ἐστίν is a customary present: "is" (CSB, HCSB, NASB, NRSV, NIV, NET). Several versions convert the subject to a verb: "we do not wrestle" (ESV, NKJV, KJV). The present tense describes an ongoing state (W, 521–22). The struggle that faces the believer is ongoing.

Syntactical Nugget: What do believers struggle against? The remainder of the verse identifies the struggle. Paul begins with a negative statement: "our struggle is *not* against blood and flesh." Most English versions invert the order: "flesh and blood" (except the NRSV and LEB), perhaps to retain the English idiom. The phrase is both hendiadys and metonymy, idiomatically referring to the human enemies (cf. GNT). The conjunction "but" (ἀλλά) contrasts the negative statement and describes a spiritual struggle. Paul repeats the preposition πρός four more times throughout the verse giving a series of opposition. The repetition of the preposition without a conjunction gives the list a rhetorical effect (Robertson, 566). The first two elements, rulers and authorities (ἀρχάς and ἐξουσίας), might refer to human rulers, but due to the contrast, Paul most likely has spiritual or angelic beings in mind (Hoehner, 826). Paul refers to rulers and authorities earlier in the book. In Ephesians 1:21, he states that God has given Christ authority over these rulers; in Ephesians 3:10, Paul proclaims his message to them. At this point, they appear antagonistic. The third opponent is "the world ruler of this darkness" (τοὺς κοσμοκράτορας τοῦ σκότους τούτου). The Greek word κοσμοκράτωρ is a *hapax legomenon*, occurring once in the New Testament. It means "world-ruler," generally referring to spiritual beings that have some part of the universe under control (BDAG, s.v. "κοσμοκράτωρ," p. 561; cf. Arnold, 447–48). The fourth element "spiritual forces in the heavens" (τὰ πνευματικὰ τῆς πονηρίας ἐν τοῖς ἐπουρανίοις) most likely refers to a comprehensive description of the spiritual elements confronting the believer (Arnold, 448–49; Lincoln,

444–45; Best, 594; Osborne, 226). The exact identity of this opposition is difficult to determine, but Paul clearly delineates spiritual forces actively attacking the Christian community. Earlier in Ephesians, he states that maturity is essential for the Christian body so that we might confront these forces (Eph. 4:14). He makes the same point more explicitly here.

Text-Critical Nugget: Is the struggle against "us" (ἡμῖν) or "you" (ὑμῖν)? A number of significant Alexandrian ($\mathfrak{P}^{46}$ and B) and Western (D, F, G) manuscripts replace the first-person plural pronoun ("us") with the second-person plural pronoun ("you"). The reading with the first-person plural pronoun is found in Alexandrian manuscripts (ℵ, A, 1739, 1881), as well as Byzantine manuscripts (K, L, 𝔐). Besides having slightly better external evidence, it is more likely that a scribe would change the text to the second-person plural pronoun to agree with the second-person nouns that run throughout this section (Metzger, 542; Hoehner, 824 n. 2).

6:13a διὰ τοῦτο: The Greek word τοῦτο is a neuter singular accusative from the demonstrative pronoun οὗτος. The pronoun with the preposition διά expresses a causal relation to the preceding context (Runge, 2010, 48). **Syntactically**, διὰ τοῦτο introduces an independent conjunctive clause: "*Therefore*, take up the whole armor of God" (διὰ τοῦτο ἀναλάβετε τὴν πανοπλίαν τοῦ θεοῦ). **Semantically**, διὰ τοῦτο expresses cause: "therefore" (ESV, RSV, NRSV, NIV, NASB, NKJV) or "for this reason" (NET, CSB). The HCSB translates the clause as "This is why." The conjunction refers to the previous two verses and the believer's struggle against these spiritual opponents (vv. 11–12).

ἀναλάβετε: The Greek word ἀναλάβετε is a second-person plural aorist active imperative from the verb ἀναλαμβάνω that means "to take up." The verb can refer to taking up weapons (BDAG, s.v. "ἀναλαμβάνω" 2, p. 66). **Syntactically**, ἀναλάβετε functions as the main verb of the independent conjunctive clause introduced by διὰ τοῦτο. The subject is implied by the verb: "you," referring to the readers. The direct object is the "whole armor of God" (τὴν πανοπλίαν τοῦ θεοῦ). Paul makes a similar statement in verse 10. **Semantically**, ἀναλάβετε is a constative aorist: "take up" (ESV, RSV, NRSV, NET, CSB, HCSB, NASB, KJV, NKJV) or "put on" (NIV, NLT). It describes the action of the verb as a whole (W, 557–58). The aorist imperative gives the command a sense of urgency (W, 720). The aorist imperative contrasts with the present imperative that began this section: "be strengthened" (ἐνδυναμοῦσθε). The aorist verbs describe how the believer is strengthened.

6:13b ἵνα: The Greek word ἵνα is a conjunction that means "that" in this context to express purpose (BDAG, s.v. "ἵνα" 1, p. 475). **Syntactically**, ἵνα introduces a dependent conjunctive clause "*that* you might be able to resist in the evil day" (ἵνα δυνηθῆτε ἀντιστῆναι ἐν τῇ ἡμέρᾳ τῇ πονηρᾷ). The entire clause functions adverbially, modifying the main verb of the sentence: "take up" (ἀναλάβετε; v. 13a). **Semantically**, the ἵνα marks the clause as a purpose clause: "that" (ESV, RSV, NKJV, KJV) or "so that" (NRSV, NIV, NET, CSB, HCSB, NASB). The clause states the purpose for which the believer needs to take up the full armor of God.

δυνηθῆτε: The Greek word δυνηθῆτε is a second-person plural aorist passive subjunctive from the verb δύναμαι that means "to be able to" or "be capable," introducing an aorist infinitive (BDAG, s.v. "δύναμαι" aβ, p. 262). **Syntactically**, δυνηθῆτε functions as the main verb of the dependent conjunctive clause introduced by ἵνα. The subject is implied by the verb: "you," referring to the Ephesian believers. **Semantically**, δυνηθῆτε is a constative aorist: "you may be able" (ESV, RSV, NRSV, NIV, NET, CSB, HCSB, NKJV). It describes the action of the verb as a whole (W, 557–58).

ἀντιστῆναι: The Greek word ἀντιστῆναι is an aorist active infinitive from the verb ἀνθίστημι that means "to resist," particularly within the context of opposition (BDAG, s.v. "ἀνθίστημι" 2, p. 80). **Syntactically**, ἀντιστῆναι introduces a dependent adverbial infinitive clause functioning as the direct object of the main verb "you might be able" (δυνηθῆτε). **Semantically**, the infinitive functions as a complementary infinitive, completing the verbal idea of the previous verb (δυνηθῆτε): "that you may be able *to withstand*" (ESV, RSV, NRSV, NKJV; cf. NIV, NET, CSB, HCSB, NASB, NLT; W, 598–99). Along with the previous verb, the aorist tense is constative, describing the action of the verb as a whole (W, 557–58).

> **Lexical Nugget**: What does Paul mean by the "evil day"? The prepositional phrase "in the evil day" (ἐν τῇ ἡμέρᾳ τῇ πονηρᾷ) is temporal. The reference is debated. Paul could be describing an intense day of evil prior to Christ's return. Most English translations bring out this notion by rendering the phrase as a point in time: "in that evil day" (ESV, RSV, CSB, HCSB, NASB) or "on that evil day" (NRSV, NET), the NIV renders it "when the day of evil comes." The problem is that Paul seems to be describing the present life of the believer. It could refer to the current present age, which Paul describes as evil (Thielman, 423; Lincoln, 446). Finally, it could refer to a specific time in the life of the believer. Earlier, Paul exhorted the readers to redeem the time, because "the days are evil" (Eph. 5:16), suggesting that the believers are living in these evil times, but experience this evil more intensely at different times in their life. The final two views are not mutually exclusive. Paul probably has both of these in mind (Osborne, 228; Hoehner, 834; Arnold, 450).

[6:13c] καί: The Greek word καί is a conjunction that means "and" (BDAG, s.v. "καί" 1bδ, pp. 494–95). **Syntactically**, καί introduces a dependent conjunctive clause: "*and* having conquered all things" (καὶ ἄπαντα κατεργασάμενοι). **Semantically**, καί is a coordinating connective: "and" (ESV, RSV, NRSV, NIV, NET, CSB, HCSB, NASB, NKJV, KJV). The conjunction connects the following infinitive clause with the preceding one (Hoehner, 834).

κατεργασάμενοι: The Greek word κατεργασάμενοι is a masculine nominative plural aorist middle participle from the verb κατεργάζομαι that means "to achieve" or "accomplish" (BDAG, s.v. "κατεργάζομαι" 1, p. 531). **Syntactically**, κατεργασάμενοι introduces a dependent participle clause. It functions adverbially, modifying the following infinitive: "to stand" (στῆναι). The direct object is "all things" (ἄπαντα). **Semantically**, the aorist tense indicates that the action of the participle is antecedent with the action of the main verb. Hoehner classifies this participle as cause: "*because* you have done all things." The believer is able to stand because they have made the necessary preparations (Hoehner, 836). However, it might be best to interpret the participle as temporal: "*after* you have done everything" (NIV, NLT; Arnold, 450). The participle clause describes the preparation for battle. It looks forward to the next sentence (vv. 14–17), which describes the armor of God in detail.

στῆναι: The Greek word στῆναι is an aorist active infinitive from the verb ἵστημι that means "to stand up against" or "resist" (BDAG, s.v. "ἵστημι" B3, p. 482). **Syntactically**, στῆναι is a dependent adverbial infinitive functioning as the direct object of the main verb "you might be able" (δυνηθῆτε), along with the infinitive ἀντιστῆναι ("to resist"). **Semantically**, the infinitive functions as a complementary infinitive, completing the verbal idea of the main verb (δυνηθῆτε): "that you may be able … *to stand*" (NIV, NET, RSV, NKJV, KJV; cf. ESV, NRSV, CSB, HCSB, NASB, NLT; W, 598–99). The aorist tense functions as a constative aorist, which focuses on the action of the verb as a whole (W, 557–58).

[6:14a] οὖν: The Greek word οὖν is a conjunction that means "therefore" or "consequently" (BDAG, s.v. "οὖν" 1b, p. 736). **Syntactically**, οὖν introduces an independent conjunctive clause: "*therefore* stand" (στῆτε οὖν). **Semantically**, οὖν is inferential: "therefore" (ESV, RSV, NRSV, NET, CSB, HCSB, NASB, NKJV, KJV) or "then" (NIV). The conjunction draws out the implications for Paul's previous command. The believers should strengthen themselves so that they can withstand the attacks from the evil one (Hoehner, 837; Arnold, 451).

στῆτε: The Greek word στῆτε is a second-person plural aorist active imperative from the verb ἵστημι that means "to stand" or "resist" (BDAG, s.v. "ἵστημι" B4, p. 482). **Syntactically**, στῆτε functions as the main verb of the independent conjunctive clause introduced by οὖν. The subject is implied by the verb: "you," referring to the Ephesian believers. **Semantically**, στῆτε is a constative aorist, describing the action as a whole: "stand" (ESV, RSV, NRSV, CSB, HCSB, NKJV, KJV) or "stand firm" (NIV, NET, NASB). The NLT offers a more interpretive translation: "stand your ground." The aorist tense describes the action of the verb as a whole (W, 557–58). The aorist imperative gives the command a sense of urgency (W, 720). Paul uses a form of this verb three times in verses 11–13, each describing the purpose of the main verb: the believer is to be strengthened in order to withstand attacks from evil. At this point, "standing" becomes the main verbal idea (vv. 14–16). The following participles describe how the believer withstands these attacks.

6:14b περιζωσάμενοι: The Greek word περιζωσάμενοι is a masculine nominative plural aorist middle participle from the verb περιζώννυμι that means "to gird oneself." The idea of "girding suggests preparation for some activity" (BDAG, s.v. "περιζώννυμι" 2c, p. 801). **Syntactically**, περιζωσάμενοι introduces a dependent participle clause. It functions adverbially, modifying the main verb: "stand" (στῆτε). The direct object is "your waist" (τὴν ὀσφὺν ὑμῶν). **Semantically**, Hoehner classifies this participle as expressing cause: "*because* you have girded your waist" (Hoehner, 838). But it probably best expresses means: "*by* girding your waist" (W, 629; Arnold, 451; Merkle, 214; cf. NET). Since the participle modifies an imperative, the participle itself carries an imperatival notion. The prepositional phrase "with truth" expresses means.

> **Lexical Nugget**: What does "truth" mean? The idea of "girding your waist with truth" is parallel to Isaiah 11:5: "and he will be girded around his waist with righteousness and truth" (καὶ ἔσται δικαιοσύνῃ ἐζωσμένος τὴν ὀσφὺν αὐτοῦ καὶ ἀληθείᾳ). Even though there is no object in the Greek text, several English translations insert "belt," such as the NIV: "with the belt of truth buckled around your waist" (cf. ESV, NRSV, NET, HCSB, CSB, NLT). This is the first in a series of objects that describe the "full armor of God" (cf. v. 13). Truth is an important theme throughout the letter of Ephesians. Paul commands believers to put away falsehood and lead a life of truth (Eph. 4:25; cf. 5:9). But he can refer specifically to the gospel as "the word of truth" (Eph. 1:13). In Ephesians 4, he reminds the believers that they have learned the truth as it relates to "putting on the new self" (Eph. 4:21–24). He certainly has the broader meaning in mind, but he most likely refers to the more general idea of the gospel (Arnold, 452).

6:14c καί: The Greek word καί is a conjunction that means "and" (BDAG, s.v. "καί" 1bα, p. 494). **Syntactically**, καί introduces a dependent conjunctive clause: "*and* put on the breastplate of righteousness" (καὶ ἐνδυσάμενοι τὸν θώρακα τῆς δικαιοσύνης). **Semantically**, καί is a coordinating connective: "and" (ESV,

RSV, NRSV, NASB). Because Paul gives several participles, each separated by καί, most English versions omit the conjunction (CSB, HCSB, NASB, NIV, NET).

ἐνδυσάμενοι: The Greek word ἐνδυσάμενοι is a masculine nominative plural aorist middle participle from the verb ἐνδύω that means "to put on," "wear," or "clothe oneself" (BDAG, s.v. "ἐνδύω" 2a, p. 333). **Syntactically**, ἐνδυσάμενοι introduces a dependent participle clause. It functions adverbially, modifying the main verb "stand" (στῆτε; v. 14a). The direct object is "the breastplate of righteousness" (τὸν θώρακα τῆς δικαιοσύνης). **Semantically**, like the previous participle (vv. 14–16) it is best understood as a participle of means: "*by* putting on the breastplate of righteousness" (NET). Since the participle modifies an imperative, it also carries an imperatival notion. Paul most likely draws this image from Isaiah 59:17, and the prophet's description of a divine warrior "putting on righteousness as a breastplate" (καὶ ἐνεδύσατο δικαιοσύνην ὡς θώρακα). The concept of righteousness refers to the objective relationship between the believer and God. Because of Christ's death, believers are righteous before God (cf. Rom. 3:21–24; 5:1). Paul most likely refers to a subjective understanding as well. Throughout the second part of the letter, he encourages believers to pursue righteousness as a response to what God has done (Witherington, 2007, 352; Schreiner, 2001, 304).

6:15 καί: The Greek word καί is a conjunction that means "and" (BDAG, s.v. "καί" 1ba, p. 494). **Syntactically**, καί introduces an independent conjunctive clause: "*and* by binding your feet" (καὶ ὑποδησάμενοι). **Semantically**, καί is a coordinating connective: "and" (ESV, RSV, NIV, CSB, HCSB, NASB, NKJV, KJV). Because Paul is offering a series of participle phrases, some versions omit the conjunction (NET, NRSV).

ὑποδησάμενοι: The Greek word ὑποδησάμενοι is a masculine nominative plural aorist middle participle from the verb ὑποδέω that means "to tie" or "bind," or "to put on" with regard to footwear (BDAG, s.v. "ὑποδέω," p. 1037). English versions render the participle a number of ways: "having shod" (RSV, NASB, NKJV), "sandaled" (CSB, HCSB), "as shoes for your feet, having put on" (ESV; cf. NRSV, NLT), or "by fitting your feet" (NET; cf. NIV). **Syntactically**, ὑποδησάμενοι introduces a dependent participle clause. It functions adverbially, modifying the main verb: "stand" (στῆτε; v. 14a). The direct object is "feet" (τοὺς πόδας). **Semantically**, like the previous participles in verse 14, ὑποδησάμενοι is best understood as a participle of means: "*by* binding your feet." Since the participle modifies an imperative, it also carries an imperatival notion.

Semantical Nugget: What does it mean to "bind your feet with preparation"? Rather than refer to shoes or boots, Paul uses the prepositional phrase "with preparation" (ἐν ἑτοιμασίᾳ) to point to what believers should put on their feet. The preposition ἐν expresses means. The object is ἑτοιμασία, which means "readiness" or "preparation" (BDAG, s.v. "ἑτοιμασία," p. 401). Even though the verbal form is used throughout the New Testament, the noun is a *hapax legomenon*, occurring only once. The RSV renders the object of the preposition literally: "with the equipment," referring to that which would equip the soldier, but this is an odd phrase. It is best to understand the object metaphorically: the believer should be ready. The genitive τοῦ εὐαγγελίου is an objective genitive. Preparation is for the gospel (Arnold, 454; Hoehner, 843). The genitive τῆς εἰρήνης is content or objective—this is the message of peace (Arnold, 455; Hoehner, 843). In Ephesians 2, Paul states that as a result of Christ's death, believers have peace with one another as well as with God (Eph. 2:14–15, 17). Ironically, the image presents peace as a tool of war. The phrase seems to refer to Isaiah 52:7. The LXX renders the phrase "as an hour on the mountain, as the feet of the one who brings the good news of peace" (ὡς ὥρα ἐπὶ τῶν ὀρέων, ὡς πόδες εὐαγγελιζομένου ἀκοὴν εἰρήνης). However, Paul seems to use the image differently than the prophet. Isaiah refers to the proclamation of God's victory over the nation's enemies, whereas Paul describes the believer withstanding attacks from evil (Thielman, 426). How does this change impact Paul's image? Paul cites Isaiah 52:7 in Romans 10:15 to describe the proclamation of the gospel. Because of Paul's usage and the background of Isaiah, Arnold argues that Paul envisions the believer actively proclaiming the gospel (Arnold, 455). However, the context does not explicitly refer to gospel preaching. The other parts of armor seem to describe defensive pieces of armor (Thielman, 426). Hoehner states: "It is the believers' 'surefootedness' in the tranquility of the mind and security of the heart in the gospel of peace that gives them the readiness to stand against the devil and his angelic hosts" (Hoehner, 844).

6:16a ἀναλαβόντες: The Greek word ἀναλαβόντες is a masculine nominative plural aorist active participle from the verb ἀναλαμβάνω that means "to take up" particularly in reference to weapons (BDAG, s.v. "ἀναλαμβάνω" 2, p. 66). **Syntactically**, ἀναλαβόντες introduces a dependent participle clause. It functions adverbially, modifying the main verb in verse 14: "stand" (στῆτε). The direct object is "the shield of faith" (τὸν θυρεὸν τῆς πίστεως). Unlike the other participles in this section, Paul omits καί and places a prepositional phrase before the participle. **Semantically**, like the previous participles in verses 14–15, ἀναλαβόντες is best understood as a participle of means: "*by* binding your feet." Since the participle modifies an imperative, it also carries an imperatival notion.

Syntactical Nugget: What does the prepositional phrase "in all things" (ἐν πᾶσιν) mean? The prepositional phrase could refer to all of the other parts of the armor: "above all *these other parts*, take up the shield of faith." Most English versions render the phrase this way, for example, "With all of these" (NRSV); "In addition to all this" (NIV; cf. NLT, NASB); or "besides all these" (RSV). Most commentators understand the phrase this way (Hoehner, 845; Thielman, 427; Lincoln, 449; Barth, 771). On the other hand, the prepositional phrase could be rendered "in all things," referring to all circumstances. This is the normal way to understand the phrase (1 Tim. 3:11; 2 Tim. 2:7; 4:5; Titus 2:9; BDAG, s.v. "πᾶς" 1dβ, p. 783). The CSB renders the phrase "In every situation"; the ESV renders it "In all circumstances." Since this is consistent with Paul's usage elsewhere, it is the better understanding of the phrase (Arnold, 456; Larkin, 161; Merkle, 216).

6:16b ᾧ: The Greek word ᾧ is a masculine singular dative from the relative pronoun ὅς that means "whom" or "which" (BDAG, s.v. "ὅς" 1a, p. 725). **Syntactically**, ᾧ introduces a dependent adjectival relative clause "with *which* you are able to extinguish all the fiery arrows of the evil one" (ἐν ᾧ δυνήσεσθε πάντα τὰ βέλη τοῦ πονηροῦ τὰ πεπυρωμένα σβέσαι). The antecedent of the pronoun is "the shield" (τὸν θυρεόν). The pronoun functions as the object of the preposition ἐν, which expresses means: "*with which*" (ESV, RSV, NRSV, NIV, NET, CSB, NASB, NKJV; cf. HCSB). The shield provides the believer with the means of extinguishing these fiery darts.

δυνήσεσθε: The Greek word δυνήσεσθε is a second-person plural future middle (deponent) indicative from the verb δύναμαι that means, "to be able to," or "to be capable" particularly with an infinitive following (BDAG, s.v. "δύναμαι" 1aβ, p. 262). **Syntactically**, δυνήσεσθε functions as the main verb of the relative clause "with which you will be able to extinguish all the fiery arrows of the evil one" (ἐν ᾧ δυνήσεσθε πάντα τὰ βέλη τοῦ πονηροῦ τὰ πεπυρωμένα σβέσαι). The subject of the verb is implied: "you," referring to the Ephesian believers. **Semantically**, δυνήσεσθε is a predictive future, which focuses on the fact that the event will take place. Paul does not have a specific moment in the future in mind, but that this will happen after picking up the shield (Hoehner, 847; Best, 601).

πεπυρωμένα: The Greek word πεπυρωμένα is a neuter accusative plural perfect passive participle from the verb πυρόω that means "to burn" (BDAG, s.v. "πυρόω" 1a, p. 899). **Syntactically**, πεπυρωμένα is an attributive participle modifying "arrows" (τὰ βέλη). In the sentence, the participle phrase "all of the fiery arrows of the evil one" (πάντα τὰ βέλη τοῦ πονηροῦ τὰ πεπυρωμένα) functions as the direct object of the infinitive "to extinguish" (σβέσαι). **Semantically**, πεπυρωμένα is intensive perfect. The tense highlights the present results of the action of the verb (W, 574–75). Throughout the book, Paul has warned believers about the power that Satan employs against the believer. He is actively looking to destroy the believer (cf. Eph. 6:11). Paul describes these attacks as fiery arrows, making the faith of the Christian community essential (Eph. 4:5, 13–16).

σβέσαι: The Greek word σβέσαι is an aorist active infinitive from the verb σβέννυμι that means "to extinguish" (BDAG, s.v. "σβέννυμι" a, p. 917). **Syntactically**, σβέσαι introduces a dependent adverbial infinitive clause functioning as the direct object of the main verb "you will be able" (δυνήσεσθε). **Semantically**, σβέσαι functions as a complementary infinitive, completing the verbal idea of the main verb (δυνήσεσθε): "you will be able *to extinguish*" (NRSV, HCSB, NASB, NKJV, KJV; cf. ESV, RSV, NIV, NET, CSB; W, 598–99). The aorist tense functions as a constative aorist, which focuses on the action of the verb as a whole.

6:17a καί: The Greek word καί is a conjunction that means "and" (BDAG, s.v. "καί" 1bα, p. 494). **Syntactically**, καί introduces an independent conjunctive clause: "*and* you have received the helmet of salvation" (καὶ τὴν περικεφαλαίαν τοῦ σωτηρίου δέξασθε). **Semantically**, καί is a coordinating connective: "and" (ESV, RSV, NET, NASB, NKJV). Some commentators suggest that the conjunction is parallel to the previous participles, introducing the next weapon (Arnold, 459–60; Merkle, 217; Lincoln, 431). However, the shift from the participle to the aorist imperative, suggests that the imperative is parallel to the aorist imperative in verse 14a: "stand" (στῆτε) (Hoehner, 849).

δέξασθε: The Greek word δέξασθε is a second-person plural aorist middle (deponent) imperative from the verb δέχομαι that means "to take" or "grasp" (BDAG, s.v. "δέχομαι" 2, p. 221). **Syntactically**, δέξασθε functions as the main verb of the independent conjunctive clause introduced by καί. Even though Paul continues describing the armor, structurally, the imperative is parallel to the verb "stand" (στῆτε; v. 14a). The subject is implied by the verb: "you," referring to the Ephesian believers. The direct object is "the helmet of salvation" (τὴν περικεφαλαίαν τοῦ σωτηρίου) and "the sword of the Spirit" (τὴν μάχαιραν τοῦ πνεύματος). **Semantically**, δέξασθε is a constative aorist: "take" (ESV, RSV, NRSV, NIV, NET, CSB, HCSB, NASB, NKJV, KJV). It describes the action of the verb as a whole (W, 557–58). The aorist imperative gives the command a sense of urgency (W, 720).

6:17b ὅ: The Greek word ὅ is a neuter singular nominative from the relative pronoun ὅς that means "which" in this context (BDAG, s.v. "ὅς" 1dγ, p. 726). **Syntactically**, ὅ introduces a dependent adjectival relative clause: "*which* is the word of God" (ὅ ἐστιν ῥῆμα θεοῦ). The antecedent of the pronoun is somewhat debated. Even though it is neuter, it most likely does not refer to τοῦ πνεύματος ("Spirit"). It could refer to the entire phrase "the sword of the Spirit" (Best, 603).

However, a better option is that it refers to the feminine noun "sword," and that the gender of the relative pronoun shifts to neuter due to the gender of the predicate nominative ῥῆμα ("word") (W, 337–38; Robertson, 712; Hoehner, 852; Larkin, 162). The relative pronoun functions as the subject of the verb.

ἐστίν: The Greek word ἐστίν is a third-person singular present active indicative from the verb εἰμί that means "to be" (BDAG, s.v. "εἰμί" 2a, p. 283). **Syntactically**, ἐστίν functions as the main verb of the relative clause. The relative pronoun is the subject. The predicate nominative is "word of God" (ῥῆμα θεοῦ). **Semantically**, ἐστίν is an equative present: "is" (ESV, RSV, NRSV, NIV, NET, CSB, HCSB, NASB, NKJV, KJV). The sword of the Spirit is the word of God. This could have a broad referent describing Scripture, the words that proceed from God (Hoehner, 853). A better option is that this refers specifically to the gospel message. Paul has already referred to the gospel within the context (v. 15) and he regularly refers to the gospel with ῥῆμα rather than λόγος (cf. Rom. 10:8) (Thielman, 429; Lincoln, 451).

6:18a προσευχόμενοι: The Greek word προσευχόμενοι is a masculine nominative plural present middle (deponent) participle from the verb προσεύχομαι that means "to pray" (BDAG, s.v. "προσεύχομαι," p. 879). **Syntactically**, προσευχόμενοι introduces a dependent participle clause. It functions adverbially, modifying the main verb "take" (δέξασθε; v. 17a) (Hoehner, 854–55; Thielman, 432–33). Some interpreters argue that this participle, as well as ἀγρυπνοῦντες, modify στῆτε (v. 14a). These commentators argue that the imperative δέξασθε is subordinate to the imperative στῆτε (Arnold, 463; Merkle, 218; Lincoln, 451). However, it is best to see the two imperatives as parallel commands (see our comments at 6:17a). Some English versions translate the participle independently as an imperative: "Pray" (RSV, NRSV, NIV, NET, NLT, CSB, HCSB, NASB; Barth, 777). Since the participle modifies an imperative, it carries an imperatival force, but since it is grammatically dependent on a finite verb, it should not be considered independent (W, 650–52; Robertson, 1134). **Semantically**, προσευχόμενοι is best understood as expressing means by which a believer takes up the helmet of salvation: "*by praying*." The participle is modified by three prepositional phrases. The first prepositional phrase διὰ πάσης προσευχῆς καὶ δεήσεως expresses the means by which Paul makes these prayers: "through all prayers and petition." The Greek word προσευχή has a more general meaning for "prayer" (BDAG, s.v. "προσευχή" 1, p. 878) than δέησις, which means more of an urgent request (BDAG, s.v. "δέησις," p. 213). Paul probably uses both words to say "all sorts of prayers" (Arnold, 464). The second prepositional phrase "in every season" (ἐν παντὶ καιρῷ) is a temporal marker. Elsewhere Paul communicates the idea of prayer without end (1 Thess. 5:17; cf. Eph. 1:16). The final prepositional phrase "with the Spirit" (ἐν πνεύματι) could express sphere:

"in the Spirit" (ESV, RSV, NRSV, NIV, NET, CSB, HCSB, NASB, NKJV, KJV; Hoehner, 857), but probably best expresses means: "*by* the Spirit" (Arnold, 464). The prepositional phrases underscore the importance of prayer for the believer as they equip themselves to withstand the opposition. Osborne sums it up nicely: "On all occasions and with every kind of prayer, we are called to train our sight and to depend utterly on our heavenly Father" (Osborne, 235).

6:18b καὶ εἰς αὐτό: The Greek word καί is a conjunction that means "and" (BDAG, s.v. "καί" 1b, p. 494). The Greek word εἰς is a preposition that expresses purpose (BDAG, s.v. "εἰς" 4f, p. 290). The Greek word αὐτό is an accusative singular neuter pronoun from αὐτός, which means "this" in this context (BDAG, s.v. "αὐτός" 2a, p. 153). **Syntactically**, καὶ εἰς αὐτό introduces a dependent conjunctive clause: "*and to this end* by being alert" (καὶ εἰς αὐτὸ ἀγρυπνοῦντες). **Semantically**, καί is a coordinating connective: "and" (CSB, HCSB, NASB, KJV) that connects the participle phrase with the previous participle phrase (v. 18a). The prepositional phrase εἰς αὐτό expresses the purpose of remaining alert: to pray (Lincoln, 453; Arnold, 465; Hoehner, 858).

ἀγρυπνοῦντες: The Greek word ἀγρυπνοῦντες is a masculine nominative plural present active participle from the verb ἀγρυπνέω that means "to look after" or "care for" (BDAG, s.v. "ἀγρυπνέω" 2, p. 16). The verb literally means to "lie awake" (LSJ, s.v. "ἀγρυπνέω," p.16). The verb can be used eschatologically, to watch out for the second coming (Mark 13:33; Luke 21:36; Thielman, 434). **Syntactically**, ἀγρυπνοῦντες introduces a dependent participle clause. It functions adverbially, modifying the main verb in verse 17a: "take" (δέξασθε), parallel with the previous participle προσευχόμενοι. Like the previous participle, several English versions render the participle as an imperative: "keep alert" (ESV, RSV, NRSV; cf. NIV, NET, CSB, HCSB, NASB). Nonetheless, it is best to understand the participle as a dependent participle (see our discussion in v. 18a). **Semantically**, ἀγρυπνοῦντες is a participle of means by which the believer takes up the helmet of salvation: "*by* being alert." Paul modifies the participle with three prepositional phrases. The first prepositional phrase ἐν πάσῃ προσκαρτερήσει καὶ δεήσει expresses manner: "*with* all perseverance and petition." The second prepositional phrase περὶ πάντων τῶν ἁγίων expresses advantage: "*on behalf* of the saints." The final prepositional phrase in verse 19 καὶ ὑπὲρ ἐμοῦ communicates the same idea—that they pray for Paul specifically. The following ἵνα clauses (vv. 19b–20) give his specific prayer requests.

6:19b ἵνα: The Greek word ἵνα is a conjunction that means "that" in this context (BDAG, s.v. "ἵνα" 2ca, p. 476). **Syntactically**, ἵνα introduces a dependent conjunctive clause "*that* a word might be given to me when I speak" (ἵνα μοι δοθῇ λόγος ἐν ἀνοίξει τοῦ στόματός μου). The clause functions substantively as the direct object of the participle προσευχόμενοι (v. 18a).

Semantically, ἵνα introduces the content of Paul's prayer (Hoehner, 862; Turner[1], 103–4; Larkin, 165).

δοθῇ: The Greek word δοθῇ is a third-person singular aorist passive subjunctive from the verb δίδωμι that means "to give" or "to produce" (BDAG, s.v. "δίδωμι" 4, p. 242). **Syntactically**, δοθῇ functions as the main verb of the dependent conjunctive clause introduced by ἵνα. The subject is "word" (λόγος). The indirect object is "me" (μοι), referring to Paul. **Semantically**, δοθῇ is a constative aorist: "may be given" (ESV, RSV, NRSV, NIV, NET, CSB, HCSB, NASB, NKJV, KJV). It describes the action of the verb as a whole (W, 557–58). The verb is a divine passive, suggesting that God is the agent who gives this word. The Greek word λόγος carries the idea of an oral speech—an "utterance" (RSV, NASB, NKJV, KJV) or "message" (NRSV, CSB, NET) (BDAG, s.v. "λόγος" 1aβ, p. 599). Knowing the gospel, Paul probably does not mean actual content, but rather divine guidance in when to speak or how to say it (cf. Mark 13:11; Luke 21:14–25; Arnold, 466).

> **Lexical Nugget**: What does Paul mean by "when I open my mouth" (ἐν ἀνοίξει τοῦ στόματός μου)? The preposition ἐν is a temporal marker and should be translated "when" (NRSV, NET, CSB, HCSB; cf. NIV). The Greek word ἄνοιξις is an *hapax legomenon* that means "the act of opening" (BDAG, s.v. "ἄνοιξις," p. 85). The genitive στόματος is an objective genitive ("open my mouth"). The phrase is a Hebrew idiom for speech (Turner[2], 84, 92). The Old Testament can speak of God opening a speaker's mouth (Exod. 4:12; Num. 22:28; Ps. 50:17; Ezek. 3:27; 29:21; Hos. 9:7). The phrase implies some divine utterance (Hoehner, 862).

6:19c γνωρίσαι: The Greek word γνωρίσαι is an aorist active infinitive from the verb γνωρίζω that means "to make known" or "reveal" (BDAG, s.v. "γνωρίζω" 1, p. 203). **Syntactically**, γνωρίσαι introduces a dependent infinitival clause. The entire clause "to make the mystery of the gospel known" (γνωρίσαι τὸ μυστήριον τοῦ εὐαγγελίου) functions adverbially, modifying the verb δοθῇ ("a word might be given"). The direct object is "the mystery" (τὸ μυστήριον). The genitive τοῦ εὐαγγελίου is best understood as a genitive of apposition: "the mystery, *namely* the gospel" (cf. Eph. 5:32). In Ephesians 3, Paul refers to the reconciliation of Jews and Gentiles as the mystery (cf. Eph. 3:3–6; see Theological Nugget at 3:3a). The concept of "mystery" refers to divine revelation (see Theological Nugget at 1:9a). **Semantically**, γνωρίσαι expresses result: "*so as to* make known the mystery" (W, 594; Robertson, 1090; Hoehner, 862). The prepositional phrase "in boldness" (ἐν παρρησίᾳ) expresses manner.

6:20a οὗ: The Greek word οὗ is a neuter singular genitive from the relative pronoun ὅς that means "which" in this context (BDAG, s.v. "ὅς" 1a, p. 725). **Syntactically**, οὗ introduces a dependent adjectival relative clause "for which I am bound in chains" (ὑπὲρ οὗ πρεσβεύω ἐν ἁλύσει). The antecedent could be "mystery" (μυστήριον) (Hoehner, 863), "gospel" (εὐαγγελίου) (Arnold, 468), or the infinitival clause (Larkin, 165). Since "gospel" is the closest to the pronoun, it is most likely the antecedent. However, since it is in apposition to "mystery," there is very little difference in meaning (Merkle, 220). The pronoun functions as the object of the preposition ὑπέρ. Hoehner states that the preposition conveys that the gospel is the reason for his imprisonment (Hoehner, 865); however, it may simply mean that Paul is an ambassador *for* the gospel (Arnold, 468; BDAG, s.v. "ὑπέρ" 2, p. 1031; cf. ESV, RSV, NRSV, NIV, NET, CSB, HCSB, NASB, NKJV, KJV).

πρεσβεύω: The Greek word πρεσβεύω is a first-person singular present active indicative from the verb πρεσβεύω that means "to work as an ambassador" (BDAG, s.v. "πρεσβεύω," 861). **Syntactically**, πρεσβεύω functions as the main verb of the relative clause. The subject is implied by the verb: "I," referring to Paul. **Semantically**, πρεσβεύω is a customary present: "I am an ambassador" (ESV, RSV, NRSV, NIV, NET, CSB, HCSB, NASB, NKJV, KJV). The present tense describes an ongoing state, namely that of Paul's ambassadorship (W, 521–22).

> **Semantical Nugget**: What does the phrase "in chains" (ἐν ἁλύσει) mean? The prepositional phrase "in chains" (ἐν ἁλύσει) expresses sphere. The phrase metaphorically refers to Paul's imprisonment (BDAG, s.v. "ἅλυσις" 2, p. 48). The image is paradoxical. An ambassador would have been appointed as a high-ranking official to represent the senate or even the emperor. In order to speak on behalf of the government that they represent, they never would be faced with the kind of incarceration in which Paul suffered. This would have given them the freedom to speak boldly, which is part of Paul's request (vv. 19c, 20b) (Arnold, 468; Hoehner, 864).

6:20b ἵνα: The Greek word ἵνα is a conjunction that means "that" in this context (BDAG, s.v. "ἵνα" 2ca, p. 476). **Syntactically**, ἵνα introduces a dependent conjunctive clause "*that* a word might be given to me when I speak" (ἵνα ἐν αὐτῷ παρρησιάσωμαι). The clause functions substantively as the direct object of the participle προσευχόμενοι (v. 18a). **Semantically**, ἵνα introduces the content of Paul's second request. His first request is that God gives him the words to speak. This request is that he speaks these words boldly.

παρρησιάσωμαι: The Greek word παρρησιάσωμαι is a first-person singular aorist middle subjunctive from the verb παρρησιάζομαι that means "to speak freely" or "fearlessly" (BDAG, s.v. "παρρησιάζομαι" 1, p. 782). This is the verbal cognate of the noun παρρησία (v. 19c). **Syntactically**, παρρησιάσωμαι functions as the main verb of the dependent conjunctive clause introduced by ἵνα. The subject is implied by the verb: "I," referring to Paul. **Semantically**, παρρησιάσωμαι is a constative aorist: "I may speak boldly" (NET, NASB, NKJV, KJV). It describes the action of the verb as a whole (W, 557–58). The prepositional phrase "in it" (ἐν αὐτῷ) expresses sphere. The antecedent of the pronoun is the relative pronoun in verse 20a, a reference to the gospel.

6:20c ὡς: The Greek word ὡς is a conjunction that means "as" in this context (BDAG, "ὡς" 1a, p. 1103). **Syntactically**, ὡς introduces a dependent conjunctive clause "*as* it is necessary for me to speak" (ὡς δεῖ με λαλῆσαι). The entire clause functions adverbially, modifying the verb "I may speak boldly" (παρρησιάσωμαι). **Semantically**, ὡς expresses a comparison: "as" (ESV, RSV, NRSV, NIV, NET, CSB, HCSB, NASB, NKJV, KJV). The conjunctive clause gives the request a sense of solemnity. Paul's use of δεῖ suggests that this is a divine prerogative. This is not just his request, it is a "divine necessity" (Arnold, 468).

δεῖ: The Greek word δεῖ is a third-person singular present active indicative from the verb δεῖ that means "it is necessary," indicating that a general event should occur "because it is fitting" (BDAG, s.v. "δεῖ" 2a, p. 214). **Syntactically**, δεῖ functions as the main verb of the dependent conjunctive clause introduced by ὡς. **Semantically**, δεῖ is a customary present: "it is necessary." Most English versions treat the accusative pronoun με as the subject: "as I ought" (ESV, RSV, NASB, NET) or "as I should" (NIV, CSB, HCSB). The present tense describes an ongoing state (W, 521–22). Every time Paul speaks the gospel, he should do so with boldness.

λαλῆσαι: The Greek word λαλῆσαι is an aorist active infinitive from the verb λαλέω that means "to talk" or "speak" (BDAG, s.v. "λαλέω" 2aβ, pp. 582–83). **Syntactically**, λαλῆσαι introduces a dependent infinitival clause. The entire clause "speak" (λαλῆσαι) functions adverbially, modifying the main verb δεῖ ("it is necessary"). The subject of the infinitive is the accusative pronoun με, referring to Paul. **Semantically**, λαλῆσαι is a complementary infinitive. It completes the thought of the verb "it is necessary" (δεῖ).

EPHESIANS 6:21–24

Big Greek Idea: Paul closes the letter by commending Tychicus, a trusted servant who ministers to the church, to provide an update of his circumstances, and by praying that God gives them peace, love, faith, and grace.

Structural Overview: Paul signals the end of his letter with the conjunction δέ: "*Now.*" The end of the letter serves two parts. In the first part, Paul commends Tychicus to the readers, who will give a report on Paul's situation (Eph. 6:21–22). As the letter carrier, Tychicus would have been in the best position to provide an update. His imprisonment was due to the accusation of bringing Gentiles into the temple—even one from Ephesus (Acts 21:29)! It would have been natural for the believers in Ephesus to hear what has transpired, which would encourage their hearts. Tychicus most likely carried a letter to the church at Colossae (Col. 4:7). Presumably, since Onesimus, the runaway slave, accompanied him (Col. 4:9), he also delivered a letter to Philemon. In Colossians 4:7, he gives Tychicus the same role, to give the church an update.

In the second part of the conclusion, Paul gives a two-part benediction. Both phrases follow a similar pattern: neither phrase contains a conjunction or a verb. We have to supply some form of εἰμί. First, he wishes that the readers receive peace and love from God the Father and Jesus Christ. Second, he wishes that they receive grace. Both "peace" and "grace" are placed at the beginning of the clause for emphasis. The benediction mimics Paul's initial wish for health: "grace and peace to you from God our Father and Lord Jesus Christ" (Eph. 1:2).

Two details about how Paul closes out Ephesians stand out. First, there are no personal greetings in Ephesians, which he normally includes (cf. Rom. 16:1–16). This omission might be due to the fact that it was a circular letter, so the audience would have been larger. Regardless, this gap does not necessitate that Paul is unknown to the community. Tychicus would have been able to relay any personal greeting. The second detail is that he normally delivers a benediction in the second person. In Ephesians, he gives the benediction the third person: "Peace be to *the brothers and sisters.*" Again, this might be due to the letter's broader audience (Thielman, 438–39).

Outline:

> Paul commends Tychicus to the readers to give a report about Paul's situation (vv. 21–22)
> Paul ends his letter with a benediction wishing the readers peace and grace (vv. 23–24)

Clausal Outline for Ephesians 6:21–24

^{6:21a} **Ἵνα** δὲ **εἰδῆτε** καὶ ὑμεῖς τὰ κατ᾽ ἐμέ, (τί πράσσω),
^{6:21a} <u>Now **that**</u> you also **might know** about my circumstances (<u>what</u> I am doing),

^{6:21b} πάντα **γνωρίσει** ὑμῖν Τυχικὸς ὁ ἀγαπητὸς ἀδελφὸς καὶ πιστὸς διάκονος ἐν κυρίῳ,
^{6:21b} Tychicus, the beloved brother and faithful servant in the Lord, **will make known** all things to you

[Τυχικὸς (v.21)]

^{6:22a} <u>ὃν</u> **ἔπεμψα** πρὸς ὑμᾶς εἰς αὐτὸ τοῦτο
^{6:22a} **I am sending** <u>him</u> to you for this very reason

^{6:22b} **ἵνα γνῶτε** τὰ περὶ ἡμῶν
^{6:22b} **so that you may know** about our circumstances

^{6:22c} <u>καὶ</u> **παρακαλέσῃ** τὰς καρδίας ὑμῶν.
^{6:22c} <u>and</u> that **he may encourage** your heart.

^{6:23} Εἰρήνη [**εἴη**] τοῖς ἀδελφοῖς καὶ ἀγάπη μετὰ πίστεως ἀπὸ θεοῦ πατρὸς καὶ κυρίου Ἰησοῦ Χριστοῦ.
^{6:23} Peace and love [**be**] to the brothers and sisters with faith from God the Father and the Lord Jesus Christ.

^{6:24} ἡ χάρις [**εἴη**] μετὰ (πάντων τῶν ἀγαπώντων) τὸν κύριον ἡμῶν Ἰησοῦν Χριστὸν ἐν ἀφθαρσίᾳ.
^{6:24} Grace [**be**] with (all of those who love) our Lord Jesus Christ in incorruptibility.

Syntax Explained for Ephesians 6:21–24

^{6:21a} δέ: The Greek word δέ is a conjunction that means "but" (BDAG, s.v. "δέ" 2, p. 213). **Syntactically**, δέ is in the postpositive position, introducing an independent conjunctive clause: "*Now* that you might know the things concerning me" (Ἵνα δὲ καὶ ὑμεῖς εἰδῆτε τὰ κατ᾽ ἐμέ). **Semantically**, δέ is transitional, marking a change of topic: "now" (RSV) or "so" (ESV, NRSV, NIV, NET, CSB, HCSB) (W, 674). Some versions translate the conjunction as "but" (NASB, NKJV, KJV). Paul uses the conjunction to transition to the final section of the letter.

ἵνα: The Greek word ἵνα is a conjunction that means "that" in this context (BDAG, "ἵνα" 1aδ, p. 475). **Syntactically**, the conjunction ἵνα introduces a conjunctive dependent clause. The entire clause "that you might know about my circumstances" (ἵνα δὲ καὶ ὑμεῖς εἰδῆτε τὰ κατ᾽ ἐμέ) functions adverbially, modifying the main verb of the sentence in the following clause "will make known" (γνωρίσει). **Semantically**, ἵνα marks the clause as purpose: "so that" (ESV, NRSV, NIV, NET, CSB, HCSB). The clause expresses the reason for Tychicus's report—so that the Ephesians might learn about Paul's circumstances.

εἰδῆτε: The Greek word εἰδῆτε is a second-person plural perfect active subjunctive from the verb οἶδα that means "to understand," "recognize," or "experience" (BDAG, s.v. "οἶδα" 1b, p. 693). **Syntactically**, εἰδῆτε functions as the main verb of the dependent conjunctive clause introduced by ἵνα. The subject is "you" (ὑμεῖς), referring to the Ephesian readers. The direct object is the phrase "the things about me" (τὰ κατ᾽ ἐμέ). The article makes the prepositional phrase substantival. The ESV translates the phrase "how I am" (cf. RSV, NRSV, NIV, NLT); the CSB translates it "about me"; and the NET translates it "my circumstances" (NASB; cf. BDAG, s.v. "κατά" B6, p. 513). **Semantically**, εἰδῆτε functions as a perfect with a present tense force (W, 579–80). Just as Paul has received news about the church (cf. Eph. 1:15), he hopes to relay information about his situation to them.

τί: The Greek word τί is an indefinite pronoun from the word τίς that means "what" or "what sort of" (BDAG, s.v. "τίς" 1αβ‏ב‏, p. 1007; W, 345–46). **Syntactically**, τί introduces a clause in apposition to τὰ κατ᾽ ἐμέ. It functions as the direct object of the verb: "I am doing" (πράσσω). Several versions translate it "what I am doing" (ESV, RSV, NRSV, NLT; Best, 614). Since they probably know his circumstances, the phrase might best be translated as "how I am doing" (NASB, NET, NKJV, KJV; Hoehner, 868; Arnold, 479). The CSB translates the phrase as "the news about me."

πράσσω: The Greek word πράσσω is a first-person singular present active indicative from the verb πράσσω that means "to be situated" (BDAG, s.v. "πράσσω" 1a, p. 860). **Syntactically**, πράσσω functions as the main verb of the clause introduced by τί. The subject is implied by the verb: "I," referring to Paul. **Semantically**, πράσσω is a customary present: "I am doing" (ESV, RSV, NRSV, NIV, NET, NASB, NKJV, KJV). The present tense describes an ongoing state (W, 521–22).

6:21b γνωρίσει: The Greek word γνωρίσει is a third-person singular future active indicative from the verb γνωρίζω that means "to make known" (BDAG, s.v. "γνωρίζω" 1, p. 203). **Syntactically**, γνωρίσει functions as the main verb of the independent conjunctive clause introduced by δέ (v. 21a). The subject is Tychicus (Τυχικός). The nominative phrase "the beloved brother and faithful servant in the Lord" (ὁ ἀγαπητὸς ἀδελφὸς καὶ πιστὸς διάκονος ἐν κυρίῳ) is in apposition to Τυχικός. The direct object is "all things" (πάντα). The indirect object is "you" (ὑμῖν), referring to the Ephesian readers. **Semantically**, the future tense functions as a predictive future, which looks forward to a time when Tychicus will deliver the letter.

> **Lexical Nugget**: Who is Tychicus? Tychicus was most likely the letter carrier, presumably the same person who carried Colossians (Col. 4:7). Rather than give an extensive list of greetings, Paul leaves it for Tychicus to greet those in both Ephesus and Colossae. There is little to know about him, though it appears that he is one of Paul's most trusted assistants. He was from Asia, and possibly Ephesus (Acts 20:4). Though it is not clear if he journeyed with Paul to Jerusalem prior to his arrest, he was with Paul in Rome. He thought about sending him to Titus in Crete (Titus 3:12). Finally, he sent him to Ephesus (2 Tim. 4:12). Tychicus could have delivered up to five letters for Paul: Ephesians, Colossians, Philemon, 2 Timothy, and Titus (Hoehner, 870). Paul calls him "beloved brother and faithful servant" (ὁ ἀγαπητὸς ἀδελφὸς καὶ πιστὸς διάκονος). In Greek, this is an example of the Granville Sharp rule, where one article governs two nouns joined together with καί (W, 270–72). This is no insignificant description. In light of the fact that several abandoned Paul throughout his ministry, the fact that Tychicus was available for Paul at the end of his ministry is encouraging.

6:22a ὅν: The Greek word ὅν is a masculine singular accusative from the relative pronoun ὅς that means "who" (BDAG, s.v. "ὅς" 1a, p. 725). **Syntactically**, ὅν introduces an adjectival relative clause "whom I send" (ὅν ἔπεμψα). The antecedent of the pronoun is Tychicus. The pronoun functions as the direct object of the verb "I send" (ἔπεμψα). Because of the syntax, most English translations begin a new sentence with verse 22 and translate the relative pronoun as a personal pronoun: "I am sending him" (NRSV, NIV, CSB, HCSB).

ἔπεμψα: The Greek word ἔπεμψα is a first-person singular aorist active indicative from the verb πέμπω that means "to send" (BDAG, s.v. "πέμπω" 1, pp. 794–95). **Syntactically**, ἔπεμψα functions as the main verb of the relative clause. The subject is implied by the verb: "I," referring to Paul. **Semantically**, ἔπεμψα functions as an epistolary aorist. Even though the action has not occurred—Paul is still writing the letter—he portrays the action from the readers' point of view (W, 562–63; Lincoln, 465; Merkle, 224). Because of this, the aorist is best translated: "I am sending" (NRSV, NIV, CSB, HCSB), not "I have sent" (ESV, RSV, NET, NASB, NKJV, KJV, NLT). The prepositional phrase εἰς αὐτὸ τοῦτο conveys the notion of purpose: "for this very reason" (BDAG, s.v. "εἰς" 4f, p. 290).

6:22b ἵνα: The Greek word ἵνα is a conjunction that means "that" in this context to express purpose (BDAG, s.v. "ἵνα" 1aε, p. 475). **Syntactically**, ἵνα introduces a dependent conjunctive clause "*that* you might know the things concerning me and that he might encourage your heart" (ἵνα γνῶτε τὰ περὶ ἡμῶν καὶ παρακαλέσῃ τὰς καρδίας ὑμῶν). The entire clause functions adverbially, modifying the verb of the relative clause: "I am sending" (ἔπεμψα; v. 22a). **Semantically**, the ἵνα clause expresses purpose: "so that" (NASB) or "that" (ESV, RSV, NIV, NET, NKJV, KJV).

γνῶτε: The Greek word γνῶτε is a second-person plural aorist active subjunctive from the verb γινώσκω that means "to know" or "learn of" (BDAG, s.v. "γινώσκω" 2a, p. 200). **Syntactically**, γνῶτε functions as the main verb of the dependent conjunctive clause introduced by ἵνα. The subject is implied by the verb: "you," referring to the Ephesian believers. The direct object is the clause "the things concerning us" (τὰ περὶ ἡμῶν). The article makes the prepositional phrase substantival. **Semantically**, γνῶτε is a constative aorist: "you may know" (ESV, RSV, NRSV, NIV, NET, NASB, NKJV). It describes the action of the verb as a whole (W, 557–58). Paul reiterates his comments from verse 21, but he changes the pronoun from first-person singular to first-person plural. Not only does he want them to know about his own circumstances, but the circumstances of the other believers in his community.

6:22c καί: The Greek word καί is a conjunction that means "and" (BDAG, s.v. "καί" 1bδ, p. 494). **Syntactically**, καί introduces a dependent conjunctive clause: "*and* that he may encourage your heart" (καὶ παρακαλέσῃ τὰς καρδίας ὑμῶν). **Semantically**, καί is a coordinating connective: "and" (ESV, RSV, NIV, NET). The conjunction introduces the second purpose for sending Tychicus.

παρακαλέσῃ: The Greek word παρακαλέσῃ is a third-person singular aorist active subjunctive from the verb παρακαλέω that means "to comfort," "encourage," or "cheer" (BDAG, s.v. "παρακαλέω" 4, p. 765). **Syntactically**, παρακαλέσῃ functions as the main verb of the dependent conjunctive clause introduced by καί. It is the second part of the purpose clause introduced by ἵνα in 6:22b. The subject is implied by the verb: "he," referring to Tychicus. The direct object is "hearts" (τὰς καρδίας), a metaphor describing the inner being of a person, the center of their emotions (BDAG, s.v. "καρδία" 1bε, p. 509). **Semantically**, παρακαλέσῃ is a constative aorist: "he may encourage" (ESV, RSV, NIV, NET). It describes the action of the verb as a whole (W, 557–58). Paul offers a similar statement in Ephesians 3:13—by providing the details of his situation, he hopes that they might not lose heart.

6:23 [εἴη]: The Greek word εἴη is a third-person present active optative from the verb εἰμί (BDAG, s.v. "εἰμί" 3c, p. 284). **Syntactically**, the ellipsis [εἴη] is the main verb of the asyndeton clause. The subjects are "peace" (εἰρήνη) and "love" (ἀγάπη). The indirect object is "the brothers" (τοῖς ἀδελφοῖς).

Since the audience is mixed, the reference is "brothers *and sisters*" (BDAG, s.v. "ἀδελφός" 2a, p. 18; cf. CSB, NIV, NET, NLT). **Semantically**, the ellipsis [εἴη] is a gnomic present, describing a general statement (W, 523–25). The clause is modified by two prepositional phrases. The first prepositional phrase "with faith" (μετὰ πίστεως) expresses association (BDAG, s.v. "μετά" 2f, p. 637). Even though peace and love are emphasized, faith is closely related. The second prepositional phrase "from God the Father and the Lord Jesus Christ" (ἀπὸ θεοῦ πατρὸς καὶ κυρίου Ἰησοῦ Χριστοῦ) conveys the notion of source. Both peace and love are important themes throughout Ephesians. Paul begins the letter by wishing his readers peace (Eph. 1:2). Christ's death gives them peace (Eph. 2:15, 17; cf. 6:15). Peace holds the community together (Eph. 4:3). Likewise, love is the basis of God's salvation (Eph. 1:4; 2:4). Because of this love, believers should love one another (Eph. 1:15; 4:2, 15, 16; 5:2).

6:24   [εἴη]: The Greek word εἴη is a third-person present active optative from the verb εἰμί (BDAG, s.v. "εἰμί" 3c, p. 284). **Syntactically**, the ellipsis [εἴη] is the main verb of the asyndeton clause. The subject is "grace" (χάρις). **Semantically**, the ellipsis [εἴη] is a gnomic present, describing a general statement (W, 523–25). The prepositional phrase "with all those who love the Lord" (μετὰ πάντων τῶν ἀγαπώντων τὸν κύριον) expresses association. The phrase follows the pattern of the first half of the benediction (v. 23), but here μετά expresses an association with other believers (BDAG, s.v. "μετά" A2aγ ℷ, p. 636). Besides peace, love, and faith (v. 23), grace also plays a significant role in the book. God saves the believer as an act of grace—"for it is by grace you are saved" (Eph. 2:5, 7, 8). He ends the book in a similar manner as the beginning, by wishing grace and peace on his readers. Here, however, he reverses the order.

ἀγαπώντων: The Greek word ἀγαπώντων is a masculine genitive plural present active participle from the verb ἀγαπάω that means "to cherish," "to love," or "to have affection for" (BDAG, s.v. "ἀγαπάω" 1aβ, p. 5). **Syntactically**, ἀγαπώντων is a substantival participle functioning as the object of the preposition μετά. The direct object of the participle is "the Lord" (τὸν κύριον). **Semantically**, ἀγαπώντων is a customary present: "love" (ESV, RSV, NRSV, NIV, NET, CSB, HCSB, NASB, NKJV, KJV). The present tense describes an ongoing state (W, 521–22). The substantival participle refers to all of the believers. The phrase expresses the close association that these Ephesians have with all the believers.

> **Syntactical Nugget**: What does the prepositional phrase "in incorruptibility" (ἐν ἀφθαρσίᾳ) modify? The object of the preposition is ἀφθαρσία meaning "incorruptibility" or "immortality," referring to a state not subject to decay (BDAG, s.v. "ἀφθαρσία," p. 155). The syntax of the preposition

impacts the meaning of the object. First, Arnold argues that the prepositional phrase modifies χάρις. This suggests that either this grace is incorruptible or perhaps incorruptibility is associated with grace (Arnold, 482–83; Osborne, 241; cf. NLT). Paul uses the preposition in a similar way in Ephesians 6:2 (Robertson, 588–89). The position of the prepositional phrase makes this view difficult. If Paul intended the phrase to modify χάρις, he would have placed it earlier in the sentence (Thielman, 446). Second, it could modify the final phrase "our Lord Jesus Christ." This view takes advantage of the fact that the prepositional phrase immediately follows. This requires that we translate the preposition as sphere. Baugh suggests this translation: "our Lord Jesus Christ, who *dwells in incorruptibility*" (Baugh, 576). The problem with this view is that the object, φθαρσία, suggests a state of being, not a location (Hoehner, 876). Finally, it could refer to the participle τῶν ἀγαπώντων. This suggests that the Ephesians love the Lord Jesus Christ with an incorruptible love. Most English translations render the prepositional phrase as an attributive adjective: "with undying love" (NRSV, NIV, NET) or "incorruptible love" (NASB, ESV) (Thielman, 447–48; Hoehner, 877).

Text-Critical Nugget: Does Paul conclude the letter with "amen" (ἀμήν)? Several Byzantine manuscripts (𝔐, K, L), some secondary Alexandrian manuscripts (104 and 1739^c), and a key Western manuscript (D) add ἀμήν at the end of the letter. On the other hand, the majority of our Alexandrian manuscripts (𝔓^{46}, ℵ, A, B, 33, 81, 1175, 1739*, 1881) and Western manuscripts (F and G) omit the ending. Paul seems to end Romans (16:27) and Galatians (6:18) with this word; however, this variant appears at the end of each of his letters. The fact that the omission is found in most of our earlier manuscripts in both the Alexandrian and Western texttype suggests that the omission is a better reading. It would have been routine for a scribe to add the liturgy at the end of each book, suggesting that it is secondary.

Ephesians: Interpretive Translation

PAUL'S GREETING TO THE EPHESIAN CHURCH

1:1Paul, an apostle of Christ Jesus by the will of God, to the saints who are in Ephesus and the faithful in Christ Jesus; 2grace and peace to you from God our Father and the Lord Jesus Christ.

GOD'S BLESSING

3Blessed be the God and Father of our Lord Jesus Christ, who blesses us with all spiritual blessing in the heavenly places in Christ 4because he chose us in him before the foundation of the world so that we should be holy and blameless before him in love 5while predestining us for adoption through Jesus Christ to himself according to his pleasurable will 6for the praise of his glorious grace, which he gave to us in the beloved. 7In whom we have the redemption through his blood, the forgiveness of our trespasses according to his rich grace, 8which he lavished on us in all wisdom and insight, 9by making known to us the mystery of his will, according to his pleasure, which he intended in him 10for the administration of the fullness of time, namely to bring all things together in Christ, the things in the heavens and the things on the earth in him. 11In him we have also obtained an inheritance because we were predestined according to the plan of the one who works all things according to the will of his desire 12so that we, the ones who have already hoped in Christ, might be for the praise for his glory. 13In him you also, when you heard the word of truth, the gospel of your salvation, in whom also, when you believed, you were sealed with the promised Holy Spirit, 14who is the down payment of our inheritance until the redemption of the possession for the praise of his glory.

A PRAYER OF THANKSGIVING

15For this reason, after hearing about your faith in the Lord Jesus and your love for all of the saints, 16I do not cease giving thanks on your behalf while remembering you in my prayers, 17that the God of our Lord Jesus Christ, the glorious Father might give to you spiritual wisdom and revelation in knowing him 18since the eyes of your heart have been enlightened so that you may know what is the hope of his calling, what is the wealth of the glorious inheritance from him among the saints, 19and what is his surpassingly great power for us who believe according to the working of his strong might. 20He exercised this power in Christ by raising him from the dead and by seating him at his right hand in the heavenly places 21high above every rule and authority and power and dominion and every name which is called upon, not only in this age, but in the age to come. [22]And he put all things under his feet and he appointed him as the head over all things to the church, [23]which is his body, the fullness of the one who fills all in all.

A New Life—Sinners Saved by Grace

[2:1]And even though you were dead in your trespasses and sins, [2]in which you once walked according to the age of this world, according to the ruler over the authority of the air, over the spirit who is now working in the sons of disobedience [3]among whom also we all behaved once in the lusts of our flesh, by carrying out the will of the flesh and mind, and we were children destined for wrath because of our nature, even as the rest were; [4]but God, because he is rich in mercy, because of his great love, with which he loved us, [5]and even though we were dead in our trespasses, he made us alive with Christ—you are saved on the basis of grace—[6]and he raised us with him and he seated us in the heavenly places in Christ Jesus [7]so that he might show his surpassing wealth of grace in kindness toward us in Christ Jesus in the coming age. [8]For you are saved on the basis of grace through faith; and this is not from yourselves; it is a gift from God; [9]it is not from works, so that no one can boast. [10]For we are his workmanship, because we have been created in Christ Jesus for good works, which God prepared beforehand so that we might walk in them.

A New People—Jews and Gentiles Brought Together in Peace

[11]Therefore, remember that once you—Gentiles in the flesh, the ones called "uncircumcised" by the so-called "circumcised," done by hand in the flesh—[12]that you were at that time without the Messiah, by being alienated from the citizenship of Israel and strangers of the covenants of promise, by having no hope and godless in the world. [13]But now in Christ Jesus you, who were once far off, have been brought near by the blood of Christ. [14]For he is our peace, the one who has made both groups into one and destroyed the dividing wall, the partition, which is the hostility, in his flesh, [15]by making the law of commandments in ordinances powerless, so that he might create in him one new person from the two, as a result making peace [16]and so that he might reconcile both into one body to God through the cross, by killing the enmity in it. [17]And when he came, he proclaimed the good news of peace to you who were far off and peace to those who were near, [18]for through him we both have access in one Spirit to the Father. [19]So then, you are no longer strangers and aliens, but you are fellow citizens with the saints and members of the house of God, [20]because you have been built on the foundation, namely the apostles and prophets—Christ Jesus himself being the cornerstone, [21]in whom the whole building, by being joined together, grows into a holy temple in the Lord, [22]in whom also you are being built together into a dwelling place for God by the Spirit.

Paul's Ministry to Proclaim the Mystery of Christ

3:1For this reason, I Paul, a prisoner of Christ Jesus on behalf of you, the Gentiles—2if indeed you have heard of the administration of God's grace, which was given to me for you, 3that the mystery has been made known to me according to revelation, just as I previously wrote in short, 4according to which, when you read, you are able to understand my insight in the mystery of Christ, 5which was not made known to the sons of men in other generations as it has now been revealed to his holy apostles and prophets by the Spirit, 6that the Gentiles are fellow heirs, fellow members of the body, and fellow partakers of the promise in Christ Jesus through the gospel 7of which I became a servant according to the gift, namely God's grace, which was given to me according to the working of his power. 8This grace was given to me, the very least of all of the saints, to proclaim the good news of the unfathomable wealth of Christ to the Gentiles, 9and to enlighten all people what is the administration of the mystery which was hidden for ages in God, who created all things, 10so that the multifaceted wisdom of God might now be made known to the rulers and authorities in the heavenly places through the church 11according to his eternal purpose, which he accomplished in Christ Jesus our Lord, 12in whom we have boldness and access with confidence through faith in him. 13Therefore, I ask that you not be discouraged because of my suffering on your behalf, which is your glory.

Benediction: A Prayer to Be Strengthened by God

14For this reason, I bow my knees before the Father, 15from whom every family in the heavens and on the earth receives its name 16that he grant you, according to his glorious wealth, to be strengthened with power through his Spirit in your inner being, 17that Christ might dwell through faith in your hearts; because you have been rooted and established in love 18that you may be able to comprehend with all the saints what is the width and length and height and depth 19and to know Christ's love for you, which surpasses knowledge; and that you might be filled to all of the fullness of God. 20Now to the one who is able to do above all, infinitely more than what we ask or think according to the power that works in us, 21to him be the glory in the church and in Christ Jesus in every generation forever and ever, amen.

Walk in Unity to Achieve Maturity

4:1Therefore, I, a prisoner in the Lord, urge you to walk worthy of the calling by which you were called, 2with all humility and gentleness, with patience, by bearing one another with love, 3by making every effort to keep the unity of the Spirit in the uniting bonds of peace. 4There is one body, and there is one Spirit, 5just as you have also been called in one hope of your calling; there is one Lord; there is one faith; there is one baptism; [6]there is one God and Father of all, who is over all and through all and in all. [7]But grace was given to each one of us according to the measure of the gift of Christ. [8]Therefore it says: "While ascending on high, he took prisoners captive; he gave gifts to people." [9]Now what does "he ascended" mean except that he also descended to the lower parts, namely the earth. [10]The very one who descended is also the one who ascended above all the heavens so that he might fill all things. [11]And he gave some as apostles, some as prophets, some as evangelists, and some as shepherds and other teachers [12]for the equipping of the saints for the work, that is, the ministry for the building up of the body of Christ, [13]until we all attain to the unity of faith and the knowledge of the Son of God, to the complete person, to the measure that is Christ's full stature, [14]so that we are no longer infants being tossed by the waves and being carried about by every wind of doctrine, by craftiness of man, by trickery in deceitful schemes; [15]but by practicing the truth in love, that we may grow in him in all things, who is the head, Christ, [16]from whom the whole body, joined and held together by every supporting ligament according to the working capacity of each individual part, makes the body grow so that it builds itself up in love.

WALK IN HOLINESS

[17]Therefore, I say this, and I testify in the Lord, that you no longer walk just as the Gentiles also walk in the futility of their minds, [18]with the result of being darkened in their understanding, with the result of being alienated from the life that God gives, because of the ignorance that is in them due to the hardness of their heart [19]who, because they have become callous, gave themselves over to sensuality for the practice of all uncleanliness with greed. [20]But you have not learned Christ in such a manner, [21]if indeed you heard about him and were taught in him, just as the truth is in Jesus, [22]that you put off the old self who is corrupted according to the former behavior according to the desires from deceit, [23]but you are being renewed in your spirit, your mind, [24]and you put on the new self who is created according to God's likeness in righteousness and holiness from truth. [25]Therefore, since you have put away falsehood, let each of you speak the truth with their neighbor, because we are members of one another. [26]Be angry and do not sin, do not allow the sun to set while you are angry [27]nor give the devil an opportunity. [28]The one who steals must no longer steal, but rather must do work by producing what is good with his own hands, so that they may have something to share with the one who has need. [29]Do not let any unwholesome word come out of your mouth, but whatever is good for the edification of the need let it come out, so that it may give grace to those who hear. [30]And do not grieve the Holy Spirit of God, in whom you were sealed for the day of redemption. [31]Let all bitterness, anger, wrath, shouting, and slander be put away from you with all wickedness. [32]But be kind to one another, compassionate, by forgiving one another just as also God forgave us in Christ.

WALK IN LOVE

[5:1]Therefore be imitators of God, as beloved children, [2]and walk in love, just as also Christ loved us and gave himself up for us as an offering and sacrifice to God for a fragrant offering. [3]But also do not let sexual immorality, any uncleanliness, or greediness be named among you, because it is not proper among the saints, [4]nor let obscenity, foolish talk, or sarcastic ridicule be named, which is not fitting, but rather let thanksgiving be named. [5]For you certainly know this, that every immoral, unclean, or greedy person, that is an idolater, does not have an inheritance in the kingdom of Christ and God. [6]Let no one deceive you with empty words, for because of these things, the wrath of God comes upon the sons of disobedience.

WALK IN LIGHT

[7]Therefore do not become partners with them; [8]For you were once darkness, but now you are light in the Lord; as children of the light, walk—[9]for the fruit of light is in all goodness, righteousness, and truth—[10]by testing what is pleasing to the Lord. [11]And do not participate in the unfruitful works of darkness, but rather expose them. [12]For even to say the things done by them in secret is shameful, [13]but all things that are exposed by the light become clear, [14]for all things that are made clear are light. Therefore it says:

> "Get up, sleeper,
> and rise up from the dead,
> and Christ will shine on you."

WALK IN WISDOM

[15]Therefore, watch carefully how you walk, not as the foolish, but as the wise, [16]by making the most of the opportunity, because the days are evil. [17]For this reason, do not become foolish, but understand what is the will of the Lord. [18]And do not get drunk with wine, in which is debauchery, but be filled by the Spirit [19]with the result of speaking to one another with psalms, hymns, and spiritual songs, with the result of singing and with the result of making music with your heart to the Lord, [20]with the result of giving thanks always for all things in the name of our Lord Jesus Christ to God and Father, [21]with the result of submitting to one another in the fear of Christ.

HOUSEHOLD RULES 1: WIVES AND HUSBANDS

[22]Wives, submit to your own husbands as you submit to the Lord, [23]because the husband is the head of his wife as Christ also is the head of the church, he is the savior of the body. [24]But as the church submits to Christ, thus also wives submit

to their husbands in all things. [25]Husbands, love your wives, just as Christ also loved the church and gave himself up for her, [26]so that he might sanctify her by cleansing her with the washing of the water by the word, [27]so that he might present the church to himself as glorious, not having a spot, wrinkle, or any such thing, but that she might be holy and blameless, [28]thus husbands also ought to love their wives as they love their own body. He who loves his wife loves himself. [29]For no one ever hates his own flesh, but nourishes and cherishes it, just as Christ also nourishes and cherishes the church, [30]because we are members of his body. [31]For this reason, a man shall leave his father and mother and be joined to his wife, and the two will become one flesh. [32]This mystery is great, but I am speaking about Christ and about the church. [33]Nevertheless, each of you, love his own wife as he loves himself, and the wife should respect her husband.

Household Rules 2: Children and Parents

[6:1]Children, obey your parents in the Lord, for this is right. [2]Honor your father and mother, as it is the first commandment with a promise, [3]that it may be well for you and you will live long in the land. [4]And fathers, do not anger your children, but bring them up with discipline and instruction from the Lord.

Household Rules 3: Slaves and Masters

[5]Slaves, obey your humanly masters with fear and trembling in sincerity of your heart, as you obey Christ, [6]not by being watched as people pleasers, but as slaves of Christ, by doing the will of God from your heart, [7]by serving with goodwill as you are serving the Lord and not men, [8]because you know that each of you, whether slave or free, if you do something good, will receive this back from the Lord. [9]And masters, do the same to them by stopping your threats, because you know that also their Lord and yours is in heaven and there is no partiality with him.

Strength to Withstand Spiritual Attack

[10]Finally, be strengthened in the Lord and in his mighty strength. [11]Put on the whole armor of God so that you can stand against the schemes of the devil [12]because our struggle is not against blood and flesh but against the rulers, against authorities, against world rulers of this darkness, against the spiritual forces of evil in the heavens. [13]For this reason, take up the whole armor of God, so that you may be able to withstand in the evil day and after you have done everything, to stand. [14]Therefore, stand by girding your waist with truth, and by putting on the breastplate of righteousness, [15]and by binding your feet with the preparation of the gospel of peace, [16]in all things, by taking up the shield of faith, with which you will be able to extinguish all of the fiery arrows of the evil one [17]and take the helmet of salvation and the sword of the Spirit, which is the word of God,

[18]by praying through all prayers and petitions, in every season by the Spirit and to this end by being alert with all perseverance and all petition concerning the saints [19]and for me that a word may be given to me when I speak to make known with boldness the mystery of the gospel, [20]for which I work as an ambassador in chains, that I may boldly proclaim about it as it is necessary for me to speak.

A Final Greeting and Wish for Peace

[21]Now that you also might know about my circumstances, what I am doing, Tychicus, the beloved brother and faithful servant in the Lord, will make known all things to you. [22]I am sending him for this very reason, so that you may know about our circumstances and that he may encourage your heart. [23]Peace and love be to the brothers and sisters with faith from God the Father and the Lord Jesus Christ. [24]Grace be with all of those who love our Lord Jesus Christ in incorruptibility.

Figures of Speech in Ephesians

FIGURES OF SPEECH INVOLVING COMPARISON

1. <u>Simile</u>, or Resemblance: a declaration that one thing explicitly (by the presence of "like" or "as") resembles another.

    Ephesians 5:1 "Therefore be imitators of God <u>as</u> beloved children"

    Ephesians 5:15 "Therefore, watch out how you walk, not <u>as</u> the foolish, but <u>as</u> the wise."

2. <u>Metaphor</u>, or Representation: a declaration that one thing is or represents another.

    Ephesians 1:14 "<u>The Holy Spirit</u> is the down payment." (CSB)

    Ephesians 2:20b "<u>Christ Jesus himself being</u> the cornerstone"

    Ephesians 5:23 "The <u>husband is</u> the head of the of the wife."

    Ephesians 6:20 "<u>I am</u> an ambassador in chains."

3. <u>Hypocatastasis</u>, or Implication: a declaration that implies the comparison.

    Ephesians 6:13 "For this reason take up <u>the whole armor of God</u>, so that you may be able to withstand in the evil day."

4. <u>Allegory</u>, or continued Metaphor and Hypocatastasis: a continued comparison by representation or implication.

    Ephesians 5:14 (and the extended description of someone asleep):
    "Therefore, it says: "Get up, O sleeper,
    and rise up from the dead,
    and Christ will shine upon you.""

5. <u>Proverb</u>: a wayside saying in common use, a specific illustration to signify a truth of life.

    Ephesians 5:5 "For you certainly know this, that every immoral, unclean, or greedy person, that is an idolater, does not have an inheritance in the kingdom of Christ and God."

Ephesians 5:29 "No one ever hates his own body, but nourishes and cares for it"

6. <u>Personification</u>: the giving of human characteristics to inanimate objects, ideas, or animals.

Ephesians 2:3 "among whom also we all behaved once in the lusts of our flesh, by carrying out <u>the will of the flesh and the mind</u>."

7. <u>Anthropomorphism</u>: the representation of God in the form of, or with the attributes of man.

Attributing human actions to God
Ephesians 1:5 "God <u>decided in advance to adopt</u> us into his own family" (NLT)

Attributing a location to God
Ephesians 1:22 "And he (=God) put all things <u>under his feet</u> and he appointed him (=Christ) as the head over all things to the church"

Attributing human circumstances to God
Ephesians 1:18 (God's wealth): ". . . so that you may know . . . what is the wealth of the glorious inheritance from him" (cf. Eph. 2:4, 7; 3:8, 16).

8. <u>Idiom</u>: a fixed expression that cannot be understood grammatically from its component parts, but it has an understood and set meaning.

Ephesians 1:18 "Enlighten <u>the eyes of my heart</u>" (or to give understanding)

Ephesians 3:8 "the <u>unfathomable</u> (literally 'unsearchable' or 'untraceable') wealth of Christ to the Gentiles"

Ephesians 2:2 "sons of disobedience" (or those characterized by disobedience; cf. 5:6; 2:3)

Ephesians 6:19 literally, "that a word be given to me <u>at the opening of my mouth</u>" (or 'when I speak')

FIGURES OF SPEECH INVOLVING SUBSTITUTION

1. <u>Metonymy</u>, or Change of Noun: the change of a word naming an object for another word closely associated with it.

a. When the cause is stated but the effect is intended (instrument for product):

Ephesians 2:12 "that at that time you were without the <u>Messiah</u> (or the hope associated with the Messiah)."

Ephesians 2:16 "and so that he might reconcile both into one body to God through <u>the cross</u> (or the instrument that killed Christ), by killing the enmity in it."

b. When the effect is stated by the cause is intended (reverse of the above):

Ephesians 2:11 "Therefore, remember that once you—Gentiles in the flesh, <u>the ones called "uncircumcised"</u> by <u>the so-called circumcised</u>, done by hand in the flesh"

Ephesians 2:13 "But now in Christ Jesus you, who were once far off, have been brought near by <u>the blood of Christ</u> (or Christ's sacrificial death)" (cf. Eph. 1:7)

Ephesians 2:17 "And when he came, he proclaimed the good news of peace to you <u>who were far off</u> (those where spiritually separated from God)"

c. When the subject is stated for an attribute or adjunct of it (metonymy of subject):

Ephesians 2:3 "among whom also we all behaved once in the <u>lusts of our flesh</u> (or our desires)"

Ephesians 4:20 "But you have not learned <u>Christ</u> (or Christian teaching about Christ) in such a manner"

d. When the attribute or adjunct that pertains to the subject is put for the subject (metonymy of adjunct; opposite of the previous):

Ephesians 2:2 "in which you once walked according to the <u>age of this world</u> (or according to the customs of this world)" (cf. Eph. 6:12)

Ephesians 3:14 "For this reason, <u>I bow my knees</u> (or pray) before the Father."

Ephesians 6:16 "…by taking up the shield of faith, with which you are able to extinguish all of the <u>fiery arrows of the evil one</u> (or spiritual attacks)."

2. <u>Synecdoche</u>, or Transfer: the exchange of one idea for another associated idea (the metonymy deals with nouns, the synecdoche with closely related ideas).

   a. The genus is put for the species (general for specific):

       Ephesians 6:22 "<u>Wives</u> (literally, 'women') submit to your own <u>husbands</u> (literally, 'men') as to the Lord."

   b. The species is put for the genus (specific for the general):

       Ephesians 4:13 "until <u>we all attain</u> (literally, 'come into') the unity of faith and the knowledge of the Son of God, to the complete person, to the measure that is Christ's full stature."

       Ephesians 4:17 "Therefore, I say this, and I testify in the Lord, that you no longer walk just as the <u>Gentiles</u> (or unbelievers) also walk in the futility of their minds."

       Ephesians 6:4 (possible) "And <u>fathers</u> (or both fathers and mothers) do not anger your children."

   c. The whole is put for the part (this may be a lexical consideration):

       Ephesians 2:21 "in whom the <u>whole building</u> (or every part of the organization), by being joined together, grows into a holy temple in the Lord."

       Ephesians 3:15 "from whom <u>every family</u> (or all of creation both on earth and in heaven, including divisions of angels) in the heavens and on the earth receives its name"

   d. The part is put for the whole:

       Ephesians 1:22 "And he (=God) put all things under <u>his (=Christ's) feet</u> (referring to Christ's position in relationship to other authorities)"

       Ephesians 4:28 "The one who steals must no longer steal, but rather must do work by producing what is good <u>with his own hands</u> (through physical labor)."

       Ephesians 6:12 "because our struggle is not against <u>blood and flesh</u> (or a physical problem as opposed to a spiritual one)."

3. <u>Hendiadys</u>, or Two for One: two formally coordinate terms express a single concept in which one of the components defines the other (see also verbal hendiadys in Lambdin).

> Ephesians 1:8 the wealth of his grace, "which he lavished on you, with all <u>wisdom and insight</u>."

> Ephesians 2:1 "And you—being dead in your <u>trespasses and sins</u>"

> Ephesians 3:12 "in whom, we have <u>boldness and access</u>"

> Ephesians 5:2 just as Christ "gave himself for us as an <u>offering and sacrifice</u>"

> Ephesians 5:29 "For no one ever hates his own flesh, but <u>nourishes and cherishes</u> it"

4. <u>Euphemism</u>: The substitution of an inoffensive or mild expression for an offensive one:

> Ephesians 2:13 "you have been brought near by <u>the blood of Christ</u>"

> Ephesians 5:2 "just as Christ loved us and <u>gave himself up for us</u>."

5. <u>Apostrophe</u>: a turning aside from the direct matter to address others (who or which may not actually be present):

> Ephesians 3:1–2 "For this reason, I Paul, a prisoner of Christ Jesus on behalf of you, the Gentiles—if indeed you have heard of the administration of God's grace, which was given to me for you." Paul outlines his current ministry to the Gentiles in verses 2–13; he picks up his prayer again in verse 14.

6. <u>Hyperbaton</u>, or Transposition: the placing of a word out of its usual order in the sentence for the sake of emphasis.

> Ephesians 1:4–5 (possible, see Syntactical Nugget at 1:4b) "<u>In love</u> he predestined us for adoption to sonship through Jesus Christ, in accordance with his pleasure and will" (NIV)

> Ephesians 3:17b–18 (possible, see Grammatical Nugget at 3:17b) "<u>because you have been rooted and established in love</u>, that you may be able to comprehend with all the saints what is the width and length and height and depth."

7. <u>Antimereia</u>: the use of one part of speech for another.

> Ephesians 1:6 "for the praise of his <u>glorious grace</u> (literally, 'glory of grace')"

> Ephesians 2:2b "…over the spirit who is now working in <u>the sons of dis-</u><u>obedience</u> (or those who are characterized with disobedience)" (cf. Eph. 2:4; 5:6, 8)

8. <u>Type</u>: a divinely prefigured illustration of a corresponding realty (called the antitype).

> Ephesians 5:31–32 "For this reason, a man shall leave his father and mother and be joined to his wife, and the two will become one flesh. This mystery is great, but I am speaking about Christ and about the church."

9. <u>Symbol</u>: a material object substituted for a moral or spiritual truth.

> Ephesians 5:8 "For you were once <u>darkness</u> (or characterized by immoral-ity), but now you are <u>light</u> in the Lord (or characterized by righteousness)"

10. <u>Irony</u>: the expression of thought in a form that conveys its opposite.

> Ephesians 6:20 "for which I work as <u>an ambassador in chains</u>, that I may boldly proclaim about it as it is necessary to speak." An ambassador would not have been imprisoned, but free to represent their own country.

FIGURES OF SPEECH INVOLVING ADDITION OR AMPLIFICATION

1. <u>Chiasm</u>: a form of parallelism in which there is the inversion of terms in the second half of the verse.

> Ephesians 2:8–9a "for you have been saved through faith
> and <u>this is not from you</u>
> **It is a gift of God**
> <u>It is not from works</u>."

> Ephesians 4:22–24 "you <u>put off</u> the <u>old self</u> who is corrupted according to the former behavior according to the desires from deceit **but you are being renewed in your spirit, your mind** and you <u>put on</u> the <u>new self</u> who is creat-ed according to God's likeness in righteousness and holiness from truth."

Ephesians 5:23–24 "The <u>husband</u> is the head of the <u>woman</u>
just as <u>Christ</u> is the head of the <u>church</u>
he is the savior of the body,
but as the <u>church</u> submits to <u>Christ</u>,
thus also the <u>wife</u> should submit to her <u>husband</u> in all things."

2. <u>Repetition</u>: the repetition of the same word or words in a passage (many varieties).

Ephesians 4:8–11 "Therefore it says: 'While <u>ascending</u> on high, he took prisoners captive; he <u>gave</u> gifts to men.' Now what does 'he <u>ascended</u>' mean except that he also <u>descended</u> to the lower parts, namely the earth. The very one who <u>descended</u> is also the one who <u>ascended</u> above all the heavens so that he might fill all things. And he <u>gave</u> some as apostles, some as prophets, some as evangelists, and some as shepherds and other teachers."

3. <u>Anaphora</u>, or Like Sentence Beginnings: the repetition of key words or lines at the beginning of successive predications.

Ephesians 4:4–6 "<u>There is</u> one body,
and <u>there is</u> one Spirit,
just as you have also been called in one hope of your calling;
<u>there is</u> one Lord;
<u>there is</u> one faith;
<u>there is</u> one baptism;
<u>there is one God and Father of all, who is over all and through all and in all</u>."

Ephesians 6:12 "our struggle is not <u>against</u> blood and flesh
but <u>against</u> the rulers,
<u>against</u> authorities,
<u>against</u> world rulers of this darkness,
<u>against the spiritual forces of evil in the heavens</u>."

4. <u>Inclusio</u>: the rhetorical device in which a literary unit begins and ends with the same (or similar) word, phrase, or clause. It is a framing device, stressing the theme.

Ephesians 2:1–2, 10 "And even though you were dead in your trespasses and sins, in which <u>you once walked</u> according to the age of this world.... For we are his workmanship, because we have been created in Christ Jesus for good works, which God prepared beforehand <u>so that we might walk in them</u>."

Ephesians 3:2, 7 "if indeed you have heard of the administration of <u>God's grace, which was given to me</u> for you ... of which I became a servant according to the gift, namely <u>God's grace, which was given to me</u> according to the working of his power"

Ephesians 4:22, 25 "...that you <u>put off</u> (literally, 'take off') the old self who is corrupted.... Therefore, since you have <u>put away</u> (literally, 'take off') falsehood"

5. <u>Polysyndeton</u>, or Many Ands: the repetition of the conjunction.

   Ephesians 1:21 "... high above every rule
      <u>and</u> authority
      <u>and</u> power
      <u>and</u> dominion
      <u>and</u> every name which is called upon, not only in this age, but in the age to come"

6. <u>Anabasis</u>, or Gradual Ascent: an increase of sense in successive lines.

   Ephesians 1:20 "He exercised this power in Christ by raising him form the dead and by seating him at his right hand in the heavenly places high above every rule and authority and power and dominion and every name that is called upon, not only in this age, but in the age to come."

7. <u>Hyperbole</u>: exaggerated theme for the purpose of emphasis or heightened effect (more is said than is literally meant).

   Ephesians 3:19 "to know the love of Christ, which surpasses knowledge" (Paul prays that the Ephesians come to know the love of Christ, which is so great, that it is unknowable)

FIGURES OF SPEECH INVOLVING OMISSION OR SUPPRESSION

1. <u>Ellipsis</u>: The omission of any element of language that technically renders a sentence to be 'ungrammatical,' yet the sentence is usually understood in context.

   Ephesians 3:18 "that you may comprehend with all what is the width and length and height and depth [of God's love]" (See Syntactical Nugget at 3:18c for a discussion on the possible referents.)

2. <u>Aposiopesis</u>, or Sudden Silence: the breaking off from what is being said (in anger, grief, deprecation, promise etc.) with sudden silence.

   Ephesians 3:1 "For this reason, I Paul, a prisoner of Christ Jesus on behalf of you, the Gentiles—"

3. <u>Erotesis</u>, or Rhetorical Questions: the asking of questions without expecting an answer (to express affirmation, demonstration, wonder, exultation, wishes, denials, doubts, admonitions, expostulations, prohibitions, pity, disparagements, reproaches, lamentations, indignation or absurdities).

   Ephesians 4:9 "In saying, 'He ascended,' what does it mean but that he also descended into the lower regions, the earth?" (ESV; cf. NET, CSB, NIV)

4. <u>Meiosis</u>, or Belittling: a belittling of one thing to magnify another (also called <u>litotes</u> or understatement).

   Ephesians 4:17 "Therefore, I say this, and I testify in the Lord, that you no longer walk just as the Gentiles also walk in the futility of their minds"

5. <u>Tapeinosis</u>, or Demeaning: a lessening of a thing in order to increase it.

   Ephesians 2:5a "and <u>even though we were dead in our trespasses</u>, he made us alive with Christ"

   Ephesians 3:8 "This grace was given to me, <u>the very least of all the saints</u>, to proclaim the good news of the unfathomable wealth of Christ to the Gentiles."

6. <u>Anacoluthon</u>, or Non-sequence: a breaking off of the sequence of thought, a change from a construction which has been begun already, to one of a different kind (especially after a long parenthesis).

> Ephesians 1:13 "in whom you also, when you heard the word of truth, the gospel of your salvation, in whom also, when you believed, you were sealed with the promised Holy Spirit."

> Ephesians 2:1–3 "And even though you were dead in your trespasses and sins, in which you once walked according to the age of this world, according to the ruler over the authority of the air, over the spirit who is now working in the sons of disobedience among whom also we all behaved once in the lusts of our flesh, by carrying out the will of the flesh and mind, and we were children destined for wrath because of our nature, even as the rest were…."

> Ephesians 2:11–12 "Therefore, remember that once you—Gentiles in the flesh, the ones called 'uncircumcised' by the so-called circumcised, done by hand in the flesh—that you were at that time without the Messiah…."

Bibliography

Abbott, T. K. 1909. *A Critical and Exegetical Commentary on the Epistle to the Ephesians and to the Colossians.* ICC. Edinburgh: T&T Clark.

Aland, B. et al. 2012. *Novum Testamentum Graece.* 28th ed. Stuttgart: Deutsche Bibelgesellschaft.

Aland, K. et al. 1963. *Novum Testamentum Graece.* 25th ed. Stuttgart: Deutsche Bibelgesellschaft.

______. 1993. *Novum Testamentum Graece.* 27th ed. Stuttgart: Deutsche Bibelgesellschaft.

Arnold, C. E. 1989. *Ephesians: Power and Magic, The Concept of Power in Ephesians in Light of Its Historical Setting.* SNTMS 63. Cambridge: Cambridge University Press.

______. 2010. *Ephesians.* ZECNT 10. Grand Rapids: Zondervan.

Barnett, P. 1993. "Apostle." *DPL,* 45–51.

Barth, M. 1974a. *Ephesians 1–3: A New Translation with Introduction and Commentary.* AB 34. Garden City, NY: Doubleday.

______. 1974b. *Ephesians 4–6: A New Translation with Introduction and Commentary.* AB 34a. Garden City, NY: Doubleday.

Bateman IV, H. W. 2013. *Interpreting the General Letters: An Exegetical Handbook.* HNTE. Grand Rapids: Kregel.

Bateman IV, H. W. and A. C. Peer. 2017. *John's Letters: An Exegetical Guide for Preaching and Teaching.* Big Greek Idea. Grand Rapids: Kregel.

Bauernfeind, O. 1964. "ἀσέλγεια." TDNT 1:490.

Baugh, S. M. 2015. *Ephesians.* EEC. Bellingham, WA: Lexham.

Bedale, S. 1954. "The Meaning of κεφαλή in the Pauline Epistles." *JTS* 5:211–15.

Best, E. 1998. *A Critical and Exegetical Commentary on Ephesians.* ICC. Edinburgh: T&T Clark.

Blass, F., A. Debrunner, and R. W. Funk. 1961. *A Greek Grammar of the New Testament and Other Early Christian Literature.* 3rd ed. Chicago: University of Chicago Press.

Bock, D. L. 1994a. "'The New Man' as Community in Colossians and Ephesians." Pages 157–67 in *Integrity of Heart, Skillfulness of Hands: Biblical and Leadership Studies in Honor of Donald K. Campbell*. Edited by Charles H. Dyer and Roy B. Zuck. Grand Rapids: Baker.

______. 1994b. "A Theology of Paul's Prison Epistles." Pages 299–331 in A *Biblical Theology of the New Testament*. Edited by Roy B. Zuck and Darrell L. Bock. Chicago: Moody.

Bratcher, R. G. and E. A. Nida. 1993. *A Handbook on Paul's Letter to the Ephesians*. UBS Handbook Series. New York: United Bible Societies.

Bruce, F. F. 1984. *The Epistles to the Colossians, to Philemon, and to the Ephesians*. NICNT. Grand Rapids: Eerdmans.

Bruce, F. F. and E. K. Simpson. 1957. *The Epistles to the Ephesians and the Colossians*. NICNT. Grand Rapids: Eerdmans.

Bullinger, E. W. 1986. *Figures of Speech Used in the Bible: Explained and Illustrated*. Grand Rapids: Baker.

Burer, M. H. and J. E. Miller. 2008. *A New Reader's Lexicon of the Greek New Testament*. Grand Rapids: Kregel.

Burton, E. D. 1898. *Syntax and the Moods and Tenses in New Testament Greek*. 2nd ed. Edinburgh: T&T Clark.

Campbell, C. R. 2008. *Basics of Verbal Aspect in Biblical Greek*. Grand Rapids: Zondervan.

______. 2012. *Paul and Union with Christ: An Exegetical and Theological Study*. Grand Rapids: Zondervan.

Carson, D. A. 1996. *Exegetical Fallacies*. 2nd edition. Grand Rapids: Baker.

Comfort, P. W. and D. P. Barrett. 2001. *The Text of the Earliest New Testament Greek Manuscripts*. Wheaton, IL: Tyndale.

Conzelmann, H. 1971. "συνίημι κτλ." *TDNT* 7:888–96.

______. 1974. "φῶς κτλ." *TDNT* 9:310–58.

Danker, F. W., W. Bauer, W. F. Arndt, and F. Wilbur Gingrich. 2000. *A Greek-English Lexicon of the New Testament and Other Early Christian Literature*. 3rd ed. Chicago: University of Chicago Press.

Delling, G. 1964. "ἀργός κτλ." *TDNT* 1:452–54.

______. 1968. "πλήρης κτλ." *TDNT* 6:283–311.

______. 1972. "ὕμνος κτλ." *TDNT* 8:489–503.

Dockery, D. S. 1993. "New Nature and Old Nature." *DPL*, 628–29.

Dunn, J. D. G. 1998. *The Theology of Paul the Apostle*. Grand Rapids: Eerdmans.

Fanning, B. 1990. *Verbal Aspect in the New Testament*. OTM. Oxford: Clarendon.

Fee, G. D. 2007. *Pauline Christology: An Exegetical-Theological Study*. Peabody, MA: Hendrickson.

———. 2018. *Jesus the Lord according to Paul the Apostle: A Concise Introduction*. Grand Rapids: Baker Academic.

Fitzer, G. 1971. "σφραγίς κτλ." *TDNT* 7:939–53.

Foerster, W. 1964. "ἀρέσκω κτλ." *TDNT* 1:455–57.

Fowl, S. E. 2012. *Ephesians: A Commentary*. NTL. Louisville: Westminster John Knox.

Gombis, T. G. 2005. "Cosmic Lordship and Divine Gift-Giving: Psalm 68 in Ephesians 4:8." *NovT* 47:367–80.

———. 2010. *The Drama of Ephesians: Participating in the Triumph of God*. Downers Grove, IL: InterVarsity Press.

Grundmann, W. 1964. "ἀγαθός κτλ." *TDNT* 1:10–18.

Guthrie, G. H. and J. S. Duvall. 1998 *Biblical Greek Exegesis: A Graded Approach to Learning Intermediate and Advanced Greek*. Grand Rapids: Zondervan.

Hagner, D. A. 2012. *The New Testament: A Historical and Theological Introduction*. Grand Rapids: Baker Academic.

Harris, M. J. 2012. *Prepositions and Theology in the Greek New Testament: An Essential Reference Resources for Exegesis*. Grand Rapids: Zondervan.

Harris, W. H. 1994. "The Ascent and Descent of Christ in Ephesians 4:9–10." *BSac* 151:198–214.

———. 1998. *The Descent of Christ: Ephesians 4:7–11 and Traditional Hebrew Imagery*. BSL. Grand Rapids: Baker.

Hawthorne, G. F., R. P. Martin, and D. G. Reid, eds. 1993. *Dictionary of Paul and His Letters*. Downers Grove, IL: Intervarsity Press.

Hodges, Z. C. and A. L. Farstad. 1985. *The Greek New Testament according to the Majority Text*. 2nd ed. Nashville: Nelson.

Hoehner, H. W. 2002. *Ephesians: An Exegetical Commentary*. Grand Rapids: Baker Academic.

Holmes, M. W. 2010. *The Greek New Testament SBL Edition*. Atlanta: Society of Biblical Literature; Bellingham, WA: Logos Bible Software.

Hurtado, L. W. 2018. *Honoring the Son: Jesus in Earliest Christian Devotional Practice*. Snapshots. Bellingham, WA: Lexham.

Jeremias, J. 1964. "γωνία κτλ." *TDNT* 1:791–93.

Jongkind, D. and P. J. Williams. 2017. *The Greek New Testament: Produced at Tyndale House*, Cambridge. Wheaton, IL: Crossway.

Keith, C. 2011. *Jesus' Literacy: Scribal Culture and the Teacher from Galilee*. LNTS 413. LHJS 8. New York: T&T Clark.

Klauck, H. 2006. *Ancient Letters and the New Testament: A Guide to Context and Exegesis*. Waco, TX: Baylor University Press.

Köstenberger, A. J., B. L. Merkle, and R. L. Plummer. 2016. *Going Deeper with New Testament Greek: An Intermediate Study of the Grammar and Syntax of the New Testament*. Nashville: B&H Academic.

Kruse, C. G. 1993a. "Servant, Service." *DPL*, 869–71.

______. 1993b. "Virtues and Vices." *DPL*, 962–63.

Kubo, S. 1975. *A Reader's Greek-English Lexicon of the New Testament and A Beginner's Guide for the Translation of New Testament Greek*. Andrews University Monographs 4. Grand Rapids: Zondervan.

Larkin, W. J. 2009. *Ephesians: A Handbook on the Greek Text*. BHGNT. Waco, TX: Baylor University Press.

Lenski, R. C. H. 1937. *The Interpretation of St. Paul's Epistles to the Galatians, to the Ephesians and to the Philippians*. Columbus, OH: Wartburg.

Liddell, H. G., R. Scott, and H. S. Jones. 1996. *A Greek-English Lexicon*. 9th ed with revised supplement. Oxford: Clarendon Press.

Lincoln, A. T. 1990. *Ephesians*. WBC 42. Dallas: Word.

Lohse, E. 1968. "πρόσωπον κτλ." *TDNT* 6:768–780.

Louw, J. P. and E. A. Nida, eds. 1989. *Greek-English Lexicon of the New Testament: Based on Semantic Domains*. 2nd ed. New York: United Bible Societies.

MacDonald, W. G. 1986. *Greek Enchiridion: A Concise Handbook of Grammar for Translation and Exegesis*. Peabody, MA: Hendrickson.

Merkle, B. L. 2016. *Ephesians*. EGGNT. Nashville: B&H Academic.

Metzger, B. M. 1997. *Lexical Aids for Students of New Testament Greek*. 3rd ed. Grand Rapids: Baker.

Metzger, B. M. and B. D. Ehrman. 2005. *The Text of the New Testament: Its Transmission, Corruption, and Restoration*. 4th ed. Oxford: Oxford University Press.

Michel, O. 1967. "οἶκος κτλ." *TDNT* 5:119–59.

Montanari, F. 2015. *The Brill Dictionary of Ancient Greek*. Translated and edited by Madeleine Goh and Chad Schroeder. Boston: Brill.

Morris, L. 1993. "Redemption." *DPL*, 784–86.

Moule, C. F. D. 1959. *An Idiom Book of the New Testament Greek*. 2nd ed. Cambridge: Cambridge University Press.

Moulton, J. H. and G. Milligan. 1930. *The Vocabulary of the Greek Testament: Illustrated from the Papyri and Other Non-literary Sources*. Grand Rapids: Eerdmans.

Mounce, W. D. 1996. *A Graded Reader of Biblical Greek*. Grand Rapids: Zondervan.

______. 2009. *Basics of Biblical Greek Grammar*. 3rd ed. Grand Rapids: Zondervan.

Muddiman, J. 2001. *The Epistle to the Ephesians*. BNTC. Peabody, MA: Hendrickson.

O'Brien, P. T. 1993a. "Benediction, Blessing, Doxology, Thanksgiving." *DPL*, 68–71.

______. 1993b. "Letters, Letter Forms." *DPL*, 550–553.

Osborne, G. R. 2017. *Ephesians: Verse by Verse*. Bellingham, WA: Lexham.

Porter, S. E. 1993. "Holiness, Sanctification." *DPL*, 397–402.

______. 1994. *Idioms of the Greek New Testament*. 2nd ed. BLG 2. Sheffield: JSOT Press.

Richards, E. R. and B. J. O'Brien. 2016. *Paul Behaving Badly: Was the Apostle a Racist, Chauvinist Jerk?* Downers Grove, IL: InterVarsity Press.

Roberts, M. D. 2016. *Ephesians*. Story of God Bible Commentary. Grand Rapids: Zondervan.

Robertson, A. T. 1934. *A Grammar of the Greek New Testament in the Light of Historical Research*. Nashville: Broadman.

Robinson, J. A. 1907. *St. Paul's Epistle to the Ephesians: A Revised Text and Translation with Exposition and Notes*. 2nd ed. London: Macmillan.

Robinson, M. A. and William G. Pierpont. 2005. *The New Testament in the Original Greek: Byzantine Textform, 2005.* Southborough, MA: Chilton.

Rosner, B. S. 2013. *Paul and the Law: Keeping the Commandments of God.* NSBT. Downers Grove, IL: InterVarsity Press.

Runge, S. E. 2010. *Discourse Grammar of the Greek New Testament: A Practical Introduction for Teaching and Exegesis.* Peabody, MA: Hendrickson.

Schreiner, T. R. 2001. *Paul, Apostle of God's Glory in Christ: A Pauline Theology.* Downers Grove, IL: InterVarsity Press.

Scott, J. M. 1993. "Adoption, Sonship." *DPL*, 15–18.

Simpson, B. I. 2015. *Translating Ephesians Clause by Clause: An Exegetical Guide.* Leesburg, IN: Cyber-Center for Biblical Studies.

Stott, J. R. W. 1979. *The Message of Ephesians: God's New Society.* BST. Downers Grove, IL: InterVarsity Press.

Stowers, S. K. 1986. *Letter Writing in Greco-Roman Antiquity.* LEC 5. Philadelphia: Westminster.

Taylor, R. A. 1991. "The Use of Psalm 68:18 in Ephesians 4:8 in Light of the Ancient Versions." *BSac* 148: 319–36.

Thielman, F. 2007. "Ephesians." Pages 813–33 in *Commentary on the New Testament Use of the Old Testament.* Edited by G. K. Beale and D. A. Carson. Grand Rapids: Baker Academic.

———. 2010. *Ephesians.* BECNT. Grand Rapids: Baker Academic.

Turner, N. 1963. *Grammar of the New Testament Greek: Volume 3 Syntax.* Edinburgh: T&T Clark.

———. 1965. *Grammatical Insights into the New Testament.* New York: T&T Clark.

———. 1976. *A Grammar of the New Testament Greek: Volume 4 Style.* Edinburgh: T&T Clark.

Wallace, D. B. 1996. *Greek Grammar beyond the Basics: An Exegetical Syntax of the New Testament.* Grand Rapids: Zondervan.

Witherington III, B. 2007. *The Letters to Philemon, the Colossians, and the Ephesians: A Socio-Rhetorical Commentary on the Captivity Epistles.* Grand Rapids: Eerdmans.

Zerwick, M. 1963. *Biblical Greek: Illustrated by Examples.* Translated by Joseph Smith. SubBi 41. Rome: Pontifical Biblical Institute.

Nugget Index

GRAMMATICAL NUGGETS

SYNTACTICAL NUGGETS

"

SEMANTICAL NUGGETS

Lexical Nuggets

THEOLOGICAL NUGGETS

TEXT-CRITICAL NUGGETS